A Diplomacy of Hope

A Diplomacy of Hope

Canada and Disarmament,
1945–1988

ALBERT LEGAULT AND
MICHEL FORTMANN

Translated from the French by
DEREK ELLINGTON

McGill-Queen's University Press
Montreal & Kingston • London • Buffalo

© McGill-Queen's University Press 1992
ISBN 0-7735-0920-8 (cloth)
ISBN 0-7735-0955-0 (paper)

Legal deposit third quarter 1992
Bibliothèque nationale du Québec

Printed in Canada on acid-free paper

This book is a translation of *Une diplomatie de l'espoir;
Le Canada et le désarmement 1945–1988*, published by
Les presses de l'université Laval in 1989.

This book has been published with the help of a
grant from the Social Science Federation of Canada,
using funds provided by the Social Sciences and
Humanities Research Council of Canada, and with
a grant from the Department of National Defence.

Canadian Cataloguing in Publication Data

Legault, Albert, 1938–
    A diplomacy of hope: Canada and Disarmament,
    1945–1988
    Translation of: Une diplomatie de l'espoir.
    Includes bibiographical references and index.
    ISBN 0-7735-0920-8 (bound) –
    ISBN 0-7735-0955-0 (pbk.)
    1. Disarmament – History – 20th century.
    2. Arms control – History – 20th century. 3. Canada –
    Foreign relations – 1945–   . I. Fortmann, Michel.
    II. Title.

JX1974.L55413 1992   327.1'74'0971   C92-090378-9

Typeset in Baskerville 10/12
by Caractéra production graphique inc., Quebec City

Contents

Tables and Figures

Foreword

Cynics have tended to regard the pursuit of arms control and disarmament agreements as the modern day equivalent of the search for the philosopher's stone. Arms controllers have been derided as alchemists – fruitlessly engaged. For others, arms control and disarmament is a Holy Grail to be pursued single-mindedly. To them, Government arms control and disarmament policy and negotiators have failed fundamentally because they have succeeded in bureaucratizing the process while failing to achieve significant progress in reducing arms.

Like all caricatures, these serve a rhetorical purpose more than they serve the truth which, as often is the case, lies somewhere in between. The doggedness with which successive Canadian Governments have pursued arms control and disarmament does represent, as the title of this book implies, a victory of hope over pessimism. But it also reflects a calm, rational political analysis that tells us arms control and disarmament are fundamental to enhancing the security and prosperity of the people of Canada. In an interdependent world, Canadian and Western security cannot be achieved at the expense of anyone else's. In that context, arms control and disarmament are essential.

Arms control alone does not bring peace; it has to be fully integrated into the political process. Albert Legault and Michel Fortmann provide an invaluable service to serious students of arms control by consistently placing arms control and disarmament talks and initiatives firmly in the context of their contemporary international events.

This close relationship frequently raises the question of which comes first, better political relations or arms control? Perhaps the answer doesn't exist or doesn't matter, because both are essential if we are to achieve a secure peace.

Today, the hope and the persistence with which Canada has pursued arms control finally seem vindicated. Changes of an unforeseen scope are taking place in the former Soviet Union. If these changes persist, the next decade could well see unprecedented progress in arms control and disarmament.

The USA/USSR agreement on intermediate-range nuclear forces and the 35-nation Stockholm Agreement on Confidence- and Security-Building Measures in Europe are already in place. Hopes are high and prospects are good for early agreement on conventional forces and strategic nuclear arms. If these agreements are reached, the focus of East-West relations will change fundamentally from what it has been during the 43 years covered by this volume. The events and negotiations researched so painstakingly and chronicled so thoroughly in these pages will then be important as history and not as precedent.

Albert Legault and Michel Fortmann are to be highly commended for this book. The Department of External Affairs is proud to have been associated with their effort, both by having provided access to its archives and files, and by having contributed financially through the Disarmament Fund. The research has been thorough and has been complemented by an exhaustive program of interviews. Most important, the history of Canada's participation in arms control and disarmament is put firmly into its proper context of international relations.

This is not an "official" history. It is the work and responsibility of the authors. They have brought their own points of view and their own judgements to their research. This too enhances the value of the book – the authors have been able to take their distance from events; they are more objective in their judgements than the participants and policy-makers could ever hope to be.

No history of Canadian arms control policy on the scope of this book has previously been attempted. This work should serve for many years as a valuable tool for students of Canadian foreign policy, of arms control and disarmament negotiations, and of international relations.

From the comfortable hindsight of spring 1992, it is humbling to note that Si Taylor, in his August 1989 Foreword to the French edition of this book, had already grasped the revolutionary nature of the changes then underway as the architecture of the Cold War disintegrated around him. Next he zeroed in on what is now generally seen as a key security issue of the post Cold War era: the proliferation of weapons of mass destruction – nuclear, chemical and biological – throughout the four corners of the Earth.

What he – along with all the rest of us – did not foresee, however, was the scale of the impact on the United Nations of the demise of the Cold War. For the liberation of the Security Council from the paralysis of the "permanent five" veto meant that the United Nations was able, in its response to Iraq's 1990 invasion of Kuwait, to act collectively to counter aggression, that is, to act as its creators had intended – for virtually the first time in its then 45 year history.

And alongside this renaissance of the United Nations was an equally significant political transformation among its member States. For the first time a majority of UN member States are democratic with the result that the United Nations – in 1992 – is actively promoting democratic values. Peacekeeping is becoming peacemaking. The stalemate of Cyprus – where blue-helmeted Canadian soldiers have kept the two sides at bay for over 27 years – has now given way to the Cambodian model. There, the United Nations will not only deploy peacekeepers but will operate as the *de facto* interim government during the period of transition to multiparty democracy.

Does this mean that arms control and disarmament negotiations are now feasible but irrelevant – as some have vociferously announced? On the contrary. What it really means is that regional disputes as diverse and difficult as the Westerns Sahara and the Korean peninsula can now be tackled through multilateral processes which focus both on the military dimensions – on the type and quantity of armaments and the requirements for guaranteeing security in its traditional sense – and on security in its broader sense, taking into account social, economic and environmental needs as well; in short, the full spectrum of human needs.

In the post Cold War era, where myriad new instabilities have replaced the horrendous, yet familiar, devil of the Cold War nuclear standoff, the role of multilateralism and of multilateralists is needed as never before. Bernard Wood, in his final annual statement as Chief Executive Officer of the Canadian Institute for International Peace and Security, wrote in January of 1992:

All available testimony from foreigners tends to corroborate the view that the traditional Canadian role in the world – together with its model of pluralism and tolerance at home – remains as constructive and important as ever, and if anything should be strengthened.

A Diplomacy of Hope, in its careful record of the past 43 years of Canadian arms control policy and practice, records the hopes of the post-war generation of Canadian diplomats. It also serves to quietly mark the passing of the torch to a new generation of constructive multilateralists struggling to bring stability to the waning years of the twentieth century.

Peggy Mason
Canadian Ambassador for Disarmament
Ottawa, April 1992

Preface

The present work is the first in-depth study on the history of Canadian diplomacy in the area of arms control and disarmament. The study was made possible only through the assistance of the Department of External Affairs which made its records available to us. We have been able to cite foreign texts which appeared during the postwar period up to 1969, but not beyond because of the 30-year rule of diplomatic discretion which applies in the case of foreign nations. In this regard, Chapter 3 in particular reveals the great tensions which existed between the allies. For the last 20-year period, we were forced to use stylistic devices: either a question which, in most cases, constitutes an affirmation; a paraphrase in the case of Canadian Cabinet decisions; or, a metaphor in instances where a description would hurt some or offend others.

Generally, we have tried to deal with the major negotiations on arms control and disarmament, in which Canada has participated since 1945, in a manner which we hope will make them more intelligible for the reader. These negotiations were many and varied, but may be categorized under the following thematic headings: The Atomic Energy Commission of the United Nations (UN), the Commission for Conventional Armaments (UN), the Disarmament Commission (UN) and the work of its Subcommittee, the sectoral negotiations on the Arctic and the de-nuclearization of Central Europe during the late 1950s and early 1960s, the Ten-Nation Committee on Disarmament, the Eighteen-Nation Committee on Disarmament, the Nuclear Non-Proliferation Treaty, the negotiations on chemical and biological weapons, the negotiations on banning nuclear tests, the negotiations on the use of outer space, Mutual and Balanced Force Reductions (MBFR), the Conference on Security and Cooperation in Europe (CSCE), and the Stockholm negotiations at the Conference on Disarmament in Europe (CDE). The latter three themes in particular were the responsibility of Michel Fortmann. The only themes that have not been treated in detail are the major bilateral negotiations between the United States and the Soviet Union – the negotiations during the Strategic Arms Limitation Talks (SALT I and SALT II) and the Nuclear and Space Talks (NST) – although we have, on occasion, lifted the corner of the veil whenever these major issues were interactive with the others.

The main element of the arms control and disarmament process that we have not treated exhaustively is the peace initiative of former prime minister Trudeau. Several aspects of this initiative have, however, been examined when dealing with Canadian actions in the Special Sessions of the United Nations devoted to disarmament (Chapter 9), when considering the Canadian position on the use of outer space (Chapter 10) and when allowing ourselves a few indiscretions based on information obtained in some interviews. The main reason for omitting the Trudeau peace initiative, if indeed it is omitted, is that we refrained from seeking access to the records of either the Prime Minister's Office or the Privy Council. The second element that we have not dealt with is the Sea-Bed Treaty of 1971. There are several reasons for this omission. The first is that all the aspects of this topic have been examined in depth in the doctoral thesis of Michael Tucker which is cited in the Bibliography. The second reason is that this matter was not one which provoked lengthy and difficult negotiations on the international diplomatic stage, even though the main States that were interested in this Treaty were the superpowers. In short, we had to make a choice. There was simply not enough time or space.

A few cautions are in order. The present book makes no claim to theoretical analysis. For example, the chapter on the bees and the ants would appear to be more far-reaching than a simple description of bureaucratic phenomena. We have intentionally focused on diplomatic history *per se*. In many instances, the complexity of the issues, the richness of the texts or again the pluralism of opinion provides a more interesting backdrop than the somewhat dry or simplistic models to which we have become accustomed in the study of political science or international relations. In this regard, we leave it to the reader to form his own judgements. Sometimes we have cited authors or made mention of the major trends in arms control and disarmament, but we have only laid prime emphasis on these trends in the general conclusions.

A word on terminology is also in order. The expressions "Defence Department" or "National Defence" have been used indiscriminately to mean the Department of National Defence. In the body of the text we speak of arms control and disarmament. Arms control is understood in a broad general context which embraces the policies of disarmament, which themselves are linked to the more general problems of international security.

In order to provide the reader with a better understanding of the major issues of the negotiations, we have attempted to popularize the scientific and technical aspects. In most instances all the technical explanations necessary to a sound understanding of the issues have been included. This is the case as much for nuclear physics as for international law. Throughout, we have strived to set Canadian actions in the international context of the era, so that the reader may appreciate the fact that Canada is, or was, only one actor amongst many. The pacifists will perhaps accuse us of having been too influenced by rational analysis, and the military strategists of having been too swayed by diplomatic reason. We accept this criticism from the outset, for our study is positioned at the crossroads of two schools of thought which we designate, in the Conclusion, as the "peace through force" school and the "peace through law" school.

Albert Legault
Michel Fortmann

Acknowledgments

This work has benefited from a generous grant from the Canadian Institute for International Peace and Security, formerly directed by Geoffrey Pearson and presently by Bernard Wood. We have also received generous financial support from the Department of External Affairs.

We are also particularly indebted to all those who participated in the research itself, specifically in perusing the mass of official documents and proceedings on arms control and disarmament. Our thanks are due – ladies first – to Françoise Fâché, Francine Lecours, Agnès Marcaillou, Geneviève Roy and Noëlle Willems, and – gentlemen second – to Gaétan Blais, William George, Thierry Gongora, Jean-François Bussières and Jean-François Thibault. We are equally indebted to our colleagues Istvan Szoghy of the Physics Department and Jean-Yves Chagnon of the Geology Department for their invaluable comments on the technical aspects of the manuscript.

Within the Department of External Affairs, our warmest thanks are due to Dacre Cole of the Historical Section, without whose assistance some important texts might have escaped our attention, as well as to his director, John F. Hilliker, who has always given us his full support. In addition, the Departmental Library gave us access to texts that were impossible to find elsewhere.

Amongst the senior officials, we wish to thank all the officers and managers who took such care in reading the texts and who, in several instances, provided invaluable clarification. In this context, we wish to thank John J. Noble, Ralph Lysyshyn, Ron Clemenson, Ian

Mundell, Gordon Vachon and Patricia Cocker. Special thanks are also due to Suzanne and Gilles Caron who assisted us in Ottawa in perusing the records.

We are deeply grateful to our translator, Derek Ellington, not only for faithfully and scrupulously rendering the French manuscript comprehensible to the English reader, but also for editing and revising the text, for proofreading the final manuscript and for producing the consolidated index.

Finally, we also wish to convey our gratitude to McGill-Queen's University Press, and in particular to Joan McGilvray, its Coordinating Editor, and to Philip J. Cercone, its Director, for facilitating the publication of this book.

Albert Legault
Michel Fortmann

Acronyms

ABC	America-Britain-Canada
ABCA	America-Britain-Canada-Australia/New Zealand
ABM	Anti-Ballistic Missile
ACDA	Arms Control and Disarmament Agency (U.S.)
ACIS	Arms Control Impact Statement (U.S.)
AEC	Atomic Energy Commission (UN)
also	Atomic Energy Commission (U.S.)
AECB	Atomic Energy Control Board
AECL	Atomic Energy of Canada Limited
AHG	Ad Hoc Group (NATO)
ALMV	Air-Launched Miniature Vehicle
AMU	Atomic Mass Unit
ANF	Atlantic Nuclear Force (NATO)
ARPA	Advanced Research Projects Agency (U.S.)
ASAT	Anti-satellite
AVLIS	Atomic Vapor Laser Isotope Separation
BBC	British Broadcasting Corporation
BC	Bacteriological (Biological) and Chemical
BTWC	Biological and Toxin Weapons Convention (Convention on the Prohibition of the Development, Production and Stockpiling of Bacteriological (Biological) and Toxin Weapons and on Their Destruction)
BW	Bacteriological (Biological) Warfare
CANADARM	Canada Arm on the Space Shuttle
CANDU	Canada Deuterium Uranium

CAS	Committee on Assurances of Supply (IAEA)
CBM	Confidence-Building Measure
CBW	Chemical and Biological Warfare
CCA	Commission for Conventional Armaments (UN)
CCD	Conference of the Committee on Disarmament
C³I	Communications, Command, Control and Intelligence
CCOS	Chairman, Chiefs of Staff
CCSBMDE	Conference on Confidence- and Security-Building Measures and Disarmament in Europe (see CDE)
CD	Committee on Disarmament (1979 – 1983)
also	Conference on Disarmament (1984 –)
CDA	Combined Development Agency
CDE	Conference on Disarmament in Europe (see CCSBMDE)
CDT	Combined Development Trust (ABC)
CERN	*Centre européen de recherches nucléaires* (European Nuclear Research Centre)
CFE	Conventional Armed Forces in Europe
CIDA	Canadian International Development Agency
CIIPS	Canadian Institute for International Peace and Security
CIRUS	Canadian Indian Reactor (US was probably meant to indicate that the U.S. supplied heavy water to India)
CMEA	Council for Mutual Economic Assistance
CND	Campaign for Nuclear Disarmament
COPUOS	Committee on the Peaceful Uses of Outer Space (UN)
CORRTEX	Continuous Reflectometry for Radius versus Time Experiments
COSPAR	Committee on Space Research (ICSU)
COSPAS	Soviet equivalent of SARSAT
CPC	Combined Policy Committee (ABC)
CPSU	Communist Party of the Soviet Union
CSBM	Confidence- and Security-Building Measure
CSCE	Conference on Security and Cooperation in Europe
CST	Conventional Stability Talks
CTB	Comprehensive Test Ban
CTS	Communications Technology Satellite (ESA)
CW	Chemical Warfare
CWC	Chemical Weapons Convention
DC	Disarmament Commission (UN)
DEA	Department of External Affairs
DEW	Distant Early Warning
DNA	Deoxyribonucleic Acid
DNACPOL	Directorate of Nuclear and Arms Control Policy
DND	Department of National Defence

DPC	Defence Planning Committee (NATO)
DRB	Defence Research Board
DSS	Directorate of Strategic Studies
DWG	Disarmament Working Group
EAEC	European Atomic Energy Community (see EURATOM)
EDC	European Defence Community
also	Export Development Corporation
EDIP	European Defence Improvement Programme (NATO)
EEC	European Economic Community
EMR	Department of Energy, Mines & Resources
ENDC	Eighteen-Nation Disarmament Committee
ENMOD	Environmental Modification
EOPP	Earth Observation Preparatory Program (ESA)
ERIS	Exo-atmospheric Reentry-vehicle Interceptor Subsystem (SDI)
ERS-I	European Remote Sensing satellite
ESA	Environmental Sciences Agency (U.S.)
also	European Space Agency
EURATOM	European Atomic Energy Community (see EAEC)
EXOS-D	Japanese scientific satellite (physics of the magnetosphere and polar auroras)
FAO	Food and Agriculture Organization (UN)
FEL	Free Electron Laser (SDI)
FOBS	Fractional Orbital Bombardment System
FRG	Federal Republic of Germany
FSS	Full-Scope Safeguards (IAEA)
GCD	General and Complete Disarmament
GDR	German Democratic Republic
GEODE	Experiment on fabrication of materials in space (Sweden)
GLCM	Ground-Launched Cruise Missile
GNP	Gross National Product
GNT	Guidelines for Nuclear Transfers (IAEA)
GRU	*Glavnoe Razvedyvatel'noe Upravlenie* (Main Intelligence Directorate of the Soviet General Staff)
GSE	Group of Scientific Experts (seismic verification)
HERMES	French space shuttle
HOE	Homing Overlay Experiment (SDI)
IAEA	International Atomic Energy Agency
IAF	International Astronautical Federation
IAU	International Astronomical Union
IBM	International Business Machines
ICBM	Intercontinental Ballistic Missile

ICRASL	Institute and Centre for Research on Air and Space Law (McGill University)
ICRP	International Commission on Radiological Protection
ICSU	International Council of Scientific Unions
IDC	Interdepartmental Committee
IDO	International Disarmament Organization
IFRI	*Institut français des relations internationales* (French Institute of International Relations)
IHE	Insensitive High Explosive
IISS	International Institute of Strategic Studies
ILO	International Labour Organization
INF	Intermediate-Range Nuclear Forces
INFCE	International Nuclear Fuel Cycle Evaluation
INFCIRC	Information Circular (IAEA)
INTERBALL	Magnetospheric studies project (USSR)
IPIC	Image-Processing and Interpretation Centre (ISMA)
IRBM	Intermediate-Range Ballistic Missile
ISDE	International Seismic Data Exchange
ISIS	International Satellite for Ionospheric Studies
ISMA	International Satellite Monitoring Agency
ISU	International System of Units
IUPAC	International Union of Pure and Applied Chemistry
IVO	International Verification Organization
JBMDS	Joint Ballistic Missile Defence Staff
JDC	Joint Disarmament Committee
JDWG	Joint Disarmament Working Group
JDWP	Joint Disarmament Working Party
JERS-I	Earth Resources Satellite (Japan)
JIC	Joint Intelligence Committee
JPC	Joint Planning Committee
JPS	Joint Planning Staff
JS	Joint Staff
KAL	Korean Air Lines
KANUPP	Karachi Nuclear Power Plant
KMP	Key Measurement Points (IAEA)
LANDSAT	Earth observation (remote-sensing) satellite
LASA	Large Aperture Seismic Array (U.S.)
MAD	Mutual Assured Destruction
MAS	Mutual Assured Survival
MBA	Material Balance Area (IAEA)
MBFR	Mutual and Balanced Force Reductions
MC	Military Committee (NATO)
MCSC	Military Chiefs of Staff Committee (UN)

MHV	Miniature Homing Vehicle
MIRV	Multiple Independently-Targetable Reentry Vehicle
MIT	Massachusetts Institute of Technology
MLF	Multilateral Force (NATO)
MLIS	Molecular Laser Isotope Separation
MOS-I	Maritime Observation Satellite (Japan)
MPC	Maximum Permissible Concentration (radioactivity)
MPT	Multilateral Preparatory Talks
MRBM	Medium-Range Ballistic Missile
MSAT	Mobile Services Satellite
MUF	Material Unaccounted For (IAEA)
NAA	North Atlantic Assembly (NATO)
NAC	North Atlantic Council (NATO)
NATO	North Atlantic Treaty Organization
NFZ	Nuclear-Free Zones
NGO	Non-Governmental Organization
NNA	Neutral and Non-Aligned (nations)
NOFUN	No First Use of Nuclear Weapons
NORAD	North American Aerospace Defence
NORESS	Norwegian Regional Seismic Array
NORSAR	Norwegian Seismic Array
NPG	Nuclear Planning Group (NATO)
NPT	Nuclear Non-Proliferation Treaty (Treaty on the Non-Proliferation of Nuclear Weapons)
NRC	National Research Council
NRRC	Nuclear Risk Reduction Centers
NSC	National Security Council (U.S.)
NSG	Nuclear Suppliers Group (also known as London Group or Club of London)
NSS	National Seismic Stations
NST	Nuclear and Space Talks
NTM	National Technical Means (surveillance satellites)
NWS	North Warning System (NORAD)
OAU	Organization of African Unity
OLYMPUS	Communications technology satellite (ESA)
OOG	Out-of-Garrison Activities
OPANAL	*Organismo para la Proscripción de las Armas Nucleares en América Latina y el Caribe* (Treaty for the Prohibition of Nuclear Weapons in Latin America – Treaty of Tlatelolco)
OPP	Other Physical Principles (SDI)
ORAE	Operational Research and Analysis Establishment
OS	Outer Space

OSI	On-Site Inspections
PAXSAT	Canadian satellite for observation of arms agreements
PCC	Political Consultative Committee (WPO)
PCSL	Political Committee at the Senior Level (NATO) (see SPC)
PERMREP	Permanent Representative (NATO)
PJBD	Permanent Joint Board on Defence
PNE	Peaceful Nuclear Explosions
PNET	Peaceful Nuclear Explosions Treaty (Treaty on Underground Nuclear Explosions for Peaceful Purposes)
PRC	Peoples' Republic of China
PSDE	Payload and Spacecraft Development and Experimentation Program (ESA)
PTBT	Partial Test Ban Treaty (Treaty Banning Nuclear Weapon Tests in the Atmosphere, in Outer Space and Under Water)
RADARSAT	Radar Satellite
RAF	Royal Air Force (U.K.)
RAPP	Rajasthan Atomic Power Plan
RCMP	Royal Canadian Mounted Police
RSTN	Regional Seismic Test Network (U.S.)
RW	Radiological Weapons
SAC	Strategic Air Command (U.S.)
SACEUR	Supreme Allied Commander Europe (NATO)
SALT	Strategic Arms Limitation Talks
SARSAT	Search and Rescue Satellite-Aided Tracking program (Canada, France, U.S. and USSR)
SBKKV	Space-Based Kinetic Kill Vehicle
SDEDSI	*Société pour le développement des études de défense et de sécurité internationale*
SDI	Strategic Defense Initiative (U.S.)
SDIO	Strategic Defense Initiative Organization (U.S.)
SEATO	South East Asia Treaty Organization
SHAPE	Supreme Headquarters Allied Powers in Europe (NATO)
SIOP	Single Integrated Operational Plan (U.S.)
SIPRI	Stockholm International Peace Research Institute
SPACECOM	Space Command (U.S.)
SPC	Senior Political Committee (NATO) (see PCSL)
SPETSNAZ	*Voïska Special'nogo Naznačenija* (Soviet Special Purpose Forces)
SPOT	Satellite Probatoire d'Observation de la Terre (French Geodesic Satellite)
SSEA	Secretary of State for External Affairs
START	Strategic Arms Reduction Talks

TNDC	Ten-Nation Disarmament Committee
TNT	Trinitrotoluene
TRR	Taiwan Research Reactor
TTBT	Threshold Test Ban Treaty (Treaty on the Limitation of Underground Nuclear Weapon Tests)
TTCP	The Technical Cooperation Program (ABCA) (formerly the Tripartite Technical Cooperation Program (ABC))
UAR	United Arab Republic
UARS	Upper Atmosphere Research Satellite (U.S.)
U.K.	United Kingdom
UNEF	United Nations Emergency Force
UNGA	United Nations General Assembly
UNISPACE	United Nations Conference on the Exploration and Peaceful Uses of Outer Space
UN	United Nations
UNIDO	United Nations Industrial Development Organization
UNO	United Nations Organization
UNSCEAR	United Nations Scientific Committee on the Effects of Atomic Radiation
UNSSOD	United Nations Special Session on Disarmament
U.S.	United States (of America)
USSR	Union of the Soviet Socialist Republics
VELA	U.S. satellite for remote sensing of nuclear tests (from the Spanish term *vela*, meaning "watch")
VIKING	Swedish space science satellite
WESTAR	Teleseismic Data Exchange Satellite
WEU	Western European Union
WG	Working Group
WHO	World Health Organization
WIND II	French wind-imagery device designed to be integrated with UARS
WMO	World Meteorological Organization
WP	Warsaw Pact
also	Working Party
WPO	Warsaw Pact Organization
WWSSN	World Wide Standardized Seismograph Network

A Diplomacy of Hope

1   The Bees and the Ants

The Succession Dance mimes the accession of Emperor Shun in
peaceful conditions. All was in harmony in heaven and earth.
The War Dance, on the other hand, depicts the accession of the
warlike Emperor Wu, who came to the throne by overthrowing
the Yin ... Confucius spoke of the Succession Dance as being
perfect beauty and at the same time perfect goodness; but of
the War Dance as being perfect beauty, but not perfect goodness.

David Payne, *Confessions of a Taoist on Wall Street*

The world has witnessed a series of major disarmament talks over
the past few decades. They were not conducted in a vacuum of
isolation, but were closely coupled to the international climate prevailing at the time. Clearly, they must be viewed in that context. Only
then is it possible to analyze the essentials of the various proposals
and to understand and appreciate the several positions adopted by
the Canadian Government.

We would not pretend to be cognizant of all that has occurred
during the development of Canada's approach to the disarmament
debate. Our perusal of the copious records has, however, yielded
some insights on certain activities, particularly at the base of the
bureaucratic pyramid where ideas and public servants abound. Sometimes we were able to uncloak the superstructure of the pyramid to
discover that Cabinet does, in fact, occasionally take decisions. We
are not aware of all these decisions, for those taken during the last
20 years are still shrouded in secrecy. On the whole, however, we have
enough to write a book ...

In the absence of a proper backdrop it would be misleading to
bring to centre stage the essentials of the statements, plans and
actions intrinsic to the disarmament debate. First, we must pose the
questions: Who were the main players involved? How did they
behave? How did they organize their interrelationships, and how did
they negotiate? In other words, how do governments arrange and
establish their linkages within both the international system and the
national system?

We shall not attempt to introduce new ideas on the "roles" or perceived "roles" assumed by Canada in formulating or developing her foreign policy, since much has already been written on the subject. One can identify three basic approaches in the development of Canadian foreign policy. There is, of course, the functionalist approach which was characteristic of Canadian diplomacy following the Second World War. John W. Holmes was, and remains, its greatest proponent. The functionalist approach holds that Canada, being neither a significant nor insignificant power, must specialize in those "niche areas" of international diplomacy where Canadian expertise and influence can be brought to bear. During the 1950s and especially the 1960s, the notion of Canada as a "middle power" or "broker" in the international system thus emerged. This notion pertained largely to a style of foreign policy based on the perception of a "role" voluntarily assumed by Canada or accorded to her by other nations within the international system. Lester B. Pearson, John W. Holmes and Peyton Lyon were undoubtedly the most eloquent representatives of this approach.[1] Rightly or wrongly, this approach was often denounced in later years on the basis that it "over-estimated" Canada's diplomatic potential. Its strongest supporter was the internationalist, Louis Sabourin, who always maintained that Canada enjoyed a flawless reputation abroad while her image at home was tarnished or under-appreciated.

The second approach, adopted by people like Stephen Clarkson[2] and Thomas C. Hockin,[3] was just the opposite. They went so far as to claim that Canada's foreign policy reflected only her internal policy, in that the qualities of moderation and mediation found within the system of federal-provincial relations were simply mirrored on the international scene. Again, it was more a matter of political "style" – the international projection of a national personality, as Clarkson wrote – in which form was favoured over substance.

The third approach, which we hesitate to categorize, might be called the "idealist" school, which is founded on moral considerations. Michael Tucker first called it the "activist" school, pertaining to a style of Canadian diplomacy characterized by moral imperatives.[4] Generally, this kind of idealism in Canadian diplomatic objectives was apparent during times when strong political personalities, such as Howard Green or E.L.M. Burns, were personally committed to the pursuit of peace. This political style can certainly be attributed to cultural traits inherited from history, education or upbringing. At the same time, it is impossible to discount the qualities of leadership displayed by ministers and advisors which shape the general orientation of a nation's foreign policy.

Throughout this book we shall have the opportunity to revisit many of these schools of political thought that are manifest to some degree or other in the evolution of Canadian policy on disarmament and arms control. For the moment, however, we believe that we should focus first on the organization of decision-making within the Canadian Government on issues of disarmament and arms control. Traditionally, the main players involved have been the Secretary of State for External Affairs and the Minister of National Defence. How were the relationships established between them? Strangely enough, and with due respect, the manner in which the Departments of External Affairs and of National Defence respectively conduct their affairs is often reminiscent of the behaviour of bees and ants. As we shall see later, this analogy is perhaps more appropriate than might appear at first sight. Before explaining it further, a few words on policy and strategy are necessary.

GOOD AND BAD MARRIAGES: POLICY AND STRATEGY

The Munich situation in 1938 was a small masterpiece of ambiguity. When does peace actually begin? When does it end? Hitler knew, but not Chamberlain. History has taught that democracies and totalitarian regimes alike wage total war tenaciously and ferociously. Democracies have almost always held the view that peace begins when the cannons stop, but the totalitarian regimes have been more realistic. Clausewitz, and later Lenin, argued that war "is a continuation of politics by other means". The truth is that peace is contained in war and that war is contained in peace, for otherwise it would be impossible to move from war to peace or from peace to war.

Actually, things are not quite that simple. The great leaders of antiquity were both strategists and statesmen: Pericles, Alexander the Great and Caesar, to name but a few. In more recent times, the same could be said of Napoleon or of Stalin. Stalin was named Commissar for War in 1941, Marshal of the USSR in March 1943 and Commander-in-Chief in 1945. The practice of combining the functions of policy and strategy is still evident today. The President of the United States is the Commander-in-Chief of the U.S. armed forces. In the Soviet Union, the General Secretary of the Communist Party is also the Commander-in-Chief of the great armies of the nation – or indeed, the armies of the Eastern nations. This duality of function does not exist in Canada, for presumably at some point in our nation's history there was royal confusion and the Governor General became the Commander-in-Chief.

James Eayrs reminds us that: "There is a natural antipathy between diplomatists and militarists ("militarists" as Shakespeare used the word) ... [which] arises out of the incompatibility of their respective missions ...: the diplomatist's to keep the peace, the militarist's to win the war".[5] Things have changed since the time of Shakespeare. Politicians have judged for ages that military matters are too serious to be left to the sole discretion of the military. In latter years, the trends of public opinion have come to the fore, with slogans such as: "no incineration without representation!" Seemingly, there is a move towards progressive democratization of the strategic debate.

Marshal Foch, delivering his famous eulogy for Napoleon in 1921 in *Les Invalides* stated: "above war, there is peace". The logical inverse would be "below peace, there is war", but that would betray Foch's thought. Foch meant to say that above and beyond war there must be a search for peace. But between peace and war there are many stages. A border incident is less serious than limited war, which is less severe than general war. General war, in turn, is less catastrophic than nuclear war.

There are both good and bad marriages between strategy and policy. Good marriages are formed when strategy and policy converge. When there is a divergence between them the result is inevitably a bad marriage. Evidently, one cannot make an omelette without breaking eggs, but one can break eggs without making an omelette. The Israelis learned this in 1956 when, after conducting a brilliant military campaign in the Sinai, they won the war but lost the peace. There is little doubt that the United States was capable of wiping out Vietnam, but decided not to do so, in part because of the vigilance of the American people who chose not merely to listen but to make their voices heard.

Nowadays, strategy and policy tend to have the same ends, but they use different means to achieve them. In the early 1960s, the Minister of National Defence, Douglas Harkness, sought to ensure Canada's security by equipping the Canadian Armed Forces with nuclear weapons. Howard Green, then Secretary of State for External Affairs, was categorically opposed to this idea. In Green's opinion, the only way to ensure Canada's security at the time was to check nuclear proliferation. Although the strategies adopted by the two departments were different, they served the same political end, namely to ensure the security of Canada. This issue proved to be the downfall of the government of John Diefenbaker, who was incapable of deciding between two such diametrically opposed and contradictory views. Policy should resolve contradictions, not exacerbate them, although some journalists and politicians seem able to concoct

Machiavellian schemes at will to serve their own purposes. Moderation is a good thing, but it can easily be buried in excess.

How could two individuals, as sincere and loyal as Harkness and Green arrive at such contradictory positions? This question leads in to the essential topic of this chapter: the bees and the ants.

THE BEES AND THE ANTS[6]

Matters as serious as peace and war cannot be totally explained by genetic or biological determinism. Reasoning by analogy, however, through the use of mental pictures, frequently has virtues which cannot be rivalled by the most scholarly of arguments. It is said that one picture is worth a thousand words, and everyone is free to interpret it as he will.

We recognize immediately the dangers of over-generalization. The behavioural pattern of diplomats is not always analogous to that of bees, any more than the behavioural pattern of the military is analogous to that of ants. Anthills and beehives nevertheless have many things in common. For instance, they are remarkable architectural entities which house intense social activities and organizational structures whose secrets still defy human understanding. Both the Department of External Affairs and the Department of National Defence are highly developed organizational structures that are buzzing, or rather teeming – to avoid any injustice to the military – with ideas for programs, strategies and policies.

In many ways, the life of a diplomat is similar to that of a bee, although the useful lifespans of diplomats and bees are, of course, different. Whereas the career of a diplomat can frequently span thirty years, the worker bee lives for only some thirty days. On the other hand, a queen bee can live for about five years, which is roughly the same duration as a Cabinet minister's mandate. Throughout its life, the bee performs successively the roles of hive-cleaner, nurse, wax-maker, guard and nectar-gatherer. In his early career, the diplomat generally keeps and cleans house, in that he reads through despatches in order to classify and sort the information. Subsequently, the diplomat learns how to digest the information, reproduce it in accessible form and feed it to the proper authorities. Later, he participates in developing policies and in establishing networks or honeycombs of information. As his career evolves, the diplomat becomes the division director who safeguards information and transmits it only to reliable persons. In this way, he guards against intruders and prevents them from getting too close to things that most of the time have already been revealed by the media. Ultimately, the diplomat may be named ambassador to one country after another. In this role he is required to keep his department informed of the plots that are hatching in other hives, and to return for consultations in Ottawa, either stuffed with nectar or laden with pollen, as the case may be.

Interestingly enough, it seems that the honey-producing bee is still one of the few insects that serves man's peaceful purposes best. Legend has it that, of all the government departments, the Department of External Affairs is the one that serves peace best. Rather than destroy this marvellous legend, we shall concede that the diplomatic "bees" are producers of peace.

In contrast, and again according to legend, the Department of National Defence does not appear to be a major producer of peace. Indeed, it is a major consumer of products rather than a producer. So it is with the ants. The ant is one of the rare insects to take great care of aphids, and it even raises them as food for the larvae. In analogous vein, the Department of National Defence nurtures its military industries whose products it later consumes – naturally, only if war breaks out ...

Ants, like bees, are marvellous architects. They build nests, fortifications – in a word, anthills. No minute detail escapes them when they are excavating and building. They are peaceful by nature, but deadly in combat, particularly when the colony is threatened. They also display important military qualities. When wounded, they help each other. They are excellent navigators and take their bearings, just like the bees, from the sun. They communicate through sounds, and also by means of antennas. When on the move, they can cause considerable agricultural damage by attacking in columns or in swarms.

The number of epithets that apply to the ant is prodigious. The ant is generous, prudent, wise, diligent, active, attentive, laborious, industrious and indefatigable. And not to leave out the immortal La Fontaine, the ant is above all provident. Although ants are considered harmful to agriculture, it must be remembered that they destroy large numbers of other harmful insects. Ants, it is said, are quite short-tempered and touchy on territorial issues. Consequently, they maintain security at the boundaries of their colonies to provide protection for the workers inside – their visible product is security.

Unlike honey, security is not a consumable product. It simply allows work to be performed in safety. Obviously, security is always relative. Insects know by instinct that it is dangerous to conduct construction operations in the open if security is lacking at their borders. The providers, namely the workers, see to the security needs of the entire colony.

At this stage one might ask how the bees and the ants evolved, or how the Department of External Affairs and the Department of National Defence evolved. According to some, insect evolution still remains a mystery. It appears to be "polyphyletic", that is, there is no common origin between species. We poor humans are still prisoners of a monophyletic hypothesis, whereby man, it is said, is descended from the apes. What will become of man in millions of years, and why did the ape remain as it is?

Equally, little is known about human institutions. The most erudite works[7] talk of the three most important activities that can be traced back to earliest antiquity, specifically farming, warring and praying. Clearly, evolution is a rather slow process. Even today, man continues to produce food, make war and pray for peace.

What part does genetic and biological determinism play in the behaviour and habits of insects? To what extent does the Department of External Affairs, or the Department of National Defence, conform to established codes of behaviour? As for the insects, we shall have to wait until the geneticists succeed in unravelling all the secrets of their heritage. As far as human behaviour is concerned, the rules of play are infinitely more complex. Humans think, reflect, feel and create. Since antiquity, therefore, a great deal of caution has been used in describing their behaviour. Humans have an infinite capacity for putting on appearances – a problem that is scarcely encountered by insects.

PSYCHOLOGICAL MAKE-UP AND STRATEGIES OF NEGOTIATION

The question of whether psychological make-up reflects human values or vice-versa is difficult to answer. If we pursued this issue, we would be faced with the awesome problem of studying the very basis of knowledge. Obviously, we shall avoid following this path. Instead we shall adopt certain premises and admit that psychological make-up depends on a number of factors including education, the environment, history, human experience and lifestyle. Neither do we intend to establish the relative order of importance of these factors, but we must recognize nevertheless that there are linkages between them. First, we postulate that there are two possible extremes of behaviour, which for convenience we shall denote as "playing" and "refusing to play".

Playing, in all its forms, involves an actor relative to a system. This was the main contribution of Crozier and Friedberg[8] to political science. Those who decline to play are not hermits, mystics or individuals on the fringe of society, but simply those who prefer to engage in the noble activities of exchanging views, making observations, discussing or criticizing without entering actively into the play. Otherwise there would be few professors. In the final analysis, whether one enters the play or not is a personal choice which everyone must weigh for himself.

This dichotomy between thought and action is not the only dilemma, for even in action there is a range of motives which underlie behaviour. This, then, is our second observation. Among the players there are both strategists and pacifists. Strategists cannot make mistakes without, at the same time, losing their credibility. Throughout history, strategists have been advisors to royalty or governments. But we should not be too restrictive, since strategists are to be found everywhere. They include economists, political scientists, consultants, bureaucrats – in short all those who try, by reason of State, to maximize the benefits and advantages to the State. Strategists are nationalists at heart. Pacifists, on the other hand, seek primarily to be internationalists. Their main concern is not to maximize benefit to the State, but rather to promote, through all possible means, international peace based on equality, respect for social justice and a better distribution of wealth.

Strategists clearly have a wide range of research tools at their disposal. They also benefit from the generosity of government which extends support whenever possible. The research tools employed by strategists include operations research, systems analysis, game theory, meta-games, canonical analysis, and so on. Whether by intent or not, all political science departments produce young, budding strategists. With a curriculum that focuses on the balances of power, and how they can be exploited or contained, it is hardly surprising that the most lively debates occur among political scientists or those trained in sociology, the mother of political science.

Those involved in the play must never play with their eyes closed. Otherwise they are exposed to the risk of bitter defeat. In the military field, a good knowledge of the rules of play is indispensable to a healthy understanding of the laws of deterrence. We shall restrict ourselves to two brief examples. The first concerns the world of 1945, that of the atom, and the second concerns the world of 1983, that of Star Wars. The atom completely revolutionized the rules of play, and nations could not use it in warfare without risking total destruction. They were forced, therefore, to use deterrence as an instrument of competition. Since then the superpowers have sought to rid themselves of this straightjacket which they had blithely donned without being truly aware of its constraints. As for our second example, it is clear that the embryo of Star Wars is in full gestation. The United States is unilaterally trying to impose on the Soviets a new definition of the nuclear rules of play. We are, however, still far from the impregnable and invincible fortresses that tomorrow's technology promises.

Irrespective of his field of study, the strategist, who is today's somewhat more scientific counterpart of the sorcerer and soothsayer of yesteryear, should in time be able to recognize at what point and to what extent the dynamics of a system shifts from a familiar earlier world to a relatively unknown new world.

Once the two extremes which motivate the players have been identified, what can be said of their origins? Space does not permit a detailed in-depth examination of this problem. We shall, therefore, treat the subject in the briefest way.

Two fundamental trends are at the origin of pacifism. The first is clearly the rejection of violence as a means of resolving conflict. If one is optimistic, he can believe that history is full of promise for the future. The second trend is the direct heir of revolutionary and egalitarian Christianity which preaches the sharing of earthly resources. The laity had found a new formula: social justice. The pacifists, therefore, had to right the wrongs of society, naturally in a non-violent way, and correct the incredible deviations of the system. In defence of the pacifists it should be said that the capabilities of societies to settle their differences in a peaceful way are greater today than in the past. People are now beginning to detest violence. From watching television it is not clear whether, in today's society, violence is repressed rather than restrained. Fortunately, psychologists tell us that it is all a matter of education ...

The origins of strategy can be retraced just as easily. Its two roots are diametrically opposed to those of pacifism. Strategy is not of Christian origin. It is the direct result of positivism, and derives from the world of empiricism and scientific enquiry. Its importance today is comparable to that of economics when it first appeared in the 18th Century. The second root of strategy lies in the industrial revolution, which continues to nourish it even today. Admittedly, the terminology has changed a little. Nowadays, the terms post-industrial revolution and technetronic revolution are used. For some, however, the changes and the rates at which they occur are concertinaed at such a speed that technology has become the only driver of their thinking. They live and think like "PacMan" – that marvellous electronic bug –

incapable of casting a glance on history. Such people are incorrigibly myopic.

This leads us to the third issue: what can be expected to occur between the two antagonistic extremes of action, and how can negotiation strategies be developed based on the underlying premises? Specifically, how can negotiation models be developed that can shed even a little light on disarmament and arms control. In this regard, thank God, insects are still of precious assistance. If we accept the basis of the foregoing analysis, two extremes of attitude can be clearly distinguished, namely, cooperation and non-cooperation. These two extremes, considered in their pure state, correspond to the following two models:

1   the warlike ant (non-cooperation);
2   the peaceful bee (cooperation).

The first strategy, that of non-cooperation, implies that one endeavours to cede nothing that belongs to him, and attempts to obtain things not yet in his possession. In other words, it is a question of maximizing gains and minimizing losses. The economists use the word monopsony to describe this situation where one player has a monopoly over one commodity. The second strategy, that of cooperation, implies that the player who practises it seeks cooperation first and foremost before any other objective. Here again, economics is of considerable help. This situation is similar to that which ideally should exist between a parent company and its subsidiaries. In the real world it is rare to encounter either one of these two situations. Most often the situation is characterized by mixed strategies, namely:

3   the hybrid of bee and ant (cooperation and non-cooperation).

In other words, the player behaves simultaneously as a bee and as an ant. Under this scenario we can define three subgroups: little cooperation and little conflict; a lot of cooperation and little conflict; or little cooperation and a lot of conflict.

There are, however, two other patterns that are just as fundamental and that logic tends to forget, because the intellect does not pay sufficient attention to what Hegel calls the cunning of reason. They are:

4   the ant that plays at being a bee (non-cooperation disguised as cooperation); and

5   the bee that plays at being an ant (strategy of reverse cooperation which corresponds, in fact, to a strategy of non-cooperation).

The reader will quickly recognize that these two stratagems correspond to pure exercises in propaganda.

The Baruch Plan on control of atomic energy presented by the United States to the UN in January 1946 is a good example of a strategy of non-cooperation presented in the guise of a strategy of cooperation. In effect, the Americans said to the Soviets: "What is ours is yours" (strategy of sharing or cooperation), "on condition, of course, that all your industries pass under international control" (implying "our" control). Here we have an example of the warlike ant going into action, for the Americans were basically saying "once we know the full extent of your capabilities, we shall supply you with the minimum of information and nuclear secrets that you might need". The Soviets, of course, did not take the bait. This caricature of the situation serves to demonstrate the point, but obviously lacks the shades of meaning.

Finally, there are many instances when bees play at being ants. The strategy of negotiation consists of presenting proposals that are more or less acceptable in order to shift the responsibility of refusal to the other. It is really a strategy of non-cooperation, presented with the innocent smile of someone who pretends to be cooperative. The Soviets are past masters of the art of this game. The Americans have also learned a great deal, and in this regard they are now second to none.

These last two patterns are logical inversions. These types of operation are to be found in mathematical proofs which use the technique of *reductio ad absurdum*. Negotiators did not, therefore, invent anything that was not already known by instinct. And to complicate things a little more, it should be noted that various combinations of these scenarios are also possible. Even the analysts occasionally can make neither head nor tail of it, not to mention the negotiators who, more often than not, are taken at their own game.

Aside from these fascinating preoccupations, which are the staple diet of strategists and analysts, there is yet one more fundamental problem. How can reality – what happens, unfolds and is at stake – be distinguished from intention?

Inveterate players know the answer to this question. Napoleon said: "you start, and then you see". That is one approach. After all, it is during the game that one puts his cards upon the table. Situations which at first appear desperate or without solution are suddenly redressed, some contradictions disappear, and then others appear. Such is the nature of life and, incidentally, it also provides for the analyst's livelihood.

Knowing what the other person is thinking distinguishes reflection from action. Historians reflect, sometimes too much, but undoubtedly it is necessary. They have to dissect the records, find all the pertinent documents – sometimes those concerning the wife or the mistress or alternatively the lover or the gigolo – in order to know the underlying motives of the actor or the actress. Reflection is a commendable preoccupation but, in the heat of action, one must act. Ants probably know a great deal on this subject ...

In matters of intention, then, it is normal for historians to display a good deal of wisdom. The situation is always more complex than can be imagined. The strategy of the peaceful bee practised by Chamberlain in 1938 was condemned unanimously by all strategists, because it led the world to disaster. In his defence, Chamberlain could always plead that his intentions were pure. He thought he was saving the peace, and even said so very frankly. Besides, it would probably be inappropriate to expect a true bee to behave like an ant. Khrushchev also said, when presenting a proposal to the UN, "that his hands were clean and his heart was pure". In any negotiation where the parameters of action are frozen, the web of intentions is like a Gordian knot which cannot be untangled. It is only in an action situation that one begins to see in the dark.

The Chinese have solved this age-old problem of intention. This Chapter bears in epigraph a quotation from Confucius. The answer to the problem is of a moral, rather than a scientific, nature. It concerns individual values. For after all, the dance of the ant which plays at being a bee, and of the bee which plays at being an ant, is always of perfect beauty. In both cases, however, it is not perfect goodness. Only the peaceful bee can claim perfect goodness. Alas, policy is not made solely by peaceful bees. In this world, there are many insects.

POLICY COORDINATION BETWEEN THE BEES AND THE ANTS

In principle, policy management is left to the Cabinet or its many committees which are responsible for developing the main guidelines that the Government intends to follow in its foreign relations. Most of the time, policies are defined and formulated by the administrative organizations that are functionally responsible. In the case of security and disarmament, the two main organizations are obviously the Departments of External Affairs and of National Defence.

For reasons of courtesy and discretion, only the period from 1945 to 1965 will be covered here. The period from 1965 to 1985 will be discussed separately in the context of later chapters. During the post-war period, Canadian policy was defined by a handful of individuals. They were few in number, but they formed a quality group. There was no need, therefore, for cumbersome administrative organizations. Communications were easy between New York, Washington and Ottawa. In Ottawa itself, consultations between senior officials of External Affairs, National Defence, the Combined Policy Committee (CPC) – which we shall discuss in depth in Chapter 2 – the Privy Council Office and the Prime Minister's Office were smooth and without difficulty. The creation of the UN Disarmament Commission in 1952 posed, however, the problem of creating administrative organizations capable of conceiving, analyzing and commenting on the various disarmament proposals. It was really from this moment that the problem of coordinating policy between the bees and the ants arose.

We shall not spend too much time describing the administrative structures themselves. After all, they are only empty shells in which people and thinkers work. It is more important to know the reasons for the creation of these organizational structures, the officials that worked in them and the objectives that they were supposed to meet. These issues will be discussed subsequently. We shall restrict ourselves here solely to a description of the organizational structures that existed between 1952 and 1965.

In May 1953, after countless discussions and following a proposal from the Department of External Affairs, the Department of National Defence created a Working Party (WP). This Working Party was responsible for "preparing joint working papers and assisting the Department of External Affairs in matters of disarmament". The Working Party consisted of a representative from each of the three services (Army, Navy, Air Force), a representative from the Defence Research Board (DRB), one or two representatives from the Department of External Affairs and a representative from the Atomic Energy Control Board (AECB). In the event of differences of opinion within the Working Party, the Cabinet Defence Committee was to make the final decision, but the question was first referred to the Joint Chiefs of Staff Committee. The Joint Chiefs of Staff were thus able to review any contentious issue before it was referred to the Cabinet Defence Committee.

In 1956, the Working Party was dissolved and replaced by a series of agreements under the terms of which were created: a Joint Disarmament Committee (JDC), a Joint Disarmament Working Group (JDWG), and the position of Permanent Military Advisor to the Canadian Delegation to the UN.

Representation on the first two organizations was provided by the Department of National Defence, the Department of External Affairs, the Defence Research Board and the Atomic Energy Control Board. The essential difference between the two organizations was the level at which representation was provided. In the case of the first committee, representatives from the Department of National Defence were drawn from the Joint Planning Committee (JPC) which reported directly to the Joint Chiefs of Staff Committee. In the case of the second committee, the military representatives were drawn from the Joint Planning Staff (JPS) which reported directly to the Joint Planning Committee (JPC).

In April 1959, in response to a letter from the Under-Secretary of State for External Affairs, the Chairman of the Joint Chiefs of Staff Committee, General Charles Foulkes, proposed that the two structures created in 1956 be abolished and replaced with a single organization to be known as the Joint Disarmament Working Group.

The position of Permanent Military Advisor was maintained. At this point, the difference between the former committees and the new one was difficult to discern, since the latter had the same representation (the three services, DRB, DEA and AECB). Moreover, the reporting relationship was not really changed, for this Group reported through a coordinator to the Joint Chiefs of Staff Committee. In short, the Department of National Defence wished to constitute a small working group on a non-permanent basis, whose status could be reviewed at any time in the future.

On 21 January 1961, at its 654th meeting, the Joint Chiefs of Staff Committee delegated responsibility for coordinating activities relating to disarmament within the Department of National Defence to the Joint Ballistic Missile Defence Staff (JBMDS). The terminology was obviously peculiar. Even the most obtuse mind would have difficulty with this name. In July 1961, the JBMDS became the Directorate of Strategic Studies (DSS). This organization still functions today, but no longer reports to the Joint Chiefs of Staff Committee.

Immediately following the war, Canadian policy in the Department of External Affairs was coordinated directly through the Office of the Under-Secretary of State. Coordination was first the responsibility of John Starnes, and later of Marcel Cadieux. When Cadieux left the Office of the Under-Secretary to take up new duties within the Personnel Bureau, he continued to concern himself with atomic energy issues. On 17 January 1949, R.G. Riddell of the UN Division proposed that responsibility for these issues should come under the Defence Liaison Division.[9] The Acting Under-Secretary, Escott Reid, agreed to this proposal. In the meantime, the Economic Affairs Division continued to be responsible for sales of uranium abroad.

Shortly afterwards, however, the UN Division became the main administrative unit responsible for developing Canadian policies on disarmament. This was confirmed in a memorandum from the Under-Secretary of State dated 12 January 1953. Since the issues discussed within the UN Disarmament Commission and the Collective Measures Committee had become "primarily political and only military to a small degree", they would come under the UN Division. This situation lasted until 1959, at which time the UN Division tried to acquire responsibility for monitoring sales of uranium abroad. In 1960, enormous pressures were brought to bear to establish an actual Disarmament Division. In this regard, Lieutenant-General E.L.M. Burns won his case. In June 1961, the Disarmament Division was created. Administratively speaking, this Division was just like all the other Divisions of the Department of External Affairs. Its director, however, reported to the Disarmament Advisor to the Government of Canada, in this instance General Burns.

The Lazy Ant

On 13 May 1952, Escott Reid wrote to the Chairman of the Joint Chiefs of Staff to advise him of progress within the UN Disarmament Commission, stating: "we shall shortly have to take a position on several of the issues discussed". On 3 June 1952, Commodore H.E. Rayner replied: "the most appropriate organization for discussing the issues that you have raised is the Joint Planning Committee (JPC)". Until then, there was no problem. Things started to look different, however, on 8 August 1952 when the Department of External Affairs proposed a "New Approach" intended for submission to the Disarmament Commission. That was going too far. One month later, on 9 September 1952, the Joint Planning Committee claimed that it was unable to make an in-depth study of all these issues because, quite simply, the Committee had a full load of work.

The issue of policy coordination, however, remained. How could Canada play a more active role in the disarmament discussions and also obtain good advice on the kind of proposals that should be presented? At its meeting of 6 November 1952, the Joint Planning Committee proposed that an Interdepartmental Committee (IDC) be established. On 11 December 1952, the Deputy Chiefs of the Defence Staff concurred in this proposal. It was ratified on 8 April 1953. On 15 May 1953, the Secretary of State for External Affairs presented a note to the Cabinet Defence Committee recommending the establishment of the said Committee "to facilitate, as necessary, rapid assessment of the political and military merits and of the implications of any proposal" that might be presented to the Disarmament Commission.[10] However, on 28 May 1953, the Chiefs of Staff rejected the proposals of the Deputy Chiefs. There would be no Interdepartmental Committee, but simply a Working Party. The Working Party would be responsible for "preparing joint working documents and assisting the Department of External Affairs on disarmament issues". No explanations for this about face are to be found in the records of either the Department of National Defence or the Department of External Affairs. It remains as a matter of conjecture.

The most plausible theory is that the Chiefs of Staff did not wish to ascribe too much importance to the discussion of disarmament issues. To create an Interdepartmental Committee at the Deputy Minister level would only emphasize the importance of the issue. A simple Working Party would be unobtrusive and would give the military all the necessary lead time to react to any request that it judged unusual. Three things are certain. First, the Armed Forces would do their duty as long as they were required simply to comment on the proposals of others. In this regard, the ant was not overly lazy. Second, when the ant had to be involved in the preparation of Canadian plans it quickly became lazy. Under these circumstances, the poor ant was simply overworked. Third, it felt no need whatsoever to discuss all these trivial details for they could have detrimental effects on the morale of the Armed Forces. The Joint Planning Committee was very clear on this matter in its report of 8 January 1953 to the Chiefs of Staff:

The front pages of Canadian newspapers would feature stories of Canada's disarmament proposals, and on the inside pages would appear the usual recruiting advertisements for the Navy, Army and RCAF. The recruiting campaigns of all services would undoubtedly suffer. Quite apart from recruiting, the morale of the armed services would also suffer if it were felt that the Canadian Government were sponsoring disarmament proposals. To overcome a drop in recruiting, it might be necessary for the services to spend more money on recruiting campaigns and even raise the rates of pay in order to maintain the forces required to fulfil NATO commitments.

The least that can be said is that this reasoning was disarmingly simple. In a memorandum of 9 January 1953 to his superior M.H.

Wershof, John G.H. Halstead, attached at the time to the Defence Liaison Division, tried to keep both parties happy. Essentially, he stated that it was unfortunate that the question of consultation procedures had been raised at the very time that Canada wished to present a "New Approach" to the Disarmament Commission. "Although purely coincidental", he added, "it gave the impression that we were satisfied with their collaboration [the Armed Forces] up to now, but that we were dissatisfied with their comments on a Canadian draft proposal." "It would perhaps be wise at this stage", Halstead concluded, "not to push things much further."

In his memorandum of 21 April 1953[11], Morley Scott of the UN Division spelled it out. "Our attempt", he said, "to bring the Canadian Forces to play a greater role in disarmament has generally failed. Confronted simultaneously with a New Approach and a New Machine [consultation procedure], the military disposed of the former by deciding that it could not be considered unless the New Machine was set up, and disposed, for sometime, of the New Machine by resolving to consider its implications." Concerning the New Approach, Scott stated that the French liked it well enough, but that the British and American comments were clearly discouraging. "Now that we have asked the Armed Forces to give us their comments on the New Approach", Scott continued, "we would be seen in a bad light if we did not send them the comments that we have received from allied countries." "The difficulty", Scott concluded, "would be to explain why we had not done so earlier."

Actually, Scott had no cause for concern. Other allied forces had already advised the Department of National Defence of their views on the Canadian "New Approach". In defence of the Joint Chiefs of Staff Committee, it should be noted that, at the time, the war was raging in Korea, and Washington was pressing Canada to send a combat brigade to Europe. About one year after the proposal to establish improved consultation between the two departments, the meeting of the Working Party finally took place on 23 June 1953. Three days later, Wershof reported to the Under-Secretary that the meeting went "very well".

The Absent-Minded Bee

Roughly one year later, on 4 November 1954, Harry Jay of the UN Division, in a memorandum to his superior Saul Rae[12], stated that neither William Barton (then the Atomic Energy representative) nor Geoff Bruce (Joint Planning Committee) were satisfied with the way that work was progressing in the Working Party:

Both John Holmes and M.H. Wershof have already noted in the margin of one of Rae's memoranda dated 9 April, that it would undoubtedly be desirable to establish a coordinating committee at a much higher level. I strongly doubt whether such a solution would be more satisfactory, for the problem is to bring these people to demonstrate much greater technical expertise on political issues.

In any event, a whole series of questions were to be submitted to this Working Party as a result of all the discussions within the Disarmament Commission.

It should be remembered also that, in 1955, the "Geneva spirit" led to cautious optimism for East-West *rapprochement* on a number of contentious issues. Western proposals to the UN were being tabled in rapid succession. On 12 January 1956, the Under-Secretary of State resumed discussions with General Foulkes on the question of coordinating disarmament policies between the two departments. Jules Léger insisted on the "need for increased cooperation on a continuing basis ... through the establishment of joint study groups or other groups".[13] Léger felt, moreover, that it would be desirable to obtain a "positive contribution" from these groups in order to facilitate the work of the Canadian Delegates to the UN. On 19 January, General Foulkes politely replied to the effect that disarmament issues were indeed of great importance. He insisted, however, "that any organization which is set up to deal with disarmament questions be within the framework of the present Chiefs of Staff organization".[14] An unsigned note in the margin read as follows: "I don't agree in principle." Who was deceiving whom? Was it simply a way for the Chairman of the Joint Chiefs of Staff to reaffirm his role on these issues?

Foulkes' letter expressed the position held by the Department of National Defence on these problems very well. First, as Foulkes noted, the Joint Planning Committee (JPC) was responsible for policy recommendations to the Chiefs of the three services. The Committee could, therefore, recommend what "our policy should be". Second, the kind of continuity sought in the consultations could be provided by the Joint Planning Staff. After all, that was its role. Foulkes could hardly have expected to be taken seriously. It was about as credible as if Dr. Morgentaler were suddenly to lay claim to the status of advisor to the pro-life organizations. Finally, Foulkes suggested that disarmament issues should first be channelled through the Department of National Defence to the Joint Planning Staff, and then through the Military Advisor to the Canadian Delegation.

The hierarchical relationship between the two groups was thus affirmed. If the problem were purely technical, the JPS would deal with it. On the other hand, if the problem fell outside the traditional political bounds, it would be referred to the Joint Planning Committee. This view was confirmed by the JPS at its meeting of 6 February 1956, and by the JPC at its meeting of 14 February 1956. Meanwhile, George Ignatieff, who was the Acting Director of the Defence Liaison Division, tried to obtain some additional clarification. In a letter to John W. Holmes, dated 30 January 1956, Ignatieff reported on the four points that had been discussed with the JPC that same day:

a   that special representation would be added to both the Joint Planning Staff and the Joint Planning Committee when they were considering disarmament questions and, in addition, that our representations would be altered on these bodies when they were considering disarmament matters; I was assured by Brigadier Rothschild that this was quite acceptable to the Chiefs of Staff;

b   that the agenda of these bodies should be so arranged as to permit proper consideration of disarmament questions; this was also agreed;

c   that as far as the point of contact on disarmament matters is concerned, Brigadier Rothschild said that he preferred that it be either himself or Captain Lucas on the understanding that advice on the military aspects of disarmament had to be within the Chiefs of Staff framework and that he or Lucas would be most likely to get quick reactions from the Chiefs of Staff;

d   that as regards the provision of a Permanent Military Advisor, the consensus was that it seemed to involve a full-time job.

Ignatieff continued that Brigadier Rothschild had assured him that "nothing was rigid except that the advice on the military implications of disarmament had to be put forward on the authority of the Chiefs of Staff as the military advisors to the Government".[15]

The Department of External Affairs obviously had no desire to engage in parochial disputes. After all, it could not start to question the mandate of every department. Clearly, the main role of the Department of National Defence was to advise Government on matters of military security. It was also patently obvious that the Department of External Affairs was responsible for formulating Canadian policy in the various fora of negotiation around the world. In his wisdom, therefore, Jules Léger did not pursue the issue. Four objectives were of foremost importance to him: to force the Department of National Defence to study these problems; to broaden DND's horizons by ensuring adequate representation from other departments (Atomic Energy of Canada, the Defence Research Board, External Affairs); to bring in various experts depending on the nature of the discussions; and, finally, to have an input in establishing agendas for the discussions.

Under-Secretary of State Léger informed General Foulkes, in a letter dated 16 February 1956, that he was largely in agreement with his proposals. Léger also stated that he appreciated the offer of the Department of National Defence to provide a Permanent Military Advisor to the Canadian Delegation, and added, somewhat candidly:

You will be interested to know that, in addition to making arrangements for participating in the work of the JPS and the JPC on disarmament, we have appointed Saul Rae as Special Advisor on Disarmament ... Geoffrey S. Murray, advisor to Canada's Permanent Mission in New York, will also participate in the preliminary discussions that will be held in London between the four Western powers. It would, therefore, be useful if your Permanent Military Advisor could be present at these discussions before the talks open.

In one fell swoop the hierarchies were re-established and the Department of External Affairs recovered its leadership role for disarmament proposals. In public administration it is sometimes necessary to create positions and, in the process of creating them, to eliminate others. It fell to naval Captain M.H. Ellis, Director of Naval Intelligence in Halifax, to be named the first Permanent Military Advisor to the Canadian Delegation to the Disarmament Commission.

The deliberate absent-mindedness of the bee left, on paper, a totally confused situation. After countless revisions the terms of reference of the committees were finally defined. In its report of 20 April 1956 to the Chiefs of Staff Committee[16], the JPC stated that the 1952 Working Party (WP) was henceforth dissolved and replaced by the Joint Disarmament Committee (JDC) having the following mandate: "The Joint Disarmament Committee will be responsible to the Chiefs of Staff Committee for reviewing and recommending Canadian policy on disarmament." The Joint Disarmament Working Group (JDWG) was responsible to the Joint Disarmament Committee for examining these problems on a continuing basis. It was also responsible for responding to requests from the Military Advisor if they fell within the general framework of previously defined policy. Finally, the Permanent Military Advisor was responsible for providing advice to the Canadian Delegation. He was an ex-officio member of the Joint Disarmament Working Group. Any extraordinary issue was to be referred to the Chiefs of Staff Committee.

The terms of reference of the Joint Disarmament Committee were evidently problematic. Whether one liked it or not, they gave the impression that it was the responsibility of the Chiefs of Staff Committee to define Canadian policy on disarmament. Obviously, responsibilities in this area can only be shared. In theory, the ant emerged victorious from this battle with the absent-minded bee. Actually, the Department of External Affairs continued, no less, to act as it saw fit. The victory of the Department of National Defence remained unreal and transitory, particularly when a centralizing bee appeared on the scene a few years later.

The Centralizing Bee

In the late 1950s, the issue of policy coordination in the area of disarmament came to the fore both within the Department of External Affairs itself and in its interaction with the Department of National Defence. Other departments became increasingly involved since atomic energy again moved into the spotlight on the international scene. The questions were twofold: how to use nuclear energy for peaceful purposes, and how to allow the North Atlantic Treaty Organization (NATO) to modernize its tactical nuclear forces in order to neutralize the crushing superiority of the conventional forces of the Warsaw Pact? The turning point was reached in the mid-1950s: in 1955 the first tactical nuclear weapons were introduced into NATO's arsenals and, in 1957, the International Atomic Energy Agency (IAEA) was created in Vienna.

Scientific cooperation in the field of nuclear energy had assumed many complex dimensions. Amongst them were the issues of increased cooperation in regional organizations such as the European Atomic Energy Community (EAEC or EURATOM) and the European Nuclear Research Centre (CERN), the development of nuclear power stations to produce electrical energy, the use of nuclear explosions for industrial purposes (for example, oil extraction from the Athabaska tar sands), and the network to be established between various organizations to ensure much closer liaison between science and policy. In the fall of 1958, the British created an administrative service responsible for studying the dual problems of disarmament and atomic energy.

In Canada, Jack A. McCordick, liaison officer with the UN Division, proposed in a memorandum to John W. Holmes dated 17 February 1959[17] that a division for studying interrelated questions of science and disarmament (Science Liaison and Disarmament Division) be established. In July 1957, Arnold Smith in London had already informed McCordick of actions that the British intended to take in this regard. In February 1959, George Ignatieff provided McCordick with an update of Smith's report. In his memorandum to Holmes of 17 February, McCordick wrote:

I began thinking about these matters early in 1957 from the vantage point of the Defence Liaison Division. A circumstance which stimulated my interest was my attendance at a couple of meetings of the Interdepartmental Committee on the Economic Aspects of Defence, which were called to discuss Canada's policy on the export of uranium ... At these meetings there was a good deal of reference to "clean and dirty nuclear weapons" and "strategic and tactical nuclear weapons", made with an air of understanding by officials who apparently really only had vague ideas of exactly what they were talking about on these specific points ... As far as our own Department was concerned, I felt that there were important gaps in our knowledge ... The increase of appreciation of science and technology ... is not the principal reason for my suggesting some organizational changes in the Department. Indeed, the foregoing is by way of a preamble to the nub of the matter which is a functional need. This need, which by itself would, in my opinion, justify an increase in staff and a reorganization of responsibilities, concerns our handling of several important subjects: disarmament, outer space and atomic energy ... Arthur Campbell has prepared a draft memorandum with which I am in substantial agreement, although I would modify some details. I attach a copy of this draft.

It is not enough for most of us nowadays to feel that we qualify for the avant-garde and have the *Zeitgeist* by the tail if we subscribe to *Encounter*, know which end of an abstract painting is 'up', and almost manage a convincingly positive reaction to CBC première performances of discordant new compositions ...

It seems to me that we should consider setting up before long a new Division which might be called the 'Science Liaison and Disarmament Division' ... I would suggest an initial establishment of five or six officers.

For his part, Arthur Campbell, in his memorandum of 13 February, proposed the creation of a separate Disarmament Division, using the same kinds of argument as those of McCordick. Campbell, however, had in mind an organization similar to that which had just been established in Washington for integrating issues of disarmament and nuclear energy, and which reported directly to a Special Assistant to the State Department. The difference between the two proposals was, therefore, rather slim. McCordick said essentially that issues of disarmament and space belonged to the UN Division, while those of atomic energy belonged to the Economic Affairs Division. It was a matter, therefore, of integrating all of these dimensions under the umbrella of science and technology, and of establishing a distinct section on questions of disarmament within the UN Division. Campbell argued essentially for the establishment of a Disarmament Division separate from the UN Division. The Division would be directed by an official having the rank of ambassador. This question was not without importance for it reappeared abruptly several years later when, following the personal recommendation of John W. Holmes, General E.L.M. Burns was nominated to head the Canadian Delegation within the Ten-Nation Committee on Disarmament.

The following hand-written note by John W. Holmes appears in the margin of McCordick's memorandum: "I think we should proceed to put forward these proposals immediately." In March 1959, it was decided to implement these new proposals effective 1 April 1959. In this way, the embryo of the Science Liaison and Disarmament Division was formed within the UN Division.

At about the same time, on 13 February 1959, the Under-Secretary of State, Norman A. Robertson, resumed discussions with General Foulkes. Essentially he asked General Foulkes to ensure that questions of disarmament would be discussed on an on-going basis. In a letter from the Permanent Military Advisor to the Chairman of the Joint Chiefs of Staff dated 11 March 1959, Squadron Leader R.J. Mitchell expressed the view that there was no need to create a permanent group since it would have little on its agenda. Mitchell thought, however, that there was a considerable number of subjects that the Chiefs of Staff Committee could study, for instance nuclear-free zones, space, bacteriological and chemical weapons and the general problem of force reduction. On 22 April 1959, Foulkes replied to Robertson proposing the dissolution of two groups created in 1956, the JDC and the JDWG. According to Foulkes, this organization "had not been very effective because of more pressing planning problems".[18] Repeating broadly the arguments that he had made to Léger in 1956, Foulkes recognized "the important nature of any disarmament proposal", and consequently proposed the establishment of a Disarmament Working Group (DWG).

Nowhere did he state why this new group would have any more time than the two previous groups constituted in 1956 (the JDC and the JDWG) to work on problems that it was required to study. In addition, Foulkes proposed that the Permanent Military Advisor be physically located in the offices of the Department of External Affairs where, in Foulkes' view, most of the proposals originated. In other words, Foulkes politely said to Robertson that the Department of National Defence had many other fish to fry and that it was up to the Department of External Affairs to do the bulk of the work.

Top-ranking civil servant Robertson was not deterred. On 12 June 1959, Robertson wrote to Foulkes:

The main purpose of my letter of February 13 was to raise the question whether a group in the Department of National Defence might have responsibility for initiating studies in areas which might be broadly designated in advance, in addition to providing answers from time to time to problems raised by this Department. As I read the draft terms of reference for the Joint Disarmament Working Group attached to your letter, it seems to me that the emphasis is still upon providing responses to specific questions, which would essentially be a continuation of the existing arrangements.

Would you be prepared to consider including in the terms of reference a responsibility to initiate technical and military studies in the disarmament field especially in methods of verification, inspection and other forms of control?

Should some such revision of the terms of reference of the JDWG commend itself to you, it might be desirable to consider whether "permanent military advisor" would be the most apt designation for the concerned officer of your staff. What I have in mind is that he would be the logical person to propose to the JDWG, after consultation as appropriate with this Department, the areas and priorities of the studies to be made ... It will be apparent that if the JDWG is to operate, even on a trial basis along the lines I have suggested, the "disarmament staff officer" is likely to devote the greater part of his time to the coordination and stimulation of the studies under way within the Department of National Defence.

In short, the Department of National Defence was cordially invited to set to work so as to ensure that the officer assigned to disarmament satisfactorily completed his assigned tasks. The new terminology proposed by Robertson (JDWP) was obviously aimed at making Foulkes understand clearly that the Department of External Affairs was first and foremost responsible for disarmament issues but that this question could not be studied without the assistance of the Department of National Defence, particularly when technical issues were involved.

In order to simplify matters for the reader, it may be useful at this point to summarize briefly all the changes that occurred in the coordination mechanisms between 1952 and 1959. In May 1953, a Working Party (WP) was created which reported to the Cabinet Defence Committee through the Joint Chiefs of Staff Committee. The WP was dissolved in 1956 and replaced with two other committees, the Joint

Disarmament Committee (JDC) consisting of representatives of the Joint Planning Committee (JPC), and the Joint Disarmament Working Group (JDWG) consisting of representatives of the Joint Planning Staff (JPS). In 1959, General Foulkes proposed that the JDC and the JDWG be abolished and replaced with a single committee, the Disarmament Working Group (DWG), which Robertson in turn called the Joint Disarmament Working Party (JDWP). This was little more than a play on words for, starting in 1959, the coordinating group between the two departments continued to be known as the Joint Disarmament Working Group (JDWG). In 1960, the Department of National Defence created the Joint Ballistic Missile Defence Staff (JBMDS) which, in 1961, was made responsible for the coordination of disarmament issues within the Department. Thus, we are left with five different acronyms (WP, JDC, JDWG, DWG and JDWP) to designate a single interdepartmental committee for coordinating arms control and disarmament issues.

The approach of the Canadian Chiefs of Staff from 1952 to 1959 thus consisted of establishing and dissolving committee after committee, claiming that pressing requirements prevented them from embarking on important disarmament issues and refusing, for all practical purposes, to follow up on the idea of constituting a permanent group for consultations between the two departments. There were exceptions to this rule, as we shall see in the chapters that follow. For instance, the questions concerning prevention of surprise attack or of the Arctic becoming an "open skies" zone, that is, open to mutual inspections, were the subjects of countless studies within the military establishment. DND did not refuse totally to undertake studies, but rather was strongly selective concerning the issues that the Department was prepared to study. This attitude started to change during 1959 and 1960. At about that time, the Department of National Defence no longer had a choice. The epoch of the lazy ant had passed. The Department of National Defence could always continue to "put spanners in the works" *vis-à-vis* the Department of External Affairs, but it was not in DND's interests to act in that way, for the simple reason that circumstances had changed.

In mid-1959, Sydney Smith died prematurely, and was replaced by Howard Green. Within the Department of National Defence – in October 1960 – Douglas Harkness replaced General George R. Pearkes who had been named Lieutenant Governor of British Columbia. Along with Harkness and Green came the shadowy seeds of discord that led in 1963 to the fall of the Diefenbaker Government which was elected in 1958. Howard Green was "Mr. Disarmament". For Green, Canada had "only friends and no enemies". Stursberg describes him as "a tall spare man, amiable and at the same time austere, a non-drinker and non-smoker with a strong sense of integrity".[19] It would be tempting to say that he had too many good qualities for his time. Harkness was "Mr. Decision". He abhorred never-ending discussions in Cabinet and the multitude of meetings imposed by Diefenbaker on everything and nothing. On important issues " ... we would have two Cabinet meetings a day almost continuously for a week or more".[20] Green wanted to force the decision for a non-nuclear Canada; Harkness for a nuclear Canada. The Department of National Defence was supported by Robert Bryce, a valued advisor to Diefenbaker and a number of previous governments. Green had the support of a solid Under-Secretary of State, Norman A. Robertson.[21] At this stage, the only thing at stake was to win the support of Prime Minister Diefenbaker. Knowing the obstinacy and the fierce tenacity of the legendary Diefenbaker, that were equalled only by his strong taste for procrastination, it is not difficult to anticipate the events that were to follow ...

Important discussions took place in November 1959 between Foulkes, Robertson and Burns. One months later, General E.L.M. Burns was named Disarmament Advisor to the Government of Canada. And on 11 March 1960, General Burns was accredited by the Foreign Minister in London, Selwyn Lloyd[22], as Head of the Canadian Delegation to the Ten-Nation Disarmament Committee in Geneva. This accreditation by London obviously stemmed from the fact that Great Britain was one of the five founding nations of the Ten-Nation Committee.

In Ottawa, things took an urgent turn. The Department of National Defence recognized that unless it gave its support to the Department of External Affairs it could be completely by-passed. On 4 December 1959, General Foulkes' assistant, Air Commodore R.C. Weston, wrote to J.A. McCordick, Director of the UN Division:

It is my understanding that, in recent informal discussions between Mr. Robertson, General Burns and General Foulkes, it was agreed that this Department would undertake to assist in preliminary study of such disarmament questions as your Department may wish to raise at this stage ... For this purpose it has been decided to make available at this time a small staff headed by Brigadier D.A.G. Waldock, in lieu of reactivating the Joint Disarmament Working Group.[23]

The Department of External Affairs thus obtained what it had fought for since 1952: the constitution of a working group on disarmament in the Department of National Defence. DND nevertheless held fast, for Weston terminated his letter by talking of a "temporary" working group on disarmament whose mandate could be reviewed from time to time. With this proviso, the Department of National Defence cautiously embarked on the path towards studying disarmament.

Strictly speaking, these developments settled the controversy that had raged between the two departments concerning the decision-making structures. In the Department of External Affairs, however, the need for reform was felt. The Department had to define the relative importance of the Canadian Delegation in Geneva and its terms of reference. It fell upon Green to deal with the first task, and upon Burns to deal with the second.

On 8 December 1959, Robertson sent Minister Green a memorandum on the "appropriate" organization for the Permanent Delegation to Geneva.[24] It stated that, in the past, the Delegates to the various fora for negotiation had been "borrowed" from various organizations. Thus, for the Disarmament Commission and its Subcommittee, Canada's Delegates had been drawn from the Permanent Mission in New York, from the High Commission in London, from the Canadian embassies in Moscow and Bonn or from other Missions in Europe. The same procedure had been followed for Canadian participation in the Conference of Experts on Methods of Detecting Nuclear Explosions in 1958, and in the Conference of Experts on Surprise Attack. Robertson judged that it was time to end this "borrowing of officers" since "their regular functions have not been properly executed." He proposed, therefore, to provide the Geneva Delegation with "an organization which can function effectively over an extended period."

That same day, Green sent a memorandum to Cabinet reflecting on the *ad hoc* organization that had previously existed. In order to ensure better continuity and operation of the Geneva Delegation, Green proposed to enlarge this Delegation to fifteen members[25] at an annual cost of 150,000 dollars. This proposal was ratified by Cabinet.

The remaining problem concerned the links and the hierarchy that should exist between the Geneva Delegation, the Disarmament Section in Ottawa which, it will be recalled, formed part of the UN Division, and General Burns himself. The centralizing bee was none other than General Burns. It took him over a year and a half to realise his objectives. A former military career officer, General Burns was born in Westmount on 17 June 1897. He carried arms during the First World War and commanded the 5th Canadian tank division in Italy during the Second World War, for which he won the

Distinguished Service Order of the British Empire in 1944. He subsequently won fame as the first Commander of the UN Emergency Force (UNEF) in Suez in 1956. Writer, soldier, scholar, negotiator and bureaucrat, General Eedson Louis Millard Burns passed away on 13 September 1985, at the age of 88. His much-awaited official biography is being written by Professor Michael Tucker of Mount Allison University.

The nomination of Burns as Disarmament Advisor to the Government of Canada in March 1960 coincided with the opening of the Ten-Nation Committee talks in Geneva. Unfortunately, the talks were of short duration. The U-2 incident in May 1960 caused the Paris Summit to be aborted. In June 1960, the five Eastern European Delegations withdrew from the Ten-Nation Committee. It was only with the opening of the Conference of the Eighteen-Nation Committee on Disarmament in March 1962 that East-West multilateral negotiations resumed. The interruption of the work of the Ten-Nation Committee did not prevent the UN General Assembly from playing a very active role in disarmament throughout 1961. Some resolutions which were supported by Canada caused a serious rift to develop between the Departments of National Defence and of External Affairs. This aspect will be discussed below.

In July 1960, Burns fought to keep his disarmament team "intact". He deplored the nomination of Campbell to New Delhi, and insisted on having public servants experienced in disarmament join his team. On 23 November 1960, Burns told Robertson of his desire for some major changes, specifically the establishment of a separate Disarmament Division. In his memorandum of 6 December 1960 to Green, Robertson wrote:

General Burns has suggested that, in preparation for future negotiations on disarmament, the Department should establish a separate Disarmament Division which would come under his direction when he was in Ottawa.

At this time it is very difficult to forecast what the future course of disarmament negotiations may be ... No decision is likely to be reached on any of these matters until the new United States Administration is firmly installed. In all these circumstances, the Department should be quite capable of dealing with disarmament questions with the existing organization in the United Nations Division.

At the same time, it might be useful to make a start on the kind of studies which General Burns has in mind. My thought is that in the period following the current meetings of the Assembly, General Burns might wish to give further direction to the studies carried out in the Department of National Defence. He might also suggest some lines of approach to officers in the Disarmament Section of the United Nations Division.

I recommend that no further action be taken for the time being on the suggestion made by General Burns. We might review the situation early in the new year. If you agree, I propose to reply to General Burns in the sense of this memorandum.[26]

In the margin of this memorandum, Green wrote "O.K.". Burns was not discouraged, since he had the support of his Minister. He returned to the attack in a letter to Robertson dated 23 January 1961.[27] Burns reported on his visit to Washington and recounted his discussions with McCloy on the importance of the Arms Control and Disarmament Agency (ACDA). He mentioned that ACDA was thinking of increasing the number of public servants responsible for studies on disarmament from 40 to 90. Burns insisted that unless the Disarmament Division was well staffed, Canada would be incapable "of developing healthy policies on defence, security and disarmament in coordination with other government departments". "We shall also be unable", he added, "to make specific contributions to disarmament proposals unless such a priority is reflected in our organization and personnel."

In a lengthy memorandum attached to this letter, Burns specified the functions that this organization should undertake:

The function of the Division would be to study and prepare, for the Minister's information or decision, matters relating to Canada's disarmament policy; to prepare instructions for and receive reports from negotiating missions; to correlate questions of disarmament policy with other departmental divisions and, with the Department of National Defence and other departments concerned, to be a central point for disarmament information; to coordinate any Canadian research on disarmament; to prepare briefs for ministerial statements for answers to parliamentary questions; to prepare, in cooperation with the Information Division, material on disarmament and Canada's policy relating thereto for the information of the public; and to appoint representatives at conferences and seminars on disarmament, etc.

In the event of a difference of opinion ... between the proposed Disarmament Division and other divisions of the Department coordination should be effected at the Under-Secretary level ... Coordination with the Department of National Defence on disarmament matters, when agreement is not reached by direct conversation, should be at the Privy Council level.

The objectives of General Burns were clear. He wanted to establish a Disarmament Division with a high political profile that would be well staffed and would have the capability of formulating broad policies on disarmament, security and defence. In the event of conflicting objectives between the two departments, the Privy Council would intervene. That was asking a great deal, given that Canada's system of government is parliamentary rather than presidential. In the United States, the National Security Council (NSC) fulfils these functions. Unfortunately, this organization has had a rather disastrous history in contributing to u.s. foreign policy development, "Irangate" being only one of the most publicized of the whole dark series. The brilliant contribution of ACDA was short-lived. Within the space of a few short years, the Agency was discredited by a succession of u.s. presidents.

General Burns' memorandum did, however, have one saving grace, in that it served to focus attention on a problem that, until then, had never been resolved to anyone's satisfaction. A little later, on 25 April 1961, Burns commented on the disarmament organization proposals prepared by George Ignatieff:

I am sorry that I must disagree rather emphatically with your organization proposals ...

In order to follow a single and effective disarmament policy, there should be one person or organ responsible for knowing what this policy is and seeing that all measures initiated by this Department are consistent with the policy on this subject. It is an elementary tenet of good organization that responsibility for any specific kind of action should be clearly defined and allocated to one person or organ, not spread among several.

In your proposed organization, the Disarmament Advisor, as far as I can see, has no function or responsibility except to "initiate studies". The responsibility for initiating instructions to the Canadian Representative on NATO in regard of disarmament is given to the Defence Liaison Division, and instructions to the Canadian Representative in the United Nations is made the responsibility of the United Nations Division. It is true that these divisions are supposed to "consult" the Disarmament Advisor. However, if it is desired to maintain consistency in Canadian disarmament policy, suggestions for action concerning disarmament to be taken by the Canadian Representatives to NATO, the United Nations or by other missions, should be drafted in the first place in a central Disarmament Division and pushed to the appropriate division of the Department for despatch to the intended recipient. Of course, the other divisions concerned could refer the drafts back to the Disarmament Advisor with suggestions for changes, or a redraft as they might see fit ...

Instructions from the Minister in regard to action to be taken on disarmament matters should come down through the Under-Secretary to my office ...

With regard to the answering of letters and preparation of statements, answers to questions in the House, I would feel that eventually this also should be the responsibility of the Disarmament Division or group, but until a suitable officer to cope with this duty can be found, I would agree for this work to continue in the UN Division. I should, however, like to be consulted in regard to any statements to be made or answers to questions in the House.[28]

Following a meeting between Burns, Ignatieff and the other directors of the divisions concerned, a working document prepared by E.W.T. Gill and dated 1 June 1961 was sent to the office of Under-Secretary Robertson. It proposed that responsibility for nuclear weapons tests[29] and disarmament issues be transferred from the UN Division to the Disarmament Division, and that subsequently responsibility for arms export issues and atomic energy safeguards be transferred from the Economic Division to the Disarmament Division.

The responsibilities of the Disarmament Division included those mentioned above and listed in an appendix to the letter from Burns to Robertson of 23 January 1961. In addition, the Disarmament Division would be responsible for assisting the Disarmament Advisor in the exercise of his duties. This latter responsibility was justified in light of two basic options mentioned in the introduction of the working document prepared by E.W.T. Gill:

• One possibility is to designate the unit as "Office of the Disarmament Advisor" or "Disarmament Delegation". In this case the Disarmament Advisor would be the working head of the unit.
• Another alternative is to set up a Disarmament Division headed by the senior officer in the Disarmament Advisor's staff which would be responsible to the Disarmament Advisor but which would in other respects function as an ordinary Division. This second option would appear to have more merit than the first.

Concerning coordination between the various departmental divisions, the Advisor would report to the Under-Secretary through Ignatieff, who had been specifically designated by the Under-Secretary. As for coordination with other departments, an Interdepartmental Committee would be formed which would report to the Clerk of the Privy Council. This Committee would be made up of representatives from the Departments of National Defence, External Affairs, Finance and Defence Production. The new organization was to become operational on 1 June 1961.

Burns, the good general that he was, won on all fronts. He obtained everything that he had wanted. The support of Green was clearly indispensable to Burns although there is no reference to this in any of the records that we consulted. At first, Robertson did not see the usefulness of creating a separate Disarmament Division, and Ignatieff was tasked to develop a new organizational proposal, which was subsequently torn to shreds by Burns. Finally, Ignatieff was appointed as the responsible person through whom Burns would report to the Under-Secretary. Five months later, on 22 November 1961, the new Director of the Disarmament Division, K.D. McIlwraith, sent a brief report[30] to Burns on progress in studies undertaken within his division. These studies concerned:

1   Prevention of Further Dissemination of Nuclear Weapons.
2   Biological, Chemical and Radiological Warfare.
3   A Nuclear-free Zone in Europe.
4   Control of Rocket Testing and Space Vehicles.
5   Relationship between Conventional Armament Reduction and Military Manpower Reduction.
6   First-Stage Reduction of Long-Range Weapon Delivery Systems.
7   Methods of Exercising Control over Strategic Vehicles.
8   Possible Canadian Membership in a Subcommittee for Studies on Nuclear "Cut-Off".
9   Peacekeeping Machinery.
10 Character of Top Executive Echelon of the International Disarmament Organization (IDO).
11 Control of Traffic in Armaments.
12 Forecast of Attitude of "Neutral" UN Members on Items 9 & 10.

The centralizing bee clearly had a lot on its plate; enough, in fact, to keep several departments busy at once – the main one being the Department of National Defence.

The Ant Goes to War

Diefenbaker rose to power in 1957 as leader of a minority government. His hour of glory came in 1958 when his government was re-elected with an overwhelming majority. He was a colourful, fierce, impulsive individual, an assailant of the superpowers and a defender of minorities. Diefenbaker was close to the people and distrustful of the powers of others. He disappeared from the political scene, betrayed and abandoned by his own, incapable of resolving the great policy contradictions of his time.

His biographer, Munro, states that he never agreed with John F. Kennedy[31], but Granatstein gives a different impression.[32] The first "JFK-Dief" meeting was marvellous, but the others were disastrous. At a Cabinet meeting on 6 December 1960, the glaring and impossible legacy of the contradictions in his policy came to light. It was decided:

1   That the Canadian Delegation at the United Nations should vote in favour of the "Irish Resolution" ... along the lines suggested by the Secretary of State for External Affairs, but with the last sentence changed to read: "If, however, there is no significant progress in this field in the immediate future we will reconsider our position on the temporary measures which are proposed in this resolution".

2   That only the Prime Minister should make public statements regarding Canadian policy in respect of nuclear weapons ... other Ministers should, when it is necessary to refer to Canadian policy in these matters, quote the Prime Minister or use the same wording.

3   That discussions (or "negotiations") with the u.s. Government concerning arrangements for the essential acquisition of nuclear weapons or war-heads for use by the Canadian Forces ... may proceed.

5   That Canadian Ministers should recognize that the Government has agreed, at the meeting in December 1957 and at other times, and is morally bound, to equip the Canadian Forces under NATO command with ready-to-use nuclear weapons, if and when they are necessary.

7   That preparations should continue to enable the Canadian Forces ... to be ready to use nuclear weapons to be acquired from the United States under joint control arrangements if and when the adoption of these weapons is considered necessary.

The meeting brought to light three false premises. First, Diefenbaker reserved the right to decide alone on nuclear issues, when in reality he was incapable of making decisions. Second, it was thought that the differences between the Departments of External Affairs and of National Defence could be resolved through concessions, but this proved to be impossible. Both Green and Harkness threatened to resign if one gained ascendancy over the other. Politicians had not become accustomed to the somewhat perverse but realistic "double track" policy of re-arming while talking of peace. Third, in the absence of perfect wisdom, the warlike ant could not co-exist with the peaceful bee. Harkness eventually resigned. The Diefenbaker Government fell in the spring of 1963, and Pearson's Liberals took power the following June.

The ant profited from this set of circumstances. In June 1963, the Department of National Defence drafted a veritable declaration of war on the Department of External Affairs. What had happened in the meantime, that is, between 1960 and 1963? In 1960, the

Department of National Defence started to sharpen its knives. Green was intractable; Burns even more so. The Department of National Defence had to contend with two adversaries. Burns was particularly tough because he was a former military officer who was perfectly familiar with the rules of strategy, deception and subterfuge, and who enjoyed, moreover, the respect of his peers.

On 12 January 1960, at its 653rd meeting, the Chiefs of Staff Committee defined the role of the Department of National Defence in matters of disarmament. Departmental responsibilities were defined as follows:

a   to advise and support the Department of External Affairs;
b   to advise the Government concerning the strategic and technical impli-
    cations of specific disarmament proposals;
c   to advise the Government concerning the detailed military implications of
    particular proposals in terms of the Canadian Forces and defence budget.

On 23 September 1960, the Chairman of the Joint Chiefs of Staff, Air Marshal F.R. Miller, wrote to Air Vice-Marshal Hendrick in Washington that in future it would be desirable for all disarmament issues to be "handled through your office to mine rather than pass through normal service to service channels".[33] Miller took this step towards centralization in light of the quarrels that existed between the various services at the time. On 25 October 1960, Dr. Zimmerman, Chairman of the Defence Research Board, wrote to Miller that as long as no pressing issues emerged from negotiations at the UN, the Department of National Defence would be in a position to respond to the needs of the Department of External Affairs. He doubted even that it would be desirable to increase the staff of the Department of National Defence in this area as long as Canada was not involved in substantive issues as opposed "to political discussions of a propaganda nature". On 1 March 1961, Zimmerman modified his position. He still considered it unnecessary to create special groups as long as the areas of research had not been defined, but he nevertheless proposed to Miller that an interdepartmental group should be created "to combine inputs from the Political, Economic, Scientific and Military factions as studies progress". Zimmerman continued: "It seems to us that such a group ... could provide an efficient means for achieving a well balanced position on the complex problems to be faced in the future." This request was undoubtedly the basis for the creation of the Directorate of Strategic Studies in July 1961.

On 2 March 1961, Miller jumped at the opportunity and wrote to Robert Bryce, the Secretary to the Cabinet, advising him of

Zimmerman's reticence concerning the real room for manoeuvre that was available to Canada. Zimmerman had told Miller the previous day that Canada could do little, but that it should make the necessary efforts "to understand the problems, appreciate the proposals and evaluate the situations developing abroad". In concluding his letter to Bryce, Miller nevertheless stretched Zimmerman's words somewhat, stating "DRB do not feel that they are justified in instituting any Canadian Research Program aimed at the disarmament problem". Centralization obviously had merit. The Chairman of the Chiefs of Staff Committee was thus in a position to revert to the strategy practised by his predecessor at the beginning of the 1950s – that of the lazy ant.

Throughout 1961, negotiations on disarmament made life difficult for Miller. We shall return to this topic in subsequent chapters. For now, however, we shall restrict ourselves to the main individual cases. The Chiefs of Staff Committee took issue with the four following resolutions:

• the Indian resolution of September 1961;
• the African resolution of November 1961;
• the Swedish resolution of November 1961;
• the resolution of the "neutrals" of October 1962 on the halting of nuclear tests.

These resolutions concerned the issues of non-proliferation of nuclear weapons, nuclear-free zones, prohibition of indirect transfers of nuclear weapons to third party countries, and haiting of nuclear tests. The idea of non-proliferation obviously clashed head on with the strategies of the Department of National Defence. DND felt that any support for this kind of resolution would undermine any attempt to equip the Canadian Forces in Europe with nuclear weapons. Within the limits of defined policy, the issue was Europe and not yet Bomarc, which Diefenbaker did not even want to hear about.

On 13 February 1961, Harkness sounded the alarm. In a letter to Green, he said that Burns, in his preliminary statements before the Plenary Committee (the Ten-Nation Committee), "should only talk about halting the production of fissile material and not about issues of non-proliferation". On 17 October 1961, he went further:

We are not happy about the Canadian position that seems to be developing whereby Canada is moving from the position of supporting a test ban with adequate inspection to one where we are prepared to support a test ban without insurance that it will be enforced ... in other words a test ban at any price.

Even the u.s. President got involved. On 20 October, in a letter to Diefenbaker, John F. Kennedy wrote:

Dear Mr. Prime Minister,

To my distress I have learned that your Government intends to support in the General Assembly this year a resolution ... calling for an unverified moratorium on nuclear weapons tests.

Should Canada cast its vote in favour of a moratorium this year, it will be tantamount to Canada's abandoning the Western position at Geneva on this issue ...

Mr. Prime Minister, I cannot overemphasize my concern in this matter and for the reasons I have advanced above and in the interest of a vital Western solidarity ... I hope you will reconsider this decision to cast an affirmative vote for a resolution which can only damage, and damage seriously, the Western position on an essential issue of Western security.[34]

Perhaps Kennedy would not have taken such pains had he been aware of Diefenbaker's penchant for storing letters sent to him by foreign heads of State under his mattress and leaving them there for months until a reply was finally sought and the staff discovered his secret. In any event, all this happened two days before the Cuban missile crisis and Washington's urgent request that the Canadian Forces be put on alert. In light of Cabinet's belated response to Washington's request, the odds are that, on a subject as minor as Kennedy's earlier letter, Diefenbaker was in no hurry to reply.

On 18 October, Harkness received a reply from Green. Dissatisfied with Green's response, Harkness wrote to Diefenbaker on 26 October stating that he wished to discuss this matter "personally" with him or, alternatively, if he found it "more appropriate", to have the matter referred to Cabinet.

Several months later, after Harkness resigned, the Governor General dissolved Parliament at Diefenbaker's request. The circumstances surrounding the resignation of Harkness are vividly described by Granatstein.[35] On 26 June 1963, the Joint Staff (js) produced its register of grievances which contained a mixture of flattery, meanness and the most scathing denunciations of Burns.[36] Only the main extracts will be reproduced here. The document starts by stating the role of the Department of National Defence on disarmament issues (discussed above) and continues:

DND also had a separate responsibility towards the Government which was in parallel with that of External Affairs. It was important, therefore, that

DND should so conduct its affairs that it would speak with the same voice towards the Government and External Affairs.

... It was considered that during 1960, DND had been able to exert an appreciable influence at the official level in the Department of External Affairs, and often to modify their approach to disarmament to take account of defence implications.

Unfortunately, this desirable state of affairs began to rapidly deteriorate when disarmament negotiations were reactivated in March 1962 in the forum of the Eighteen-Nation Disarmament Conference.

... It has seemed that External Affairs has tended to approach disarmament in the role of international peacemaker, backing unrealistic initiatives at the expense of NATO solidarity and without due regard for the interests of Western security. In fact, some of the positions taken had been so clearly unrealistic that they have discredited Canadian diplomacy and could be considered rather crude attempts to combine our NATO membership with a policy of *de facto* neutralism.

DND protests and efforts to modify these policies are well documented. ... In all these contentious matters, there was almost no substantive discussion between the two responsible government departments ... It was quite common for instructions to be sent to the chief negotiator, General Burns, to make proposals or table resolutions or amendments to resolutions, not only without consulting DND, but without even sending information copies of the relevant telegrams to DND. Conversely, it has not been uncommon for General Burns to recommend initiatives or proposals on disarmament matters with strong security connotations without sending information copies to DND ... An important example of this is the memorandum submitted by General Burns for the Ottawa ministerial meeting (11 June 1963) ... Such a brief should have been prepared in consultation with DND ... [*À propos* this memorandum] Fortunately this new Government is well versed in world problems including NATO strategy and disarmament, but suppose the leadership of the country had been in more naïve hands!

In addition, the Burns' memorandum called for the consideration of measures which, as he is aware, are considered by the best military advice available to him to be contrary to the interests of Western security. It is interesting to speculate how such advice rendered on short notice ... might have been used by a less experienced minister for External Affairs ...

It is concluded that the present Canadian Government organization for disarmament is satisfactory, but that there is a lack of coordination in the making of major policy decisions.

It is recommended that major policy proposals or decisions which cannot be agreed at the Under-Secretary of State/CCOS/General Burns level be referred to the Cabinet Defence Committee for decision.

This document should obviously be classified in the annals of diplomatic imbecility. It brought nothing to the resolution of policy coordination problems, and proposed no more than a return to the position adopted by Foulkes in 1952. The document is interesting, however, because it reveals the frame of mind of the high-ranking military officers of the time.

The military dreamed, lived and breathed for a nuclear capability. This obsession obviously drove the paranoiac ant to believe that everything which moved and thought differently from itself was hostile. In defence of the ant, it must be acknowledged that, on many occasions, its advice was sought and then ignored. This frustrating situation was hardly conducive to social adaptability ...

There is a strange irony in politics. The incoming Liberal Minister of National Defence, Paul Hellyer, undertook to implement his party's policy of integration of the Canadian Armed Forces effective 1 August 1964. Total unification followed several years later. The Under-Secretary of State then had to deal with a civilian – the Deputy Minister of National Defence.

As for Canadian disarmament policy, General Burns had to climb down. The Pearson Government had been elected on the promise that it would respect the commitments undertaken by Canada. The Canadian Forces would be equipped with nuclear weapons to the great displeasure of the Québec wing of the Liberal Party. Trudeau, Marchand and Pelletier amongst others undertook later to dismantle in part what the Pearson Government had accepted *en bloc*. The good intentions of the Pearson Government were not at issue; it simply had to preach less ostentatiously ...

2 Canada Caught in the Squall, 1945–1952

> How can two parties, content to be deaf, see each other without being seen?

From 1945 until the time that the UN Disarmament Commission was created in 1952, the influence of Canadian policy was felt more through Canada's involvement in the "cultural ferment" of the international system than through her disarmament proposals *per se*. The system was experiencing profound upheaval; it was the period of the great squall.

THE MAJOR TRANSFORMATIONS

Transformations were occurring at all levels of the system. The major transformation was obviously the division of the world into two blocs, and this occurred for three reasons. First and foremost, there was a wide divergence of ideology. Western ecumenicalism, with all its traditions of freedom and economic liberalism, stood opposed to Soviet messianism, which was at once doctrinaire, authoritarian and sensitive to criticism. Second, there was the nuclear reality. The awesome destructive power of the atom cast a cloak of terror over the international legal and organizational structures that had been designed with so much care by the founding fathers of the Charter of San Francisco. Then there was the inability of the Allies (United States, United Kingdom, France and the USSR) to reach agreement on a common policy *vis-à-vis* Germany. In Asia, Japan had neither been divided nor occupied in the same way as Germany. Ultimately, with the advent of the Korean War, the world was crystallized into two closed universes that were totally opaque, each obsessed with mistrust of the other.

The second transformation occurred at the level of Western inter-relations. In 1947, the United Kingdom was on the verge of bankruptcy. In the Mediterranean, Truman sped to the aid of Greece and Turkey. Perhaps the most afflicted region throughout history, the Mediterranean was often referred to by Churchill as one of the "two blocked nostrils" of the Soviet giant, the other being the Baltic Sea. In 1948, on the advice of Secretary of State Marshall, Truman decided to rebuild the economic foundations of Europe. America was all-powerful, and Europe's principal creditor. Ernest Bevin, British Foreign Minister, actually heard of the existence of the Marshall Plan from the BBC. America did not consult – she decided.

Following the war, Europe no longer occupied a central position within the international system. From that time on, the tempo of change was set by the powers flanking Europe, specifically the United States and the USSR. It took several years before the void in the system created by the collapse of Europe was filled. Only in the early 1950s did the sworn enemies of yesteryear, Germany and Japan, become the favoured allies of tomorrow. Historians refer to this important change with a great deal of tact, using expressions such as "reversal of the alliances". The changes in the West also affected Canada, which was caught between the decline of the British Empire and the sudden emergence to the south of an eagle with atomic claws. Canada's former allies, apart from the USSR, remained the same. Canada could only survive by continuing to support the principles of a new international order under the aegis of the United Nations, and by developing multilateral relations with other nations both within the Commonwealth and within NATO – Canada had been one of NATO's main architects.

The third transformation concerned fundamental strategy. In 1945, the United States alone had the atomic bomb. This monopoly gave the Americans considerable peace of mind, and in some respects they became less preoccupied with the positions of their allies. In 1949, the monopoly was broken. From then on, there were two super-powers: strategic bipolarity had been established. The threat was global, but still not immediate and imminent. Following the explosion of the world's first nuclear device in 1945, it took a full twelve years before the key enabling technology emerged. In 1957, with the appearance of the intercontinental ballistic missile, a spatial dimension was cast over the international system that made the threat sudden, unexpected and immediate.

As Jean-Paul Sartre said, "humanity now was in control of its own mortality". Although these events occurred beyond the timeframe considered in this Chapter, they are stressed at this point because of their influence on post-war strategy. The launch of Sputnik 1 in 1957 heralded the dawn of the militarization of space. From a strategic standpoint this first launch gave birth to the concept of "Star Wars" aimed at countering ballistic missiles in flight. Although it seems unlikely that a system to provide total protection against ballistic missiles will be deployed in the foreseeable future, some form of limited ballistic missile defence may see the light of day.

The fourth transformation, in 1945, was the re-orientation of Canadian perspectives in light of Canada's particular geographic situation. Faced with the possibility of war between the superpowers, Ottawa became quickly aware of Canada's vulnerability. In 1945, the Department of External Affairs sent a document to the Cabinet Defence Committee which stated:

Canada is still most unlikely to be involved in other than a general war, and general war can only originate in disputes between great powers. The basic Canadian policy should therefore be to do our part to make general war less likely and to maintain a reasonable degree of preparation as reinsurance ... In the long view, the most important factor in determining Canadian defence policy must be the estimates of the outbreak of general war ... We must take into account estimates reached by the United States and the United Kingdom.[1]

The desire to avoid a catastrophic war between the major powers was the cornerstone of Canada's "middle of the road" position – a position intermediate between those developed by the superpowers. This position was adopted in 1945, and reiterated as a basic postulate of the 1971 White Paper on Defence. Canada assumed this stance whenever possible or whenever the occasion arose. The peace initiative of Pierre Elliott Trudeau, developed almost forty years later, was little more than a "return to the basics" of Canadian foreign policy.

The fifth and final important transformation concerned national sovereignty. Canada sought to be master of her own territory. With the development of the sea routes and railroads in the latter half of the 19th century, Canada became acutely conscious of her east-west dimension. The Second World War served to confirm the strategic importance of the Great Lakes and the sea routes from the ports of Montreal, Halifax and St. John's for transporting men, supplies and equipment to Europe. At the same time, Canada recognized the strategic importance of the north-south dimension. In August 1940, following the Ogdensburg Declaration, the Permanent Joint Board on Defence (PJBD) was constituted. During the war, the Crimson route was established across Hudson Bay, Baffin Island and Greenland for transporting reinforcements to Europe, while the aerial corridors of the Northwest and Alaska were used to send aircraft to the USSR and to China. In 1953, the Distant Early Warning (DEW) line was built. In 1957, the North American Aerospace Defence (NORAD) Agreement was signed to consecrate the military bond between Canada and the United States. This bond was established *nolens volens* during the Second World War. The vows of the NORAD Agreement are renewed roughly every five years, which allows both parties to the marriage to extol its virtues or bemoan its shortcomings.

CONTROLLING THE ATOM

From time immemorial, nuclear energy has been at the very origin of our universe. According to Carl Sagan, if the whole timeframe of the universe were compressed into one calendar year, humanity would first appear on Earth on 31 December of that year. Clearly, the universe was inhospitable to any form of human life until the very recent past.

Intense nuclear radiation is lethal for members of the animal kingdom, except for certain species such as reptiles and insects which seem to be more resilient than other species. In recent times, the residents of Chernobyl felt the effects of nuclear death rays. Forty years earlier, the Japanese had experienced the nuclear inferno, first at Hiroshima, and then at Nagasaki.

Were the secrets of the universe really unravelled in 1945? Some thought so at the time, and still think so today. Undoubtedly, nuclear energy has remarkable applications, whether in medicine, in food preservation or in supply of electricity. To cite but one example, France nowadays produces more than 50 percent of its electricity from nuclear power stations. In Canada, the corresponding proportion is 15 percent, but this lower figure is largely due to the fact that Canada has a vast reserve of hydro-electric resources.

In military parlance, the atomic bomb is referred to as the A-bomb. The term is something of a misnomer, since the energy is released from the atomic "nucleus". A more exact term would, therefore, be nuclear bomb. Even the most powerful chemical explosion cannot compare with the power of a nuclear explosion. The standard of explosive nuclear yield is expressed in equivalent tonnes of trinitrotoluene (TNT). An atomic bomb might have an equivalent yield of 1 kilotonne (Kt), or 1,000 tonnes of TNT. The hydrogen bomb (H-bomb) has a yield expressed in megatonnes (Mt), or 1 million tonnes of TNT. The most powerful nuclear explosion to date was detonated by the Soviets in 1961 and had a yield of 58 megatonnes. There are no theoretical limits to the power of a nuclear explosion. The only limitations are imposed by the practical considerations of size, volume and safety.

Control of atomic power can be viewed as a revolutionary breakthrough on two counts, since it holds not only the promise for peaceful applications but also the potential to be used as a deterrent in times of conflict. In 1945, even though there seemed to be some kind of willingness to share the benefits of peaceful applications of the atom amongst all nations, there was no guarantee that the sharing of atomic secrets would prevent potentially belligerent nations from using the atom to further their aspirations towards domination and political expansion.

Some observers felt that nuclear power should be purely and simply abolished. According to an ancient Chinese proverb, "he who wants to make an axe keeps the model at hand (Mencius)". Many have asked whether the atom can be "disinvented". But is it logical to assume that those nations which possess nuclear arsenals and which vow to destroy them will not be tempted to rebuild them subsequently? Control of the atom clearly opens up the possibility for abuse and, for this reason, the dangers of nuclear proliferation continue to be discussed today. The two extremes which characterize the nuclear debate arose frequently in 1945 in all discussions on the control of atomic energy.

The first official East-West texts which addressed these issues were the Declaration of Washington on 15 November 1945 and the Moscow Communiqué of 27 December 1945. President Harry S. Truman, Prime Minister Clement Attlee and Prime Minister Mackenzie King, the three partners who shared in the Manhattan Project, met in Washington to discuss, among other things, the steps to be taken following the Gouzenko affair[2] and the international actions that should be pursued to control the atom. The purpose of the discussions was clearly twofold: "to prevent the use of the atom for destructive purposes" and to "promote its use only for peaceful purposes". In Moscow, where Canada was not represented, Foreign Ministers Byrnes, Bevin and Molotov agreed to recommend to the General Assembly of the United Nations, a study on the possible creation of a commission that would be responsible for studying the problems resulting from the discovery of atomic energy. Such a commission would report to the Security Council of the UN. As Jean Klein aptly observed, the veto posed a problem even before the commission was established.[3]

The Atomic Energy Commission

It goes without saying that the collective conscience of all the States represented within the UN would be reflected in the very first resolution adopted by the General Assembly. Resolution number 1, adopted on 24 January 1946, created the United Nations Atomic Energy Commission. It was charged with making recommendations to the Security Council:

- for extending between all nations the exchange of basic scientific information for peaceful ends;
- for control of atomic energy to the extent necessary to ensure its use only for peaceful purposes;
- for the elimination from national armaments of atomic weapons and all other major weapons adaptable to mass destruction;
- for effective safeguards by way of inspection and other means to protect complying States against the hazards of violations and evasions.

The UN Atomic Energy Commission comprised all members of the UN Security Council including Canada, even though Canada was not a member of the Security Council at the time. The Commission presented its first report on 31 December 1946, its second report on 11 September 1947 and its third on 17 May 1948. The Commission was dissolved by the General Assembly on 11 January 1952.

Two days after the official opening of the work of the Commission, on 16 June 1946, the American Delegate, Bernard Baruch, tabled the substance of the U.S. proposals. The Baruch Plan drew on the previous work of the Acheson-Lilienthal Commission, but went further. The Americans wanted to add "teeth" to the proposed Commission. In general terms, the Baruch Plan called for the establishment of an International Authority on atomic energy development. According to Jozef Goldblat, this Authority would have the following responsibilities:

Managerial control or ownership of all atomic energy activities potentially dangerous to world security; with the power to control, inspect and license all other atomic activities; as well as with the responsibility to foster the beneficial uses of atomic energy. In particular, the Authority was to conduct continuous surveys of supplies of uranium and thorium and bring these materials under its control, and to possess the exclusive right both to conduct research in the field of atomic explosives and to produce its own fissionable material. All nations were to grant the freedom of inspection deemed necessary by the Authority. The United States stressed the importance of immediate punishment for infringements of the rights of the Authority, maintaining that there must be no veto to protect those who violated their agreements not to develop or use atomic energy for destructive purposes.[4]

Annex 2 of the 3rd Report of the Commission[5] contained a superb review of the nature, jurisdiction, powers and functions of the proposed 1945 Authority.

The USSR made its own position known in a document tabled before the Commission on 19 June 1946. The document was, in effect, a "draft international convention aimed at prohibiting the production and use of atomic weapons for mass destruction".[6] The States party to this convention "undertook never to use atomic weapons under any circumstances, neither to produce nor stockpile such weapons, and to destroy, within three months following the entry into force of this convention, all their stockpiles of atomic weapons, whether in production or in development". Any violation of this convention would be considered as "a crime against humanity".

In short, the United States proposed a system for international control of the atom containing effective safeguards together with an undertaking that the Authority would conduct research only for peaceful purposes. The Soviet Union insisted on total prohibition of all nuclear weapons, and their destruction within a three-month period. Under these circumstances there was a total impasse. Despite allied reticence, the U.S. proposal was adopted. Subsequently, following the adoption of the first report of the Commission on 31 December 1946, all further discussion was precluded. There was no longer the possibility of any agreement between the superpowers. The negotiations which ensued will be discussed in a later section.

CONTROL OF ARMED FORCES AND WEAPONS REDUCTIONS

Following every major war the international community has tried to rebuild the international order on new foundations. In some instances, it was the will of the victorious State that prevailed. Imperialistic States, in their time of power, imposed their own laws, political structures and customs. The modern European structure emerged following the Treaty of Westphalia, signed in 1648, at the end of the Thirty-Year War. The two victorious powers, France and

Table 1
The UN Atomic Energy Commission

Origins: Declaration of Washington, 15 November 1945; Moscow Communiqué, 27 December 1945.

Creation: Resolution of 24 January 1946, adopted unanimously by the General Assembly of the United Nations.

Mandate: Formulate proposals to the Security Council for:
• fostering the exchange of scientific information;
• controlling atomic energy;
• eliminating atomic weapons from military arsenals;
• establishing an effective inspection system.

Composition: All members of the UN Security Council together with Canada who was not a member at the time. Between 1946 and 1949 the composition was as follows:
Canada, China, U.S., France, U.K., USSR and:

Argentina (1948–49)	Cuba (1949)	Poland (1946–47)
Australia (1946–47)	Egypt (1946–49)	Syria (1947–48)
Belgium (1947–48)	Mexico (1946)	Ukraine (1948–49)
Brazil (1946–47)	Netherlands (1946)	
Colombia (1947–48)	Norway (1949)	

Commission Reports:
• 1st Report, 30 December 1946, AEC/18/Rev. 1, 10 in favour, 2 abstentions (USSR and Poland);
• 2nd Report, 11 September 1947, AEC/26, 10 in favour, 1 against (USSR), 1 abstention (Poland);
• 3rd Report, 17 May 1948, AEC/31/Rev. 1, 9 in favour, 2 against (Ukraine and USSR).

Dissolution of the Commission: Res. 502 (VI) of 11 January 1952. The USSR had already withdrawn from the Commission on 19 January 1950.

Sweden, became the guardians of religious freedom in Europe. The Treaty of Westphalia constituted the first international charter guaranteeing religious freedom.

During the last two centuries, the world has experienced three distinct international systems. First, the system that was established at the Congress of Vienna in 1815 following the Napoleonic Wars which had subjected Europe to fire and the sword. Second, the League of Nations which appeared following the First World War. Third, the United Nations Organization (UNO) which replaced the defunct League of Nations whose credibility had been ridiculed by the rise of fascism and naziism in Europe.

The current international system is a direct descendant of the three anterior systems. The Congress of Vienna gave birth to the idea that nations would meet relatively frequently to prescribe the destiny of the international system. In the United Nations Organization, this prime responsibility falls upon the major powers of the system and is embodied in Article 24 of the Charter which states that the Security Council has "the principal responsibility for maintaining peace and international security". From the League of Nations came the concept of parliamentary diplomacy and its resulting consequences which established the standards and codification of international law. Finally, from the United Nations Organization came the pressing need to "preserve future generations from the scourge of war". These words in the Preamble of the UN Charter have a particular significance for rising generations which are eagerly grasping for a lasting and peaceful international order.

In 1945 the issues of disarmament and arms control ran into a series of difficulties, the most important of which were political in nature. Other difficulties arose in connection with the Charter itself and with the collective security system envisaged at the time.

The concept of "all for one" against an aggressor, which is the basic principle of collective security, only has meaning if the main States within the system think along the same lines. This was the main virtue of the system established by the Congress of Vienna following the Napoleonic Wars. Unfortunately, this concept was no longer viable within the climate of distrust that developed in 1945. Moreover, it was still too soon to talk about the "equalizing atom", an expression that General Pierre Gallois used several years later. Control of the atom was tantamount to the right of veto. In other words, it was unthinkable that the entire international community could succeed in aligning itself against the United States which, at that time, held the monopoly on atomic weapons.

Clearly, the atom was a power to be reckoned with, but its secrets were still a mystery to those who drafted the Charter. The provisions of the Charter were obviously written with the firm intention of ensuring arms control. These provisions were very clear: the Security Council would be responsible for ensuring international peace and security. Article 43 of the UN Charter requires member nations to place their national armed forces at the disposal of the Security

Council. These forces report to a UN Military Chiefs of Staff Committee which in turn reports to the Security Council.

Under Article 11 of the Charter, the General Assembly was empowered to study "the principles governing disarmament and regulation of armaments and to make appropriate recommendations". The Security Council was obviously not devoid of responsibility, since under Article 26 it was also charged with "establishing an arms control system". There was, therefore, a considerable overlap of jurisdiction concerning disarmament and weapons reduction. There was no confusion over legalities, but the dynamics of negotiations proved to be particularly complicated.

In December 1946, the General Assembly adopted a resolution on "the principles governing control and general reduction of armaments". Whether the priority was conventional disarmament or nuclear disarmament remained an open question. Throughout the negotiations, the United States justifiably insisted on the need to differentiate between the respective jurisdictions of the Atomic Energy Commission and the Commission for Conventional Armaments. The United States insisted that the atomic issue should assume priority, while the USSR continued to insist on the need to link the two issues.

The Commission for Conventional Armaments

A few weeks before the Security Council received the first report of the Atomic Energy Commission, the UN General Assembly adopted, on 14 December 1946, a resolution on "the principles governing general control and reduction of armed forces". This resolution invited the Security Council to study the issue and to ensure that control would be "observed by all member States and not just unilaterally by certain member States". On 13 February 1947, the Security Council accepted this recommendation and created the Commission for Conventional Armaments.

Six months later, on 8 July 1947, the Security Council approved the work plan of the Commission. This work plan included six items, the first four of which are the most important. The Commission for Conventional Armaments was required to make recommendations to the Security Council on regulations governing "armaments and armed forces" within its jurisdiction (item 1), and to formulate concrete proposals (item 4). It was required to examine and define general "principles" related to these issues (item 2), and to propose "safeguards" aimed at protecting nations against evasions or violations of the regulations (item 3). This latter item was only touched

Table 2
The Commission for Conventional Armaments

Origins: Resolution of the United Nations' General Assembly [Res. 41 (1)], 14 December 1946.

Creation: Resolution of the UN Security Council (S/268/Rev. 1/Corr. 1), 13 February 1947.*

Mandate: To make recommendations according to the established work plan.

Composition: Members of the Security Council. For the period 1947–49, see Table 1. Canada became a member of the Security Council on 1 January 1948.

Commission Reports: 1ˢᵗ Progress Report, 12 August 1948, (S/C. 3/27), together with two resolutions S/C. 3/24 and 25;
2ⁿᵈ Progress Report, 17 August 1948, (S/C. 3/32/Corr. 1). This report was not adopted by the Commission, and there was no follow-up.

Main Resolutions of the General Assembly concerning the Commission: Res. 192 (III), 19 November 1948 (this resolution amended the Commission's mandate);
Res. 300 (IV), 5 December 1949.

Dissolution of the Commission: 30 January 1952, by the Security Council. The USSR had already withdrawn from the Commission on 27 April 1950.

---

* Resolution S/268 stipulated that "issues falling within the jurisdiction of the Atomic Energy Commission, under resolutions of the General Assembly dated 24 January and 14 December 1946, are excluded from the Commission's mandate".

upon during the work of the Commission, and discussion was essentially focused on items 1 and 2.

Of main value were the Commission's efforts to define weapons of mass destruction and to link regulatory proposals to the broader framework of international security. The Commission's first resolution was embodied in its second progress report to the Security Council, dated August 1948. This resolution, which was adopted by 9 in favour versus 2 against (the USSR and the Soviet Socialist Republic of the Ukraine), essentially stated:

That the Commission considered that all armaments and armed forces, except atomic weapons and weapons of mass destruction, fall within its jurisdiction and that weapons of mass destruction should be defined to include atomic explosive weapons, radioactive material weapons, lethal chemical and biological weapons and any weapons developed in the future which have characteristics comparable in destructive effect to those of the atomic bomb or other weapons mentioned above.[7]

This definition of weapons of mass destruction is probably the first official characterization to be found in United Nations' texts. The second resolution contained in the second report of the Commission concerning security/disarmament reiterated that general control could only be effected within "an atmosphere of international trust and security". Paragraph 3 of this resolution specified the conditions necessary for such trust:

- the entry into force of an effective system of agreements in conformity with Article 43 of the Charter;
- the establishment of an international atomic energy control system;
- the signing of peace treaties with Germany and Japan.

Thus, since 1945, the Western nations introduced nothing new into the debate by constantly linking trust and security, whether through the Harmel report of 1967, the MBFR negotiations, the CSCE or the CDE. The UN introduced nothing new either, since all the problems had already been discussed at length during the time of the League of Nations.

In 1948, the main Soviet and Western proposals on control of armed forces and armaments were tabled before the General Assembly. In September 1948, as a first step in armaments reduction, the Soviets proposed[8] that the members of the Security Council reduce by one-third all their land, naval and air forces during the course of one year, and prohibit unconditionally the use of atomic weapons, which the Soviets considered to be "aggressive". According to Jean Klein, this proposal was unacceptable to the West "since a proportionate reduction of armed forces and armaments would have maintained the overwhelming superiority of the communist camp in conventional armaments, while the prohibition of atomic weapons would have deprived the Western world of an instrument on which its security depended".[9] On 19 November 1948, following a Belgian initiative, the Western nations succeeded in passing Resolution 192 (III) by 43 votes against 6 with one abstention. This resolution required that the Commission would formulate proposals within its working plan "for the accumulation, verification and publication ... of complete information to be provided by the member States concerning their conventional manpower and armaments". This proposal for a "survey" and disclosure of information on military manpower essentially constituted the Western response to the Soviet proposal for proportionate reduction by one-third of the armed forces of the permanent members of the Security Council. The Soviet Union opposed this resolution on the pretext that it ignored atomic issues.

The French Delegation expended a great deal of effort in refining this proposal. Several important documents[10] were produced in July 1949 and adopted by the Commission. Faced with the refusal of the USSR to discuss this issue before the Security Council, the General Assembly finally recommended, through Resolution 300 (IV) of 5 December 1949, that the Security Council "study this issue ... through the Commission in conformity with its work plan". Several months later, the USSR withdrew from the Commission on the pretext that the Western countries refused to exclude from the UN the Chinese representative from the Kuo-ming-tang following the victory of Mao Tse-tung.

CANADIAN DIPLOMATIC ACTIONS

Foundations

In 1945, Canada was ready to participate in the development of a new international order, but not just any international order. Canada distrusted the former system and looked towards better tomorrows. Ottawa was not in favour of the idea of regional regroupings that might recreate power blocs or associations having conflicting interests. The world espoused by Ottawa, somewhat naïvely, was one of international cooperation in a world community where the veto would not exist and where law and equality would be respected.

Canada was not receptive to the ideas of Churchill, who thought in terms of a Council of Europe, a Council of Asia and, for that matter, a Council of the Pacific. In 1944, at the Commonwealth Conference in London, Mackenzie King challenged the views of the old British lion. King contended "that the seas do not divide and that the peace and prosperity of the world are indivisible". "It would not be wise", he continued, "to encourage the peoples of the world to return to their illusions about their ability to live in continental isolation."[11] Anthony Eden, the Foreign Office and the Department of External Affairs were no doubt encouraged by this conference and derived some comfort from the similarities of views expressed by Canadian and British diplomats alike.

Churchill no longer talked of regional Councils; the defence of the Commonwealth was entrusted to others. Lord Halifax, British Ambassador in Washington, caused some concern for Canadian diplomats when, in Toronto in January 1944, he referred to the Commonwealth as a fourth power, and then in New York in November of the same year, he characterized it as the third vertex of a triangle in which the USSR and the United States comprised the other two vertices. Canada had no interest in witnessing the reconstitution of opposing blocs.

King's vision of the world was one of cooperation between the allies that would also extend to the USSR through the United Nations. In common with many others, King condemned the right of veto of the superpowers. But King was not present at Yalta. The British, Americans and Soviets decided the course of future events. But this did not prevent King from claiming a veto right of sorts for Canada. An isolationist at heart and a fierce defender of Canadian interests, King could not accept the idea that the Security Council could demand armed contingents from the member nations of the United Nations without consultation. King wrested the terms of Article 44 of the Charter from U.S. Secretary of State Edward Stettinius.[12] If the Security Council wished to call upon military contingents from a member State it should invite such member to participate in the deliberations of the Security Council. King and ex-General McNaughton, who had become Head of the Canadian Delegation to the United Nations, surely did not have to consult each other on that issue. Both had experienced the dark period of conscription in Canada. McNaughton in particular never appreciated the views of the British military high command (especially those of Montgomery) which sought to use the Canadian Armed Forces in Europe as "detached units". For both King and McNaughton, it was a matter of preserving Canadian sovereignty and political control of the Canadian Armed Forces by the Canadian Government.

Concerning collective security, Canada saw the United Nations Organization as the only salvation. In a speech delivered in Toronto in March 1944, Lester B. Pearson, who was to become Under-Secretary of State for External Affairs in 1946, stated: "The collective system which was spurned in peace has proven to be our salvation in war ... There is no other way to win the peace. If we want it badly enough, we can secure it."[13] When the chips were down and the superpowers were unable to reach agreement, either in New York or elsewhere, Pearson and St-Laurent tried to convince King of the need for a regional alliance. NATO was thus born. This was another paradox of Canadian diplomacy. It was easy to understand, for neither the United Nations Organization nor the world conformed to the image which Canada envisaged. Historians and political scientists speak of functionalism: do not clash head on with political problems, and utilize all cooperative mechanisms that are likely to foster progress. In her dealings with the UN, Canada accepted the views imposed by the superpowers. When the superpowers met with failure, Canada was content with "selective security", a term aptly used by Inis Claude in his book *Swords into Ploughshares*, to mean the collective security provided by alliances.

In the great post-war squall, Canadians were also concerned with the Moscow-Washington axis. John W. Holmes admirably summarized the climate conducive to the effectiveness of Canada's foreign policy.[14] "Canada best achieves its objectives" he said, "when the mood is relaxed and generous". The situation was not, however, easy to deal with. How could Canada assert her point of view as a middle power? Canada did not like to be thought of as either a Patagonia or a Panama, and she shared a border with a powerful giant State, confident of itself and of its resources. As Holmes noted, the Americans had "plenty of arrogance". He diplomatically added that the problem was not so much the arrogance of the United States but rather the immense disparity of power that existed between the two countries. To borrow the expression of Paul Valéry, Canada could never refer nostalgically to the United States as "the presence of things absent". Rather, the tendency has been to talk of the "omnipresence" or, in less kindly terms, of the "intrusive presence".

Although at times Canada remained reticent, she closed ranks with other Western allies at the moment of truth. In December 1946, when the United States forced the USSR to lay its cards on the table through the plan devised by the "redoubtable" Baruch, Canada supported Washington in concert with all the other Western allies. At that time, a lengthy discussion took place between King and St-Laurent. On 28 December, King recorded the substance of this discussion in his diary:

Much better to have no agreement at all than one which would admit of subterfuges and interpretations that would fail to effect the real purpose of achieving peace. It would be like building a structural piece on quicksand. What was needed was the solid rock of complete truth and understanding.[15]

Through her diplomats and politicians, Canada spared no effort to bring the Soviet Union around to her way of thinking. The effort proved to be in vain, despite the subterfuges and ingenuity of Canadian diplomacy. The USSR was intractable concerning the right of veto. Again, when it was no longer possible to give the USSR the benefit of the doubt, Brooke Claxton, then Canadian Minister of National Defence, spoke out to denounce Soviet policy. In a speech delivered on 9 February 1948, he declared: "The Soviet Union's use of the veto twenty-three times ... cannot be interpreted as evidence of her determination to make the United Nations an effective body for world co-operation. She has expanded her official borders since the end of the war so as to take in the whole or part of eight different countries having an area of 274,000 square miles".[16]

Generally, Ottawa was not too concerned about Soviet behaviour. Few in the political community felt that the Soviet Union had warlike intentions or a true capability to declare war on the West, at least for another four or five years. All historians agree that the major turning point was the 1948 *coup* in Prague which led to the annexation of Czechoslovakia, the ancient bastion of democracy in Eastern Europe. Two years earlier, Hume Wrong, Canadian Ambassador in Washington, and one of the pillars of post-war Canadian diplomacy, expressed a judgement on Soviet policy very similar to that of George F. Kennan. In a memorandum dated 28 June 1946, Wrong wrote:

Soviet policy is defensive. While there is a resemblance in technique between the diplomatic practices of the Kremlin and those used by Hitler, it would be most misleading to push the comparison far. For instance, the Soviet Government completely controls one seventh of the earth's surface and already possesses, unlike Nazi Germany, a vast field for internal development. The Russian peoples also do not share the German illusion that they are a master race.[17]

Dale C. Thomson, the biographer of St-Laurent, wrote that, following very lively discussions in the United Nations, the Prime Minister allegedly went to shake hands with Molotov, then Soviet Foreign Minister, to assure him that there was no reason why Canada could not enjoy as amicable a relationship with her neighbour across the Arctic as with her neighbour to the south.[18] History sheds no light on the feelings of Molotov at the time, although undoubtedly he was highly gratified.

In 1945 Canadian policy had little in the way of foundation, save for a strong determination to promote a new international order while, at the same time, protecting Canadian interests. There was no question of blindly following the lead of the United Kingdom and certainly no intent to align Canadian policy with British ideas for the defence of the Commonwealth. Canada also stood apart from the post-war quarrels between the United Kingdom and the United States. Canada had no wish to offend the sensibilities of the USSR, but at the same time sought the favours of the United States. As for the operation of the world security organization, Canada lacked influence but not ideas. Despite her wishes, Canada was unable to impose her views. Hume Wrong was perfectly conscious of this in 1944. On 13 May, in a letter to L. Dana Wilgress, Canadian Ambassador in Moscow, Hume Wrong wrote that it would be a waste of Canada's time to attempt to develop or impose her ideas on a world security organization, adding: "We should, however, be in a position at least to decide what is not acceptable to us, and to advocate changes to accord with our interests, through appropriate channels, in the plans of the Great Powers."[19] Canada was, therefore, conscious of her own limitations in influencing disarmament negotiations within the UN.

Canada and the Atomic Energy Commission

The Atomic Energy Commission met for the first time on 14 June 1946 in New York. Bernard Baruch and Andrei Gromyko were its co-chairmen. Depending on one's perspective, the useful work of the Commission lasted for three days or for six months. On 16 June, the United States tabled its proposal to create an International Atomic Energy Control Authority. Three days later, on 19 June, the Soviets presented their own proposal, embodying a draft convention aimed at prohibiting the production and use of atomic weapons. The Soviets made no comment on the American proposal. At the end of his speech, Gromyko stated, however, that he would oppose any form of tampering with the right of veto of the major powers. On 30 December 1946, the first report of the Commission was adopted by its members. One day later, the Security Council – which comprised the same members as those of the Commission – in turn adopted this report, but this time against the wishes of the USSR and Poland.

In a penetrating and sound judgement, Eayrs observes that the Commission, after only two meetings, had reached "instant deadlock".[20] It should be recognized, however, that the initial position adopted by the Soviet Union was subject to negotiation and modification. On 31 December, the die was cast; there was no turning back.

Throughout the summer of 1946, all negotiators became clearly aware that the Commission was about to box itself in. On 26 June,

Pearson reported that Baruch was just as inflexible as Gromyko. On 1 August, Hume Wrong sensed the impasse that was shaping up. It was clearly important to avoid a break with the USSR, but if that should happen, it was better after, rather than before, the Paris Peace Conference.[21] On 29 October, Soviet Foreign Minister Molotov accused the United States of using their proposal to acquire "monopoly of the atom". That proved to be the final straw. Baruch decided that he would oblige the Soviets to speak openly. On 5 November, the White House authorized him to force the debate. On 13 November, Baruch introduced a resolution to form a Subcommittee[22] of the Commission which would be charged with completing its work before 20 December. In the same vein, on 5 December he insisted that the whole report be finished by 20 December and that it be submitted to the Security Council by 31 December at the latest. The U.S. ultimatum was respected. The allies, one by one, moved to support the American position.

Canada's essential contribution to the work of the Commission was threefold. First, Canada assigned one of her most competent experts in atomic energy to the Commission. Second, Canada tried in every way possible to mollify the fierce opposition exhibited by the Soviet Union at the U.S. proposal to deny the right of veto within the atomic energy control authority. Third, Canada paid particular attention to the rights of nations to develop atomic energy for peaceful purposes. Each of these elements will be discussed more fully below.

On 27 March 1946, the Cabinet Defence Committee appointed General Andrew George Latta McNaughton as Canada's representative to the UN Atomic Energy Commission. King made this decision personally. Several years earlier, during the war, King had thought of appointing McNaughton to the position of Governor General, but when Defence Minister Ralston placed the King Cabinet in difficulties on the conscription issue, King replaced him with McNaughton. McNaughton attempted on two occasions to win a seat as a Liberal candidate in the ridings of North Grey, Ontario and Qu'Appelle, Saskatchewan, but was unsuccessful. In June 1945, McNaughton presented his resignation to King, who was not too reluctant to accept it, since McNaughton had shown little flair for politics.

In September 1946, a few months after his nomination to the UN Atomic Energy Commission, General McNaughton assumed the chairmanship of the Atomic Energy Control Board of Canada. In January 1948, he became Head of the Canadian Delegation to the UN. At that point, Canada had taken her seat as a member of the Security Council, and McNaughton became the Security Council

Chairman. Subsequently, General McNaughton was appointed Chairman of the Joint International Commission – a euphemism coined to describe an organization for u.s.-Canada cooperation – and Co-Chairman of the Permanent Joint Board on Defence (PJBD). On 11 July 1966, General McNaughton passed away, leaving behind his wife Mabel, and the legacy of one of the most brilliant military, political and diplomatic careers that Canada has ever known. Subsequently, only one person has been able to claim comparable stature – General E.L.M. Burns – another military career officer, whom Tucker describes as a "true Renaissance man".[23]

John Swettenham, McNaughton's biographer, describes him as one of the great gunners of the Canadian Army during the First World War. McNaughton was also a scientist who, according to Swettenham, worked on the development of the diode which, in conjunction with British work, led to the development of radar. In 1935, McNaughton's scientific research was recognized through his appointment as President of the National Research Council (NRC). When he resigned from NRC he was replaced by another renowned scientist, C.J. Mackenzie who developed the Chalk River nuclear laboratories.

When King named McNaughton to the Atomic Energy Commission, he was advised that other nations had delegated scientists, politicians or diplomats. As King noted in his diary, McNaughton was "all three". McNaughton was assisted at the Commission by a handful of diplomats, including George Ignatieff who undoubtedly had the subtlest of minds. This was not the first occasion on which McNaughton was favoured with the assistance of brilliant men. In 1932, Lester B. Pearson worked with him at the Disarmament Conference in Geneva. In his memoirs, Ignatieff, just like the official biographer of McNaughton, held certain reservations about McNaughton's diplomatic abilities. In the middle of a session at the United Nations, McNaughton allegedly rose to his feet to repudiate a statement that had just been made by a Canadian representative. History says nothing about whether McNaughton subsequently made amends.

As Ignatieff recalls, McNaughton who, when incensed, would stand with piercing brown eyes and eyebrows askew, had the necessary moral fibre to stand up to the formidable Baruch. As President Truman's advisor, Baruch found few historians who would come to his defence. Swettenham, quoting *Time Magazine*, described Baruch as "a millionaire at 30, a celebrated national figure at 50 ... and a legend by the time he was 70".[24] Ignatieff displayed an obvious dislike for Baruch. When he visited Baruch in his "palatial mansion",

Ignatieff was not impressed with a portrait of Baruch flexing his muscles, neither with the inflexibility of his character nor his ostentatious taste for richness and power.[25]

In early June 1946, Baruch told McNaughton privately that it was absolutely essential to control atomic energy from "its birth to its death". McNaughton was the first to appreciate the merits of the American proposal. Nevertheless, when Washington tried to force the issue, McNaughton opposed it. He asked for more time, and tabled amendments to the u.s. proposal. He went so far as to remain silent on the third item – the issue of the right of veto – contained in the resolution proposed by Baruch on 5 December. In light of the u.s. ultimatum that the Commission's work be finished by 20 December, McNaughton had no option but to respond. On the preceding day, negotiations between Ignatieff, McNaughton and Eberstadt, who was a member of the u.s. Delegation, led to a few minor changes but the Americans would not yield on the essential points. Canada thus gained a few days' grace. As Eayrs put it so well: "even though the United States was ready to confront the Soviet Union it was quite another thing to subject an ally to the same treatment".[26] During the last week of December, the differences between Canada and the United States were leaked to the *New York Times* and the *Globe and Mail*. The principal players were on the alert. McNaughton learned of the directives of King and St-Laurent: the u.s. proposal had to be supported, for after all it was better not to reach agreement at all than to arrive at a hybrid solution.

u.s. intransigence had created many divisions within the Canadian Delegation. Escott Reid considered u.s. behaviour to be quite unacceptable. Ignatieff felt the same way but judged that, in the final analysis, the u.s. position had to be supported. In his memoirs, Ignatieff regretted that he had not finally come around to Reid's way of thinking. Had it not been for Ottawa, McNaughton would probably have derived machiavellian delight from saying *nyet* to Baruch. These aspects are obviously of little consequence today. With or without the Canadian vote, the Baruch Plan would have been passed, and the Soviet position would not have changed one iota.

The proposals made by McNaughton immediately preceding the acceptance of the Commission report bring us to our second point – that of the right of veto. McNaughton maintained that it was not necessary to mention the right of veto specifically in the conclusions of the Commission's report. It was sufficient to say, for instance: "there shall be no legal right whereby a wilful violator of the terms of the treaty or convention shall be protected from the consequence of violation of its terms".[27] Baruch took a lot of persuading. He accepted the Canadian amendment, but added four words which essentially negated its intent. These four words were "by veto or otherwise", which were inserted between "no legal right" and "whereby". We had thus turned full circle.

In his book, Eayrs reproduces the text of the briefing note prepared for the members of the Commission by Escott Reid on 20 December 1946 in anticipation of the in-camera meeting planned for 27 December.[28] The two main paragraphs read as follows:

Any such violation [of the Treaty] would be likely to make other Members of the United Nations feel that they are released from their obligation under the Charter not to threaten or use force against that delinquent State. The mere existence of the "veto" in the Security Council would make no practical difference. If there came about a situation where it was generally felt that it was necessary to take armed measures against a great power which was threatening the peace of the world, those armed measures would be taken – veto or no veto.

Thus, under present circumstances, little would be gained by trying to persuade each of the permanent members of the Security Council to give up its veto over the imposition of military sanctions against a State found to be committing serious violations of the convention or conventions on atomic energy.

Canadian thinking demonstrated a political realism which left nothing to be desired. This same clarity and political realism is to be found in the speech delivered by St-Laurent on 4 December 1946 before the Political Committee of the United Nations:

I am not at all repulsed nor frightened by the existence of the veto in the Security Council ... If it is necessary that there be an international agreement, it will be necessary for each State which will become a party to that agreement to give its assent thereto ... If ever sanctions were taken against a major State it would correspond to an absolute war situation, irrespective of whether the recalcitrant State had decided to use its right of veto or had opposed a Council decision through the use of force.

In other words, with or without the right of veto, the majority of members of the Security Council would be unable to take action against a major power. History has proven the correctness of the Canadian view. The only exception was the action of the United Nations in Korea, when the USSR was absent from the Security Council. In fact, the UN provided the only legal basis on which the United States could intervene in a war of aggression by North Korea against South Korea. Most jurists agree on this point. The legal basis for the UN action in Korea could not have been in any way the decision of the Security Council since it did not respect the rule of unanimity of permanent members but rather Article 51 of the Charter which provides for the right to collective or self defence.

The third area in which Canada concentrated her efforts concerned the right to develop the atom for peaceful purposes. On 17 December 1945, one month and two days after the Washington Declaration, Canada's Prime Minister, Mackenzie King, stated before the House of Commons that the problems of development and control of the atom were intimately interconnected. "Up to a certain point" he said, "the processes for releasing atomic energy are the same whether that purpose is an industrial, commercial or humanitarian use, or whether it is that of mass destruction". Thus, even in 1945, the problem of Peaceful Nuclear Explosions (PNE) arose, together with the inability of distinguishing a priori between the two uses of the atom in the absence of a strict control system. Scientific and technical experts supported this conclusion in the first report of the Commission.

John W. Holmes was correct in noting that the Washington Declaration was really aimed at resolving this problem and not, as others claim, at consolidating the triumvirate of atomic cooperation comprising the United States, Great Britain and Canada.[29] The nuclear genie emerged from the bottle in 1945, and mankind has struggled since to find a way of making it go back. Obviously, it is more easily said than done.

The Commission repeatedly stumbled over this difficulty throughout its work. On several occasions, Canada argued in its statements and interventions on the need to develop the atom. As both Holmes and Eayrs point out in their books, this attitude dates back to the position held by Canada at the time of the trilateral meeting in Washington. In December 1946, this issue came up again in a rather strange way.

During the months of November and December 1946, the General Assembly started its deliberations on the famous resolution of 14 December. This resolution, together with the Security Council resolution of 13 February 1947, led to the creation of the Commission for Conventional Armaments. The first signs of the difficulties to come appeared in a number of Canadian statements. On 29 November 1946, Dana Wilgress stated before the Political Committee that it was not sufficient, as the Soviets had proposed, "to prohibit the production and use of atomic energy for military purposes". Control mechanisms would have to be established to ensure that the atom was developed only for peaceful purposes. In a speech delivered on 4 December 1946, St-Laurent took the opportunity to stress the essential link between the two aspects of the problem.

In a memorandum from Lester B. Pearson to the Prime Minister, dated 3 December 1946, but which was never sent[30], the following summary appears. There were three proposals on the negotiating table: 1. a Soviet resolution which proposed establishing a single commission for controlling atomic energy and for limiting and reducing armaments and armed forces; 2. a Canadian amendment to the Soviet proposal; and 3. a draft u.s. resolution.

The Canadian amendment, in its final form, incorporated three proposals contained in an Australian amendment. It recommended "that the first step towards general regulation and reduction of armaments should be the negotiations for this purpose making available to the Security Council armed forces as provided in Article 43 of the Charter". The Canadian proposal argued that mechanisms for the control of atomic energy would be the responsibility of the Commission according to its mandate. The final paragraph of this memorandum is the most important:

If proposals for the control of atomic energy ... are incorporated completely in the general plans for the reduction and regulation of armaments, as the United States proposal would appear to do, the Atomic Energy Commission might thus be circumvented. The Soviet and the United States proposals would also make the inspection and control procedure subject to the veto of permanent members of the Security Council. In his teletype[31], General McNaughton has indicated his apprehension over this trend in the disarmament discussions.

McNaughton was not concerned here with the right of veto, but the confusion that could result from the overlapping of responsibilities for the establishment of a system for controlling both atomic energy and conventional armaments. Confusion was obviously the objective sought by the Soviet Union which had insisted since the beginning of the year on the prohibition of atomic weapons as a prerequisite to any reductions in conventional armaments. It proved to be a most effective manoeuvre, as evidenced by the confused despatches between Ottawa and New York. Canada was first to draw Washington's attention to this issue which, in the final analysis, was only one of mandate. Clearly, the mandate had to be precisely defined in order to avoid unfortunate confusion in the future. Paragraph 8 was, therefore, added to the resolution of 14 December 1946, to the effect that "nothing contained herein shall change or restrict the resolution of the General Assembly of 24 January 1946 which created the Atomic Energy Commission". In its resolution of 13 February 1947, the Security Council stated in a more explicit manner that issues falling under the jurisdiction of the Atomic Energy Commission "are excluded from the jurisdiction of the Commission for Conventional Armaments".

In all these discussions on procedure and mandate, the Canadian Government was obviously most concerned with the issue of peaceful uses of the atom. In a note to St-Laurent, dated 12 December, R.G. Riddell stated: "The Canadian Delegation does not consider satisfactory paragraphs 2 and 3 of the proposed [U.S.] resolution, and have moved amendments which provide specifically for the control of atomic energy for peaceful purposes, and not merely for the prohibition of atomic weapons".[32]

It fell to Dana Wilgress to present the Canadian concerns[33] before the Subcommittee of the Political Committee on 12 December. In essence he said the same thing. Canada could not accept a "restrictive" interpretation of the resolution establishing the Atomic Energy Commission. It was not sufficient to provide for a control system solely for prohibiting nuclear weapons. It was equally necessary to control the development of the atom for peaceful purposes. Canada thus reverted to the fundamental position held at the Washington Conference. Canada won her case, but history did not reflect it until the time of the creation of the International Atomic Energy Agency in Vienna. The resolution of 14 December also reflected Canada's point of view, for paragraph 6 stated: "atomic energy should be controlled to the extent necessary to ensure its use for purely peaceful purposes".

Canada's interventions within the Atomic Energy Commission thus conformed to the main line of Canadian policy. It was defined by a handful of individuals who, for the most part, had a solid and realistic knowledge of the international system. Canada's influence was, therefore, much greater than that which might have been expected from such a small number of individuals. The majority of Canadian diplomats read carefully and write well. Others act and negotiate astutely.

General McNaughton was an outstanding diplomat, and all historians recognize the important role that he played in 1946. There was no lack of Canadian testimony to this effect, whether it came from King, St-Laurent, Holmes or Ignatieff. He was accorded the same kind of recognition by his peers, including the British Delegate to the Commission, Sir Alexander Cadogan, and the French Delegate, Baron Guy de la Tournelle.

Paradoxically, the Canadian position on the right of veto was at once clear yet ambiguous. Canada detested the veto but accepted it when it was agreed and embodied in official texts. Ironically, Canada claimed a right of veto indirectly through Article 44 of the Charter. When this right of veto obstructed agreement on the Baruch Plan, Canada made every effort to reconcile the Soviets by downplaying the importance of u.s. insistence. This was understandable for, strictly speaking, the United States did not seek a right of veto but rather the absence of a right of veto concerning the establishment of an atomic energy control system. In other words, the United States was not prepared to leave the ussr even the possibility of exercising a "preventative" right of veto. The Canadian argument was perfectly logical. The ussr would not be penalized by renouncing this "preventative" right of veto since, after all, the Soviet Union would preserve such right through the powers of the Charter if ever the Council decided to impose sanctions. The Canadian position made sense. It differentiated between the effective right to use the veto and the freedom not to use it when not required by circumstances.

The Soviet position was just as defensible. The Soviets had no wish to discuss the issue *ad nauseam*: "We have what we have, and no one will take it from us!" No legal arguments that Canada could advance would change the basic problem, since the Security Council could take no important decision without Soviet consent. The position adopted by the Soviets was perfectly defensible for if they had accepted the Canadian arguments, the un would have set in motion a mechanism for institutionalized control which the ussr obviously could not support. This is clear today, but perhaps it was not so clear at the time.

These considerations perhaps explain the scepticism that the United Kingdom exhibited *vis-à-vis* the control of nuclear energy for peaceful purposes. According to Ignatieff, Ernest Bevin had little faith in the American plan and liked it even less.[34] "What would the world think today", Bevin told Ignatieff, "if at the time of Faraday's discovery of electricity, the United Kingdom had proposed a system to internationalize means of production and management of electrical power?". The argument obviously made sense, except that atomic energy was not electricity even though electricity could be produced using nuclear reactors. All things considered, the Baruch Plan was probably no more credible at the time than President Reagan's proposal to share u.s. technology in the area of strategic defence with the Soviet Union. In 1965, McNaughton spoke of the Baruch Plan as "insincerity from start to finish".

Canada and the Commission for Conventional Armaments

Before describing Canadian actions on control and reduction of armaments, a few words may be appropriate on documentary sources, personalities, the international environment and the

Canadian political context. The disarmament problem, as it was called at the time, was particularly complex since it involved innumerable commissions, committees and organs of the United Nations. Amongst French authors, Jean Klein gives the most complete and succinct account of the situation. Amongst English texts, there are two reports in the official Canadian records which provide full accounts of the first phase of negotiations, one by J.A. Gibson dated 21 April 1947, and another, unsigned, that was probably authored also by Gibson, dated 24 June 1947. The most complete account covering the 1947–49 period is that prepared by Pierce-Goulding of External Affairs for Arnold Smith, which was transmitted to John W. Holmes by John Starnes of the Canadian Delegation on 7 September 1949. These documents are available in the archives of the Department of External Affairs.[35]

In the context of personalities, it will be recalled that the United States undertook a review and revision of its foreign policy in early 1947. According to the Canadian report of 24 June 1947: "Byrnes had just been replaced as Secretary of State by General Marshall; Mr. Baruch, together with all his principal advisors had resigned from the United States' Delegation to the Atomic Energy Commission; and Senator Austin had just taken over his duties as principal Delegate of the United States to the United Nations". In Canada, St-Laurent, of whom King wrote: "He would be my choice in a moment, were he not of the minority in both race and religion"[36], became Prime Minister on 15 November 1948. According to Jean Chapdelaine[37], King really had no other choice. St-Laurent was recognized as (the) King's "*dauphin*", or heir apparent, and King had no wish to choose either Howe or Gardiner. Ilsley remained a contender since he had been named Acting Prime Minister while King was resting in Virginia. But King did not want him either. Lester B. Pearson was not yet in the race, even though he assumed the portfolio of External Affairs following the confirmation of St-Laurent as Prime Minister. Pearson was faithfully supported in his duties by such men as Marcel Cadieux, John W. Holmes and George Ignatieff. Arnold Heeney of the Privy Council, who was King's constant advisor, maintained his position until 1949. At that time, he was replaced by Norman A. Robertson, who held the position until 1952, while Heeney became Under-Secretary of State for External Affairs in March 1949.

As for the international situation, it was far from promising. In December 1947, the Berlin Conference was leading nowhere. Bevin confided to Marshall that he expected nothing more from the Soviets, and for good reason. In January 1948, there was a turn for the worse in Czechoslovakia. The *coup* in Prague took place on 25 February. In June 1948, the Berlin blockade caused major upheavals and it was not lifted until May 1949. In August 1949, the U.S. monopoly was broken. Throughout this period, Canada took cover behind a shield of well-considered caution. From 1947 onwards, King took refuge in his pre-war position of isolationism. As a result, as far as Berlin was concerned, Canada had provided "not a bag of flour or a box of powdered milk or eggs ... Canada had neither helped to run the blockade nor helped to end it".[38] In early 1950, the Soviet Union withdrew from all the main organs of the UN. In June of the same year, the Korean War broke out. As U.S. General Omar Bradley observed, to be involved in Korea was "to fight the wrong war in the wrong place at the wrong time with the wrong enemy." In any event, irrespective of who was the enemy, the international system experienced a severe shake-up.

Profound changes also occurred in Canadian policy. Eayrs summarized these changes in rather ornate style: "It may thus be concluded that by the fall of 1947 there existed within the policy community of Canada a consensus that the time was approaching when it would be prudent and expedient to create a Western security alliance of some kind to meet the threat of Soviet imperialism and to prevent the outbreak of a war."[39] Consensus thus existed. The House of Commons voted unanimously in favour of Canada's membership in the United Nations. The House also strongly supported the creation of NATO by a vote of 185 in favour with 1 abstention.

Canada also accepted the right of veto of the major powers. Canada did not merely accept alliances, she insisted on them. Above all, this was intended to bring about a change of heart within the U.S. Congress which slept warmly in its bed of isolationism, disturbed only occasionally by the proddings of Senator Vanderberg. Canada was actually one of the main architects of NATO. Canada recognized that the collective security system of the United Nations was paralysed, and thus reverted to the provisions of Article 51 of the Charter. That being said, Canada continued to defend the United Nations valiantly, through statements, diplomacy and efforts to impart some realism into the tiresome American and Soviet monologues.

The Way Ahead. During the 1948 to 1949 period, the West was faced with three fundamental questions. Should the Soviet Union be backed against the wall? Should the Soviet Union be forced to lose face? Should negotiations be broken off or resumed?

It was impossible to think that the Soviet Union could be backed against the wall. Baruch had tried it before, but without success. The

Western bloc admittedly had a large majority in the United Nations, but the USSR, even in a minority position, was able to resist through procedural manoeuvres and, to borrow and expression used by Philip Noel Baker, through the "extravagances"[40] of its discourse. Soviet diplomacy was aggressive, hard, categoric, inflexible and intolerant. The Soviet countenance was unable to raise a smile ... until Gorbachev arrived on the scene.

From time to time, Moscow walks away and slams the door. This occurred in 1950. Why continue negotiations when the Soviets had rejected Baruch or when the international situation had deteriorated to the point where agreement was clearly no longer possible? The reasons were evident. Some believed that it was still possible to bring the Soviet Union around to their way of thinking. At stake was the future of the United Nations, the very concept of the international system and the pursuit of an admittedly uneasy dialogue but one which had no substitute. Canada feared that the Soviet Union would withdraw from the United Nations, and thus dash so many genuine hopes. The Soviets had to be kept at the negotiating table.

Obviously, Moscow's appetite was not whetted by the menu on the table. The Soviets were not especially enthralled with the idea of opening their borders to an army of foreign inspectors. For the Soviet Union, the prospect of allowing its uranium mines and its nuclear industries to pass under international control was totally foreign to the concept of a Soviet State founded on secrecy, love of country and the consolidation of socialism. And when the time came for the Soviets to disclose information on their military manpower and their armed forces they resisted tenaciously, as if Baruch himself had forced open the door of the Kremlin to unveil its secrets. One can only speculate on what might have been found. All the tactics employed by the USSR were probably aimed at intimidating the West, at keeping the West occupied in interminable discussions abroad, at consolidating the territorial gains won during the war, and at stabilizing a regime for which incredible and superhuman sacrifices had been made in the name of the homeland.

The former Director of Soviet Affairs at the *Quai d'Orsay* wrote:

The USSR is the very contradiction of a State. It seeks to be at once extraordinary and ordinary, different and similar, and espouses simultaneously two policies, one of revolution through a unified and disciplined communist movement and the other of State interest through traditional military and diplomatic means ... Most non-communist leaders have difficulty reconciling the simultaneous existence of contradictory doctrines. If they meet with intolerance, they anticipate war, and if they encounter coexistence, they believe that their problems are solved. They are wrong on both counts.[41]

The West found itself in a difficult position. The socialist camp refused to open its doors or to discuss any of the proposals presented by the West. The United States decided to exploit the immense psychological advantage of propaganda that the circumstances presented, and there was nothing shameless about that. In the long term it might have brought others around to the u.s. way of thinking. The tactic obviously had little effect against such a strong adversary, especially one that was equally agile at the game. In this context, the responsibilities were shared equally between both camps, even though the moral values advocated by the United States were obviously more transparent than the somewhat coarse and boring obstructionism practised by the Soviet Union.

Canada's problem was that of assuming the appropriate posture in this dangerous game. As in most situations, there were two extremes and an intermediate position. The extreme of saying nothing and doing nothing, or savouring in silence the power and virtues of a democratic system, was rejected immediately. At the other extreme, there was the approach which consisted of being more Catholic than the Pope, and of providing advice on how better to exploit power and prestige.

Between these two extremes was the expedient of moderation. It goes without saying that Canada elected to remain faithful to her historical moderate approach. There was, however, one personality who came to break this tradition, an individual by the name of Escott Reid whom Eayrs considered as "the most deserving of mention in despatches".[42] As Eayrs observes, "Escott Meredith Reid was ... a genuine scholar and intellectual". He wrote well and had a clear and perceptive mind. In the circumstances at hand, Reid was a true strategist.

A brief history of negotiations is warranted to set the scene better. Canada became a member of the Commission for Conventional Armaments when she took her seat at the Security Council on 1 January 1948. In February 1948, there was a storm in a teacup between John Starnes of the Canadian Delegation and Frederick Osborn of the u.s. Delegation. Osborn intended to consult members of the Canadian Delegation on an informal basis on the issue of "safeguards" under item 3 of the work plan of the Commission which was approved in July 1947. He suggested that the United States had no real intention of discussing these problems in depth, particularly since the u.s. military was hardly enthralled with the idea of engaging in such discussions. In a note to R.G. Riddell dated 24 February 1948, B.M. Williams of the United Nations Division stated that if the United States intended to use this issue as a propaganda argument "it would probably be useful to know whether we wish to be part of this process".

In the meantime, consultations took place between the French, British, American and Canadian Delegations on the u.s. working paper. Following a meeting on 20 February, John Starnes received a telephone call from Osborn who was obviously furious. In recounting his conversation with Osborn, Starnes stated:

He [Osborn] said that he understood that we had referred the matter to our Government, and this had been contrary to his understanding of the manner in which it had been agreed the discussion should proceed. Without pause he went on to say that he must ask me to immediately return the document which had been handed to us under a misunderstanding. It was not, he explained, an official u.s. document ... He even went on so far as to ask me if I had made a copy of it! (At that time, we hadn't). With constraint, I pointed out that while I naturally should be very glad to comply with his request, he could not very well prevent General McNaughton from reporting to the Department of External Affairs on any matter that he felt fell within his purview ... Needless to say, under cover of a short letter, I returned the two copies by special messenger the same evening.[43]

This incident probably reflected Osborn's lack of experience and the fact that the u.s. administration had probably not authorized him to discuss the proposed work plan officially. But that was not the end of the matter. On 20 March, Escott Reid wrote a letter to Arnold Heeney, Secretary to the Cabinet, which stated:

There is not the slightest chance now of an international agreement on the reduction and limitation of armaments. The important thing, therefore, is for the Western powers to use the disarmament discussions as a stick to beat the Soviet Union with or as a weapon in the political warfare which is now going on. I have, therefore, suggested amendments to the working paper on safeguards and to the u.k. resolution on general principles. It seems to me that the same considerations apply to the work of the Atomic Energy Commission.

   The report [of the Commission] should make it crystal clear in the simplest possible language to the peoples on our side that the Western countries on the Commission want to abolish the atom bomb immediately, and are willing to accept all the necessary invasions of national sovereignty. They have been prevented from achieving this objective by the obstruction of the Soviet Union. The Soviet Union has refused to agree to the effective international inspection which alone will make an international agreement to abolish the bomb anything more than a pious Briand-Kellogg peace pact.

The refusal of the Soviet Union to agree to effective international inspection means that the world must rest under the terror of the atom bomb. It also means that the world will not be able to reap to the full the benefits of the higher standard of living for all the toiling masses of the world which would result from the full use of atomic energy for peaceful purposes.[44]

On the same date, Reid sent another note to the UN Division. "The important thing", he argued, was that "the Western powers should win a propaganda victory. We should take a leaf from Litvinov's book[45], and not worry too much about declaring our firm intention to accept substantial reductions in national armaments and effective international inspection."

On 22 March, Marcel Cadieux replied to Reid. Even if the discussions were to continue, he wrote in essence, it would not reduce the disagreements between the East and the West and the Treaty would still not be signed. After receiving this letter, Reid made a marginal note: "This is irrelevant to my argument; I meant a treaty drafted by the non-Soviet group". Cadieux continued with his analysis and exposed the essentials of his position. "Rather than continue these discussions, which would lull the people of the world into believing that something is being done about the control of atomic energy, the UK, the USA and Canada now propose to report that there is no point in continuing such discussions in view of the attitude of the USSR." In this regard, Cadieux obviously had in mind the tabling of the third and final report of the Atomic Energy Commission.

On 12 May 1948, B.M. Williams of the United Nations Division sent a long note of explanation to R.G. Riddell on the reasons why the West should suspend discussions within the Commission on issues pertaining to item 2 of the work plan:

There can be no progress in disarmament in the absence of confidence-building measures; it would perhaps be more difficult to suspend discussions later; the same reasoning applies to the discussion of safeguards, and even if these issues were discussed, they would not necessarily result in a lengthy indictment against the USSR. Our best efforts should be directed towards strengthening the United Nations so that it may fulfil its high purpose ... It is doubtful whether continuation of the work of the Commission at this time would assist in this regard. It is unlikely that the differences of opinion concerning safeguards can be resolved.

Once again, Escott Reid did not agree with this approach. In a handwritten marginal note, Reid summarized the issue of safeguards: "the point is whether further discussions would help Western governments to persuade their peoples that they are prepared to cooperate in a reasonable disarmament scheme but the Russians are not".

The Canadian position was close to that of the British, who considered that there was little more to be gained from such discussions. London went much further, however, for the Foreign Office was ready to terminate the work of the two Commissions as well as discussions bearing on the UN Military Chiefs of Staff Committee. For its part, the United States wanted to pursue these discussions. France was of the same opinion, and French Delegate de la Tournelle held that even though discussions on control of atomic energy had reached an impasse, such was not the case concerning the discussions on reduction of conventional armaments. The United States were willing to discuss safeguards, but there was no question of discussing item 4. In other words, there was no question of making concrete proposals on disarmament.[46]

In August 1948, when the second report of the Commission for Conventional Armaments was discussed, Canada sought to include a statement made previously within a working group. Ukrainian representative Manuilsky objected. When McNaughton cleverly proposed that this same statement should be repeated before the Commission, the Ukrainian representative withdrew his objection. In a memorandum to Ignatieff, dated 29 September 1948, Escott Reid in Paris returned to the attack. He proposed that the United States should declare its willingness to accept an international inspection system for both its atomic weapons as well as its nuclear reactors, adding: "However, since there is not the slightest chance of the Russians accepting international inspection, the Americans will be taking no risks in making such a promise". This was the point at which Reid's keen strategy became blunted.

On 29 October, when Reid proposed amending the draft Soviet resolution on proportionate reductions in armed forces, R.G. Riddell asked the opinion of G.K. Grande, today a journalist with the *Ottawa Citizen*. On 3 November 1948, Grande replied:

It is true that in the United Nations an amendment can amend anything with anything. It is even possible, for example, for someone to amend the phrase: "Whereas the peoples of the world are all hungry" so as to make it read: "Whereas none of the peoples of the world are at all hungry".

Therefore, it must be admitted that it is technically possible to submit any kind of amendment to any kind of a proposal.

Is it not better tactics from a purely propaganda point of view to have the original Soviet proposal go down to resounding defeat in the Assembly and then have an entirely separate resolution carried by a large majority? Surely this would be better than proposing amendments to a Soviet resolution which, stripped of all substance, might well be adopted by the majority. In any event, it is doubtful whether the Soviet bloc would sit complacently by while the Soviet resolution is entirely changed. No doubt other amendments, restoring its original meaning, would be introduced by the Ukraine, Byelorussia, Poland, etc., etc. The result would, in my opinion, be a hopeless mess.

R.M. Macdonnell, a member of the Canadian Delegation to the UN General Assembly, which at the time was sitting in special session in Paris, confirmed the soundness of Grande's judgement. Macdonnell argued that it was impossible to make changes to the Soviet resolution that would be acceptable to the West. In Macdonnell's view, the Soviets had lost the diplomatic battle: "I believe that Reid is pessimistic. The Canadian Delegation has carried its share ... and the Soviet Union is the villain of the piece."

On the whole, although Canada closed ranks with her allies, she did not engage in a pure battle of propaganda. It is difficult to imagine what more Canada could have done. The international situation allowed Canada, in common with all the other nations, no freedom of action either through her influence or public opinion.

The resolution of 19 November 1948 marked a new phase in the war of words which continued to be waged on all fronts. This resolution required "the receipt, verification and publication of all information on military manpower and weapons" of all States. In February 1949, the Soviet Union voiced its opposition to the discussion of this issue before the Security Council. The United States, therefore, referred the problem back to the Commission for Conventional Armaments which, thus empowered with a new mandate, in turn created a committee charged with studying an allied proposal presented by France on 26 May 1949.

The Issue of Military Strength.   In 1949, the disarmament negotiations became nothing more than a game. Each side moved its pawns forward and set up lines of defence while attempting to circumvent and eliminate the forces of the other. The opponents watched each other closely; there was always the chance that one side could make a mistake. In this game, a mistake could be costly, but the risks were worth it. As Churchill had said, "the USSR is a mystery shrouded in enigma". Every attempt had to be made to penetrate this engrossing mystery using all possible means.

The socialist camp showed little interest in the game, but it would be going too far to say that the Western powers were playing the game alone. After all, each opponent sought to win the respect and sympathy of other nations. At stake was the credibility of the forces of democracy pitted against the heroic hermetism of an autistic bloc. It was a strange riddle: How can two deaf parties, content to be deaf, see each other without being seen? Ten years later, two factors intervened to solve it. First, the emergence of satellite technology allowed the supposedly hard of hearing to hear a little better and, at the same time, to benefit from "celestial vision". Second, there was an improvement in communications due largely to the media and the specialized institutes which delighted in publishing information that the military authorities had, until then, attempted to conceal.

In 1949, the superpowers had neither eyes nor ears in space. They had to manage with the little at their disposal. They tried to maximize the advantage from their available resources without going too far, for then it would have been difficult to back down subsequently. Each camp had to decide what it wanted the other to reveal without divulging too much in return.

The initial positions of both sides were summarized in a short report of the Department of External Affairs dated 14 March 1949. For the United States, the issue involved three aspects: personnel, materiel and verification procedures. Personnel was to include regular, reserve and para-military forces. Materiel had to include a breakdown of naval forces, land forces (tanks, artillery, infantry) and combat aircraft. In order to verify the accuracy of the information received, the control procedures had to include general access to information through random "spot checks" that would be defined by common agreement rather than by a "search procedure" established by States party to the Treaty.

The British position on personnel was similar to that of the United States. As far as materiel was concerned, the British considered that there should be no breakdown of weapons by category – tanks, infantry, artillery – or by geographic deployment. The inspection mechanisms had to be adequate to satisfy any inspector that he was checking the records that were actually in use. Clearly, if the British proposals had been adopted, some States would have been strongly tempted to establish artificial accounting systems. Neither were the British prepared to allow access to information concerning rations, pay supplies and clothing since such information could imply geographical distribution of military forces, particularly land and air forces.

For Canada there was little at risk, for her forces were already minimal. If the proposal to reduce her military forces by one-third had been adopted, Canada would have quickly found herself with an army equivalent numerically to the current police forces of New York City. In a letter to Ignatieff, dated 26 February 1949, Holmes observed that Canada's forces represented no more than 5 percent of the maximum held by Canada during wartime. According to Holmes, the following figures pertained:

Maximum Levels (in wartime)	(736,081)	Existing Levels (February 1949)	(39,898)
Navy:	95,277	Navy:	7,753
Army:	495,804	Army:	18,145
Air Force:	215,000	Air Force:	14,000

In March 1949, the Department of External Affairs sought to sound out the Canadian military on the developments occurring within the United Nations. On 29 March, Heeney, who had become Under-Secretary of State for External Affairs that same month, wrote to the Chairman, Joint Chiefs of Staff, General Charles Foulkes, requesting his comments on the u.s. proposal. Heeney, who was present at the Joint Chiefs of Staff meeting, asked that the possibility for release of information on materiel be preserved, since such provisions were already included in allied draft proposals. If the ussr were to accept the u.s. proposal, the West would have to reciprocate in kind. At the Joint Chiefs of Staff meeting held on 28 March, the Committee agreed to release a tabulation of Canadian military forces, information on the length of service of enlisted military personnel, and all the necessary documents to allow verification of the overall tabulation of military personnel.

Little progress was made before 5 May. On that date, Holmes asked Heeney to obtain the opinion of the Joint Chiefs of Staff on three matters: the extent of McNaughton's freedom to negotiate with the allies; the substance of the u.s. and French proposals; and the question of assigning an expert to the Commission's Subcommittee responsible for studying these matters. In response, the Joint Chiefs of Staff scheduled a special meeting for 28 May. The Chiefs of Staff Committee was not in favour of the French proposal because it included a clause to release information on "holdings of warlike stores". Earlier, on 11 May, the Joint Chiefs of Staff had opposed this kind of approach, stating: "To date, Canadian holdings have not been disclosed even to the United States and the United Kingdom. If the USSR accepted these proposals it would mean that Canada would be required to table certain information which, to date, the Minister of National Defence has not given to Parliament." On 28 May, the Joint Chiefs of Staff rejected the French proposal, supported the U.S. proposal and agreed to delegate a Canadian military expert to the Subcommittee.

The U.S. proposal did not include provisions applicable to weapons under development or to "laboratories, test and experimental centres". Obviously, the Americans had in mind the guided missiles on which they were then working. For their part, the British also preferred the U.S. proposal to the French proposal. Nash, who replaced Osborn in the U.S. Delegation, considered that the French proposal was inadequate as far as control and verification was concerned. Nevertheless, the Americans were liberal-minded since they voiced no objection to Soviet inspections in Guam, recognizing that it would not involve any disclosure of the distribution of U.S. military forces in the Pacific.[47] The French Government authorized de la Tournelle to withdraw the clause from the French proposal that worried many of the military: "The tabling of information on manpower engaged in manufacturing conventional armaments and also figures indicating the production of raw materials and certain finished products having a bearing on the potential of the conventional armaments industries". At the time, the French were interested in what is known today as the industrial "input-output" picture invented by the economist Leontieff. In matters of disarmament, forward-thinking is admissible but should not be flaunted!

At its 448th session on 8 June, the Joint Chiefs of Staff Committee authorized General McNaughton to pursue negotiations with the allies on an interim basis while awaiting a decision to be made a few weeks later by the Cabinet Defence Committee. At its 11 May meeting, the Cabinet Defence Committee had proposed that a phased approach be taken to the disclosure of information. In this way, the goodwill of the Soviets could be tested at each step before proceeding to the next. Should the Soviets accept this proposal, there was always the possibility of backing down. Holmes realized that this proposal had no chance of being accepted. Nevertheless, he conscientiously advised the Canadian Delegation in New York of this new proposal. In a letter to Under-Secretary Heeney, dated 26 May, Holmes stated that "although the United Kingdom representative, speaking personally, saw some merit in the proposal, the general feeling of the meeting appears to have been that to offer to exchange information by stages would be to reduce the propaganda value of the joint paper."

On 26 May, France tabled its proposal before the third session of the General Assembly held in Paris. France, like other nations, was interested in disarmament issues. The French proposal obviously conformed to the rules of the game. It was clearly of Franco-Anglo-American inspiration, without any Canadian flavour, aimed at opening the doors to the Soviet camp while keeping the doors of the West tightly closed. Musset was right: doors have to be either open or closed.

On 18 July, the French proposal received approval from the working group by eight votes to three. On 1 August, the Commission endorsed the proposal and transmitted it to the Security Council.[48] In the ensuing discussions of the Security Council, the USSR attempted a final manoeuvre on 14 October by introducing a resolution[49] requesting States to disclose information both on their conventional weapons and on their atomic weapons. In New York, Arnold Smith negotiated with the u.s. Delegation on the tabling of a Canadian amendment aimed at responding to the Soviet request. The Canadian amendment would recognize the essential link between conventional and atomic weapons on condition that the USSR accept in each case the verification procedures proposed by the West. Following lengthy debate, the United States opposed the Canadian proposal. Discussions within the Security Council ended with the 39th Soviet veto. The deaf remained deaf, but the blind of the West never abandoned hope of being able to see ...

ATOMS FOR WAR OR FOR PEACE?

Close cooperation within the American-British-Canadian (ABC) triangle dates back to the Québec Conference in 1943. The classified discussions of this meeting were finally published in 1954 through common agreement between all parties involved. At this meeting, the three powers agreed to pool their resources to perfect the atomic bomb, known under the code name of the Manhattan Project or, as the British chose to call it, Tube Alloys. At this same meeting it was decided to establish a Combined Policy Committee (CPC). On 13 June 1944, the Combined Development Trust (CDT) was created, which became, following the entry into force of the MacMahon legislation in 1946, the Combined Development Agency (CDA).

In Canada, on 27 March 1946, Cabinet authorized the establishment of the Advisory Panel on Atomic Energy, a commission of high-level political advisors responsible for studying "the problems of national and international use and development of atomic energy". Most of the important decisions on atomic energy were taken within this Panel which was composed of a small group of influential individuals. The Prime Minister participated in discussions within this Panel whenever the circumstances so required. In August 1946, Canada created the Atomic Energy Control Board (AECB) responsible for monitoring the development of "prescribed substances" for peacefully-oriented medical or industrial research. The AECB had neither the jurisdiction nor the functions of the u.s. Atomic Energy Commission.

The Canadian Advisory Panel on Atomic Energy reported to the Under-Secretary of State for External Affairs. In 1949, this responsibility was transferred to the Defence Liaison Division which, together with the UN Division, assumed considerable importance within the Department of External Affairs. The decision to transfer responsibility from the Office of the Under-Secretary to the Defence Liaison Division did not imply any increased military interest in the issues under discussion. It was simply an administrative restructuring of the reporting relationships of an organization whose secret nature had become less imperious.

All the historians who reflected on the documentation of the Second World War and of the post-war period were categoric in their assessment of the Canadian nuclear option. The option had never been taken seriously. At least, the records reveal nothing to the contrary. Nor is there anything in the records consulted by the authors to refute this assessment. Amongst all the governmental organizations involved in atomic research, only the Chalk River laboratories would have had the requisite capability to develop atomic weapons. But according to all the historians, there was never any such intent. The Minister who was most involved in nuclear matters, C.D. Howe, the "Minister of Everything", was quite definite on this question. On 5 December 1945, he declared in the House of Commons: "We have not manufactured atomic bombs, we have no intention of manufacturing atomic bombs".[50]

The authors have not consulted, nor have sought to consult, the records of the Defence Research Board (DRB) in this regard. Logically, DRB was the only organization in which astute minds could have developed the political and military rationale for producing an atomic arsenal for the defence of Canada. Certainly the records of the Combined Policy Committee for the period 1948–1954 clearly indicate that Canada had no intention of embarking on such a path. On 9 November 1949, Prime Minister St-Laurent stated before the CPC:

"We did not want to make bombs, neither to have title to them nor to use them".[51] This line of thinking was faithfully followed in all the discussions of the CPC. Some events, however, caused Canada to lose some of her innocence in nuclear matters. The Canadian nuclear contribution was not direct, but indirect.

In 1946, the MacMahon legislation put an end to the superb allied collaboration within the ABC triangle. The United States had no intention of sharing nuclear secrets with any other power. The United States could not, however, penalize the allies that had exhibited such unfailing loyalty in the Manhattan Project. There was more to it than just that: how could the United States demonstrate its goodwill in cooperative ventures aimed at using atomic energy for peaceful purposes? The Combined Development Trust (CDT), known later as the Combined Development Agency (CDA), became little more than an agency for allocating mining resources. Nevertheless, a means had to be devised for continued information exchange. In January 1948, the U.S. Atomic Energy Commission, under the direction of Admiral Strauss, established a *modus vivendi* through Article 6 which reads as follows:

It is recognized that there are areas of information and experience in which cooperation would be mutually beneficial to the three countries. They will, therefore, cooperate in respect of such areas as may from time to time be agreed upon by the CPC and insofar as this is permitted by the laws of the respective countries.[52]

The text was silent on the right of consultation concerning the use of atomic weapons, which was established in the 1943 Québec Agreements. It is now known that British Air Marshal Maitland-Wilson was informed by the CPC on 4 July 1945 of the U.S. decision to use the A-bomb against Japan.[53] On the same occasion, C.D. Howe, who participated in this same meeting, was also informed. Two other Canadians were also advised, C.J. Mackenzie and Prime Minister Mackenzie King. King was not particularly enthusiastic about using the atomic bomb against the Japanese people, and would have much preferred that it be used against Nazi Germany.

Between 1948 and 1954, Canada faced three particular problems within the CPC. The first concerned Canada's trade position on the production of fissile material. The second resulted from the somewhat ludicrous idea of storing British atomic bombs in Canada. The third problem concerned the possibility of conducting nuclear tests on Canadian territory. The two latter problems are well documented by the renowned British specialist, Margaret Gowing, in her books on atomic collaboration between the allies. The Canadian perspective on these issues is discussed below.

The difficulties of finding a fair and equitable means of distributing uranium resources during the war are elaborated in the *Documents on Canadian External Relations*.[54] Canada did not play a significant role in the CDT or its successor, the CDA, because C.D. Howe reserved the right to sell Canadian uranium to the customers of his choice. Canada, therefore, avoided any involvement in Anglo-American disputes over distribution of uranium resources. In practice, however, Canada preferentially sold her uranium to the United States as a *quid pro quo* for 20 tonnes of heavy water, valued at 2 million dollars, provided by the Americans during the war.[55] Any good physicist, knowing the reaction capacity of the first Canadian nuclear reactor at Chalk River, could easily calculate the amount of plutonium produced by Canada during the war. The Chalk River facility was partly experimental, but also had a production capability. John W. Holmes rightly observed that Canadian production of plutonium during the war did not provide the only source of supply for the Americans, who obtained significant amounts of radioactive minerals from the Congo.[56] At the same time it must be recognized that the Congo could not supply irradiated fuels since it had no nuclear industries. Whether the plutonium in the bomb dropped on Japan was of Canadian or American origin is a question that remains unanswered. It is a fact, however, that only the Americans possessed a reprocessing plant at that time capable of recovering plutonium from irradiated fuels. And the Americans surely must have used all the plutonium available to them to produce the atomic bomb which, in 1945, was an unique device.

In all fairness, it must be admitted that C.D. Howe's main interest was in the development of Canadian industrial capability and trade with the United States. This was his essential rationale for developing the Canadian nuclear industry. Canada's plutonium production capability depended on the supply of heavy water which came from the Trail Smelter Company in British Columbia, a company situated in Canada but controlled by American interests. But Canada's nuclear industry was not totally at the mercy of the United States. First, the U.S. was developing the graphite rod as a moderator in the nuclear reaction, while Canada used a heavy water moderator. Unless the United States decided to develop a comparable heavy water system, Canada could continue to count on its heavy water supply from British Columbia. Second, Canada's Chalk River facility was comparatively efficient and produced plutonium at a rate three times greater than that of the U.S. reactor.[57] But early in 1950, C.J. Mackenzie warned that Canada's first experimental reactor was facing obsolescence and could cease to be functional within five years. Thought should therefore be given to constructing a second reactor. There was, however, no way of anticipating the future directions to be taken by the United States. Would the Americans develop their own heavy water system, or would their reserves of plutonium meet their expected needs? On 1 February 1950, Mackenzie advised the CPC that he was still not ready to present Canada's decision.

During 1950, two events occurred which completely changed the nature of the problem. First, the allies were negotiating a new five-year tripartite agreement. The Americans were particularly anxious to prevent the British from manufacturing nuclear bombs. Negotiations were aimed at defining the conditions for cooperation in developing atomic energy both for peaceful and military purposes. The United States was unwilling to reveal secret information, but was willing to exchange information on condition that the reciprocal party was engaged in "parallel research". Canada took no part in the re-negotiation of agreements on nuclear weapon production, but asked to be kept informed on weapons' characteristics so as to develop "defensive measures" against them, particularly for civil defence purposes. The tripartite cooperative agreement was signed on an interim basis. It was, however, short-lived. On 2 February 1950, Klaus Fuchs was arrested. In the words of an American authority cited by Eayrs[58], "No one ... knew more about fission bombs than James Tuck, then at Oxford ... The co-holder (of a top secret "Disclosure of Invention") was ... Klaus Fuchs".

The second event resulted from the evolution of U.S. nuclear strategy: the Pentagon decided to develop nuclear bombs for tactical use. Gordon Arneson of the U.S. State Department informed Canada and Britain of this new line of thinking on 11 November 1950. All atomic bombs would be manufactured in the United States. In exchange for British plutonium, the Royal Air Force (RAF) would be equipped with U.S. nuclear bombs. Conceivably, this turn of events influenced Canada's decision to build a second heavy water reactor at Chalk River.[59] Henceforth, Canada was assured of a market. The price of Canadian plutonium would be indexed to the price of heavy water, while the price paid by the British for South African uranium would be indexed to the price paid by the United States for Canadian uranium. From then on, the imperious needs of defence were served by cartelization and mercantilism. Canada profited from the arrangement – the same can hardly be said for Britain.

The United States was not particularly enthusiastic about the possibility that Britain could develop her own nuclear weapons.

According to Eayrs[60], a number of individuals including Byrnes, Patterson (Secretary of War), Acheson and Groves (father of the Manhattan Project), were worried not only about security *per se*, but also about the vulnerability of the British Isles to acts of sabotage, theft and terrorism. There was some justification, therefore, in allowing the British to construct their nuclear weapons on Canadian soil. When this issue was raised within the CPC, Lester B. Pearson voiced no opinion. Later, the Americans adopted the "store-British-bombs-in-Canada" proposal. According to Eayrs, it seems that Canada conditionally approved this proposal on 29 September 1949.[61] Perhaps this is an over-simplification, for discussions in the CPC continued throughout 1949 and part of 1950. Canadian approval-in-principle was accorded later, and in a somewhat indirect manner.

According to the minutes of the CPC, the proposal to store British bombs in Canada was made during the visit of the U.S. Secretary of Defense, Louis Arthur Johnson, to Ottawa in the summer of 1949. Preliminary discussions took place during September, but the issue finally came to a head in November. Omond Solandt, Chairman of the Defence Research Board, expressed the view that the British had little confidence in the ability of the U.S. Congress to declare war sufficiently rapidly in times of crisis. For his part, C.D. Howe felt that there was nothing particularly original in the proposal, given that Britain had stockpiled picrates in Canada during the Second World War. Air Vice-Marshal Frank Miller made the proposal more palatable by revealing information received from Washington to the effect that the United States was willing to share proprietary rights to their atomic bombs with the British. Arnold Heeney found the storage-in-Canada proposal unacceptable unless it were accompanied with a clause justifying it on the grounds of common defence of the Atlantic Alliance. But the Prime Minister held firm to the position that Canada would not manufacture, possess or use atomic weapons, nor would she be party to any agreement which would make Canada the "custodian" of the atomic bombs of other countries. In December, Miller added another page to the annals of history. In his view, the problem was strictly theoretical, since U.S. atomic bombs could only be supplied to the British under the "agreed strategic concepts" provisions of the Atlantic Alliance. It would take time for the British to reach the quotas prescribed by the Atlantic Alliance. Time was not, therefore, critical. But was it? In one sense, the concept was credible, for in 1950 atomic bombs could not be produced like candy. In another sense, it was not totally honest. On 12 December 1949, the NATO Defence Planning Committee agreed upon a strategic concept for the integrated defence of the North Atlantic area. The outcome of the meeting was that the United States would assume primary responsibility in wartime for initiating a nuclear attack. Only Denmark opposed this decision, apparently as a matter of principle, since for the Danes, atomic weapons could not be included in the context of strategic defence.

Was it possible that, at the CPC meeting of 9 November 1949, Miller was unaware of U.S. intentions to establish "bases for SAC [Strategic Air Command] bombers" on Canadian territory? St-Laurent was opposed to any such suggestion. Miller contended that the United States would never use such bases to launch an attack, since the United States would use them "only in case of emergency, should existing flight plans be modified". Later, U.S. plans became perfectly clear[62], and they totally contradicted Miller's statement. From that point on, the problem was twofold: How could Canada respond to the proposal to store atomic weapons on Canadian territory and at the same time allow the Americans to establish SAC bases on Canadian soil? On 1 February 1950, the CPC advanced the working hypothesis: "It is agreed that bombs shall be stored in the United States, the United Kingdom or Canada in accordance with agreed strategic concepts". Canada and the United Kingdom thus received the short end of the stick. Clearly, the only purpose of the proposal that Canada should store British atomic bombs was to ensure that the United Kingdom would not develop her own. SAC bases in Canada obviously were an integral element of the U.S. strategic concept. Canada could have resisted the proposal to store bombs on her territory, and she could have denied the unilateral U.S. request to establish SAC bases on her soil. But Canada found it difficult to deny both requests. In August 1949, the Soviets tested their first nuclear bomb. In June 1950, North Korea launched an offensive against South Korea, and towards the end of 1950, Minister of National Defence Claxton received Cabinet approval to pursue discussions with the United States aimed at establishing U.S. bases in Goose Bay and at Harmon airport. Secret agreements to that effect were signed in May 1952, and discussions opened shortly afterwards on the common defence of North America. In 1957, NORAD was born – it had already been conceived in the 1950 agreements.

In the summer of 1950, Britain's Dr. William Penney, Chief Superintendent of Armament Research and in charge of British atomic bomb production, paid a visit to Canada aimed at finding a suitable site for British nuclear tests. Eayrs used the expression "an innocent abroad" to characterize Penney's trip. Margaret Gowing refers to a feasibility study jointly prepared by Penney and Solandt on that subject, but Solandt, in his correspondence with Eayrs, denies the existence of any such study, stating: "As I recall it, the Canadian attitude toward the whole idea of [a] nuclear weapon program was so negative that it was not pursued beyond the informal discussion stage".[63] Solandt was right. The minutes of the CPC reflect these discussions, but make no mention of an Anglo-Canadian report.

The situation was actually more complex. There was not only one "innocent abroad", for the Americans were also looking for new test sites. The Penney Report observed that, from Britain's perspective, the ideal site would be the western side of Hudson Bay, south of Churchill in Manitoba, where the shallow waters would best suit British test requirements. The Penney Report considered that 200 scientists, 50 technicians and 100 industrial workers would be needed to conduct the first test of what Penney might have described as a British bomb. In his report to the CPC, Solandt talks of 500 personnel and a total cost of 5 million dollars.[64] As far as the Americans were concerned, the Eniwetok Atoll in the Pacific was no longer suitable, and their attention was turning towards Alaska and the Aleutian Islands. There was no talk of sites in Canada. Scientific and military staffs were, however, justifiably concerned with means of detection and the effects of nuclear bombs, since civil defence had become a priority issue. At that time, Canada was developing techniques to determine the characteristics and levels of radioactivity in air samples, and thus identify the types of test devices. Shortly afterwards, during the 1950s, Canada succeeded in developing her own means of detection. In 1951, the watchword was cooperation and collaboration. It was then learned that "the MacMahon Act prevented the U.S. Atomic Energy Commission from actually giving us the results obtained at their observation stations in northern Canada".[65]

Nevertheless, the United States put on a good appearance. Canada would receive half of the information collected by U.S. sensors, together with a full description of U.S. analytical methodology.

In 1951, the British engaged in informal discussions with the Australians on the same issue. The British Admiralty was interested in "simulating the explosion of a clandestine bomb introduced by a ship in port". C.J. Mackenzie observes that there was little chance that the Americans would support such a proposal. It goes without saying that Canada was not too unhappy that it now became Australia's turn to be exposed to the extravagant demands of the British. None of these proposals was followed up, and the discussions always remained purely informal. It is difficult to assess how Canada might have reacted if all these proposals had materialized. The only available indication is contained in a statement made by the Secretary to the

Cabinet, N.A.R. Robertson, to the CPC at its 11 November 1950 meeting:

> The only condition on which the Canadian Government might consider such a proposal sympathetically, would be if both the U.S. and the U.K. governments were to ask us to establish a joint testing area on the grounds that it were close enough to both countries for administrative convenience and economy, and yet a sufficiently remote area where there would be a minimum of dislocation to the life of the area. We should not, however, initiate any program or proposal for the establishment of an atomic proving ground in Canada.

At the time, there was no systematic opposition to establishing a nuclear test facility in Canada. The mere fact that it was discussed indicates that any such proposal would not necessarily have been rejected. Nevertheless, reticence ran high. If a pact with the Devil was really necessary, it would have to be made in the name of the Atlantic Alliance. When surrounded by "innocents", it is perhaps better to lose one's virginity in a series of steps rather than in one fell swoop.

For others, the question did not even arise. Ignatieff, for instance, in an interview with the authors, claimed that Canada lost her virginity at the time of the Québec Accords in 1943. According to Ignatieff, Mackenzie King's thinking on the nuclear issue could be summarized in the succinct phrase: "Hear no evil, think no evil, do no evil!" Saying is easier than doing, but Canada achieved the opposite: doing without saying. Still, Canada's sin was no more than venial, for she did little more than participate in the war effort against the forces of fascism and naziism. In 1950, Canada again found herself caught up in the turn of events. The name of the game was now the fight against communist totalitarianism, under the cover of an alliance that she herself had helped to found. The U.S. nuclear umbrella was deployed, and the winds of the squall intensified ...

3 The Pilgrim's Staff and the Blind Man's Cane

... feet sliding in the clinging mud, despite the aid of steel-tipped staffs, on the steep slopes of the paths.

Pierre Loti, *Ramuntcho*

For the Europeans, the problems posed by conventional forces and atomic weapons are inextricably intertwined. This is probably true for the Soviets also. It is less true for the Americans, who hardly feel threatened by the presence of military forces massed at their borders. When the question of negotiating the elimination of intermediate-range nuclear forces arose in 1987, the good sense of the Europeans prevailed. There could be no question of eliminating INF without suitable provisions to neutralize, or compensate for, the significant numerical superiority of the Warsaw Pact conventional forces.

It was in 1950, as the war raged in Korea, that the international system entered a period of great tension. Military research was at its peak. Within the space of five years, two new technologies – the thermonuclear warhead and the intercontinental ballistic missile – came to revolutionize strategic thinking. In each case, the superpowers had to adapt quickly. The Americans were the first to test the H-bomb in November 1952, followed by the Soviets less than one year later (August 1953), just a few months after the Korean armistice was signed. Stalin's death in 1953, the resolution of the Indochina issues in 1954, the Geneva Summit in 1955, the discrediting of Stalinist doctrine in 1956, and the major disarmament talks all contributed to the first real East-West *détente*. Nevertheless, the 1957 revolution in ballistics technology completely changed the u.s. perception of the Soviet threat. The great American "island" suddenly became vulnerable. The nuclear threat, previously far removed yet absolute, became immediate and global. The world trembled while

America reflected for, to modify Metternich's well-known phrase, when America sneezes, Europe catches cold.

In the early 1950s, the United States produced very few proposals on the control of atomic energy. The State Department was "short of ideas". The United States still considered that it must adhere to the majority plan (Baruch plan). France thought otherwise. Why not entrust the matter to an international control organization which would allow the various nations to develop at least their own nuclear power stations on condition that all other nuclear elements fell under international control? In January 1953, Ike Eisenhower, former Supreme Allied Commander Europe (SACEUR), replaced Harry Truman as President of the United States. Several working groups were established to review the main elements of the Baruch plan. In December 1953, President Eisenhower proposed his "Atoms for Peace" plan.

In the area of general conventional and nuclear disarmament, the Europeans carried the pilgrim's staff. The road was long and arduous, strewn with pitfalls. Against all obstacles, the Europeans came forward with global disarmament plans, the best known of which is the famous Anglo-French Memorandum of June 1954. In 1955, American Delegate Stassen "held in reserve" the American position on all the proposals previously discussed within the Subcommittee of the Disarmament Commission in London. From that time on, there was a move away from disarmament *per se* towards arms control. The American sneeze disrupted dialogue in the Subcommittee. For the Europeans, the Subcommittee was no longer viable. Europe, rightly or wrongly, caught cold. The French continued to press for support of their disarmament proposals.

The trend towards arms control became more pronounced in 1957 with the spectacular launch of the first Soviet Sputnik. Europe had to cast aside its pilgrim's staff. From that point on, the United States was left with only the blind man's cane. It was essential to penetrate the Iron Curtain, to see the other side and to know what was going on. The result was the "Open Skies" proposal of 1955 and the creation of the Conference of Experts on Prevention of Surprise Attack in 1958. Ironically, the 1957 technology which made nuclear war possible was the very technology which, from 1960 onwards, transformed blind nuclear terror into a half-visible threat, at least for the Americans. Through satellites, territories that were previously closed became open and military forces took shape on ordnance survey maps. The large military industrial complex, whose existence had been one of the jealously guarded State secrets, became visible for all to see.

THE DISARMAMENT COMMISSION AND ITS SUBCOMMITTEE[1]

When the Disarmament Commission was established in January 1952, it inherited all the problems that had been under discussion between 1945 and 1950. How was it possible to control atomic energy and at the same time reduce and regulate conventional armaments? As early as 1950, the General Assembly of the United Nations, through its resolution 496(V), proposed a study to assess the appropriateness of combining the mandates of two previous agencies, the Atomic Energy Commission and the Commission for Conventional Armaments. The following year, the Committee of Twelve proposed the creation of such a combined agency within the Security Council. In January 1952, in conformity with its resolution 502(VI), the General Assembly created, under the aegis of the Security Council, a Disarmament Commission charged with developing proposals "for the regulation, limitation and balanced reduction of all armed forces and all armaments". In April 1952, the Disarmament Commission established two working groups, one charged with studying the issue of "regulation of all armaments and armed forces", the other with studying the issues of "disclosure and verification of information on all armaments" (including atomic weapons).

All the above issues were the subject of intense negotiation in 1952. During the following year, the Disarmament Commission held only one session. In its third report, which was innocuous and hence supported unanimously, it expressed the hope that the recent events (end of the war in Korea and change of government in Washington) "would create a more propitious atmosphere for the reconsideration of the disarmament question". In November 1953, the United Nations General Assembly (UNGA) proposed the creation of a "Subcommittee of the main powers involved" which would be responsible for undertaking an independent study to find an acceptable solution to the problem of disarmament. On 19 April 1954, the Commission followed up on the proposal, and created a Subcommittee comprising five powers, namely the Big Four and Canada. This Subcommittee met intermittently mostly at Lancaster House in London throughout the period between May 1954 and September 1957. In total, the Subcommittee held 157 working sessions. The structure, mandate and main activities of the Disarmament Commission and its Subcommittee are given in Table 3.

In the course of its work, the Commission examined various proposals, the more important of which were:

Table 3
The Disarmament Commission and Its Subcommittee

THE DISARMAMENT COMMISSION

Creation: Resolution 502(VI), 11 January 1952, (42 votes versus 5, with 7 abstentions).

Mandate: "To prepare proposals ... for the regulation, limitation and balanced reduction of all armed forces and all armaments, for the elimination ... of weapons of mass destruction, and for the effective international control of atomic energy ..."

Composition: The eleven member States of the Security Council plus Canada.

Commission Reports:
- 1st Report, 29 May 1952, DC/11;
- 2nd Report, 20 August 1953;
- 3rd Report, 9 October 1954, DC/20;
- 4th Report, 29 July 1954, DC/55.

THE FIVE-POWER SUBCOMMITTEE

Origin: Resolution 715(VIII), 28 November 1953, (54 votes versus 0, with 5 abstentions).

Creation: By the Commission on 19 April 1954, (9 votes versus 1, with 2 abstentions).

Mandate: To seek, in private, solutions to the problems discussed within the Commission.

Composition: The Big Four plus Canada.

Main dates of sessions and events connected with work of the Subcommittee:
- London: 13 May 1954 – 22 June 1954;
- London: 25 February 1955 – 18 May 1955;
- The Geneva Summit (18–23 July 1955);
- New York: 29 August – 7 October 1955;
- Four-Power Foreign Ministers' Conference (27 Oct – 16 Nov 1955);
- London: 19 March 1956 – 4 May 1956;
- London: 18 March 1957 – 6 September 1957.

- the American Plan of 5 April 1952 (DC/C. 2/1) concerning the progressive and continuous disclosure and verification of information on armed forces and armaments;
- the Soviet Plan of 19 March 1952 calling for prohibition of atomic weapons;
- the tripartite proposal (United States, France, Great Britain) of 28 May 1952 concerning the fixing of numerical ceilings for armed forces (DC/10), of which the main elements were:

USSR, U.S. and China:	Between 1 and 1.5 million men;
France and the U.K.:	Between 7 and 8 hundred thousand men;
Other States:	Ceiling less than 1% of population and at existing levels, save under exceptional circumstances;

- the French "compromise formula" of 24 June 1952, presented by Delegate Jules Moch.

In the view of Jean Klein there were three main areas of divergence within the Commission:[2]

- the disclosure of military information should have been at the start of the process according to the American proposals, and at the end according to the Russian proposals;
- conversely, atomic weapons should have been banned at the start according to the Russians, and at the end according to the Americans;
- finally, according to Washington, atomic control should have included international ownership or at least international management of all mines and factories, while for Moscow it would have comprised continuous inspection, although the details were not specified.

The main proposals discussed within the Subcommittee of Five were as follows:

- the Anglo-French plan of 11 June 1954;
- the Soviet proposal of 10 May 1955;
- the American "Open Skies" proposal presented at the 1955 Geneva Summit;
- the Anglo-French synthesis proposal of 19 March 1956;
- the American proposals of 21 March 1956, one concerning technical exchange missions and the other experimental zones for demonstrating control and inspection;
- the Soviet proposal of 27 March 1956 on reductions in conventional armaments and armed forces;

- the American proposal of 3 April 1956 on the first phase of a disarmament program;
- the Soviet proposal of 30 April 1957 (and of 20 September 1957) on aerial inspection and acceptance of geographic zones of over-flight, as well as the halting of nuclear tests;
- the Western proposals of 29 August 1957.

On 4 November 1957, the government of the USSR informed the Western world that it would no longer participate in the work of the Subcommittee unless the Commission were radically changed. That same month, following an Indo-Canadian proposal, the General Assembly enlarged the composition of the Commission to twenty-five members. In 1959, all the member States of the United Nations were included. The Commission continued to meet until 1965. It then fell into oblivion until 1978 when it was reactivated at the First United Nations Special Session on Disarmament (UNSSOD I). After that, the Commission became purely a forum for discussion and met for roughly three weeks annually.

On the whole, the period between 1954 and 1957 was one of change and adaptation in which hopes were born and dashed, with the Western world experiencing one disappointment after another. Europe insisted on balanced and controlled disarmament even though the United States no longer believed in it, while the USSR, which was undergoing profound internal change, tried every means to exploit any differences between Western nations.

CANADA AND THE DISARMAMENT COMMISSION

The UN Disarmament Commission was created in 1952. It was quite normal that Canada should be a participant because the Commission had inherited all the issues discussed within the former Atomic Energy Commission and the Commission for Conventional Arma-ments. Canada's role remained, however, rather unobtrusive. Ottawa had insufficient resources to exert much weight, in terms of both its analytical capability and its influence within the international system.

Canada's Overall Position

The records show that on many occasions it was not possible to separate basic issues from propaganda. As early as February 1952, Canada hovered between an "active approach and a passive approach". Lester B. Pearson, Secretary of State for External Affairs, in a despatch to the Canadian Embassy in Washington dated 29 February 1952, concluded that he would prefer the Commission to "do nothing rather than to have it engage in polemic exchanges". On 25 April 1952, in a despatch from Ottawa to David M. Johnson, Canada's Permanent Representative to the United Nations, the same theme recurred: it would be better to have the Commission go into hibernation rather than allow it to become a forum for propaganda. On that same date, Canada's Representative admitted that his role in the discussions had not been one of "leadership".

The Canadian Representative's assessment of the situation as a whole at the Commission and of its key figures is interesting in several respects. Johnson confirmed that the Western powers were unanimous on the importance of maintaining the linkage between nuclear and conventional weapons. Since Canada had no experience in maintaining vast military establishments, Johnson considered that Canada should focus on influencing issues concerning control of atomic energy rather than on those bearing on reductions in conventional weapons. Although he was correct in his judgement of basic issues, he was incorrect in his assessment of the nature of events that would follow. Up to December 1953, the proposals that were presented to the Commission largely reiterated the majority plan. At that time, the Americans decided to present their "Atoms for Peace" proposal, and Canada was not even consulted. Furthermore, when Canada did put forward a proposal in August 1952, it concerned a "new approach" to the issue of conventional force reductions.

As for personalities, Johnson considered that the French Delegate, Jules Moch, was one of the most effective debaters in the Commission, commenting that "Mr. Moch has been making remarkably lucid and comprehensive studies of the situation as a whole". This was a fair judgement but one which apparently did not apply to the American Delegate, Benjamin V. Cohen, of whom he wrote:

Although his querulous manner of speaking does not carry much weight, he has been more effective in his private talks with other Delegations in which he has demonstrated his sincerity and his readiness to listen carefully to other points of view.[3]

Concerning procedures, Canada wanted the Commission's discussions to be held in camera. According to Escott Reid this position was strongly held by External Affairs' Minister Lester B. Pearson.[4] In actual fact, it was first proposed by British Delegate Gladwyn Jebb, and supported by the Dutch Delegate, Von Balluseck. Due to a mistake by the Chairman of the Commission, the British position was linked to an amendment that Canada was presenting at the time. The Canadian amendment did not survive long. Cohen did not systematically oppose it, but he argued that before the amendment came into effect the Soviets and Americans should first present officially their initial proposals for negotiation. The Canadian amendment was defeated in April by one vote. There was no further discussion until the time of the final draft of the Commission's second report in October. When the Secretariat asked the principal Delegations to summarize the content of their main proposals with a view to preparing the report, Canada dropped its insistence on in-camera discussions on condition that the Soviets relinquish their arguments on the need for public debate. Thus, there is no mention of the issue of public or in-camera debate in the Commission's second report.

Still in the context of procedural issues, the Canadian Peace Congress asked for a hearing before the Commission in July 1952. In a despatch to Ottawa dated 18 July, Johnson stated that this would bend the rules of procedure, but that the Secretariat had no wish to quarrel with the Canadian Peace Congress. Johnson was wrong on this point since, according to the Charter of the United Nations, any Non-Governmental Organization (NGO) has the right to argue its case before the United Nations. This error was corrected in a telegram dated 19 August that was signed simply "The Canadian Delegation", and which read: "Contrary to what the Secretariat had told us last month, the rules of procedure of the Disarmament Commission do not exclude the appearance of a non-governmental Delegation before the Commission". All's well that ends well.

On the whole, the best document on Canada's overall position in the Commission can be found in a despatch from the Secretary of State for External Affairs dated 9 May 1952 addressed to Canada's Permanent Representative to the United Nations. It was, in fact, prepared the previous day by an affable and serious man, John G.H. Halstead, Director of the Defence Liaison Division. It reads, in part, as follows:

Whether we like it or not, the two main aspects of this task [substance and propaganda] cannot be separated.

It will not be sufficient for the Western powers merely to take a dogmatic stand on their previous position ... Any real progress toward the goal of disarmament can be measured only by the extent to which agreement can be achieved between the Soviet Union and the Western powers. It should therefore be the main objective of the Canadian Delegation to bring about such agreement ... In this connection we should bear in mind, as I stated in

Committee 1 of the General Assembly on November 21, 1951, that there must be a balance of risks and safeguards on both sides ...

It would scarcely be appropriate for Canada, with its limited experience in the maintenance of large military establishments, to prepare in detail a general disarmament plan, but we might contribute to such a plan with respect to atomic control.

We therefore intend to re-examine the provisions of the majority plan concerning ownership and operation of facilities with a view to working out possible modifications on those points ...

I should therefore like to see the Disarmament Commission's committees operate like the Four-Power Subcommittee established by Committee 1 of the recent General Assembly, and not like most of the "secret" discussions which are being conducted at Panmunjom where the practice has been to tell the press everything, thus foregoing the advantages of secret diplomacy.

We must face the fact that progress there [the work of the Commission] depends in large part on the broad balance of power in the world between the Western powers and the Soviet Union and its allies ... Our purpose in building defensive strength in association with our allies in NATO is not only to deter and, if necessary, to defeat aggression, but also to reach such a position of strength that the Soviet Union will wish to negotiate with the Western world.

These instructions clearly summarized Canada's position: moderation, prudence, mediation, search for a serious atmosphere of discussion, and modest contribution to debate, within the framework of a more general policy wherein Canada remained a faithful ally of the Western world.

Canadian Reaction to the Tripartite Proposal

The Anglo-Franco-American proposal of 28 May 1952 for reducing armed forces was the product of collective allied efforts. The Tripartite Proposal had its origins in an American draft, but the draft contained so many uncertainties and so little balance that it would scarcely have escaped harsh Soviet criticism. The original text was "wordy and repetitious", and the main force reduction formula was "buried in the middle of the paper".[5] The reaction of the British representative on the U.N. Military Chiefs of Staff Committee, General Dimoline[6], was similar to that of Delegates Moch and Jebb. He had no hesitation in telling Cohen that the American proposal had no "balance". On 25 April 1952, Johnson advised Ottawa that the American proposal basically advocated the following manpower levels for the force structures of the main blocs:

- Western powers: 5,231,000 men
- Middle East and India: 3,487,000 men
- Eastern powers: 3,873,000 men.

In the figures proposed for the two Germanies, it is interesting to note that West Germany was allowed 500,000 men compared with 170,000 for East Germany. The British and the French efforts to modify the American proposal resulted in the Tripartite Proposal of 28 May 1952 (see above). This proposal advocated a million and a half men each for the USSR and the United States, thus providing a better balance. Global thresholds of between 700,000 and 800,000 men each were proposed to meet the defence requirements of the home countries and colonies of both Britain and France. The United States carefully avoided any possible discussion on the manner in which the respective forces of these two nations would be distributed.

The formula for sizing the armed forces of all other States was one percent of population except under special circumstances. This formula, which was written into the original American proposal, obliged the Canadian government to examine the Tripartite Proposal of 28 May a little more closely. Even at the time when the American proposal was being discussed, Johnson in New York made it known on 25 April that it would allow for an expansion of the Canadian Forces.

On 30 May, Escott Reid asked the Chairman of Canada's Joint Chiefs of Staff for his advice on the Tripartite Proposal. On 23 June, the Department of External Affairs informed the Canadian Delegation in New York that this advice had still not been received. The same day, D. Wilgress of the Department of External Affairs, in a briefing note to the Joint Planning Committee, raised three specific questions:

1   Do you agree with the intention of the proposal, which is "to reduce the possibility and fear of successful aggression" and "to avoid a disequilibrium of power dangerous to international peace and security"?
2   Is it necessary or desirable in the proposed "working formula" to make a distinction between the armed forces of the five major military powers and those of all other States?
3   Should Canada be prepared to accept the Tripartite Proposal?

On 9 July, in response to the initial request of 30 May, the Joint Planning Committee stated that "the proposal for numerical limitation of personnel in the armed forces is but one aspect of the overall disarmament question, and that the success of disarmament measures will be dependent on the working out of a suitable formula for control". This point of view was endorsed by the Joint Chiefs of Staff on 17 July. Military advice can hardly be described as excessively verbose.

On 21 July, the Department of National Defence provided its response to the three above questions to the Department of External Affairs. To the first question, the Chiefs of Staff answered in the affirmative. To the second, they accepted the validity of maintaining a distinction between the armed forces of the five major powers and those of all other States, but concluded "it is doubtful if agreement would ever be reached if such an attempt were made. Therefore, a different formula is needed for the remaining States". To the third question, which more directly affected Canada, the Chiefs of Staff answered affirmatively, but added:

The present service strength in Canada including active reserve forces and the RCMP is 162,039. Present ceiling is 231,454. A reduction in both the present strength and the ceiling would be necessary to reduce the forces below the one percent figure. This would have to be a balanced reduction of the three services. The reduction figures for each service could be determined at a later date if there were any indications that the Tripartite Proposal would be accepted.

The opinion of the military was not the most judicious, since on 31 May 1952 the breakdown of Canadian military strength was as follows:

Active strength:	103,587
Regular forces:	97,834
Reserves:	57,452
	155,286
RCMP	5,753
Grand total	162,039

The opinion given by the Chiefs of Staff on 21 July did not satisfy the Department of External Affairs. On 12 August, External Affairs posed two more questions. How could reductions in the various services be made, and what weapons systems should each service possess? These additional questions were posed at a time when two new initiatives were being discussed. The first was a Canadian initiative proposing a "new approach" for balanced reductions in military strength. This aspect will be dealt with in the following section. The second initiative, proposed by the Americans, was an addendum to the Tripartite Proposal of 28 May. It was tabled on 12 August partly in response to the general Soviet criticism that the Tripartite Proposal was aimed only at justifying the "swollen" levels of current strengths, but mainly in response to the particular complaint of Delegate Malik that the Western proposal made no specific mention of existing force levels for the naval and air elements nor the manner in which reductions in these services would be effected. The addendum essentially proposed that the superpowers come to a negotiated agreement on the force level issue, that regional conferences be held to include the participation of States having military forces deployed in the regions in question, and that all the agreements be incorporated into a draft treaty for approval by all States within the framework of a world conference on disarmament. There could not have been a better way of burying the issue. At all events, it was at this particular point in time, when the addendum to the Tripartite Proposal was tabled, that D. Wilgress chose to pose his two additional questions to the Chairman of the Chiefs of Staff.

On 19 August, the Joint Planning Committee acknowledged that the Tripartite Proposal "could only have minimal effect" on Canada since the reserves were included in the total force strength figures presented previously. In 1952 Canada's population was 13.8 millions, which in principle allowed her to maintain a total force strength of 138,000. The Joint Planning Committee also took the position that any force reduction formula should take account of a number of geographic, economic and industrial factors and that, in any case, it should not prevent States from increasing military strength to the maximum in time of war. This proposal was eminently sensible, but it hardly responded to the concerns of the Department of External Affairs. On 22 August, the Committee added that a general reduction formula was not feasible and that any reductions would depend on our obligations to NATO and the United States.

On 26 August, the Cabinet Defence Committee intervened and authorized the Canadian Delegation to act on the basis of the following principles:

a   the Canadian Government agrees with the intention of the Tripartite Proposal that numerical limitations on the armed forces of all militarily important States is an essential element of any disarmament program;

b   the Canadian Government agrees with the necessity in such limitations of making a distinction between the armed forces of the five major military powers and those of all other States;

c   Canada would be prepared to accept, as part of a general disarmament plan, the ceiling which the Tripartite Proposal would impose on Canadian armed forces (either less than one percent of the population or less than current levels); and

d   the numerical limitation of armed forces is but one aspect of the disarmament question and the success of disarmament would be dependent upon the working out of a suitable formula for control.

Canada was no more inclined to discuss the Tripartite Proposal than any other power in the Commission. The United States had no wish to make compromises or to grant concessions until the Soviets demonstrated their willingness to negotiate.[7] French Delegate Moch was reminded of the u.s. position during private discussions with B.H. Bechoeffer of the State Department at the beginning of May.[8] The main aim of these discussions was obviously to prevent Moch from tabling his proposal for three stage reductions, which he did, in any case, on a private and informal basis in June. The United States, through its affiliation with the Tripartite Proposal, sought to "draw public attention to Soviet mass armies rather than the United States' atomic bombs".[9] This struggle for public opinion continued throughout the period of the Commission's work in 1952. The British position was clear from the time that the October report was developed. B.H. Robinson, then Second Secretary of the Canadian High Commission in London, wrote to the Under Secretary of State for External Affairs on 4 September informing him of the content of a telegram sent from the British Foreign Office to New York, which included the following:

I consider the most important outcome of the proceedings of the Disarmament Commission up till now to be the contrast between the constructive and sincere efforts of the Western powers to lay a practical basis for disarmament, as evidenced by the working papers they have submitted, and the purely propaganda reiteration of the slogans, which he has refused to amplify, by the Soviet Delegate ... Finally, I should prefer the Assembly's resolution, while continuing the Disarmament Commission in being for another year, to do no more than request the Commission to continue its discussions on the basis of the working papers already before it and to formulate further working papers of similar nature.

The British Foreign Office showed the way. A seemingly endless succession of proposals appeared over the next five years.

The Canadian Proposal for a New Approach

In a memorandum to External Affairs' Minister Pearson dated 14 August 1952, Assistant Under-Secretary of State L.D. Wilgress focused attention on the dilemma faced by the Western powers in the Disarmament Commission. Quoting from a British document, Wilgress re-stated the argument that Western security depended on atomic weapons. The capability for nuclear deterrence should not, therefore, be relinquished "until a very late stage in any disarmament process". The major powers "should even avoid consideration by the Disarmament Commission of any concrete or substantive proposals for a firm program, a timetable, or a draft treaty". This did not prevent the British from preparing a draft treaty which finally was not tabled for fear that the French be tempted to follow suit.[10] The British managed, however, to include the essentials of their proposals in the Commission's second report, while the French, as early as 24 June 1952, proposed their own formula for compromise. Obviously, Canada was not satisfied with this situation, and contemplated a "new approach" to remove this dilemma for the Western powers. As Wilgress wrote, a "horizontal" rather than "vertical"[11] approach should be proposed for the components of a disarmament program. His suggestion was, therefore, to start with a first manageable "slice" which would cover, in the first stage, all the essential elements of a disarmament program. This approach would include the following elements:

a   the balanced reduction of armed forces (the Tripartite Proposal for the numerical limitation of armed forces might serve to cover this element of the "first slice");
b   the balanced reduction of conventional armaments;
c   the initial steps in the establishment of an effective international control of atomic energy to ensure the eventual prohibition of atomic weapons (for this purpose it will undoubtedly be necessary to re-examine the United Nations majority plan with a view to working out possible modifications of those provisions dealing with ownership and operation of facilities);
d   the disclosure and verification of sufficient information on armed forces and armaments, including atomic weapons, to enable the "first slice" to be carried out (the first stage of the United States proposal – the 2 April proposal – on this subject might be adapted for this purpose); and
e   the establishment of an embryo international control organ with sufficient staff and authority to ensure the implementation of the "first slice".

The Canadian formula was obviously not without interest. Its intent was similar to that of a statement made later by Jules Moch: "no disarmament without control, no control without disarmament, but all disarmament that can be controlled". The Canadian formula also attempted not to offend British or American sensibilities and demonstrated profound political realism.

The proposal ran into problems, both from within and without, and died before the ink was even dry. In Ottawa, the Department of External Affairs naturally asked for the opinion of the Department of National Defence. In his correspondence of 25 August, L.D. Wilgress noted that Canada's silence on the Tripartite Proposal was due mainly to remaining doubts that required further study (the Cabinet Defence Committee reached a decision only on the following day). On 4 September, the Canadian Ambassador in Washington, Hume Wrong, signalled that, in accordance with directives received, he would refrain from discussing Canada's "new approach" with the State Department. At that point in time, discussions on the "new approach" were confined to other allied Delegations in New York.

On 30 September, the Joint Planning Committee declined any further participation, stating that insufficient resources were available to study the "new approach". One week earlier, on 23 September, James George of the Canadian Delegation made no attempt to mince his words in a personal letter describing the situation to John G.H. Halstead in Ottawa. In it, he asserted that nothing ever happened in Ottawa unless all those involved agreed with the assumptions of their superiors, and in turn with the superiors of their superiors, adding whimsically that in the Department of National Defence:

It is never possible to reach agreement because that first paragraph with which every Chiefs of Staff study must start – assumptions – cannot ever be cleared ... In our Department we seem to work on the less tidy but probably more practical premise that the assumptions, if any, may emerge from the study rather than the other way around.

James George was right, for on 6 November the Joint Planning Committee essentially declared: "no structures, no advice". The lazy ant was snowed under.[12] On 14 November, the Deputy Chiefs of Staff concurred in the view of the Joint Planning Committee, adding, somewhat audaciously that before proceeding further they would have to know the extent to which the Chiefs of Staff were prepared to engage in discussions on disarmament. The patience of External Affairs had already been exhausted. In a sharp note dated 26 December, G. de T. Glazebrook of the Defence Liaison Division essentially said that if the military did not intend to give an opinion, they should come right out and say so – and as soon as possible. In the same note to R.A. MacKay, Glazebrook nevertheless added: " ... it seems that they are not satisfied with this way of solving the problem".

All these difficulties led to the creation in 1953 of the Joint Disarmament Working Party (JDWP), the history of which has already been described in Chapter 1. The Canadian proposal went no further, as the "new approach" met with resistance from the allies. The Americans, who were the first to oppose it, considered that the "new approach" was unsatisfactory from a propaganda standpoint.[13] According to Hume Wrong, R. Gordon Arneson of the u.s. State Department thought that the Soviets would use this proposal to publicly accuse the West of insincerity, since the Western nations themselves had proposed a one-third reduction in the force strengths and numbers of weapons of the superpowers. In addition, the United States were reviewing their position on disarmament following the creation of a group of experts led by Secretary McGeorge Bundy (the main achievement of this group later proved to be the "Atoms for Peace" proposal). The United States sought increased consultation with their allies and the final *droit de regard* "before such complex proposals were exposed to discussion in a wider forum and to negotiation with the Soviet Union". In short, the Americans thanked the Canadians for their efforts, while telling them that they were not the least interested in doing anything in the circumstances of the time.

The comments of the other Delegations in New York were hardly more encouraging, except for those of the French which, in any event, were few. Jacques Tiné of the French Delegation said simply that he had no doubt that the *Quai d'Orsay* as well as Moch (who at the time was travelling in the French provinces) would welcome the Canadian initiative. Tiné added that although it was not a "great leap forward" it was a step in the right direction.[14] The British and American Delegations repeated the arguments that had been advanced in Washington on the importance of the propaganda element, adding that "no amount of work on a first slice alone will overcome the fundamental Soviet objection that the West is only interested in collecting intelligence data and not in prohibiting weapons of mass destruction which we reserve for some final and, they say, never-to-be-reached stage". B. Cohen admitted that he had tried to separate the various elements of a disarmament program, but had met with objections from the Pentagon. Cohen concluded that the three services would never agree on how the forces within a given total threshold should be distributed. There is no need of further elaboration. David M. Johnson ended his despatch by noting that there was little advantage in submitting a new approach before an armistice convention could be held in Korea.

The irony was that both the French and the Canadians thought along similar lines. Conceivably, their efforts might have succeeded, had it not been for the isolation that both France and Canada experienced, and the torpedoing of the Canadian proposal from within by the Department of National Defence. Admittedly, Washington would have been outraged by any Franco-Canadian alliance, particularly in light of the French proposal of 24 June 1952 which irritated the Americans intensely.

The French Compromise Formula of 24 June 1952

The French proposal of 24 June 1952 was strangely similar to that which the French later proposed on 11 November 1953. This is not surprising, since the compromise formula of 24 June consisted of nothing more than the personal views of French Delegate Jules Moch and a section of the Socialist Party in power at the time. In actual fact, the compromise formula of 24 June was presented, despite allied reticence, as a personal and unofficial proposal.

The compromise formula essentially specified the links to be maintained between the issues of force reduction and control of atomic energy, or what is referred to today as the non-diversion of atomic energy for military purposes. It also proposed a schedule for the various stages of disclosure and control in the process of reducing force strength and weapons. The u.s. position on atomic energy was known: Washington held that stocks of nuclear material had become so considerable that immediate disclosure was necessary. The French position was no less sensible: whether or not agreement on control could be reached, no control organization would be able to discover the extent of previous production. This was the problem that led to consultations between the Americans and the French in September 1952 on ways of resolving their technical differences. But, in fact, their differences were political. The French argued that the Baruch plan was outdated, and that some sort of alternative should be proposed. France was well aware of the economic benefits that could accrue from the exploitation of atomic energy for peaceful purposes. Controls should not apply, therefore, to nuclear power plants, but essentially to the other elements of the nuclear production cycle. Furthermore, all the discussions on production of thermonuclear weapons only served to reinforce the growing importance of the atom to the nuclear powers.

At the initiative of the French, discussions were held between France and the United States in September 1952. Canada was informed of the content of these discussions on the understanding that no information would be communicated to any other government. In the meetings of 9 and 11 September, the American participants were Gordon Arneson and Joseph Chase of the State Department, Benjamin Cohen of the New York Delegation, and John

Hall, R.I. Spiers and Paul Fine of the u.s. Atomic Energy Commission (AEC). The French participants included two representatives of the French *Commissariat de l'énergie atomique*, Francis Perrin, Commissioner, and Bertrand Goldschmidt, Director of Chemical Operations, both of whom were involved in the development of the Baruch Plan in 1945. The third French participant was Jacques Tiné from the French Delegation in New York. The minutes of these meetings run to nine pages and only confirm the theses previously discussed.

The strange aspect of these consultations was not so much that, at the end, the two parties left convinced of their differences in political opinion, but rather that each considered that there was nothing new to discuss. In other words, both parties were convinced that there were no new elements that could be proposed. It seems too that this was the secret design of the State Department throughout, namely to convince the other party that nothing should be done. Nevertheless, France put forward a proposal that "quotas of fissile material" be put in escrow, as the American AEC had done for some groups. According to some sources, the French initiative could have been a first step towards establishing a world government, an idea that was apparently cherished by Delegate Jules Moch. At the same time, a new group of consultants was established to find a long-term solution to these problems. It was chaired by Dr. Robert J. Oppenheimer, and McGeorge Bundy acted as Secretary.

The French initiative did not fall upon deaf ears, although the United States never believed in the virtues of world government. The change in American policy was influenced by three factors. First, the election of President Eisenhower who, under Truman, was already party to the secret of the disarmament negotiations. Second, the signing of the Korean armistice and, third, the testing of the first Soviet H-bomb in August 1953. In these circumstances, it was no surprise that the Americans made their "Atoms for Peace" proposal in December 1953. According to the minutes of the 9 September meeting, it was the brainchild of the French, and of Bertrand Goldschmidt in particular. Unfortunately, in their proposal of 11 November 1953, the French did not pursue the content of their earlier private discussions with the Americans.

As far as reductions in armed forces and weapons were concerned, relations between France and the United States were particularly difficult. Moch proposed his plan of 24 June on a personal basis. He had little other choice, given the virtually unanimous barrage of opposition that he faced from the other Delegations. The Americans were the first to systematically oppose any proposal for a draft treaty, arguing that this should not be presented until all the other problems had been resolved. In addition, the French plan insisted on disclosure followed by verification. The United States insisted that both operations be pursued simultaneously, otherwise the West would risk total disclosure while the East would doubtless present reports filled with blank sheets. Moreover, no one in Washington thought that a three-stage proposal would suffice to solve all the problems linked to atomic energy. In terms of conventional force reductions, the American view was that the French proposal did not contain sufficient guarantees.

Consultations between the allies extended for over a year. The allied Delegations agreed not to present a new proposal at the fall Session of the General Assembly. In September 1952, the French Embassy instructed M. de Laboulaye in Ottawa to ask the Canadian Government to examine the French proposal carefully. On 20 April 1953, France made further representations. On this occasion, the French Ambassador himself directly approached the Assistant Under Secretary of State for External Affairs, Jules Léger. This was followed on 24 April 1953 by another visit, this time from the Secretary of the Embassy, M. Rouillon.

On 18 April 1953, the United States advised Canada that, according to information received at their Embassy in Paris, the French proposal was more of an initiative by Jules Moch than the *Quai d'Orsay*. In the very words of the *Quai d'Orsay*, the reception accorded to the Moch proposal was "ostensibly warm but actually cool". On 16 and 25 April 1953, the statements of President Eisenhower and of *Pravda* left it clear that no agreement could be envisaged and no disarmament process could start until the major policy issues concerning Korea and Germany had been resolved. The Canadian position was clearly specified on 13 May 1953 following a meeting between External Affairs' Minister Pearson and the French Ambassador. Canada intended to support Western unity if the United States and Great Britain persisted in their opposition to the French proposal[15], but Canada had no objection to these matters being raised publicly in the Disarmament Commission, since Delegate Moch had already discussed the essence of his proposal before the Commission on 24 June 1952. On 25 May Canada's views were passed to de Laboulaye who, strangely enough, commented that Moch would no doubt be pleased to hear that the Canadian Government had been consulted. It was learned through de Laboulaye that Parodi, Secretary General at the *Quai d'Orsay*, partly backed Moch who, incidentally, was opposed to ratification of the draft treaty on the European Defence Community.

On 2 July, the Defence Research Board (DRB) expressed the judgement that the French proposal did not go to the heart of the matter, at least as far as issues on control of atomic energy were concerned.

Neither was it understood why biological and atomic weapons were considered to comprise a separate category of weapons of mass destruction, nor why chemical weapons were not specifically mentioned. On 3 July 1953, the Joint Disarmament Working Party (JDWP) summarized its position, stating specifically that the proposal:

a   would fail to provide for the simultaneous disclosure and verification ... in the three stages recommended;

b   would place Canada and the Western powers in an undesirable position, when compared to the present numerical superiority of the forces of the Soviet Bloc, once the levels of the armed forces and the military expenditures, disclosed and verified in accordance with Article 5, could not be exceeded pursuant to a decision of the Security Council;

c   would remove atomic weapons from the arsenals of the Western powers even before the first reduction of armed forces and non-atomic weapons had been implemented;

d   would only provide for the permanent control of atomic energy plants and research laboratories at the completion of all three stages of disclosure and verification instead of simultaneously with the prohibition of use and manufacture of biological and atomic weapons.

The Working Party recommended, therefore, that the Department of External Affairs be advised that the proposal was "unacceptable from a military standpoint" and that no changes to the proposal should be attempted. In short, the French proposal was unacceptable. These objections were redrafted in diplomatic language and transmitted to the French "unofficially". The Canadian position was so close to the American and British positions that it could scarcely have influenced Jules Moch who, persisting in his ideas, proposed a compromise formula to the General Assembly on 11 November 1953. This proposal was, in almost every respect, similar to the proposal that had been rejected outright by the three other allied Delegations. Moch may have been stubborn, but at least he believed in what he proposed. In contrast, the other Delegations persisted in presenting proposals, for propaganda purposes, in which they did not believe. France could have been the "steel-tipped staff of America in the sticky mud of disarmament". It was not a time, however, for disarmament but for rearmament.

CANADA AND THE SUBCOMMITTEE OF FIVE

The Subcommittee of Five undertook its most important work during 1954 and 1955. The period marked what may be justly called the great European period of the Subcommittee, since the main issues of the time concerned Europe. It was already known in NATO, following the private discussions between Acheson and Adenauer in 1950, that the defence of Europe was impossible without the participation of the Federal Republic of Germany (FRG). In the spirit of the Brussels Treaty, the Europeans sought to organize their defence on a European basis, and the concept of a European Defence Community was, therefore, considered. Unfortunately, on 30 August 1954, it sank into oblivion following the withdrawal of the item on Treaty ratification from the agenda of the French National Assembly. The London and Paris Agreements of September and October 1954 removed the problem posed by Germany. The Western European Union (WEU) was created (replacing the Brussels Treaty of 1948), while the FRG was authorized to participate in the defence of the North Atlantic Treaty Zone. In 1955, the FRG became a full member of NATO.

1953 witnessed the death of Stalin, the election of a new administration in Washington, the cessation of hostilities in Korea and the breaking of the monopoly on the thermonuclear bomb that the Americans had held briefly since 1952. As far as control of atomic energy was concerned, Washington held stubbornly to the Baruch Plan. Gordon Arneson of the State Department considered that control of nuclear energy had become all the more necessary now that Moscow possessed the H-bomb. The image of the two "scorpions in a bottle" progressively emerged. The trend towards bilateralism was essentially complete by August 1955 when U.S. Delegate Stassen played down all the previous American statements made before the Subcommittee in London. At the same time, the United States introduced their first tactical nuclear weapons in Europe. The "New Look" strategy was that of a nuclear-based European defence.

The 1956–1957 period was one of East-West bilateral dialogue. Although the Europeans participated, the real issues centred on arms control and plans for partial disarmament. We shall return to this topic later in Chapters 5 and 6.

The Question of Canada's Participation in the Subcommittee

From 1945 up to the present, Canada has participated in all the discussions on disarmament, except those that were strictly bilateral in nature. In 1945, Canada was the fourth military power in the world in terms of manpower and materiel, an ally of the United States and Great Britain in the Manhattan Project and a respected member of the UN Atomic Energy Commission and the Commission for Conventional Armaments. For these reasons, Canada's participation in the work of the Subcommittee of the Disarmament Commission would have made perfect sense, but it was far from an established fact in 1954.

The creation of the Subcommittee of Five – the Big Four and Canada – resulted from a British proposal which was accepted on 19 April 1954 following the rejection of a Soviet proposal for the participation of China, Czechoslovakia and India. Actually, as early as November 1953, consultations between France and India led to the proposal for a "restricted committee" within the Disarmament Commission. No nation was specifically cited in the 28 November resolution, but the resolution was directly inspired by an Indian text[16] in which Canada was expressly mentioned. The British were not particularly enthusiastic about the Indian proposal because it implied that the proposed organization would study exclusively nuclear disarmament issues. Moreover, Great Britain, which had already recognized the Peoples' Republic of China (PRC), had not abandoned hope of creating a Subcommittee of Five on which the PRC would be represented.

Such was the situation in early April 1954 when negotiations on the subject resumed. In the interim, for various reasons, the Western powers came to support Canada's participation in the work of the Subcommittee. The United States refused even to consider China's participation, while Great Britain decided, rightly or wrongly, that Canada's participation might prove useful in the event of "wobbling on the part of the French".[17] For once, "perfidious Albion" was not completely wrong.

Neither Cabot Lodge nor Pierson Dixon wanted to sound out the Soviet Delegation on the possibility of Canada being nominated. The strategy adopted, therefore, was to have Canada withdraw if faced with clear opposition from the Soviets or in the event that the USSR insisted on nominating an Eastern Bloc country.[18] It was also known from the New York Delegation that the Soviets were no more enthusiastic than necessary in supporting China's nomination and that they were ready, in the final analysis, to fall back on India's choice.

External Affairs' Minister Pearson, recalling prior discussions with his counterpart Krishna Menon on India's proposed amendment of November 1953, was reluctant to press for Canada's nomination without India's support for the British proposal which contained a similar list of candidate countries. India's support for the British proposal came in April 1954, and Canada then had greater freedom to manoeuvre. The Soviet Delegate complained, with some degree of humour, that Canada would be "the State Department's spokesman" in the Subcommittee. The USSR knew full well that Czechoslovakia's nomination had no chance of being accepted by the West. Despite threats by the Soviets that they would not participate in the work of the Subcommittee if they were not completely satisfied with its composition, Vychinski nevertheless attended the first official meeting of the Subcommittee in New York on 23 April.

Finally, it should be mentioned that Canada considered the possibility of standing down in favour of India or Czechoslovakia if, by so doing, it would enable the Big Four to reach consensus. Nevertheless, the instructions approved by L.B. Pearson and sent to the Delegation on 15 April were that:

... we should continue to support the U.K. resolution, and should resist attempts to broaden membership of the Subcommittee to include non-members of the Disarmament Commission. This would involve voting against all three proposed additional members (if they are voted on together), and if voted on separately, voting against Communist China and Czechoslovakia, and abstaining on India, as the government which originally suggested private talks and on general political grounds.

Courtesy has its responsibilities!

The composition of the Subcommittee remained a more or less closed issue until November 1957 when the Subcommittee became dormant. However, during the time that the Subcommittee was active, several member nations of the Disarmament Commission complained about the lack of information provided by the Subcommittee to the Commission, the short timeframes given to the Commission for examination of Subcommittee reports and the little consideration accorded to proposals submitted by the Commission for study within the Subcommittee. In November 1954, India suggested broadening the composition of the Subcommittee by granting the status of "participating consultants" to certain nations. When India privately approached Canada on this matter, Canada's response was negative.[19] In matters of diplomacy, the practice is not always to "send the elevator back down".

In April 1954, the Italians also sought to change the composition of the Subcommittee so that they could be better integrated in discussions on European security. In 1955, India bitterly complained that her proposals on nuclear disarmament and on halting nuclear tests were not discussed in the Subcommittee despite assurances that such proposals would be considered. In this regard, Canada did not attempt to out-herod Herod and was no more faithful than the other members of the Subcommittee. The Subcommittee did not want to hear about the "Menon factor", or any other proposal coming from outside.

In retrospect, there is no doubt that this Subcommittee was, and remained, throughout all its deliberations, a highly select and exclusive club in which the USSR found itself completely isolated. Even so, this did not prevent the USSR, often with the more or less involuntary help of the French Delegate, from exploiting differences between the Western nations. It was not surprising that, as more and more countries expressed their fears and anxieties at the development and proliferation of nuclear weapons, there were increasing pressures to broaden the membership of the Subcommittee. As well, the other nations were ever ready to "parade" their views before the United Nations, especially at the ritual annual meetings of the General Assembly. There are occasions, however, when the rules of secret diplomacy should prevail, particularly on issues as important as nuclear war and nuclear peace. In 1954 and 1955, talk of disarmament intensified as both blocs continued to rearm.

Canada and the Proposals Discussed in 1954 and 1955

On a subject as broad as the work of the Subcommittee, it is not possible to cover everything. The records are extensive and the shades of meaning are often of interest only to experts. In addition, Canada did not play a significant role in formulating proposals. Canada frequently remained silent, lacking either policy or adequate analytical means to make her influence felt. Because of her moderate approach, Canada was sometimes able to lessen the differences between Western nations. On the other hand, when Canada came head to head with American interests, she often preferred to leave the floor to the French or the British. Whether this was an acknowledgement of impotence remains a matter of conjecture. By the end of 1955, N.A. Robertson, the Canadian representative on the London Subcommittee, went so far as to wonder whether Canada should withdraw.

It was only with the reorganization of the Joint Disarmament Working Party in May 1956[20] that Canada was able to conduct serious studies on the main proposals under discussion in London. Ironically, from that time on, Canada's role became increasingly unobtrusive. This was especially evident in 1957 when the studies were mainly of a technical nature and some were never tabled. 1957 was also the year when the Diefenbaker government came to power. We shall return to this aspect later.

Of all the proposals discussed in 1954 and 1955, two stand out: the Anglo-French Memorandum of 11 June 1954 and the Soviet proposal of 10 May 1955.

The Anglo-French Memorandum proposed a more or less parallel reduction of conventional and atomic weapons subject to some previously established means of control. The reductions were to be effected in three phases, as described by Klein:[21]

- Immediate ban on the use of weapons of mass destruction, except in the case of defence against aggression; creation of an international control organization and a simultaneous "freeze" on the levels of force strengths, conventional weapons and overall military funding;
- Subsequent cutbacks in conventional force strengths and conventional weapons by one-half of the total proposed reductions or, in other words, by one-half of the difference between the force levels previously registered and the final inclusive levels agreed upon. Once these reductions were completed, there would be a complete halt in the manufacturing of nuclear weapons;
- Implementation of the final phase of reductions in forces and conventional weapons, to be followed by an unconditional ban on the use of weapons of mass destruction and a progressive transformation of nuclear stocks from military to peaceful purposes.

The Soviet plan of 10 May 1955, which was to be implemented over two years (1956 and 1957), envisaged two stages:[22]

- In the first stage, the five Powers – the United States, the Soviet Union, China, the United Kingdom and France – would reduce their armed forces and armaments by 50 per cent of the difference between the levels at the end of 1954 and the ceilings of 1 million to 1.5 million men and 650,000 men, respectively. A world conference would establish ceilings for the other countries. Simultaneously with carrying out the 50 per cent of the agreed reduction of armed forces, States possessing nuclear weapons would undertake to discontinue tests of nuclear weapons and assume obligations not to use them except for purposes of defence against aggression when a decision to that effect was taken by the Security Council. Finally, some of the military bases in the territories of other States would be eliminated.
- During the second stage, the second half of the reductions would be carried out. When 75 per cent of the total reduction had been completed, a complete prohibition of the use of nuclear weapons would come into force. These weapons would be destroyed simultaneously with the last 25 per cent of the reduction of armed forces.

With regard to nuclear weapons, the Anglo-French proposal comprised three stages: prohibition of use (except for defence against aggression), manufacture and possession. The Soviet plan, on the other hand, made provision for two stages: prohibition of the use (except for defence against aggression) and then unconditional prohibition. There was, therefore, consensus on the first stage – conditional prohibition of the use of nuclear weapons.

With regard to control, the Western proposal insisted on the operations being simultaneous. The Soviet plan, in its draft treaty form, referred to setting up, on a reciprocal basis, "control posts at major ports, at railway junctions, on main highways and at airfields". In other words, the control posts would be land-based. In addition, control would be exercised progressively. On the other hand, on-site observations of reductions in conventional forces would not be made during the first stage. In this respect, even if the Soviet plan did not satisfy the Western nations, it showed progress since, for the first time, the Soviets seemed to admit the principle of on-site inspection.

With regard to reductions in conventional forces, there was also some progress. Moscow gave up its claims to fractional reductions (through percentages) and accepted that an agreement be negotiated on the basis of reciprocally assigned ceilings. Actually, the Soviet plan of 10 May 1955 was a response to the modification made, on 19 April 1955, to the Anglo-French proposal of June 1954. In April 1955, the French and the British agreed to propose a ban on the manufacture of nuclear weapons once 75% of the first reductions in conventional weapons had been completed.

The British agreed to this major revision to the joint memorandum only when they "became convinced that the French would go ahead with their plan even at the cost of accepting amendments from the Russians to obtain their support".[23] Canada, for her part, wanted to support this compromise formula, especially since she had accepted the first Anglo-French proposal of June 1954. The United States, however, opposed the compromise formula but did not object to its being tabled. In view of the u.s. reticence, Canada abstained so that the United States would not find itself in a position of isolation within the Subcommittee. The Canadian Delegate limited himself to saying "that in his personal view he did not see any reason why the Canadian Government could not support it".[24] In matters of prudence and diplomacy, and also pause for reflection, it is difficult to do any better.

In the spring of 1955, therefore, there seemed to be a progressive resorption of the cancerous tumour which had gnawed at East-West relations since 1945. The Soviets called for unconditional prohibition of atomic weapons followed by reductions in conventional forces, while the West countered with a call for conventional weapons' reductions followed by the elimination of nuclear arms. It seemed that both sides wished to appear conciliatory.

On the other hand, reference to the record of negotiations quickly reveals the extent of the East-West conflict, as well as the profound differences that separated the Western powers themselves. From London, N.A. Robertson stressed that true leadership came from Selwyn Lloyd and Jules Moch. Both, he wrote, had great negotiating capability and showed the greatest patience and persistence in smoothing out difficulties and in appeasing the unending suspicions of Delegate Malik. On 20 July, the Delegation in New York judged that the Anglo-French proposal still represented the best document tabled to date on the question of disarmament, and viewed it as a "major advance" in the Western position. On 29 July, a telegram from the Delegation in New York announced the already-known fact that the United States was paying only lip service to the Anglo-French proposal. In the Disarmament Commission, the u.s. Delegate stated that American support "would not necessarily include an endorsement of every detail of the memorandum". In addition, Gordon Arneson told Canada that, in view of Soviet opposition, there was little chance that the European proposal would be as strongly supported as the majority plan in 1948.

In August, the Americans were somewhat displeased with Moch's declarations in the General Assembly. Moch, who characterized himself as "an impenitent optimist" and "dangerously candid", considered that the Baruch Plan was clearly obsolescent and that the United States Delegation was "putting the cart before the horse". He invited the Soviets to "take a step forward", an action which he felt was above reproach. The Americans, however, considered such optimism as premature, being predicated on a false image of Moscow.[25] On 1 September, a message from New York announced an American about-face. The United States, from that time on, were ready to endorse the Anglo-French proposal of control and the principle of maintaining permanent or continuous discussions on disarmament.

Two factors explained the about-face in the American position. The first was u.s. dismay at the French rejection of the European Defence Community Treaty and u.s. apprehension of the prospect of a Franco-Soviet alliance, particularly when it was learned that the Soviet Ambassador in Paris had "told Parodi that Moscow would make proposals close to the views of Mr. Moch".[26] The second factor concerned the u.s. interpretation of the Anglo-French proposal, Washington considering that only the Lloyd version of the proposal was acceptable but not the Moch interpretation.

Essentially, Moch considered that the clause prohibiting nuclear weapons except for defence against aggression constituted in itself a new proposal from the Western Bloc. The British viewed the clause differently, considering that it resulted quite simply from the right of legitimate defence embodied in the Charter of the United Nations. The clause did not, therefore, represent anything new. The difference here was evidently rather slim, but for the u.s. it was significant because a new proposal would have opened up discussion on new issues. The Americans had no wish to discuss new issues, particularly those on the global prohibition of nuclear weapons and the halting of nuclear tests. The American National Security Council (NSC) was opposed to any halting of the tests, "even on a temporary basis".

Under-Secretary Jules Léger summarized the Canadian position in a memorandum to Minister Pearson dated 1 October. Léger stated that it was in Canada's interest to promote disarmament, to recognize that it depended on establishing a climate of trust and to admit that the only way of eliminating atomic war was to eliminate war itself. He went on to summarize the u.s. objections to the Anglo-French proposal as follows:

- the United States does not want even a conditional ban on the use of nuclear weapons separate from the comprehensive disarmament treaty;
- the United States would not be satisfied with the loose type of inspections by "sampling" envisaged by Mr. Moch during the first stage;
- the United States considers it would not be compatible with its national security to accept an 80% or 90% effective plan now but preferred to maintain its position that any control plan for the "safeguarded disarmament" must be "no less effective" than the majority plan for atomic energy;
- the United States would be most reluctant to give complete data on its atomic production and plant capacities at the beginning of the second stage, before there had been a reduction of armed forces and conventional armaments.

The last objection obviously resulted from a misinterpretation of the Anglo-French proposal, and should have read "before there had been overall reductions in conventional forces". Be that as it may, the American position remained unchanged. Clearly, there had to be a treaty with a perfectly watertight inspection system, and conventional weapons had to be eliminated before nuclear ones.

It remains, however, that since 1954 the Soviets have spoken of prohibiting recourse to nuclear weapons and not prohibiting their manufacture. On 23 June 1954, Robertson summed up the Western dilemma:

The Western powers should be careful to avoid putting themselves in the position of making unilateral concessions. Perhaps the chief lesson to be learned from the London talks is that the Soviet Government does not consider the present time opportune for serious negotiations and is still seeking to derive the last ounce of propaganda advantage from its latest "Ban the Use of the Bomb" proposal. In these circumstances, it is the line of the least resistance to stand on a fixed position. This course of action can be justified by the undeniable fact that, up to the present time, the question of disarmament has been treated largely as a propaganda exercise, and that any agreement in this field is almost certainly unattainable. Although this line of reasoning is unassailable if the Cold War premise is accepted, it is just possible that it might not be true, and for this reason we cannot afford to give up too easily.

In his last sentence, Robertson could not have made the Canadian position clearer and, undoubtedly, that of France also. After first rejecting the Anglo-French proposal within the Subcommittee, the Soviets then accepted it during a meeting of the General Assembly, as a "basis for discussion". In his long memorandum of 1 October, Jules Léger considered that this gesture by the Soviets should be viewed with some reservation (they were now talking only of prohibiting recourse to nuclear weapons and not of prohibiting their manufacture). Léger also considered that the Soviet Union should be told that there was no way it "can demonstrate its sincerity, except by recording its recognition that the creation of adequate and authoritative machinery for inspection and control is not inimical to its interests". In this regard, Canada was dreaming in technicolour. It could only happen if Moscow started to think like Washington, and to date that has not happened.

In October 1954, the United States reproached Moch for maintaining privileged one-way contact with the Soviets. According to the Americans, Moch had been aware of Soviet intentions on several occasions and had known in advance the substance of the amendments that Moscow intended to propose, even before they were communicated to the West. Although these suspicions were never formally discussed with the *Quai d'Orsay* (?), the United States asked the French Government "to ensure that instructions are sent to Moch which would serve to bring his actions at the Assembly more closely in line with what are presumed to be the intentions of the French Government and the concerted policy of the three Western powers concerned".[27] Ottawa, however, was careful to avoid being unduly influenced by the American perception. After all, Ottawa could hardly check with Paris on something that had never been the subject of official representations and, in addition, had been communicated to Ottawa on a confidential basis between allies. In this same message to New York, Ottawa stated that Canada felt obliged to say that in all his declarations to the Assembly, Jules Moch was just as critical as the others (for instance, his "twenty questions" speech). The message continued: "we have had no evidence either that he was not acting in good faith or that his contacts with the Soviet Delegation in New York were out of the ordinary given his intense interest in this subject". Ottawa should have sent this message directly to Washington, rather than to the Canadian Delegation in New York ...

Canada was certainly not fooled by Washington's manoeuvre. Nevertheless, the seeds of doubt were sown, since the memorandum ended as follows: "For our own information, however, we should welcome any comments which you might wish to make on the basis of your experience of negotiations with Mr. Moch". In a telex of the same date addressed to the Canadian Ambassador in Paris, Ottawa revealed that Paul Martin (Minister of Health and Welfare at the time, but also Acting Chairman of the Canadian Delegation) had informed the Delegation of something that Moch had told him privately. Moch stated that if Vychinski came around to the idea of sponsoring, in conjunction with Canada, the resolution discussed in the General Assembly[28], he would immediately send a telegram to Mendès-France urging him to delay debate on ratification of the Paris Accords[29] on German rearmament by two months. The Ottawa-Paris telex also stated that the Canadian Delegation in New York had already been advised "that we think it would be unfortunate if a strong plea from Moch should muddy the waters and increase the hesitancy concerning French ratification". Ottawa added that Soviet diplomacy, irrespective of its changing character, would not result in a weakening of the relationships between Moch and the other Western powers. This, then, constituted the American quarrel concerning "Mochism" in the context of Canada-u.s. relations.

Another bone of contention on the subject of the Anglo-French proposal was the Australian position. The Australians sent a vehement protest to the British informing them that the proposal did not take Australian interests into consideration. At the time, Canberra was in discussion with the United States on the formation of the South East Asia Treaty Organization (SEATO). As early as 1952 the Australians had protested the Tripartite Proposal. By 1954, Australian representations were so severe that the British Joint Chiefs of Staff felt forced to study a whole series of military issues on the defence needs of South-East Asia. In October 1954, probably to make amends for the lack of British consultation with the Australians, Selwyn Lloyd encouraged Canberra to submit a resolution that would involve the Secretariat of the United Nations in the "troubled waters" of disarmament.[30]

In Canada's view, such a proposal served no useful purpose. According to Ottawa, it was not the Secretariat's function to explain the political positions of the various nations, since this would imply that it play the role of interpreter. Moreover, since the deliberations of the Disarmament Commission were published, it was difficult to see how the Secretariat could satisfactorily clarify matters that others had chosen to leave deliberately vague. Despite Canada's reticence, the instructions nevertheless read: "on balance it might be voted for although not spoken for".

On 22 November 1954, R. Harry Jay prepared a remarkable synthesis on the commonalities and differences between the Soviet Union and the West. This document is of primary interest only to the specialist and it is mentioned here solely in the interests of being faithful to the Canadian record. As a final point, it should be noted that the Department of External Affairs did not deem it useful to seek advice from the Canadian Joint Chiefs of Staff on the content of the Anglo-French memorandum, probably because Canada would be no more affected by the proposal than by the Tripartite Proposal of May 1952.

The situation was completely different concerning the Soviet proposal of 10 May 1955, which provoked a whole series of major questions in political and military circles. Did the Soviets wish to negotiate in good faith, or was it purely propaganda? Was the content of the proposals militarily acceptable?

On both points there were differences in the Canadian and British positions. The British held that the Soviet economy was in bad shape and that Moscow needed time to catch its breath. The Soviets, negotiating from a position of weakness, were ready to make concessions in order to create an atmosphere of *détente*. R.A.D. Ford, who had recently returned from Moscow, thought otherwise. "These weaknesses", he wrote on 23 June 1955, "are one of the important factors in their decision to modify their tactics in foreign policy". Concerning the Soviet proposals, he added: "The way in which they are presented … would indicate rather that they were made as part of a big diplomatic build-up without any real expectation that they would be accepted". Ford concluded that this approach was designed to indicate the kind of settlement that the Soviets wanted, and mainly to point out "that the question of Germany can only be envisaged in a general settlement including disarmament, European security, Far Eastern problems, etc."

Two days later, a telegram from the Commonwealth Relations Division confirmed this point of view: "Molotov was clearly more interested in subject of European security than in subject of German unification on which Pinay sought to focus the conversation". This comment was made in the context of the Foreign Ministers' Meeting held in San Francisco in preparation for the Geneva Summit. In this same telegram of 25 June, it was reported that "Molotov did not seem so concerned about German rearmament as about disarmament in general and the American bases in Europe and the threat of nuclear weapons in particular". This general trend is important, since it largely explains the progressive bilateralization of the debates from the summer of 1955 onwards.

In July, the Joint Intelligence Committee (JIC), which was attached to the Department of National Defence but chaired by a representative of the Department of External Affairs, examined the British military assessment of the Soviet proposal of 10 May. There were wide differences between the Canadian and British assessments. The British considered that the Soviets had made significant progress in nuclear weapons, but that they were far behind and that the gap would continue to widen. In addition, the British considered that Soviet missiles could not reach North America, and that the situation would not likely change for at least two years. Moreover, the British judged that the Soviets did not possess nuclear warheads with an explosive power of more than 1 megaton, and that their ability to cheat under a disarmament agreement would be confined to a production difference of about ten 1-megaton bombs and a hundred 5-kiloton bombs. The British Joint Chiefs of Staff thought that this quantity would be insufficient to allow the Soviets to strike a mortal blow against North America. Finally, the British considered that it would take Moscow several years to produce a propulsive unit to give their missiles a range of over 4,500 miles,* unless the Soviets made spectacular technological progress.

Ottawa believed that the British had seriously under-estimated the capability of the Soviets to strike a mortal blow against North America. The document produced by the Joint Intelligence Committee in July stated that consultations had been held with the British Joint Chiefs of Staff, but that no additional information had been provided to change the Canadian position. On the whole, it was considered that the Soviet plan would be unfavourable for the West, because although air defence would not be prohibited (the NORAD Agreement, for instance), nevertheless the West could not effectively strike at the heart of Soviet power.[31] The inability of the Americans to project their power abroad would make conventional war more likely and

---

* Authors' note: Quantities are expressed in the British system of units whenever they are quoted directly from the records, otherwise we have used the metric system.

"possible" for the Soviets. On the other hand, the ability of the Soviets
to cheat under an agreement could exert considerable influence on
tactical nuclear warfare, particularly in Europe. Moreover, given the
differences in respective political regimes, it would be much easier
to cheat in the Soviet Union than in the Western nations where
pressures to respect the agreements would be compelling.

The Canadian military establishment expressed serious reservations about the rather liberal British assessment. Canadian military
opinion was thus quite similar to the conservative judgements that
might have been heard in u.s. military circles at the time.

In the area of ballistic missiles, Canada was right. Lester B. Pearson,
in a speech delivered to NATO in the spring of 1955, said that we were
rapidly approaching an era where the acronym IBM[32] would no longer
mean only "International Business Machines".[33]

The aforegoing sums up the essence of the Canadian reaction to
the basic issues discussed in London. Throughout this period, however,
Canada entertained more than one doubt on the usefulness and functional nature of the London Subcommittee. For his part, L.B. Pearson
disliked the "frivolous" use of the Subcommittee advocated by some,
especially if the only purpose was to expose the "insincerity" of the
Soviets. That being said, Pearson himself wondered whether peace
could not be best assured, as thought Churchill, "based on each camp's
capability to destroy the other".[34] He wondered also if it would not be
best to give up all the "present proposals" and develop an entirely new
approach. In the same personal letter to Robertson, Pearson encouraged him to remain in his position in London, given his experience
in disarmament and the "interpretations that could be drawn in the
event of his replacement". Eight months later, N.A. Robertson wrote
a veritable political testament on the negotiations in London. On 21
November, he wrote to Jules Léger, Pearson's right hand man:

I have been wondering again, however, whether there is any real justification
for our membership on it. The historical basis of our association with the
Great Powers on the Committee is getting remoter and less relevant as the
years go on, and to date, we have not, so far as I know, made any useful or
distinctive contribution to its proceedings. A fifth wheel that only rattles and
squeaks now and then has not much to be said for it. I am aware of the
difficulties or perhaps the impossibility of explaining to the Subcommittee
or to Canadians the reasons for our withdrawal ... But with doubts about
the timeliness and effectiveness of the Subcommittee as such, with doubts
about the contribution which Canada can make to its work, and with doubts
about the wisdom and realism of our general approach to the problems, I do
not feel I am likely to be a very effective representative on the Committee ...

So far as my experience goes, our only opportunity of putting anything in the pot has been in the private, off-the-record discussions between the Western Delegations ... If we are serious ... we should not agree to resume discussions with the Russians on this particular topic until we have ironed out the differences and inconsistencies in our Western position and are prepared to negotiate from it with the Russians ... This opportunity may, in fact, exist, for I am told that in the Geneva Foreign Ministers' discussions, Molotov never explicitly agreed to renewed meetings of the Subcommittee. This point was to have been covered in the "Four Power Declaration on Disarmament" on which the Western countries had agreed a draft, but in the confusion of the last days in Geneva, it was never pressed to the point of Four Power agreement. I think the Western powers would be well advised to take advantage of this lacuna and refrain from fixing a time and place for the next meeting until they have tidied up and reconsidered their own positions.

There may be some murmuring in the United Nations circles if we try to postpone the fixing of a definite date for reconvening the Subcommittee. If there is such criticism, it will reflect what I believe to be a misconception of the role of the Subcommittee. It is true it is a creature of the United Nations, but it has also been a forum for negotiations between East and West on one sector of the front that separates them. From this point of view, the approach to the Disarmament problem at Geneva was more realistic ... it could be argued that meetings of the Big Four at Foreign Minister level are a closer approach to the principal object of the Security Council than anything we have had since the war.

Several of the points developed by Robertson are to be found in the records. On 27 June 1955, Marcel Cadieux wrote to John W. Holmes in the same vein. In a memorandum to Pearson dated 27 July, Jules Léger pointed out that Canada was not a great power with unlimited financial resources and that the discussions in the Subcommittee tended to revolve increasingly around European security matters:

Amongst the reasons which favour our participation is the fact that our presence constitutes a link between the Big Four and the United Nations, that sometimes we were able to reconcile differences in viewpoint between the United States on the one hand and France and Great Britain on the other, that our participation is an expression of our functional approach and that, in any case, our point of view is just as important as that of any other participating nation.

David M. Johnson also pointed out, not without reason, that there was general support for Canada's nomination in 1954 and that

Canada should not, therefore, disappoint those nations which have placed their confidence in her.

On 28 December, Jules Léger informed Robertson that he was not alone in thinking along these lines, adding: "the problem however is that both our withdrawal or the enlargement of the Subcommittee would create additional problems. The participation of India for instance would inject Menon into the proceedings ... and would also likely prejudice whatever slight prospects of success may still be available". On the question of consultations between allies, Léger agreed entirely with Robertson, adding:

At all cost we should avoid the earlier practice of hurried consultation on the last days, if not hours, which precede the meetings of the Subcommittee. The problem is that u.s. machinery is so complex and so slow that the u.s. officials can only get instructions at the very last minute and there is no real opportunity for consultation. We had this experience again on the eve of the disarmament debate in the First Committee. Lodge returned to New York from consultations in Washington and was disappointed when his Western colleagues were not prepared to accept immediately a very inadequate draft resolution to be introduced the next day.

Since late 1955, when Cadieux and Robertson expressed their doubts, a lot of water has flowed under the bridge. In August 1955, following the Geneva Conference, the Americans put "on hold" all the proposals that they had previously accepted. For them, the disarmament "escapade" was over. Moreover, they intended to take advantage of the wave of public support that the "Open Skies" proposal gained in Geneva. Although the record reveals nothing on the subject, Minister Pearson probably feared that, as the debates between the USSR and the u.s. became increasingly bilateral, he would be caught between the superpowers and the European allies. In 1955 Paul Martin prepared the first draft of his statement to the UN General Assembly, in which he commended the Subcommittee and encouraged it to continue its work. In a memorandum to L.B. Pearson on 5 December, R.M. MacDonnell was quick to point out that Martin was persuaded to change his mind during Pearson's absence, noting that this first draft "does not conform to your thinking on this subject". MacDonnell concluded that although it would have been inappropriate for Martin to criticize the Subcommittee, "he need not go out of his way to urge its continuance".[35] The fact that a subordinate was so frank about the opinions expressed by another minister implied that the Minister for External Affairs had deep convictions on the subject. Pearson always kept an eye on his colleague Martin, who often sought to take initiatives that were not always appreciated by his superior.[36] In this regard, MacDonnell probably had to act in accordance with the guidelines established by N.A. Robertson and Jules Léger.[37]

The "Open Skies" Proposal and the Canadian Arctic

At the Heads of State Conference of the Big Four held in Geneva between 18 and 23 July 1955 (Geneva Summit), President Eisenhower announced to the world his "Open Skies" proposal aimed at promoting military openness between the superpowers and at reducing the risk of war. There was instant surprise. The British and the Canadians, but not the French, were informed in mid-July of the main terms of the u.s. proposals. Again, the details are imprecise. A despatch to Ottawa from the Canadian Embassy in Washington, dated 14 July 1955, informed the Canadian Government that the United States had thoroughly re-examined its approach to disarmament. From that time on, contended the Americans, any disarmament plan had to be based on an "inspection and communications system". A.D.P. Heeney, then Ambassador to Washington, asked Stassen about the content of the proposals that the u.s. intended to present in Geneva. The only answer given to the Ambassador was that the u.s. proposals were based on a new approach that had not been discussed up to that time. Stassen added, by way of courtesy, that he would discuss it personally with Pearson who was due to arrive in Paris the following week. The fact that this despatch from Washington was marked "Secret" rather than "Top Secret" was a true indication that the information provided by Washington was very tenuous.

The Canadians were completely taken in. On 15 July, Ottawa cabled the Canadian representative to NATO: "There is little if anything new in Stassen's report ... it indicates that the United States is definitely thinking in terms other than the Baruch Plan". The Canadian records give no indication of whether the British were informed in the same way as the Canadians.

Our research has revealed nothing on the subject of the Pearson-Stassen meeting in Paris. It is known, however, that Nutting, the British Delegate to the Subcommittee of Five, talked with Stassen in Paris. A despatch from London to Ottawa, dated 27 July, revealed that Nutting was convinced that "present United States policy is opposed to any attempt to secure nuclear disarmament". Based on this information and the record of the Geneva Conference, the Canadian High Commissioner concluded:

Given the United States position, there is now no purpose to be served in trying to rewrite the Western Plan. It is out of date as it stands (having been overtaken by the Soviet proposal), the Anglo-French proposed amendments are in cold storage, the French proposal put forward by Faure at Geneva is a non-starter and the Soviet proposals will certainly not be accepted by the Americans.

A fine program, one might say, but it was not far from reality. Jean Klein, unlike many authors, quite accurately observed that, at the close of the Geneva Summit, "u.s.-Soviet antagonism was more pronounced than before" and that "progress in the Disarmament Subcommittee was in question".[38] Although Klein's observations are perfectly correct, it may be added that the Europeans continued to discuss "disarmament", while the United States opted for "arms control".

The u.s. philosophy was explicitly defined at the Foreign Ministers' Meeting held in Geneva between 27 October and 16 November 1955. Before considering the u.s. statements, the essence of Molotov's declaration of 10 November is worth noting:

Proposals relating to aerial photography and to the exchange of military blueprints are quite distinct from the problem of stopping the armaments race, and in fact are not connected with it. They would not reduce the danger of new war, nor relieve taxpayers of the heavy burden they have to bear on account of the armaments race. Insofar as it refers only to the Soviet Union and the United States, and the territories of those two States, this proposal would not prevent an attack by one country on the other ... The proposal does not provide for the extension of aerial photography and the exchange of military blueprints to those States on whose territories American military bases are being maintained and the States which are connected with the United States by military obligations under various treaties and agreements whose purpose is well known.[39]

In his response to the Soviet accusation that the "Open Skies" proposal applied only to the superpowers, John Foster Dulles argued that the ussr also had troops and bases in Eastern bloc countries, but that the bulk of the forces of both sides were located within the borders of the two sovereign States. Dulles considered that this formed a suitable starting point, but was willing to extend the u.s. proposal to American bases abroad. The u.s. Secretary of State continued: "Major aggression is unlikely unless the aggressor has the advantage of surprise ... Aerial inspection would, however, provide a warning against a great surprise attack". Aerial inspection would not solve all the problems, but it could comprise the first stage which "could mark the end of a period of arms race ... It could signal the beginning of a period of arms control". Dulles ended his address by inviting the Soviets, with tongue in cheek, to integrate their "Land Control" proposal of 10 May with the u.s. "Open Skies" proposal to provide a dual inspection system.

Some diplomats were highly sceptical of the u.s. proposal, as evidenced by M.A. Crowe's despatch from New York of 27 July. Generally, however, the Canadian Government endorsed this proposal and considered it, for want of anything better, as a first step. In a letter dated 8 August 1955, the Under-Secretary of State for External Affairs asked the Chairman of the Joint Chiefs of Staff for his opinion on the proposal since the British, he said, thought that the ussr, for tactical reasons, might want to extend the proposal to the whole of North America. The opinion of the military was important, he argued, since Canada would have to establish a position when the Subcommittee resumed its work in London.

General Foulkes was highly supportive. In his 12 August reply to the Department of External Affairs, he wrote:

It is our view that the value which would be obtained for us by a surveillance of Russian territory, particularly the parts of Russian territory which are contiguous to Alaska and the northern part of Canada, far outweigh any disadvantages to us. If some definite arrangements could be made whereby this reconnaissance could be carried out, it may be possible for us to relax somewhat on our present concept of twenty-four hour a day manning of the early warning lines, which will be a very expensive and difficult operation to carry out over a prolonged period.

With regard to Canadian airfields, I perhaps should point out that the specification and descriptions of all the present Canadian airfields are now available unclassified from the Department of Transport. Therefore, ... all the information regarding these airfields and the only data they could obtain by aerial reconnaissance would be a description of the buildings and the numbers of aircraft that might be on the runways ... As you are perhaps aware ... the only airfields which could be considered bases used by the United States are the leased bases in Newfoundland and the joint occupation of the base at Goose Bay. Care should be exercised, however, regarding any public reference to the joint occupation of Goose Bay as the use of Goose Bay by the United States Strategic Air Force has never been released to the public.

General Foulkes could have added that it was foolish to look upon the Soviets as "babes in the woods". The Europeans had no hesitation in pointing this out to the Americans when the Subcommittee resumed its work on 29 August. Apart from the fact that the

Europeans considered the u.s. plan to be perfectly unacceptable from a Soviet standpoint, they deplored the existence of a purely bilateral proposal within the Subcommittee. The Subcommittee members also found it extremely difficult to establish a link between the Eisenhower proposal and the proposals previously discussed in London. Stassen took it upon himself to point out in clear terms that indeed there was no link. The diplomatic language used was somewhat more refined: the United States held in reserve its position as previously developed in the Subcommittee. As Stassen stated, all the previous proposals tabled before the Subcommittee "have not been withdrawn, but have not been reaffirmed either". From a despatch out of New York dated 7 September, it would appear that Presidential Advisor Stassen had acted without the approval of the State Department. According to a weekly note from Ottawa dated 26 October, the statements of Delegate Henry Cabot Lodge were even less reassuring than those of Stassen. The previous proposals were not put in "cold storage" but in "deep freeze". According to the Americans, this was necessary not only because inspection capabilities could not totally exclude fraud, but also because of the "facts of life".

The dice were cast. From that time on, there were fundamental differences in philosophy between the Europeans and the Americans. Most of the reasons for these trans-Atlantic differences of opinion have been explained above. The fact that the Western nations arrived at the Geneva Summit in broken ranks did little to improve the climate. The Americans considered that they could no longer walk without the blind man's cane. In other words, to be totally reassured vis-à-vis Soviet intentions, they had to know what was happening on the other side of the border. The British, without much consultation with their allies, presented a proposal for a regional disarmament zone extending along both sides of the border of Western Europe, including the whole length of the Czech-German border. The United States had no wish to discuss it. Faced with vehement protests from the FRG and opposition from the u.s., the Eden plan was only half-heartedly supported by the British in the Subcommittee. Henceforth, they only talked of a first "exercise" to study mechanisms for control and inspection. As for the French proposal to reduce military budgets, only the Soviets lent an attentive ear.

In October, the Eden proposal was resurrected in the studies that were undertaken by the Supreme Allied Commander Europe (SACEUR) and approved by the NATO Standing Group. As a result, the Eden proposal came under further attack. The zone to be considered would have to extend between 200 and 300 miles on each side of the border, and would contain chains of radars with overlapping beams.

Thus, Soviet radars could be located in the FRG and Western radars located in Poland.[40] The Eden zone thus became the Eisenhower zone. As for the plan of President Faure, all the Western chancelleries considered that it was presented for internal political reasons and had no chance of success whatsoever. France intended, at all costs, to limit German forces to a ceiling of 300,000 men in accordance with the proposals previously presented. The United States, however, wanted Germany to have 500,000 men. It may be noted that one of the objectives of the Anglo-French memorandum of June 1954 was aimed specifically at preventing German rearmament since it called for a manpower freeze effective 31 December 1954. Jules Moch, who had chaired a Commission of the French National Assembly which was hostile to the idea of a European army, was personally opposed to the European Defence Community. In this regard, whether one liked it or not, there was convergence of interest between France and the USSR.

In the wake of the events of 1955, it is no surprise that Western differences came into broad daylight. The Soviets missed no opportunity to exploit the Western differences, stating that they accepted the concept of land control stations within the framework of controlled disarmament, but that they refused the principle of aerial inspection. This was the essence of Bulganin's letter of 23 September 1955 to the Western powers.

Despite all Stassen's efforts to obtain support from his European peers on the Subcommittee, the "Open Skies" proposal was not accepted as a formal Western proposal. Moch had no desire to make the "Open Skies" proposal another Baruch plan. European resistance remained fierce. In this regard, Canada was no warmer than France or Great Britain, but preferred to leave the responsibility with the Europeans.[41] In fact, the Secretary of State for External Affairs considered that the initiative should be taken by Great Britain and France. The allies nevertheless rallied around the U.S. proposal when the General Assembly met.

These events led to the compromise formula that was tabled by Great Britain on 2 December before the First Committee, and which was countersigned by the United States, France and Great Britain. The major powers were invited to resume discussion and, as a matter of priority, to seek agreement based on the Eisenhower and Bulganin plans. They were encouraged to conclude feasible disarmament agreements with adequate safeguards as early as possible. Delegate Nutting had no hesitation in saying privately that feasible agreements meant more than verifiable agreements. After many amendments, the main content of this resolution was adopted by the First

Committee on 12 December, and ratified by the General Assembly on 16 December.[42]

The Eisenhower plan was thus far from dead. Following the suggestion that the "Open Skies" proposal be extended to include u.s. bases abroad, the Canadian Joint Chiefs of Staff were again asked to review the matter. On 21 October, General Foulkes repeated the content of his letter of 12 August, without any addition. In November, it fell upon R.A. MacKay to revive the "Open Skies" plan in Canada. MacKay, who was attached to the Office of the Under-Secretary of State for External Affairs, was at the time posted to New York. Paul Martin, who was also in New York, informed MacKay of his concerns at the appearance of the Intercontinental Ballistic Missile (icbm). MacKay prepared a report for Martin dated 1 November in which he wondered whether it would be appropriate to seek reciprocal agreement to prohibit the installation of launch platforms for ballistic missiles north of the 60th parallel. The objective would not be to establish a precise boundary, but rather to encourage the creation of a semi-demilitarized zone on each side of the Pole. MacKay was perfectly aware of the problems that this could pose for the United States, since the Strategic Air Command (sac) was about to seek authorization for refuelling its aircraft in Frobisher, or perhaps Whitehorse, as well as in one or two bases north of 60° latitude. "Without being alarmist", he wrote, "we might insist that there be no such refuelling bases established north of a certain line if we had in mind a general agreement with the Russians".

This draft proposal was sent to Jules Léger on 5 December 1955. Three days later, with admirable swiftness, Léger informed MacKay that his proposal had been studied by a committee comprising members of the armed forces, the Defence Research Board and the Atomic Energy Control Board. Léger's response stated that, for technical reasons, it appeared that MacKay's proposal did not meet the desired objectives.

The arguments of the review committee essentially concerned four aspects. First, it was unlikely that the Soviets would accept any demilitarization south of latitude 70° N, since the Soviet strategic air forces were based near Murmansk (latitude 69° N) in the West, and in Markovo (latitude 65° N) in the East. Leningrad (latitude 60° N) is about a hundred miles further north than Fort Churchill. Second, it was doubtful whether the range of the missiles was an important factor since, by installing missiles in the north there was a gain of only some 10 to 15 percent (the arc over the Pole above latitude 60° N is 3,600 nautical miles long). The missiles envisaged at the time would have a range of 5,000 miles. Third, if the Americans wanted to install missiles in the North, they would probably position them in Alaska. Fourth, the path followed by the ballistic missiles would most probably be the Iceland-Greenland trajectory in the East and the trajectory above the Aleutian Islands in the West.

In view of these considerations, Léger asked MacKay to refrain from making any political remarks on the proposal. Léger informed External Affairs' Minister Pearson of the content of the proposal, and sent him copies of all the correspondence with the following note: "If the USSR are not prepared to compromise on any of the outstanding disarmament schemes, it would hardly be worthwhile to introduce another one which may have even broader implications than, for instance, the Faure plan". In this instance, Léger was wrong. The MacKay plan would certainly have been easier to discuss than the Faure plan. No matter, the die was cast. In the margin of Léger's note, L.B. Pearson wrote: "I am inclined to agree with the position taken by the interdepartmental group on this matter".

There is a twofold irony in all that. First, whenever a proposal was formulated in Washington, Canada considered that there was "more to be gained than lost", but when conceived by a Canadian civil servant it was without interest. It is true that from a technical standpoint, the MacKay proposal was not of great interest. There are still no launch installations for ballistic missiles in the Canadian far north. There are, however, many in the far north of the Soviet Union. Second, as MacKay stressed, the purpose of the proposal was to engage the Soviets in political negotiations. This was precisely the purpose pursued in 1957, but without success, when it was proposed that studies be undertaken on the feasibility of establishing experimental zones of aerial inspection, amongst which was the Canadian Arctic. No man is a prophet in his own country!

Canada and the Proposals Discussed in 1956 and 1957

All kinds of events and developments occurred during 1956 and 1957. The events in Suez and Hungary served to reaffirm U.S. leadership within the Atlantic Alliance, and also pointed up the limits of Western solidarity. On the other hand, they also demonstrated the helplessness of the United States when the Soviets decided to act within their own sphere of influence. The spectacular launch of the first Sputnik in October 1957 boosted the confidence of the Soviets who henceforth sought to be treated on an equal basis with the Americans. After that, the roles were reversed. The Soviets were willing to wait until international circumstances were favourable before they would negotiate, an approach which was hardly conducive to the granting of even the least concession to the West.

History of Proposals.   The climate for disarmament was not good. At the beginning of the period (19 March – 4 May 1956) of the Subcommittee's work in London, the differences between the allies seemed irreconcilable. There were two conflicting basic approaches. The Europeans, reverting to the mandate of the Subcommittee, advocated plans for general disarmament, while the Americans responded strongly with their theories of "arms control". For their part, the Soviets tried to satisfy the Americans while keeping the focus on the regional disarmament proposals of the Europeans.

At the time of the Geneva Summit, President Eisenhower tried to include control and inspection proposals as priorities on the agenda. When the Soviets refused, the Americans agreed to downplay their demands in exchange for a Soviet promise not to pursue the issue of prohibition of nuclear weapons.[43] Actually, this *modus vivendi* prevented neither the Americans nor the Soviets from talking respectively about control and prohibition of nuclear weapons. Prohibition was mentioned seven times in the Soviet document tabled at Geneva!

The Soviet plan of 27 March 1956 did, however, satisfy the Americans. It contained four proposals, the first two of which made no mention of nuclear weapons. The first proposal was to freeze manpower, weapons and military expenditures starting 31 December 1955, and to establish ceilings of 1 to 1.5 million men for the superpowers, 650,000 for France and Great Britain, and 150,000 to 200,000 for the other nations. The second proposal concerned only the control organization and the means of inspection. Apart from defining the "objects to be controlled" the proposal mentioned that aerial inspection could be envisaged as a "means of control". The third proposal was to establish a restricted zone in Central Europe where nuclear weapons and forces would be excluded. Finally, the fourth proposal provided for the immediate halting of thermonuclear tests and the exclusion of nuclear forces or weapons from German soil. Delegate Moch said rightly that the first two proposals dealt only with "obsolescent or soon to be obsolescent" military materiel.[44]

France and Great Britain tabled their joint proposal on 19 March 1956. It was a revised version of the Anglo-French memorandum of 11 June 1954, and comprised a three-stage plan for general and controlled disarmament.

As was the case for the document of 19 April 1955, the three-stage proposal was a product of last-minute intervention by the British. The British feared that Moch would table his draft of September 1955, about which both the Americans and the British had serious reservations. In addition, Lloyd considered that the risks of a French move towards the Soviet camp were running too high. Accordingly, he proposed changes to the Moch proposal, deleting reference to the Faure plan and suppressing the plan for inspection on German borders. Moch agreed to make a distinction between limitation and strict prohibition of nuclear tests. This, then, was the context in which the Anglo-French plan of 19 March 1956 was presented.

In a note to External Affairs' Minister Pearson of 21 March, Jules Léger summarized the main provisions of the plan as follows:

The first stage calls for a freeze of the levels of armaments and armed forces and for a prohibition of the use of nuclear weapons except in defence against aggression. During this initial stage, a control agency and inspection procedures are to be set up along the lines foreseen in the Eisenhower and Bulganin proposals. Initial steps in agreed reductions in armed forces and conventional armaments are foreseen.

During the second phase, there is to be a limitation of nuclear tests and further reductions in armed forces and armaments.

The third stage provides for the prohibition of nuclear test explosions for military purposes, further reductions in armed forces, the complete prohibition of the manufacture and use of nuclear weapons.

The clause prohibiting nuclear tests was originally envisaged as part of the second stage. Under pressure from Stassen during the preliminary meetings, Moch agreed to insert it as part of the third stage.[45] During these preliminary consultations, the French and the British also agreed not to raise the matter of the previous ceilings of 1 to 1.5 million men for the superpowers. U.S. policy was extensively revised, and from that time on the force levels of the superpowers were set, for "illustrative" purposes, at 2.5 million men.

The Anglo-French proposal was inherently complex, particularly concerning the transition from one stage to the next, which implied an automatic veto given that the rule of unanimity applied. It also proposed a complex control organization (an International Disarmament Organization composed of an Assembly and an Executive Committee). Despite its complexity, the proposal had merit in that, at least, the traditional approach of balanced, controlled and gradual disarmament was retained intact. In addition, it was a real attempt to synthesize all the proposals that had been previously discussed. The Achilles heel of the Anglo-French proposal was, of course, its high degree of complexity.

The United States presented its working documents on 21 March, and its main proposal on 3 April. The working documents aimed at the prior creation of:

• technical exchange missions, and
• an experimental zone for demonstrating control and inspection.

The main u.s. proposal provided for a first stage in which the two study proposals of 21 March would be implemented and the suggested military ceilings of 2.5 million men for the superpowers and 750,000 for France and Great Britain would be established. In addition, the proposal called for prior notification of anticipated troop movements on foreign soil. Some fifteen other clauses followed containing incidental mention of monitoring and possible limitation of nuclear tests. The first phase was open to discussion, while the other points were subject to subsequent negotiation.

This plan was even more complex than the Anglo-French proposal. It contained some nuclear and conventional elements, but its main thrust was towards opening borders through the use of mobile inspection teams and inspection zone "pilot" projects.

When the time came to prepare the report on the deliberations of the Subcommittee, Stassen insisted that, if there were compromises to be made, they should bear on proposals 1 and 2 of the Soviet statements of 27 March, on the first two stages of the Anglo-French plan of 19 March, or on the first phase of the u.s. proposal of 3 April.[46] For the Americans, therefore, there was no question of discussing prohibition of nuclear tests.

A few days before the Subcommittee completed its work, the Western nations tabled several documents to improve their propaganda advantage, including the one of 4 May which was countersigned by the Big Four.

The situation in London was so twisted that one is led to wonder whether the Soviets and the Americans had not reached prior agreement on the general content of the discussions within the Subcommittee. Only a historian with access to the archives of both superpowers would be able to answer the question. In any event, excluding nuclear issues from disarmament discussions is rather like putting the cart before the horse. As the Soviets privately admitted, their proposal on conventional disarmament was aimed only at meeting the expectations of the British. At the Foreign Ministers'

Conference in Geneva, MacMillan had in fact talked about "partial" disarmament.

Conversely, assuming that it made sense at the time to discuss conventional disarmament, there can be no doubt that the proposal of 14 May 1956 by the USSR to reduce Soviet forces by 1.2 million men invalidated all prior discussion in the Subcommittee. In due course, this was recognized by all participants. The British, who were the first to understand it, tried desperately to present an alternate formula on 7 June 1956.[47] Nutting hoped to reach agreement before 25 June on a one-phase disarmament formula and, to that end, asked that discussions be held in New York. Nutting hoped that if agreement could be reached, the proposal could be discussed during the meeting of the Disarmament Commission scheduled for July.

The State Department issued a clear refusal to this British initiative, questioning whether the Foreign Minister's trip would even be "productive". Undoubtedly, the State Department broke the rules of hospitality, but considered that there was no alternative. U.S. thinking was clearly expressed in the telegram of 20 June:

The specific points in your plan which are not acceptable to the United States are the same as have caused the United States and the United Kingdom differences in the past, notably:

a   the United States insists that limitations on test explosions [authors' note: these limitations concerned the quantity and volume of nuclear explosions] must proceed *pari passu* with limitations on the production of nuclear weapons;

b   the extent to which the President's proposals for aerial inspection should be given precedence in any disarmament proposals;

c   the amount of nuclear disarmament which should be included in the first phase; and

d   the mechanism of control.

Meanwhile, the letter from Marshal Bulganin to several NATO nations dated 6 June blamed the Western powers for the impasse in negotiations. Preliminary consultations between the recipients of the letter, followed by additional consultations within NATO, resulted in a virtually unanimous reply from an undivided Western camp.

On 5 July, during debate in the Commission, Minister Paul Martin made a noteworthy speech. The impasse in the work of the Disarmament Commission was so complete that no vote had been taken on any of the three main resolutions on the agenda. The only new element in the debate was that Gromyko accepted, on 16 July, the ceiling of 2.5 million proposed by the United States as a basis for discussion. The work of the Subcommittee thus resumed in 1957.

Description of the 1957 proposals is limited here to those elements that are essential to an understanding of Canadian policy during that year. The main subjects discussed can be grouped under three main headings: 1. suspension of nuclear tests; 2. reduction in armed forces; and 3. establishment of inspection and control zones. Canadian policy on suspension of nuclear tests is the subject of a separate chapter in this book and discussion of this topic is, therefore, postponed. Under the other two groupings, two marathon proposals should be singled out: the Soviet proposal of 20 September 1957 which essentially mirrors that of 30 April, and the Western proposal of 29 August 1957.

The brief comparative review of these two proposals which follows is based on a document prepared by M.F. Yalden of the United Nations Division of the Department of External Affairs, dated 1 November 1957. The Western position on conventional force reduction was as follows:

Force Levels

- The USSR and the USA, and France and the U.K. will reduce their armed forces to 2.5 million and 750,000 respectively as a first step ... The levels of forces for other States will be determined later.
- In two subsequent stages the USSR and the USA, and France and the United Kingdom will reduce their forces to 2.1 and 1.7 million, and to 700,000 and 650,000 respectively, (force levels for other States will be specified at the same time through negotiation with them), provided that at each of these two stages: a) compliance with the provisions of the convention has been verified, and the control organ has been expanded as necessary to verify further reductions; b) there has been progress towards the solution of political questions; and c) other essential States have become parties to the convention and accepted force levels in relation to the above.

Armament Levels

- During the first stage of force reductions, France, the U.K., the USSR and the USA will place agreed quantities of specified types of armaments in depots within their own territories, and under the supervision of an international control organization.

- On the conditions outlined in a, b, and c, the States will undertake further armaments reductions, on the understanding ... that the armaments of no State will be permitted to exceed the levels so fixed.

The provisions of the Soviet proposal of 20 September were as follows:

Force Levels

- The Soviet Government still considers its April 30 proposals to be satisfactory (reduction to 1.5 million for the USA, USSR and China, and to 650,000 for the U.K. and France). However, it is willing to agree to reductions to 2.5, 2.1 and 1.7 million men for the USA, the USSR and China, and to 750,000, 700,000 and 650,000 for the U.K. and France, subject to the following understandings: a) force levels will include personnel employed by the armed forces as civilians "but engaged in servicing military equipment and installations"; b) the disarmament agreement will cover all three stages; agreement on subsequent reductions will be simultaneous with agreement on first reductions; and transition from one stage to another will not be "dependent on any conditions which are not stipulated in the agreement itself".

Armament Levels

- Although the Soviet Government considers that a 15 percent reduction in armaments "would be most expedient" during the first stage, it "agrees in principle" with the proposal to reduce arms through the reciprocal submission of specific lists.
- At the same time, it should be stipulated that agreement on this method of armaments reductions would not "delay the implementation of the provisions of the agreement which relate to the reduction of armed forces and military budgets".

The proposals from both the Soviet Union and the West contained an important clause on the prohibition of recourse to nuclear weapons. For the West, the obligation was passive, namely the use of nuclear weapons was prohibited except for individual or collective self-defence. For the Soviets, prohibition was absolute – all States had to formally renounce the use of nuclear weapons under any circumstances and in any form ("including air bombs, rockets of any range with atomic or hydrogen warheads, atomic artillery, and so forth").

Oddly enough, these proposals read like insurance policies, peppered with escape clauses. They are also more significant in terms of things unstated as opposed to things stated. The provisions of these texts were relatively simple, however, compared with the provisions of the clauses governing the establishment of control and inspection zones. Concerning aerial inspection, the Western proposal of 29 August prescribed two general inspection zones, namely zone A (covering the Western hemisphere and the Soviet Union), and zone B (covering Europe). Within these two general zones it was possible to choose specific inspection zones, but on condition that one of the two alternatives within zone A was agreed upon first. Thus, the proposal for the zone of the Western hemisphere and the Soviet Union was:

- all of North America north of Mexico in exchange for all of the Soviet Union;
- all of the territory north of the Arctic Circle of the Soviet Union, Canada, the u.s. (Alaska), Denmark (Greenland) and Norway, and all of the territory of Canada, the u.s. and the ussr west of 140° W longitude, east of 160° E longitude and north of 50° N latitude, together with all the remainder of Alaska and the Kamchatka Peninsula and all of the Aleutian and Kuril Islands.

Once one of these specific zones was agreed upon, the alternative choice for Europe was:

- an area bounded in the south by 40° N latitude, in the west by 10° W longitude and in the east by 60° E longitude [authors' note: in other words, all of Europe less southern Spain, Sicily, Greece and Crete, but including the British Isles and the European part of Russia up to the Urals];
- or a more limited zone ... provided that it included a significant part of the Soviet Union and other countries of Eastern Europe.

It could well be argued that the dice were loaded, recognizing that the first option in zone A was unthinkable at the time, and that the second option was infinitely more favourable to the West than to the East. Canada was not slow to discover this fact.

Despite their reticence, the Soviets had decided early in 1957 to lend support in the First Committee to the eleven nations that wanted to focus particular attention on the Eisenhower plan. Thus, in their draft of 30 April they proposed that two specific zones be studied, comprising, as described by Klein:[48]

- two wide zones of equal area (7,100,000 km²), one located in North America (western United States and Alaska) and the other in Asia (eastern Siberia, Kamchatka, Sakhalin);
- a European zone encompassing all the territories of the NATO nations (excluding Portugal, Greece and Turkey), the Warsaw Pact countries, part of Bulgaria and a strip of the Soviet Union.

In terms of means of control, the differences between the two proposals were equally substantial. On 29 August, the West demanded the establishment of land control posts at main strategic points, as well as the constitution of mobile control teams. The land posts were to be established "without restriction to the limits of the zones of aerial inspection". In addition, the zones covered by the land posts could not be less than those subjected to aerial inspection. On the same date as the Western proposal was made, a note was drafted for the Canadian Joint Chiefs of Staff which reads as follows: "the emphasis placed on the constitution of mobile teams within the aerial inspection zones is new ... This idea became part of current U.S. thinking following the visit of Secretary of State Dulles to Ottawa and London in July".[49] Finally, the nations would undertake to provide, within three months of the agreement coming into force, "inventories of their fixed military installations and numbers and locations of their military forces and designated armaments within the agreed inspection zone".

During the first phase, the Soviets planned to establish control posts at strategic points (ports, railway junctions, highways) excluding airfields, inspection of which would only be permitted during the second and third stages of force reductions in connection with relevant measures "for the final prohibition of atomic and hydrogen weapons and their elimination from the armaments of States". Concerning force reductions in Europe, the USSR demanded that the forces of the Big Four in Germany be reduced by one third. The proposal of 20 September, however, contained a new element: "or some other agreed level". Aerial inspection was mentioned only in connection with the two zones suggested in the Soviet proposal of 30 April.

To be faithful to history, it should be noted that the Western proposal of 29 August was brushed aside by Gromyko on the very day that it was tabled in London. On 16 September, Moscow officially rejected the proposal, a few days prior to submitting its own proposal of 20 September to the Secretary General of the United Nations.

Canadian Reactions.   During 1956 and 1957, Canada's main contributions to the work of the Subcommittee were confined to N.A. Robertson's participation in the discussions, to a few notes on Canadian experience on monitoring and control in Indochina, a few attempts at mediation and the production of a number of increasingly lengthy technical reports. From the standpoint of political strategy, Canada attempted to avoid being caught up in the disputes between the u.s. and Europe. Generally, the Canadian position was closer to u.s policy than to Anglo-French policy. It should be added that Robertson personally proposed several initiatives to Ottawa, but without success.

The main issues concerned the procedures to be followed and the consultations to be maintained between the allies. The West Germans and then the Italians insisted on being kept abreast of the negotiations in London. Britain and Canada, with strong support from the United States, considered it normal to keep the FRG in the picture on issues of prime importance to that nation by means of diplomatic channels through London. On that issue, Moch waged a quixotic battle. He claimed, with perfectly defensible logic, that the Germans in particular had no right to examine the proposals tabled in London. After all, the Subcommittee was an organization of the Commission which in turn was a "creature" of the United Nations. In matters of allegiance, there was no doubt where Moch stood.

The quarrel arose during the time that the Anglo-French proposal of 19 March 1956 was in preparation. The Germans made formal representations about the proposal to the British who were embarrassed when the news broke in Bonn. It meant that Bonn had been informed in advance, which implied "an especially privileged relationship which not even the other members of the Disarmament Commission enjoy".[50]

This epic battle was, however, an exercise in futility, for it was learned that Great Britain gave "briefings" on a more or less regular basis to Australia, New Zealand and South Africa, while information was occasionally given to Ceylon, India and Pakistan. On 4 April, following a conversation between the Italian Ambassador and John W. Holmes, Italy requested access to the same privileged information from Canada. Holmes, with his usually masterful diplomacy, stated: "Speaking for myself, I did not think that we would want to accord any favours to the Germans which we did not also accord to Italy, although it might be possible that as German territory was specifically included in the Soviet proposal some special discussions with the Germans might be necessary on this aspect of the question".[51]

At all events, from 1955 onwards, debate on these issues became increasingly multilateral. Lester B. Pearson created a precedent that year by informing the North Atlantic Council of the content of discussions in the Subcommittee. Subsequently, this practice was followed regularly. For instance, when the time came for Canada to respond to Bulganin's letter of 6 June 1956, Jules Léger even proposed to Pearson that the letter be first submitted to NATO. Actually, the British, French and Americans had done the same thing. According to the records, this allowed the British to revise substantially their draft letter. Léger, therefore, took a lot of precautions. He reminded Pearson of his duties within the Committee of Three[52], as well as of his plea for increased consultation within NATO.[53] History does not indicate whether Pearson appreciated Léger's note. In the margin, Pearson had written "I agree in the circumstances but it is silly for the Council to occupy themselves with the details of the draft".

Four aspects of the debate within the Subcommittee during 1956 are worth recording, specifically the attempt at mediation between the American and European positions by N.A. Robertson, the Canadian reactions to the Anglo-French proposal of 19 March, the Soviet proposal of 27 March and the u.s. proposal of 3 April.

At the time of the first preliminary meetings in London, the State Department's Howard Myers, chief u.s. advisor to Stassen, was gloomy and pessimistic. Following discussions between Stassen and Moch on 13 March, Myers reported that "in many years of working on disarmament, he had never heard a French representative indicate that it was unnecessary to consult his own government on proposals and comments as significant as those advanced by Mr. Stassen".[54] Essentially, Stassen was asking that the u.s. proposal on aerial inspection be included in the first phase of the Anglo-French proposal. Obviously this was asking a lot. Nutting was not happy but, at Moch's insistence, he remained firm. The Americans judged, therefore, that they would have to present separate proposals. In addition, Stassen stated that he was in possession of "fairly substantial" reports, without mentioning how he obtained them, which indicated that the Soviets were attracted by the idea of aerial inspection zones. Rae stressed in his report that Robertson and Stassen thought that the Subcommittee might not be the best forum for negotiation, adding "We are thinking of subsequently directing the consideration of United States proposals into a bilateral framework". Léger stated on 20 March that he found this idea "realistic and useful", but it was never considered seriously. Canada was not enthralled with the idea of bilateralism. It was observed only that, should the idea come to fruition, it would have to be handled with extreme care over a relatively long period.

Robertson tried to convince Stassen that if the U.S. renounced a global disarmament plan it would only fuel the arguments of the opposition. Stassen understood the Canadian position, but repeated that he would insist in future negotiations on the priority of aerial inspection, and on the need to reach agreement on "limited and practical" means. Robertson asked Stassen whether it would be possible to include his general proposal on aerial inspection into the more general framework of partial means of inspection envisaged in the first phase of the Anglo-French plan. In other words, he was asking the United States to accept the same suggestion, cast in a different form, that the U.S. had asked Moch to accept. In light of his reservations concerning the whole Anglo-French proposal Stassen refused to take the bait.[55] There was no further discussion because, one week later, the Americans firmed up their position.

The Anglo-French proposal posed serious problems for Canada. In a note to External Affairs' Minister Pearson dated 20 March, Léger stated that Canada had essentially three options: "we could express our general agreement with the Anglo-French approach; our agreement with specific features of both plans; the view that there is a broad agreement on the most important initial steps and the hope that they provide a sufficiently large and realistic basis for an agreement with the Soviet Union". One day later, a second note stated that U.S. reticence "may stem from the uncertainty in the Pentagon as to the desirability of subscribing even in theory to the principle that under certain circumstances the nuclear deterrent might be abandoned". Léger added that the Department of National Defence had no basic objection to the plan, and that Canada had abstained until then from supporting it given the uncertainty that prevailed in Washington. He went on to say that, in the previous year, Canada had only partly supported certain Anglo-French initiatives, because the United States had refused to close ranks. "For the moment", he wrote, "we think that we should continue to abstain from any action which could isolate the United States within the Subcommittee". Presumably, this is what the Minister wanted to hear.

There were lengthy discussions between the allies on the clause prohibiting recourse to nuclear weapons. This debate was covered in our earlier discussion of the Lloyd and Moch interpretations of the first Anglo-French memorandum. The British had no problem with the clause, because no clause could replace article 51 of the Charter of the United Nations. The United States wanted Moch to provide a "qualified" interpretation of the clause of non-recourse in the form of a "suspension" clause. No one ever solved the problem, not even the Americans in their draft treaty which followed on 2 August 1957.

Clearly, the thesis of self defence embodied in article 51 of the U.N. Charter constituted the ultimate qualification. After all, no healthy person should be obliged to die against his will. It was curious, therefore, that Canada attempted to make proposals in this regard.

Three problems naturally arose in connection with this issue. The first concerned propaganda. The Soviets wanted to prohibit recourse to nuclear weapons, but recourse to force was already prohibited in the Charter. What more could be asked? A solemn declaration! The Americans wanted none of it. They had no faith in the Briand-Kellogg pact, or in any moral declaration that was not accompanied with a system of controls and safeguards that would render the very threat of recourse to nuclear weapons impossible. In other words, to eliminate the threat would require the elimination of nuclear weapons. And to eliminate nuclear weapons would require disarmament. And to accept disarmament would require trust and a system of control. There was a strong element of propaganda in all that. The Russians adopted the scenario of a bee playing the role of an ant, in that they attempted to use the cover of a seemingly laudable proposal to transfer the responsibility for failure to reach agreement to the other party.

The second problem concerned the defence of third parties. If a third party country were attacked, and the United States came to its defence, would the United States be acting in self defence? Could Europe be considered as U.S. territory (Kennedy's famous *Ich bin ein Berliner*)? Perhaps, if one is talking of Berlin or of France. But what of Korea, Israel or some other country? At the time, the Americans could not conceive of defending their allies without nuclear weapons. Prohibition of recourse to nuclear weapons had, therefore, to be qualified. But to qualify prohibition is to render the very concept invalid.

The third problem concerned the psychological advantages of deterrence. If one party formally renounced the use of nuclear weapons, then the other party would not fear the threat of nuclear retaliation. If the fear of retaliation were to be a moderating influence on the second party, then the first could not make a unilateral declaration to the effect that, whatever the circumstances, it would not use nuclear weapons. In a climate of non-disarmament, renunciation of recourse to nuclear weapons by a nuclear-weapon State would be tantamount to acknowledging that, although it possessed the means, it had no right to use the means. That would be perfectly alright given that all States thought the same way, but nothing is less certain. And the only way of being certain would be to disarm all States. Thus, we have turned full circle.

In his first telegram to London dated 5 April, Marcel Cadieux of the United Nations Division proposed linking the prohibition of recourse to nuclear weapons to reductions in conventional forces. The provision prohibiting recourse to nuclear weapons except for reasons of self defence would remain as defined in Phase One of the Anglo-French proposal but would become unconditional in the event of agreement on reduction of conventional forces. The idea was to maintain the clause restricting recourse to nuclear weapons to self defence in a nuclear war, but to remove it in a situation of conventional war where conventional force reductions had been made. The telegram was, however, so worded as to imply that prohibition would be unconditional and absolute if reductions in armed forces were to occur. William Barton asked that this ambiguity be removed. George Ignatieff of the Defence Liaison Division considered that Canada could not go beyond the clause contained in Phase One of the Anglo-French proposal. John W. Holmes, who had copies of the correspondence, told Cadieux that he was not sure that he understood the sense of the proposal, and asked for a meeting of the three players. The ambiguity was eliminated in a second telegram sent to London on 9 April.

It would be superfluous to add that this Canadian proposal went unheeded. Not only were the two telegrams somewhat incomprehensible – they are not the most elegant pages of the Canadian archives – but the proposal did not respond at all to either the first or the second points discussed above. In addition, the Soviets would have been only too happy to accept a proposal of this type, given their numerical superiority in conventional forces. It is interesting to note that Marcel Cadieux, who wanted to go beyond the Anglo-French proposals and meet the Soviets halfway, was also the same person who made another rather curious suggestion on 28 March. In order to pull the thorn from the feet of the Americans, who were accused by the Soviets of conducting illegal nuclear tests on their island possessions in the Pacific, Cadieux advanced the notion: "I suppose the possibility that Canada's waste lands in the North might be suggested as alternative testing grounds should also be examined".[56]

Ottawa, in common with the other chancelleries, studied the implications of the Soviet proposal of 27 March. The first reaction came from R.A. McGill in a memorandum prepared for the Minister on 28 March. He wondered, and not without reason, whether the Anglo-French proposal had not become obsolete, since neither the u.s. nor the ussr discussed prohibition of nuclear weapons from that time on. "This new development", he concluded, "may shift attention directly to the u.s. and the ussr and to the possibility of agreement between them without much reference to the elaborate schemes propounded by Moch and Nutting". This judgement was obviously premature, but there was nothing at the time to prevent anyone from thinking that the Russians and the Americans had much more to say to each other than might appear from the official minutes of the negotiations.

Concerning Soviet intentions, the Canadian Joint Chiefs of Staff considered that the USSR was not the plaintiff in the case. Future increases of any amount in the power of U.S. nuclear stockpiles would not induce the Soviets to make concessions. Even though the Soviets were in a difficult economic situation and short of manpower due to the low birthrate during the Second World War, such considerations were not "sufficiently great to outweigh their military and security objections to the cardinal Western conditions of effective inspection and control".[57] These assessments were close to those of the Americans, who considered that the Soviet proposals were used "as instruments of foreign policy, regardless of any desire to reach real agreement or not".[58] The United States viewed the Soviet proposal as an attempt to "obstruct" German rearmament. All Western observers were in agreement on this point. A careful reading of the text of the proposal, especially parts 3 and 4, shows this to be true.

George Ignatieff of the Defence Liaison Division reiterated that the defence of Europe was unthinkable without nuclear weapons. There was no question, therefore, of accepting a plan which was aimed at the "neutralization of Germany".[59] He thought, however, that the plan should be studied with the greatest of care. On that point, John W. Holmes was in agreement. He stated that the text of the Soviet proposal contained concessions that Molotov had made in private at the time of the Foreign Ministers' Conference in Geneva, particularly on the possible use of aerial inspection as a means of control.[60] Cadieux, like Holmes, felt that attempts should be made to negotiate on those points of the proposal that seemed acceptable. In short, Canada should continue to pursue the objective of working for disarmament as a permanent principle of foreign policy, and no proposals should be accepted which were "disproportionately contrary" to Canadian interests. The proportions that were acceptable or unacceptable were not, however, specified.

During 1956, the main Canadian statement to the Subcommittee was made by Norman A. Robertson on 23 April.[61] Robertson spelled out, in substance, the whole Canadian approach to the issues under negotiation at the time. We were at a turning point, he claimed, and time was running out. We had to ask ourselves whether it would not be better "to accord greatest priority to implementing the 'initial measures' rather than to withdraw on an acknowledgement of failure". These 'initial measures' were obviously the aerial inspection means proposed by the Americans. "Although we might wish to press", he continued, "for the implementation of a comprehensive program which would fit neatly into an international convention, to be concluded at some future date in a happier world, ... there are compelling reasons for trying to reach agreement now on the measures that can be made effective in the immediate circumstances". The language could not have been clearer. Disarmament would be cast aside in the absence of possible agreement. From then on, every priority had to be given to small steps that were possible and realizable. Specifically, negotiations on limiting nuclear tests "would have to take place in the context of other measures of disarmament under effective control". As noted in Chapter 9, the year 1956 marked the first turning point in the evolution of Canadian policy on the suspension of nuclear testing. In the area of force reductions, Robertson advocated that the Big Four accept the figures advanced by the United States. As for the other States, a compromise should be worked out based on the respective figures suggested by the United States and the USSR. It was Robertson at his best. It seems that he made his statement without seeking too much assistance from Ottawa. The telegram from Cadieux, which was countersigned by Holmes, started as follows: "We are glad that you made the suggestions outlined in your telegram ... the time was ripe for a proposal that the possibilities for a limited first stage agreement should be explored".[62]

Within the Subcommittee, however, the time was not yet ripe. The international situation did not lend itself to the realization of agreements based on reciprocal trust.

With regard to the other aspects of the u.s. proposal of 3 April, the Canadian Joint Chiefs of Staff accepted, of course, the new military manpower figure of 2.5 million suggested by the United States. On 23 March, General Foulkes sent a telex to his counterpart, Smith, in the United Kingdom, informing him that, on a *pro rata* basis by population, Canada – whose population was roughly 10 percent that of the United States – would be satisfied with a ceiling of 250,000 men. It was obviously easy to say in the circumstances, since a disarmament plan would have effectively permitted a doubling of Canadian military manpower at the time. Foulkes added that if it were necessary to revert to the previous 1 percent formula within the Subcommittee, another basis for the calculation would have to be found, since it was deemed that the level of Canadian military manpower should not fall below a ceiling of 150,000 men. Replying to another question that Smith had posed in an earlier telegram, Foulkes stated that, on 31 March 1945, Canadian military manpower stood at 761,041 (the army alone accounted for almost half a million men).

In the framework of examining u.s. proposals for technical exchange missions and for constitution of demonstration zones, the Department of National Defence supported the u.s. proposals and found it "reasonable and appropriate"[63] for Canada to provide representatives and military personnel to technical exchange missions. The Joint Disarmament Working Group, on the other hand, had to study the issue of the "mandate" of these teams as well as the issue of their composition. On 2 August, following an expression of dissatisfaction with the progress of these studies, the Working Group was encouraged to go back to work. On 18 September, it was learned that the issues had been left in abeyance in view of other more pressing priorities which faced the Joint Disarmament Working Group. This was certainly true, since the Working Group toiled relentlessly on the issue of limiting nuclear testing. On 12 December, there was general agreement that this issue should be pursued, and this was reconfirmed at the meeting of the Joint Planning Committee on 5 February 1957. Subsequently, nothing further was heard about this issue, simply because it was subsumed in the more general study of prevention of surprise attack.

The only document available to the Canadian Delegation on the issue of technical exchange missions was a report on Canadian experience sent on 16 April to the Indochina Commission. This two-page document covers about ten points in connection with the mandate, composition, nationalities represented, questions of freedom of movement, logistics, communications, interpretation, chairmanship, testimony and local laws. Its content could hardly be expected to contribute to the debate on an issue which, in any case, was judged by Ottawa to be of "doubtful effectiveness".[64]

The London Subcommittee, which Moscow viewed as a "futile"[65] organization, terminated its work at an impasse. The Soviets judged the Anglo-French proposal as a camouflaged attempt by the West to retain its nuclear arsenals indefinitely. As for the u.s. proposal, the Soviets judged that it was not even linked to any disarmament measure. The debates which followed in the Disarmament Commission in July were hardly more encouraging. The report of 26 July from E. Ronald Walker, the Australian Ambassador to the un, to his minister in Canberra, R.G. Casey, is most eloquent:

Theoretical disarmament is still a part of current disarmament discussions because France does not have so much a disarmament policy as a disarmament personality, Mr. Moch. Moch, refusing various important portfolios as French Governments come and go, has dedicated himself to the idea of disarmament ... The trouble with Moch is that his tactics are often dangerous while his mastery of the immensely complicated technology of disarmament is so overwhelming that no one in his own country, and very few outside it, are capable of arguing with him ... Nutting really believed in doing nothing in the circumstances, Moch only believed in his own magnificently coordinated "synthesis", the United States Task Forces under Stassen were already rumoured to be moving on to fresh studies (while Lodge insisted on taking over the public presentation of a position he knew little about), and Canada seemed mainly concerned, after making a distinguished contribution in London [authors' note: the Ambassador undoubtedly had access to different records from ours!], with preserving some bonds of agreement with all three ... Nutting told me of the great difficulty he had in getting his "One-Phase" plan through Cabinet and of the objections that had been raised on nuclear weapons by the United Kingdom Chiefs of Staff.[66] ... Nutting told me that the United Kingdom had not been able to get their partners' agreement[67] to his plan in time to present it in the Commission ... Martin's statement of 5th July was perhaps the most impressive individual contribution to the debate.

The Australian Ambassador had certainly mastered the art of making friends. His observations on Moch are interesting in that they perhaps reflect the Anglo-Saxon perceptions held of the French Delegate at the time. We have been unable to find any comment on such perceptions in the Canadian record.

Martin's statement of 5 July was made in the climate of anxiety created by a declaration of the Soviets on 14 May 1956 to reduce unilaterally their military manpower by 1.2 million men. The West had talked for twenty years about disarmament and suddenly the Soviets decided to deliver the goods. In early June, in response to this propaganda gesture and in an attempt to prevent any further deterioration in the situation, Nutting submitted to the allies his "One Phase" disarmament proposal. Paul Martin also attempted to attenuate Soviet propaganda by declaring:

Unilateral reductions outside the framework of international agreement providing for suitable controls can do far less to restore confidence than smaller reductions executed within an agreement providing the necessary safeguards. In other words, disarmament means agreed reductions; but unilateral reductions do not necessarily mean disarmament.

Martin's statement was a noteworthy summary of the specific negotiations in London and of Canadian policy in general. But one person in particular – R.A.D. Ford, of the Europe Bureau – was most unhappy with this approach.

Ford considered that the West should have stressed the point that Soviet reductions would have been more appropriately made ten years earlier when the West demobilized its forces, at which time the USSR continued to maintain its divisions in Europe at a level five times greater than that of the West. In addition, Ford considered that the West should take advantage of the period of de-Stalinization, which marked the beginning of a climate of new trust, to invite the USSR to contribute to disarmament efforts and improved relations between States.[68] It was too late at the time to change Martin's statement, but nothing was lost since Ford's arguments comprised the essence of the Canadian reply to Marshal Bulganin's letter of 6 June which was sent to a number of Western nations.

Robertson, for his part, undertook two personal initiatives during 1956. He raised the question in Ottawa of whether the Arctic would be an appropriate zone for consideration under the U.S. proposals for inspection zones. Rae, in his 5 April letter from London to Ottawa, informed George Ignatieff that Robertson had raised the question the previous day. Possibly the suggestion was made by Stassen to Robertson in private. Rae informed Robertson, however, that the suggestion had been made previously by MacKay but that no favourable conclusion had ever been reached. The *status quo* remained. Robertson was right, for in 1957 Canada received an official request from the U.S. to include the Canadian Arctic in the proposed inspection zones.

The other proposal by Robertson, to control arms exports, was never pursued either. The proposal, which was made on 7 April, did not stem from conviction but simply from Robertson's opinion that Canada's contribution to the work of the Subcommittee had been rather small and that some means had to be found to remedy the situation. The argument he used was not lacking in good sense. If the first phase of the Anglo-French proposal were accepted, there would likely be sufficient means of control to allow serious study of the problem. Ottawa took note with interest ...

In 1957, Canada's role in the Subcommittee was somewhat subdued. At the moment when the work resumed in London, the electoral campaign was in full swing in Canada. In June 1957, Diefenbaker formed a minority government. By November he was already musing over new elections. In March 1958, he was re-elected with an overwhelming majority.

Canada made a few noteworthy contributions in London, especially in the area of means of control[69], but there was not much further progress. In the wings, however, things were happening. On 13 February, Cadieux wrote to Captain F.W.T. Lucas informing him of the u.s. request to include the Canadian Arctic in the inspection zones.

The question was put to Cabinet on 4 April. Stassen wanted to know whether the Canadian Government was ready to accept responsibility for the region which might be assigned to Canada within the North American zone. In addition, Ottawa was asked whether Canada would be willing to sponsor the initiative in the Subcommittee. Two zones had been proposed, one covering North America and the other covering Europe. The North American zone covered Alaska, part of the Yukon and the Northwest Territories, all of British Columbia except its southeast extremity, and extended southwards to Portland, Oregon. The Soviet counterpart extended in the west to the port of Magadan and included the Kamchatka Peninsula and eastern Siberia to the south of Sakhalin.

The European zone covered virtually all of Scandinavia, but excluded Great Britain. Its western border passed in a southerly direction close to Amsterdam, Brussels and Dijon to a point near Lyon. Its eastern border passed just to the west of Leningrad and Kiev to a southerly point west of Odessa. In this way, Germany and most of Central Europe would be covered, but the designated zone excluded Moscow, Paris and London. Within these zones, it was not planned to perform inspections using land control posts, but this was unimportant because acceptance of these plans was linked to the implementation of the first phase of conventional force reductions which, in turn, required the use of land control posts.

The Department of External Affairs had strong doubts about whether these plans could succeed, observing: "we would gain more than we would lose". The Department was reluctant to be the sole sponsor, but agreed to countersign the proposal with the United States. Cabinet approved the proposal on condition that it be discussed within NATO before being submitted in London.

This proposal was never tabled because, in the meantime, Stassen was entertaining other ideas. Possibly the Pentagon or the State Department caused him to change his mind or, more probably, NATO insisted that the European zone coverage should extend eastwards from Paris as far as Moscow. The records do show, however, that Stassen had held private talks with his Soviet counterpart, and that new zones were proposed. As for the European zone, suffice it to say that the changes involved movement of the boundaries a few degrees to the east and a few degrees north. Canada, however, was required to open up all her territory. Canada once more accepted – honour to whom honour is due! The Department of External Affairs nevertheless had serious misgivings, viewing it simply as a return to the "Open Skies" proposal which now included Canada in order to satisfy Moscow's demand for zones of equal size. Canada's approval on 10 June gave the u.s. some elbow room. The Western powers could thus table their proposal of 29 August. Debate resumed in Canada on the issue during the review on means for preventing a surprise attack.

Canada's contribution to the matter of conventional force reductions was rather slim. Ottawa was content to comment on formulas proposed by the Europeans. France proposed the "Points System", while the u.k. advocated the "Standard Manpower Group Plan". The French formula involved assigning points according to the types of weapon in a nation's arsenal. The British formula called for fixing the levels of weapons according to conventional manpower groups (division, battalion, combat group, etc). Canada felt little need to study these issues which had little relevance in the Canadian context.

Reference was made previously to the telex sent by Foulkes in March 1956 to his counterpart Smith in England. For Canada to become party to an agreement on force reductions, it was first necessary to establish a preliminary basis as a starting point. On 26 July, Foulkes wrote to the new Minister of National Defence proposing the following ceilings for the three stages of reduction envisaged in the Western proposals:

- 1st stage: 250,000 men
- 2nd stage: 215,000 men
- 3rd stage: 175,000 men.

The Department of External Affairs was not too enthusiastic about this approach. Aside from the fact that Canada's military manpower was already lower than the figure established for the third stage, there seemed to be no relation between these figures and Canada's security requirements. The military was sent back to the drawing board. The first concession came on 14 January 1958, with a proposal that the new ceilings be established at 205,000, 170,000 and 135,000 men respectively. These figures were conditional, however, on the Reserves and auxiliary forces being excluded.

On 27 January 1958, G.B. Summers of the United Nations Division spelled it out: "Nevertheless, it is our view that our disarmament policy should be a disarmament policy and not one which would seek to legalize increases above the existing levels". Moreover, Summers noted that the Soviet proposal of 18 March 1957 was very clear in this regard. Another meeting of the Joint Disarmament Working Group was held in March 1958. There was a total impasse. In effect, the decision was made not to make decisions, as evidenced by the following recommendations:

a   that in principle Canada should not seek, as an initial ceiling under a disarmament agreement, force levels which would be above those authorized at the time by the Canadian Government;
b   that no attempt should be made at the present time to decide what reductions in Canadian force levels could be accepted as a result of a disarmament agreement;
c   that the Working Group continue to keep this matter under review and submit more definite recommendations at an appropriate time.

It must be acknowledged that, at the time, it was not easy for the bees and the ants to live together. In some respects, it was as difficult to negotiate with the Minister of National Defence as with Moscow. General Foulkes was just as intransigent on the issue of arms reductions. In his letter of 26 July to Pearkes, he argued that Canada could not accept reductions during the first stage since her military forces were defensive and barely adequate to meet her needs. In a prior letter to Jules Léger, the strategy adopted was more subtle. On 5 July, Foulkes advised him that L.D. Wilgress was aware of the fact that, independent of the disarmament issue, Canada's increased commitments to the defence of North America under NORAD might necessitate a reduction in Canada's commitments in Europe. In effect, this constituted a veiled threat that, if too much were asked in the area of disarmament, Canada's participation in NATO would be brought into question. It goes without saying that these issues, which were important at the time, have little bearing on today's reality.

Concerning the 1954–1957 period, the last word belongs to John W. Holmes:

Being on this Subcommittee with the great people was pretty "heavy stuff". I was always somewhat sceptical and even more so today. There was so little we could do. We felt the need to be totally responsible but we simply did not have the independent sources of information. The Americans were always so busy getting agreement in Washington that they were unable to let us know their policies until about 24 hours before the meetings began in London. We could be procedurally useful and tried hard to be, and it was very useful to us to be on an intimate basis with such people as Jules Moch. It was not easy, however, to take initiatives. I don't think the parties concerned deliberately intended these sessions to be farcical or to be a game of musical chairs, as we called them ... It may be worth bearing in mind that one of the persistent embarrassments we had over disarmament discussion was that none of the proposals for reduction ever discussed were of a size which would have reduced the Canadian forces at all. I remember particularly during the period of the five-nation Subcommittee that one of our tactical disadvantages was that we could never offer a reduction in exchange for anything.[70]

Whether we like it or not, the work of the Disarmament Commission and its London Subcommittee served, at least, to de-mystify an undertaking that concerned disarmament in name only.

4 Things Told and Things Untold

Everyone agrees that a secret should be inviolate, but ... most of
the time we ask only ourselves what should be told and what
should not be told ...

La Rochefoucauld, *Réflexions diverses*

But remember that no one catches me off-guard, don't pride
yourself on having surprised me; I face the situation head-on.

Jean-Paul Sartre, *Huis clos*

"Face the situation head-on", so as not to be caught off-guard. That
was exactly the philosophy adopted by the Americans in the late
1950s when they initiated reconnaissance missions over Soviet territory from Pakistan and elsewhere. These operations continued until
1 May 1960 at which time the U-2 flown by American pilot Francis
Gary Powers was forced down by a SAM-2 missile, and Powers was
exposed to world criticism by the Soviet Air Command. On 1 July,
another U.S. aircraft was shot down over the Barents Sea. Two years
earlier, in April 1958, Soviet Delegate Sobolev presented a formal
complaint to the Chairman of the UN Security Council, Henry Cabot
Lodge, declaring that the Soviet Union vigorously protested the
overflights of Soviet territory by U.S. reconnaissance aircraft.

The U-2 incident aborted the Paris Summit scheduled for May
1960. Nevertheless, in 1960, as in 1959, the United States continued
to maintain its same firm attitude, namely, that in the absence of
Soviet cooperation, the Americans were justified in adopting whatever "unilateral measures" were necessary to minimize the risks of
surprise attack. These measures included U.S. reversion to the time-
honoured concept of "aerial inspection".

Europe was acutely concerned with similar preoccupations. In the
mid-1950s, tactical nuclear weapons had been introduced into
Western nuclear arsenals. Clearly, the West had no choice but to
resort to their deployment in order to neutralize the overwhelming
superiority of Soviet conventional forces. By 1960, the situation had

changed. Somehow, the West had to compensate for the "missile gap". Washington thought of making NATO the fourth world nuclear power, by equipping its forces with intermediate-range nuclear weapons. In face of allied resistance – from France in particular – the plan was abandoned in 1963 in favour of a NATO Multilateral Force (MLF) which, in turn, experienced its demise in 1965 under President L.B. Johnson. On each occasion, there were fears that the FRG would entertain the nuclear option. Emerging technology also created new uncertainties which had to be addressed.

The need to protect against the scenarios of first strike and surprise attack was paramount on both sides. Plans for "disengagement" in Central Europe resurfaced. The West essentially held to their proposals of 27 August 1957. For its part, the Warsaw Pact adopted the Rapacki Plan which was first discussed in the UN General Assembly on 2 October 1957, formalized on 17 February 1958 and then revised and amended on 6 November 1958. In 1960, Canada undertook the study of a new secret "disengagement" plan under the direction of General E.L.M. Burns, a man who had just been named Disarmament Advisor to the Canadian Government. The study continued for over a year, but without any final outcome.

Meanwhile, between 10 November 1958 and 18 December 1958, the Conference of Experts on the Prevention of Surprise Attack met in Geneva. It was aimed at minimizing the risks of war between the superpowers and at settling the issues of "control and inspection" in Central Europe. There was, however, no mention of the role of the FRG.

All the proposed plans were a total "flop". The Soviets were no more inclined to discuss the Arctic in 1959 than they were in 1955 or 1957. For all practical purposes the Rapacki Plan was doomed following the first Soviet ultimatum on Berlin on 28 November 1958, while the Burns Plan never saw the light of day. In 1958, international attention turned towards the Middle East and the crisis in Lebanon while, in 1960, Cuba and the Congo expanded East-West rivalries throughout the breadth of the North-South dimension. Conditions were hardly favourable for negotiation of serious agreements, except perhaps for the tripartite discussions aimed at negotiating a nuclear test ban. These issues are considered separately in Chapter 10.

The present Chapter is concerned essentially with Canada's position vis-à-vis the three aforementioned topics, namely, aerial inspection zones in the Arctic, the Rapacki Plan and the Burns Plan. A few words are also appropriate on the Geneva Conference of Experts on the Prevention of Surprise Attack.

"OPEN SKIES" OVER THE CANADIAN ARCTIC

Following the complaint registered by Soviet Delegate Sobolev before the Security Council on 18 April 1958, the United States proposed, on 29 April, that an aerial inspection zone be established in the Arctic whose limits would be more or less those proposed by the Western powers on 27 August 1957.[1] A report[2] prepared by the Department of External Affairs to the Joint Intelligence Committee (JIC), dated 13 May 1958, stated: "both Dulles and Lodge asserted privately that the proposal was advanced seriously, and not only for propaganda purposes".

Despite the acrimony of the debate within the United Nations, there was some measurable progress. The Soviet complaint was directed essentially at the conduct of the Strategic Air Command (SAC), and there was no mention of the use of Canadian territory by U.S. reconnaissance aircraft. Sweden, like Canada, supported the U.S. proposal, but Canada refused to be a co-signatory. C.A.R. Ritchie, Canadian Delegate to the Security Council, stated that Canada was "not wedded to the particular zone proposed".[3] At the time, Ritchie felt that his stand was appropriate, for he was Chairman of the Security Council when the United States tabled its proposal. The Eastern bloc seemingly wanted to avoid confrontation, but after some hesitation the West called for a vote. It was met with a Soviet veto of the 2 May 1958 resolution. Several aspects of this resolution warrant particular attention:

- the international character of the proposed inspection system;
- the mandatory requirement to provide prior notification of over-flights;
- the need for radio-surveillance for all flights; and,
- the establishment of fixed ground-control stations.

On 26 May 1958, General Foulkes wrote to the Secretary to the Cabinet, R.B. Bryce, to advise him of Canada's earlier commitments concerning inspection zones. This unusual procedure is perhaps explained by Prime Minister Diefenbaker's keen interest in Arctic matters. Foulkes stressed that up to that time Canada had accepted the principles of: 1. establishing international teams of observers on Canadian soil; 2. authorizing overflights of Canadian territory by foreign aircraft; and 3. contributing manpower and aircraft towards the development of an inspection system.

Attached to the letter from Foulkes was a report prepared by the Chiefs of Staff dated 14 May. It contained several new elements. The Soviets had 28 airfields within the Arctic Circle capable of accommodating medium or heavy bombers, as opposed to 9 comparable airfields for the West. In addition, the Soviets had 150 smaller airstrips as opposed to 46 for the West. The report also pointed out that weather conditions in the Arctic permitted aerial photography for only 50 percent of the time. Foulkes also noted that, from an inspection standpoint, the proposal obviously favoured the West, despite the fact that the DEW (Distant Early Warning) Line would be visible for all to see. Because the DEW Line stations "would be accurately located and their capabilities carefully estimated" by the Soviets, Canada would have to adopt a new security policy to avert disclosure of their exact locations. These arguments obviously carried little weight, since they were equally applicable to the location of the Soviet radar stations.

The important element of the report was the expression of uncertainty concerning the effectiveness of the inspection system. The Chiefs of Staff could offer no viable solution, since no information was available to permit serious study of the issue. As early as 1957, at the time of the review of Western proposals, the Joint Disarmament Working Group had identified a series of points to be raised with U.S. Delegate Stassen.[4] They included the operational altitude and speed of surveillance aircraft, the type of surveillance equipment, the speed of processing photographic imagery, the information that photographic imagery could yield in targeting enemy objectives, and so on. By 1958, the circumstances had hardly changed. A joint meeting with U.S. experts was, therefore, necessary.

The meeting of experts was convened in Washington for 19 and 20 August 1958. Both sides sought an open and frank exchange, and the discussions were, therefore, informal. The U.S. team was led by Philip Farley who was assisted by L.D. Weiler, both of the State Department, together with a bevy of specialists under the direction of Dr. G. Kistiakowsky of Harvard. The Canadian team was led by S. Rae, Canadian Ambassador in Washington, assisted by Philip Uren, Squadron Leaders R.J. Mitchell and C.R. Milne, and Group Captain C.E.D. Armour.

The meeting produced no unexpected conclusions. The warning time would amount to minutes or days, depending on whether ballistic missiles or bombers were used. Any disruption of the communications system would be disastrous. Inspection zones established in the Arctic or in Europe would be inadequate to prevent surprise attack from other quarters – particularly the maritime approaches. As well, innumerable countermeasures could be used to disguise an attack as part of routine operations. Perhaps the only surprise which emerged from this meeting was the breadth of the control measures suggested by the United States. These measures were aimed at controlling not only the three main weapon system platforms, namely bombers, missiles and submarines, but also the supply lines from Soviet factories to the weapon deployment areas. Altogether, these inspection and control proposals would require a complement of 35,000 personnel. To meet the Arctic requirement, the Pentagon estimated a need for two squadrons of RB-47s, one based at Thule and the other based in Alaska, together with a complement of 740 ground personnel, of which some 250 personnel would be assigned to mobile teams and some 80 to 100 to communications groups. The manner in which these proposals would be presented to the Soviets was not specifically defined, but it was generally felt that an approach similar to that used during technical discussions towards agreement on a nuclear test ban might be appropriate.

On 29 August, General Foulkes advised the Minister of National Defence, George R. Pearkes, of the outcome of the Washington meeting. Pearkes, with Canadian interests in mind, asked Foulkes to enquire whether the United States would be willing to purchase Canadian CC-106 transport aircraft to perform the aerial inspection mission. On 3 September, Foulkes replied that he doubted very much whether the Americans would be interested in the CC-106 aircraft, since none were operational in the u.s. and the Americans lacked a repair and maintenance capability.[5] Moreover, he added, the inspection system would be established under the auspices of the United Nations, and each member State would be asked to contribute personnel and equipment on an individual basis.

The Conference of Experts on the Prevention of Surprise Attack (10 November to 18 December 1958) afforded the opportunity for the Department of National Defence to further its work on the prevention of surprise attack. The Canadian studies were essentially limited to conditions peculiar to the Arctic. Some excellent technical studies were conducted on methods of reconnaissance[6], the problem of telecommunications in polar regions[7] and on fixed and mobile ground control stations.[8] The technical report on telecommunications in particular was a true *tour de force*, and is still valid today.

The report on reconnaissance methods concluded that five bases[9] would be required to provide complete aerial coverage of the Soviet Arctic, using aircraft of 5,000 nautical mile range. Conditions for reconnaissance operations over the Soviet Arctic would be most favourable between the months of February and May when brightness would be maximal and cloud cover minimal.

The Canadian participants at the Geneva Conference of Experts on the Prevention of Surprise Attack included Air Commodore W.W. Bean, Squadron Leaders K.R. Greenaway, W.C. Maclean and R.J. Mitchell, and two scientists from the Defence Research Board, T.A. Harwood and John Laskoski.[10]

Klein summarizes the impasse encountered at this Conference extremely well.[11] The crowning achievement for the West had to be the definition of the "general technical characteristics of systems to reduce the threat of surprise attack", while for the Soviets, "it was dominated by the preoccupation to prevent the outbreak of war in the traditional sense of the word".[12] The West discussed technical issues, while the Soviets sought to discuss political issues. There was a total deadlock. The report to the Secretary General of the United Nations clearly reflected the prevalent state of thinking.[13] Despite the efforts of the Soviet Union and some Western nations to revive this Conference, it was not to be. The United States was completely opposed to it. As Klein observes, the most modern weapon system – the intercontinental ballistic missile – could not be subjected to inspection and control.[14] The only recourse was to seek other means of stabilizing deterrence. In part, this was the problem addressed by the Ten-Nation Committee on Disarmament when it was constituted one year later.

In view of these circumstances, one might ask whether the discussions served any useful purpose. First, they allowed both the East and West to express their mutual fears and intents. Second, they at least allowed both sides to distinguish between the essentials and the requisite non-essentials. The essentials consisted of avoiding a nuclear holocaust, while the requisite non-essentials consisted of employing all available means to find common ground for agreement. In this context, 1955 marked the beginning of bilateral debate between the USSR and the United States and, by the end of the 1950s, both sides were committed to restricting membership of the nuclear club to those nations having nuclear weapons at the time. Clearly, France was not pleased with this development. China, too, was a major preoccupation for the USSR. There is reason to believe that the Chinese problem was an important determinant in the Soviet decision to enter into discussions with the West in 1958 on a nuclear test ban treaty. Finally, it must be recognized that the aggregate of these discussions caused the various military establishments to become increasingly aware of the pressing need for arms control. This was not an unimportant aspect, at least for Canada.

This latter aspect largely explains Canadian policy on aerial inspection zones. Canada was reluctant to support U.S. plans. All possible means were used to avoid the appearance of being too closely associated with U.S. plans or U.S. draft resolutions tabled at the United Nations, for fear that Canada might be accused of supporting unfair propaganda levelled against the Soviets. John W. Holmes clearly recognized the difficulty: How could Canada change her position on this issue, having supported it both in the United Nations and in NATO? In Holmes' words, "having staunchly supported the project in the Security Council, it would be embarrassing to announce now that we realize it is inequitable".[15]

N.A. Robertson was more direct. He had just been appointed Under-Secretary of State for External Affairs. Robertson was endowed with the advantage of a long memory. In a letter to General Foulkes dated 13 February 1959, Robertson pointed out that on several occasions while he was in London and Washington[16] he had stressed the need for Ottawa to undertake studies within the general framework of Western policy "without necessarily waiting for the authorities in Washington to produce initial papers". He also expressed regret that studies frequently had been undertaken only at the last minute "under the pressure of deadlines established by imminent conferences while the other problems [had] not been considered at all". In another vein, Robertson advised Foulkes that a number of U.S. studies had been undertaken during Stassen's time in office, but that he had no means of gaining access to them. Accordingly, he invited the Department of National Defence to establish a study group that could respond to the priorities set by the Department of External Affairs.[17] Indications are that the State Department also sought similar support from the U.S. Department of Defense. At least, that was the impression gained by General Burns when he was in Washington in 1960. Conceivably, the diplomatic officials in both countries might have supported each other in their efforts to secure the collaboration of their respective military colleagues.

Robertson was not alone in his criticism of the Department of National Defence. Other officials in the Department of External Affairs had voiced the same criticism for upwards of a year. C.J. Marshall was not one to mince his words. In a letter to Campbell, he stated that no one, of course, could predict the final Canadian Government position on inspection in the Arctic, but "it would seem highly desirable that a group of people who have some real understanding of the factors involved be given an opportunity to make a thorough study of the question".[18] He did not go so far as to label the military as incompetent, but it amounted to the same thing. It was obvious, he added, that a surprise attack could arise in many ways[19], but "surely it would be folly to write off the idea of inspection because it cannot hope to cope with ICBMs or rockets launched from submarines". After all, Marshall continued, the military had spent 600 million dollars for the DEW Line and 200 million for the Mid-Canada Line for inspection purposes, even though those systems were far from perfect.

On 20 June, Marshall came back to the attack.[20] He did not understand the figures provided by the Department of National Defence. Why would it take 10,000 personnel and 700 aircraft to operate an effective inspection system in the Arctic? Was it necessary to patrol 600,000 square miles every two weeks? Marshall was willing to accept exaggeration, but not fantasy. He claimed that the DND estimates were completely unrealistic, since first of all it would take at least a year to construct a base in the Arctic. In a note to Summers, dated 17 July, Marshall repeated the same arguments. Photographic inspection of all the vast empty spaces of the Arctic was definitely unnecessary. All that was required was to "verify the work of ground inspection in built-up areas and to check for possible activity in locations outside existing settlements". Marshall concluded that studies should be conducted by appropriate experts. The joint meeting in Washington confirmed the correctness of Marshall's reasoning. In a letter to Defence Minister Pearkes, dated 7 August, General Foulkes stressed that the Canadian estimates were only of a "preliminary nature".

Overall, the records indicate that the Department of National Defence was less than lukewarm to the idea of "open skies" over the Canadian Arctic. One can only wonder whether the figures produced by the Department of National Defence were deliberately aimed at inducing the politicians to abandon a proposal which they could only support half-heartedly. Moreover, it appears from other sources that military staffs were concerned that the costs of inspection would be debited directly from their budgets. By deliberately inflating the figures and stressing the immediate priorities of air defence, the military could be assured that there would be no additional money available for other ventures. This obviously is the point of departure from the realm of the untold to that of speculation ...

Following the failure of the Paris Summit in May 1960, President Eisenhower stated that the United States was still committed to the "open skies" proposal. Diefenbaker, after meeting with Eisenhower, informed the House on 6 June: "I said that such a proposal, if and when advanced in the United Nations, should have co-sponsors and that Canada would join in sponsoring an appropriate resolution in that regard".[21] Diefenbaker went further than his predecessors, perhaps because he realized that this proposal would fall into oblivion. Satellites were to replace the U-2 ... .

THE RAPACKI PLAN

Since 1956, the Supreme Allied Commander Europe (SACEUR) had been preoccupied with ways of preventing a surprise attack in Europe. The concept of East-West overlapping radar systems has been discussed previously.[22] The Western proposals of 27 August 1957 were tabled following the completion of a NATO study on these issues. In June 1957, the North Atlantic Council prescribed that any proposal presented should at least meet the following six criteria: 1) the measures devised should be imaginative; 2) they should be perceived as a first step in alleviating tensions; 3) they should not prejudice the interests of the FRG; 4) they should be self-consistent and independent of any other proposal; 5) they should be practical; and 6), if accepted, they should lead to other agreements for European security.[23]

Paradoxically, it was Poland that responded to the NATO challenge with the Rapacki Plan, which met all the NATO criteria, even though German interests were not fully accommodated. The Polish Foreign Minister, Adam Rapacki, first spoke of his plan before the General Assembly of the United Nations in October 1957. He advocated a nuclear-free zone in Central Europe encompassing the two Germanies, Czechoslovakia and his own country, Poland. Manufacture and possession of nuclear weapons would also be excluded in this zone. Rapacki's proposal was considered with some interest by the United Kingdom, Canada and several other NATO countries. Nevertheless, it was rejected by NATO at the ministerial meeting in Paris in December 1957. Neither the FRG nor the United States would entertain any suggestion that West Germany should be disarmed against its will. On the other hand, "Prime Ministers Gerhardsen of Norway and Hansen of Denmark, on 16 December, as well as Foreign Ministers Selwyn Lloyd of Britain on 23 December and Sydney Smith of Canada[24] on 29 December argued that the Rapacki Plan be seriously studied".[25]

Poland submitted its proposals through diplomatic channels in December 1957, and they were officially recorded in Poland's memorandum of 17 February 1958. The first article reiterated the argument for a nuclear-free zone comprising the two Germanies, Poland and Czechoslovakia, and sought the assurance that there would be no recourse to the use of atomic weapons against any country within this zone. The second article concerned the obligations of the Big Four which occupied these countries.

Two of these obligations were very clear. Nuclear weapons, including any associated materiel or equipment, should not be located in the nuclear-free zone, and such weapons should not be used against any country within that zone. The third article concerned "broad and effective" controls, predicated on ground-based and aerial techniques. The control organization could include representatives appointed by NATO or the Warsaw Pact, as well as national representatives from other States that were not party to either of the alliances. Finally, the fourth article required that all these obligations be unilaterally binding, and that they be officially registered in an agreed national capital.

The Rapacki Plan was at least self-consistent, and could stand on its own merits. Despite the fact that the Eastern territories of this zone were much larger in area than that of the FRG, the Plan was severely criticized by the West. Britain voiced Western objections as follows:

- the Plan was strategically disadvantageous in view of the Soviet capacity to concentrate large forces close to the zone;
- effective control and inspection would be difficult to secure;
- the Plan might lead eventually to the withdrawal of United States' forces from Europe;
- disengagement of any form might increase rather than lessen the risk of conflict by creating an area of uncertainty, and a problem of "re-entry";
- the Plan would tend to stratify the existing division of Europe and would involve some recognition of East Germany ... ;
- it was undesirable to discriminate against troops of any individual country, specifically Germany.[26]

Although Britain acknowledged the validity of some of these arguments, she considered that, on the whole, "the dangers in the Rapacki Plan have been exaggerated and its merits underestimated". In general, the most serious arguments against the Rapacki Plan concerned the fear of U.S. disengagement from Europe and the repercussions of the ostracism that Bonn displayed towards the German Democratic Republic (GDR). "The creation of a special nuclear-free zone in Europe would have led to the *de facto* recognition of the GDR and would have affected the broader concept of deterrence".[27]

The thrust of U.S. criticism was centred, first, on the fact that NATO could only compensate for Soviet conventional superiority through the deterrent effect of tactical nuclear weapons and, second, that the

Plan was flawed from the standpoint of effective control. The first point will be discussed in the following section that deals with the Burns Plan. Concerning the second point, the inspection techniques under the Rapacki Plan left much to be desired. The Plan only repeated principles that had been agreed upon in previous negotiations for aerial and ground inspection, without prescribing specifics. Article 3 of the Polish memorandum simply stated that: "the details and forms of the implementation of control can be agreed upon on the basis of the experience acquired up to the present time". This was a minor concession in light of the NATO requirements developed in June 1957.

Apart from the six criteria previously mentioned, the Polish document required that control posts be established to cover all of Europe from the Atlantic to the Urals. Strangely enough, the "absolute minimum" included the Rapacki zone together with the Benelux countries and part of Denmark. The Rapacki Plan might only have been an insidious attempt by the East to beat the West at its own game. There is nothing on the record, however, to prove or disprove this hypothesis. In any event, the Rapacki Plan responded perfectly to Soviet preoccupations *vis-à-vis* the issue of West German tactical nuclear re-armament.

NATO insisted that aerial inspection should be as extensive as ground inspection. Control should comprise the exchange of information on the location, composition and nature of the existing and planned military forces; verification of information received; periodic reports of fixed and mobile inspectors and airborne teams; freedom of communication of autonomous systems; freedom of access to significant military installations, excluding private buildings; and, denial of access to nuclear stockpiles. As a minimum, 3,000 inspectors would be required, excluding personnel assigned to radar surveillance and aerial inspection.

Irrespective of the designated zone, it was recognized that the proposed control methods could not ensure protection against surprise attack from outside the agreed inspection zone. It was concluded that: "This fact does not invalidate the merit of the system proposed, which undertakes no more and no less than a reduction of the chance of surprise attack".

On 6 November 1958, partly in order to respond to Western criticisms concerning Eastern numerical conventional superiority, Poland revised its proposal on "disengagement". This time, the plan was a little closer to the proposals discussed previously within the Subcommittee of the Disarmament Commission. The main proposal of the Rapacki Plan was retained, namely that of a nuclear-free zone in Central Europe, as defined in the previous plan. At the same time, conventional forces would be "frozen" at existing levels. During a second phase, following discussions on force reductions, nuclear weapons would be totally eliminated and conventional forces would be reduced to agreed levels. One of the principal merits of the Rapacki Plan thus disappeared, since specific arms control measures were then linked to the problem of conventional force reduction.

These changes were never discussed in the West. A few weeks later, the first Berlin crisis negated any possibilities for favourable dialogue that might have existed previously. On 11 May 1961, a note from the Europe Bureau to Ignatieff concluded: "Since Gomulka was actually present with Khrushchev when he issued the ultimatum on 28 November 1958[28], it is to be assumed the ultimatum was intended, as some Polish official remarked, to be a 'state funeral' of the Rapacki Plan".

Canadian military reaction to the Rapacki Plan was contained in a document dated 29 January 1958.[29] It was a classic response. First, it emphasized that such a plan would deprive the NATO ground forces of their nuclear support. Second, it stated that a nuclear-free zone would not be meaningful, since intermediate-range missiles could be launched from Turkey or Northern Scotland. The clause prohibiting manufacture of nuclear weapons, which was embodied in the Brussels Treaty and the London and Paris Accords of 1954, presented no problem provided that the West would not be deprived of German engineering competence. This provision was clearly superfluous, because both the West and the East never hesitated to use German scientific expertise in support of their military programs. Finally, it should be noted that, at the time, possible changes to the Rapacki Plan were being contemplated, such as the prohibition of deployment of all atomic weapons around the world, except those deployed by u.s. and Soviet forces. Such a change would have rendered the Rapacki Plan impotent, and denied the expectations of the FRG which sought an increased role in the Atlantic Alliance by deploying tactical nuclear weapons on its territory.

THE BURNS PLAN

The Burns Plan was never tabled, but it is interesting in many respects. It demonstrated the difficulties of individual intervention within the bureaucracy. Both Mackay and Robertson, in turn, encountered internal problems when they attempted to establish special arms control provisions for the Arctic. General E.L.M. Burns, as Disarmament Advisor to the Government, was more fortunate. He had the advantage of being able to address the Privy Council directly, a privilege that none of his successors was to enjoy. He also held the trust of External Affairs Minister Green, a man of unparalleled austere principle, who made no secret of his anti-nuclear views. Burns was a military career officer who could claim expert knowledge of the subject at hand.

In June 1960, the Soviets withdrew from the Ten-Nation Committee on Disarmament. Negotiations collapsed. At that point, Burns introduced his plan to make the whole of Europe a nuclear-free zone. Burns submitted his plan in a letter dated 29 August 1960[30] to several officials of the Department of External Affairs, specifically G.S. Murray, R.H. Jay and J.H. Taylor. Taylor was later to become the Under-Secretary of State for External Affairs, a position he still held in 1988. The Plan was under study for over a year, during which period the Kennedy Administration came into office in the United States. Kennedy's election reopened the whole question of U.S. strategy within NATO. The Burns Plan became the subject of discussion between the Department of External Affairs (in particular, the Disarmament Division) and the Department of National Defence. It was only in 1961 that the Disarmament Division came under the control of General Burns, but the Department of External Affairs still considered it as no more than a purely administrative unit.[31]

Finally, it would be remiss not to record General Burns' way of thinking. He disliked nuclear weapons, and made his position clear in his book *Megamurder*. He was opposed to the U.S. proposal to make NATO an independent nuclear power, and expressed this view strongly in private correspondence with N.A. Robertson dated 4 July 1960[32], stating: "I think that the Canadian Government must decide whether it wants disarmament in nuclear weapons, or whether it is in favour of rearming NATO with them with all that that implies. In short, its defence policies and disarmament policies must be compatible". That was all very well, but Burns ventured into the realm of policy that was properly the prerogative of Cabinet and not that of a Policy Advisor.

In August 1960, Burns prepared a nine-page document which summarized his thinking. Essentially, it contained four points:

- agreement to a nuclear-free zone in Europe under international control;
- achievement of agreed force ceilings and levels of conventional armaments as between NATO and the Warsaw Pact;
- gradual expansion of the initial zone until only the retaliatory nuclear-carrying forces of the USA and the USSR remain in being;

• gradual reduction of the USA and USSR retaliatory forces ... until general and complete disarmament has been achieved.

The Burns Plan introduced certain new elements. It proposed general and complete disarmament and the idea of international control under the aegis of the UN. On the other hand, it contained no innovative ideas on the issue of linking a nuclear-free zone with conventional force reductions. In this regard, it conformed to the Rapacki Plan, but went further by suggesting rough numerical parity of conventional forces.

From a general philosophical standpoint, the Burns Plan constituted a return to the Anglo-French position of the early 1950s, which advocated general and complete disarmament. It was not necessarily incongruous, for the major powers progressively reverted to this position. The McCloy-Zorine agreement-in-principle, developed in September 1961, perhaps afforded the best example of the return – at least in words if not in action – to the notion of general and complete disarmament. Burns wanted the major powers to adopt a strategy of "minimum deterrence", based essentially on nuclear retaliation from forces deployed outside the nuclear-free zone, which would be gradually phased out within the framework of a global disarmament program.

The nuclear-free zone proposals of Burns were nevertheless somewhat complex. The first phase involved the delineation of a zone free from any ballistic missile launch platforms, which would extend for 1,500 miles on each side of the East-West demarcation line, ranging from Iceland to the Ural Mountains. Burns recognized that, as far as the West was concerned, the nuclear-free zone would encompass vast maritime regions, while the Soviet zone would comprise a land mass of much greater significance from a sovereignty standpoint. He proposed, therefore, that the zone would extend from the Western borders of Europe – excluding Great Britain but including Spain and Portugal – to the Eastern borders of Poland, including Byelorussia and the Ukraine. Within this zone, all launch platforms would be subject to strict control, particularly aircraft capable of carrying atomic weapons. Further, all atomic artillery would be totally prohibited.

Burns avoided any reference to British nuclear forces, but insisted that no Intermediate-Range Ballistic Missiles (IRBMs) be based in Europe. He hoped that with the replacement of U.S. B-47s with B-52s there would be no further need of American bases in Spain. Finally, tactical nuclear missiles would be eliminated from the designated nuclear-free zone. Methodologically, the Plan held certain promise, at least as far as nuclear launchers were concerned. Nothing was mentioned concerning conventional forces, save for a general need to pursue conventional force reductions; the Plan was essentially geared towards limiting nuclear weapons.

Clearly, the implication was that the agreed reductions would allow the West to resist any Soviet attack using purely conventional forces. In other words, it was a matter of reducing conventional forces to levels that would preclude the possibility of reaching the nuclear threshold. General Burns had already arranged to have this question raised before the Joint Chiefs of Staff Committee through a letter from the Under-Secretary of State for External Affairs to the Department of National Defence. Air Marshal F.R. Miller, who had just replaced General Foulkes, replied to the Under-Secretary on 29 September.[33] Miller stated that Soviet forces at the time comprised some 3.6 million men. Parity would require a reduction in Soviet forces to 1.7 million men, equivalent to 0.81 percent of the Russian population. Comparable reductions for the West would involve 700,000 men. He added that the essential criterion was not manpower but the firepower afforded by the armaments at their disposal. Miller concluded his response as follows:

The devising of an acceptable system has exercised some of the best brains since World War 1 ... I suppose the simple answer to your question would be to list current NATO armament goals, and to stipulate that the Warsaw Pact countries should not exceed these. Such an answer might be too simple to command serious attention.

Following the election of the Kennedy Administration in the United States, the Joint Chiefs of Staff responded to the Burns' proposal in a thirteen-page document, dated 1 March 1961, based on a text prepared by the Joint Ballistic Missile Defence Staff.[34] The conventional force situation was not as serious as previously thought. It was estimated that the FRG would have 12 divisions by the end of 1961. Given some success in Algeria, the French could add a further two or three divisions. In total, NATO forces could comprise about 30 divisions as prescribed by the NATO Military Committee in its document MC 70. But such figures were no more than a presumption, and the Joint Chiefs of Staff concluded that: "It is worth pointing out that the NATO strategy is already moving in the direction of de-emphasis upon nuclear weapons ... The Burns' Plan is obviously incompatible with the present agreed strategy of NATO".

The problem of verification and control of launchers was extremely difficult, particularly since solid propellants came to replace liquid propellants. As far as aircraft were concerned, the problem was no less difficult, for they were perfectly capable of delivering nuclear weapons. The same was true of artillery pieces which could be used in either a conventional or nuclear role, despite General Burns' reservations on this matter. In addition, following the events in the Congo, serious doubts arose concerning the effectiveness of a control organization under the aegis of the United Nations.

Air Marshal Miller, without repeating all these arguments, replied directly to Burns on 6 March 1961:

At this time, a major review of NATO strategy is taking place ... and the new administration has set up the "Acheson Committee" specifically for this purpose ... There is some evidence of a trend towards increased reliance upon conventional forces and decreased reliance upon the use of tactical nuclear weapons ... The U.S. "Bowie Report" is understood to have made recommendations along those lines ...

The proposals are subject to some question in detail from the military viewpoint. However, until the current review of NATO strategy has been completed, it is difficult to comment in detail upon the proposals since the two are closely interdependent. Moreover, the chief value of the proposal at this time lies in its broad concept. Pursuing it in detail, much of which is likely to be irrelevant and inaccurate, is likely to produce more disadvantages than advantages at this stage.

In short, Burns was invited to postpone further study of his plan. The Europe Bureau was far from convinced that the Soviets would accept nuclear parity in the nuclear-free zone context.[35] F. Yalden of the Disarmament Division was not about to lay down his arms. He realised that the extent of the nuclear-free zone was, in itself, a problem. As he wrote on 23 June 1961:

If we were to claim a small Rapacki-type nuclear-free zone, the French would oppose it, since we would thus create, to use their own terminology, a "zone of special limitations", which would constitute in itself a form of discrimination in Europe. The Germans would also object. On the other hand, if we selected too large a zone, the Soviets would pretend that they would be obliged to withdraw a significant part of their forces, while the United States would maintain their Polaris submarines and other weapon systems within striking distance of the Soviet Union. In the final analysis, any zonal scheme will either be difficult to "sell" to our allies or sufficiently biased to be unacceptable to the Soviet Union.[36]

Yalden considered that the 1,500 mile zone was too large and that the Rapacki zone was too small. He suggested, therefore, a zone[37] that would extend from the region eastwards of Paris to the Eastern borders of Poland. The North-South limits of the envisaged zone would extend, in the West, from the Massif Central to the North Sea, and in the East from Transylvania to the Lithuanian border. On 30 June, General Burns, without regard to Yalden's note, made the following proposals to Miller:

a   the ban on nuclear weapons be confined to tactical as opposed to strategic weapons;
b   the geographical area of the ban be confined to the land area of Western and Eastern Europe, less the USSR;
c   conventional forces in Western and Eastern Europe (less the USSR) be frozen at about current levels;
d   strategic weapons in Europe be treated within the overall pattern of the East-West balance of strategic delivery vehicles rather than in a regional scheme.[38]

This was an interesting proposal in many respects. L.J. Byrne of the Disarmament Division had already proposed to Burns on 20 June 1961 that the nuclear ban should only apply to tactical nuclear weapons. In addition, Byrne argued that the firepower of field artillery based in the FRG should be less than 155 mm calibre. Yalden supported Byrne's proposals, considering that they offered a number of advantages. First, there was no reference to Germany *per se*, and only longitudes and latitudes were mentioned. It could not, therefore, be argued that the proposal was directed against Germany. Second, Germany would not have tactical nuclear weapons. Third, the "freeze" on conventional forces would be enforced when the French divisions from the Algerian war were re-deployed in Central Europe. Fourth, NATO nuclear deterrence would be guaranteed by strategic nuclear weapons, and the French nuclear weapon program would not be affected.

Point b) of Burns' letter obviously raised a number of problems. Aside from the fact that the geographical area of the proposed zone would necessarily deprive NATO of its tactical nuclear weapons, a circumstance which DND considered potentially "disastrous", it would force NATO to adopt an "all or nothing" nuclear strategy in the event of conventional war in Europe. This was precisely what the Americans were attempting to avoid with their strategy of "flexible response". Their aim was clearly to delay recourse to tactical nuclear weapons as long as possible without precluding their possible use or jeopardizing U.S. doctrinal precepts.

The Disarmament Division clearly did not agree. In a memorandum[39] to Burns dated 31 August, Byrne presented the following arguments. First, tactical nuclear weapons afforded no advantage, whether used defensively or offensively. Second, in the context of the Berlin crisis, they would not increase Western fire-power, since they were purely defensive in nature and would not "enable us to fight our way into Berlin". Third, the use of such weapons would lead to uncontrollable war, since "control over such a conflict would be much less than the control that the Kaiser had over the military situation once the mobilization of German forces had started prior to World War 1".

Byrne was obviously well versed in history. And he was right: no expert seriously considered that tactical nuclear warfare could be "controllable". If NATO, and the FRG in particular, wanted to deploy tactical nuclear weapons, it would be to deter warfare rather than to engage in battle. Had Byrne and Yalden been more cognizant of the arguments and discussions which took place in Europe at the time, they would perhaps have realized that the only response that the West could make to the Rapacki Plan consisted of a proposal to make Central Europe a nuclear-free zone, outside of which the West would have been free to deploy tactical nuclear weapons. A. Philip and André Fontaine made these suggestions independently.[40] Their suggestions probably would not have satisfied the Americans, who were concerned that acceptance of such proposals would have entailed withdrawal from Europe, but the suggestions were nevertheless "open to debate".

Point c) was no more than a return to the most current version of the Rapacki Plan. Point d), on the other hand, anticipated the difficulties that the West would encounter twenty-five years later in negotiating the "zero option" on long-range nuclear theatre weapons. The INF (Intermediate-Range Nuclear Forces) Agreement was concluded within the overall context of East-West strategic weapons, even though such weapons were referred to as "tactical" in nature. It was only under pressure from the United States, in late summer 1987, that Chancellor Kohl accepted the withdrawal of the NATO Pershing 1A missiles.

That being said, it remains that the situation in 1988 was far from that which Burns had wished in 1961. The "low pressure" zone that Burns had sought in Central Europe still remains a "high pressure" zone, bristling with thousands of tactical nuclear weapons. However, none has sufficient range to reach the USSR. It is a first step towards the concept of a "European sanctuary". Although the possibility of limited nuclear warfare has not been eliminated, given that the great powers still retain their strategic weapons, nevertheless there have been many significant changes in Europe. The British and French strategic nuclear forces still exist, and have even been strengthened to ensure a "nucleus of deterrence" for European security. Moreover, U.S. nuclear forces still remain in Europe. U.S. maritime forces assigned to SACEUR still accounted for some 400 nuclear warheads, comprising a non-negligible retaliatory threat. When all is said and done, the question raised by Christian Herter in 1959 on the prospect of conflict in Europe has not really changed. It is impossible to foretell whether the United States would be prepared to risk their "all" in the defence of Europe. In the meantime, France and the United Kingdom have continued to strengthen their independent nuclear capability. As well, the political circumstances are also totally different. Germany has settled its differences with the Eastern European countries, the Conference on Security and Cooperation in Europe (CSCE) has confirmed the inviolability of European borders, and Honecker's visit to Bonn in the late summer of 1987 has reaffirmed the existence of two separate German "Republics". The old doctrines of Ulbricht in the West and of *Abgrenzunz* in the East are no more than empty shells.

The Burns Plan was never discussed in the West. L.J. Byrne was opposed to such discussions, arguing that "DND might persuade the Government to adopt a different policy". There is nothing in the record to indicate that the Canadian Government would have supported the Burns' Plan, but Byrne continued: "[such a change in policy] could result in our papers being used against us; for this reason most of my colleagues are opposed to this course".[41] All this being said, Washington would hardly have blinked an eye, even if this initiative had been communicated ...

At the time, all plans for denuclearization would have met with stiff opposition. France would have automatically rejected the concept of a strictly European nuclear-free zone. A "Rapacki" zone would also have been rejected out of hand by West Germany, not to mention the United States whose strategy was contingent upon the deployment of tactical nuclear weapons. Having assessed the various proposals in 1962, the British were very clear:

But the antipathy of our allies to any proposals smacking of disengagement is so marked that we could not afford to advance our views in the present circumstances. The Germans are especially concerned that such schemes should not gain currency at the disarmament talks and their objection to them has been the chief reason for their insistence that any Berlin negotiations should be conducted on a "narrow" basis. The French have also expressed suspicion and apprehension ...

In order to reassure our allies, we have said several times in the preliminary negotiations that we should resist any Russian attempts to discuss any measures of regional limitation of armaments.

On 12 April 1962, Ignatieff forwarded the British report to Burns, stating that the views of the British were not so far removed from those held by Burns, and suggested that Burns might invite the British, on an informal basis, to air their viewpoint either before NATO or the Eighteen-Nation Committee on Disarmament.[42] Ignatieff's suggestions went unheeded. Although the idea of a nuclear-free zone was still under consideration by the Eighteen-Nation Committee, it was mainly in the context of Western proposals on "non-dissemination" or "non-proliferation" of nuclear weapons for regions other than Europe.

In retrospect, the Burns' Plan had little chance of success. It was an isolated initiative, negotiated at a relatively low level in Government circles and lacking the support of Canada's allies. From a strategic standpoint, its merits were somewhat limited. Politically, the Plan was either ahead of its time or else totally superseded by the proposals under discussion. On that point – and on that point only, for otherwise the judgement would be too harsh – Burns was either a man of the past or of the future, but hardly a man of his time ...

5 The Catechesis of Perseverance: Canada and the Ten-Nation Committee on Disarmament

Tell me what hope my master can derive from perseverance.

Corneille

World hope for general and complete disarmament was never more prevalent than during 1959 and 1960. On 17 September 1959, the United Kingdom presented a comprehensive proposal on general and complete disarmament to the General Assembly of the United Nations. This was followed on 18 September by a comparable proposal from the Soviet Union. At Camp David, the superpowers agreed that disarmament "was the most important issue facing the world today". Several months before, in July 1959, at the Big Four Conference on Berlin, the foreign ministers decided to resume, on an equal representation basis, the disarmament talks that had been suspended since 1957. This decision provided the foundation underlying the 7 September 1959 resolution of the UN Disarmament Commission to create the Ten-Nation Committee on Disarmament.

The Ten-Nation Committee comprised membership from Canada, France, Great Britain, Italy and the United States for the West, and Bulgaria, Czechoslovakia, Poland, Romania, and the USSR for the East. In effect, the two East-West Alliances comprised the negotiating parties. The Ten-Nation Committee was not really a UN organization – it was brought into being by the Big Four. Its relationship with the UN could be inferred from the various resolutions of the United Nations, especially the resolution of 10 September 1959 which invited the Ten-Nation Committee to report to the Disarmament Commission. The General Assembly of the United Nations, in its resolution 1378 (XIV) of 20 November 1959, requested that the issue of general and complete disarmament "be studied and resolved as soon as possible".

The Ten-Nation Committee started its work on 15 March 1960 in Geneva. The Committee was short-lived. On 29 April, its work was interrupted to accommodate the Paris Summit. Negotiations resumed on 7 June, but were terminated on 28 June following the hurried withdrawal of the Warsaw Pact members on the previous day. During its brief existence, the Ten-Nation Committee considered three proposals: the Western proposal of 16 March 1960; the Soviet proposal of 7 June 1960 which was presented to Western chancelleries on 2 June and tabled at Geneva on 7 June; and, the u.s. proposal of 27 June tabled immediately following the Soviet withdrawal from the Committee. For a long time, the Soviets refused to recognize this u.s. proposal, since it was presented in their absence subsequent to their withdrawal.

The failure of the Paris Summit in May 1960 was one of the most striking events of the Cold War. It occurred in the wake of a Soviet announcement that a u.s. U-2 reconnaissance aircraft had been shot down over Soviet territory. When Khrushchev met with Eisenhower at Camp David in September 1959, he was already well aware of u.s. intrusive overflights of the ussr. The two superpowers agreed nevertheless on the paramount importance of general and complete disarmament. André Fontaine believes that Secretary of State Herter closed the door on Khrushchev by attempting to justify u.s. reconnaissance flights over Soviet territory following the U-2 incident.[1] From that time on, Khrushchev maintained that there was little to be gained from further discussions with Eisenhower, whom he later judged to be lacking in political will, and fit only to run a "kindergarten".

The work of the Ten-Nation Committee spanned the period between the two Berlin crises, from the time of the first ultimatum in November 1958 to the erection of the Berlin Wall in August 1961. Discussions took place during the most difficult period of the Cold War, when Washington pondered over its capability to inflict a retaliatory strike if ever the Soviets struck first. The first u.s. nuclear submarines became operational only in 1960 and the first Minuteman tests were conducted only on 1 February 1961. The Cuban crisis occurred in 1962; the United States knew then, both through its observation satellites and the Penkowski affair – which was only disclosed later – that the Soviets were unprepared to fight a war and, in any event, would not engage in conflict over Cuba.

As far as Europe was concerned, the United States was considering making NATO the fourth nuclear power in the world. German Minister of Defence Strauss even went to Washington to ask that Polaris missiles be made available to NATO. In Asia, Communist China was of the view that the Western powers would make no concessions to

Table 4
The Ten-Nation Committee on Disarmament

Origin: Declaration of July 1959, Conference of Foreign Ministers on Berlin
(Conference extended from 11 May 1959 to 5 August 1959).

Created: 7 September 1959, through formal recording by the Disarmament
Commission.

Mandate: To promote general and complete disarmament under a system
of effective international control.

Composition: Canada, France, Great Britain, Italy and the United States for
the West; Bulgaria, Czechoslovakia, Poland, Romania, and the USSR for the
East.

Commenced operations: 15 March 1960:
• 1st Session: 15 March to 29 April 1960:
• 2nd Session: 7 to 28 June 1960.

Adjourned indefinitely: 28 June 1960.

Main proposals presented:
• Western proposals of 16 March 1960;
• Soviet proposal of 7 June 1960;
• U.S. proposal of 27 June 1960.

Moscow, and this might have been part of the reason for the Soviet
withdrawal from the Ten-Nation Committee. It is known today that,
following the secret meeting of the Central Committee in Moscow in
December 1959, the Soviets decided to reduce their conventional
military forces by one third.[2] Moscow had been quick to understand
the reality of the nuclear era – defence had to be based on the forces
of deterrence. In mid-1961, following the Berlin crisis and diverse
internal upheavals in the Soviet Union, Khrushchev reversed his
decision to reduce Soviet conventional forces. Early in 1960, Soviet
military manpower was estimated at 3.6 millions. By July 1960, the
figure stood at 3 millions, but then increased to 3.8 millions before
decreasing, in 1962, to the earlier 1960 level.

The finest hours of the Khrushchev era occurred between 1960
and 1962, from the time of the aborted Paris Summit to the 1962
Cuban missile crisis. It was during this period, in January 1961, that
the young and fiery U.S. President John F. Kennedy came into office.

Though the climate changed, Khrushchev remained his invariant self. The meeting of the "two Ks" in Vienna in the summer of 1961 left the u.s. President convinced that only a firm attitude towards the ussr could put an end to its erratic behaviour. In the un, there was a state of crisis. Violence had erupted in the Congo and Secretary General Dag Hammarskjöld came under intense attack from Khrushchev, who demanded that Hammarskjöld be replaced by a "troïka" or "triumvirate" that would represent the three worlds, namely, the socialist, the capitalist and the neutral blocs.

THE PRELIMINARY TALKS

During February and March 1960, the five Western powers met first in Washington and then in Paris in order to prepare the Western proposal for presentation in Geneva on 16 March 1960. Larry Weiler of the u.s. State Department said later that this proposal was "a scissors and tape effort". In the view of one Soviet observer, it was "clearly a generalized compromise which defied understanding to an expert".[3] This was hardly an exaggerated description. The fact is that the u.s. proposal was inspired by Selwyn Lloyd's plan which was presented to the General Assembly of the United Nations on 17 September 1959. Canada and Italy stated that they would not be tabling alternative plans, and the ensuing discussions took place mainly between the u.s., the u.k. and France.

The u.s. contemplated a disarmament plan in two stages, while the u.k. envisaged a three-stage plan. The first stage of the British plan would be limited to the following: 1. ratification of the agreements that could ensue from the three-party negotiations on suspension of nuclear tests; 2. establishment of the International Disarmament Organization (IDO); and 3. collection of information on the levels of manpower and armaments prior to effecting force reductions. The British claimed that they were following up on proposals advocated by the French, who considered that restricting weapons systems was more important than reducing military manpower *per se*. Weapons that were withdrawn would be impounded in depots under the control of the IDO. The first stage would also include provisions for prior notification of space launches as well as provisions for holding conferences aimed at preventing surprise attack, at establishing a system to ensure the peaceful uses of space and at defining the role of the IDO in accordance with measures agreed during the first stage.

During the second stage, there would be further reductions. A world conference on disarmament would be convened in order to establish the levels of armaments of the other powers, to reinforce the authority of the IDO, to end the production of fissile materials, to reduce military stockpiles and transfer them progressively to IDO control, to undertake studies aimed at prohibiting biological and chemical weapons as well as other weapons of mass destruction and, finally, to develop other measures linked to those implemented during the first stage.

During the third phase, the manufacture and use of all weapons of mass destruction, whether biological, chemical or nuclear, would be prohibited and all stockpiles totally eliminated. All military manpower would be reduced to levels compatible only with the requirements of internal security and of obligations under the Charter of the United Nations.[4] There would be no political preconditions in moving from one stage to the next, except that everything would have to be conducted under effective international control. No schedule was established for completion of these three stages.

France opposed the British proposals on the grounds that they contained little that was new or original. The French insisted on three specific points. First, nuclear delivery vehicles should be eliminated during the first stage. Second, the approval of the UN Security Council should be secured before moving from one stage to the next. Third, a schedule for the various stages should be established to reflect the latest Soviet proposal of September 1959 which envisaged a timeframe of four years for completion of the overall disarmament process.

The Western proposals were tabled in Geneva on 16 March, subsequent to discussion and approval by the North Atlantic Council. They conformed essentially to the British proposals, the only major concession granted to France being the elimination of the missile component of delivery vehicles during the second stage. There was no mention of the UN Security Council. Instead, the powers of the IDO and its relationship with the UN were to be defined following a "joint study" by the Ten-Nation Committee. No fixed schedule was established for the transition between one phase and the next. The objective was general and complete disarmament, which would be accomplished "by phased and balanced reductions" to be verified by an appropriate international organization.

During the first stage, conventional manpower would be reduced to 2.5 millions for both the USSR and the United States, then to 2.1 millions during the second stage, while in the third and final stage only those forces necessary to meet the requirements of internal security or obligations under the UN Charter would be retained.

During the first stage, a number of studies would be conducted concerning the peaceful uses of outer space and the implementation of agreements to provide for prior notification of launches of space vehicles as well as agreements aimed at bringing to a halt the production of fissile material for military purposes.

During the second stage, provisions would be introduced to prohibit the placing in orbit of weapons of mass destruction, to halt the production of fissile materials and to convert some existing quantities to peaceful uses. There was no mention of submarines or aircraft. In the third stage, weapons would be reduced to levels compatible with the requirements of internal security, while all weapons of mass destruction would be eliminated and the use of space would be dedicated solely to peaceful purposes.

Other clauses concerned the prevention of surprise attack and the conduct of other studies. The final element of the Western plan was the constitution of an international police force aimed at ensuring world peace based on respect for international law.

In short, the West proposed a diversity of measures which would have kept an army of specialists busy for decades. The proposal had not the least chance of being accepted without discussion of each minute detail. Only in this way could the pieces be fitted together to form a jigsaw puzzle which, once assembled, would constitute the beginnings of a coherent and sensible plan.

DYNAMICS OF THE NEGOTIATIONS

From the outset, the USSR held firm to its general and complete disarmament plan of 18 September 1959. It had, at least, the merit of simplicity. The first two stages of the plan concerned only conventional force reductions. In the first stage, military manpower would be reduced to 1.7 millions for the USSR, the United States and the Peoples' Republic of China, and to 650,000 for France and Great Britain. During the second stage, all armed forces would be released, and the military bases abroad would be closed down. The third stage would consist of the elimination of weapons of mass destruction, and the destruction of existing stockpiles. The verification organization would have free access to those items under its control. Control would be progressive and would depend on the degree of disarmament achieved during each stage.

Overall, the Soviet plan was quite inadequate because the most important weapons – nuclear weapons – would not be eliminated until the final phase. Nevertheless, it took account of the perpetual Western criticism that the West could not deprive itself of nuclear weapons as long as the Socialist bloc held an overwhelming numerical conventional superiority. By reducing conventional forces on both sides to agreed or acceptable levels during the first phase, it was possible that both sides might eventually agree during the second phase on minimal nuclear deterrence levels, and finally might eliminate nuclear weapons altogether if a climate of mutual trust could be established. The world was far from achieving that in 1960. Moreover, the Soviet Union steadfastly refused to subject its forces to the scrutiny of any verification organization that would be acceptable to the West.

When the Ten-Nation Committee started its work, there was a repetition of the classic scenario of previous negotiations. The United States wanted to negotiate "piecemeal", while the Soviets demanded overall acceptance of their plan. The Soviets insisted on negotiating the principles of disarmament in conformity with Resolution 1378 (XIV) which they believed would lead to agreement on an official treaty. On 24 March, General Burns concluded that "sooner or later we shall probably have to state clearly that a complete plan to be executed within a specific period is not now negotiable".[5] On 31 March, Moch made it clear that the Soviet plan could not be accepted as the sole basis of negotiation.

On 4 April, Ottawa informed Burns that External Affairs agreed with this line of thinking, but that under no circumstances should Canada "sit back" or give the impression that she was willing to "let the Summit do it". On the same day, Burns described the atmosphere of the negotiations. In his view, u.s. Delegate Frédéric Eaton had little experience in these matters, whereas Moch and Ormsby-Gore were shrewd negotiators: "It seems that when one or other of these colleagues proposes a line of action or a change in our existing tactics, Eaton's reaction is generally negative or he opts for procrastination".[6] Burns deplored the lack of u.s. leadership. Admittedly, American diplomacy at the time was largely influenced by the Europeans. Eaton reported directly to President Eisenhower who, during the last months of his mandate, had no intention of rocking the boat ...

It was left to Moch, on 23 March, to spell out the six points of East-West agreement[7], but he received little direction or clarification concerning the timing of control measures or the extent of disarmament. On 12 April, Zorine advised Eaton that he should not view all the Soviet proposals which would be presented within the coming days as constituting the "final Soviet position". Zorine was probably waiting for instructions from Moscow, and undoubtedly his intention was to keep the talks going until the session ended on 29 April. At about that time, the British decided that discussion on the Soviet document had lasted long enough, and that the time had come to subject it to critical examination.

On 26 April, Moch thus deemed it necessary to present, on behalf of the five Western Delegations, a document delineating the principles and conditions for achieving general and complete disarmament. He maintained that four conditions were necessary to any agreement:

• disarmament should proceed by stages;
• nuclear and conventional disarmament should proceed hand-in-hand;
• control should be continuous and effective;
• negotiations should proceed progressively.[8]

The Eastern bloc was obviously not impressed. They considered it to be an "eleventh-hour" document. Three days later, work was suspended in the hope that the Paris Summit would provide new directions for negotiation.

There was indeed a new basis, but not the one that had been expected. Following the U-2 incident the Cold War was at its height and, when the Committee resumed its work on 7 June, the Soviets found nothing better to present than a new plan for general and complete disarmament which Khrushchev had in his pocket at the time of the aborted Paris Summit.

The initial Western reaction was that the new Soviet plan was nothing more than propaganda. Nevertheless, the 7 June plan did respond to some concerns, particularly those of the French who argued for control of delivery vehicles and the right of the UN Security Council to approve transitions from one phase to the next. In this regard, the Soviet proposal was rather clever, but all the other points were unacceptable.

The 7 June plan disposed of the four-year schedule but proposed that during the first phase, which would last for between 1 and 1½ years, all nuclear delivery vehicles would be eliminated while conventional force reductions would be deferred to the second phase. No one seriously believed that nuclear weapons could be eliminated in such a short period. In addition, the Soviet proposal only reinforced Western fears that defence against an opponent equipped with numerically superior forces would be impossible without nuclear weapons. As well, the Soviet plan called for the elimination of all foreign bases and equipment during the first stage, which was tantamount to demanding the withdrawal of U.S. forces from Europe.

In mid-June, Canada announced her "package" approach in a speech delivered by Green at the North Atlantic Council meeting in Istanbul. The Canadian package consisted in retaining the most positive elements of the proposals tabled by both sides in order to establish a framework for negotiation. At that point, Eaton flew to Washington to receive new instructions. He returned with a brand new plan which required the approval of the allies and of NATO before being tabled. It was an exercise in futility, because the Soviets withdrew on 27 June. To save face, the Americans tabled their plan in the absence of the Eastern bloc.

On 21 June, Polish Delegate Naszkowski informed Burns that there was nothing more to expect from President Eisenhower, particularly since Khrushchev had lost all confidence in him. Whether or not this was some kind of warning is difficult to know. In his report of 30 June, Burns concluded that the Soviets had made a "mockery" of Poland's chairmanship. Mr. Naszkowski, Burns wrote, " ... spoke in Russian rather than, as he had done until then, in French" during the session when the Eastern bloc withdrew from the Committee. Conceivably, the Poles had insufficient time to translate the note that they had received from the Soviets. According to Burns, the decision to withdraw was taken during the weekend of 25/26 June, at the meeting of the Communist Party representatives in Bucharest.

THE CANADIAN POSITION

This section is not limited to Canadian initiatives solely within the Ten-Nation Committee. The issue of general and complete disarmament concerned not only the West, but also the United Nations which played an increasingly active role in the search for solutions. UN efforts were aided by Soviet diplomacy which was aimed at introducing draft disarmament proposals into all of the UN organizations. The Soviet Union was not merely content with having ended the work of the Ten-Nation Committee, but also threatened to withdraw from the First Committee of the United Nations if support for its disarmament proposals was not forthcoming. The 15th Session of the General Assembly ended in deadlock. Throughout 1961 there were continued efforts to encourage the resumption of disarmament talks. Canada was far from inactive in this area, undoubtedly because of the boundless energy of the Secretary of State for External Affairs, Howard Green.

Areas of Canadian Diplomatic Intervention

The strong points of Green's diplomacy can be summarized as follows:

1   Strengthen the UN;
2   End the nuclear threat;

3   Broaden the base for disarmament and negotiate to the bitter end.

Strengthening the UN. Concerning points 1 and 3, Canadian policy fluctuated between political realism and blind idealism. Canada, whose loyalty to the UN had never been challenged, was justifiably concerned that the Ten-Nation Committee was not created by the United Nations. Canada used all possible means to define clearly the role of the Ten-Nation Committee in implementing the disarmament agreements that might result from the Geneva negotiations. On a number of points, Canada won her case. Ottawa was wrong, however, to imagine that the negotiations would in any way progress better by creating an advisory subcommittee within the Disarmament Commission, particularly given the mutual mistrust that existed between the superpowers. We shall return to this issue in a subsequent section.

On the question of strategy in the negotiations, Howard Green made his position known at the beginning of the preparatory work in Washington. In a document prepared on 21 January 1960, the Under-Secretary of State for External Affairs, N.A. Robertson, defined the parameters of Canadian policy. The emphasis was as follows:

1   The ultimate object is to achieve the maximum of disarmament and reduction of military forces which can be verified and controlled, and which is compatible with the maintenance of adequate security against aggression.
2   Disarmament must be accomplished in stages. However, the first stage ... should include a substantial measure of disarmament.
3   An international organization to verify and control disarmament ... is necessary. It preferably should be an organ of, or linked to, the United Nations.
4   A comprehensive plan for the prevention of surprise attack should be developed ... Priority should be given to developing means for exercising control over missiles capable of delivering nuclear weapons or other weapons of mass destruction.
5   The nations should agree not to use artificial earth satellites as carriers of nuclear or other offensive weapons.
6   Reduction of conventional armaments should be effected in terms of weapons and equipment, rather than in terms of numbers of effectives.
7   As national armaments are reduced, an international authority should be built up, disposing of military force capable of restraining aggression. The international authority preferably should be within the framework of the United Nations.
8   Production of fissile material for weapons should be stopped ...

9   The manufacture and use of biological and chemical weapons in massive warfare should be banned.

This was clearly not a comprehensive plan, but a pragmatic position developed largely by General Burns during his previous conversations with the allies. The emphasis was on the creation of concrete measures, on the control of missiles, as well as on the creation of an international police force and a control organization, both of which would report to the United Nations. These nine general principles were considered by Cabinet and approved on 25 January 1960.[9]

One month later, on 29 February 1960, a second memorandum was submitted to Cabinet. It pointed out that the u.s. plan had been subjected to persistent criticism from General Burns and the French and British allies. It argued again that Canada should insist on better linkages between the United Nations, the control organizations and the peacekeeping organizations envisaged in the disarmament plans. The memorandum advised Cabinet that, through Canada's perseverance – and undoubtedly that of France also, although France was not specifically mentioned – the United States had accepted to include a clause in the Western plan concerning the conversion of fissile materials to peaceful purposes. The Americans had conceded this point on condition that a common Western position could be developed. It was never to happen. France, for obvious reasons, expressed the view that the date of entry into force of this clause be specified, and later expressed displeasure that it was not. The objections of Paris went unheeded. It is difficult to know what tomorrow will bring ...

The recommendations to Cabinet argued that the control and peacekeeping responsibilities of the un be better specified. Should the Canadian demands not be incorporated in the Western plan, General Burns would be authorized: 1) to state that Canada would reserve her position; 2) to express his dissatisfaction; and 3) to retain the right to explain Canada's reservations in this regard if ever the Western plan were made public. One might question the usefulness of such a Memorandum to Cabinet, given that it concerned essentially the strategy of negotiation for which the Secretary of State for External Affairs has full authority. This authority is accorded to him, irrespective of the turn of events, and discretion in such matters is essentially his prerogative.

Green typically operated in this manner, considering it his duty to inform Cabinet regularly of Canada's position, whether he was in Ottawa or in Washington. Despite conflicts that existed between the Department of External Affairs and the Department of National Defence, the bureaucratic procedure of interdepartmental consultation was regularly maintained, at least during the period of negotiations in the Ten-Nation Committee and for over a year within the United Nations Organization. Characteristically, Green ensured that the instructions between Geneva and Ottawa were scrupulously respected.

On 1 March[10], George Murray of the UN Division reported that Canada had been assured by the United States that her concerns were indeed valid, and that the Western plan would include mention of the role of the UN. The deficiency in the Western plan would, therefore, be corrected. It was as far as the United States was prepared to go, since Western positions were divided on that subject. Canada wanted the UN to play a greater role in both control and peacekeeping, two issues that were regularly mentioned in despatches under the headings "International Disarmament Organization" and "Peacekeeping Machinery". France was willing to give some role to the United Nations, but insisted that the powers of the Security Council be strictly respected – no more, no less. The British, for their part, were in no hurry to make a pronouncement, mainly for tactical reasons, since they considered that it was first necessary to develop a common Western position on basic problems before undertaking studies on verification and peacekeeping mechanisms.

On some points, the Canadian position prevailed. The role of the UN would be defined during the Phase 1 studies. Development of the means for ensuring control over missiles was also mentioned, but as a Phase 2 priority, and this concession was largely due to the insistence of Delegate Moch who, since 1959, had made it a point of honour to defend this view. The issue of converting fissile materials to peaceful purposes was also included in the Western plan, but only in the context of studies to be undertaken during Phase 1 leading to agreements in Phase 2.

The role of the UN was discussed only occasionally within the Ten-Nation Committee. The Soviets acknowledged the importance of the UN in establishing control mechanisms, but were extremely reticent to discuss the establishment of an international police force, particularly following the events in the Congo. The subject was raised again in April by Italian Delegate Cavaletti. It subsequently transpired, to his great embarrassment, that he had based his arguments on a document prepared by France during preliminary discussions in Washington. At the time, there was no clear distinction between the control organ and the possible mechanisms that should be established to ensure maintenance of peace and order in a disarmed world. Cavaletti's statement subsequently led Dragan Protitch of the UN Secretariat to draft a lengthy document for "personal information" purposes on the indispensable role of the UN in the disarmament process. Actually, it appears that the document was originally drafted by Canadian William Epstein who was also attached to the UN Secretariat. According to this document, if the UN were not accorded this role, it would lead to an incredible mix-up. The actual term used in the text was "minimish", a contraction of minimize and mishmash. If nothing else, this neologism was not lacking in colour.

In the margin of the transmittal memorandum covering the Protitch document, George Murray, Director of the UN Division wrote: "The memo was written by William Epstein (ours) – they (the UN Secretariat staff) do not know my previous underlings! I doubt whether it reflects a *considered* Secretariat view and, if it does, they should sit down and reconsider".[11] The Cavaletti incident was sufficiently serious to lead Ritchie, in New York, to wonder whether the UN Secretary General should not be invited to address the Ten-Nation Committee. In Ottawa, Norman A. Robertson was of the same opinion. It would give Dag Hammarskjöld the opportunity to defend the UN viewpoint, and to specify more precisely the role that he felt the UN should play in matters of disarmament.

Following the meeting between Ritchie and Hammarskjöld on 6 April, it was learned that the Secretary General and Wilcox, of the U.S. State Department, had previously discussed the role of the UN. In Geneva, Zorine had not challenged the role of the IDO, but rather the peacekeeping role of the UN. The Soviets held that the UN Charter was perfectly adequate, and that the West was simply trying to replace the UN with a parallel organization. The Secretary General revealed that the Eastern Delegations privately sought a control organ that would be subsidiary to the UN. The telegram of 6 April did not specify whether the control organization would be a "specialized institution" – in the sense of a "subsidiary organization" –, the General Assembly itself or the Security Council. From the standpoint of the right of veto, these three possibilities posed three totally different problems.[12]

In any case, the Secretary General was doubtful about accepting an official invitation from the Ten-Nation Committee. He stated that the matter would undoubtedly be discussed during the meeting of Foreign Ministers scheduled for mid-April in Washington. Also, he planned to visit General de Gaulle in Paris on 26 April. He suggested that perhaps he could take advantage of his visit to Paris to make a brief stop in Geneva a few days later. Such a trip would be of a less official nature, and would require only short notice. Things went no further since, following Paris and the failure of the official Khrushchev-Eisenhower meeting (which never took place), there was a return to the purgatory of the Cold War years.

In a telegram to New York, dated 5 April, J.H. Taylor clearly spelled out the Canadian position. Canada envisaged a dynamic, rather than static, relationship between the control organ and the UN which would progressively evolve as agreements were reached. Unquestionably, priority had to be given first to constituting the control organ, and subsequently to constituting the peacekeeping organization. In the meantime, studies were required, since it was scarcely possible to specify every detail with a single stroke of the pen.

Before discussing the anti-nuclear policies of Green, it would be appropriate first to mention the relationship which existed at the time between the Department of National Defence and the Department of External Affairs. The problems of policy coordination between the two Departments has already been discussed in Chapter 1. The conflict became open knowledge following the Cuban missile crisis. The Ten-Nation Committee nevertheless sought detailed studies from the Department of National Defence on the problems of disarmament. For his part, Burns had no hesitation in requesting studies of all kinds from the Department of National Defence. Apart from the ten subjects mentioned in Chapter 1, another ten or so were added to the list. One item in particular was drafted at the request of Burns, who was intensely interested in the issues of surprise attack and controls governing delivery vehicles.[13] In fact, Burns considered the possibility of "mandatory inclusion of destructive devices" on nuclear missiles so as to avoid a nuclear exchange triggered by accident or misunderstanding.

In response, General Foulkes – or rather his subordinates – "concocted" an incomprehensible document in which the only intelligible phrases were the following:

Aside from measures taken to ensure the invulnerability of retaliatory forces, we believe that any scheme for further reducing the risk of accidental firing is impractical. Almost every feasible method of reducing this risk is being employed by the USA and probably also by the USSR.[14] Negotiations and verification would involve disclosure of operational and technical detail, which is unacceptable.

It is both practical and desirable to negotiate an agreement for prior notification of the launching of relatively small numbers of experimental missiles ... to ensure that they are not mistakenly identified as an attack. This is clearly in the interests of both sides.

We believe that a scheme for self-destruct mechanisms should not be pursued for the following reasons:

a   reliability of mechanism;[15]
b   limited period of effective control;

c   vulnerability to enemy action;
d   it might encourage irresponsible attitudes towards launching of deterrent
forces and therefore increase the risk of war by miscalculation.

To summarize, we believe that the proposed schemes are:

a   dangerous on strategic grounds;
b   impractical on technical grounds.[16]

And to add to the confusion, Foulkes sent Burns the following
telegram on 17 March:

Joint Staff comments relate to destruct mechanisms in general and are not
wholly applicable to destruct devices which would be inactive in the event of
intentional launch.
Additional safety measures may have some merit, although we consider
effective measures are already taken to prevent accidental launching.
If this idea is pursued we believe that it could most appropriately be the
subject of a gentleman's agreement between the u.s. and the ussr in their
mutual interest. This would avoid a difficult problem of inspection.
The kind of accident which worries us would occur as a result of misin-
terpreted warning or a garbled message. Such a destruct mechanism would
not solve this problem.[17]

The military certainly came up with some surprises, and one is left
to wonder whether they had the opportunity to consult with their
counterparts in Washington. This about-face was indeed welcomed,
but proved to be of little value to Canada's Disarmament Advisor. He
had the right to expect more discerning advice from his peers.

Ending the Nuclear Threat.   The disagreement between the Department of National Defence and the Department of External Affairs
concerning Canada's possible acquisition of nuclear weapons in the
context of both NATO and NORAD has been discussed in Chapter 1.
Within External Affairs, Green held firmly to his position. General
Burns also detested the prospect of Canada acquiring nuclear
weapons. This coherence of viewpoint within the Department of
External Affairs clearly favoured the development of strong policies
to prevent the proliferation of nuclear weapons, to establish "de-
nuclearized zones", as discussed in Chapter 4, and to contribute
directly or indirectly towards discouraging recourse to the threat of
nuclear weapons or to their possible use. In this regard, N.A. Robertson, Under-Secretary of State for External Affairs, proved himself

a model public servant. Whenever difficulties arose, he always proffered an objective viewpoint. His Memoranda to Cabinet were always substantive. And when the time came to make decisions, particularly concerning the Irish Resolution, Robertson aligned himself with the views of his Minister.

Green's first opportunity to present concrete proposals on ending the nuclear threat occurred in April 1960, at the time of the NATO Foreign Ministers' Conference in Istanbul. Green had hoped that, by the same occasion, Burns might present a report on the state of negotiations within the Ten-Nation Committee. Both France and the United Kingdom categorically opposed the presentation of any such report. Green paid no heed to that, and decided instead to make his advisor a full member of the Canadian Delegation to Istanbul! Green spoke little about disarmament, but much of the "No First Use" proposals, arguing that merely because Zorine had first surfaced such a proposal, there was no justification for dispensing with it, and if the proposal were to be considered seriously, why not extend its scope to include chemical and biological weapons? The British and French Delegations could have argued that this proposal had been tabled previously, and that there was no merit in reconsidering it. Green was nevertheless correct in pointing out that the Soviets could have become victims of their own proposals, and could even have been placed in an awkward position: " ... since their strategy may not [have been] so firmly based on a refusal to use nuclear weapons first".[18]

On 11 May, Ross Campbell in Geneva raised the issue once more, proposing the following strategy to the Minister: Since the Western Delegations have always insisted on the fact that their countries would never be the first to initiate a war of aggression, there is little to be gained by following up on the Zorine proposal. "Such a proposal might be of interest", Campbell added, "if we were able to establish a record of Western pronouncements on that subject, which we cannot do in Geneva". Geoffrey Murray, of the UN Division, had no hesitation in expressing his personal view. In a marginal annotation on Campbell's letter he wrote: "I am not impressed with this approach".[19]

The Geneva Delegation was going around in circles. At the end of May, the British Defence Minister, Harold Watkinson, visited Ottawa. He reportedly declared that the NATO Armed Forces should necessarily possess nuclear weapons, and that " ... the Western Powers should not make any commitment prohibiting the use of nuclear weapons in retaliation against an attack on a massive scale with only conventional arms". In a letter to G. Murray of the UN Division, dated

31 May, Burns wrote: "Did Watkinson really say that? And if so, is the Canadian Government in agreement with this position? ... As far as I know, such a position would be contrary to Mr. Green's views". Concerning Watkinson's statement on recourse to nuclear weapons to counter a massive conventional threat, Burns observed: " ... it would appear to be moving in the contrary direction to what Mr. Green, at any rate, would like ... so far as I can recollect from what he said on the subject in Istanbul".[20]

Obviously, Ottawa could not respond to the points raised by Burns in Geneva since, from 1958 to 1963, the Diefenbaker Government lacked the moral fibre to make a decision on the nuclear issue. In the UN, however, Green waged a fierce battle during negotiations on resolutions concerning non-proliferation of nuclear weapons. Only the details of the Canadian position on the most important resolution – the Irish Resolution which was approved on 20 December 1960 – will be discussed herein.

In September, the Canadian Government became aware of the difficulties that it faced. For Green, there was no question of Canada accepting nuclear weapons in support of her collective defence obligations. In 1957, the Cabinet had already made a decision in principle on the issue, but Green was totally opposed to the furtherance of that Cabinet decision. The position of the Department of National Defence was totally at variance with that of Green. This conflict explains the Cabinet decision taken on 16 September 1960: "[Concerning the Irish Resolution, the Canadian Delegation must] base its substantive position on the fact that the Canadian Government has no intention of lowering its defensive guard pending the promise of satisfactory progress towards disarmament". This was pure gibberish.

It fell upon Robertson to interpret the Cabinet decision, if only because of his involvement in drafting the Memorandum to Cabinet. In his instructions of 21 September to the Canadian Delegation, he stated: "I take this to mean that the Cabinet has authorized the Delegation to take a stand on the Irish Proposal in the context of general disarmament, but not in isolation".[21] In other words, if progress on disarmament was not supported by international initiative, Canada would reserve her position on the issue. Canada was unable to take a unilateral decision, but was prepared to support the Resolution within a framework of general consensus.

The Irish Resolution contained two proposals. The first proposal called upon the nuclear powers to voluntarily declare a moratorium on nuclear weapons with the aim of preventing other States from acquiring control. This proposal was hardly controversial, since the nuclear powers clearly had no intention of relinquishing such control to any other State. The second proposal had broader implications: non-nuclear-weapon States should also be required to declare, on a temporary and voluntary basis, that they would not try to acquire nuclear weapons by other means. The Irish Resolution contained the essence of the fundamental provisions of the Non-Proliferation Treaty (NPT) which was signed in 1968. Canada, as a member of NATO and NORAD, faced the prospect of being accused of duplicity or hypocrisy by voting in favour of the Irish Resolution while simultaneously equipping her military forces with nuclear weapons.

When consulted on these issues, the military authorities concluded, not without reason, that it might be possible to support the Irish Resolution on condition that the words "not try to acquire" be replaced by "not try to acquire control of".[22] In the eyes of the military, it was possible to kill two birds with one stone. Canada could thus vote in favour of the Resolution without prejudicing her defence capabilities. The Defence Liaison Division of the Department of External Affairs proposed other minor changes, but there was overall agreement on this approach. An amendment would be proposed and, if rejected, Canada could vote on individual paragraphs and abstain on contentious issues.

On 1 November, the Department of External Affairs prepared two texts explaining the rationale underlying Canada's two possible courses of action. If Canada decided to vote in favour of the Resolution, it would be argued that, in the absence of any permanent agreement on disarmament, interim measures aimed at constraining nuclear proliferation would be preferable to inaction. If, on the other hand, Canada elected to withdraw support, the argument would be that, in the absence of any permanent, universal and non-discriminatory agreement, Canada would abstain. Whatever Canada's decision, the Department of External Affairs could advance a plausible argument. Because of the proliferation of resolutions advanced at the time – some 13 in total – there was reason to expect that none would be put to the vote. Review of these proposals could be postponed until the following session of the General Assembly, or referred to the UN Disarmament Commission.

On 1 December, Robertson submitted his Department's conclusions to Prime Minister Diefenbaker. Essentially, they comprised the points outlined above. Robertson's communication stated: "Having considered the problems from the standpoint of both National Defence and NATO, the Secretary of State for External Affairs has decided that Canada should vote in favour of the Irish Resolution".[23] On that same date, Diefenbaker placed the issue before Cabinet. The Cabinet voted for abstention.

Green issued specific orders that the Canadian Delegation should not be apprised of the Cabinet decision. He sought first to appeal to Cabinet, for several reasons. On that same day, New York advised that the NATO Scandinavian countries, comprising Denmark, Iceland and Norway, had been instructed to support the Irish Resolution. Norway, in particular, had received instructions to vote in the same way as Canada, on the assumption that Canada would vote in favour of the Resolution. Green's Parliamentary Secretary, Nesbitt, who was also an influential member of the Canadian Delegation, asked that the work of the UN First Committee be temporarily adjourned in order to allow consultations to take place between the various Delegations. These new developments served to tip the scales. On 5 December, Cabinet reversed its decision.[24] Canada would now vote in favour of the Irish Resolution.

On 20 December 1960, Canada registered her vote. The Irish Resolution, co-signed by Ghana, Japan, Morocco and Mexico was carried by 68 votes. 26 other nations abstained – Canada was not one of them.

Broadening the Base of Disarmament and Negotiating to the Bitter End.   During the period between the breakdown of negotiations in the Ten-Nation Committee in June 1960 and the 16th Session of the United Nations in the fall of 1961, Canadian policy was somewhat idealistic and contradictory, and hence rather unrealistic. It was essentially founded on the sole hope that negotiations would continue, a hope that clearly derived from Green's particular set of values. Necessarily, Soviet sensibilities had to be accommodated, the base of disarmament had to be broadened, and public opinion had to be placated since disarmament issues concerned humanity-at-large. Evidently, there were many difficulties. First, Canadian diplomacy met with Allied resistance. Second, Prime Minister Diefenbaker was renowned for his unpredictable policies, as exemplified in an incisive speech before the General Assembly. Third, there were the problems posed by the weighty bureaucratic procedures of the UN. In addition, profound differences existed on fundamental issues. Clearly, the questions of who should negotiate, and what should be negotiated, were paramount issues confronting Canadian diplomacy at the time. Green was faced with a plethora of problems, not the least of which concerned the mandate, nature and composition of the negotiating organizations.

At the opening session of the Ten-Nation Committee, Green clearly expressed the basis of his thinking: "Our participation will be wholehearted, serious and energetic, and in line with our conviction that something can and should be achieved from the Geneva talks".[25] At the NATO Foreign Ministers' Meeting in Istanbul, Green repeated the same theme, arguing for a united declaration on "No First Use" of nuclear weapons or of any other weapons of mass destruction.

On 15 June, Green informed the House of Commons on his "package" strategy elaborated in Istanbul. In his view, no opportunity should be lost in exploring all possible avenues of negotiation. The Geneva negotiations concerned neither two nor ten nations, but all the nations of the world. During the debates in the First Committee and in the General Assembly in the fall of 1960, Green made numerous statements on the urgent need to resume the interrupted dialogue. On 3 November, the *Globe and Mail* carried a lead article entitled: "Mr. Green's Biggest Duty", which advocated that "Mr. Green should stay in New York to continue working towards this end for as long as he can. What is more important to him, to Ottawa, to the world, than disarmament?" In the fall of 1961, Green met with Adlai Stevenson of the U.S. Delegation to the UN. At that meeting, Green asserted that any U.S. tactics which would isolate NATO nations from the "majority opinion" within the UN could only make it more difficult for the U.S. to solicit allied support within NATO on important issues.[26] Stevenson thanked Green for his frankness, but pointed out that the U.S. had no desire to be isolated from its allies.

Green had no hesitation in advocating independent postures in instances where disarmament proposals generally conformed to his own views. But whenever a common Western position was called for, Green fought for Western solidarity. As a typical example, when negotiations broke down in Geneva, French Delegate Couve de Murville advised the Canadian Delegation that France was not especially "dismayed". Canada was puzzled by the French reaction. The French did not like the U.S. plan which was tabled at the last minute on 27 June 1960, particularly since it made no provision to accommodate French insistence that delivery vehicles should be eliminated in Phase 1. Canada was not specifically concerned with that particular point, but felt that the U.S. Plan had to be supported as a matter of priority, since it provided the only common and possible position that the West could adopt when discussions resumed within the General Assembly.

Canada decided to seek support directly from the President of the French Republic. Couve de Murville subsequently complained about this manner of proceeding, for it gave the impression that relationships between Ottawa and the *Quai d'Orsay* left something to be desired. Canada could equally have argued that this procedure was adopted because the French Ambassador was absent for a month. In actual fact, the procedure was perfectly deliberate, since Ottawa considered that President de Gaulle had the final word in shaping French policies on disarmament. And Ottawa was probably right. Michel Dupuy in Paris was charged with delivering the Canadian note dated 13 July to General de Gaulle. It contained three points.

The first point was that Canada had not insisted in the past on a substantial reduction of armed forces in the initial stages so as not to create difficulties for France. This was indeed the case for at the height of the Algerian war France was unwilling to accept military manpower levels below 750,000 and, for this reason, the Western plan of 16 May made no mention of manpower levels for Britain and France. In view of this consideration, Canada asked France to show more understanding by not insisting that "nuclear disarmament be included in the initial stages of the new Western plan". The second point was somewhat more delicate, since in effect it asked the French to bring their thinking into line with that of the Americans. The Canadian Government could not see "how a greater priority could be accorded to the destruction of nuclear warheads and delivery vehicles without compromising the essentially logical approach taken in the American plan". France could have replied that Canada had little imagination. The importance of this second point can only be fully appreciated in relation to the third:

Division amongst the Western powers could prevent us from obtaining the support of third party States on which we must rely if we are to take desirable initiatives at the forthcoming debates within the United Nations or elsewhere ... For this reason, Canada believes that the West should seek a meeting of the eighty-two member Commission[27], not for the purpose of censuring the USSR but to demonstrate to the world their willingness to negotiate seriously. Whether the debate takes place within the Commission on Disarmament or the General Assembly, the West must present a united front.

The French reply to these points was already contained in a previous note from the French President to Khrushchev dated 30 June. Canada might have taken the trouble to read it! Not only did France clearly express her position on delivery vehicles, but also on matters of procedure:

You speak now, Mr. Chairman, of bringing the disarmament debate before the General Assembly of the United Nations. Such was our intent in any case, and this occurs every year. But you know as well as I that the only practical manner of discussing such issues is within the much more confined circle of countries which are mainly involved and are technically competent.

France was not alone in her thinking on such matters. Neither Britain nor the United States were eager to resume negotiations. For his part, the Secretary General of the United Nations considered that matters should be allowed to settle before re-opening the debate. But according to G. Murray of the UN Division, Green thought otherwise: "The Minister's view is that delay tends only to dissipate whatever advantage the West might have gained from the crude action taken by the Soviet Union in breaking off the talks".[28] Canada and the United States wanted to reconvene the Disarmament Commission, while Britain and France squarely opposed the idea.[29]

On 26 September, Prime Minister Diefenbaker threw fuel on the fire. Unlike Green, who had always tried to avoid offending Soviet sensitivities, Diefenbaker stated before the whole General Assembly that there could be no double standards in matters of colonialism. Responding to Soviet demands that States be free to choose their own political regimes, Diefenbaker asked about the situation in Lithuania, Estonia, the Ukraine and other countries in Eastern Europe. Undoubtedly, Diefenbaker's remarks were motivated by Canadian internal politics; they would have been better received in Saskatoon. Concerning the breakdown of negotiations in Geneva, Diefenbaker stated: "Mr. Khrushchev, in a gigantic propaganda drama of destructive misrepresentations, launched a major offensive in the Cold War while giving lip service to the United Nations which would be destroyed by his proposal for a triumvirate". With regard to the Arctic, Diefenbaker asked the Soviet leader why he had taken no action on the U.S. proposal for aerial inspection zones if indeed he believed, as firmly as he claimed, in peace and disarmament. The records give no indication of Green's reaction to the speech of his Chief. But there is no doubt that the speech contained views that were diametrically opposed to those held by Green at the time.

Canada's position of "negotiating for the sake of negotiating" was reflected in a resolution presented to the First Committee when it resumed its work on 17 October 1960. This draft resolution received the support of 19 cosignatories. It was revised in December[30] and then vanished into thin air when, later that month, the Chairman of the First Committee, Claude Corea of Ceylon, decided to carry over all controversial draft resolutions to the 16th session (Green tried to resurrect it in 1961 despite the fact that his subordinates pointed out that its content was outdated and superseded). The Canadian-Swedish-Norwegian resolution was one of this group of deferred resolutions. As a result, only three resolutions on the nuclear issue were put to the vote in the General Assembly, and the Irish resolution was the one supported by Canada.

The Canadian resolution surfaced in a very specific context. First, the USSR insisted that the "principles of disarmament" be the subject of separate discussion. Second, there was pressure from the neutral countries and the USSR to expand the composition of the organ for negotiation, namely the Ten-Nation Committee. In an attempt to obviate these difficulties, Canada proposed in her draft resolution that the participating countries in the Ten-Nation Committee "resume their negotiations at the earliest possible date". In this regard, all the Western nations knew full well that no negotiations could start until the new Administration was in place in Washington. Canada's position was, therefore, hardly realistic. The Canadian draft resolution also proposed that an Advisory Committee be established within the Disarmament Commission. The Advisory Committee would study the "principles of disarmament", formulate proposals, receive reports from the negotiating organization, proffer advice and make recommendations. Here too, the Canadian position was simply unrealistic. To believe that "the principles" underlying the disarmament programs of the major powers would be defined by other States was akin to believing that the Moon is made of "Green" cheese. Neither the United States nor the USSR would give Green that pleasure. They took it upon themselves to define these principles which emerged one year later within the framework of the McCloy-Zorine Agreement of 20 September 1961.

As for the composition of the Advisory Committee, Green thought essentially in terms of neutral States or simply States other than those represented on the Ten-Nation Committee. He believed that Canada should not be a member of the Advisory Committee.[31] This was in keeping with Green's ideas that the other States should have a voice in disarmament. For his part, John H. Halstead thought that, in addition to the Ten-Nation Committee, an Advisory Committee could be formed composed of neutral States and other States that were not represented. Since the Negotiating Committee, just as the Ten-Nation Committee, was established at the wish of the four major powers which existed at the time, Halstead saw no reason why an Advisory Committee could not be constituted within the United Nations comprising membership from nations that were not aligned with either the East or West military alliances.[32] Also, J.H. Taylor thought that it would not be a bad idea to invite India – "this disinterested vendor of unsolicited advice in the Cold War" – to be a member of the Committee. This might lead India to reflect on her problems with Communist China and Pakistan.[33]

Participation by the neutral States in the disarmament process had long been integral to Canadian thinking, but not in the way understood by the Soviets. In an analysis of the Ten-Nation Committee, General Burns noted the lack of strong chairmanship.[34] A Chairman from a neutral country could provide much greater continuity and facilitate better progress in the Committee's work. The French were not opposed to this proposal, and even considered nominating Bindt of Switzerland as a candidate. The Soviets pointed out in private discussions[35] that such a proposal would open the door for participation of the neutral countries in the Negotiating Committee.[36] In any case, irrespective of Burns' proposal, the Soviets wanted the neutrals to be represented in the East-West organ of negotiation.

With this in mind, Green proposed broadening the base of disarmament. He spoke by telephone with Christian Herter on 14 October. On 28 October, Heeney, Canada's Ambassador in Washington, advised Robertson that the allied reaction to Green's suggestion was rather cool. Murray, of the UN Division, reported on 3 November that the allies were not exactly enthusiastic, but neither was there a "spirit of rebellion".[37] This was indeed true, for the British had already suggested, perhaps in order to suppress the Canadian proposal, that "technical study groups" be constituted within the Disarmament Commission. They subsequently told the Canadians that they had no objection to Canada's resolution provided that it would not give rise to other, more controversial, resolutions. For the British, it was a polite way of advising the Canadians that they thought little of Canada's resolution. The French, for their part, firmly maintained that the Committee should be kept in its original form, namely that membership should be restricted to ten nations, although they had no objection to having a neutral Chairman.

Canada continued to work relentlessly to find other cosignatories and, at her insistence, last-minute changes were made following negotiations with the United States. The final version of the draft resolution no longer referred to an Advisory Committee but to an *Ad Hoc* Committee of the Disarmament Commission. The *Ad Hoc* Committee would not be responsible for making recommendations but rather for studying "ways and means" to foster the resumption of negotiations using available documentation, including the "principles of disarmament" discussed in the Ten-Nation Committee together with the views expressed by the member nations during the concurrent session of the General Assembly. The proposals advanced in the final version were, therefore, rather far removed from those espoused by Green.

This last-minute compromise had no effect on the general situation, because the Canadian resolution, along with nine others, was never put to the vote. In early 1961, bilateral talks between the United States and the USSR led to agreement in principle for a meeting between Kennedy and Khrushchev in Vienna. During these talks, the question of holding a United Nations Special Session on Disarmament in the same European capital was also discussed. Dialogue between the superpowers resumed. The United States, with its new dynamic team, was prepared to accept a number of compromises in order to resume discussions on disarmament. The Americans even considered a ten-ten composition for the new organ of negotiation, comprising the ten original members of the Committee together with ten other neutral countries.

In the fall of 1961, the McCloy-Zorine agreement in principle was signed, largely to dissipate the unbearable atmosphere created by the Berlin crisis. There was a gradual move towards early resumption of the talks and towards the creation of the Eighteen-Nation Committee on Disarmament, which began its work in 1962.

6 The Nuclear Threat: From Dread to Denial

An abrupt solution of continuity is needed, a break with current practice.

Henri Bergson, *Le rire*

Events in Cuba in 1962 caused a threefold crisis: a crisis in the international system, a bipolar crisis and a nuclear crisis. The threat of nuclear war became immediate, and the world stood at the brink of nuclear annihilation. The two superpowers saved face through the compromise of a *quid pro quo*: the endurance of socialism in Cuba in exchange for the withdrawal of Soviet missiles.

From 1962 to 1969, East-West relations felt the brunt of this major crisis. Means had to be found to ease bipolar relations and to stabilize the situation in Europe. Steps had to be taken so that nuclear weapons, which for the major powers were a source of both dread and security, would be transformed, for the other nations, into a source of perpetual and deliberately agreed denial.

Two agreements signed in 1963 served to ease the general situation. One was the treaty banning nuclear weapons' tests in the atmosphere, in space and under water, and the other was the agreement to install a "hot line" to provide direct communications between Washington and Moscow. It soon became clear, however, that Europe was not about to allow the new U.S. leadership to dictate its destiny. In December 1962, John F. Kennedy and Harold MacMillan met in Nassau to consider an emergency plan to protect the independence of the British nuclear forces. The Skybolt project had been cancelled, and the British strategic bombers no longer had a useful role. The Multilateral Force (MLF) was thus born in a climate of American improvisation and British humiliation. The concept called for a certain number of nuclear submarines to be passed under NATO control to provide the foundation for a nuclear "European pillar", which would be capable in conjunction with u.s. forces of ensuring its own defence, provided that there was concomitant progress in European integration. De Gaulle refused to take the bait. On 13 January 1963, France responded with a double veto: "No" to the MLF and "No" to Britain's entry into the European Common Market. As de Gaulle subsequently explained, Britain had chosen, in Nassau, to trade her birthright for "a plateful of Polaris".

The MLF was mainly conceived to integrate the British and French forces within the Atlantic Alliance, forces which u.s. Defence Secretary Robert S. McNamara found "obsolescent, deficient and dangerous". France's refusal rendered the MLF a "lame duck". The British then proposed an Atlantic Nuclear Force (ANF). Unlike the MLF, which involved the addition of new nuclear delivery vehicles, the ANF would be formed by grouping existing tactical nuclear air forces under NATO control. Germany was not satisfied with this proposed solution, and it served only to re-focus debate on the MLF which the Soviets found distasteful. In order to satisfy Germany, McNamara proposed the creation of a "nuclear committee" within NATO, which would allow the FRG to participate in nuclear planning. Kennedy died in November 1963, Khrushchev was deposed in 1964 and, in 1965, Johnson buried the MLF project following personal representations made by A. Wohlstetter of Chicago and R. Neustadt of Harvard in the Gilpatrick Report.[1] The door to nuclear denial was then open.

Within the Eighteen-Nation Committee on Disarmament, the Americans and the Russians agreed to table a common draft proposal on nuclear non-proliferation. Thereafter, events moved quickly in Europe. The FRG Peace Note of 1 March 1966 opened the door for East-West dialogue. The West Germans could no longer be considered as the "spoilsports". The Harmel Report of 1967 provided a new basis for discussion on European security. The West proposed that negotiations be held on MBFR, thinking that the Soviets would refuse to participate in such discussions. In similar fashion, the Soviets proposed the opening of a Conference on European Security, which became the CSCE in 1973. Each of the two blocs was caught at its own game. Both sets of discussions took place, and they marked the opening of a new era of *détente* between East and West.

The rest of the world did not remain inactive. The Cuban missile crisis alerted the whole world to the extent of nuclear proliferation that would result if nations allowed foreign nuclear weapons to be based on their soil. Proposals for "de-nuclearized zones" abounded, while actions were progressively taken to follow up on the recommendations of the Irish Resolution. Nuclear proliferation had to be halted, and a new legal instrument had to be established to ensure control. The need to meet this objective became even more pressing in light of the fact that France had conducted her first nuclear tests in the Sahara desert in 1960 and that China had commenced testing in the Lob Nor Lake region in October 1964. Following the signing of the Partial Test Ban Treaty in 1963, emphasis was placed on seeking agreement to ban nuclear tests totally. This was the climate in which negotiations proceeded in the Eighteen-Nation Committee in Geneva between 1962 and 1969.

ORIGIN AND EVOLUTION OF THE EIGHTEEN-NATION COMMITTEE

On 20 December 1961, the General Assembly of the United Nations adopted Resolution 1722 (XVI) through which it "accepted" the decision of the major powers to create the Eighteen-Nation Committee on Disarmament (ENDC). On the basis of a common declaration made by the major powers on 21 December 1961, it was recommended that negotiations take place on "general and complete disarmament". In addition to the original members of the Ten-Nation Committee, eight other non-aligned nations would participate in the negotiations, namely, Brazil, Burma, Ethiopia, India, Mexico, Nigeria, Sweden and the United Arab Republic (UAR). Point 8 of the common declaration of 20 September 1961 obliged the member nations "to reach widest possible agreement as early as possible".

The Eighteen-Nation Committee started work on 14 March 1962 in Geneva with the participation of foreign ministers. The Committee met more or less regularly until August 1969. On 26 August 1969, at its 431st meeting, the Eighteen-Nation Committee was expanded by eight additional members to become the Conference of the Committee on Disarmament (CCD). The Eighteen-Nation Committee was actually a Seventeen-Nation Committee because France never participated. France was nevertheless involved unofficially in several consultations held in the caucus of the five Western powers. The present Chapter is concerned only with the discussions held in the Eighteen-Nation Committee during its existence, namely from 1962 to 1969.

Depending on one's point of view, the achievements of the Committee were either considerable or meagre. Three aspects deserve mention. First, although proposals for general and complete disarmament were discussed, primarily during the first two years of the Committee's existence, discussion essentially centred on collateral, or partial, measures of disarmament. In this regard, although the Committee ratified the Partial Test Ban Treaty and the agreement to install a "hot line" between Washington and Moscow, these initiatives actually arose as a result of negotiations outside the Eighteen-Nation Committee. The second point relates to the consequences of multilateral diplomacy. The addition of the neutral countries to the Ten-Nation Committee was a stabilizing factor. During the course of discussions in 1962, the Soviets tried to persuade the neutrals to break off negotiations within the Eighteen-Nation Committee following the resumption of u.s. nuclear testing in the atmosphere, but the neutrals refused. During discussions on most of the proposals, the neutrals tried to play a mediating role and their influence in tempering the shameless diplomacy exercised by the Soviets at the time was not insignificant. Third, the Committee initiated discussions on the Treaty banning the placing of nuclear weapons or other weapons of mass destruction on the sea-bed and the ocean floor, and the subsoil thereof (Sea-Bed Treaty), and also initiated discussions on banning biological and chemical weapons, but it was left to the ccd to complete and finalize these agreements. Strictly speaking, the only important agreement that emerged from the Eighteen-Nation Committee was the Nuclear Non-proliferation Treaty which was signed in 1968 and which entered into force in 1970. Whether the Committee achieved much or little is, therefore, a matter of opinion, since it might be argued that this Treaty would have evolved in any case, irrespective of the involvement of the Eighteen-Nation Committee.

In matters of procedure, the deliberations of the Eighteen-Nation Committee lacked realism. Shortly after the Committee was formed, it was decided to create: 1. a Plenary Commission specifically responsible for studying the overall problems of general and complete disarmament; 2. a Committee of the Whole, involving all participating nations, responsible for studying progressive measures leading to general and complete disarmament and the reduction of international tensions; and 3. a Restricted Committee, comprising membership from Great Britain, the United States and the ussr, responsible for studying the issue of halting nuclear testing. The distinction between the Plenary Commission and the Committee of the Whole clearly represented an attempt to solve the difficult problem of the chicken and the egg: should the issue of disarmament be approached from the standpoint of the whole or of the particular? It was hoped that progress would be facilitated by entrusting the Committee of the Whole to study partial measures of disarmament. This Committee met when the Eighteen-Nation Committee was not in plenary session.

Table 5
The Eighteen-Nation Committee on Disarmament

Origin: Soviet-American agreements of fall 1961.

Created: Resolution 1722 (XVI). The General Assembly "adopted" the Soviet-American common declaration.

Mandate: To promote general and complete disarmament under a system of effective international control, based on the common declaration of 20 September 1961.

Composition: Canada, France, Great Britain, Italy and the United States; Bulgaria, Czechoslovakia, Poland, Romania and the USSR; Brazil, Burma, Ethiopia, India, Mexico, Nigeria, Sweden and the UAR.

Evolution: Expanded to become the Conference of the Committee on Disarmament (CCD) on 26 August 1969, following the addition of Japan and Mongolia (3 July) and of Argentina, Hungary, Morocco, Netherlands, Pakistan and Yugoslavia (7 August).

Dates of Sessions:

1962	1966
14 March to 15 June	25 January to 10 May
16 July to 7 September	14 June to 25 August
26 November to 20 December	
1963	1967
12 February to 21 June	21 February to 23 March
13 August to 30 August	18 May to 14 December
1964	1968
21 January to 28 April	18 January to 14 March
9 June to 17 September	16 July to 28 August
1965	1969
27 July to 16 September	18 March to 23 May
	3 July to 30 October (CCD)

The dates of the ENDC sessions given in Table 5 relate only to meetings of the Plenary Commission. The work of the Restricted Committee will not be discussed since Canada was not involved and

Canada's position on halting nuclear testing is covered in Chapter 9. One final point is worth noting: Canada made the proposal that the Eighteen-Nation Committee be co-chaired by the United States and the USSR. Although this obviously complicated the setting of agendas, it promoted greater administrative continuity in the discussions.

Concerning general and complete disarmament, the main proposals tabled before the Eighteen-Nation Committee were confined to the following:

- the Soviet proposal of 15 March 1962;
- the U.S. proposal of 18 April 1962.

These proposals were revised several times during the years that followed. In this regard, the major debates centred on the following issues:

- elimination of delivery vehicles;
- reduction of military manpower;
- measures conducive to reducing tensions and avoiding the risks of war;
- the International Disarmament Organization and the peaceful settling of differences.

None of these proposals was overly original. The U.S. proposal[2] of 18 April 1962 was inspired by the proposal tabled by President Kennedy on 25 September 1961 before the General Assembly of the United Nations, a proposal which in turn had been drawn almost directly from the U.S. proposal tabled before the Ten-Nation Committee on 27 June 1960 when the Soviets were absent. In like manner, the Soviet proposal[3] of 15 March 1962 was based on the Soviet memorandum of 26 September 1961. During discussions in the General Assembly in the fall of 1962, it became most apparent that the member nations, and the neutrals in particular, were interested primarily in partial measures of disarmament, especially those concerning non-proliferation and the halting of nuclear testing, and not by the insoluble problem of general and complete disarmament. The West's only interest in these proposals stemmed from the desire to constitute a legal working group to conduct in-depth studies on issues concerning the International Disarmament Organization and the peaceful settlement of differences.

As for partial measures of disarmament, the issues discussed in the Eighteen-Nation Committee included[4], amongst others:

- prohibition of warmongering propaganda (May 1962);
- reducing the risks of war breaking out as a result of an accident (United States, 12 December 1962);
- reduction of military budgets (Brazil, Sweden and others, 1963);
- creation of observation posts and means of avoiding surprise attack (United States, January 1964, and USSR, 1964);
- verifiable freeze on strategic nuclear delivery systems (United States, January 1964);
- halting production of fissile materials for military purposes (United States, January and June 1964);
- destruction of bombers (United States and USSR, 1964);
- concluding a non-aggression pact (USSR, February 1963, January 1964 and December 1964);
- prohibition of overflights by aircraft carrying nuclear weapons (USSR, February 1966);
- regional disarmament (United States, 1966);
- prohibition of use of nuclear weapons (Ethiopia and others, 1961);
- halting of manufacture of nuclear weapons, reduction and destruction of stockpiles (USSR, 1966).

The variety was indeed substantial. No attempt will be made to summarize all the proposals on partial measures of disarmament although, in the sections that follow, brief reference will be made to them whenever necessary to bring Canadian diplomatic actions into sharper focus. Before leaving the subject of partial measures of disarmament, it may be noted that from 1963 onwards the main items included the designation of de-nuclearized zones, means for preventing nuclear proliferation and a total ban on nuclear testing. Canada, supported by other nations, introduced into the debates the issues of non-militarization of space and the elimination of biological and chemical weapons. These two issues are treated in Chapters 10 and 8 respectively, and are therefore only touched upon in the present Chapter.

CONTINUITY OF CANADIAN POLICY (1962–1969)

The work of the Eighteen-Nation Committee spanned a period which saw three successive Canadian governments in office. Green's term as Secretary of State for External Affairs ended in 1963. Following the defeat of the Diefenbaker government on the nuclear issue in the summer of 1963, Lester B. Pearson became Prime Minister and

appointed Paul Martin to replace Green as Secretary of State for
External Affairs. In 1968, a new Liberal government was elected
under the leadership of Pierre Elliott Trudeau. Despite all these
internal upheavals, the Canadian position changed little on the main
issues of disarmament. Burns remained Canadian Advisor on Disarmament until 1969. In March 1969, he was replaced in the CCD
by George Ignatieff. Earlier, in 1966, Basil H. Robinson, the former
right arm of Diefenbaker, had been named Assistant Under-
Secretary of State for External Affairs. The role of Norman A.
Robertson faded. Here again, the disappearance of a man impassioned with the problems of disarmament did not produce a fundamental re-orientation of Canadian policy, which continued to
emphasize the urgent need for mediation. This seemed to be the
underlying theme of Canadian policy during the 1960s.

That being said, there was nevertheless an important change when
Pearson took over from Diefenbaker. Pearson was elected on the basis
of his stated intent not to follow through on the previous Canadian
commitments on defence issues. Canada would, however, continue to
support all proposals aimed at curbing nuclear proliferation. All this
happened as though the issue of equipping the Canadian Armed
Forces with nuclear weapons had been strictly one of internal policy.
Canada had reservations about the MLF. Burns had no hesitation in
stating aloud what many silently thought: Germany should not have
access to nuclear weapons capable of reaching Soviet territory, even
though the MLF in itself was no more of a reprehensible instrument
of proliferation than that which Canada had accepted either through
NORAD or through NATO. The records are quite clear on this point.
No contradictions are to be found between fundamental Canadian
defence policy and the position maintained by Ottawa in the fora of
multilateral discussion.

1963 obviously marked the year when the Department of National
Defence attempted to settle the score with the Department of
External Affairs.[5] Norman A. Robertson kept an eye open for
trouble. Paul Martin, with his extensive experience with the Canadian
Delegation in New York, supported his Under-Secretary. The Department of National Defence gradually came into line. It would continue
to support the Department of External Affairs in the search for
disarmament agreements. Canadian foreign policy was revised in
1968 under the Trudeau government. Trudeau was quite simply an
antimilitarist, distrustful of the military, and above all totally opposed
to nuclear weapons. All these factors served to ensure continuity
between the policies of Green and those which might be characterized as Pearson-Trudeau. We shall return to the issue of Canadian

internal policy in our general conclusions. For the moment, however, it should be stated that Canadian parliamentarians, even from the time of Diefenbaker, were pro-disarmament, pro-North-South and pro-United Nations. As well, Pearson had no hesitation in denouncing U.S. policy in Vietnam, even though Johnson had told him to stop "pissing on his carpet". (Johnson, of course, was a Texan!). Trudeau thus provided only an additional voice to Western leadership on disarmament issues, at least when he had the time or when he judged, as in 1984, that the Cold War was anachronous. The Green period is characterized by Michael Tucker as one of "activism" and the Martin period as one of "loyal ally"[6] within the Atlantic Alliance. It is only true in part. The terminology is reminiscent of that pertaining to Kennedy-de Gaulle. When de Gaulle stated that France was admittedly a difficult but loyal ally, Kennedy replied that France was "rather more difficult than loyal". Evidently, it is all a matter of degree. On disarmament issues, Canada has been difficult at times and less difficult at other times, but she has never let down her guard.

On the other hand, though "activism" well describes some of the elements of Green's policy, the 1962–1963 period was one of great agitation, especially as a result of Green's determination to pursue negotiations at all costs. Despite all odds, Green consistently opposed any adjournment in the work of the Eighteen-Nation Committee. Green's approach was similar to the process that follows the conclave to elect a Pope. There was no question of suspending the discussions until the white smoke of peace floated over the city of Geneva. It corresponded to the most simplistic idealism.

Three examples suffice to illustrate the point. In May 1962, the question of adjourning the work of the Eighteen-Nation Committee arose. Green met with Burns in Athens and directed him to seek the support of the neutral countries to oppose the adjournment.[7] The effort was in vain, and the discussions were suspended on 15 June. At the summer session, it was the neutrals that sought an adjournment to allow time for consultations. Green considered that there was insufficient justification. On 24 July, he pressed for the work to continue concurrently with the 17th Session of the General Assembly. It was clearly too much to ask. The Geneva session was adjourned on 7 September ... In January 1963, Arthur Dean resigned as Head of the U.S. Delegation, and the United States asked that the session scheduled for January 1963 be postponed until February. The Americans consulted with the Soviets and with their allies. In his note of 8 January, Robertson wrote that postponement was a "foregone conclusion". Green reacted again. As early as the following morning, he telegraphed his opposition to this new delay.[8] The Secretary of State had but one idea in mind: to pursue negotiations until the finishing touches could be put to a program of general and complete disarmament. Such a program is still being discussed today.

The change in government in the spring of 1963 led to no fundamental reversal in Canadian policy. In 1961, during the interval between the final adjournment of the Ten-Nation Committee and the inaugural meeting of the Eighteen-Nation Committee, Burns prepared a Memorandum to Cabinet. The document, which was signed by Green on 13 February 1961 and approved by Cabinet the following day, was entitled "Disarmament: Canadian Policy 1961". On 28 May 1963, Paul Martin signed a draft document intended for Cabinet. It was entitled "Canadian Policy on Disarmament and on the Halting of Nuclear Tests". Only the most important aspects of these two documents are considered below.

Both texts stressed the need for general and complete disarmament under strict international control. Both stated that, until such an objective was attained, Canada's security would continue to be based mainly on the principle of collective security within NATO. In the area of conventional force reductions, "approximate parity" had to be maintained by both sides. The need to plan for "phased reductions" in delivery vehicles was reiterated, for it was recognized that the total elimination of these vehicles would have to be realized over many stages given that the superpowers would only agree to such a program in a climate of overall disarmament. Both documents called for the Americans to insert a clause prohibiting bacteriological and chemical weapons during the second phase of their plan. The documents also recommended that international agreements be developed and adopted to prevent the spread of nuclear weapons and to establish de-nuclearized zones, subject to verification and approval by the States located in the zones in question.

The differences in the two documents were, for the most part, contingent. For example, in the first document, it was argued that Canada could support the one-treaty approach demanded by the Soviets, but solely as a means for negotiation, since all the "phased" elements, or those required to occur in stages in the Western plans, should reappear in the one-treaty proposal. The problem of withdrawal of foreign bases could also be treated on a separate basis in any phase of a disarmament proposal, whenever a *quid pro quo* could be struck with the opposing bloc. In face of U.S. opposition on these two points, the freedom of manoeuvre accorded to Burns by Cabinet disappeared immediately. The issue of non-militarization of space appeared in the second document in the form of a proposal to prohibit the placing in orbit of weapons of mass destruction.

Concerning the halting of nuclear tests, it was stressed that Canada should maintain as "flexible" a position as possible. The recommendation stated that "Canadian representatives ... should avoid taking a public position which would appear to press the u.s. or the u.k. to agree to Soviet proposals which would be politically too difficult for them to accept". Here there was a difference in tone, but on the whole the shades of meaning between the two documents were accidental and rather slim. The continuity in the approach, admittedly, stemmed from the fact that Burns was largely involved in the drafting of both documents.

The document of 28 May 1963 was not approved immediately, for it was at that juncture that the Department of National Defence produced its unfortunate document of 26 June 1963 which was a full tilt attack against General Burns.[9] On 30 July 1963, Paul Hellyer, the youthful and fiery Minister of National Defence, put matters to the test. In a letter to External Affairs Minister Martin, Hellyer stated that disarmament policy and defence policy should be compatible. Paul Martin had already said as much in the House, and there was nothing in Hellyer's statement, therefore, to cause alarm. However, Hellyer appended to his letter a series of lengthy comments, which he claimed to be his own, and which constituted a denunciation of the draft document of 28 May before it was sent to Cabinet.

Hellyer's comments substantially stated that the allies had not been consulted on Green's declarations in March and April 1962 concerning the prohibition of placing weapons of mass destruction in orbit, that Canada should work closely with the allies on the non-proliferation issue and that it would not be opportune to insist on the establishment of de-nuclearized zones in Europe. On the issue of general and complete disarmament, Hellyer stated that only the American draft treaty was defensible and that Canada should support it. On the whole, Hellyer argued that Canada should not deviate from u.s. policy.

On 20 August, Robertson wrote to Martin:

Having studied National Defence comments in detail, I am greatly concerned to find that they reflect a line of thinking which – if it were accepted – would have the effect of preventing the Government from exercising any independence of judgement with respect to policies and proposals in the related fields of disarmament, collateral measures and the cessation of nuclear weapons' tests.[10]

In the margin next to this sentence, Paul Martin wrote "Noted". Robertson continued:

Carried to its logical conclusion, this would mean that any Canadian suggestions which are at variance with United States views should neither be
communicated to officials of any government other than the United States
Government nor urged too strongly on the United States Government itself
... These quotations[11] clearly demonstrate the excessively cautious and essentially negative attitude of our colleagues in National Defence. What is perhaps not so readily apparent is that they also tend to misrepresent the true
nature and purpose of many of the positions that we have recommended in
the draft memorandum to Cabinet.

In the margin, Martin noted "Of course" and "I agree". Martin
then asked that Canada's position be put on record through a letter
to this effect.[12] On 13 September the letter was prepared[13], and
addressed to "My Dear Colleague". It repeated essentially the same
themes developed earlier by Robertson and undoubtedly also by K.D.
McIlwraith of the Disarmament Division. Martin left the door open,
however, since he sought to arrange a meeting between the Assistant
Deputy Ministers of both departments to review the policy elements
in the Memorandum to Cabinet "in light of important events" that
had occurred, specifically the Partial Test Ban Treaty.

This procedure of consultations between Assistant Deputy Ministers subsequently characterized relations between the two departments. In addition, Hellyer lost interest to some extent in
disarmament issues and became preoccupied with unification of the
Canadian Armed Forces. It was rather ironic, since the first set of
comments that Hellyer sent to Martin were likely prepared by his
Chiefs of Staff Committee, which he subsequently set about dismantling. Even though the records do not indicate whether this famous
Memorandum to Cabinet was ever approved, the Canadian position
remained in conformity with the aims and objectives established by
the Department of External Affairs in the spring of 1963.

Two important events occurred in 1968: the Nuclear Non-proliferation Treaty was signed, and Trudeau assumed power. Both events
led the Department of External Affairs to undertake an in-depth
review of foreign policy. The need first arose following the signing
of the Nuclear Non-proliferation Treaty, which had been expected as
early as 1967. Inevitably, the key question was to determine which
aspects of Canadian efforts should receive greatest attention in the
years to follow. An in-depth review of Canada's foreign policy was also
required with the arrival of Trudeau as Prime Minister. The studies
were conducted during 1967 and 1968. Early in 1969, it was concluded
that debate should focus primarily on issues surrounding defence and
NATO. In March 1969, the Disarmament Division prepared a lengthy

Memorandum to Cabinet to ensure that these issues would not be lost in the defence debate, and also to define better the directives that should be given to Canada's representatives in the CCD.

In February 1967, B.H. Robinson, on behalf of the Under-Secretary, signed a comprehensive document on Canadian objectives in the areas of disarmament and arms control. Amongst the long-term objectives appeared the desire to involve the Peoples' Republic of China in the major discussions on disarmament. The document acknowledged that Canada should make continuing efforts to consolidate progress in arms control, but recognized that it was unlikely that, during a long period of *détente*, the same priority could be accorded to measures aimed at reducing the risks of accidental war and to proposals facilitating the exchange of declarations on non-aggression and non-recourse to the use of force to settle differences. It was stated nevertheless that these objectives should not be dismissed altogether.

Amongst the priorities which would require discussion and which promised some measure of success were the following:[14]

• a treaty on the global halting of nuclear tests;
• an agreement to prohibit the deployment of Anti-Ballistic Missiles (ABM);
• the constitution of disengagement zones and reciprocal reductions in military manpower;
• support for the constitution of nuclear-free zones in Latin America, Africa and elsewhere;
• curbing the arms race in regional zones.

Burns was delighted with this initiative and asked that a more detailed document be prepared for the approval of the Minister. He also asked that greater priority be placed on the prohibition of ABM systems than on a Comprehensive Test Ban (CTB), arguing that the superpowers would logically continue underground testing specifically to evaluate nuclear warheads for the ABM mission.[15] Finally, Burns was anxious to know whether *détente* would cause the Canadian Government to abandon its objective to achieve general and complete disarmament.

Burns was reassured on this latter point since the objective was retained in later documents. A Memorandum to Cabinet prepared on 14 March 1969 acknowledged that it was too early to comment on the content of the Sea-Bed Treaty and the proposal to ban bacteriological and chemical weapons, because discussions on these issues were still at the preliminary stage. The document included, however, three other essential aspects. First, in the context of ABM systems, given Canada's geographical location and her interest in maintaining the stability and balance of nuclear deterrence, it was desirable that the Strategic Arms Limitation Talks (SALT) be held "at the earliest possible date". Second, it was recommended that Canada shift from her former position on a CTB, which held that no treaty was viable without verification, so that she could progressively support the development of an overall treaty for which verification could be effected using data supplied by seismic detectors. The document stated, however, that such an approach should only be pursued provided that *détente* continued. Meanwhile, Canada should not inform other governments of her possible change in position. Third, the issue of non-proliferation was also important. Canada still had a good number of bilateral obligations which could place her in an awkward situation *vis-à-vis* the terms of the Nuclear Non-proliferation Treaty. The Memorandum recommended, therefore, that greatest attention be paid to this issue and that each case be studied on the basis of "its particular merits". In addition, the need for Canada to take initiatives in the area of Mutual and Balanced Force Reductions (MBFR) was stressed, mainly following studies on verification techniques that were in progress at the time.

Throughout the document, there was a remarkable degree of continuity in Canadian thinking on disarmament. This Memorandum resulted from a Canadian Government revision of disarmament policy, but it is difficult to know what part the Canadian Delegation in Geneva played in its development. A note to Minister Mitchell Sharp, dated 23 April 1969, stressed the importance of keeping the Canadian Cabinet fully informed of the position of the Department.[16] On 26 June 1969, most of the recommendations were adopted by the Canadian Cabinet, with the reservation, however, that the development of Canadian policy on a CTB be linked to the achievement of considerable progress in the SALT negotiations.

In retrospect, the continuity in Canadian policy was without question due to men like Burns and Robertson, and also to the experience gained by Martin in the Canadian Delegation to the UN. Neither should one forget the constant efforts of Green in support of the Advisor on Disarmament to the Canadian Government. Green's efforts in this regard were significant. For example, in 1968 the bureaucrats responsible for personnel conducted an evaluation of the Disarmament Delegation in Geneva. They concluded that Canada's Delegation had a greater complement of staff, in relative terms, than was considered necessary by the other participating nations.[17] B.A. Keith presented a summary[18] of his report to the Under-Secretary on 31 August 1968, and Arthur G. Campbell had to re-establish the facts on 24 October 1968. In his report to M.N. Bow of the Disarmament Division, Campbell was very clear. His report essentially dealt with the role of the Advisor on Disarmament to the Canadian Government. Since the position of Advisor was established under the Diefenbaker government, it would have been very difficult for the Liberals to abolish it without being accused of profound disinterest in disarmament. The Liberals had never considered abolishing the position, but experience shows that it is difficult to reverse decisions on matters judged essential by the public once such decisions have been taken. In this respect, the Liberals repaid the Conservatives in kind, for in 1985 the Conservatives inherited a comprehensive disarmament structure as a result of both Prime Minister Trudeau's peace initiative and the creation, in 1984, of the Canadian Institute for International Peace and Security (CIIPS).

There is no doubt that, throughout Green's term as Secretary of State for External Affairs, the bureaucratic conflicts between the Departments of National Defence and of External Affairs, were at their worst. The indomitable, reactionary, conservative and retrograde Minister of National Defence was pitted against an abrupt, idealistic and progressive Minister Green. Diefenbaker's inability to cut the Gordian knot can be viewed in two ways. Either it allowed Green elbow room, which could only have inflamed the conflicts between the two departments, or it allowed one man's will to imbue the bureaucracies with a sure sense of leadership in the absence of strong direction from Cabinet. The consequences of this conflict clearly show that the truth of the matter lies somewhere between these two hypotheses.

Areas of Canadian Intervention in the Eighteen-Nation Committee

The essential issues discussed within the Eighteen-Nation Committee pertain to the three subjects discussed above: non-proliferation of nuclear weapons, cessation of nuclear tests and partial disarmament measures. The first two subjects will be discussed in Chapters 7 and 9. The present discussion is limited to issues of general and complete disarmament, and to Canadian action in respect of partial measures.

Before discussing these issues, we should make mention of the role played by Burns on procedural matters. As early as 1960, Burns insisted that the negotiating organization should have administrative continuity. On 19 January 1962, during consultations between the allies on the Eighteen-Nation Committee, Burns proposed[19] that consideration be given to the possibility of adopting a co-chairmanship procedure for the ENDC similar to that followed for the 1954 Laos Conference which had been co-chaired by Eden and Molotov. Burns was authorized to negotiate with the allies on this possibility. The British, who preferred alternating chairmanship, eventually came around to supporting the Canadian proposal. The Americans, for their part, had no problem with Burns' formula, since it would give them better control over the agenda and over the dynamics of negotiations with their own allies. The proposal also gave the West the opportunity to take a united stand against any renewed attempt by Moscow to establish a troïka.

The United States asked Burns to inform the Soviets of this initiative, and Burns complied through his *aide-mémoire* of 3 March 1962 to the Soviet Ambassador in Ottawa, A. Aroutunian. From prior informal discussions with Soviet officials, the Canadians were already aware that the Soviets had previously described the procedure followed for the Laos Conference as "useful".[20] In addition to the co-chairmanship proposal, the March memorandum also contained a proposal to alternate the chairmen on a daily basis (Chairman of the Day). Only the first proposal was finally accepted.

Another procedural aspect concerned the Dainelli incident. In February 1962, Dainelli, a member of the Italian Delegation, wanted to publish an article in the *Communita Internazionale*. Green was not especially pleased with this article, since it stated that Canada's policy, previously inspired by Pearson, suffered now from a "particular doctrinal flexibility", oscillating between Green's "utopic" views and a more technically coherent policy.[21] Canada's protests in Rome would likely have had little effect if the article had not been written by an Italian official who had little regard for Green's reputation. In view of Canada's protests, it was decided that the incriminating paragraph would be deleted.

As a final point, mention should be made of the consultations with the FRG. Since the time of the Ten-Nation Committee, the FRG had asked to be kept regularly informed on the negotiations, and even sought regular "round table" discussions. The allies were opposed to this suggestion, especially since the FRG was likely to be the party principally concerned in most of the issues discussed. Following consultations with the allies, Canada decided to adopt a "firm but polite attitude" initially, with a view to involving the FRG as an ally subsequently, in comparable manner to the approach taken by the London Subcommittee of the Disarmament Commission which treated the FRG as a partner to be kept "informed" through diplomatic channels. The same procedure was adopted in respect of the Eighteen-Nation Committee. Despite that, and largely for internal political reasons, the FRG had no hesitation in reprimanding Burns for his statement on the MLF in 1965. Burns had taken the liberty of saying that the MLF proposal was hardly consistent with the Canadian Government's objectives on non-dissemination. The German press seized upon the affair, but the storm was quickly quelled after the interventions of J. Starnes, Canada's Ambassador in Bonn.

In 1968, and again in 1969, the FRG asked to be included amongst the new members which would be added to the Eighteen-Nation Committee to form the CCD. Canada and the United States supported West Germany's candidacy in the hope that France and China would also join the discussions in Geneva. The West proposed an arrangement under which Hungary's participation in the CCD would be accepted by the West as a *quid pro quo* for the participation of the FRG. The Soviets found the Western proposal unattractive, and at first rejected it, but subsequently agreed to reconsider if the participation of the GDR were substituted for that of Hungary. The Soviet counter-proposal was unacceptable to the West, and the two Germanies were excluded from the talks.

General and Complete Disarmament

The issue of general and complete disarmament was as much a preoccupation for Burns as for Green. Canada expended a good deal of effort in tidying up the proposals under discussion, and was active both in consultations between allies and in discussions within the Eighteen-Nation Committee.

In a speech on disarmament given at the National Defence College in Kingston[22], Robert Sutherland recalled the words of Lord Palmerston concerning Schleswig-Holstein: "Only three men have ever understood this matter: the Prince Consort who is dead, a German professor who has gone mad, and myself – but I have forgotten".

The proposals submitted in 1962 were similar to those that were discussed during the 1950s. They differed only in that the emphasis was placed on disarmament and on the procedure for managing the international system in a disarmed world. Such an academic and theoretical approach had little chance of succeeding, at least in the 1960s. Discussions in the Eighteen-Nation Committee never centred on anything beyond negotiation of the clauses in Phase 1 of the various proposals. Admittedly, much time was devoted to discussions on the International Disarmament Organization and on maintaining the peace, but the efforts were in vain. As early as the summer of 1962, the British contemplated packaging together a series of measures that could be negotiated separately and progressively. This approach was shared by the Americans, but kept secret to avoid exposing the West to increased criticism from the Soviets. The USSR surely would not have missed the opportunity of proclaiming to the world that such an approach demonstrated the West's lack of interest in the issue of general and complete disarmament.

On 27 June 1962, Canada submitted a lengthy 12-page document delineating the main elements of Canadian policy on general and complete disarmament.[23] On the whole, Canada accepted the basic document tabled by the Americans in Geneva, although some minor changes were proposed and clarification was sought on a number of issues including the following: Was the expression "fixed launching platforms" devised to exclude mobile launchers? Were civilians included in the definition of "armed forces" and would it not be better to specify a fixed percentage that should be included? Would it not be better to use the Soviet phrase "purposes other than peaceful uses" rather than the phrase "purposes other than use in nuclear weapons"?

In addition, Canada disliked the expression "norms of international conduct" which could invite criticism because it might be interpreted as meaning norms imposed from the outside. As well, Canada wanted discussion on the issue of prohibition of recourse to nuclear weapons, but the Americans would not agree since they had already withdrawn such a clause from Phase 2 of their previous preliminary proposal as a result of the reticence expressed by their main European allies.[24] In the end, the Canadian document and the allied discussions that followed in Washington led to no meaningful changes in the u.s. draft treaty.

Within the Eighteen-Nation Committee, Canada submitted several documents which synthesized and compared the two proposals that were tabled.[25] Only the essentials of these proposals will be highlighted.[26] The two proposals envisaged a three-stage process of general and complete disarmament. The Soviets wanted the process to be spread over five years, as opposed to four in their original plan, and insisted that the plan be accepted in totality from the outset. The Americans, for their part, envisaged that the first two stages would each extend over three years and that the third stage would be defined at the time of signing the treaty.

Concerning conventional force reductions, the proposals were as follows:

AMERICAN PROPOSAL OF 18 APRIL	SOVIET PROPOSAL OF 15 MARCH
Stage 1	*Stage 1*
u.s. and ussr: 2.1 million men. Other States, unless otherwise specified: 100,000 men or the equivalent of 1 percent of the population.	u.s. and ussr: 1.9 million men (1.7 million in original plan). Other States: to be determined.

AMERICAN PROPOSAL OF 18 APRIL	SOVIET PROPOSAL OF 15 MARCH
Stage 2	*Stage 2*
u.s. and ussr: 1.05 million men. Other States: to be determined according to a percentage formula to be defined.	u.s. and ussr: 1 million men. Other States: to be determined.
Stage 3	*Stage 3*
Maintenance of forces needed solely for internal security; and creation of un police force.	Disbandment of armed forces and reserves; and maintenance of light weapons needed for internal security.

As for delivery vehicles and nuclear weapons, the two proposals were diametrically opposed. The United States proposed progressive stepwise reductions: 30 percent in the first stage, and 35 percent in each of the two following stages. The Soviet Union, on the other hand, suggested that all delivery vehicles be eliminated during the first stage. This provision was subsequently changed following Gromyko's acceptance of the "nuclear umbrella" concept during discussions in the 17th Session of the General Assembly. In other words, in was agreed that a "minimum deterrent" was necessary at the time to meet international security needs. Other changes submitted to the Eighteen-Nation Committee reinforced the idea that nuclear weapons might be retained until stage 3, but the conditions for implementation of these proposals were never defined. The Soviets also required the dismantling of all foreign bases and the withdrawal of all foreign-based troops during the first stage.

The United States, in turn, broadened considerably the scope of the first stage by proposing: the halting of production of fissile materials for military purposes, transference of certain quantities of fissile materials to non-military use, exchange of military missions and establishment of observation posts, prior notification of launching of missiles or space vehicles, prohibition of transfer of nuclear weapons to non-nuclear States, cessation of nuclear testing under effective international control and prohibition of the placing in orbit of weapons of mass destruction. The Soviets proposed essentially similar clauses on the latter three points, except that there was no mention of control in connection with the cessation of nuclear testing.

The aims on both sides were clear. The United States proposed percentage reductions in delivery vehicles, which would have placed the USSR in a position of inferiority since the United States possessed many more launchers than the USSR. The Soviet Union demanded the withdrawal of all U.S. forces from Europe and Asia, which was obviously unacceptable for the United States. The Soviets soon realized that their proposal to eliminate delivery vehicles within a 15-month period was not feasible and, for this reason, softened their position by suggesting the concept of a "nuclear umbrella" which was also being considered by many Western specialists. At the time, the concept was in the realm of fantasy. Nowadays, especially after Reykjavik and the incident at Chernobyl, there is a gradual return to the concept of "minimum deterrence". In sum, the proposals on both sides were totally at variance, and therefore unacceptable. As a result, the discussions increasingly focused on partial measures of disarmament.

On the issue of delivery vehicles, the Canadian Chiefs of Staff quickly understood the significance of the Soviet proposal. On 2 April 1962, Air Marshall F.R. Miller responded to a telex from Burns in Geneva as follows: "In summary, the Soviet proposal if carried out in good faith would ensure to the USSR the domination of the Eurasian land mass and if carried out in bad faith would ensure the domination of the world".[27]

In his memorandum of 3 May to the Minister, Burns elaborated on the Soviet position:[28]

In practice, the Soviet Delegation has been endeavouring, with some appreciable measure of success, to have the Conference consider the Soviet draft treaty, article by article, as a basis of discussion ... This has placed the U.S.A. Delegation in a defensive position psychologically and tactically ... The Soviet Delegation has maintained that all the disarmament measures contained in the Soviet draft treaty are interrelated and interdependent and cannot be considered in isolation from each other. This seems to be particularly relevant ... with regard to the elimination of nuclear delivery vehicles, the dismantling of foreign military bases and the withdrawal of foreign troops from alien territories, and the demilitarization of outer space, all of which must take place simultaneously.

...

This explains the persistent opposition of the USSR to the establishment of working groups or separate subcommittees.

In response to the British representative, Michael Wright, who compared the American proposal to a three-legged stool – disarmament, verification and maintaining the peace[29] –, Soviet Delegate Zorine observed that only four-legged seats are stable. The replacement of

Zorine by Tsarapkine in the summer of 1962 introduced a little more flexibility into the negotiations, but on the whole it was clear that the United States and the Soviet Union were no more interested in disarmament than a fly is interested in a spider. In 1970, when the Department of External Affairs took stock of all these negotiations, it was concluded that there was no better way of maintaining the sanctity of the *status quo* than to hold talks on general and complete disarmament.[30]

On 22 November 1962, Burns and the Department of External Affairs tried to obtain some details from their counterparts in the Department of National Defence on ways of progressively eliminating delivery vehicles and nuclear weapons while maintaining an approximate military balance between the two blocs. A lengthy document was prepared by the Joint Chiefs of Staff[31] on 6 December 1962. The Department of National Defence obviously supported the percentage reduction approach since it favoured the West. This approach was contrary to the one adopted by the West during the 1950s. During those years, the West argued for reductions on the basis of numerical thresholds which were to be determined, while the Soviets argued for percentage reductions which, at the time, was to their advantage. It was only during the SALT discussions that the United States and the Soviet Union agreed to negotiate on the basis of equivalent asymmetric reductions, or numerical thresholds, acceptable to both parties.

The December document prepared by the Department of National Defence expressed reservations concerning the "minimum deterrent" concept favoured by Burns, emphasizing with good reason that "the price of American nuclear disengagement from Europe is a substantial indigenous European nuclear capability". Overall, the document did not respond to the questions raised by Burns and the Department of External Affairs. Most of the opinions expressed were of a policy nature. In addition, the document held that Geneva was only an exercise in propaganda and that solutions to the problems "could be achieved only by private diplomacy involving primarily the Great Powers". Although DND was right in this regard, the document was of little use to Burns who had to defend himself in the lion's den. On 21 March 1963, Burns tried again to obtain more practical advice from DND, but in vain.

In the context of general and complete disarmament, an Italian proposal afforded the Western powers the opportunity to create a group of legal experts responsible for conducting studies on the organization for disarmament and on maintaining the peace in a disarmed world. By the summer of 1964, the working group had held five study sessions. The discussions were often confused for lack of a precise agenda or prior policy conditions which, of course, could only be defined in a framework of true disarmament. The group did, however, solicit the services of leading international jurists, including A.E. Gotlieb of Canada, H.D. Darwin and D.N. Brinson of the United Kingdom, G. Arangio-Ruiz and Giovanni Battaglini of Italy as well as George Bunn, Richard Gardner and Steven Schwebel of the United States. The main mandate of the group was to study the role, structure and decisional procedures which should govern the operations of the International Disarmament Organization (IDO) as well as the issues of maintaining the peace and of peaceful settlement of differences.

Although some of the issues identified were rather theoretical, they still exerted an impact on debates within the Eighteen-Nation Committee. For instance, there was the question of whether it was necessary, in the context of disarmament, to modify Article 103 of the Charter. This Article stated that in the event of conflict of interpretation between the provisions of the Charter and those of other agreements, the former would prevail. Also, there was the question of whether the "norms of international conduct" proposed by the United States were consistent with the Charter. In this regard, the debates in the Eighteen-Nation Committee, in which Canada played an essential role, showed clearly that only the provisions of the Charter could be legally enforced, and that there could be no question of according legislative responsibility to the IDO. The Department of National Defence supported the Soviet perspective on this point, stating: "It is most unlikely that there could be in present circumstances any meaningful agreement to refrain from indirect aggression and subversion ... All forms of influence, including cultural influence and economic assistance, are in some sense aggression".[32]

There was also the question of whether the issue of maintaining the peace, which the United States wanted to institute in the context of general disarmament, should be based on Article 43 of the Charter or based, as Canada wished[33], on national contingents voluntarily assigned to the UN Peacekeeping Force. In one of his reports[34], Burns stressed that, at the 55th Meeting of the Eighteen-Nation Committee, U.S. Delegate Arthur Dean had rejected Article 43 as constituting an adequate legal basis because, at San Francisco, the Article had not been conceived within the framework of general and complete disarmament. Burns could also have added that this article was formulated and drafted before the advent of nuclear weapons on the international scene.

Another question was whether the UN could avail itself of nuclear weapons to ensure its ability to maintain the peace in a disarmed world. Britain did not want to hear of it, India neither, and Green even less. The United States thus found itself rather isolated on this issue. The work of this group of experts, as interesting as it was, will not be discussed herein. Suffice it to say that it greatly facilitated the achievement of a common perspective in Western Delegations, and contributed significant arguments to counter the objections raised by the Soviets. The studies produced by the group were also of interest to the Committee of Thirty-Three which was constituted in the late 1960s to strengthen the UN mechanisms for maintaining the peace.

McIlwraith applied himself to the full on the issue of maintaining the peace.[35] "In a disarmed world", he wrote, "will the leopard change its spots?" He denounced, with good reason, the "extreme and dogmatic" postures adopted by the two sides in Geneva. In his view, the issues of new procedure relative to the traditional obligations of the Charter constituted a chicken-and-egg problem, since it raised the question of "whether men's standards can be changed by legislation, or such legislation can only be brought into being when people are ready for it". He concluded that only a middle-of-the-road position was defensible, and that the issues of maintaining the peace and of peaceful settlement of differences should be approached from this perspective. The Soviet proposal held that, in a disarmed world, only "light firearms"[36] should be retained, while the American proposal called for the constitution of a force that "no State could challenge". In considering these two positions, McIlwraith argued:

We may have to accept, first, that the peace force would require sufficient armaments to put down a local conflict not involving the great powers and, second, to provide some measure of deterrent against any illegitimate design that might be conceived by a great power itself. At the same time, we must face what seems to be a fact of life that the world would not remain disarmed if one or more of the great powers were determined to resort to force, and we should therefore not delude ourselves into thinking that the peace force could maintain the *status quo* in such circumstances.

This, in just a few words, summarized the whole problem of general and complete disarmament. Today it is no easier to answer the following three questions than it was in the early 1960s. Theoretically, how can a police force deter a great power? With what weapons should an international force be equipped in order to prevent, for example, a recurrence of the Iran-Iraq conflict? And what would happen, even given the most optimistic assumptions, if a great power decided not to respect the agreed commitments? Raymond Aron contends that, after each war, the combatants rise up from their ruins to re-amass the means of destroying each other, and then propose that a disarmament conference be convened.[37] Even if the argument is not carried this far, it is clear that the issue of peaceful settlement of differences can only be approached in the context of a change in mentalities, as claimed by advocates of the pacifist school. Reykjavik and the events that followed seem to indicate that there is a general change in thinking on the issue of nuclear weapons. The prevailing view is that nuclear weapons are unusable and make no sense from a military standpoint, except perhaps in the context of deterrence. Although many authors challenge the validity of these views, the general opinion is that the number of nuclear weapons should be reduced to the lowest possible level as a matter of utmost urgency. But inevitably other questions will arise: What will future technology bring and, in the changing environment, will the opposition to certain weapons which exists today prevail tomorrow?

On the issue of maintaining the peace, Burns sought permission from Ottawa to make a statement[38] before the ENDC in Geneva. Given his experience with the United Nations Emergency Force (UNEF) and Canada's credibility in the area of peacekeeping, Burns was obviously qualified to speak with authority. The planned statement came at the height of the Congo crisis, and Ottawa considered that it would more likely aggravate interpretational conflicts than reduce them. Burns was asked, therefore, to "put on the soft pedal".[39] As well, the UN Division was in close consultation with the Americans who were preparing a working document on this subject for consideration by the four Western powers in Washington. Eventually, this matter was the subject of scattered statements within the Eighteen-Nation Committee but it was never studied in depth. In November 1962, Burns asked that this subject be studied more thoroughly. He was told, however, that if such a study were to be undertaken, it would have to focus on four aspects: 1. a comparison of the Soviet and American plans in order to identify common elements and differences; 2. a determination of the degree of consistency between the Canadian and American positions in order to propose changes deemed to be desirable; 3. a similar determination in respect of the Soviet position; and 4. a determination of the elements that should be included in a draft treaty on points that Canada would consider important, but that had been neglected both by the United States and the USSR.[40] By August 1965, the situation remained unchanged.[41]

In a memorandum addressed to the Under-Secretary[42], Burns recognized that the issue of general and complete disarmament had remained in a situation of total impasse for several years. He suggested a new approach which, if approved by Ottawa, would be submitted first to William C. Foster, Director of the Arms Control and Disarmament Agency (ACDA) in Washington, and subsequently to the British and the Italians. His text was entitled "General and Complete Disarmament". The title is misleading, for Burns returned to the ideas of "balanced reductions", minimum deterrence and the designation of de-nuclearized zones. Aside from his proposal to broaden the nuclear-free zone as far as Minsk[43], Burns essentially repeated his ideas of June 1960.[44] He wanted all these elements to be included within Phase 1 of the American draft treaty which would then include, apart from the aspects of non-proliferation: 1. a verifiable freeze on delivery vehicles followed by the destruction of elements that were not essential to the maintenance of credible deterrence, such as earlier generation bombers; 2. broadening of the Rapacki zone up to Minsk so as to eliminate tactical nuclear weapons; 3. modified proposals to limit the production of fissile materials; and 4. budgetary control on equipment, personnel and military installations. This was actually a grouping of partial measures, some of which had been under discussion for a long time within the Eighteen-Nation Committee. On the following day, Burns insisted that arms trade with Third World countries should also be publicized.

D.M. Cornett of the Disarmament Division, in a note to B.H. Robinson, observed that such a modification would imply a totally new structure for Phase 1 of the American proposal[45], and added: "We limited ourselves in the past to proposing minor modifications to this draft treaty ... I cannot see how we could reconcile these suggestions with the U.S. proposal for a three-phase treaty". In this regard, Cornett was correct. The order of the day was no longer general and complete disarmament, but nuclear non-proliferation. In addition, most of the issues raised by Burns had already been discussed within the Eighteen-Nation Committee under the framework of partial measures.

Partial Measures of Disarmament

The priority areas for Canada were non-militarization of outer space, cessation of nuclear testing and nuclear non-proliferation. These priorities were established under the Diefenbaker government at the time when the Eighteen-Nation Committee was starting its work. They resulted largely from discussions between Burns and Green.

By the time that the work of the Eighteen-Nation Committee was nearing completion, Canada pressed even harder for two other topics, specifically prohibition of biological and chemical weapons as well as conclusion of the Sea-Bed Treaty. Apart from these major themes, Canada devoted much attention to the study of three other issues: de-nuclearized zones, nuclear-free zones and control of conventional weapons. These issues will be treated below, but some mention of the other issues would first seem appropriate.

One issue of some importance for Canada was that of non-militarization of space. The Americans were outraged by Green's statement of 27 March 1962.[46] Secretary of State Green discussed it privately with the u.s. Ambassador to Ottawa, T. Merchant, on 3 April 1962.[47] The Americans reproached the Canadians for not having been consulted. Moreover, the Canadian proposal made no provision for specific functions in respect of verification. Green pointed out advisedly that his statement should be regarded as just that, and not as a proposal. After all, he continued, his 28 March statement suggested only that the most promising aspects of the two treaties relating to non-militarization of space be formalized. Subsequently, Arthur Dean of the u.s. Delegation in Geneva stressed that the Eighteen-Nation Committee should study the issue of outer space as soon as possible, but the Soviets responded that the subject could only be discussed in the context of general and complete disarmament.[48] In June 1962, Burns was charged with supporting the Indian proposal which called for the co-chairmen to prepare amendments for inclusion in the two draft treaties.[49] The Eighteen-Nation Committee made little progress in this regard. For this reason, Paul Martin, in his 26 March 1964 intervention[50], dropped the issue of outer space from his list, and laid emphasis on the seven topics[51] which he felt would receive favourable consideration in the negotiations.

Canada also accorded particular effort to making an inventory of all the proposals presented by both sides between 1958 and 1963 which were aimed at preventing surprise attack. The resulting document[52] was tabled in Geneva on 16 August 1963. An important element of this document concerned the establishment of observation posts, and was the subject of much discussion within the Committee. It was proposed that two, and perhaps four, such posts be established on Canadian territory.[53] To complement the network of observation posts, the United States proposed an exchange of military missions between the two blocs. The Minister of National Defence thought little of this proposal which he considered "would only put even greater strain on already inadequate Departmental resources".[54] It must be admitted that the American proposal was aimed mainly at undermining the Soviet demand for withdrawal of military forces from foreign bases by legitimizing the role of each of the alliances in the areas of inspection and exchange of military information. Canada nevertheless considered that this proposal could lead to an "assurance" against surprise attack.

On the issue of halting fissile material production, the British tabled a document[55] which was viewed by Canadian scientists and by the Department of National Defence with much reservation. The proposal was deemed neither plausible nor realizable unless it were adopted at a very late stage in the disarmament process after all the verification systems were in place. It was treated with caution, because Canada lacked broad experience in this area. At most, Canada ventured to put forward a few suggestions, but there was no subsequent follow-up. For example, if reactor fuels were subjected to prolonged radiation, it would be more difficult to produce plutonium from them for military purposes. Alternatively, the use of reflectors in natural uranium reactors could be prohibited in order to reduce the possibility of producing plutonium from the spent fuel. The separation of isotopes using chemical processes could also be prohibited.[56] Canada's suggestions were sound, but negotiations in this area started only much later following the establishment of the International Nuclear Fuel Cycle Evaluation (INFCE).[57]

On broader political issues, Canada followed closely the position adopted by the NATO allies. For instance, Burns stated that the Soviet non-aggression pact proposal of February 1963 fell outside the scope of the Eighteen-Nation Committee and should be discussed in the wider context of major European political issues.[58] On the matter of maintaining a "nuclear umbrella" to provide some form of deterrence during the various stages of disarmament, Burns tried unsuccessfully to obtain clarification from the Soviet Delegation.[59] Because the subject of "minimum deterrence" was of high interest to Burns, he supported the UAR request that a working group be created to study the relevance of maintaining nuclear deterrence on the path to disarmament.[60] This working group was never constituted.

Concerning military budgets, the Soviets proposed a reduction of 10 to 15 percent across the board. Burns, who was conscious of the difficulties that such a proposal might pose, called for standardization of the manner in which budgetary data was presented. Unlike the other Western Delegates, he was not opposed to the Soviet proposal, but thought that the reductions should not apply equally to all States.[61] In 1964, when the United States proposed the destruction of a certain number of B-47 bombers in exchange for the destruction of an equivalent number of Soviet Tu-16 bombers, Burns asked that such an agreement be linked to the u.s. proposal for a "verified freeze" on the number of delivery vehicles. The British and the Americans advised Burns that they would consult each other on the matter.[62] Notwithstanding this reassurance, they returned with similar proposals in 1966. Nothing concrete emerged from all these talks, except the feeling of helplessness experienced by the non-superpower members of the Eighteen-Nation Committee.

Preliminaries to the Non-Proliferation Treaty. Canadian efforts on the issue of non-proliferation of nuclear weapons may be conveniently separated according to two policy themes: first, the establishment of de-nuclearized zones in Europe and, second, the delineation of nuclear-free zones in other parts of the world. The first theme was mainly discussed within the Eighteen-Nation Committee, while the second, although considered in the ENDC, was largely discussed in UN deliberations.

Developments in respect of the first theme can be studied by reference to the historical sequence of proposals made by Delegates of the Eastern bloc. On 28 March 1962, at the first meeting of the Committee of the Whole, the Poles revived the Rapacki plan with a slight modification to the effect that, during the first phase, nuclear forces would be "frozen" in the region in question, and then progressively eliminated during the second phase. On 28 December 1963, Gomulka sounded out the Western Delegations on this amended proposal. By 29 February 1964, the Poles felt that they were on sufficiently solid ground to make the following proposals: 1. a freeze on all nuclear weapons in the region defined in the Rapacki plan of 1957–1958; 2. prohibition of production, introduction or importation of nuclear weapons in the region in question; 3. the provision of "safeguards" governing the operation of nuclear facilities in the region; and 4. the introduction of control posts at strategic points to prevent the installation of new nuclear weapons in the zone in question.

In 1965, a new version of the Gomulka plan was presented. The new plan, better known under the name of its author, Professor Manfred Lachs, consisted of the former proposals together with the three following additional elements. First, the idea of "control" would include, from that time on, the "capacity to commit the use" of nuclear weapons. Second, the zone under consideration would not cover any Soviet territory. In light of the ever-increasing range of nuclear delivery vehicles, the West hardly took the proposal seriously. Third, the Lachs Plan called for voluntary acceptance of "safeguards" provided under the auspices of the International Atomic Energy Agency (IAEA). By 1966, Poland, Czechoslovakia and the FRG were ready to accept such controls.

Overall, the Polish proposals were clearly structured to achieve three objectives: 1. to prevent modernization of NATO's nuclear forces; 2. to foil plans for the MLF; and 3. to ensure that the FRG would not acquire autonomy to select military objectives for the atomic weapons based on its territory. Another overall objective, ever present but never admitted, was to induce the FRG to recognize the GDR in a formal treaty without any considerations or concessions from the East. However, the boundaries drawn up at the end of the Second World War were only officially recognized following the *Ostpolitik* of Chancellor Brandt and the agreements reached in the Conference on Security and Cooperation in Europe (CSCE).

Following consultations in NATO, most of the allies responded to the Soviet note of 29 February 1964 in similar vein. Western strategy was to express regret at the inadequacies of the plan and to lay the blame on the Poles. It was a way of inviting the Poles to be more specific about their ideas. The first reason put forward was that if the freeze on nuclear weapons did not apply to those on Soviet territory, it would deprive the West of any possibility of retaliation with tactical nuclear weapons. It was a weighty argument that the East did not attempt to counter. Second, it was stressed that since the freeze applied only to nuclear weapons, it would be more substantive if linked to the Western proposal for a "verified freeze" on delivery vehicles. It was a skilful way of putting the ball back in the court of the Eastern nations in an attempt to induce them to consider a Western proposal with all the elements of control that such a proposal would entail. Third, it was pointed out that inspection would be asymmetric because of the asymmetries in inspection zones.[63]

In this regard, Canada had no wish to take a lead over her Western allies. Burns tried to link the issue of de-nuclearization with that of conventional force reductions, but no one supported this strategy. As early as 5 March 1963, the Canadian Joint Chiefs of Staff produced a report on the inequity of the Soviet proposal for conventional force reductions in Europe. The same argument reappeared later in the MBFR talks. Even if the Soviets withdrew 22 divisions from Central Europe, the West would have its back to the sea without any defence in depth, while the Soviet Union would possess a vast territory in which to mobilize her forces and transport them, in the event of war, to the Western front. The Department of External Affairs refused to accept this argument on the grounds that any withdrawal would require verified destruction of military hardware.[64] This implied, however, the acceptance of on-site inspection, which was inconceivable at the time.

Canada was much more imaginative on the issue of nuclear-free zones in other regions of the world. A number of proposals were tabled, both before and after the Cuban missile crisis. Ironically, the two resolutions which received most attention by Canada were introduced before the Cuban crisis. One was resolution 1652 (XVI) concerning Africa and the other was resolution 1664 (XVI) from Sweden. Both were presented towards the end of 1961 prior to the start of deliberations within the Eighteen-Nation Committee. The first resolution called for Africa to be declared a de-nuclearized zone where nuclear testing, stockpiling or transportation of nuclear weapons would be banned. France was clearly the foremost target of this resolution, having conducted nuclear tests in the Sahara since 1960. The Swedish resolution was more subtle. It called for the Secretary General to conduct a study on the circumstances in which non-nuclear nations might refuse to accept foreign nuclear weapons on their soil. This was clearly problematic for NATO and for NORAD.

Canada abstained in the vote on the first resolution for political reasons in deference to French sensitivities. The Canadian Joint Chiefs of Staff adopted a strange if not indifferent attitude. In a letter dated 3 October 1962 to the Under-Secretary of State for External Affairs[65], the Chairman of the Joint Chiefs of Staff voiced no objection to the draft resolution, adding that no circumstances would likely arise in the future to change this opinion. In other words, as far as the French strike force was concerned, "there is no consideration relating to Western security or to Canadian national interests". Indeed, there was more to be gained than to be lost by supporting this proposal. It was recognized that France could approach South Africa for permission to conduct guided weapon tests over the vast expanse of that country, but this apparently caused no concern for the Canadian military. In the context of de-nuclearization, it was stressed that European zones should be kept distinct from other zones. The Joint Chiefs of Staff concluded that, as long as this distinction prevailed, Africa would be of little relevance, even for the British and the Americans who had bases on that continent. It was, at the very least, a shortsighted judgement, incomprehensible in the context of overall Western security, and took no account of the growing strategic importance of this vast territory in relation to the Middle East. This was probably the only instance when Green received such unexpected and unconcerned support from the Department of National Defence.

In contrast, the Swedish resolution led to fierce conflict between the Departments of External Affairs and of National Defence. In the end, Diefenbaker came out in favour of the position of National Defence. Events unfolded in three stages. Initially, Under-Secretary Robertson, sensing the danger, proposed a compromise formula to Green. Harkness had stated that although Canada had until then abstained from acquiring nuclear weapons, steps were being taken to acquire modern delivery systems and to train military personnel in their use. Robertson's compromise consisted of accepting the suggestions of National Defence in the following form:

My Government must, of course, continue to reserve its right to adopt such measures for the preservation of Canadian security, as might be considered necessary in the light of international developments.[66]

Afterwards, Green accepted his Under-Secretary's proposal, but prefaced it with the following phrase: "My Government earnestly hopes that no changes in its present policy will be required … ". In so doing, Green assumed a right that properly belonged to Cabinet. Defence Minister Harkness rightly denounced this attitude in his letter of 12 March to Diefenbaker[67], and demanded that the phrase be removed.

Later, in a note to the Prime Minister dated 16 March, Robertson supported Green. He pointed out to Diefenbaker that the proposed formula was already a compromise and that if Green's phrase were removed, the Secretary General might interpret Canada's position as hardly consistent with the long-time support that Canada had expressed "for measures to limit the further spread of nuclear weapons".[68] The note was returned from the Prime Minister's office to External Affairs with the following hand-written annotation by B.H. Robinson: "The Prime Minister wants the underlined phrase [that added by Green] deleted". On 21 March 1962, William Barton, Acting Head of the Canadian Delegation in New York, handed the Canadian response to the Swedish proposal to Secretary General S. U Thant. It contained the Harkness-Robertson compromise formula – Green had just lost an important battle.

Shortly after the Cuban missile crisis, there was a proliferation of proposals on nuclear-free zones. On 29 April 1963, five Latin American countries voted in favour of a proposal to make the whole of South and Central America a nuclear-free zone, along the lines of that submitted by Brazil in November 1962. This proposal led to the Treaty of Tlatelolco, named after the suburb of Mexico City where it was signed on 14 February 1967. On 20 May 1963, the Soviets proposed that the Mediterranean be declared a de-nuclearized zone. This proposal was clearly aimed at denying u.s. Polaris submarines access to the Mediterranean. In Geneva, it was deemed to be nothing more than "shameless propaganda".[69] On 28 May 1963, Finland's President Kekonnen, proposed a de-nuclearized zone for Scandinavia, but it received "little response".[70]

The Department of National Defence was not opposed to the Latin American proposal of November 1962 on condition that it would not conflict with u.s. commitments in the region.[71] At first, the Canadian military felt that the base in the Bahamas might be problematic, but subsequently withdrew this reservation. The Department of External Affairs was clearly delighted with the proposal. As far as the Mediterranean was concerned, Prime Minister Pearson stated in the House on 22 May 1963 that he would be interested to see whether the Soviets were ready to include the Black Sea in their proposal. Pearson concluded that it would be premature to say more about the proposal until it had been considered by NATO. The Soviet proposal had no chance of success. McIlwraith of the Disarmament Division observed that the Soviet proposal was quite different from earlier proposals in that it included "a large area of the high seas".[72] Concerning the Kekonnen plan, Canada's Ambassador to Finland stressed, in a despatch[73] from Helsinki dated 12 June 1963, that Finland was well aware that its proposal would be flatly refused by the other Scandinavian countries. According to the Ambassador, if Finland had developed the proposal autonomously, it was perhaps aimed at reminding the Soviets that no (Soviet) threat should originate from Scandinavia. The Ambassador was unable to determine, however, whether Finland developed the proposal alone or acted as an envoy of the USSR.

On the whole, Canada's position on the de-nuclearization issue was founded on three rather uncontroversial principles: 1. the proposal had to be acceptable to all the States comprising the free zone; 2. provisions for verification had to be established to ensure respect for commitments; and 3. no unilateral advantage for a State or group of States was to result from the implementation of such proposals.[74]

Control of Conventional Weapons. In the area of general and complete disarmament, General Burns proposed, in correspondence to the various departments in Ottawa dating back to the summer of 1962, that a comprehensive study be undertaken on the issue of transfer of conventional weapons. There were three specifics in his proposal: 1. that the IDO conduct a study on this issue during the first phase of disarmament; 2. that military transactions be subject to compulsory registration with the IDO, either during phases 1 or 2, and that a clause be inserted into draft treaties to this effect; and 3. that transfer of weapons be prohibited during phases 2 and 3 without the authorization of the IDO or any other appropriate organization.

This proposal is interesting from more than one standpoint. First, it is just as relevant today as at the time. Second, it was markedly different from the proposals presented by the United States and the USSR in 1962. Third, it represented the views of a middle power that was not involved in the arms trade and unlikely to be affected by the application of restrictive controls.

Burns failed to gain allied acceptance for his ideas. In a well-written ten-page document, the Canadian Joint Chiefs of Staff laid emphasis on the difficulties surrounding such a proposal.[75] It was argued that the arms trade was, above all, a phenomenon associated with the Cold War. Nowadays one might argue that this phenomenon depends essentially on the extent of regional conflict and on the absorption capacity and credit rating of the receiver countries. The document emphasized further that a NATO committee was studying this issue in anticipation of a ministerial meeting to be held in Istanbul in the spring of 1960. The conclusions reached by this committee were hardly reassuring, and may be summarized as follows: the proposal is not without interest if it restricts the freedom of action of the USSR, but there must be no restriction of the kind for Western zones covered under bilateral or multilateral agreements! In other words, the only acceptable rule was that of a double standard.

The Burns proposal also raised the whole question of the status, role and powers of the IDO on matters of control, constraints, decisions and the standards to be established for determining whether or not a country should be authorized to receive arms. These issues have never been resolved. The Canadian Joint Chiefs of Staff were of the view that negotiations between supplier nations would more likely lead to agreements than the development of a draft treaty. This observation was not unfounded, for bilateral negotiations between the Americans and the Soviets were held on this issue during the 1970s. In addition, the Chiefs of Staff stressed that the developing countries might interpret the Burns proposal as an attempt to keep them in a permanent state of technological inferiority. On the whole, they rightly believed that such proposals would have little effect on Canadian security. They felt, however, that there was no particular reason why Canada should not take such an initiative even though, *a priori*, its chances of success seemed very slim, adding that all these efforts would only lead to interminable and futile discussions.

There was no follow-up to this proposal. Nevertheless, it was one of the most substantive proposals developed by Burns throughout his term as Advisor on Disarmament to the Canadian Government.

His efforts were not totally in vain, for the Maltese Delegation, apparently without consulting anyone, tabled a draft resolution before the First Committee of the 20th Session of the UN General Assembly which invited the Eighteen-Nation Committee to study the degree of "publicity" that should be given to conventional arms dealing. In his report to the Under-Secretary of State for External Affairs, Burns stated that, in the event of general disarmament, it would be necessary to study means for controlling arms trade with the Third World.[76]

On 6 July 1967, Burns raised this issue again in the Eighteen-Nation Committee.[77] He extended the scope of the proposal made by President Johnson in June 1967 concerning public disclosure of arms exports to the Middle East. Burns argued that all arms deliveries should be reported to the UN, whether the shipments were made to the Middle East or to any other region of the world. In 1968, Denmark presented a draft resolution calling for mandatory registration with the UN of any transaction in conventional armaments. The Minister for External Affairs, Mitchell Sharp, supported this proposal in his speech to the UN on 9 October 1968, arguing the need for an arms trade "register". At the same time, he praised the USSR for its proposal to implement "measures for regional disarmament and arms reductions in the various regions of the world, including the Middle East". The Danish draft resolution was finally withdrawn in face of stiff opposition from certain Third World countries.

The issue resurfaced again in the CCD, and it is still discussed today. Towards the end of the 1980s, France even proposed the creation of an "observation post" to monitor arms trade operations. The ideas of Burns, the old military career officer, still live on ...

7 Canada and the Non-Proliferation Treaty

> Thank you very much. Now I understand. Non-proliferation is
> really not an obstacle to some proliferation.
>
> P.E. Trudeau, Handwritten note, 28 January 1969

Few subjects in the area of arms control have caused so much ink to flow as that of the Nuclear Non-Proliferation Treaty, which was signed on 1 July 1968. The Treaty entered into force on 5 March 1970, and since then three Conferences have been convened to review its operation. These Review Conferences were held in 1975, 1980 and 1985. A fourth Review Conference will be held in 1990. In 1995, twenty-five years after the entry into force of the Treaty, a conference will be convened "to decide whether the Treaty shall continue in force indefinitely, or shall be extended for an additional fixed period or periods". In accordance with Article X of the Treaty, this decision shall be taken by a majority of the Parties to the Treaty.

Viewed retrospectively, the Treaty has been relatively successful. Under the terms of Article IX of the Treaty, a nuclear-weapon State is defined as one which has "exploded a nuclear weapon or other nuclear device prior to January 1967". Since 1967, therefore, nuclear proliferation could not be legally recognized without a change to the definition given under Article IX of the Treaty. India, regardless of her nuclear status, cannot be considered as a nuclear power under the terms of the Treaty, even though in May 1974 India exploded a nuclear device for so-called "peaceful" purposes. At the time that the Treaty was signed, five States had already exploded a nuclear weapon: the United States, the USSR, the United Kingdom, France and the Peoples' Republic of China. As of 1989, only the first three of these five States had signed the Non-Proliferation Treaty.

Israel too is thought to possess the "bomb", while opinion is divided on whether South Africa possesses it also. It is known, however, that Sweden came within a hair's breadth of acquiring a tactical nuclear weapon during the 1960s, and that Pakistan, Argentina and Brazil have the potential to develop nuclear weapons. Several other States, including Iraq and Libya, might also have lost their virgin status as non-nuclear States had it not been for the constant efforts by the international community to curb nuclear proliferation. This observation does not, in any way, constitute an endorsement of the military action taken by Israel against the Iraqi nuclear centre at Tuwaitha in 1981.

The Treaty, with some of its obscurely-worded articles, undoubtedly reflects the requirements perceived necessary at the time by its authors. For the three nuclear-weapon States party to the Treaty, it was essentially a question of maintaining the *status quo*. Nuclear weapons are a source of both security and dread, and the aim of the three nuclear-weapon States party to the Treaty was to prevent other States from acquiring them. The Preamble to the Treaty expresses it well: the danger of nuclear war must be averted. The only way of achieving this objective is to freeze the *status quo* and to do everything possible to ensure that other States use the power of the atom strictly for peaceful purposes. The nuclear-weapon States party to the Treaty undertook not to transfer to any recipient whatsoever control over nuclear weapons. Clearly, their intentions were never otherwise. At the time, however, France had acquired a nuclear-weapon capability and considered it unfair to prohibit other States from acquiring one. The Peoples' Republic of China had previously been severely ostracized for developing a nuclear-weapon capability, but had no intention of supporting the perpetuation of nuclear hegemony enjoyed by the major powers. As early as October 1964 China conducted a nuclear test in the Lob Nor desert. This event served to strengthen the resolve of the superpowers to reach agreement on the nuclear issue.

Following the Cuban missile crisis in 1962, the major powers became acutely aware of the dangers of nuclear war. There were no valid grounds that could induce the major powers to be drawn into the nuclear abyss. In this situation, management of the "brinkmanship" policy necessarily had to be duopolistic. Following the extreme tensions of 1962, the Moscow-Washington "hot line" was installed and the 1963 Partial Test Ban Treaty was concluded, serving to pave the way for a policy of conciliation. Subsequently, u.s. Defense Secretary McNamara set about establishing the rules of play between the major powers. Moscow was withdrawn from the list of u.s. strategic targets under the SIOP (Single Integrated Operational Plan), for if the opponent's political hierarchy were decimated in a nuclear war there would be no one with whom to negotiate. From that time forward, the USSR and the PRC appeared as two distinct adversaries on the ordnance survey maps. The concept of flexible response was introduced into strategic doctrine so that in a wartime scenario each situation could be assessed on its own merit and maximum control could be exercised in the conduct of military operations.

These new concepts caused quite a stir within the Atlantic Alliance which, at the time, was seized with the worst difficulties of strategic coordination. The meeting between MacMillan and Kennedy in the Bahamas in December 1962 helped the British to save face through U.S. cooperation which allowed Britain to purchase Polaris missiles. France, at the end of the 1950s, was unable to secure the same degree of cooperation from the United States for equipping her submarines. Faced with a reticent Congress and a finicky defensive attitude on the part of the Atomic Energy Commission and the Joint Committee on Atomic Energy, France decided to pursue the "adventure of the bomb"[1] alone, particularly following McNamara's suggestion that France should renounce it. The FRG, which was led to believe by the Kennedy Administration that there were grounds for "nuclear sublimation" in the context of a European nuclear force integrated within the Atlantic Alliance, became a staunch defender of the MLF (Multilateral Force) proposal. By the summer of 1964, the MLF proposal was already in a state of demise. Britain had elected a Labour government under the leadership of Harold Wilson, who promptly announced that Britain would not participate in the MLF proposal. Even in 1963, under the previous MacMillan government, Britain had tried to replace the MLF proposal with its own ANF (Atlantic Nuclear Force) proposal.

The Americans, for their part, were divided on which route to follow. In 1964, Johnson promised Chancellor Erhard that everything possible would be done to constitute the MLF before the next meeting of the North Atlantic Council scheduled for December of that year. In December, Rusk met with de Gaulle, and the outcome was that under no circumstances should West Germany be given "access" to nuclear weapons. Furthermore, de Gaulle made it clear to his ally across the Rhine[2] that he would abrogate the Franco-German Cooperation Treaty of 1963 if ever the FRG were to participate in the MLF. The constitution, in November 1964, of a study group led by Roswell L. Gilpatrick on the dangers of proliferation, and the intensification in 1965 of bilateral discussions between the U.S. and USSR on the same subject, marked the beginnings of a new American policy. The

MLF was "sacrificed on the altar of non-proliferation"[3]. The U.S. Department of Defense and the Arms Control and Disarmament Agency (ACDA) supported this new policy. It was only much later, after March 1966, that the State Department agreed to remove the famous hypothetical clause on the European nuclear option from Article I of the draft Non-Proliferation Treaty. At about the same time, a new government was formed in Bonn and the Peace Note of March 1966 was produced. These two events opened the way for the tabling of a binding draft Treaty before the Eighteen-Nation Committee on Disarmament in Geneva.

The Non-Proliferation Treaty essentially resulted from the largely bilateral manner in which the major strategic debates were managed. With the presentation of the Harmel Report in December 1967 and the opening of the CSCE and MBFR twin conferences in the fall of 1973, a new form of inter-alliance management was superposed on East-West relations. This was an important development, for it then became clear that sound management of East-West relations was only possible when bilateral and multilateral endeavours were perfectly coordinated. When the Reagan Administration took office in the early 1980s there was a significant break in continuity. The resumption of bilateral strategic dialogue in 1985 led to the signing of the Intermediate-Range Nuclear Forces (INF) Treaty in June 1988 and paved the way for the new Strategic Arms Reduction Talks (START). If the Atlantic Alliance can coordinate its policies, the START negotiations could be accompanied by new inter-alliance multilateral discussions on reductions in conventional weapons.

The terms of the Non-Proliferation Treaty are especially significant for the non-nuclear-weapon States. Not only do they provide for access by such States to the potential benefits of peaceful nuclear research, but also to the potential benefits of any peaceful applications of nuclear technology, including nuclear explosions, which will be made available to them "on a non-discriminatory basis" (Article V). The non-nuclear-weapon States can only obtain these benefits, however, "under appropriate international observation". The International Atomic Energy Agency (IAEA), created in 1957 and located in Vienna, is responsible for verifying the fulfilment of the obligations assumed under the Treaty "with a view to preventing diversion of nuclear energy from peaceful uses to nuclear weapons or other nuclear explosive devices" (Article III). Under Article II, the non-nuclear-weapon States undertake not to seek, manufacture or otherwise acquire nuclear weapons. The nuclear-weapon States, on the other hand, have a reciprocal obligation to share the benefits of research on peaceful applications with non-nuclear-weapon States.

The nuclear-weapon States are also bound, under Article VI, "to pursue negotiations in good faith on effective measures relating to the cessation of the nuclear arms race at an early date and to nuclear disarmament".

The main provisions of the Non-Proliferation Treaty can thus be summarized in just a few lines, apart from Article IV which remains particularly ambiguous. The first part of Article IV recognizes the "inalienable right" of all of the Parties to the Treaty to use nuclear energy for peaceful purposes "without discrimination". It is stressed in the second part of Article IV, however, that the Parties should cooperate in the further development of the applications of nuclear energy for peaceful purposes, "especially in the territories of non-nuclear-weapon States Party to the Treaty". Cooperation with States Non-Signatory to the Treaty is, therefore, not forbidden, since the word "especially" constitutes an encouragement and not an exclusion. Several States which were suppliers of nuclear technology (including Canada for a while) continued, and some still continue today, to cooperate with States Non-Signatory to the Treaty under safeguards set forth by the IAEA. Such cooperation is in the economic interests of the recipient States.

GROWING CIVIL AND MILITARY IMPORTANCE OF THE ATOM

The first means of exercising control over the atom was secrecy. The allied nations that were associated with the Manhattan Project were rapidly and successively ousted from the nuclear domain as a result of the drastic restrictions imposed by the United States on the development of nuclear energy. Only two nations, Canada and Great Britain, partially escaped the U.S. policy of secrecy. The situation in respect of Canada has been discussed in Chapter 2. Great Britain more or less succeeded over the years in maintaining some form of cooperation with the United States, although at some points it was essentially dependent on the particular ties developed between the two leaders of these nations, especially during the MacMillan-Kennedy era. It was a favoured relationship perhaps, but at all events cooperation was maintained.

There were various stages in the growth of the atom's civil importance. Prior to the signing of the Non-Proliferation Treaty, nations sometimes engaged in nuclear research for industrial reasons – as did France, for instance, in the mid-1950s – but also for reasons of prestige or security. The impetus for conducting nuclear research for peaceful purposes came in 1963 with the development of nuclear reactors to supply electrical power. In that year, the u.s. Department of Energy announced the development of the 650-megawatt (MW) Oyster Creek nuclear power station at a cost of 91 million dollars. Although estimates of demand proved to be overly optimistic there was nevertheless sufficient business to fill the order books of the u.s. nuclear industry. Ten years later, the 1973 oil crisis quadrupled the price of petroleum and the demand for uranium and for nuclear-generated electrical power soared.

In 1979, the incident at Three Mile Island provided food for thought. Again, in April 1986, the Chernobyl incident confirmed to humanity-at-large the extent of ecological disaster that can result from a nuclear accident. Since 1980, the search for mechanisms to ensure the safety of nuclear reactors has intensified. In 1987, three international conventions were established under the auspices of the IAEA: the Convention on Early Notification of a Nuclear Accident, the Convention on Assistance in the Case of a Nuclear Accident or Radiological Emergency, and the Convention on the Physical Protection of Nuclear Material.

By 1987, over 400 nuclear power plants were operating in 26 countries, and they accounted for about 16 percent of the world's electrical power production. 19 of these plants were located in Canada. As of 31 December 1986, the industrialized nations accounted for 92.9 percent of the total electrical power generated by nuclear reactors throughout the world, while the developing countries accounted for the remaining 7.1 percent.[4] Canada (4.1%) ranked sixth amongst the industrialized nations, after the United States (30.9%), France (16.3%), the USSR (10.1%), Japan (9.4%) and the FRG (6.9%). In the fall of 1988, the equivalent electrical power of the world's nuclear reactors was estimated at 306,544 MWe. It was also estimated that by 1990 the number of nuclear power plants would reach 480. By the year 2000 the equivalent electrical power capacity of nuclear installations worldwide will likely be between 480,000 and 600,000 MWe.[5] Nuclear reactors will account for some 16 to 18 percent of the electrical power production of the industrialized nations, although for some individual nations, notably France, Belgium and Sweden, the figure already exceeds the 50 percent mark.

In 1986, the IAEA conducted over 2,000 inspections in 53 countries and in the four nuclear States which have voluntarily accepted the application of the Agency's safeguards for their civil installations. In 1988, negotiations led to agreements with India and the Peoples' Republic of China. The Agency's control activities expanded considerably as new responsibilities were assigned following the signing of the Tlatelolco Treaty in 1967, the ratification of the Non-Proliferation Treaty (NPT) by EURATOM in 1975 and by Japan in 1976, and the conclusion of the Treaty on a Denuclearized Zone in the South Pacific (Treaty of Rarotonga) which entered into force in December 1986. Of the 131 non-nuclear-weapon States party to the NPT on 31 December 1986, 78 have signed safeguard agreements with the Agency. Many of these States, however, have nuclear research programs of such little consequence that safeguard agreements with the Agency are unnecessary.

Concerning military applications, there is no need to recount the historical developments in the nuclear programs of the major powers. Our sole purpose here is to bring into focus the close relationships which exist between the increasing civil use of the atom and the development of nuclear weapons. Many factors have contributed to the interrelationship between civil and military nuclear activities, such as the lifting of the veil of secrecy surrounding the atom for reasons of industrial development, the freedom to disseminate scientific information, the oil crisis and the development of new technologies.

A State can accede to the status of a nuclear power by first developing a so-called "atomic" bomb which can then be used as a "detonator" for the so-called thermonuclear bomb, or H-bomb. The only known fissionable materials that can be readily used to produce a nuclear explosion are plutonium 239 and uranium 235. Neither one of these materials exists in a free state in nature, and they must be manufactured artificially. Plutonium 239 can only be produced by irradiating the fuel in a reactor for a certain period of time. The irradiated fuel is then withdrawn and processed chemically in a retreatment plant to isolate the plutonium from the other irradiated materials. Subsequently, the plutonium must be "enriched", a process which is extremely difficult and which requires a great deal of technological prowess. Enrichment consists of increasing the proportion of the plutonium 239 isotope relative to other plutonium isotopes, especially the 240 isotope which tends to disintegrate spontaneously thus causing control problems in nuclear detonations.

Uranium 235, on the other hand, occurs in very small proportions (0.7%) in natural uranium, most of which consists of the 238 isotope. The yellow natural uranium cake must first be chemically converted to uranium hexafluoride, which is produced in a gaseous state. The gas is compressed in successive "cascades" where the lighter atoms (U-235) are progressively separated from the heavier atoms (U-238). In order to develop an atomic bomb, the proportion of uranium 235 must be enriched to the 90 percent purity level or over. Such isotope enrichment plants consume enormous amounts of electricity and are difficult to camouflage, if only because of the number of high tension lines required to supply these installations.

The oil crisis of the 1970s and the appearance of new enrichment technologies[6] served to renew debate on the need to develop "breeders"[7] and to control "reprocessing" plants and "sensitive" technologies. Questions were also raised on whether some fuels should be "denatured", some types of nuclear configurations prohibited (some reactors produce plutonium better than others) and some production methods internationalized, all with the aim of minimizing the dangers of nuclear proliferation that could result from further development of such enabling technologies.

For all the above reasons, the International Nuclear Fuel Cycle Evaluation (INFCE) Conference was convened in October 1977. The Conference ended in failure in February 1980, when it was agreed that no miracle technological solution was in sight. The issues were political in nature, but the technical conclusions provided food for thought: by the year 2000 the indirect production of plutonium by diverting reactors could reach 250,000 kg annually, or a quantity sufficient to produce 50,000 bombs of the Nagasaki type. The Conference served, however, to highlight the paramount need to strengthen nuclear safeguards governing the export of fissile materials and so-called "sensitive" technologies. It also clearly demonstrated the transatlantic tensions which already existed at the time that the NPT was negotiated. The fundamental question was how to prevent nuclear proliferation while satisfying the needs for security of energy supply to third-party nations. In June 1980, the IAEA constituted the Committee on Assurances of Supply (CAS) in order to address this issue.

These developments clearly influenced the expansion of nuclear safeguards by the IAEA. These matters will be examined in the third section of this Chapter. For the moment it may be noted that, by the end of 1986, Agency safeguards were in force at 485 installations and 414 other locations. The cost of administering these safeguards amounted to 38 million U.S. dollars, or 35 percent of the overall Agency budget. In total, the Agency was responsible for safeguards applicable to 158 tonnes of plutonium, 13 tonnes of enriched uranium, 22,000 tonnes of weakly enriched uranium and 33,000 tonnes of raw materials.[8] These figures are somewhat misleading, since they only include the materials in those installations that the nuclear States have voluntarily accepted to put under IAEA control.

The control exercised by the IAEA is only as strong as the weakest link in the verification process. Nevertheless, one of the greatest attributes of the Agency is the power to deter nations from diverting nuclear technology to military purposes. In this regard, the nations of greatest concern are those which have refused to sign the NPT. A variety of preventative measures are progressively being introduced, and many States are now calling for the introduction of Full-Scope Safeguards (FSS). Although such safeguards could not be forcibly imposed, they could cause non-signatory nations to reflect more seriously on the consequences of non-adherence to the Treaty.

BRIEF HISTORY OF NEGOTIATIONS

As early as 1958, Ireland was foremost amongst nations seeking to avert the dangers of nuclear proliferation. On 4 December 1961, Ireland succeeded in having its Resolution 1665 unanimously adopted at the Sixteenth Session of the UN General Assembly. The extensive scope of this resolution – and of the one that followed on 20 December – has been discussed in Chapter 6. Resolution 1665 called upon nuclear-weapon States never to relinquish, or transfer to any recipient whatsoever, control over their nuclear weapons. Fortunately, the United States could accommodate this resolution, for it left the door open for Washington to proceed with its plan for greater sharing of the responsibilities for nuclear strategy within the Atlantic Alliance.

Negotiations on the NPT were limited to a small group of nations comprising the United States, the United Kingdom, Canada and Italy.[9] This allowed most of the policies to be coordinated within the Eighteen-Nation Committee and later within the North Atlantic Council. Between 1967 and 1968, the FRG found itself completely isolated, for Bonn held certain reservations concerning the Treaty, which Paris did not share.[10]

Two significant events occurred between 1961 and the time that the first U.S. draft treaty[11] was tabled in Geneva on 17 August 1965. In July 1964, the Organization of African Unity (OAU) declared[12] that weapons' development should be banned under an international treaty to be developed by the United Nations Organization. Then, on 15 June 1965, the UN Disarmament Commission introduced a resolution[13] calling for all States to accord special attention to the problems of non-proliferation and "certain associated measures". This suggestion contained the essence of the obligations to be assumed by the nuclear powers to negotiate "in good faith" (Article VI of the NPT) towards ending the arms race.

The first version of the U.S. draft proposed that no nuclear-weapon State should transfer nuclear weapons "into the national control" of any non-nuclear-weapon State, either directly or through any military alliance, and should avoid any step that would lead to an "increase in the total number of States and other organizations having independent power to use nuclear weapons". The famous "European option" was thus affirmed. The United States could pursue the MLF proposal provided that autonomous control was not ceded to a group of States or to any independent organization. In short, as far as the Americans were concerned, the MLF proposal would not create a centre of independent nuclear power, and the United States would still be able to exercise its right of veto over the use of U.S. nuclear weapons (any change to this right of veto would have required a change in the U.S. Atomic Energy Act).

The USSR was staunchly opposed to the U.S. formulation, especially as the United Kingdom had suggested that, in theory, it left open the possibility that a group of States could use nuclear weapons in consequence of "a majority decision".[14] On 24 September 1965, in the UN General Assembly, the USSR responded to the U.S. proposal. Any transfer of nuclear weapons from a nuclear-weapon State to a non-nuclear-weapon State should be prohibited, and such States or groups of States would be denied "the right to participate in the ownership, control or use of nuclear weapons".[15] Even these restrictions on nuclear weapons did not totally satisfy the USSR, which sought to prohibit "control over them or over their emplacement and use" by units or members of the armed forces of any non-nuclear-weapon State. The USSR thus claimed a *droit de regard* over the sharing of nuclear responsibilities within NATO and the means of Western defence.

In the meantime, Italy tabled a draft declaration of unilateral renunciation[16] before the Eighteen-Nation Committee which would be binding for any non-nuclear-weapon State within a predetermined period, on condition that similar declarations would be forthcoming from a certain number of other non-nuclear-weapon States within six months following the signing of the declaration. Essentially, Italy proposed a moratorium whereby the non-nuclear-weapon States would accept the IAEA safeguards or "other international safeguards" in respect of their nuclear activities. Although not specifically stated, the "other international safeguards" related to those of EURATOM. The Italian initiative was also known as the Fanfani proposal.

For their part, the Neutral and Non-Aligned (NNA) nations of the Eighteen-Nation Committee considered that the NPT was not an end in itself, but part of a broader framework for disarmament which would include a total ban on nuclear testing, in conformity with the Committee's mandate. This particular point was developed mainly by Nigeria. Sweden also came to adopt this point of view, adding that the production of all fissile materials for military purposes should be prohibited. These conditions were developed by the Neutral and Non-Aligned nations in order to pressure the nuclear powers to sign arms control agreements in return for the assurances of non-nuclear-weapon States not to acquire, manufacture or possess nuclear weapons.

In the First Committee of the United Nations, Canada and the United Kingdom supported the u.s. draft proposal, while recognizing that it could be improved and "even more tightly drafted" to preclude any downstream or hypothetical loophole. The British thus demonstrated that they had no particular affection for the "European option". On 23 November 1965, the General Assembly adopted the draft resolution of eight nations[17] – the Neutral and Non-Aligned members of the Eighteen-Nation Committee – which outlined a series of principles governing the development of the NPT, including the absence of loopholes, the commitment to an acceptable balance of mutual responsibilities and obligations between the nuclear-weapon States and the non-nuclear-weapon States, and the implementation of acceptable provisions to ensure the effectiveness of the Treaty. The eight NNA nations later repeated the essential provisions of this resolution in a common memorandum[18] submitted to the Eighteen-Nation Committee on 19 August 1966.

On 21 March 1966, in light of allied reticence and the rebukes of the USSR – which warned that the MLF could have "grave and perhaps irreparable consequences" – Washington modified the first version of its draft treaty.[19] The original clause prohibiting transfer of control was retained, but Article IV of the revised version specified that "control" understood the "means, right or ability to fire nuclear weapons without the concurrent decision of an existing nuclear-weapon State". This clause still did not satisfy the USSR since, in the context of non-transfer of control, the expression "or to any association of non-nuclear-weapon States" was conserved, which left the door wide open for the implementation of any theoretical "European option". There was even talk in some circles of a "federal nuclear option" which, from the standpoint of international law, raised the question of the right of succession of States.

By the end of 1966, discussions were no longer anything more than artificial. Washington had decided, within the context of a nuclear-sharing strategy, to go no further than to create the McNamara Committee, which was transformed, at the close of the North Atlantic Council meeting in December 1966, into the Nuclear Planning Group (NPG). The federal nuclear option was no longer a possibility. But it was not until 24 August 1967 that the United States and the USSR tabled two identical[20] but separate drafts of Articles I and II of the NPT. These two articles constitute the body of the treaty:

- Article I
  Each nuclear-weapon State Party to the Treaty undertakes not to transfer to any recipient whatsoever nuclear weapons or other nuclear explosive devices or control over such weapons or explosive devices directly or indirectly; and not in any way to assist, encourage or induce any non-nuclear-weapon State to manufacture or otherwise acquire nuclear weapons or other nuclear explosive devices or control over such weapons or explosive devices.

- Article II
  Each non-nuclear-weapon State Party to the Treaty undertakes not to receive the transfer from any transferor whatsoever of nuclear weapons or other nuclear explosive devices or of control over such weapons or explosive devices directly or indirectly; not to manufacture or otherwise acquire nuclear weapons or other nuclear explosive devices; and not to seek or receive any assistance in the manufacture of nuclear weapons or other nuclear explosive devices.

No definition of what constitutes a "nuclear weapon" is given anywhere in the Treaty, unlike the Treaty of Tlatelolco which includes a definition under Article 5. The reason relates essentially to the difficulty encountered at the time concerning the request of the non-nuclear-weapon States not to be left ignorant of progress in peaceful nuclear explosions. The Treaty of Tlatelolco prohibited any device capable of liberating its energy in an uncontrolled way[21], whereas the Atomic Energy Act of the United States based the definition of a nuclear weapon on the "presumed intent" to develop such a weapon. Thus, according to Willrich, "the Plowshare devices can be excluded from the definition of a nuclear weapon under American law, but appear to be covered under the Treaty of Tlatelolco".[22] It should be added that, according to Article 18 of the Tlatelolco Treaty, States were permitted to use nuclear explosions for peaceful purposes under some circumstances. In practice, however, most States subsequently adopted the position that it was not possible to distinguish between explosions for peaceful purposes and explosions for military purposes. This interpretation would be confirmed in the text of the NPT.

Article I of the NPT does not forbid the pursuit of cooperative nuclear programs between nuclear-weapon States, except of course that it does not allow the direct transfer of nuclear weapons or nuclear devices. Neither delivery systems nor propulsion systems are covered under the Treaty. On 14 March 1968, the u.s. State Department declared that nuclear propulsion systems for maritime vessels did not fall under the Treaty, adding that a nuclear-propelled submarine was not a "weapon". Consequently, nothing in the Treaty "would prohibit the provision of nuclear fuel for this purpose".[23]

Article II is very clear on the form of assistance or aid that non-nuclear-weapon States may receive. No assistance may be received in the manufacture of nuclear devices for military purposes, but there is no caveat on assistance in the development of nuclear energy for peaceful purposes on condition that non-nuclear-weapon States accept the safeguards of the International Atomic Energy Agency (IAEA) as prescribed in Article III. The first version of the u.s. draft specified that the non-nuclear-weapon States party to the Treaty should undertake not to "grant such assistance" to third-party States as would enable them to manufacture nuclear weapons. In this regard, the co-authors of the Treaty have made various statements designed to carry "some weight"[24], but neither these statements nor the official texts of the articles cover the assistance that non-signatories, such as Israel and South Africa, might elect to provide to each other. Similarly, each non-nuclear-weapon State party to the Treaty undertakes not to seek or receive any assistance whatsoever in the acquisition or manufacture of nuclear weapons or other nuclear explosive devices, but there is no mention of the assistance that a non-nuclear-weapon State might contemplate receiving from a non-signatory State. Article III (2) commits States party to the Treaty not to export forbidden items, such as source or special fissionable material, unless they would be subject to safeguards, but there are no provisions for everything that falls below this threshold. Efforts were made subsequently to eliminate these loopholes through directives from the Zangger Committee and the London Group.

The problem of nuclear safeguards addressed in Article III was only resolved following lengthy negotiations in the Eighteen-Nation Committee. It was not until 18 January 1968 that the United States and the USSR tabled their separate but identical[25] drafts on the provisions of Article III of the NPT. Following minor modifications to these drafts, a third set of identical but distinct[26] drafts were tabled on 11 March 1968. The final text of the NPT was tabled in Geneva on 10 June 1968, the UN General Assembly gave its support on 12 June, and the NPT was opened for signature by the States on 1 July. The Treaty entered into force on 5 March 1970. Table 6 provides a brief summary of the main steps leading to the signing of the NPT.

Table 6
List of Main Resolutions and Proposals on NPT

RESOLUTIONS:

Res. 1665 (XVI)	Irish proposal on non-dissemination of nuclear weapons, 4 December 1965.
Res. 224 (CD)	Resolution of the Commission on Disarmament on "Associated Measures", 15 June 1965.
Res. 2028 (XX)	Eight-Nation proposal on principles governing the development of the NPT, 23 November 1965.
Res. 2373 (XXII)	UN General Assembly (UNGA) approves draft treaty, 12 June 1968.
Res. 255 of UN Security Council	Resolution of Security Council on safeguards, 19 June 1968.

PROPOSALS:

United States:	First draft treaty containing Articles I and II ENDC/152 (17 August 1965).
Italy:	Fanfani Proposal ENDC/157 (14 September 1965).
USSR:	Soviet draft treaty submitted to UNGA A/5976 (24 September 1965).
United States:	Second draft treaty containing Articles I and II ENDC/152/Add.1 (21 March 1966).
Eight-Nation Memorandum:	ENDC/178 (19 August 1966).
U.S. and USSR:	Separate but identical draft treaties containing Articles I and II ENDC/192 (24 August 1967). ENDC/193 (24 August 1967).
U.S. and USSR:	Separate but identical draft treaties, specifically on Articles I, II and III ENDC/192/Rev.1 (18 January 1968). ENDC/193/Rev.1 (18 January 1968).
U.S. and USSR:	Final draft of Non-Proliferation Treaty ENDC 225/(Annex A) (11 March 1968).
Treaty Opened for Signature:	1 July 1968
Entry into Force:	5 March 1970 (in Canada)
States Party to the Treaty on 31 Dec. 1987:	134

In its final form, Article III consists of four paragraphs. In the first paragraph, each non-nuclear-weapon State Party to the Treaty undertakes to accept safeguards as set forth in an agreement with the IAEA. These safeguards pertain to the peaceful nuclear activities of the said State. Paragraph 2 of Article III reads as follows:

Each State party to the Treaty undertakes not to provide: (a) source or special fissionable material, or (b) equipment or material especially designed or prepared for the processing, use or production of special fissionable material, to any non-nuclear-weapon State for peaceful purposes, unless the source or special fissionable material shall be subject to the safeguards required by this article.

It took several years before the drafters of the treaty agreed on the true meaning of Article III 2b. Not until the Zangger Committee and the London Group met were the new directives issued.[27] Paragraph 3 of Article III states that the system of safeguards should not hamper the economic or technological development of the Parties to the Treaty. Paragraph 4 covers the issue of signing safeguard agreements with the IAEA, either individually or together with other States, and was aimed primarily at ensuring consistency between the safeguard requirements of the IAEA and EURATOM.

The difficulties encountered in developing Article III stemmed simultaneously from East-West problems, divergent viewpoints within the Atlantic Alliance and the pressures of the nuclear industry. Lawrence and Larus claim that, during the period of negotiations between 1965 and 1967, "neither the United States nor the USSR viewed the implementation of a system of safeguards or verification to be an issue of major importance".[28] This judgement is not totally accurate. According to Pendley, Scheinman and Butler, Soviet reticence concerning safeguards began to dissipate in 1963 and by 1965 was replaced with open support.[29]

In this context, all authors agree that it was the West's sacrifice of the MLF that drew Soviet support for the draft NPT.[30] Whether the USSR was more preoccupied at the time with nuclear proliferation *per se* or with the risks of German vengeance still remains an open question. But there is no doubt that profound changes were taking place in the international system at the time. Many authors believe that the Chinese factor was conducive to the softening of the Soviet position on safeguards in 1963, since Moscow expected that the first Chinese nuclear explosion[31] would take place in 1964. In that same year, the MLF proposal unleashed controversy within the Alliance. In addition, the United States started conducting more extensive

military operations against North Vietnam following the breakdown
of the truce at the end of 1965. The Soviet-American deadlock was
broken in 1965, and undoubtedly the two elements which weighed
most heavily in the Moscow-Washington balance were the MLF and
Vietnam.

In mid-1967, a second deadlock was broken between Moscow and
Washington[32] on the issue of Article III. It was due to a *quid pro quo*,
to borrow the expression used by Willrich[33], whereby in exchange
for Soviet agreement on a generalized system of nuclear safeguards
applicable to non-nuclear-weapon States party to the Treaty, EURATOM
would reach agreement with the IAEA in conformity with the terms
of Article III (4) of the NPT. This provision was approved by the
North Atlantic Council and, according to Kramish, was presented to
the EURATOM nations as a *fait accompli*.[34] Actually, the United States
had previously insisted on the formulation "equivalent nuclear safeguards", which everyone understood to mean those of EURATOM.
Throughout 1966, the USSR repeated to anyone who would listen
that only the "exclusive safeguards" of the IAEA[35] would be acceptable
under the NPT, although the 1965 Soviet draft contained no wording
to this effect.

The evolution of U.S. policy was rather lengthy and laborious. The
NPT was largely the result of the efforts of ACDA. Within the State
Department, the efforts of the Bureau of European Affairs were
obviously aimed at promoting integration of the European community and consequently at protecting the system of safeguards developed by EURATOM. Early in 1967, Secretary of State Rusk stated that
although the United States had no problem as far as the credibility
of EURATOM safeguards were concerned, some signatories[36] would
perhaps not be too happy "to have to depend on safeguards developed internally by EURATOM".[37] Pendley, Scheinman and Butler credit
President Johnson with breaking the American-Soviet deadlock in
mid-1967. Faced with an increasing barrage of internal criticism over
the failure of the United States in Vietnam, President Johnson apparently decided to yield to the demands of Moscow. The Soviets judged
that the EURATOM safeguards were aimed at camouflaging the
vengeful intentions of the FRG and constituted nothing more than a
system of self-inspection.

The FRG found Johnson's about-face difficult to accept. In a note
dated 25 March 1966, the FRG strongly stated that it intended to
protect the special status of EURATOM, even though it was not opposed
to the safeguards established by the IAEA governing the supply of
nuclear materials to third-party States, on condition that the same
rule would apply to all nations. Six months later, in September 1966,

Czechoslovakia, Poland and the GDR offered to submit all their nuclear installations to IAEA control provided that the FRG would do the same. At the time, the FRG found this proposal unacceptable, for it refused to recognize the GDR. Without really believing in the feasibility of the idea, the FRG proposed that Western and Eastern States should make unilateral declarations to their respective alliances to the effect that they would not seek to acquire nuclear weapons, and that their commitments would be subject to "adequate control". This initiative was to be lost in the mists of time.

These dealings were doubtless painful at the level of East-West and trans-Atlantic relations, and they led to two forms of particular discrimination. The first resulted from the asymmetry of obligations between the nuclear-weapon and non-nuclear-weapon States. The non-nuclear-weapon States had to submit all their nuclear activities to IAEA safeguards, while the nuclear-weapon States were subjected to no such control. Western States were reticent for a number of reasons. The first, and most obvious, was that the USSR had no intention at the time of accepting the IAEA safeguards. Why should the United States and Great Britain, not to mention France which had not participated in the negotiations, be prepared to accept two different standards for nuclear-weapon States? Second, and equally obvious, why should nuclear industries and governments submit to servitudes on uranium imports? The transactions between the United States and Great Britain at the time were free from any kind of control. This was not the case for France, since Canada, much to the displeasure of the Canadian nuclear industry, had decided in 1965 to impose safeguards on uranium exports. For France, the situation was especially dramatic.

The meeting between de Gaulle and Pearson in January 1964 ended in bitter failure. According to some sources, de Gaulle threw Pearson a line by observing that their respective countries had many "national interests" in common. Pearson replied that Canada was, in fact, above all an "internationalist" country.[38] The gulf between de Gaulle's appeal to Franco-Canadian bilateralism and the multilateralist response of Pearson was not conducive to possible sales of Canadian uranium to France, particularly in light of Paul Martin's opposition to nuclear proliferation which, in practice, constituted opposition to the grand designs of Paris. There were also a number of other reasons which militated against such nuclear collaboration. For example, Stephen Roman, the President of Denison Mines, was from the same constituency as Pearson.[39] Roman, a Catholic immigrant, had little support from Cabinet, and his proposal to export uranium to France was summarily dismissed.[40]

Both London and Washington were reluctant to accept the IAEA safeguards. But two of the main allies, Japan and the FRG, stated that they would adhere to the Treaty on the express condition that the civil nuclear installations of the nuclear-weapon States would also be subject to IAEA safeguards. In early 1967, President Johnson acceded to the wishes of the allies. It was not until December 1985 that the Soviets agreed to accept this same condition.

The European nations, which mostly supported the principle of European integration, were affected by a second form of discrimination. It occurred as a result of U.S. support for the principle of universally agreed safeguards advocated by the Soviets, and the allies were thus obliged to bend to Moscow's demands. The U.S. position remained substantially firm, although some flexibility was displayed. The State Department was prone to favour the EURATOM system of safeguards, and the Atomic Energy Commission considered that there was no conflict between the two parallel systems of safeguards. The State Department finally concluded that the two systems were "equally effective".[41] Ultimately, a compromise was reached: the EURATOM system of safeguards would have to meet the control requirements of the IAEA. In other words, EURATOM could maintain its own control system provided it met the standards of the IAEA. The final American-Soviet compromise was thus to provide for the negotiation of a separate agreement between the IAEA and EURATOM in Article III.4. The fact that a nuclear-weapon State was part of EURATOM posed particular problems. It was for this reason that EURATOM-IAEA negotiations only started in 1971. EURATOM ratified the NPT in 1975, and Japan followed suit in 1976.

Before discussing the specific problem of nuclear safeguards, two other important elements of the negotiations should be mentioned: the issue of security assurances, and the issue of peaceful nuclear explosions. Concerning security assurances, some States made significant efforts to induce nuclear-weapon States to protect the security of non-nuclear-weapon States against the possible threat of the use of, or recourse to, nuclear weapons by adversary States. The issue was resolved, however, only outside the Treaty by the adoption of Resolution 255 on 19 June 1968 by the UN Security Council. The assurances embodied in this Resolution[42] were worth no more or less than those pertaining to any Security Council resolution. In other words, the assurances depended on the degree of unanimity reached by permanent members of the UN Security Council on actions to be taken or coercive measures to be adopted under Chapter VII of the Charter. It is worth noting also, that there is no accepted definition of aggression within the UNO.

The deliberations in Geneva were very clear on this point. No nuclear-weapon State wanted to be committed to act in a prescribed way in situations for which it was impossible to predict all the outcomes. Secretary of State Rusk hastened to declare before the u.s. Foreign Affairs Committee that such a resolution would involve no "additional commitments" over and above those which existed at the time.[43] In 1966, when negotiations took place in the Eighteen-Nation Committee, the USSR proposed that a clause be inserted in the Treaty to the effect that nuclear-weapon States could come to the aid of non-nuclear-weapon States Party to the Treaty which did not have nuclear weapons based on their territories.[44] This proposal was never followed up.

As for peaceful nuclear explosions, the United States, along with other Western nations, quickly pointed out that it was technically impossible to distinguish between such explosions and others conducted for military purposes. Even research and development in this area was prohibited by the provisions of the Treaty, at least for non-nuclear-weapon States Party to the Treaty. This aspect of the Treaty could be considered as discriminatory or otherwise, depending on one's point of view concerning the benefits of explosions conducted for peaceful purposes. Ideally, nuclear-weapon States would provide the IAEA with a data bank and an effective means for managing a service on nuclear explosive devices for peaceful purposes. Aside from the fact that such an arrangement could constitute some form of transfer of nuclear technology, which was categorically forbidden by the Treaty, no nation appeared to be interested in the possibility apart from Japan, which attempted to show that such devices for peaceful applications could technically exist.[45] As indicated in Chapter 9, a number of impressive experiments were conducted by the USSR in this area. For its part, the United States leaned towards the view that such experiments were not productive and that the dangers were greater than the benefits which could accrue. Although the question remained theoretically open, it was definitely closed from a political standpoint.

EVOLUTION OF INTERNATIONAL NUCLEAR SAFEGUARDS

The legal structure underlying the system of nuclear safeguards had its roots in a number of initiatives: the Charter which constituted the IAEA, the system of safeguards developed by the IAEA in fulfilling its mandate, the legal provisions of the NPT and the master agreement that had to be signed with the IAEA by States party to the Treaty.

This latter master agreement was complemented with a supplementary secret agreement between the signatory States and the Agency.

The procedural process required that a State first sign the Treaty, then ratify it, subsequently sign an agreement with the IAEA, and finally enter into a supplementary agreement which, from a technical standpoint, was the most important element. Efforts were made to standardize the requirements of this supplementary agreement through the use of a common form. Unfortunately, technical descriptions necessarily varied from one country to another, which presented obstacles in the path towards standardization.

The terms "proliferation" and "non-proliferation" did not appear in the statutes of the IAEA. The Agency was established as a result of the Eisenhower "Atoms for Peace" proposal, and its aim is to promote peaceful applications of atomic energy and ensure that potential applications will not be diverted to military purposes. The IAEA was established as an autonomous organization. Although it formed part of the family of international organizations, it was not established as one of the specialized institutions of the United Nations. It developed numerous cooperative agreements with both intergovernmental organizations[46] and specialized United Nations institutions[47], not to mention the 19 Non-Governmental Organizations[48] (NGO) which were accorded an advisory status.

Although the IAEA is the official watchdog of the Non-Proliferation Treaty, the Tlatelolco Treaty (OPANAL – Organismo para la Proscripción de las Armas Nucleares en América Latina y el Caribe – Agency for the Prohibition of Nuclear Weapons in Latin America) and the Rarotonga Treaty (de-nuclearization of the South Pacific), its mandate is of broader scope, embracing all aspects of the development of atomic energy for peaceful purposes. For this reason, the structure of nuclear safeguards applied by the IAEA is extremely complex. These safeguards form a tangled web of rights and responsibilities which need to be harmonized, respected and, in some cases, balanced.

The first system of safeguards developed by the IAEA dates back to the Information Circular (INFCIRC/26) of 1961. This document resulted from the lengthy negotiations which took place between April 1958 and January 1961. The negotiations were particularly fierce, and pitted the relatively homogeneous Western group of seventeen nations against the Eastern countries led by the USSR and supported by India. Some nations maintained that the IAEA safeguards were essential and should be supported by a tight control system. Others held that cooperation should be based on a simple promise of non-diversion of atomic energy to military purposes, arguing that the principle of on-site inspection violated the territorial sovereignty of States. The first set of IAEA safeguards did not, therefore, result from consensus but from a majority decision by its Board of Governors.[49]

This original set of safeguards was subsequently revised on two occasions, first in 1966 to cover reprocessing facilities, and again in 1968 to include nuclear fuel plants. The revised version (INFCIRC/66/Rev.2) is still valid today. It encompasses "all main facilities of the nuclear fuel cycle except enrichment plants"[50] using gaseous diffusion. Some gas centrifuge facilities were, however, subject to safeguards.[51] At the Board of Governors meeting in February 1982, the Director General of the IAEA indicated that INFCIRC/66/Rev.2 was open to review.

In order to fulfil its obligations under the NPT, the IAEA prepared its famous Blue Book (INFCIRC/153/Amended) which was adopted by its Board of Governors in 1970. Debate still continues over the relative merits of the two documents, INFCIRC/66 and INFCIRC/153. Some authors claim that the definitions of "objective technical conditions" specified in the first document are not as stringent as those specified in the second.[52] The safeguards contained in the IAEA INFCIRC/66 would thus be applicable to States non-signatory to the NPT, while those specified in INFCIRC/153 would only apply to States party to the NPT.[53] Other authors contend that the system of IAEA safeguards should be dynamic in nature.[54]

The final word likely belongs to L.W. Herron, Director of the Legal Services Division of the IAEA in 1982, who declared that "the Director General would not recommend to the Board a new agreement which did not contain provisions additional to those expressly foreseen by INFCIRC/66". These new provisions would include a formal declaration of non-diversion of nuclear materials to explosive applications, the introduction of confinement and monitoring techniques, the signing of supplementary agreements, express provisions for legal authority covering future generations of fissionable materials, provisions governing transfer of technology and heavy water, and so on. In short, despite the differing legal implications of INFCIRC/66 and INFCIRC/153, the IAEA made a systematic attempt to ensure consistency of contractual commitments irrespective of the legal structure which governed them.

Negotiations continued within the IAEA, due mainly to the sustained efforts of Japan and the FRG, often in conflict with States that were still committed to the INFCIRC/66 safeguards. According to R. Imai, it was critical to win the support of the United Kingdom. As Imai stated:

The "Findings of the Safeguards Committee" as reported to, and later adopted by, the Agency's Board of Governors was thus a revision of the original safeguards system. Although it was not called a revision, and although no one pronounced the decease of [INFCIRC/66 Rev.2], it was clearly understood that all of the safeguards agreements to be entered into the IAEA under the NPT would be based on the new concept.[55]

Japanese negotiator Imai wondered whether the drafters of the Treaty had the IAEA INFCIRC/66 safeguards in mind when they insisted that such safeguards be embodied in the Treaty itself. This question remains unanswered, but the system of safeguards was renegotiated at length and finalized in INFCIRC/153. The document was developed in accordance with the "systems analysis" approach advocated by the German Nuclear Centre at Karlsruhe, which laid emphasis on Material Balance Areas (MBA), Key Measurement Points (KMP) and the differences between material imports and exports, namely Material Unaccounted For (MUF). This systems approach afforded the advantage of minimizing the human factor, which many States sought to eliminate since they considered that the IAEA system of safeguards was no more than a pretext for industrial espionage.

Paragraph 28 of INFCIRC/153 called for the "timely detection" of diversion of "significant quantities" of nuclear materials. In other words, it was aimed at "deterrence of diversion by creating the risk of early detection". In 1970, the IAEA was in no position to define either the period that would be considered "timely", or the amount of material that would be considered "significant". In 1975, the IAEA created a Permanent Advisory Group on Safeguards charged with addressing these problems. Enormous progress was made through the implementation of a computer-based continuous detection system, known under the name of Recover.[56]

These developments notwithstanding, the Nuclear Suppliers Group met between 1975 and 1977 in part to eliminate any discriminatory practices in the application of safeguards. Even in September 1974, the list of nuclear materials subject to IAEA safeguards had been significantly expanded following the publication of INFCIRC 209 of the Zangger Committee and the guidelines of the London Group, which comprised the nuclear supplier countries. These initiatives were endorsed by the IAEA towards the end of 1977 and published in INFCIRC 254 in January 1978. The Guidelines for Nuclear Transfers (GNT) developed by the London Group reflected essentially the provisions previously established by the Zangger Committee, but they went much further, particularly in respect of so-called sensitive technologies. These guidelines served to define the explicit content of Article III (2b) of the NPT.

Thus, the Non-Proliferation Treaty which exists today is no longer the treaty that many States thought they had signed in 1968. In the first place, INFCIRC/66 was renegotiated. Then the Zangger Committee proposed a new list of materials which would be subject to safeguards. Finally, in 1978, the IAEA adopted the list of additional materials developed by the London Group during the course of its meetings held between 1975 and 1977. The Treaty has remained in a state of continual evolution ever since, and most of the loopholes have been eliminated one by one. This surely is indicative of the increasing maturity of the international community. Furthermore, the London Group has allowed States non-signatory to the Treaty, such as France, to participate in the development of a new international order.

CANADA AND NUCLEAR NON-PROLIFERATION

Canadian policy on non-proliferation was at once firm, yet flexible and versatile. Firm, in that Ottawa believed it contrary to Western security interests for other nations as technologically advanced as Canada to acquire independent nuclear weapons. Flexible, in that Canada recognized the difficulties posed by the MLF within the Atlantic Alliance, and versatile, in that when it became apparent that all her demands could not logically be satisfied, she finally supported the draft treaty tabled in Geneva by the superpowers. Canada's efforts were aimed as much at the prevention of weapons proliferation within the alliances as at their proliferation between States.

Canada, the MLF and Non-Proliferation

One of the most thorny problems that faced Canada was the issue of vertical proliferation within the Atlantic Alliance. In 1964, the question of Canada's acquisition of nuclear warheads under U.S. control to meet her NORAD and NATO commitments was resolved. The Diefenbaker Government was brought down over this issue in 1963 and, during the electoral campaign[57], Pearson's Liberals maintained that Canada should respect her prior commitments.

Canada's 1964 decision to honour her commitments towards the United States was taken during the period of the MLF negotiations. At the time, Canada did not appear to be particularly preoccupied with any objections raised by other States in respect of her foreign policy. On 5 January 1964, Prime Minister Pearson declared before the House of Commons that the Government had no intention of accepting "a nuclear role that would make Canada a nuclear power". Canada's acceptance of u.s. nuclear warheads should, in no way, be construed as a move towards nuclear proliferation. Yet Pearson was not in favour of the MLF proposal, considering that it would increase the risks of vertical proliferation within NATO by providing other Western allies with the means of acquiring nuclear weapons, under so-called "double-key" control, to meet the needs of Western defence.

The MLF proposal represented a quantitative and qualitative leap of gigantic proportions in comparison with the proposal made in the late 1950s to deploy tactical nuclear weapons on FRG territory. At the time, the range of such tactical nuclear weapons extended only to the territories of the Eastern European nations, and the territory of the Soviet Union was not threatened. On the other hand, the MLF concept linked the FRG, for the first time in its history, with a weapon system that could deliver a mortal blow against the Soviet Union from the depths of the sea. Admittedly, the threat to Soviet territory was posed several years earlier by the Thor and Jupiter missiles which were installed in Turkey, Italy and the United Kingdom. These missiles had been installed to counter the "missile gap" perceived by the United States following the Soviet launch of Sputnik I in 1957. For whatever reasons, the Western missile systems were dismantled following the Cuban missile crisis. In all events, the Soviets took a very dim view of the prospect of European collaboration with the United States under the MLF proposal to install nuclear missile systems on European soil that would be capable of reaching Soviet territory. In the early 1980s, the very same scenario reappeared when the United States introduced Pershing and cruise missiles into Western Europe. This action served to bring the USSR back to the negotiating table and, after lengthy and painful debate within the Atlantic Alliance, the bilateral INF agreements were finally signed in Washington in December 1987, which in turn led to the INF (Intermediate-range Nuclear Forces) Treaty which was ratified in May and June 1988.

Canada and the United States reached an important compromise on the MLF in Hyannis Port in May 1963 at the time of the first official meeting between President Kennedy and Prime Minister Pearson. The communique issued by the two heads of State at the conclusion of their meeting stated that they would "work together to demonstrate their belief in the Atlantic concept". The records are more enlightening: "Canada would not do or say anything which would make progress on the MLF difficult". From the outset, Canada had mortgaged her position. It was nevertheless an agreement between heads of State.[58] Neither Burns in Geneva nor the Disarmament Division in Ottawa seemed to be overly affected by this agreement-in-principle between Washington and Ottawa.

All this happened as if the matter of Canada's acquisition of nuclear weapons had largely been decided on the basis of internal policy considerations, which were then totally forgotten when it was decided subsequently to study non-proliferation from an international standpoint. One wonders whether, in the absence of the Hyannis Port agreement, Canada would have supported the argument before the Eighteen-Nation Committee in Geneva that the MLF did not involve some form of nuclear proliferation. Since Canada had just acquired nuclear weapons under a formula of dual control, it would have been difficult for her, even if she had so wanted, to support a radically different position in respect of her European allies. Canada could not adopt a double standard in this matter but, at the same time, she was under no obligation regarding the MLF. Canada found an elegant solution to this dilemma by simply stating that: "the Prime Minister has indicated that Canada is not interested in adding to existing responsibilities and commitments".[59] The adoption of this position ended any possible participation by Canada in the MLF, despite Canada's insistence in Geneva that the MLF proposal did not constitute some form of proliferation.

Canada's position was essentially pro-NATO and anti-MLF, and it was sustained right up to the time of the signing of the nuclear Non-Proliferation Treaty. First, Canada stated that although she had sufficient capability to develop her own nuclear weapons, she had renounced this option under the framework of her commitments towards NATO and NORAD. Canada thus moved towards becoming the lead nation that could "play a useful independent role as a middle power".[60] Second, Canada would support the principles embodied in the Irish Resolution which she believed were fundamental to any non-proliferation policy. Canada would dissociate herself from the famous "European option" as soon as it appeared possible to do so without offending the United States. Third, Canada would fully support the suggestion for greater sharing of nuclear responsibilities within the Atlantic Alliance. There would be no further talk of the MLF, but rather of the constitution of a planning committee or, as McNamara called it, a "select committee" which, in December 1966, would become the NATO Nuclear Planning Group.

By the summer of 1964, the Disarmament Delegation in Geneva was fully aware of Soviet manoeuvres to prevent any form of nuclear proliferation through military alliances, either direct or indirect. The concern was that Moscow would support or initiate draft resolutions in the UN aimed at blocking the Western proposal. In Geneva it was held that such resolutions "would prohibit not just MLF, but other NATO sharing arrangements as well, and the West would have to oppose them firmly".[61] One year later, just one week before the first U.S. draft treaty was tabled in Geneva, Paul Martin sent a letter to the High Commission in London observing that the U.S. draft treaty "was not entirely free from an element of dissemination"[62], and that efforts should be aimed at preventing dissemination rather than attempting to legislate for eventualities which were after all some distance away and which might never materialize. The need to maintain Western unity was also of paramount concern to External Affairs' Minister Martin who maintained that potential NATO solutions should not be pre-judged. In addition, Martin contended that if the responsibility-sharing plans came to fruition it would be up to the member nations to demonstrate that there would be no dissemination.

Meanwhile, in early 1965 in Geneva, Burns clearly defined his position. In a memorandum to the Secretary of State for External Affairs, entitled "Non-dissemination: 1965 or Never", General Burns posed the essential question: What is stalling the negotiations on non-proliferation? In his view, as he wrote on 23 February 1965, "it is the U.S. plan to create the MLF within NATO". For this reason, he urged Paul Martin to give Canada's non-dissemination objectives precedence over those pertaining to the MLF. He was well aware, however, of the problems that such an approach might create in Canada's relations with the FRG. He therefore proposed the formation of a strategic council within the Atlantic Alliance consisting of the three nuclear powers and the FRG "which would control the targeting and use of nuclear weapons in the European theatre". In addition, he suggested that the MLF proposal be set aside until March 1966, by which time the negotiations on non-proliferation would either have failed or succeeded.

The ideas of Burns were really not new. On 17 November 1964, in a lengthy telegram to the main Canadian missions abroad, the Department of External Affairs insisted on the need to avoid a crisis within the Atlantic Alliance, to adopt a policy of "no confrontation with, or exclusion of, France", to "devise ways for a greater sharing in nuclear strategy that would allow Germany to play an appropriate part in decisions involving German national security" and to encourage the Allies to assume a greater share in the military costs of the Atlantic Alliance in return for a greater involvement in the strategic planning process.

At the North Atlantic Council meeting held in Ottawa in May 1963, it was decided that the British V-bombers as well as three Polaris submarines would be assigned to SACEUR whose Second-in-Command would be a European. At its June 1964 meeting, the North Atlantic Council decided to integrate its Nuclear Planning Group within the Standing Group. This decision was taken by the NATO Military Committee, and was aimed at encouraging other allied nations to play a greater role in the development of strategy within the Atlantic Alliance. In a telegram dated 17 November, the Department of External Affairs raised the following questions:

a   Would France consider assigning its independent nuclear forces to SACEUR on the same basis as the present USA and British forces?
b   Could the present advisory functions of the nuclear Deputy be broadened to include responsibility for nuclear co-ordination and planning?
c   In Ottawa it was agreed that a small group of allied officers should participate as SACEUR representatives in strategic planning and targeting at Strategic Air Command HQ, Omaha. Could the USA contemplate ways of increasing allied participation in strategic nuclear planning so that major governments were given a more responsible role in overall NATO nuclear deterrent?
d   Could the Nuclear Committee, which to date has played a minor role within NATO, be used as the basis for Alliance strategic planning?

Evidently, Canada was highly preoccupied with the issues of nuclear responsibility-sharing within the Atlantic Alliance and the relative role that the FRG would play in a strategic planning group. The issue of the MLF was only secondary. In this context, there was even a suggestion that it might be best to rename the proposal. This same telegram stated that the formation of a regional defence group in which neither France nor Canada would participate would not be in Canada's interest. Burns' memorandum of February 1965 only reiterated some of the thinking within the Department of External Affairs. Even so, Burns' memorandum provoked profound objections, both from the European Affairs Bureau and the Defence Liaison Division.

A.R. Menzies of the Defence Liaison Division stressed that the United States had made every effort to make the Soviets understand the real purpose of the MLF proposal. He pointed out also that U.S. Ambassador Livingston Merchant had explained in depth the objectives of the proposal to the Canadian Government. Menzies contended that the MLF was only one of the obstacles that had to be overcome before agreement could be reached on a nuclear Non-Proliferation Treaty. His argument was very clever, and can be summarized as follows: If the Soviets truly believe that the MLF proposal poses a real threat of proliferation it would be in their interests to negotiate immediately and unceasingly. Yet the Soviets have put the proposal more or less on the back burner, and apparently feel no urgency to negotiate[63] ...

The European Affairs Bureau was clearly opposed to the formation of a strategic council consisting of the three nuclear powers with which the FRG would be associated, stressing that its nature was discriminatory. There was no assurance that Italy would not seek the same status as the FRG or that France would even participate. The MLF was only one component of the strategy of the Atlantic Alliance and the British were still thinking in terms of their ANF proposal. Moreover, the Bureau argued, the nature of the future European force, either multilateral (MLF) or multinational (ANF), remained to be decided. Rightly or wrongly, A.F. Hart laid stress on the vital coupling between Europe and the United States that would result from the formation of the MLF, which would "ensure a continuing American presence and influence in Western Europe".[64]

These reactions show clearly that there was no consensus on these issues within the Department. Overall, the Prime Minister and the Secretary of State for External Affairs were rather cool or even negative towards the MLF while General Burns was squarely opposed to it. The positions adopted by the European Affairs Bureau and the Defence Liaison Division were much closer to those held by Washington and its principal allies. Given the circumstances, it is not surprising that, at the North Atlantic Council meeting in December 1964, Canada argued that the only realistic position which could be adopted was to state that "the West neither engages in the dissemination of nuclear weapons nor hesitates to negotiate seriously to prevent it".

In 1965, the United States essentially abandoned its MLF proposal. The European option still remained open in the second U.S. draft of the NPT which was tabled in March 1966, but the outcome was predictable. Clearly, the only remaining hurdle to gaining full allied support for the U.S. draft was the question of greater sharing of nuclear responsibilities within the Atlantic Alliance. This matter was subsequently resolved towards the end of 1966, and paved the way for the tabling in Geneva in August 1967 of identical but separate draft treaties by the superpowers. Other problems remained to be resolved, as discussed in the following section. In face of Soviet insistence that the MLF proposal was radically incompatible with the

Non-Proliferation Treaty, it became clear that the MLF proposal had to be declared dead. All that remained was the matter of reaching agreement between Bonn and Washington.

For their part, the Canadians tried one last initiative. In early 1966 they informed the United States that they wanted the European nuclear option clause deleted from the draft treaty. The British were of the same mind. Nevertheless, this raised a problem. It was considered that the revised version of the u.s. draft contained one remaining loophole, namely the federal nuclear option. At issue was not just the question of a simple majority vote by a group of European States, but the whole matter of the rights of succession of States. Thus, if a State within a federation elected to renounce the use of nuclear weapons or destroy its nuclear arsenal, the federation would not be denied the use of its nuclear weapons since it would inherit this right of use from the State renouncing them. Remote and theoretical as this hypothesis appeared to be, it still caused concern in Ottawa. The Disarmament Division thus proposed that the u.s. text be amended to ensure that no nuclear power could cede control over its nuclear weapons to any other State or "association of States".[65] This, of course, definitely precluded the European nuclear option, but not the federal nuclear option.

At the time, the Americans were concerned with many other problems, chiefly the French announcement to withdraw from the NATO military structure in March 1966. The Americans viewed the federal nuclear option as quite unrealistic because all discussions at the time were essentially focused on the sharing of nuclear responsibilities within the Atlantic Alliance. Britain, however, along with other smaller European nations, was not far removed from Canada in its thinking. At the end of May, Ottawa and other capitals considered approaching Washington at the "working level" to induce the United States never, under any circumstances, to abandon its right of veto over its nuclear weapons. The representations were made to ACDA in Washington.[66] The proposals for Articles I and II were thus aimed at providing "a useful contribution towards overcoming the present impasse over the text of the Non-Proliferation Treaty".[67]

Canada went no further on the issue of vertical proliferation. Subsequently, events followed their normal course. The European nuclear option and the federal nuclear option fell into oblivion. In the summer of 1967, the two superpowers tabled their proposed texts on Articles I and II of the draft NPT. One year later, the Treaty was opened for signature of the States.

In 1968, Trudeau came into office in Ottawa. As noted in Chapter 6, this provided the occasion for an in-depth review of Canadian policy on disarmament and arms control. The events in Prague in 1968 put a temporary halt to attempts at *rapprochement* between the superpowers which had started at the June 1967 meeting between President Johnson and Soviet leader Kosygin. During 1969 and 1970 the main agenda items in East-West negotiations concerned progress under SALT, which started in Helsinki 1969, and the MBFR proposals which were appearing on the horizon. This was the climate in which the Department of External Affairs urged the Prime Minister's Office to invite Cabinet to ratify the Treaty on the Non-Proliferation of Nuclear Weapons.

In a letter dated 18 December 1968, the Secretary of State for External Affairs, Mitchell Sharp, reminded the Prime Minister that Cabinet had decided in July 1968 to sign the Treaty without any reservation. Ratification was, therefore, only a matter of procedure, and Sharp proposed that a statement be made in the House to this effect. The Prime Minister made a series of handwritten notes at the bottom of this letter. Trudeau reflected on the meaning of Article II of the Treaty which prohibits the transfer of nuclear weapons to non-nuclear-weapon States, and had difficulty understanding its implications for the Bomarc installations in Canada. If they were allowed under the Treaty, would it imply that the Soviets could install their own "Bomarcs" in Cuba? Should we not take advantage of this opportunity to ask the Americans to withdraw them from Canada? And what about our nuclear forces in Europe?[68]

On 28 January 1969, Sharp responded to Trudeau's queries[69], explaining that Article II of the Treaty did not conflict with the agreements reached with the United States on 27 September 1961 concerning Bomarc and on 12 June 1961 concerning the CF-101 Voodoos. Sharp contended that, under these agreements[70], ownership of the delivery vehicles remained under Canadian control while the nuclear warheads "remained in the custody of USA military units stationed in Canada specifically for that purpose". In the upper left portion of the page, Trudeau inscribed the scathing handwritten note cited in the epigraph to this Chapter: "Thank you very much. Now I understand. Non-proliferation is really not an obstacle to some proliferation". The Department of External Affairs subsequently judged that to provide any additional explanation to the Prime Minister would only serve to strengthen his conviction that the Non-Proliferation Treaty presented no obstacle to nuclear proliferation.[71] In April 1969, Canada announced the withdrawal of her nuclear strike force from Europe. In July 1984, the last remaining Genie nuclear air-to-air missiles were retired from Canadian fighter squadrons.

Canada's Input to the Treaty on the Non-Proliferation of Nuclear Weapons

Although some elements of Canadian policy in respect of the Nuclear Non-Proliferation Treaty were to change during the course of negotiations, the main thrust concerned the following: the need for a binding agreement; the requirement for reciprocity of obligations between nuclear-weapon and non-nuclear-weapon States; the technological benefits that non-nuclear-weapon States party to the Treaty should derive in exchange for their renunciation of nuclear weapons; elimination of the "loophole" of greatest concern, the "peaceful nuclear explosion" clause; and, the security assurances that, according to some, should be accorded by the nuclear powers to the States signatory to the Treaty. Ottawa also placed great emphasis on the need to provide for partial measures of disarmament[72], considering that the Non-Proliferation Treaty was only a first step on the path to disarmament.

As for procedures, Canada pressed to have the Geneva forum recognized as the focus for NPT negotiations. Canada assumed a posture that was unsympathetic to any proposals which might weaken the universal character of the Treaty. Ottawa thus opposed the proposal of the OAU, the Fanfani proposal and the FRG proposal which called for a renunciation of nuclear weapons by NATO and the Warsaw Pact. Some circles advocated that Canada, in concert with other nations such as Sweden and India, should assume responsibility on an informal basis for negotiations leading to a binding agreement in respect of the NPT. The argument for this initiative was based on the recognition that both Sweden and India had the potential to develop nuclear weapons and, by renouncing them, they could set an example for the rest of the world. Canada maintained the position, however, that it was up to the nuclear-weapon States themselves to define what should be included in their draft treaty proposals.

Despite this stance, and at the request of General Burns, Canada prepared a discussion paper[73] on the draft treaty which was tabled in 1965 before the Group of Four in Geneva – Canada, Italy, the United Kingdom and the United States. The United Kingdom also tabled a similar document, and both were subsequently discussed and submitted for comment to the North Atlantic Council.

In the early 1960s, the Western nuclear powers considered two alternative approaches to curbing nuclear proliferation. One approach would be to encourage voluntary declarations before the United Nations, such as the statement made by the United States[74] in 1964, while the other would encourage the negotiation of a binding international agreement along the lines of the 1961 Irish Resolution.

In May 1963, Canada declared her preference for the development of an international treaty[75] for five important reasons. First, voluntary declarations by States would not ensure the establishment of control and inspection systems. Second, there was some uncertainty as to whether other nations, such as the FRG and Italy, would adhere to such declarations. Third, Canada sought a balance of rights and responsibilities between nuclear-weapon States and non-nuclear-weapon States[76], which could not be guaranteed through mere declarations. Fourth, Canada viewed the Treaty as a first step in the process of establishing concrete measures for general disarmament, an objective that Canada had emphasized since 1962 when negotiations commenced within the Eighteen-Nation Committee in Geneva. Finally, the Treaty would constitute a confidence-building measure between nations and an instrument that would promote *détente* in East-West relations.

This was the context in which Canada opposed the u.s. proposal of January 1964 calling upon nations to make unilateral declarations to counter the threat of nuclear proliferation. This aspect of Canadian diplomacy had little influence. In December 1964, the United States tabled a modified version of the Irish Resolution before the UN which laid emphasis on renouncing "acquisition of nuclear weapons" rather than on "acquiring control" over such weapons. Equally, for the aforementioned reasons, Canada could not support the Fanfani proposal, which was tabled in Geneva against her wishes. In order to preserve Western unity, it was welcomed as a "positive" proposal deserving "careful study", but neither Burns nor the Legal Bureau of the Department of External Affairs could find any merit in it. Ottawa undertook a lengthy study of the proposal and reported its findings in a document published on 8 September 1965. The report was signed by a high-ranking official who had just returned from a foreign posting.

There was justifiable concern that the Italian proposal would be viewed as a disguised[77] attempt by the Americans to return to their former policy of "voluntary declarations". The legal validity of the Fanfani proposal was also called into question. Even if the "moratorium" proposed by the Italian Government carried legal weight, in that any such declaration by States would be recorded by the UN as a treaty obligation, the fact remained that such declarations would have had little practical impact on nuclear proliferation for the simple reason that, if any non-nuclear-weapon State acquired nuclear weapons, irrespective of whether it was a signatory to the declaration, all other States would have been free to repudiate their prior declarations. Moreover, there was no guarantee that other States would impose upon themselves the ten-year moratorium advocated by Italy and, depending on the timeframe adopted by the various States, there was a distinct possibility of encountering "a farrago of interlocking obligations of uncertain period". Further, the Fanfani proposal could have created a diversion from the objectives sought in a Non-Proliferation Treaty.

Canada approached the problem of non-proliferation from a global perspective. As early as 1965, Burns advocated the development of a Canadian draft treaty that could be submitted to the Group of Four to stimulate "discussion and reflection". The Disarmament Division threw its support behind Burns. In January 1965, the Department of External Affairs, following the staffing of Burns' proposal throughout its various branches and after consultations with Burns on proposed improvements, forwarded the resulting document to the Department of National Defence for comment, noting that it would provide "an indication of Canadian thinking at the official level".[78] On the same day, the text was forwarded to George Ignatieff, Canada's Ambassador to NATO. Shortly afterwards, consultations were held within the Group of Four, with Canada's allies in the Eighteen-Nation Committee and with other governments. In July, the Canadian draft treaty, dated 31 May 1965, was reviewed by NATO. The draft contained the following six points:

a   a non-dissemination agreement proper based on the Irish Resolution (1665/XVI) which constitutes the only norm of non-dissemination that has been generally accepted;

b   the extension of IAEA safeguards to the entirety of the non-military atomic programs of all signatories, nuclear and non-nuclear alike, the IAEA Statute being the only multilaterally agreed instrument which provides a means of verifying that nuclear materials and equipment are not being diverted to military purposes;

c   a collective security guarantee in accordance with which the nuclear powers would come to the assistance of unaligned and neutral non-nuclear States in the event they are subjected to nuclear attack;

d   a complaint procedure or mechanism which, together with safeguards under b), would provide a means of verifying compliance with commitments under a), especially with regard to the ban on relinquishing control of nuclear weapons to non-nuclear States;

e   provisions for implementation or continuance of the Treaty only in the advent of a sufficient degree of universality in adherence (it is conceivable nonetheless that the adherence of France and Communist China, as nuclear powers, would not be essential provided amongst the non-nuclear signatories were included all their possible clients); and

f   sanctions in order to dissuade States from ceasing to comply with their undertakings and a limited duration for the Treaty, the purpose of which being notably to encourage the nuclear States to make tangible progress towards nuclear disarmament within that period lest the non-nuclear States change their minds.[79]

By 1965, Canada had pretty much assumed responsibility for authoring the Treaty on Non-Proliferation of Nuclear Weapons. Paragraph a) was structured to accommodate the principles of the 1961 Irish Resolution, and all of the States present in Geneva came to support it. Paragraph b) was never really accepted in the Treaty, since only the non-nuclear-weapon States would be required to subject their entire civil programs to the safeguard controls of the IAEA. The nuclear-weapon States party to the Treaty nevertheless eventually accepted voluntary safeguards for their own civil programs. It took some considerable time before this occurred, and Canada sensed the pressures that would be imposed on the nuclear-weapon States. Canada again proved to be right as far as control mechanisms were concerned. The IAEA would become the watchdog of the Nuclear Non-Proliferation Treaty. On the other hand, the Treaty made no provision for a complaint procedure to ensure that the nuclear-weapon States would not transfer control over their nuclear weapons to any recipient whatsoever. The provisions concerning the responsibilities of the major powers in paragraph e) became, after some modification, Article VI of the NPT. In this regard, Canada remained steadfastly faithful to her principle of balanced rights and responsibilities for nuclear and non-nuclear powers.

It is of little matter that Canada deliberately courted the neutral and non-aligned countries in the Eighteen-Nation Committee. Pure good sense and equity obliged Canada to maintain this position in face of all opposition. In concert with the neutral and non-aligned countries, Canada pursued her objective of imposing at least moral responsibilities on the nuclear powers for disarmament and for halting of the arms race. The Treaty did not accommodate, however, Canada's desire to link these responsibilities to a specific timeframe. Canada was also unable to press her point of view on the issue of security assurances which, as we have seen, were not covered in the Treaty but settled through Resolution 255 of the UN Security Council.

In a working document dated 27 July 1965, Canada recorded most of the allied reaction to her draft treaty. It would be improper to divulge the names of the nations concerned, but most of them, with the exception of one non-aligned country, supported the need for safeguards under the control of the IAEA. For the nuclear powers, the problem of security assurances proved insurmountable. One of Canada's neighbours found the provisions of the Canadian draft treaty far too universal in scope, as though Canada were trying to solve all the problems at once. That was in 1965. Subsequently, as a result of pressures from other allies, such as the FRG and Japan, changing attitudes and evolving u.s.-Soviet relationships, the prejudices that remained towards Canada's forefront position gradually dissipated.

The three issues that Canada judged most important were: nuclear safeguards, security assurances for the non-nuclear-weapon signatory States and peaceful nuclear explosions. Only a brief account of the developments in respect of these three issues will be given here.

Nuclear Safeguards.   Some Canadian government departments were not overly enthusiastic about the clause on IAEA nuclear safeguards. In a memorandum to Paul Martin[80] dated 17 September 1965, it was mentioned that those responsible for Canada's atomic energy programs were reticent to accept IAEA safeguards "on the grounds that it would cause them additional work and would interfere with the carrying-out of the responsibilities placed on them by Parliament". Obviously, it must be recognized that these persons would take no commitment without first knowing the American reaction and without knowing whether the safeguard program of the IAEA would adversely affect Canadian trade interests. The argument of additional administrative work is, of course, the classical excuse invented by all departments to avoid following through on any decision which they dislike.

In April 1966, it was reported that the United States had postponed the tabling of Article III of the draft treaty on Canada's insistence.[81] If the United States had tabled its proposed text for Article III, Canada would have been forced to elaborate her position. The problem was not an easy one. The British had previously distributed their first draft proposal to the allies, and neither safeguards nor assurances were included. The British, in common with some groups in Canada, were opposed to the prospect that IAEA safeguards would be extended to cover their civil activities. First, because they knew that such a proposal would be unacceptable to the Soviets. Second, because neither the British nor the Americans wanted to renounce their option of "equivalent safeguards", for fear of stifling the possibility of an integrated Europe. Third, because no nation wanted to be exposed to unfair economic competition. Other problems stemmed from purely technical considerations – some nuclear installations served both peaceful and military purposes. Every State considered that the decision to declare which of its installations were devoted to military purposes and which were not was a prerogative of national sovereignty.

The Prime Minister of Canada, in a statement on 3 June 1965, reiterated that Canada's position was to apply safeguards to all transfers of nuclear materials or equipment to other nations. During the 1966 negotiations, Canada continued to support the principle of standardization of safeguards, specifically those of the IAEA, in preference to any other regional forms of safeguard, such as those exercised by EURATOM and which were supported by the U.S. State Department as well as the European allies. In 1967, the die was cast. On 2 December of that year, the United States announced its decision to accept the IAEA safeguards in respect of all its nuclear activities except those geared to national security. Two days later, the United Kingdom made a similar declaration.

Canada was not particularly happy with the discriminatory nature of Article III which required only the non-nuclear-weapon States to subject their entire peaceful activities to IAEA safeguards. Nevertheless, Canada took some comfort in stating that, in order to improve the prospects of treaty acceptance by the Third World, "we have put forward the idea that the Western nuclear powers make unilateral declarations of intent, separate but parallel to the treaty, voluntarily to accept safeguards on their own peaceful programs".[82] In short, Canada recognized that this was the best that could be obtained, and that when it came to a choice between a universal treaty that would be rejected by the Soviet Union and a treaty that imposed safeguards only on the non-nuclear-weapon States but which was supplemented with moral commitments from the nuclear powers, there could be no further hesitation.

Security Assurances.   Canada again had to compromise on the issue of security assurances to States exposed to the threat of nuclear weapons. The difficulties that this initiative could raise were reflected in the Canadian discussion paper on non-proliferation submitted on 31 May 1965: "the terms of the nuclear guarantee indirectly constitute a prohibition on the use of nuclear weapons against non-nuclear States which would in some measure run counter to the doctrine of nuclear deterrence on which Western defence posture is predicated."

In a speech before the UN General Assembly in December 1964, Irish Minister Aiken demanded that non-nuclear-weapon States be given security assurances irrespective of whether they were threatened by conventional or nuclear attack[83], in exchange for their adherence to the Treaty on Non-Proliferation of Nuclear Weapons. The Department of External Affairs consulted with the Department of National Defence on the policy to be adopted. In January 1965, the Department of National Defence stated that it found little merit in Aiken's proposal. The assurances would, at all events, be problematic: they could only be "vague", and the more they were "universal" the less they would be credible. In a document signed by Air Vice Marshall W.W. Bean on behalf of the Joint Chiefs of Staff, it was stated categorically: "it is unrealistic to believe that any nuclear power could be expected to accept any such blanket commitment".[84] Similar views were held by the British and the Americans. Burns, nevertheless, became the spokesman for the neutral and non-aligned nations on this issue. He returned to it frequently in his correspondence, insisting that it was an essential condition to induce acceptance by the other States of the commitments provided for in the Treaty.

In 1966, Canada was doubtful whether this clause could be incorporated in the body of the Treaty. At most, "it might be possible to produce a general article which would set out the principle".[85] The United States was prepared to go no further than to assure other States that they would receive vigorous u.s. support against "any threat of nuclear blackmail".[86] Canada continued, however, to support the position held by the neutral and non-aligned countries, even when they called for the adoption of the Kosygin proposal by which the nuclear powers would abstain from the use of nuclear weapons against States which did not allow the deployment of such weapons on their territories.[87]

Canada suggested to the u.s. Delegation that "instead of trying to defeat the new initiative outright we consider proposing alternative language which would note the importance of security assurances for nonaligned nations and urge the USA and the USSR to give this question serious consideration in private talks on the treaty which are now taking place".[88] In late 1966, in light of the general support accorded to the Kosygin proposal, Canada still considered this question sufficiently important to warrant the pursuit of "a formula embracing elements of both proposals".[89] Canada was prepared to vote in favour of such a resolution[90] before the First Committee of the United Nations, even if the United States were to oppose it.[91] Several months later, Ottawa appeared to have abandoned all hope in this regard, since the Kosygin proposal was considered "propagandist" and might lead some member nations of NATO to ban the deployment of nuclear weapons on their territories.[92]

Peaceful Nuclear Explosions. In 1966, Canada, as well as Sweden, considered "that an international body such as the IAEA should establish machinery to examine the feasibility of proposed projects involving peaceful nuclear explosion, to establish the appropriate price for the service, to act as an intermediary between the user country and the nuclear country providing the nuclear device, and to supervise the project to ensure that it served peaceful purposes only".[93] Canada's intent was clearly to make the benefits of peaceful nuclear explosions available, on a non-discriminatory basis, to the non-nuclear nations. Such benefits would include, for example, the use of nuclear devices for diverting rivers or excavating for minerals or oil.

This approach seemed especially relevant at the time since the u.s. draft treaty would permit underground nuclear testing under certain conditions without, of course, violating the Partial Test Ban Treaty. The Disarmament Division considered that the u.s. draft provided a "yawning loophole". There was, however, no consensus within the Government on the potential value of such explosions. The three aspects that Canada deemed important were recorded as follows:

a   We are impressed and alarmed by the possibility of a non-aligned peaceful nuclear explosion and believe that the possibility should be precluded at an early juncture;

b   It will nevertheless be important to safeguard Canada's economic interests and this might be done [by making] specific provision for the "loan" or "rental" of a nuclear device for economic purposes by and under the control of a nuclear State and/or an international control agency ... ;

c   The incorporation of such a provision would go a considerable way assuaging non-aligned concern at the "discriminatory" nature of a measure to preclude the nuclear option.[94]

In sum, the document essentially advocated a ban on the so-called peaceful nuclear option while at the same time recognizing it as a possibility under strictly controlled conditions. The Disarmament Division wondered whether it would be better to approach these issues during discussions on the Partial Test Ban Treaty since the question had been left open in the first versions of this Treaty but then subsequently turned down by common agreement between the major powers. In the fall of 1966, however, the United States decided that peaceful nuclear explosions should be banned. Instead, the Americans talked about "nuclear explosion services". It is difficult to know whether the u.s. reversal resulted from internal policy considerations or from consultations with the ussr. Both hypotheses are probably plausible and correct. But for whatever reason, the Americans came to the conclusion, just as the Canadians, that there was no technical distinction between a nuclear warhead and a nuclear device used for peaceful purposes.

On 25 October 1966, during debate in the First Committee, General Burns took the opportunity to spell out the Canadian position, stating: "We consider that the countries not possessing nuclear weapons should give up the right to conduct nuclear explosions for any purpose whatsoever".[95] Despite the closeness of the u.s. and Canadian positions, Canada wished to avoid any position that might be construed as influential or discriminatory, and thus supported the "internationalization of nuclear explosive services" where the IAEA, without controlling these services, would nevertheless act as an intermediary between the "donor" State and the "receiver" State. Burns spoke in these terms to the First Committee on 7 November 1966. Canada also sought universal application of the IAEA safeguards, although Burns did not specifically address this matter.

During the summer of 1967, Canada considered making a statement before the Eighteen-Nation Committee inviting the nuclear powers to do more, "through a separate but parallel agreement"[96], to make the peaceful "nuclear explosive service" available to all States. In February 1968, it was disclosed that the Disarmament Division had already developed an outline of an international agreement along these lines, following consultations with other departments and agencies of interest.[97] Canada continued to work on these issues, but it must be admitted that Article V of the Treaty remains as an empty shell even today, despite its assertion that "negotiations on this subject shall commence as soon as possible after the Treaty enters into force".

Canadian Application of Nuclear Safeguards

The main decisions taken by the Canadian Government on the Treaty on the Non-Proliferation of Nuclear Weapons are listed in Table 7. Apart from the decisions to sign and ratify the Nuclear Non-Proliferation Treaty, the two most striking Canadian decisions were taken in June 1965 and, 11 years later, in December 1976. In the June 1965 decision, Canada elected to subject all uranium export sales to safeguards.[98] In the December 1976 decision, Canada decreed that nuclear transfers abroad could only proceed if the recipient State was a signatory to the NPT or had accepted the "full scope safeguards" of the IAEA. Canada went as far as possible in this matter, and encouraged other States to follow her example.

Before reviewing the events that occurred between these two salient decisions, it is worth pausing briefly to focus on the six-month delay between signing and ratifying the Treaty. At first sight, this delay

Table 7
List of Main Canadian Decisions on Nuclear Safeguards and the NPT

3 June 1965	Safeguards imposed on foreign sales of uranium.
13 February 1968	Cabinet approves Article III of the NPT.
12 July 1968	Standing Committee on External Affairs and National Defence recommends that Cabinet adopt Treaty.
17 July 1968	Cabinet approves signing of the NPT.
23 July 1968	Canada signs the Treaty on the Non-Proliferation of Nuclear Weapons.
29 October 1968	Nuclear Non-Proliferation Treaty is tabled in the House.
19 December 1968	Cabinet approves ratification of the NPT.
8 January 1969	Instruments of ratification transmitted to Depositary Governments.
5 December 1974	Cabinet announces decision on nuclear safeguards.
22 December 1976	Cabinet announces decision on conditions governing foreign sales of Canadian nuclear supplies.

would appear excessive for a country that sought to be amongst the first to sign and ratify the Treaty in order to set an example and encourage other nations to follow suit. The records shed some light on the reasons for this delay.

When Mitchell Sharp tabled the Treaty before the House he stopped short of asking for its ratification, although the request for ratification was included in the statement that his officials had prepared for him. Actually, the Minister did not want debates to move too far away from defence issues, which were provoking intense controversy, and he undoubtedly preferred to settle them as a matter of priority. As well, the Minister was advised not to ratify the Treaty before one of the nuclear powers had done so, and until the IAEA had developed a standard set of nuclear safeguards. The first condition was not difficult to meet. On 27 November 1968, Britain became the first nuclear power to ratify the Treaty. The second condition appears to have been established following consultations with the Atomic Energy Control Board. Once the Board was satisfied, and following consultations with Atomic Energy of Canada Limited (AECL) and with various government departments (Industry, Trade and Commerce; Energy, Mines and Resources; Transport; Communications), the Legal Bureau informed the Department of External Affairs that all the obstacles had been removed from the path to ratification.

The records are quite voluminous concerning the events that occurred between June 1965 and December 1976. Canada's first obligation as a signatory of the Nuclear Non-Proliferation Treaty was to sign an agreement with the IAEA. Contrary to what one might have expected, certain difficulties remained until the late 1970s. Everything looked rosy as far as the relationships between the IAEA and the Canadian Government were concerned, as well as those between the IAEA and Canadian scientists. But relationships between the IAEA and Canadian industry left much to be desired. For several years, the IAEA was dissatisfied with the balance sheets that Eldorado Nuclear provided in respect of its activities.[99] Admittedly, the 1973 oil crisis significantly affected supply and demand of uranium and Canada was accused of being party to an international cartel attempting to fix the price of uranium, probably because neighbouring States practised a policy of "dumping" Canadian uranium.[100] Under these circumstances, Eldorado Nuclear had no wish to disclose to the IAEA the true extent of its current stocks. Between 1979 and 1980, all these problems were resolved to the satisfaction of the IAEA.

The second kind of problem faced by Canada was that of standardizing all her bilateral agreements in conformity with the new safeguards approved by the IAEA[101], so that all prior contracts could be placed under IAEA control. It was a considerable undertaking. Canada had signed agreements on uranium sales with the FRG in 1957, with Switzerland in 1958, with Japan and the EURATOM countries in 1959 and with Sweden in 1962. Canada signed contracts to sell experimental reactors to India[102] in 1956 and to Taiwan[103] in 1969. As for nuclear power reactors, Canada entered into an agreement with Pakistan[104] in 1959, with India in 1962[105] and 1967[106], and with Argentina[107] in 1973. The KANUPP reactor came under IAEA safeguards in 1969, the RAPP-2 in 1971 and the Argentinean CANDU in 1974. RAPP-1 was also under IAEA control.

These issues illustrate the kinds of difficulty that all supplier nations faced. In the United States, the Nuclear Non-Proliferation Act was passed in 1978, and the Americans were thus obliged to renegotiate retroactively a good number of their prior bilateral contracts. In Canada, some contracts had to be renegotiated as early as 1965 with the imposition of controls on uranium exports.

In 1965, France obviously wanted to purchase Canadian uranium under the same conditions as those enjoyed by the United States and the United Kingdom – in other words without controls. As previously noted, Canada refused, perhaps under U.S. pressures. Canada felt a sense of frustration, and subsequently gave the United States and the United Kingdom a taste of their own medicine by standing firm on the "peaceful uses" clause.[108]

Throughout all the lengthy negotiations on the Non-Proliferation Treaty, Burns insisted that Canada should negotiate transactions only with countries that had signified their intent to adhere to the Treaty. The process of implementing this policy proved to be lengthy for, among other things, no one at the time was willing to submit to such stringent restrictions in the climate of fierce competition existing between the supplier nations.

In 1968, the Department of External Affairs prepared a Memorandum to Cabinet recommending approval of Article III of the NPT. The Memorandum contained the two following observations:

b   We would be bound to apply IAEA safeguards to all transfers of Canadian source and special fissionable materials to non-nuclear States …;

f   … it is the view of the Atomic Energy Advisory Panel and interested departments and agencies of the Canadian government that Treaty safeguards would not unduly hamper any existing or projected activity of the Canadian government or of Canadian industry in the nuclear field ….

In the early 1970s, a number of interdepartmental conflicts became apparent. Some departments considered that there had been insufficient consultation on the political and trade consequences of Canada's adherence to the NPT. In March 1971, the Disarmament Division prepared a scathing memorandum to the effect that the other departments had only themselves to blame if they had not done their homework at the time, adding that all departments had been kept regularly informed of progress in the negotiations, and that it was time that they stopped using the Department of External Affairs as a scapegoat.

This peremptory attitude solved no problems. In 1969, there were lively discussions on the interpretation of Article IV of the Treaty.[109] Following a review of Canada's foreign policy, attention turned to a re-examination of Canada's policy on disarmament and arms control. For all practical purposes, the study was completed at the end of 1968. The points at issue concerned Canada's policy towards States that had not signed the Treaty and which had no intention of signing it, and towards States such as Australia[110] which, without subscribing to the Treaty, were nevertheless willing to accept the IAEA system of safeguards.

The working document on disarmament covered a number of issues, notably SALT, MBFR and Chemical and Biological Warfare

(CBW). On the issue of non-proliferation, the document stressed the need to take account of the positions of the other supplier nations and the interests of the Canadian nuclear industry, the impossibility of specifying Article IV "[which was] deliberately drafted to mean all things to all nations"[111], and chiefly the need to make the NPT an effective instrument for curbing nuclear proliferation.

The document was revised and corrected on countless occasions, and was sent to Cabinet only on 7 May 1969. Although some "uncertainties" remained concerning the safeguard agreements that should be reached between the IAEA and the States Party to the Treaty, the Memorandum to Cabinet argued that a State's signature obviously constituted a determining policy criterion in according or refusing Canadian assistance. Until such time as the IAEA safeguards were developed, it was recommended that:

each application for assistance and/or financing for nuclear power projects should be considered on its merits and in light of all relevant circumstances, giving full weight to our obligations under the Non-Proliferation Treaty.

Canada chose a policy of least evil, for any other vanguard position would probably have eliminated any chance of survival for the Canadian nuclear industry. The nuclear explosion in India led to Canada's announcement, on 20 December 1974, of "stricter controls on the export of Canadian nuclear material, equipment, technology and heavy water to all States whether nuclear-weapon States or non-nuclear-weapon States".[112]

Although countless articles have been written on the Indian nuclear explosion, two basic facts are worth recalling.

First, all of the reports from the Canadian intelligence community[113] together with the many analyses undertaken by the Economic and Disarmament Divisions of the Department of External Affairs give no clear indication that India had any intention of proceeding with the explosion of an atomic bomb, an explosion which would be described as "peaceful" in nature. During 1967, arguments raged for months within the Canadian Government over this issue.

At the time, Canada knew that India was "optimizing production of plutonium", but the agreement on the CIRUS reactor only banned the use of the reactor or any of its products, including plutonium, for non-peaceful purposes. There were many scientific reasons that could justify India's decision to engage in plutonium reprocessing.[114] For one thing, a new generation of reactors was being developed which could operate using plutonium or thorium, and India had an abundance of thorium. Although Canada suspected that India had accumulated small stocks of plutonium, it was not known how these stocks would be used. Because of these doubts, the Canadian Government refrained from responding to a 1966 request from the Indian Government for collaboration in space.[115]

Second, it was clear both from Prime Minister Trudeau's letter to Indira Gandhi of October 1971, and from the subsequent visit to India of the Prime Minister's advisor, Ivan Head, accompanied with Michel Dupuy of the Department of External Affairs, that the Canadian Government favoured a policy of persuasion by maintaining cooperation rather than one of coercion by threatening to suspend all Canadian aid.[116] This cooperative approach promised much better chance of success than the sudden break that some advocated or wished imposed automatically. Admittedly, the initiative failed, but not through lack of goodwill on the part of the Canadian Government.

India's decision not to provide the political assurances sought by the Canadian Government was tantamount to an assertion of Indian sovereignty. The Canadian Government, having been backed into a corner, was equally free to exercise its right to suspend nuclear assistance to the Indian Government. Interestingly enough, Canada first provided nuclear assistance to India during the time that the Pearson government was in office. Although Pearson opposed the entry of Greece and Turkey into NATO in 1952 on the pretext that these nations were not democracies, he held a different view of India, arguing that all possible means should be employed to help India persevere as a democracy.

The Indian nuclear explosion reinforced Canadian efforts to impose stricter controls. The Minister of Energy, Mines and Resources, Donald MacDonald, announced on 20 December 1974 that Canada would in future demand assurances from receiver nations that Canadian assistance would not be used "to manufacture a nuclear explosive device for any purpose whatsoever, including peaceful purposes".[117] Canada was thus legally opposed to any sort of intent in this regard. From that time on, the application of safeguards was extended to cover all fissile materials, whether imported from Canada or elsewhere, that were processed in facilities supplied by Canada, as well as all fissile materials produced from Canadian source materials.[118] This essentially provided Canada with the right of "follow-up". Canada also required that safeguards be maintained on all equipment and facilities supplied throughout their useful lifetimes, as well as on facilities that might be built using Canadian technology. Other requirements included:

- a provision for fallback safeguards in the event that a situation arises where the IAEA is unable to continue to perform its safeguard functions;
- a control over the retransfer of Canadian-supplied nuclear items;
- a control over the reprocessing of Canadian-origin spent fuel, subsequent storage of the separated plutonium and enrichment beyond 20 percent U-235 of Canadian-origin uranium;
- an assurance that adequate physical protection measures will be applied.[119]

All these provisions were aimed at precluding the manufacture of a nuclear explosive device using technology, fissile materials or equipment supplied by Canada. Shortly after exploding its nuclear device, India acknowledged that the device was fabricated with plutonium from the CIRUS reactor and with uranium of non-Canadian origin. Canada could not, therefore, assume direct responsibility. Although Canadian technology was involved in producing the plutonium, the uranium came from non-Canadian sources and the heavy water was supplied by the United States. India's "peaceful" device could not have been more international in nature.

Finally, it should be noted that Canada never lost hope of persuading India of the error of her ways. Throughout the 1974–1976 period, negotiations continued in an attempt to extend the scope of safeguards applicable to the three Canadian reactors.[120] In May 1976, the Canadian Government finally concluded that it could not secure a definite promise from India not to proceed with any further so-called peaceful tests. It was only then that Canada formally ended its nuclear cooperation with India, although cooperation had been essentially suspended since May 1974. At the same time, the Americans, for policy reasons similar to those of the Canadians, declined to respond to a request from the Indian Government to supply India's reactors with heavy water. It was discreetly arranged that the USSR would supply heavy water to India, but under IAEA safeguards.

Certain aspects of the Cabinet decision of 5 December 1974 were not made public immediately. One part of the decision dealt with technical aid and assistance. In 1974, as in 1969, the question remained unsolved. In its December 1974 decision, the Government recognized, as it had done five years earlier, that the provision of aid to a nuclear country would essentially be contingent on whether that country was a party to the Nuclear Non-Proliferation Treaty. The Cabinet decision was not, therefore, a blanket refusal to provide nuclear assistance; the decision only indicated a preference. The novel feature of the decision, however, lay in the fact that Cabinet intended to provide assistance only to signatories of the Treaty.[121] In other words, Cabinet was disposed to consider requests for aid from countries party to the Treaty – there was no automatic exclusion – but, at the same time, the poor countries which were not party to the Treaty were *ipso facto* excluded.

This part of the Cabinet decision of December 1974 was kept secret for several months. The Government was concerned that by making the decision public, Canada would be exposed to the risk of competition from other States that would seize the opportunity by dismissing any legal quibbles concerning non-signatories to the Treaty. The decision would only be made public provided that other States were prepared to support Canada's approach. Opinions changed, however, following an interdepartmental meeting held on 17 April 1975 at which all the departments of interest were represented. The general view was that Canada would have little to lose by publicly exposing her position, and that there might even be benefits to be derived from adopting such a stand. As a result, at the first Review Conference on the Nuclear Non-Proliferation Treaty held in Geneva on 7 May 1975, Allan J. MacEachan disclosed the previously unannounced portion of the Cabinet decision of 5 December 1974.

The Cabinet directives of December 1974 applied to all agreements either previously reached or to be negotiated in the future. Canada clearly favoured the imposition of general safeguards, and would only conduct transactions with States whose entire nuclear activities were controlled by the IAEA, whether within the framework of the NPT or otherwise. At the time, other States were not prepared to go that far. Canada knew full well that none of the major nuclear supplier countries would follow her lead. In 1975, the international climate was changing rapidly. The first Review Conference on the Non-Proliferation Treaty was held in Geneva in May, and the Nuclear Suppliers Group (NSG) held their first meeting to find a fair balance between legitimate energy needs and international security concerns.

In 1975, Canada was concerned about possible accusations of having provided greater assistance to non-signatories than to signatories. Canada could not escape the fact that, for historical reasons, she had established special ties with certain countries in the Commonwealth and in Latin America. The announcement of Canada's decision to accord assistance only to signatories of the NPT was clearly aimed at correcting the situation and at encouraging non-signatories to sign the Treaty. Through this announcement, Canada also intended to give greater weight to Article IV of the Treaty, for it was well known that neither the IAEA nor the International Bank for Reconstruction and Development would agree to assign funds for development and technical cooperation solely on the basis of a discriminatory criterion requiring States to be signatories of the NPT. In adopting this approach, Canada was aware that she might invite recriminations from France and other countries that were interested in pursuing cooperative programs unhindered. Canada nevertheless considered that it was better to intervene than to adopt a policy of *laissez-faire*.

In December 1976, the Canadian Government opted for the hard and fast policy that Canada would, from then on, supply nuclear materials only to States signatory to the NPT or States that had accepted the application of IAEA safeguards to all their nuclear activities. A number of factors contributed to Canada's decision, including: the ratification of the NPT by the EURATOM member States in 1975, Japan's ratification of the Treaty shortly afterwards, the failure of Canada's proposal made at the first NPT Review Conference to the effect that the application of general safeguards should be the criterion for according assistance, and the impossibility of securing a formal promise from India to renounce any future "peaceful" nuclear tests. Canada's new policy was announced in the House of Commons on 22 December 1976 by Don Jamieson, then Secretary of State for External Affairs.

On the same day, Canada terminated her cooperative nuclear agreements with Pakistan "which refused to adopt retroactively new safeguards for the Karachi nuclear power plant and which refused to abandon its plans to construct a reprocessing plant ... with the help of France".[122] Between 1975 and 1977, Canada signed six cooperative agreements[123], all of which conformed faithfully to the policy enunciated by Canada in December 1974. Negotiation or renegotiation of these agreements often spanned several months.

The European Economic Community (EEC) as well as Japan posed special problems for Canada. With one exception, all the problems with the EEC were settled by the end of 1977. The outstanding issue concerned Canada's right to accord prior consent to any reprocessing or enrichment activities. An interim agreement was reached at the meeting between Trudeau and Schmidt in July 1977. This agreement led to the lifting of the Canadian embargo by the end of 1977 and to the signing, on 16 January 1978, of an interim Canada-EEC agreement on reprocessing. The provisions of this agreement were to be reviewed once the conclusions of the INFCE were tabled. The matter was finally resolved in December 1981. The provisions of the agreement included:

a description of the EC's current and planned nuclear energy program including in particular a detailed description of the policy, legal and regulatory elements relevant to reprocessing and plutonium storage. On this basis, Canada agreed that nuclear material subject to the Canada-EURATOM Agreement could be reprocessed and plutonium stored within the framework of the current and planned nuclear energy program as described and updated from time to time.[124]

The difficulties with Japan stemmed essentially from the system of double controls imposed through the involvement of both Canada and the United States, since the bulk of Canadian uranium destined for Japan was first enriched in the United States before being shipped. These difficulties were minimized to some degree through an exchange of notes between Canada and the United States[125] dated 15 November 1977 by which it was agreed that only the consent of the United States would be required in the event that Japan wished to enrich its uranium to a level in excess of 20 percent. In January 1978, the text of the Canada-Japan agreement was renegotiated to allow the resumption of uranium deliveries to Japan. This agreement was finally ratified in September 1980.

Difficulties arose also with other agreements signed between 1974 and 1977, but they largely related to the identification of the proper internal authorities responsible for technology transfer. The situation that arose in the case of Switzerland is but one example.[126] The list of agreements signed after 1977 is too lengthy to include here, and the reader is referred to other sources.[127]

THE THREE REVIEW CONFERENCES ON THE NUCLEAR NON-PROLIFERATION TREATY

This brief section aims at providing general conclusions and an overview of Canadian policy on non-proliferation matters. Under the terms of Article VIII (3), the States party to the Treaty engage to hold a Review Conference on the operation of the Treaty at regular five-year intervals. As of 1989, three Review Conferences have been held in Geneva:

Date	Chairperson	NPT Parties/ Participants	Result
5 May – 30 May 1975	Inga Thorsson (Sweden)	96/58	Final Declaration
11 Aug – 7 Sep 1980	Ismat Kittani (Iraq)	114/75	Final Document
27 Aug – 21 Sep 1985	Mohamed Shaker (Egypt)	130/86	Final Declaration

The two most significant conferences were those held in 1975 and 1985. The conference held in 1980 resulted in no Final Declaration through lack of consensus. But this is not the only criterion on which to judge the success or failure of multilateral talks. There is no legal provision which obliges participants to agree on the text of a Final Declaration. Moreover, the first Review Conference could have resulted in a lack of consensus, had it not been for the unrelenting efforts of the Canadian Delegation to draft a synthesis document in the wings that was subsequently transmitted to the Review Conference Chairperson. Inga Thorsson presented it as a general document which, in her view, represented a consensus on the overall discussion. The participating States supported her, and the Final Declaration thus emerged – this, despite strong protests from the Israeli Government that the basic rules of democracy had not been respected.[128]

In 1987, Canada's Ambassador for Disarmament, Doug Roche, discreetly acknowledged the essential role played by Inga Thorsson and William Barton during the 1975 Review Conference.[129] The Second Review Conference met with a less fortunate fate. During the preliminary work, long before the Conference opened, nasty rumours prevailed to the effect that the Second Review Conference might even be boycotted by the Group of Seventy-Seven. But nothing of the sort actually happened. Overall, a serious-minded spirit prevailed throughout the discussions of the Review Conference. Both Canada and Australia played leading roles amongst the group of Western nations. The United States and the USSR were content to play lesser roles, perhaps to allow the non-nuclear nations to vent their pent-up recriminations and frustrations at the lack of superpower progress on disarmament.

The bad humour of the Group of Seventy-Seven showed up early, for during the preliminary work they sought to elect one of their own group – the Iraqi Delegate – as chairperson rather than the Swedish representative who undoubtedly would have liked to chair the Review Conference for a second time. As the work progressed, it became clear that Mexico was increasingly asserting its influence at the expense of Sweden. The whole Review Conference was held in an unfavourable climate. Some countries were resentful towards the superpowers, the non-nuclear States still complained that the Treaty was discriminatory, while several nations thought that by adopting a hard line on Article VI – urging the superpowers to negotiate towards disarmament – they would gain concessions on Article IV in respect of liberalization of the conditions governing nuclear cooperation for peaceful purposes. These tactics only turned nation against nation and led, for all practical purposes, to the failure of the Review Conference.

One might also speculate that some Third World countries simply wanted to score points. Efforts to find a compromise continued until the final moment. One country ignored the views of its closest advisors and went so far as to propose that a working group be set up in Geneva under CCD auspices to discuss the thorny issue of global suspension of nuclear tests. The proposal was not without interest, but it met with an icy reception. The offering was described as "peanuts" – too little, too late. Admittedly, no one had a voracious appetite. Nevertheless, had it not been for the intransigence of one of the representatives, who today figures amongst the great Nobel Peace Prize winners, the eleventh hour solution might have succeeded.

In 1980, the climate for discussion was hardly favourable. One year earlier, NATO had adopted its "double track policy", the USSR had intervened in Afghanistan, a new administration assumed office in Washington and with it came a facile and aggressive rhetoric, while the Iran-Iraq conflict degenerated into a long and bloody war and there was little hope that the superpowers would negotiate "in good faith" to end the arms race.

The Third Review Conference took place in a warmer climate. The superpowers played a more active role and Third World recriminations were less violent. Above all, it now seems that the real threat of nuclear proliferation looming on the horizon was the determining factor that led the Third World to tone down its vocal resentment. For the first time, the majority of participants could work together for a common cause, that of strengthening the NPT, which was the only viable mechanism available to the international community for curbing nuclear proliferation.

Judgement is divided on the value of the three Review Conferences. The Stockholm International Peace Research Institute (SIPRI) is rather harsh in its judgement on the value of the first Review Conference, deeming that its sole success was the fact that it did not disintegrate, and that it had failed to resolve the problems critical to the NPT's survival because a number of its provisions had been circumvented.[130] According to SIPRI, the only innovation was the insistence of the Review Conference on multilateral arrangements to ensure the "physical protection" of fissile materials – a clause which Canada had already inserted in its revised policy of December 1974 – as well as the possible creation of regional centres on nuclear fuel cycles.

For her part, Canada was ready to support the idea of regional reprocessing centres. The United States, however, finally came out against this kind of proposal, even though it was strongly supported by some European countries and by senior officials of the IAEA. The purpose of these reprocessing plants was to recycle spent fuel which could then be re-used in the production of nuclear power. It was argued that regional plants, as opposed to national plants, would reduce the risk of nuclear proliferation, if only by virtue of the multiplicity of multilateral controls that could be imposed on them. The problem was that no one wanted such regional facilities. Interestingly enough, the profitability of these plants had been seriously underestimated and, even today, many are inclined to believe that reprocessing plants are nothing more than management plants for "radioactive waste".

There was no consensus on general safeguards at either the first, second or third Review Conference. Opinions were just as divided in the Western bloc, the Eastern bloc and the Group of Seventy-Seven. The principle that no nuclear transaction could take place without prior acceptance of such safeguards was, therefore, far from being adopted. The general safeguards would, of course, form part of a separate legal system distinct from that of the NPT – the difference between INFCIRC/66/Rev. 2 and INFCIRC/153 – but in practice the difference between the two systems was minor. Admittedly, from a political standpoint, such a system was not as rigid as the promise never to acquire nuclear weapons or other nuclear explosive devices which was required from the non-nuclear-weapon States signatory to the Treaty under Article II. These slight differences clearly formed the basis for the strict condition imposed by the Canadian Cabinet in its 5 December 1974 decision.

On the issue of peaceful nuclear explosions, Brazil and India naturally insisted – during the first Review Conference in particular – on the rights of States to take advantage of their benefits in conformity with Article V of the Treaty. No progress was made in this regard during any of the three Review Conferences. Canada was sensitive to the problem in 1975, but preferred to maintain the *status quo*, since any other approach could have encouraged non-nuclear-weapon States to develop an unhealthy or unjustified curiosity towards such explosions which Canada deemed, in any event, to be unprofitable. Once again, it appears that the claims of the States had been "overtaken by events". These were the very words used by the Director General of the IAEA during the second Review Conference to describe the declining interest of nations on this issue. Some nations, such as Japan, considered that it would perhaps be possible one day to distinguish between a peaceful nuclear explosion and the blast of an atomic bomb. But it remained a closed issue, and there was nothing to indicate that the matter would be reopened in the foreseeable future.

At all three Review Conferences, Article VI posed the greatest difficulty. This Article was largely responsible for the failure of the 1980 Review Conference which, according to SIPRI, had the misfortune of being held at the "wrong time". Canada's policy on Article VI during all three Review Conferences remained remarkably close to that contained in a statement made by Canadian Delegate William Barton to the CCD on 20 August 1974. "The fact that the nuclear powers will not see the error of their ways", he declared, "does not give the non-nuclear powers the right to refuse any measure aimed at preventing proliferation".[131] This statement clearly shows the fallacy of the claim that some observers made subsequent to the 1980 Review Conference to the effect that the Conference pitted the "disarmers" against the "peaceful users".

In 1980, Canada was better placed than any other country to recognize that it was not a good time for negotiation. Canada nevertheless encouraged the non-nuclear-weapon States to remind the major powers of their moral obligations under the Treaty. In 1985, Canada insisted with renewed vigour on the need for the major powers to conclude a Comprehensive Test Ban (CTB) Treaty.

On the whole, during all three Review Conferences, Canada laid greatest emphasis on efforts to strengthen the NPT, both by proposing incentives such as increased aid to countries willing to adhere to the Treaty, and by strengthening supplementary measures that might be adopted subsequently on a multilateral basis. Apart from the United States, which passed its Nuclear Non-Proliferation Act in March 1978, Canada was about the only Western nation to hold aloft the torch of general safeguards. Canada still carries that torch today. Following the third Review Conference, more and more States sought to avert the threat of nuclear proliferation, and the NPT assumed greater legitimacy. Significantly, both France and the PRC have repeatedly stated over the years that they would behave as though they were signatories to the Treaty.

The INF agreements of December 1987 and progress under START augured well for the success of the fourth Review Conference scheduled for 1990. As in the past, nations would try to strengthen the legal provisions of the Treaty itself, as well as the parallel provisions pertaining to the NPT. If the Treaty is ever modified, the changes will likely be made in 1995 when the States Party to the Treaty will decide on its future extension. Although Canada thought of proposing amendments to the Treaty in the early 1970s in order to facilitate adherence by some States, she quickly discarded this option, recognizing that opening the Treaty to amendments could result in endless debate.

8 Canada's Position on Chemical and Biological Weapons

> There are ways of curing insanity, but not irrationality.
> La Rochefoucauld, *Maximes, Réflexions morales*

Debate on the control of chemical and biological weapons was pursued with increased vigour in the late 1960s. The main factors which led the international community to intensify efforts to prohibit these weapons included the presumed use of chemical weapons by the United Arab Republic (UAR) in the civil war in Yemen (1963–67), the 1969 report of the Secretary General of the United Nations on biological and chemical weapons, the increased use by U.S. forces in Vietnam of "defoliants" and "incapacitating gases", and the new difficulties that arose in interpreting the 1925 Geneva Protocol.

The issues that preoccupied the international community can be conveniently segregated into two main periods. The first is from 1966 to 1972 when negotiations were in progress on the Convention on the Prohibition of the Development, Production and Stockpiling of Bacteriological (Biological) and Toxin Weapons and on their Destruction which was opened for signature on 10 April 1972 and entered into force on 26 March 1975. This Convention will be referred to subsequently as the Biological and Toxin Weapons Convention (BTWC). The second period is from 1972 to the present day, covering all the negotiations aimed at producing a legal control mechanism for eliminating chemical weapons, which will be referred to subsequently as the Chemical Weapons Convention (CWC).

From a legal standpoint, this division into two timeframes is not strictly correct, since most of the discussion throughout the overall period actually concerned the prohibition of both chemical and bacteriological weapons. But 1971 marked a major turning point because, for the first time, the Soviet Union and the other Eastern countries agreed to discuss each issue separately. This concession quickly led to the adoption of the BTWC within the CCD. Subsequently, the CCD turned its attention to the overall problem of negotiating a CWC, especially in light of Article IX of the BTWC which enjoined member nations to "pursue negotiations in a spirit of goodwill to reach early agreement" on a global and general ban of chemical weapons.

Actually, the real breakthrough did not occur until 1984, since bilateral negotiations on this issue had been frozen in 1980 as a result of the Soviet invasion of Afghanistan.

In accordance with the provisions of Article XII of the BTWC, the first Review Conference was held in Geneva from 3 to 21 March 1980. The second Review Conference was also held in Geneva, from 8 to 26 September 1986, at which time the Final Declaration was adopted by consensus. A third Review Conference on the operation of the BTWC was scheduled to take place before the end of 1991.

GENERAL CONSIDERATIONS

This chapter is not intended for the specialist. Any examination of the issues of chemical and bacteriological weapons presupposes, however, some minimum of agreement on the meaning of the terms that are used. There are many difficulties in this regard. To begin with, from a legal standpoint, there is no basic agreement amongst specialists. The differences in interpretation are well-known. There are those who hold that recourse to chemical and bacteriological weapons is prohibited by international customary law, and those who, on the other hand, consider that the Geneva Protocol is purely contractual in nature and binds only the signatories.

From a military standpoint, there are three problems. First, does it make sense to renounce weapons which everyone agrees are abhorrent but which everyone would nevertheless like to retain for deterrence reasons? Second, assuming that agreement could be reached on eliminating these weapons, would nations have sufficient trust in the verification procedures to follow through and actually destroy them? Third, would the fear that these weapons might spread to other countries provide an added incentive for implementing control measures which, if universally accepted, could by the same token eliminate the threat posed by chemical weapons to the security of the great powers?

Legal Considerations

All jurists agree on the main texts, declarations and conventions which constitute the normative basis of customary international law concerning the prohibition of chemical and bacteriological weapons. The St. Petersburg Declaration of 1868, which was developed by military officers rather than jurists, considers "the employment of arms which uselessly aggravate the sufferings of disabled men" to be contrary to the laws of humanity. Article XIII of the Declaration of the Brussels Conference of 1874 bans the use of "poisons or poisonous weapons". In its Declaration of 1899, the Conference of The Hague called upon nations "to abstain from the use of projectiles, the sole object of which is the diffusion of asphyxiating or deleterious gases" and, in its Regulation of 1907 concerning laws and customs of land warfare, banned the use of "poison or poisonous weapons" (article 23a) or weapons likely to cause "unnecessary suffering" (article 23b). Although most authors do not view the 1899 Declaration as binding, the United Nations War Crimes Commission in 1948 nevertheless considered it as one of the oldest generally-recognized rules confirming prohibition "of the use of poison and of material causing unnecessary suffering".

Much of the substance of these earlier declarations forms the basis for Article 171 of the Treaty of Versailles, the Peace Treaties of 1919, the Berlin Treaty of 1921, the Washington Treaty of 1922 (particularly article 5) which was never ratified, and of the Geneva Protocol of 17 June 1925: Protocol for the Prohibition of the Use in War of Asphyxiating, Poisonous or Other Gases and of Bacteriological Methods of Warfare. The two pertinent paragraphs of the Protocol read as follows:

Whereas the use in war of asphyxiating, poisonous *or other gases* [emphasis added] and of all analogous liquids, materials or devices has been justly condemned by the general opinion of the civilized world ...

[the Governments] declare that the High Contracting Parties, so far as they are not already Parties to Treaties prohibiting such use, accept their prohibition, *agree to extend this prohibition to the use of bacteriological methods of warfare* [emphasis added] and agree to be bound as between themselves according to the terms of this declaration.

It should be noted that the French text reads as follows: "*Considérant que l'emploi à la guerre des gaz asphyxiants, toxiques ou similaires ...* ", [emphasis added]. This difference between the English and French texts, both of which were official, resulted in different interpretations during the post-war period. The Protocol was ratified by the United States only in 1975. Based on the French version of the text, the United States concluded that only asphyxiating and poisonous weapons were prohibited by the Geneva Protocol. In other words, gases other than asphyxiating or poisonous gases would not be prohibited by the Protocol. In contemporary terminology, such gases might include non-lethal incapacitating gases or defoliants. The same distinction could be applied to biological weapons, given that the Protocol extended the ban on chemical weapons to bacteriological weapons. During the 1930s, the British held to the restrictive English version of the Protocol. In a note tabled at the League of Nations in November 1930 before a commission responsible for organizing a Conference on Disarmament, the British declared that the use of all forms of gas was prohibited, including incapacitating gases. During the 1960s, when the British were faced with maintaining order in Northern Ireland, they reversed their position and adopted the more liberal interpretation used by the Americans.

Essentially, the Geneva Protocol is a guarantee of no first use of chemical or bacteriological weapons, since a large number of the signatory States reserve the right to retaliate, both in kind and in degree, if attacked by weapons prohibited under the Protocol. Moreover, the Protocol is binding only between signatories and not between signatories and non-signatories. Canada, for her part, ratified the Protocol on 6 May 1930.

The Geneva Protocol gave rise to two opposing legal positions. Some maintained that recourse to chemical and bacteriological weapons was forbidden by the Geneva Protocol based on the normally recognized principles of customary international law. This was the position adopted by the General Assembly of the United Nations during the 1960s. Others held that there were escape clauses in the Protocol and that new multilateral agreements would have to be developed to eliminate them. Canada was probably right in adopting this approach since, at the time of signing the Geneva Protocol, bacteriological weapons were largely unknown, and "herbicides" did not exist. It should be noted, however, that without the differences of interpretation which existed between the French and English versions of the Protocol there would have been no legal justification for differentiating between lethal and non-lethal weapons.

The UN Secretary General, in the preface of his report on chemical and bacteriological weapons, took little account of this distinction. Among the measures advocated to strengthen world security was the recommendation that nations affirm that the Geneva Protocol applied to the use in wartime of "any chemical, bacteriological or biological agents (including tear gas and other irritants) that existed at the time or were likely to be developed in the future".[1] Many Western nations never accepted this interpretation of universal prohibition, since it constituted an unauthorized addition to the terms of the Geneva Protocol and also raised the whole question of the non-binding nature of the Protocol for those nations that were non-signatories.

The issue of differentiating between various types of weapon also arose during negotiations on the Bacteriological and Toxin Weapons Convention (BTWC) that was signed in April 1972. At that time, virtually no nation possessed bacteriological weapons, although some progress was being made in laboratory research. This research culminated some time later with spectacular breakthroughs in cloning and genetic engineering. As a result, efforts were made to close the gaps through "endogenous" transformation of the articles of the Treaty. This process was limited to confirmation of the main interpretations of the articles of the Treaty by its authors rather than actual changes that could have been achieved through the submission of proposed amendments for majority approval.

Military Considerations

Throughout history there has been a variety of debates on the military usefulness of chemical weapons, but most observers today would agree that these weapons are of limited value.

It has been estimated that there were 1.3 million casualties of chemical warfare during the First World War, including some 91,000 dead. During the Second World War, chemical weapons were not used in the European theatre except on rare occasion in Poland (apparently this was accidental) and in the Crimea. Chemical weapons were used by Italy against Ethiopia in the 1936 campaign and by Japan against China before and during the Second World War. At the end of hostilities the major powers were left with considerable stockpiles of chemical weapons. The United States had 135,000 tonnes, Germany 70,000 tonnes, Great Britain 35,000 tonnes and Japan 7,500 tonnes.[2] Most of these stockpiles were destroyed soon after the end of the Second World War, but not without some accidents and technical difficulties. Figures for the USSR are unknown, but in January 1988 the Soviet Union admitted to possessing 50,000 tonnes of chemical weapons.

It has been suggested that the Allied landings in Normandy would have been much more difficult if the Germans had used chemical weapons. In November 1944, Hitler supposedly ignored the advice of Goebbels and others who advocated the use of *Tabun* to slow the Allied advance. Conversely, there are reports that it was Hitler himself who wished to use these chemical weapons but was discouraged from doing so by his main advisors. Conceivably, Hitler may have been strongly deterred from the use of chemical weapons by the prospect of massive Allied retaliation against cities.[3] Apart from the First World War, it would appear that chemical weapons have been used mostly in conflicts where the opponents did not possess similar weapons. There are many recent examples which lend credence to the idea that these weapons are of little military value but of great strategic value as a means of deterrence.

After the Second World War, the Soviet Union accumulated vast stockpiles of chemical weapons following the takeover of German industry and the "recruitment" of German scientists. Robin Ranger goes so far as to claim that, during the 1950s, chemical weapons were the main Soviet deterrent against Western tactical nuclear weapons. At all events, experts agree today that Soviet stockpiles largely exceed those held by the Western nations, in particular the United States, Great Britain and, to a lesser degree, France. The leading British specialist on these matters, J.P. Perry Robinson, unhesitatingly asserts that recent Soviet doctrine de-emphasizes the importance of the possible use of chemical weapons.[4] Apparently, the FRG holds a similar view.[5]

Despite such statements, immense disparities exist in the ratios of resources for chemical warfare. Estimates of the stockpiles of old U.S. chemical munitions vary between 30,000 and 80,000 tonnes. According to J.P. Perry Robinson, the stocks available to the United States are larger than those indicated by some U.S. statements.[6] Some estimates claim that the Soviet potential is some 20 to 50 times greater than that of the United States.[7] Under the agreement reached by Kohl and Reagan in Tokyo in May 1986, the United States agreed to withdraw all its chemical weapons in Europe between then and 1992 in exchange for FRG support for U.S. development of binary chemical weapons. According to German statements in the Bundestag, it appears that this agreement contains four essential clauses: 1. the withdrawal of U.S. chemical weapons from the FRG between 1986 and 1992; 2. no deployment of U.S. binary chemical weapons in peacetime; 3. the requirement for close political consultation within NATO prior to any deployment; and, 4. acceptance of deployment in wartime by other NATO nations. J.P. Perry Robinson rightly concludes that this agreement corresponds to the de facto institution of a chemical weapon-free zone in all of Western Europe except France.[8]

The attitude of the U.S. Congress concerning the manufacture of binary weapons has led to a "lame duck" situation in Europe. In 1985, Congress declared that no production would occur before NATO had given its approval. On 22 May 1986, sitting in ministerial session, the Defence Planning Committee (DPC) of NATO apparently gave the green light on chemical weapons in the context of the U.S.

contribution to the NATO *Force Objectives for 1987–92*. According to the November 1986 report of the Military Committee of the North Atlantic Assembly (NAA), only Canada, the FRG and Great Britain supported this decision. This would presumably imply that the United States is left with sole responsibility for chemical deterrence within the Alliance. Conceivably, this would explain in part the French decision of November 1986 to proceed with the development of her own binary chemical weapons.

Since Great Britain destroyed its own stockpiles of chemical weapons, the United States and possibly France would be the only powers capable of exercising the right to retaliate following chemical attack. J.P. Perry Robinson asserts, probably with good reason, that an approved procedure exists within the Atlantic Alliance for chemical retaliation in conformity with the doctrine of flexible response.[9] Robinson considers, however, that the use of chemical weapons is largely problematic, particularly in light of the Kohl-Reagan agreement of 1986. In December 1987, the United States commenced production of the M-687 warhead for use in 155 mm calibre guns. The United States also started production of the "Bigeye" bomb in the fall of 1988. The effectiveness of this weapon has been questioned on several occasions. In view of the difficulties of rapidly shipping these weapons to Europe, the United States considered storing some on maritime vessels.

Little became known of the chemical warfare (CW) potential of the Warsaw Pact. At one time, the Soviets had over 80,000 officers and men trained in the use of chemical weapons. Some 45,000 of this force were assigned to Army units. These figures are obviously misleading since many of these units were trained for decontamination, reconnaissance or protection purposes. Some Soviet Special Purpose Forces, known as SPETSNAZ (*Voïska Special'nogo Naznačenija*), which were controlled by the Main Intelligence Directorate of the Soviet General Staff (*Glavno Razvedyvatel'noe Upravlenie* – GRU) could also conduct chemical missions. The Soviet Union has always denied the existence of a program to develop binary weapons, whose components, although poisonous, are relatively inoffensive when they are kept separate.

The United States was anxious to develop these weapons for two reasons: first, to establish a deterrent against the immense Soviet CW potential, and second, to force the opponent to use protective systems which would considerably slow his advance or the speed of his manoeuvres.

Outside the two main alliances, the risk of chemical proliferation seems to be mounting rapidly. No year passes without the occurrence of allegations on the use of chemical weapons by third party countries. Every year SIPRI compiles an impressive list of these presumed cases. In the 1987 Yearbook, a dozen cases were recorded for the year 1986 alone. Concern has been particularly acute since the time that independent investigators confirmed the use of chemical weapons by Iraq in its war against Iran. Western nations currently undertake detailed examinations of the export of some 35 chemical products to other countries. These examinations are conducted through the Brussels Group[10], which presently comprises 19 countries. Unlike the London Group (or NSG), which brings together the nuclear supplier nations from both the West and the East, membership of the Brussels Group is presently confined to Western nations. It appears that the USSR and certain other Eastern countries also maintain controls on the export of dual-use chemical substances (peaceful and military). Within the framework of the Chemical Weapons Convention, a control organization similar to the International Atomic Energy Agency (IAEA) might be established which would be responsible for monitoring the production as well as the export and import of certain chemical materials. It has been estimated that upwards of twenty countries[11] are in a position to produce their own chemical and bacteriological weapons. According to *Time Magazine*, 16 countries currently possess the "poor man's atom bomb", among them Iran, Iraq, Libya and Syria.[12]

Canadian Experience in Chemical Weapons

This section provides only a brief overview of the developments in Canadian policy on chemical weapons from the time of the Second World War up to 1969. Other major aspects will be discussed in a later section on Canadian policy from 1969 to the present day.

Canadian research on chemical weapons was largely conducted under the aegis of the Defence Research Board which was established in 1947. The United Kingdom and Canada were, however, already undertaking collaborative research as early as 1941 at an experimental station at Suffield, Alberta. This centre is still the main laboratory for studying methods of defence against chemical weapons. Other laboratories existed at Kingston and at Shirley's Bay and there was also an experimental station at Grosse Île, near Québec City. The latter was closed in 1946, re-opened in 1951 and closed again a little later. This was the station which developed an important Canadian vaccine against cattle plague. According to one observer, the economic spinoff from this development alone has been sufficient to justify the entire cost of Canadian research on chemical weapons during the Second World War.[13]

The appearance of the hydrogen bomb and the tactical nuclear weapon forced a review of Canadian defence policy in 1955. One committee, under the direction of Colonel R.P. Harkness, recommended that nuclear, bacteriological and chemical research be pursued for defensive purposes, particularly in the areas of protective equipment, bacteriological identification, decontamination and medical treatment. Most of the Canadian research was conducted under the Tripartite Technical Cooperation Program (TTCP) which was established in 1957 under the Bermuda Agreement between the United States, Great Britain and Canada. Coordination of chemical and bacteriological research in Canada remained the responsibility of the Defence Research Board. In 1965, with the addition of Australia and New Zealand as participants, the program was re-named "The Technical Cooperation Program". TTCP activities are coordinated through an international group known as the Washington Deputies.

Between 1960 and 1966, various "Spotcheck" exercises demonstrated that the Canadian Forces could not operate effectively in a chemical warfare environment.[14] A resulting memorandum recommended that an exercise, code-named "Vacuum", be conducted in Suffield in September 1968. It was planned as a joint exercise with the British and American forces to test Canadian protective equipment. The proposal followed in the wake of the election of the Trudeau government and was subsequent to a request from the Department of National Defence to consider the possibility of training the Canadian Forces in offensive chemical warfare. The Disarmament Division of the Department of External Affairs became increasingly concerned. Canadian opposition to these weapons was mounting, the United States was becoming bogged down in Vietnam, the Secretary General of the United Nations had asked for a study on CW issues and the CBC, in a broadcast *The Way It Is*, had alerted Canadians to the dangers of chemical weapons. The Canadian Government maintained its traditional position, namely that research should concern itself only with the defensive aspects of chemical warfare.

In a document issued by the Chairman of the Joint Chiefs of Staff dated 1 May 1963, the general principles of Canadian policy were enunciated as follows:

• Under no circumstances will Canada initiate nuclear, biological or chemical warfare;
• The Canadian Forces could be called upon to participate in a war in which nuclear, chemical or biological weapons were first used by the enemy;

• The Canadian Forces will develop the knowledge and the capability necessary to protect themselves adequately, as well as a retaliatory capability which could be brought into play rapidly if necessary.

These same common sense directives are also to be found in a letter dated 31 December 1968 from Brigadier-General H. Tellier, DND Director of Plans, addressed to the DEA Bureau of Political and Military Affairs.[15] In his letter, BGen. Tellier added that the directives were still in effect and that they had not changed since the time of unification of the Canadian Armed Forces. He also made reference to the need to study the question of training the Canadian Forces in offensive chemical warfare. This matter was probably raised in order to respond to the requirements of NATO document MC 14/3 which was approved the previous year, although this was not specifically stated. Perhaps the United States needed a sure ally to promote this idea within NATO, for it is difficult to see how Canada would claim authorship of such an un-Canadian policy. Or perhaps Canada's right to retaliate could equally justify such a request. In any event, the proposal was rejected. The situation in 1968 was, therefore, somewhat similar to that which came to exist in 1987 – the United States was virtually alone in bearing the responsibility for chemical deterrence within the Atlantic Alliance.

THE BIOLOGICAL AND TOXIN WEAPONS CONVENTION

The final version of the Convention on the Prohibition of the Development, Production and Stockpiling of Bacteriological (Biological) and Toxin Weapons and on Their Destruction – which we refer to in brief as the Biological and Toxin Weapons Convention (BTWC) – was presented to the UN General Assembly on 28 September 1971. The BTWC was opened for signature of States on 10 April 1972 in London, Moscow and Washington. Table 8 provides a list of the main resolutions and proposals on the prohibition of bacteriological and toxin weapons.

A few words of explanation are appropriate concerning terminology. The report of the UN Secretary General of 1 July 1969 defines toxins as biologically-produced chemical weapons. These toxic substances are produced by living organisms – plants, animals or bacteria – but cannot, unlike the organisms that produce them, reproduce themselves. At the request of the United States, the British accepted to add toxins to their draft convention on the prohibition of bacteriological weapons.

Table 8
List of Main Resolutions and Proposals on Prohibition
of Bacteriological (Biological) and Toxin Weapons

RESOLUTIONS:

Res. 2162 B (XXI):	Nations invited to comply with strict principles and objectives of Geneva Protocol, 5 December 1966.
Res. 2454 A (XXIII):	UN Secretary General urged to prepare concise report on the effects of possible use of chemical and bacteriological weapons, 20 December 1968.
Res. 2826 (XXVI):	UN General Assembly approves draft Convention, 16 December 1971.

PROPOSALS:

Great Britain:	Draft Convention on Prohibition of Microbiological Warfare, ENDC 231 (6 August 1968).
Great Britain:	Draft Convention on Prohibition of Methods of Biological Warfare, CCD 255 (10 July 1969). Rev. 1: (26 August 1969).
Report of UN Sec. Gen.:	Chemical and Bacteriological Weapons and the Effects of their Possible Use, A/7575 and S/9292 (1 July 1969).
USSR and Eastern Bloc:	Draft Convention on Chemical and Bacteriological (Biological) Weapons and on Their Destruction, A/7655 (19 September 1969). Modified by CCD on 14 April 1970 (CCD 285/Corr. 1) and by UNGA on 23 October 1970 (A/8136).
USSR and Eastern Bloc:	Draft Convention on Bacteriological (Biological) and Toxin Weapons, CCD/325/Corr. 1 (30 March 1971).
USSR et al., U.S. et al:	Separate, but identical, draft conventions CCD/337 (05 August 1971) USSR et al; CCD/338 (05 August 1971) U.S. et al.
Bulgaria, Canada, Czechoslovakia, Great Britain, Hungary, Italy, Mongolia, Netherlands, Poland, Romania, United States, USSR:	Convention on the Prohibition of Development, Production and Stockpiling of Bacteriological (Biological) and Toxin Weapons and on Their Destruction, CCD/353 (28 September 1971).
Convention open to signature:	10 April 1972.
Date of ratification of Convention:	18 September 1972.
Entry into force of Convention:	26 March 1975.

The Geneva Protocol talks of bacteriological weapons. Neither the British nor the Canadians like the term "biological" since man could also be considered as a "biological agent". The British, among others, have argued that the term biological encompasses more than the term bacteriological. In their first draft convention on prohibition in 1968, the British, sensing future progress in genetic engineering, talk about microbiological weapons. This terminology was not adopted, however, for some microbiological techniques do not involve genetic changes. The difficulties are circumvented by use of the terminology bacteriological (biological) weapons. The two terms are used indiscriminately in the majority of official texts.

Recombinant deoxyribonucleic acid (DNA) technology was discovered only in the early 1960s. Through transformations in DNA chains, it is now possible to produce some toxins, but not all, since many involve chemical processes or purely synthetic production techniques. This difficulty was resolved in Article 1 of the BTWC at Canada's request through the phrase "whatever the origin or means of production", in order to ensure that all microbiological and biological agents as well as toxins were covered under the terms of the Convention.

The main provisions of the BTWC are embodied in Article 1 which reads as follows:

Each State Party to this Convention undertakes never, in any circumstances to develop, produce, stockpile, or otherwise acquire or retain:

1   Microbial or other biological agents or toxins, whatever their origin or method of production, of types and in quantities that have no justification for prophylactic, protective or other peaceful purposes;
2   Weapons, equipment or means of delivery designed to use such agents or toxins for hostile purposes or in armed conflict.

Concerning prohibited weapons and agents, there is only a simple list and no definition. Nations were opposed to the publication of a list of agents that either existed or were being researched at the time. This deficiency was compensated by an extension of the prohibition to cover equipment and means of delivery.

Only research for prophylactic, protective or other peaceful purposes was allowed. The vague nature of the notion of "protection" was left open to interpretation. Where did protection start or end? The prohibition of weapons, equipment and means of delivery "for hostile purposes or in armed conflict" broadened the scope of the Geneva Protocol which dealt only with their "use in war". The phrase "for hostile purposes and in armed conflict" clearly gave the impression that the prohibition covered both interstate conflict and internal conflict. Also, "hostile purposes" was no doubt aimed at covering the possibility of terrorist attack.

Among other obligations assumed by the nations was the undertaking (Article II) to destroy, or divert to peaceful purposes, within nine months following the entry into force of the Convention, all systems or agents prohibited under Article I. A clause of non-transfer of systems or agents mentioned in Article I, which was copied from the Treaty on Non-Proliferation of Nuclear Weapons, was incorporated into the Convention (Article III). Article V made provision for consultation and cooperation between parties concerning the application of the Convention and the difficulties that could arise. Canada and Sweden insisted that the phrase "appropriate international procedures" be included in the context of the UN and in conformity with its Charter, so as to allow the involvement of the Secretary General and all the UN subsidiary organizations to which the General Assembly or the Security Council wished to delegate responsibility.

Article VI describes the means of control which basically comprises complaint and investigation. Following a complaint to the UN Security Council from a State Party to the Convention, an investigation could be undertaken. There was, therefore, no effective international control system nor any verification procedures. The Convention depended on the good faith of the Parties and on their cooperation and assistance when violations occurred. From a political standpoint, trust was strengthened through the insertion of Article V under which nations could engage in bilateral consultations.

Over the years, there have been numerous allegations that the Convention has been violated, particularly in conflicts in southeast Asia. In this context, a group of United Nations experts submitted a report on 26 November 1982 to the Secretary General.[16] The group was unable to draw any definite conclusions although the suspicions raised by the allegations could not be discounted. In Canada, an informal study by G.C. Butler in December 1981 recommended to the Department of External Affairs that a more detailed investigation be conducted. This study was followed by a second one which was largely based on information gathered from political refugees from southeast Asia. A third unofficial report noted that the first two reports displayed "a very strong possibility of recourse to chemical weapons in the region" although no definite proof had been obtained.[17] Another report, written in 1982 by H. Bruno Schiefer, then Director of the Toxicology Department at the University of Saskatchewan, stressed that the phenomena observed could not be explained on the basis of "naturally-produced illnesses". The suspicions, therefore, remained. J.P. Perry Robinson, relying on a report of President Reagan, stressed that there had been no use of chemical or toxin weapons in Afghanistan, Kampuchea or Laos in 1984, and that the number of allegations of recourse to these weapons had diminished in 1985.[18]

It should be noted that these reports were concerned only with chemical weapons. Other reports deal with biological weapons and the issue of "yellow rain" in particular. In 1982, a Canadian team formed under the aegis of the Department of National Defence was sent to Thailand. The results of the enquiry were more positive than negative[19], but the conclusions were far from clear. Other American studies were also rather inconclusive.[20] The mycotoxins that were identified might equally have been associated with honey bee faeces in the region. The same conclusion emerged from a study undertaken by the Department of National Defence in April 1986.[21] One study in particular, published in 1987, appears to be the most authoritative.[22] It should be noted in passing that the Canadian Government sent all the Canadian studies, except for that published by Norman and Purdon, to the UN Secretary General.

J.P. Perry Robinson insisted that, in the absence of proof, it would be difficult to further the debate on this issue. Experience demonstrated that the only way of compensating for the deficiencies of the BTWC was for the investigators to arrive rapidly on the site where alleged incidents took place. At the time of the first Review Conference on the Convention in 1980, the question of "appropriate international procedures" was broadened to allow nations to demand "that a consultative meeting of experts open to all member nations be convened" in a no-veto environment. At the time, Canada considered that the verification procedures were inadequate to withstand the passage of time and to prevent certain nations from becoming engaged in the production of these weapons.[23] Special effort was, therefore, accorded to matters of "cooperation and consultation" and of greater openness in the operation of the Convention.

On 13 December 1982, through Resolution 37/98 C, Sweden proposed that a special conference be held to strengthen the procedures for enforcing the BTWC. France, through Resolution 37/98 D, encouraged the UN Secretary General to investigate any activity that could constitute a violation of the Geneva Protocol and to establish a group of experts capable of intervening rapidly when called upon. Although France's proposal concerned chemical weapons, it reflected a trend towards enlarging the question of "appropriate international procedures" and entrusting a neutral party, namely the Secretary General, with these responsibilities.

The 1980 Review Conference opened in the midst of accusations against the USSR over the incidents at Sverdlovsk where an anthrax epidemic had erupted in 1979. These same accusations were repeated by the U.S. representative, Donald Lowitz, at the Second Review Conference in September 1986. The Soviet Ambassador, Victor Issraelyan, naturally denied these allegations and, for the first time, the USSR provided an official explanation – the anthrax epidemic in 1979 was due to consumption of contaminated beef. This explanation never satisfied the United States, although for some time there was a softening of the U.S. allegations. The U.S. Department of Defense, however, returned to the attack with a highly incriminating report[24] dated 24 March 1987.

The main contribution of the 1986 Second Review Conference was a broadening of the scope of Article I of the Convention. Whereas in 1980 this article was considered adequate to accommodate future scientific progress, the Final Declaration of 1986 was designed to cover all "natural or artificially produced" microbial or biological agents and toxins. From that time on, toxins or their synthetic analogues were specifically covered. This served only to reinforce the initial article which, in any event, already prohibited all agents "whatever their origin or means of production".

The Second Review Conference also proposed the constitution of an *ad hoc* group responsible for examining scientific cooperation and information exchange. This group met in Geneva from 31 March to 15 April 1987. Article V advocated the need for a consultative group that would be established "rapidly" so that, upon request, it could "study any problem" concerning the Convention within the framework of "mutual cooperation" between States Party to the Convention.[25]

CANADA'S POSITION FROM 1966 TO 1972

The question of chemical and bacteriological weapons resurfaced in international discussions in November 1966 when the Hungarian resolution was presented to the First Committee. The first draft resolution was manifestly aimed at condemning the use of chemical weapons by the United States in Vietnam. A series of amendments supported by eight other countries went so far as to demand the prohibition of recourse to these weapons "to destroy humans or their means of existence". The Western Delegations – Canada, Italy, Great Britain and the United States – presented last minute amendments which, to their great surprise, were accepted. This move was the basis for Resolution 2162 B (XXI) of 5 December 1966 which invited nations to conform strictly to the principles and objectives of the Geneva Protocol. States which were not already party to the Protocol were invited to join.

On 6 August 1968 the British tabled a working document on microbiological weapons before the Eighteen-Nation Committee on Disarmament.[26] Prior to that time, Canada had been faced with three basic political choices. The first was to update and revise the Geneva Protocol. This option was not particularly encouraging, for apart from the fact that it opened up the Treaty to a long process of amendment, there was the possibility that some States might take advantage of the opportunity either to dissociate themselves from the Treaty or to accept only its least restrictive interpretation. The second option consisted of proposing an entirely new Convention which would cover all aspects of bacteriological and chemical arms control, particularly the possession, production, destruction and non-use of these weapons. This approach scarcely seemed realistic, and Burns in Geneva quickly stated that it was simply not negotiable given the broad extent of the means of control that would be implied by such a Convention.[27]

The third option, which was supported by the British, was to dissociate negotiations on bacteriological weapons from those on chemical weapons. It was well understood that such an approach should not be viewed as a challenge to the 1925 Protocol, but rather considered as complementary to that agreement. The British, who were encouraged by the report of the UN Secretary General in July 1969, took a second step in dissociating these issues by formally tabling in Geneva, on 10 July 1969, their proposal for a Convention on the Prohibition on Bacteriological (Biological) Weapons.

This last step obviously simplified the problem. The Legal Affairs Bureau of the Department of External Affairs considered that the Geneva Protocol did not cover "defoliants" and "incapacitating" gases. The Defence Research Board was not sure that the first option was the best, since if it were adopted it could have an adverse impact on international cooperative agreements which DRB considered to be valuable for scientific reasons.[28] Under these circumstances, the Disarmament Division wondered whether it would not simply be better to leave it to each country, through unilateral declarations, to specify its own interpretation of the Geneva Protocol. As we shall see shortly, this approach was taken by the Canadian Government in its declaration to the CCD on 24 March 1970.

The British proposal did not, however, solve all the problems. If a separate Convention on Bacteriological Weapons were agreed upon, should it leave open the option of possible retaliation as in the Geneva Protocol? In other words, should the proposed Convention be an unconditional prohibition or an international instrument of no first use similar to the Geneva Protocol? The position of the military was quite clear. The Defence Research Board wanted a total prohibition on recourse to biological weapons.[29] The u.s. position, on the other hand, was somewhat illogical. The u.s. claimed that prohibition of bacteriological weapons was covered by the Geneva Protocol which was universal and non-restrictive. Canada took the opportunity to inform the United States that Washington had adopted a double standard, since it split the Geneva Protocol into two halves that could be interpreted differently depending on whether bacteriological or chemical weapons were under consideration.

In defence of the u.s. position it should be noted that the Arms Control and Disarmament Agency (ACDA) based its interpretation "on the preliminary work and the history of negotiations" of the Geneva Protocol.[30] The issue may appear somewhat academic, but it was important with regard to the prohibitions that were to be included in the Convention. If the right to retaliate in kind were denied, then research activities on bacteriological weapons were pointless. Why retain the right to conduct research on weapons which were, in any event, prohibited? The military answer to this question was that research for "protective" purposes should continue.

Meanwhile, M.K. McPhail of the Defence Research Board was named, in 1969, as a consultant to the group of experts established by the UN Secretary General to study chemical and biological weapons. Burns, in Geneva, was not too happy with this nomination. Although Burns admitted not knowing the individual, he felt it hardly appropriate that a representative of a major centre of research on chemical and biological weapons should be chosen to study the possible elimination of such weapons. Canada's choice was, in fact, perfectly justified, because the study was aimed specifically at clarifying technical issues as well as educating the public on the disastrous consequences of using these weapons.

In July 1969, the UN Secretary General produced a report which obviously posed a difficult problem for the Canadian Government.[31] Canada's support for the foreword of the Secretary General's report would have implied tacit Government agreement that the 1925 Protocol represented an accepted principle of international law and not a contractual agreement which bound only the signatories. Furthermore, the military considered that the use of some chemical weapons, particularly incapacitating gases, "could be a more humane method of control in some circumstances than the simple use of military force". It was decided that the issue should be referred to Cabinet for review. On 24 November 1969, the Department of External Affairs submitted its Memorandum to Cabinet:

We recommend that the Canadian Delegation support the recommendations of the Secretary General with the reservations that the Canadian Government considers that the use of non-lethal chemical weapons is more humane in some circumstances of war than other weapons which kill or cause suffering instead of incapacitating the opponent; that it seems illogical or unrealistic to forbid the use in wartime of the same non-lethal agents that are used in peacetime for controlling riots and that, unless these anomalies be eliminated from the international draft agreement envisaged by the Secretary General, Canada will reserve her position in this regard.[32]

This Memorandum actually followed a letter dated 15 August from Prime Minister Trudeau to Mitchell Sharp instructing him to proceed with a review of Canadian policy on the matter. As early as 3 July 1969, Prime Minister Trudeau had stated before the House that this question was being "re-examined". On 4 November 1969, a significant document was prepared entitled: "Review of Canadian Disarmament and Arms Control Policy on Chemical and Biological Warfare", but the Memorandum to Cabinet of 24 November only repeated certain elements of this review.

At its meeting of 9 December 1969, the Cabinet Committee on Foreign and Defence Policy concurred in the reservations held by the Departments of External Affairs and of National Defence, supported the British draft Convention on Biological Weapons as complementary to the 1925 Geneva Protocol and advocated that the Soviet draft Convention[33] be examined with the utmost care in order to propose changes that could make it an appropriate instrument for strengthening the provisions of the Geneva Protocol on matters of chemical warfare. Two days later, on 11 December, the full Cabinet in plenary session confirmed these decisions.

On 24 March 1970, the Canadian Delegate to the CCD, George Ignatieff, stated:[34]

Canada has never had, and does not possess, biological weapons (or toxins) and has no intention to develop, produce, acquire or stockpile such weapons in the future. Canada does not possess chemical weapons ... and has no intention of using such weapons[35] at any time in the future unless these weapons were used against her military forces or against the civilian population of Canada or her allies. This latter condition is consistent with the reservations that Canada expressed at the time of signing the 1925 Geneva

Protocol. We stand ready to formally withdraw these reservations if effective and verifiable controls can be negotiated for destroying all these stockpiles and preventing the development, production and acquisition of chemical weapons.

The Canadian position was rather subtle. Renunciation of biological weapons was absolute and without reservation. As for chemical weapons, Canada confirmed her intention not to use such weapons, which was hardly a significant pronouncement since she had none. It should be added that only the right of "retaliation" was retained in conformity with the reservations recorded by Canada at the time of signing the 1925 Geneva Protocol. Canada, therefore, went much further than the United States which held that the Protocol did not forbid recourse to non-lethal chemical weapons in wartime. Ottawa dissociated itself from Washington while admitting the practicality of the right of retaliation. In addition, Canada stated that she was ready to remove this last reservation in the event that effective and verifiable agreement could be reached.

R. Ranger claims that such a statement would have carried much more weight if it had been made by the Secretary of State for External Affairs.[36] At the same time, criticisms from within grew in intensity. Professor James Eayrs talks of the "reckless hospitality" of Canada in opening up the "gas chambers and germ tunnels" at Suffield for u.s. and u.k. research. Andrew Brewin of the New Democratic Party demanded that a Canadian decision should be taken with some urgency, arguing that it was impossible to distinguish between defensive and offensive activities, and that the media had long since seized on this issue. Ranger was not totally wrong in this matter. During talks at the United Nations, George Ignatieff asked the Prime Minister to make an opening statement to the ccd when the session resumed in February 1970. Since the Canadian statement was not approved in time, Ignatieff had to read it at the ccd. It seems too that the Prime Minister did not view this statement as a radical departure from past policy.

In his statement of 26 November 1969, President Nixon announced his intention of ratifying the Geneva Protocol without, however, renouncing "defoliants" and "herbicides". In this same statement he also renounced all methods of biological warfare. The only biological research to be conducted would be confined to immunization problems and safety measures for persons working in laboratories. In addition, President Nixon went further than the Geneva Protocol and denied himself first use of any lethal or incapacitating chemical weapon against any third party whether signatory or not to the

Geneva Protocol.[37] Nixon's statement was complemented by a second one on 14 February 1970 which prohibited the use of "toxins". The path was opened, therefore, to negotiation of a Biological and Toxin Weapons Convention. The United States was willing to make this addition to the Convention provided that the Soviets were willing to dissociate bacteriological from chemical weapons. On 30 March 1971, the Soviet Union and the socialist countries tabled their own draft Convention on the Prohibition of Biological and Toxin Weapons, undoubtedly in response to criticisms that the CCD had never, up to that time, produced any concrete measures on arms control. On 5 August 1971, two separate but identical proposals were tabled at Geneva, one by the United States and its allies and the other by the USSR and the Eastern European countries.[38] After some amendments, the draft proposal was finally sponsored by 12 nations[39] and presented to the UN General Assembly on 28 September 1971. Approval for this convention was given under resolution 2826 (XXVI). On 10 April 1972, the Biological and Toxin Weapons Convention was opened for signature of nations. By early 1987, 107 nations were party to the Convention.

Despite the significance of the Canadian statement of 24 March 1970, George Ignatieff at Geneva was far from satisfied. In fact, he had never accepted the Cabinet decision of December 1969. In private he talked about a "sell-out" of Canadian policy at the hands of the Department of National Defence. He believed that "defoliants" and "herbicides" should also have been covered by the Canadian statement. Ignatieff had no objection to the retention of "tear gas" for internal conflicts, but wanted to see a move away from the traditional rut of lethal and non-lethal gases towards the development of a list of prohibited chemical substances. This process had been rejected some considerable time earlier by the Defence Research Board which was of the opinion that such a list would be unending, continuously changing and likely to create more problems than it would solve.

At the same time, important consultations were taking place within NATO on the question of chemical weapons. Canada prepared its White Paper on Defence in 1971. Although there was mention of chemical weapons and research for defensive purposes at Suffield, there was no mention of "defoliants" or "incapacitating gases". Consultations between Canada and the United Kingdom also took place on these issues. For its part, the Department of External Affairs increasingly viewed such issues as matters of international public opinion. Also, the Department considered that the right to retaliate was a theoretical, rather than a real, option and sought to have this matter re-discussed within Cabinet independent of the White Paper on Defence.

In 1971, Cabinet agreed to reverse its decision. According to some sources, the opinion of Cabinet was changed not only by the protests of George Ignatieff but also by those of a well-known chemist, John C. Polanyi, who subsequently received the 1986 Nobel Prize for chemistry. The main elements of the Cabinet decision are contained in the Canadian statement made by Ambassador Ignatieff before the First Committee on 16 November 1971. The Canadian statement was so convoluted that the *United Nations Yearbook on Disarmament (1970–1975)* makes no mention of it and the *SIPRI Yearbook of 1972* mentions it only in a footnote![40] Few Canadians seem to be aware of this decision.

In essence, the Canadian Ambassador stated that Canada's reservations on the use of chemical agents in wartime "should be waived". Ignatieff reiterated the first paragraph of his statement of 24 March 1970 and added, in the second paragraph, that Canada had no intention at any time in the future "of using chemical weapons in wartime". This assertion was, however, contradicted by the clause "unless these weapons are used against the military forces or civilian populations of Canada or her allies". The statement also reaffirmed Canada's desire to waive her reservations in the event that an effective and verifiable agreement could be reached on chemical weapons. The only new idea was contained in the conclusion. "I think, Mr. President", continued Ignatieff, "that this statement obviously applies to all chemical and biological agents intended for use against persons, animals or vegetation". This statement had a dual purpose: first, to suppress the previous reservations concerning "tear gas" and other incapacitating agents in wartime (between States), and second, to make it clear that Canadian renunciation applied both to defoliants and herbicides. The verbal acrobatics of this statement were probably intended to obviate any perception that Canada's interpretation of the Geneva Protocol was universal and non-restrictive.

In correspondence with the authors, George Ignatieff provided an additional explanation of his perspective at the time.[41] Ignatieff wrote: "What I and a number of Delegations were concerned about was, that in taking separate action on biological weapons (originally linked in the Geneva Protocol of 1925), we would not be legitimizing chemical weapons by introducing reservations to the reaffirmation of the Geneva Protocol in deference to American prejudices on the subject". This attitude was perfectly defensible. The records of the Departments of External Affairs and of National Defence show, however, that there was a lack of consensus on these issues. In his memoirs, Ignatieff seemed to consider that policy direction on these major issues had been abandoned to the other departments that were more directly involved.[42] In retrospect, this judgement seems to be somewhat harsh.

Ignatieff's statement of 16 November 1971 was obviously only a unilateral statement of intent. In expressing the desire to renounce all reservations in the event that overall agreement on chemical weapons was reached, Ignatieff was stating the obvious. If the Protocol had provided for an inspection and control system as effective and global as that still sought today within the Chemical Weapons Convention (CWC), the parties to the Protocol would likely have expressed no reservations. Be that as it may, if agreement on a CWC is reached in the future, Canada will have to reveal the details of its 1971 decision.

THE CHEMICAL WEAPONS CONVENTION

Some observers feel that the BTWC was not a significant step forward since the member States were only committed to destroy weapons that, in any case, they did not possess. This was probably true for most countries except the superpowers. In 1969, President Nixon ordered the destruction of all U.S. biological stockpiles. The Soviet Union, on the other hand, never tabled a document in Geneva certifying the destruction of its own stockpiles.[43] The Soviet Union obviously could not do this since it had never previously admitted possessing such weapons. The Convention, nevertheless, was a considerable step towards a binding multilateral agreement. The fact that the majority of nations signed this Convention also reflected the feelings of the international community towards such weapons whose effects were difficult to control, unforeseeable and probably very difficult to counter in times of conflict. Countering these weapons would involve vaccinating the military in advance as well as whole populations, assuming of course that a biological antidote existed or could be discovered in time.

Given the rapid progress in genetic engineering, biological weapons might turn out to be infinitely more threatening than chemical weapons. But to consider, as did Sweden and Canada in the past, that the prohibition of these weapons would constitute the first effective disarmament measure since 1945 is going a bit far. Nevertheless, common sense has prevailed, both for moral and humanitarian reasons, because such weapons could easily and rapidly cause harm not only to the intended victim but equally to those nations using them.

As for chemical weapons, the situation was quite different. Since 1945 there has been considerable progress in the development of chemical agents, particularly lethal nerve gas, which could have limited use in times of conflict. In this regard, most of the incidents reported concern the alleged use of chemical weapons against countries such as Iran which had no similar means of retaliation. Since 1969, the United States has not produced chemical weapons. From the time of the Kohl-Reagan agreement in 1986, the u.s. Congress has approved the production of binary weapons, but on a very restricted basis and subject to a large number of conditions. This approach conforms with u.s. strategy which seeks to exploit chemical weapons as deterrents for as long as the opponent and other third parties do not renounce them. On the other hand, this approach is similar to the Baruch Plan of 1945, arguing that there can be no renunciation, prohibition or elimination in the absence of an effective system for control and verification of destruction of the existing stockpiles.

Negotiations on Chemical Weapons

Until 1979, negotiations within the CCD concerned three main proposals: 1. the draft Convention submitted by the socialist members of the CCD on 28 March 1972 which only repeated the main content of the BTWC[44]; 2. the Japanese working paper submitted in 1973 which became a draft Convention[45] in April 1974; and 3. the British draft Convention of 6 August 1976 which consisted of 17 articles and which was an attempt to establish a compromise between the first two proposals.[46]

Following the Moscow Summit in 1974, the superpowers agreed "to pursue a common initiative" aimed at developing a draft Convention to prohibit the most dangerous and lethal means of chemical warfare. The process was clearly conceived to avoid multilateral discussion within the CCD. In 1975 the United States ratified the Geneva Protocol with the reservations that have been outlined earlier. The superpowers engaged in technical discussions in 1976, and this was followed by a period of bilateral negotiations from 1977 to 1980. Within this negotiation framework, the first step was taken on 7 August 1979 when the superpowers submitted a joint report[47] to the Chairman of the Committee on Disarmament on progress in their bilateral consultations on chemical weapons.

In January 1980 the negotiations reached an impasse due to the lack of progress on verification issues and the repercussions of Soviet intervention in Afghanistan. Negotiations resumed in July[48], but the new Reagan Administration felt that it was pointless to continue further in view of the impossibility of reaching agreement on verification.

In 1980, the Committee on Disarmament took advantage of this impasse to create its own *ad hoc* Working Group on Chemical Weapons. Japan, Sweden and Poland successively chaired this Group until 1983 when Canada's D.S. McPhail was elected Chairman. Following a detailed review of various papers and proposals, the Working Group prepared a report[49] which contained a list of "essential provisions to be included in the draft Convention". Resolution of the impasse was due largely to Canadian diplomatic efforts which, for the first time, caused the Committee on Disarmament to move away from a strategy of deliberation and development to the true strategy of negotiation. On some issues, agreement was much closer than appeared at first sight. McPhail[50] considered that both the u.s. and the Soviet drafts[51] were especially important. The Soviet draft in particular opened, for the first time, the possibility for on-site inspection. Following a proposal from the Chairman of the *ad hoc* Working Group, it was decided to establish four subgroups whose responsibilities were as follows:

- Subgroup A: existing stockpiles;
- Subgroup B: provisions for verification and compliance with the Convention;
- Subgroup C: prohibition of use;
- Subgroup D: definitions.

In 1984, the Conference on Disarmament (which had replaced the Committee on Disarmament) created its own subsidiary organization on chemical weapons, responsible for drafting the main elements of a Convention "except for the final version". This organization became the *Ad Hoc* Committee on Chemical Weapons. The *Ad Hoc* Committee, in turn, established three working groups A, B and C which were responsible respectively for studying the scope of the Convention and the definitional problems, the problem of eliminating stockpiles and facilities, and all other issues concerning compliance with the Convention.

On 18 April 1984, u.s. Vice-President Bush submitted a draft Convention on global prohibition of chemical weapons.[52] The provisions of the draft covered development, production, acquisition, retention, transfer and destruction of stockpiles. It also provided for a mandatory inspection system through "challenge". At the time of writing, the position of the United States remains much the same, but the Soviet position has significantly converged towards that of the u.s.

On 15 July 1986, Great Britain presented an alternative approach[53] involving an inspection system that would be mandatory except in unusually rare circumstances. In such circumstances, where the right to refuse inspection might be considered legitimate, the nation under suspicion would nevertheless have to demonstrate respect for the Convention by proposing alternate methods that would satisfy the challenging nation. The Soviets obviously supported this British proposal, and this was made clear in a speech to the First Committee by Issraelyan, the Soviet representative to the UN, on 3 November 1986. On 10 November, Soviet Foreign Minister Shevardnadze accepted the British proposal as a basis for discussion. In actual fact, Soviet support for the British proposal was first expressed in July 1986 in Workshop C of the *Ad Hoc* Committee on Chemical Weapons.

On 6 August 1987, Foreign Minister Shevardnadze made an about face. In Geneva he accepted the principle of inspection by "challenge" without the right of refusal. Additional information on this subject was provided a few days later by Soviet Delegate Nazarkin.

Since then, progress has warranted cautious optimism. In a report submitted by the *Ad Hoc* Committee on Chemical Weapons in 1987, a 56-page draft Convention on Chemical Weapons was included as an annex. Many difficulties remain to be smoothed out. These fall into four categories. First, the definition of chemical weapons, and particularly the problem of "precursors", which are the components used in manufacturing binary weapons. Second, the statement concerning location of chemical installations. The Soviets and the Americans would perhaps agree to disclose these locations even before the Convention entered into force, but perhaps not France for security reasons.[54] Third, the question of verifying declared stockpiles and of verifying the halting of production of chemical weapons. Fourth, and most important, the procedures for application of means of control and verification.

Other major difficulties concern the structure of the proposed organization that would be responsible for controlling chemical activities. The main control organization envisaged was the Advisory Committee comprising all the States Party to the Convention. The Advisory Committee would meet once a year to issue general directives, elect members to an executive body and periodically review the operation of the Treaty. The Soviets wanted the Advisory Committee to operate on the basis of consensus, which would give them the right of veto, while most other nations advocated decision-making by majority vote. In some cases decisions would be based on a simple majority of the members present and voting, and in other cases on the basis of a two-thirds majority of members present and voting. The Advisory Committee would be analogous to the Board of Governors of the International Atomic Energy Agency.

The Advisory Committee would elect an Executive Board which would function as the watchdog of the Advisory Committee. It would be responsible for ensuring compliance with the Convention by the member nations, and therefore essentially for implementing and applying the verification provisions. Debate on the decision-making process for the Executive Board encountered the same difficulties as in the case of the Advisory Committee. Great Britain suggested that the Executive Board should comprise two levels. The first level would be elected by the Advisory Committee based on equitable geographic distribution of membership, while the second level would comprise representatives of those countries with the largest chemical industrial bases. A permanent Secretariat would also be established. The draft Convention would provide for the elimination of chemical weapons over a period of ten years.

The terms of reference of these control organizations obviously remain to be defined. This is not expected to cause insurmountable difficulties since they could be modelled on those which govern the activities of the IAEA. Politically, however, these organizations would go much further than the IAEA since inspection by "challenge" would be applied to any installation suspected of activities that were illegal or prohibited by the CWC.

Canadian Policy on Chemical Weapons

The efforts of the superpowers to reach agreement on the issue of prohibition of chemical weapons were reflected in the joint Soviet-U.S. statement of 19 September 1961. The two draft proposals advanced by the superpowers in 1962 for general and complete disarmament included provisions for the elimination of chemical weapons in the various planned disarmament stages.[55] The issue of the elimination of chemical weapons was also under study by the Ten-Nation Committee on Disarmament within this broad framework of proposals for general and complete disarmament. This was the time when Canada first seriously studied the problem.

On 25 July 1960, General Burns in Geneva proposed that a clause be inserted in the Soviet draft treaty of 2 June 1960, and also subsequently into the American draft, to the effect that States would "voluntarily accept" to prohibit the development and production of chemical weapons as well as their use.[56] More specifically, in Phase 1 nations would commit to take note of the Geneva Protocol, and those who were member signatories would reaffirm their adherence to it. In Phase 2, nations would declare their intention not to produce chemical or biological weapons and not to stockpile or use them. In Phase 3, the stockpiles would be eliminated. In the mind of General Burns, the whole exercise would be accomplished in the spirit of strengthening the Geneva Protocol and extending its scope to cover operations of production, development and stockpiling. During the same period, M.F. Yalden of the Disarmament Division had prepared a synthesis of the legal aspects of the Geneva Protocol.

In February 1960, the Defence Research Board initiated a study on the question of adequate means of control. Having examined the three most promising control methods (accountability for materials, detection techniques and inspection) the Board concluded that "it is extremely difficult and very doubtful that an effective system is feasible".[57] On 12 February, the Joint Chiefs of Staff made the distinction between "positive" control (certainty of detection) and "negative" control, where the probability of detection, although not large, would nevertheless exert some deterrent effect. There was reason to believe, therefore, that a proposal involving some degree of control might be acceptable. At the time there was a tendency to consider a chemical weapon as "no more effective than a large bomb". It should be noted that the notion of positive and negative control has not lost all its relevance. Negotiators today come up against the problem of defining the degree of "intrusion" which would be necessary to meet the requirements both for security and for the protection of industrial secrets. Various forms of control could be envisaged to meet these conflicting requirements.

In the final analysis, the Joint Chiefs of Staff considered that negative control would perhaps be practicable as far as chemical weapons were concerned, but impossible for biological weapons. The Joint Chiefs of Staff also felt that it might be better to abandon these discussions rather than become engaged in negotiations where the parties would be forced to reveal technical details.[58]

On 9 September 1960, the Joint Chiefs of Staff studied the Burns and Yalden proposals.[59] They considered that, during Phase 1, the Burns proposal would not create difficulties since it was equivalent to substituting a contractual obligation for an established standard practice in American policy (no first use of chemical weapons). The text stressed the legitimate needs of research while at the same time pointing out the paradox that:

"peaceful" medical research is quite likely to result in more effective BW agents and the means of propagating them, whereas attempts to develop a defence may appear very offensive. The effect of inhibiting the development of defensive measures would be to increase the military value of BW and CW. This might tempt some governments to break the agreement.

This was a highly relevant observation and corresponded to the judgements held on the BTWC by several people in the United States. At the time, Washington considered that there was no hope of reaching agreement on the BTWC. Perhaps only a Chemical Weapons Convention, negotiated to include toxins, could compensate for some, but not all, of the deficiencies of the BTWC. *A priori*, there appeared to be no legal difficulties associated with the same substance being governed by two different conventions.

In conclusion, the Joint Chiefs of Staff considered that the Burns-Yalden proposal did not conflict with the requirements of Western security. If the objective was to reach a tangible East-West agreement without paying too much attention to the meaning of such an agreement, then the proposals had certain "merit". The authors of this study went on to say that it remained to be seen whether the United States would support it. In retrospect, knowing the difficulties of present negotiations and those that surrounded the negotiations of the BTWC, it is understandable that Burns was unable to make much progress.

Burns' initiatives are interesting from more than one standpoint. In his thinking, Burns displayed all the tradition of humanitarian law. As mentioned earlier, the St. Petersburg statement was written by military officers and not by politicians. Burns disliked war, but he disliked nuclear weapons even more, and he had some deep-seated convictions in that regard.[60] His attitude towards chemical weapons was, however, much more objective.

The desire to constitute a stable international order, founded on respect for international law, and a democratic legal order where law prevails over force, led to the creation of the United Nations. This same desire underlies the quest for international cooperation founded on equality and social justice, and for establishing an international community governed by the principles of a new world that are founded on parliamentary democracy rather than the principles of *Realpolitik* which, when they collapse, lead the world to ruin and to war.

The recurring themes of Canadian policy were founded on all the hopes born in San Francisco following the Second World War. But the Cold War imposed specific constraints on these hopes. In the late 1960s, Canada nevertheless attempted to see the problems first in the context of the responsibilities of governments towards their own populations, and then towards the needs of the international community. In this context, the international community was not restricted to the countries of the East and West but encompassed all nations including those of the North and South. This perspective was never developed so fully in Canada as during the Trudeau years.

It is difficult to know whether Canada would have adopted a different attitude on bacteriological and chemical weapons if the Diefenbaker government had been in power at the end of the 1960s. On the international scene, Diefenbaker distrusted the superpowers, and on the national scene saw himself as the defender of minorities and promoter of large social projects. Only his fierce anti-communism linked to his somewhat old-fashioned provincialism distinguished Diefenbaker from successive Liberal leaders. In this regard, Trudeau was poles apart from Diefenbaker. In his soul Trudeau was a nationalist but in his intellect he was an internationalist. He could see no merit in the Cold War, nor in the use of force to resolve international differences.

The legal tradition has always been an important factor in shaping Canada's international policy. The same is true of North-South values. These factors were paramount in the development of Canadian policy at the end of the 1960s and the beginning of the 1970s. Strangely enough, they were accompanied with increased interest in all aspects of the protection of Canadian sovereignty – defence, raw materials, culture and territory.

The issue of bacteriological and chemical weapons falls squarely within the province of the age-old tradition of the law of nations and peoples, of humanitarian law and of respect for individual freedoms vis-à-vis the reason of State. Canadian policy in the early 1970s was at the crossroads of all these influences. Canada did not attempt to rule on these issues, but only to establish a balance between the legitimate security requirements of the Western world and her deep desire to eliminate bacteriological and chemical weapons.

The archival records for the period between 1966 and 1972 make for most interesting reading on chemical weapons. After 1972, the material tends to be more technical in nature. Between 1972 and 1980, when negotiations were at a standstill in Geneva, Canada reiterated her main objectives and her priority for eliminating chemical weapons. Starting in 1980, renewed interest in the problems of verification enabled the Canadian Government to state its point of view more forcefully.

At that time, the main areas of interest from a verification standpoint were underground tests of nuclear weapons, weapons in space, and chemical weapons. Overall, Canadian policy on chemical weapons was based on two fundamental requirements: first, the development of legal control mechanisms for strengthening international cooperation on the basis of justice and equity and, second, technical expertise.

Important changes occurred in the organizational framework for negotiation between 1970 and 1987. Beginning in 1969, the Eighteen-Nation Committee on Disarmament was enlarged[61] to become the Conference of the Committee on Disarmament (CCD). Five new members were admitted in 1975: the two Germanies, Iran, Peru and Zaire. In 1979, the CCD became the Committee on Disarmament composed of 5 nuclear nations and 35 non-nuclear nations. The Committee on Disarmament changed its name in 1984 to become the Conference on Disarmament. For her part, Canada attempted to develop special relations with Japan, the Netherlands, Norway and Sweden.

These developments were not inconsequential for Canadian policy. More and more, the industrial nations tabled important working documents in a forum which until then had been the preserve of Canadian expertise. In 1975, the Germans privately recognized the importance of the Canadian contribution, particularly concerning the definition of chemical weapons and of toxicity. From that time on, the FRG came to play an increasingly active role in the Committee. This was also true for a number of other countries, including France, whose role became increasingly authoritative following her return within the Geneva forum.

Table 9 lists the main documents submitted by the Canadian Government on chemical weapons between 1972 and 1987. It should be noted that several important technical documents were presented before 1980, particularly on toxicity and lethality of agents used in chemical weapons – CCD 387, 414 and 473. In these documents, Canada proposed methods for measuring the lethality of chemical agents in terms of their toxicity. For example, a toxic threshold can be defined as the probability that a chemical substance will produce death in 50% of cases, which can be mathematically expressed as a function of the rate of inhalation and the concentration of the substance. In the progress report on their bilateral negotiations in 1979, the superpowers applied these formulae to determine lethality depending on whether these substances were inhaled or absorbed by the skin.[62]

Since 1980, Canada has presented four documents on verification. Prior to 1980, Canada produced only one (CD 275), but it covered the whole spectrum of verification activities. This document was, in

Table 9
Main Texts and Documents on Chemical Weapons Presented by Canada to the Conference of the Committee on Disarmament, the Committee on Disarmament, and the Conference on Disarmament

CCD 300	Working Paper on Verification and Prohibition of the Development, Production, Stockpiling and the Use of Chemical and Biological Weapons (6 August 1970).
CCD 334	Working Paper on Atmospheric Sensing and Verification of a Ban on Development, Production and Stockpiling of Chemical Weapons (8 July 1971).
CCD 387	Working Paper on Toxicity of Chemical Substances, Methods of Estimation and Applications to a Chemical Control Agreement (24 August 1972).
CCD 414	The Problem of Defining Chemical Substances in a Treaty Prohibiting the Development, Production and Stockpiling of Chemical Weapons (21 August 1973).
CCD 433	The Problem of Defining Compounds having Military Significance as Irritating and Incapacitating Agents (16 July 1974).
CCD 434	Destruction and Disposal of Canadian Stocks of World War II Mustard Agent (16 July 1974).
CCD 473	Working Paper on Use of Measurements of Lethality for Definition of Agents of Chemical Warfare (26 August 1975).
CD 113	Organization and Control of Verification within a Chemical Weapons Convention (8 July 1980).
CD 117	Definitions and Scope in a Chemical Weapons Convention (10 July 1980).
CD 167	Verifications and Control Requirements for a Chemical Arms Control Treaty based on an Analysis of Activities (26 March 1981).
CD 173	Disposal of Chemical Agents (3 April 1981).
CD 275	Compendium of Arms Control Verification Proposals (2nd ed.) (7 April 1982).
CD 313	A Proposed Verification Organization for a Chemical Weapons Convention (16 August 1982).
CD 677	Letter dated 11 March 1986 addressed to the Secretary General of the Conference on Disarmament from the Permanent Representative of Canada to the Conference on Disarmament, transmitting a Handbook for the Investigation of Allegations of the Use of Chemical and Biological Weapons (12 March 1986).
CD 679	Identification of Chemical Substances (13 March 1986).

Table 9 (continued)

CD 689	Letter dated 10 April 1986 addressed to the Secretary General of the Conference on Disarmament from the Permanent Representative of Canada to the Conference on Disarmament transmitting a Compendium of all Chemical Weapons Documentation of the Conference during the Period 1983–1985 (11 April 1986).
CD 766	Canada and Norway: The Chemical Weapons Convention. Proposal for an Annex to Article IX concerning the Verification of Alleged Use of Chemical Weapons (2 July 1987).
CD 770	Letter dated 10 July 1987 addressed to the Secretary General of the Conference on Disarmament from the Permanent Representative of Canada transmitting a research report entitled: "Verification: Development of a Portable Trichothecene Sensor Kit for the Detection of T-2 Mycotoxin in Human Blood Samples" (14 July 1987).
CD 771	Letter dated 10 July 1987 addressed to the Secretary General of the Conference on Disarmament from the Permanent Representative of Canada transmitting compendia on chemical weapons, comprising plenary statements and working papers from the 1986 session of the Conference on Disarmament (14 July 1987).

fact, a revision of an earlier document (CD 99) which was expanded to include analyses of the various proposals on verification of chemical weapons. The Canadian Government updated the document in July 1987. It runs to three volumes.[63]

In the context of verification, Canada believed that a truly effective control system should take account of four factors: 1. equity; 2. non-discrimination; 3. reciprocity; and 4. the preservation of national sovereignty.[64] In 1980, Canada proposed a broadened system of verification that was modelled on that of the International Atomic Energy Agency (IAEA).[65] In 1984, the Canadian Ambassador, J. Alan Beesley, insisted that the creation of an effective verification organization would undoubtedly constitute "the price that had to be paid" to ensure the peace of mind of nations and to promote the development of mutual trust between them. In this, he concluded, there was no other alternative.[66]

Canadian expertise in the area of verification continued to make itself felt. In 1986, Canada published a *Handbook for the Investigation of Allegations of the Use of Chemical and Biological Weapons* (developed in collaboration with the University of Saskatchewan) which was submitted to the Secretary General of the United Nations and subsequently tabled at the Conference on Disarmament.[67] In addition, Canada tabled a compendium of all documentation on chemical weapons prepared by the Conference during the period 1983 to 1985.[68] On 20 May 1987, following a contract with the Armand-Frappier Institute of Montreal, the Secretary of State for External Affairs, Joe Clark, submitted to UN Secretary General Pérez de Cuéllar, the latest ideas on verification embodied in a report[69] entitled: "Verification: Development of a Portable Trichothecene Sensor Kit for the Detection of T-2 Mycotoxin in Human Blood Samples".

In 1986, Canada proposed that a new nomenclature[70] developed by Chemical Abstracts Service of Columbus, Ohio, be adopted in preference to that developed by the International Union of Pure and Applied Chemistry (IUPAC) which, up to that time, had been used by the *Ad Hoc* Committee. Although the new classification system did not identify the structural composition of the chemical products, it had the merit, at least, of considerably simplifying inherent difficulties in chemical nomenclature.

In July 1987, Canada and Norway presented a joint compendium on investigation techniques and procedures aimed at facilitating verification of alleged use of chemical weapons. It was suggested that these procedures be appended to Article IX of the proposed Chemical Weapons Convention.

Undoubtedly, the numerous efforts that have been made and the increased cooperation between nations in the area of control and verification will have a positive influence in slowing the threatening proliferation of chemical weapons in the future. It is unfortunate that the superpowers had to come face to face with the increasing risks of proliferation before their views really started to converge.

Canada remained faithful to her long-standing tradition of humanitarian law and reliance on technical expertise developed through cooperation with her allies since the Second World War. This is but one example of Canada's systematic attempts to promote peace as opposed to confrontation.

9 A Comprehensive Test Ban: In Search of the Grail

> But having opted for innocence, we have also opted for igno-
> rance. The former may be an asset, but the latter is not and we
> should perhaps be rather careful about displaying it.
> F.R. Miller, Chairman, Joint Chiefs of Staff, 28 April 1966

Since 1957, no single issue has so preoccupied the Disarmament and Arms Control Division of the Department of External Affairs as that of a global nuclear test ban. The superpowers have long argued that nuclear weapons must be tested if deterrence is to remain credible. Even as the world enters the 1990s, many contest this conventional wisdom. The banning of nuclear tests has always been viewed as the most effective means of "choking the oxygen supply" from the major defence research laboratories and industries which are developing the weapons of tomorrow. All nations, including the superpowers, seek a Comprehensive Test Ban (CTB). But nations are still far from agreement on its specific terms, and the gulf that separates the superpowers is still as wide as ever. The quest for the Grail continues, despite repeated frustration and failure. One can only hope that the theme of "failed resurrection" – the successive failures to reach agreement on a CTB – will no longer prevail now that bilateral talks have resumed.

GENERAL CONSIDERATIONS

Debate on the suspension of nuclear testing is characterized by a maze of uncertainties and contradictions. Any review of the issue must start with a brief account of three related topics: first, the damaging effects of ionizing radiation; second, the technological reasons underlying the never-ending arms race; and third, the difficulties intrinsic to seismic detection of underground nuclear explosions. The reader will appreciate that some technical detail cannot be avoided in the discussion of these topics.

Ionizing Radiation

Humanity is profoundly uneasy about nuclear radiation. Understandably, it stems from the mysterious nature of the atom, from recent knowledge acquired about the atom, from fear of the deadly diseases produced by radioactivity such as cancer and leukaemia which condemn their victims to certain death, from the horrors of atomic war evoked by the spectre of a Hiroshima or a Nagasaki, and from the public's general lack of knowledge about such phenomena. Overall, the public is much better informed on atomic phenomena today than earlier in the atomic age, although the lethal or noxious nature of certain types of radiation is still not fully understood.

The atom of any of the 92 elements found in nature can be thought of, in simple terms, as a miniature "solar system" consisting of a central nucleus surrounded by a cloud of orbiting electrons. The nucleus is made up of protons and neutrons, particles which have roughly equal mass but which differ in electrical charge. The proton is a positively-charged particle while the neutron, as its name implies, is uncharged or neutral. The electron carries a negative charge, equal but opposite to the charge of a proton. Since the atom as a whole is uncharged, the number of electrons orbiting the nucleus is equal to the number of protons within the nucleus. It should also be mentioned that the mass of an electron is some two-thousand times smaller than that of a proton or neutron. The bulk of the atom's mass is thus concentrated in its nucleus. Again, for the sake of simplicity, we can consider that the mass of one proton (or neutron) is 1 Atomic Mass Unit (AMU). On this scale, the mass of the simplest atom in nature – the hydrogen atom which consists of one proton and a single orbital electron – is roughly 1 AMU. The uranium atom, which is found at the upper end of the scale, has a natural mass of 238 AMU. Its nucleus, which contains 146 neutrons and 92 protons, is surrounded by 92 orbital electrons. Finally, to complete our simple picture of the atom, we should note that if we liken the nucleus to a ball-bearing located in the nave of a cathedral, the orbital electrons could be represented by grains of sand orbiting the cathedral walls.

It is important to note that all the atoms of any given element have exactly the same number of orbital electrons (and hence the same number of protons in their nuclei). Looked at in another way, this is equivalent to saying that the chemical characteristics of an element are determined by the number of orbital electrons in its atoms. The atoms of a given element can, however, have differing numbers of neutrons in their nuclei. These variants are known as "isotopes" of the element. While some isotopes of a given element are stable, others are highly unstable and are prone to disintegrate either spontaneously or through interaction with other particles. This process of spontaneous disintegration, known as radioactive decay, is characterized by the emission of so-called decay particles from the nucleus. The rate of spontaneous disintegration of an isotope is usually expressed in terms of the "half-life" of the isotope, defined as the length of time taken for one-half of the atoms in any sample of radioactive material to decay, each atom emitting a decay particle.

In general, the term "radiation" relates to a wide range of phenomena exhibited across the full range of the electromagnetic spectrum. These various types of radiation include, in order of decreasing wavelength, radio waves, microwaves, infrared radiation, ultraviolet radiation, X-rays and gamma rays. The term "ionizing radiation" refers to radiation which can strip electrons from otherwise neutral atoms which then become charged particles known as "ions". The main forms of ionizing radiation comprise alpha particles, beta particles, neutrons and, to a lesser degree, gamma rays and X-rays. Each type of ionizing radiation has its own particular properties. Atoms which emit such ionizing radiations are termed "radioactive".

Alpha particles are analogous to helium nuclei, and beta particles are analogous to electrons. Gamma rays, on the other hand, are a form of electromagnetic radiation of very short wavelength, well below that of visible light or X-rays. Gamma radiation is always associated with the alpha particle or beta particle decay process. The penetrating power of these radiations depends mainly on their type. An energetic alpha particle is stopped by the surface of the skin, and can penetrate water to a distance of only one or two centimetres. A gamma ray or neutron is capable of passing through the human body and of penetrating a block of concrete one metre thick.

Certain types of radiation in the electromagnetic spectrum can cause burns or biological damage. Such radiations include microwaves, for instance, where the heat is sufficient to burn tissue. At wavelengths below the ultraviolet, ionizing radiation can cause damage even though the heat produced in not enormous. Biological damage depends on the amount of energy absorbed at the scale of individual cells, as well as on the rate or flux of energy.

Two units are used to measure exposure to radiation, the rad and the rem. The rad measures only the amount of energy absorbed, and is equivalent to 0.01 joules per kilogram of the exposed substance. The rem – röentgen equivalent man – accounts for the *way* in which energy is absorbed, which depends on biological factors. For example, a dosage of one rad of neutrons is ten times more biologically destructive than that of one rad of X-rays. A dosage expressed in rems can thus be thought of as a measure of biological damage. A millirem (mrem), which is one-thousandth of a rem, is the base unit commonly accepted by the International Commission on Radiological Protection (ICRP). The rate of human absorption of energy is usually measured in mrem per year. According to the ICRP, public safety is endangered when human dosage exceeds 500 mrem per year (mrem/y).

In their natural environment, humans are exposed to ionizing radiations from various sources, such as cosmic radiation from space and radiation from the ground. The intensity of radiation in the natural environment varies according to local conditions. For instance, it has been estimated that each individual in Canada receives about 100 mrem/y from the ambient environment.[1] In Kerala, India, the average dose is 400 mrem/y due to the high level of radioactive thorium in the ground.[2] The dosages absorbed by ingestion or inhalation obviously depend on the kind of food or liquid that is consumed and the quality of air that is breathed. Humans are also exposed to radiation from construction materials used in housing, which contain a number of radioactive isotopes. Radiation dosages can vary from 30 to 50 mrem/y in the case of wooden construction, from 50 to 100 mrem/y for brick construction and from 70 to 100 mrem/y for concrete construction. It must be remembered too that X-radiation due to medical radiography contributes to the limits of radiation considered acceptable by the ICRP. Typically, a dose of 20 mrem is absorbed from X-rays of the entire mouth, 40 from X-rays of the lungs, 100 from X-rays of the abdomen, 300 from X-rays of the stomach and 600 from X-rays of the small intestine.

A dose equivalent to 1 mrem/y can be absorbed by persons living near a nuclear power station. On an airline trip from London to New York, a passenger can expect to absorb about 4 mrem, equivalent to the total radioactive fallout in Canada[3] in 1975. The International Atomic Energy Agency (IAEA) estimates that in 1979, the average individual absorbed the following proportions of radiation depending on source: ambient environment 67.6%, medical diagnosis and treatment 30.7%, nuclear industry 0.15%, radioactive fallout 0.6%, nuclear workplace 0.45%, other sources 0.5%.

For the sake of completeness, it should be noted that, since 1985, the International System of Units has recognized the Gray (Gy) and the Sievert (Sv) as the basic units of ionizing radiations. The Gray is the unit used for measuring the dose absorbed by any kind of material, living or inert. One Gy is equal to 100 rads. The Sievert, which is equal to 100 rems, is now used to measure the amount of radiation absorbed by human or animal tissue. A dose of 400 to 450 rems, or about 4 to 4.5 Sv in the new units, is considered lethal.[4] The ICRP tolerable threshold is thus about one-thousandth of the lethal dose. A dose of 100 to 200 rems provokes radiation sickness, but is rarely fatal. In 1954, after the tests in the Marshall Islands, 64 out of 267 persons exposed to radioactive fallout received this kind of dose.[5] There was recovery in all cases. In the nuclear industry, where the standards are ten times less stringent for the workers than for the general public, the following doses are deemed to be acceptable limits:[6]

- 50 mSv/y (5 rems/y) for the body as a whole;
- 30 mSv (3 rems) for the main blood-generating organs over any consecutive period of 14 weeks;
- 6 mSv (0.6 rem) over a two week period for the eyes or gonads (sexual organs);
- 750 mSv/y (75 rems/y) for the hands;
- 380 mSv/y (38 rems/y) for the forearms;
- 40 mSv (4 rems) for the feet or ankles over a period of two weeks.

These figures pertain to the most penetrating radiations, such as gamma rays, X-rays and neutrons. The acceptable radiation limits are higher for low energy beta rays, gamma rays and X-rays. In addition, the figures vary according to the sex of the individual.

Other units are employed to measure emission, rather than absorption, of radiation. The Becquerel (Bq), for instance, is the smallest unit and corresponds to one nuclear disintegration per second. This unit has replaced the Curie (Ci) which corresponds to 37 billion disintegrations per second. The Becquerel is increasingly used to describe the degree of activity of radioactive nuclei contained in food, milk products, drinks and the air.

Various studies have been conducted on the somatic and genetic effects of nuclear tests in the atmosphere. The somatic effects appear during the lifetime of the individual exposed, while the genetic effects appear in his descendants. Lengthy debates persist on the genetic consequences of ionizing radiations. The radiation dosage received by an individual from a nuclear explosion in the atmosphere depends on the altitude of the explosion, the distance from the point of explosion, the wind direction, the degree of protection afforded by the topographical environment, the degree of exposure of the individual and the parts of the body exposed.

A.C. McEwan[7] of the National Radiation Laboratory in Christchurch, New Zealand, has monitored the fallout from radioactive strontium 90 (the unstable isotope of mass 90 AMU) over a thirty-year period from 1955 to 1985. His observations indicated two peaks of maximum activity, one of 700 MegaBequerels per square kilometre (MBq/km²) at Milford Haven in the U.K. during the 1962–63 period, and the other of 130 MBq/km² in New Zealand during the 1964–65 period. Since 1976, beta-ray activity in the atmosphere has been below the observable threshold (0.3 MBq/m³).

Aside from radiation sickness, the most frequently reported somatic effects of radiation are leukaemia and cancer. The report[8] of the United Nations Group of Experts, drawing on a 1977 study of the UN Scientific Committee on the Effects of Atomic Radiation (UNSCEAR)[9], estimates that the total mass of fission products released by all the nuclear tests in the atmosphere between 1945 and 1976 amounted to 145 Megatonnes (Mt).[10]

Assuming two or three deaths for every 10,000 manrad[11] of collective dose received by the whole world population, the report estimates that nuclear testing will account for 150,000 premature deaths before the year 2000. The calculation is based on innumerable factors, the most important of which is the highly improbable assumption that the fallout is distributed uniformly throughout the biosphere. In the final analysis, it is not possible on the basis of such measurements to discriminate between cases of cancer caused by "natural" phenomena and those caused by exposure to the ionizing radiations produced by nuclear explosions. The figures quoted must, therefore, be treated with some circumspection and prudence.

Of all the fission products generated in the nuclear industry, the most dangerous radioactive isotopes are tritium with a half-life of 12 years, iodine 131 with a half-life of 8 days, krypton 89 and argon 41 whose half-lives vary between several hours to a few days. These products are usually present in gases. The most dangerous elements present in liquids are cesium 134 and 137 as well as cobalt 60. Tritiated water[12] also poses a threat. Oxides of tritium do not emit gamma radiation and the beta particles emitted do not penetrate far. But inhalation of tritiated water vapour or absorbtion through ingestion is extremely dangerous because tritium spreads rapidly throughout the whole human body. Fortunately, the "biological" half-life of water in the human body is only one week, because half of the water contained in the human body is exchanged every seven days. Tritium is, therefore, almost completely eliminated before it disintegrates. This is not so in the case of plutonium. The most stringent precautions must, therefore, be taken in handling these products.

The most serious nuclear accident in the history of the atom was obviously the meltdown of the core of the nuclear power plant at Chernobyl. Following the explosion of the building enclosure (this did not occur at Three Mile Island), a plume of radioactive gas and dust was observed reaching altitudes between 1,500 and 3,000 feet. This plume produced clouds of contamination at great distances. Apart from the countries of the Soviet Bloc, the two foreign countries most affected by the radioactive fallout were Finland and Sweden. It seems that the Soviets rapidly took steps to seed the clouds around Chernobyl with silver iodide to prevent excessive concentrations of radioactive debris from polluting local rainfall in the Ukraine. It was six of one and half a dozen of the other, for although the local inhabitants were affected to a lesser degree, the more distant populations received a larger share of the radioactive fallout. The repairs at Chernobyl cost the USSR at least eight billion roubles, or about sixteen billion Canadian dollars.

Atmospheric radioactive emission from the Chernobyl disaster (discounting the rare gases) reached 12 MegaCuries per day (MCi/day) on the day of the explosion, and fell to 0.1 MCi/day ten days later.[13] The intensity of the radiation at ground level from the radioactive cloud was relatively high. According to the former director of the Curie Foundation, "the intensity was of the order of 200 rads at 1 km, 30 rads at 5 km, 1 rad at 30 km and 0.1 rad at 100 km".[14] Dr. Robert P. Gale, the U.S. specialist in transplantation of spinal fluid, who arrived in Moscow following the Chernobyl disaster, estimated that the accident would cause some 12,000 cases of premature cancer.[15] Other estimates[16] range between 2,500 and 75,000 over the next 50 years, an exorbitant price to pay for an industrial accident.

In its first report to the IAEA on the Chernobyl accident, the USSR stressed the dangers "specific to nuclear installations in wartime" and asserted that the accident "made war even more absurd and unacceptable". This statement was not merely propaganda. Several Soviet studies undertaken since Chernobyl have emphasized the vulnerability of the European nuclear industrial structure, even in the event of conventional war.

Canadian studies undertaken since the Chernobyl experience suggest that all of the St. Lawrence valley would be especially vulnerable to a serious nuclear accident occurring in the Eastern United States or even in Ontario. It may be of some consolation to note, however, that the concrete structures surrounding u.s. reactors provide a much greater margin of safety than those which housed the four, 1,000 Megawatt (Mw) Chernobyl reactors.

Nuclear Tests and the Arms Race

1,645 nuclear tests are known to have been conducted[17] between 1945 and 1987, of which 487 tests were conducted in the atmosphere and 1,158 underground. The ussr and the United States account for over 80% of all the nuclear tests conducted in the atmosphere.[18] The same trend is evident in underground nuclear tests. The ussr and the u.s. account for 89%, while France, the u.k., and the Peoples' Republic of China (prc) account respectively for 8.5%, 1.6% and 0.7% of these 1,158 underground tests.[19]

The megatonnic yield of all these nuclear tests can only be roughly estimated. According to Norris, Cochran and Arkin[20], the total yield of the nuclear tests undertaken by the United States between 1945 and July 1986 was about 173 megatonnes. u.s. tests[21] undertaken before 1963 account for 80% of this total. As for the ussr, it has been estimated by Sands, Norris and Cochran[22] that Soviet nuclear tests totalled 473 megatonnes, 95% of which, representing some 452 megatonnes, were conducted prior to the 1963 treaty banning nuclear tests in the atmosphere. Altogether, the Americans and Soviets detonated a cumulative yield of 646 megatonnes during the 1945–1986 period, or about 50,000 times the explosive yield of the Hiroshima bomb.[23]

According to G. Alan Greb[24], the total yield of all underground tests has been overestimated by 20%. This overestimate is closer to 30% according to Lynn R. Sykes.[25] Included in the underground tests are 71 American tests conducted for Project Plowshares[26] between 1957 and 1973, and about a hundred Soviet tests which were conducted for peaceful purposes, mostly outside the traditional test sites at Semipalatinsk and Novaya Zemlya. The number of atmospheric and underground nuclear tests known to have been undertaken between 1945 and 1963, and between 1963 and 1987 are displayed in graphical form on Histograms 1 and 2.

In 1974, France declared that all nuclear testing in the atmosphere would be stopped. In turn, Zao Zi-Yang of China announced, on 21 March 1986, that his country would conduct no further tests in the atmosphere.[27] Since the superpowers and the u.k. ended atmospheric testing in 1963, it may be assumed that the planet will henceforth be freed of this military source of radioactivity which some observers believe is the cause of many premature deaths.

Histogram 1

Histogram of Known Nuclear Tests from 1945 to 5 August 1963

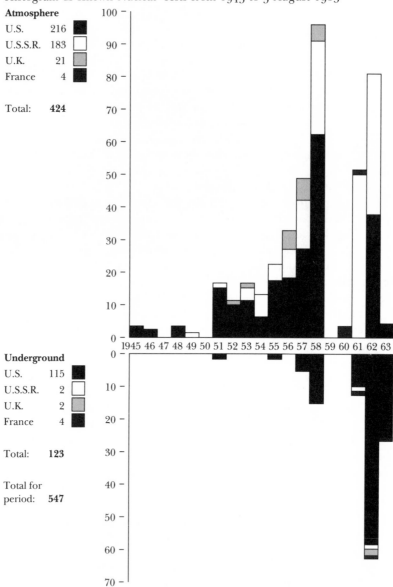

Note: The u.s. conducted at least one underwater test in each of the years 1946, 1955, and 1962; and at least two underwater tests in 1958. These tests are accounted for under the heading of nuclear tests in the atmosphere. The ussr also conducted at least one underwater test in each of the years 1955, 1957 and 1961.

Source: Table compiled from data given in Goldblat-Cox, 1988, pp. 402–404.

Number of Tests by Country and Year (Histogram 1)

		U.S.	USSR	U.K.	France
Atmospheric tests					
	1945	3			
	1946	2			
	1947	0			
	1948	3			
	1949	0	1		
	1950	0	0		
	1951	15	2		
	1952	10	0	1	
	1953	11	4	2	
	1954	6	7	0	
	1955	17	5	0	
	1956	18	9	6	
	1956	18	9	6	
	1957	27	15	7	
	1958	62	29	5	
	1959	0	0	0	
	1960	0	0	0	3
	1961	0	50	0	1
	1962	38	43	0	0
	1963	4	0	0	0
			165		
			18	(between 1949 and 1958, years unknown)	
	Total:	216	183	21	4 = 424
Underground Tests*					
	1951	1			
	1955	1			
	1957	5			
	1958	15			
	1961	10	1		1
	1962	58	1	2	1
	5 August 1963	25	0	0	2
	Total:	115	2	2	4 = 123
				Total for period:	547

* No tests in missing years

Histogram 2

Histogram of Known Nuclear Tests from 5 August 1963 to 1 July 1987

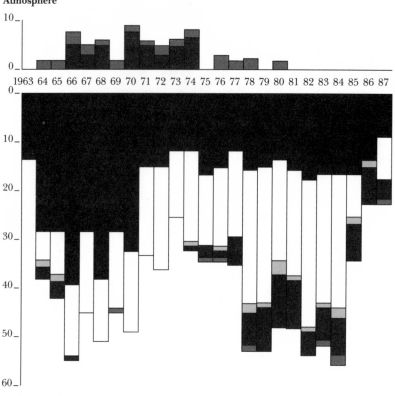

Atmosphere

Underground

Atmosphere	63	Underground	1035	Total for the period: 1098
U.S.	0	U.S.	493	
U.S.S.R.	0	U.S.S.R.	421	
U.K.	0	U.K.	17	
France	41	France	95	
P.R.C.	22	P.R.C.	8	
		India	1	

Note: Multiple explosions are counted as single explosions. U.S. figures are slightly
   high since, from 1962 onwards, all British tests have been conducted at the
   Nevada test facility.
   France stopped testing in the atmosphere in 1974.
   The PRC announced in 1986 that it would discontinue testing in the
   atmosphere.

Source: Table compiled from data given in Goldblat-Cox, 1988, pp. 402–404.

Number of Tests by Country and Year (Histogram 2)

	U.S.	USSR	U.K.	France	PRC	India	
Atmospheric tests							
1964					1		
1965					1		
1966				5	3		
1967				3	2		
1968				5	1		
1969				0	1		
1970				8	1		
1971				5	1		
1972				3	2		
1973				5	1		
1974				7	1		
1976				0	3		
1977				0	1		
1978				0	2		
1980				0	1		
Total:				41	22	=	63
Underground Tests							
1963	14			1			
1964	29	6	1	3			
1965	29	9	1	4			
1966	40	15	0	1			
1967	29	17	0	0			
1968		39	13	0	0		
1969	29	16	0	0	1		
1970	33	17	0	0	0		
1971	15	19	0	0	0		
1972	15	19	0	0	0		
1973	12	14	0	0	0		
1974	12	19	1	0	0	1	
1975	17	15	0	2	1	0	
1976	15	17	1	1	1	0	
1977	12	18	0	6	0	0	
1978	16	28	2	7	1	0	
1979	15	29	1	9	0	0	
1980	14	21	3	11	0	0	
1981	16	22	1	10	0	0	
1982	18	31	1	5	0	0	
1983	17	27	1	7	1	0	
1984	17	28	2	8	2	0	
1985	17	9	1	8	0	0	
1986	14	0	1	8	0	0	
1987	9	9	0	4	1	0	
Total:	493	421	17	95	8	1 =	1035

Total for period: 1098

A number of conclusions can be drawn from the two histograms on nuclear tests. The first, and most obvious, is that far from putting an end to nuclear tests, the 1963 Partial Test Ban Treaty (PTBT) gave new impetus to the arms race. In fact, the total number of underground tests now stands at twice the total number of tests in the atmosphere. The Treaty came after one of the most intense periods of testing, both in terms of frequency and explosive power, ever experienced since the atomic age began. Between November 1958 and September 1961, the moratorium was respected. In the 16 months that followed, the superpowers conducted over 200 nuclear tests both underground and in the atmosphere, equivalent to an explosion rate of one every 2.5 days.[28] It is a matter of speculation whether, during the moratorium, the superpowers tested various types of delivery vehicle that were in development at the time.

The second conclusion is that the Treaty was one of convenience. The tripartite Treaty of Moscow (or PTBT) was very easy to accept for the States Signatory, because they had the means to continue underground testing, despite higher costs, and so to pursue the race for technological superiority. The Americans were ready to sign the Treaty in 1962 since they had conducted 58 underground tests as opposed to 38 in the atmosphere. It should be noted, however, that in 1962 several British nuclear tests were conducted in the test facility in the Nevada desert, so that the U.S. figures are slightly exaggerated. Opinion is divided on the value of the Moscow Treaty. Raymond Aron, for example, considers it "one of the most meaningless treaties in diplomatic history".[29] In contradistinction, other observers view it as an essential first step on the road to disarmament.

There is no doubt that the superpowers wanted to avoid any further nuclear proliferation when they ratified the Treaty. For humanitarian, economic and political reasons, France and the PRC, who were non-signatories to the 1963 Treaty, later adopted the expedient of underground testing. This does not imply, however, that these two States would necessarily fall in step with the superpowers in the event of Soviet-American agreement on a global suspension of nuclear tests. The argument advanced in 1963, that the test ban would halt nuclear proliferation would, therefore, only apply in the case of those States that had not, until then, embarked on the development of atomic weapons. Even so, nothing would prevent such a State from defying international public opinion if it decided that its security had to be ensured at any cost. International pressures on such a State would certainly be strong, but they would never be more than just pressures.

The third conclusion that can be drawn from the Histograms is that the Soviet unilateral moratorium of 1985 – which was renewed five times before Moscow resumed testing in February 1987 – was declared only after the Soviet Union had completed an unprecedented series of underground nuclear tests. Having completed the majority of its tests, one superpower would obviously be in a good position to propose a moratorium to the other, which could only accept such a moratorium at the expense of its own development program.

The fourth and final conclusion is that enormous technological progress was made between 1963 and 1988. Today, the superpowers can use computer simulation techniques to eliminate the need for the large number of experimental tests which otherwise would be required to ensure statistical reliability. For the superpowers, nuclear testing now provides only minimal advantage in offensive nuclear weapon development, and such advantage is itself progressively decreasing with the passage of time.

Under these circumstances, why did the superpowers continue nuclear testing during the period from 1977 to 1986 at an average rate of 17 per year for the United States and 21 per year for the Soviet Union (see Histogram 2)? In the case of the Soviets, one can only speculate because very little information has filtered through on the scientific objectives of their nuclear experiments. As for the Americans, the information available is usually second hand, but adequate enough to provide at least a general picture of the reasons for their underground nuclear tests.

According to Norris, Cochran and Arkin[30], 75% of the 830 nuclear tests that they studied were aimed at developing new kinds of warhead. A further 10% of these tests were conducted to study the effects of nuclear weapons under water, underground or at high altitude. Although the figures vary according to author, there appears to be general agreement that between 75% and 85% of all tests conducted by the u.s. were undertaken for the reasons mentioned. J. Carson Mark[31], former Director of the Theoretical Studies Group at Los Alamos National Laboratory, estimates that 800 of the 850 u.s. tests, or 90% of the total, were conducted in support of the weapon development program. The remaining tests were conducted mainly for the following reasons: studying the effects of nuclear explosions for peaceful purposes; improving capabilities under a program known as VELA for testing the ability of satellites to detect nuclear tests; testing the safety and reliability of warheads[32], including their physical resistance to shock, storage and transportation; and, finally at developing safer devices for detonating nuclear warheads.

Experts generally seem to be in agreement on the following observations. A State that embarks on the path towards production of nuclear weapons must have at least 100 tonnes of fissile material at its disposal for use in a development program before it can expect to attain total reliability[33] of the final weapon. This amount of material is clearly very large and very expensive, particularly in view of the fact that the critical mass of an atomic bomb is about ten kilograms, depending on whether plutonium 239 or enriched uranium is used. Nevertheless, a State could probably produce a series of bombs of the Hiroshima or Nagasaki type without necessarily passing through this process of testing. The main problem is to obtain a critical reaction in an extremely short period of time, which in the final analysis depends on the implosion mechanism employed in the bomb, or alternatively the explosive mechanism used for projecting several sub-critical masses towards each other at high velocity. The shorter the timeframe, which is of the order of nanoseconds (one-billionth of a second), the greater the probability of successful yield. In this regard, even the superpowers had to undertake tests when, for reasons of safety, they decided to replace the conventional detonation mechanism in the bomb with so-called Insensitive High Explosive (IHE).[34] IHE minimizes the chance of accidental explosion of a bomb due to shock which could occur, for example, when a bomber crashes, or a munitions depot is subjected to a violent shock wave.

Testing becomes imperative when a State decides to develop a thermonuclear device. According to Westervelt[35], improving the yield-to-weight ratio is an empirical science, and no calculation or statistical projection can replace the need for actual testing. The technique of "boosting"[36] has led to improvements in yield-to-weight ratio of fission weapons by a factor of about 100. Tests of this type have been the most numerous, and by now the superpowers have likely mastered the technique.

By 1983, close to half of the 25,000 devices in the u.s. nuclear stockpile were over 25 years old.[37] Because of technological progress, the Americans decided to modernize their arsenal in order to meet the ever-changing needs of their strategy. It has been estimated that, on average, some 5 to 10 tests are needed before it is possible to proceed to "certification" of a new warhead design. This number would obviously be higher for a novice country. It is important here not to confuse the type of nuclear warhead, of which there are about a hundred in the u.s. arsenal, with the "design" itself, which relates to the type of physical configuration of the nuclear device. Although there are about a hundred types of warhead, they could probably be categorized under a dozen or so particular "designs". The United States tested the warheads of MINUTEMAN III (335 Kt) and TRIDENT II (450 Kt), as well as the B-83 strategic bomb (1.2 Mt) before the Treaty on the Limitation of Underground Nuclear Weapon Tests

— usually referred to as the Threshold Test Ban Treaty (TTBT) — entered into force on 31 March 1976. The TTBT imposes an upper limit of 150 Kt on underground nuclear tests. Prior to the entry into force of the TTBT, the Soviet Union also tested a number of warheads, specifically those for the SS-17 (mod. 2), SS-18 (mod. 1) and SS-19 (mod. 3), as well as the MIRVed[38] warheads of the SS-17 (mod. 3), the SS-18 (mod. 4) and the SS-19 (mod. 3).[39] In other words, most of the so-called modern strategic missiles in the panoply of the superpowers were tested a good ten years ago.

Current underground tests are clearly aimed at developing future weapons, the so-called third generation.[40] The new designs are based on particular physical configurations which improve the effectiveness of directed energy weapons. These tests are concerned with war in space, even though some types of test may have strategic or tactical implications. A global ban on nuclear testing would probably have little impact on the strategic and tactical capabilities of the superpowers to wage nuclear combat, but it would seriously hinder the development of anti-missile defensive weapons. Like many other legal instruments[41], the 1963 Treaty banned nuclear tests in space. The questions that now arise are: first, will States be able to re-create the vacuum conditions of outer space in an underground facility and, second, what nuclear explosion threshold will be needed to make the tests meaningful?

Unfortunately, these questions are not answered in the latest work of Goldblat-Cox. No weapon designer was present at the symposium held at Montebello in October 1986 which provided the foundation for this work, even though many scientists from the principal U.S. laboratories participated. A threshold of 150 Kt is, however, probably adequate to enable the nuclear powers to develop their future weapons, given their accumulated previous knowledge. According to Jeremy K. Leggett of the Imperial College of Science and Technology in London, even the tests of nuclear-pumped X-ray lasers, which are part of a project espoused by Dr. Edward Teller, have been conducted close to the 150 Kt threshold fixed by the TTBT.[42] Under the best "decoupling"[43] conditions, the detected power of a nuclear explosion can be reduced by a factor of 10, or even by a factor of between 50 and 100 in a low yield explosion, say below 1 Kt. One is left to wonder, therefore, whether a threshold of even 15 to 20 Kt would constitute a major obstacle to the development of directed energy weapons. According to V. Goldanskii[44] of the Soviet Academy of Sciences in Moscow, over 60% of U.S. nuclear tests conducted between 1980 and 1984 were below a threshold of 20 Kt and, of these, over two-thirds were between 5 and 20 Kt.

It seems fair to conclude that a treaty which establishes a threshold above 5 Kt is not particularly significant. Some observers claim that it would be difficult to initiate a thermonuclear explosion using an atomic detonator of less than 5 Kt. Such a low threshold would likely inhibit development of thermonuclear weapons by other nations. A treaty which restricts the number and power of nuclear tests to lower limits than those of present agreements would surely hinder research, but the superpowers could circumvent this difficulty if they were willing to pay the price. Such a treaty could nevertheless reflect the intention of the superpowers to curb the pace of development of their future arsenals. It would, therefore, be a valuable asset, and pave the way for other possible agreements.

Seismic Detection

Seismic detection is a relatively complex matter, and some prior discussion on the general principles of wave propagation would seem appropriate.

Physics teaches that any disturbance of a point in a medium is gradually transmitted to all points in that medium. When a stone is thrown into calm water, surface waves propagate in all directions. Every point on the surface of the water, at the moment that the wave reaches it, is subjected to an oscillation perpendicular to the surface, and therefore perpendicular to the direction in which the wave propagates. These surface waves are known as *transverse* waves. *Longitudinal* waves represent another type of wave motion. Sound waves are an example of longitudinal waves, where each impulse causes an oscillation of the medium in the same direction as that in which the wave is propagating. When a drummer strikes the stretched skin of his drum with a stick, the skin experiences a transverse wave motion. The sound waves set up inside the resonant chamber of the drum are longitudinal waves.

The distance between a crest or trough of a wave and the median, or centre line of the wave, is called the amplitude of the wave, while the number of oscillations occurring per unit time is called the frequency of the wave. The unit of frequency is the hertz (Hz). The period of the wave is defined as the time taken for one complete oscillation – in other words, the total time taken from the moment that the wave crosses the median to trace out a crest, then re-crosses the median to trace out a trough and finally returns to the median. In mathematical terms, the period is the reciprocal of the frequency and vice versa, namely:

$$f = 1/T \text{ or } T = 1/f,$$

where f denotes the frequency and T the period.

Our planet Earth is also a true resonant medium, but one which is far from homogeneous. For all practical purposes, the Earth is a sphere of approximately 6,500 km radius and 40,000 km circumference. The sphere consists of three parts: the crust, the mantle and the core. The crust and the mantle form the lithosphere, which is the solid part as opposed to the core which is more or less liquid (the magma) or gas. The lithosphere extends to a depth of 70 km.

A seismometer is an instrument which is secured in solid rock to record the movements of the ground both horizontally and vertically. In seismic detection there are two important kinds of wave. First, there are body waves[45], which consist of primary waves or P (*pressure*) waves, and secondary waves or S (*shear*) waves. Second, there are surface waves that can be subdivided into Rayleigh waves and Love waves. As their name indicates, body waves propagate through the whole mantle and are often reflected or diffracted by the core, thus producing a null zone at angular intervals of between 100 and 140 degrees in which seismic detection is impossible. Surface waves are produced essentially through interactions between body waves, and are transmitted on the periphery of the mantle. These waves propagate on the surface of the earth over very long distances[46], sometimes up to 10,000 km.

Body waves, particularly P-waves, travel most rapidly. They propagate in exactly the same way as sound waves, or compression waves, in the longitudinal direction. They cover a range of frequencies between 0 and 100 Hz. The S-waves, on the other hand, are transverse waves. They travel more slowly than compression waves, the speed of an S-wave being roughly 60% of that of a P-wave. An approximate estimate of the distance between a seismometer and a detected phenomenon can be obtained by studying the delay between the times of arrival of the two different waves.

Surface waves propagate at speeds of between 3 and 4 kilometres per second (km/s), corresponding to wavelengths of between 60 and 80 km.[47] They travel more slowly than body waves, but they propagate over great distances. The amplitude of a surface wave is attenuated, or diminished, as a function of the square root of the distance travelled, unlike the amplitude of a body wave which attenuates as a function of the distance itself. Thus, at great distances from the epicentre of a disturbance, the surface waves will predominate.

Nuclear explosions and earthquakes can be distinguished from each other by the relative number of body waves and surface waves that they produce. In general, an earth tremor produces more surface waves and fewer P-waves than a nuclear explosion. The primary P-wave due to a nuclear explosion is, therefore, more pronounced than that resulting from an earthquake. Also, the waves produced by a nuclear explosion are of higher frequency and shorter duration. The above general principles pertain, of course, only under reasonably well-defined conditions and in cases where the magnitudes of the disturbances are above the surrounding microseismic noise.

It is difficult to obtain seismic readings of low amplitude signals. The signal must be separated from the background noise which is produced by movements of the oceans, by the wind, by industrial activities such as dynamiting, and so on. As mentioned earlier, the earth is far from homogeneous – sound waves propagate easily in granite but less easily in sand. The greater the number of high quality seismographic stations and the easier it becomes (using triangulation or other methods) to determine the epicentre of an explosion and its magnitude.

The magnitude of an explosion or earthquake is usually measured on the Richter scale. It is a logarithmic scale, on which each successive step represents a factor of ten increase over the previous one. The largest earthquake recorded this century registered 8.9 on the Richter scale. Today, it is relatively easy to measure amplitudes less than 1 on the Richter scale. The number 4 on the Richter scale corresponds to a weak earthquake. At a magnitude of 5, the earthquake is very strong, at 7 it is disastrous and at 8 it is catastrophic. It has been calculated[48] that, under ideal conditions, 1 kilogram of TNT would correspond to magnitude 1 on the Richter scale, 10 kilotonnes to magnitude 4.5 (in granite), 20 kilotonnes to magnitude 5, 1 megatonne to magnitude 6, and 60,000 megatonnes – 60,000 megatonne bombs – to magnitude 8. There are about 700,000 earthquakes annually of magnitude 1, and about 50,000 in the range[49] between magnitudes 3 and 3.9. In this kind of environment, when the disturbances are at low amplitude, it is easy to understand the difficulty of distinguishing nuclear explosions from earthquakes.

The following four methods of concealing a nuclear explosion are described in a Department of External Affairs brochure on seismic verification:[50]

- Keeping seismic signals below the level of background Earth "noise";
- Testing in an earthquake-prone zone or creating seemingly "normal" noises at the same time to mask any explosion;
- Selecting a site so that the signal will pass through an absorbent region of the Earth's crust; or
- Partial or complete "de-coupling" of the explosion from its immediate solid surroundings, by detonating the device in a large artificial cavern.

Most earthquakes, however, cannot be confused with nuclear explosions. Underground disturbances occurring below 10 km for instance, are undoubtedly natural seismic phenomena, for no one has been able to excavate to such depths. It has been estimated[51] that 90% of all earthquakes occur at depths greater than 10 km. Moreover, if the epicentre of the disturbance (the point on the surface of the Earth vertically above the focus of the explosion or earth tremor) is geographically located in the ocean, then the disturbance would almost certainly be due to an earthquake, because the costs of constructing a nuclear test site below the ocean floor are prohibitively expensive. Therefore, discrimination techniques are required only for low-amplitude borderline cases and for tests conducted at shallow depths.

The problem of discrimination poses the greatest difficulty for seismologists in the case of an explosion which is "de-coupled" from its surrounding medium. For instance, caves such as those that have been excavated in salt mines are often used for storing gas, petroleum or radioactive waste. Such caves can also be used to camouflage nuclear explosions. In the USSR, some caves have diameters of between 10 and 100 metres, and enclose volumes between 20,000 and 1,000,000 cubic metres.[52] Cavities made previously by nuclear explosions can also be re-used to camouflage subsequent tests. The United States did precisely this in December 1966 when they tested a device of 0.38 kt (the so-called STERLING test). Among other things, this test demonstrated that, in such a cavity, the seismic signal from a nuclear explosion could be reduced by a factor of 70.[53]

In recent years, enormous progress has been made in the field of seismology, and some of the discoveries have forced a re-examination of the data from the STERLING test. Review of this data, in concert with new theoretical calculations, have led to the conclusion[54] that nuclear explosions can be "muffled" by a factor of ten in the (relatively) high frequency band between 15 and 30 Hz. The new seismographic techniques are particularly important for frequencies between 10 and 50 Hz, since waves at these frequencies propagate as far in the lithosphere as waves of lower frequency. This discovery has important implications, since seismic noise is preferentially generated in the very low frequency band of the spectrum, and therefore discrimination can be more easily effected by examining the higher frequency bands. Spectral analysis has, therefore, become an important tool for discriminating between nuclear explosions and earthquakes.

A number of discrimination techniques are commonly used. Amongst them is the technique of examining the ratio of the magnitude of body waves to the magnitude of surface waves. The value of this ratio is very different for an underground nuclear explosion from the value corresponding to an earthquake at shallow depth. The process consists of comparing the magnitude of the primary P-waves, which have a period of about 1 second, with that of the Rayleigh surface waves, which have a period of about 20 seconds. Generally, this technique permits discrimination between a disturbance produced by a nuclear explosion and one produced by a natural phenomenon, such as an earthquake.[55] Unfortunately, the differences tend to disappear in the case of earthquakes at great depth.

Techniques using the ratio of the magnitudes of body waves to surface waves, complemented with spectral discrimination at the high end of the frequency spectrum, seem to afford the most reliable means of determining the nature of terrestrial disturbances, whether due to nuclear explosions or earthquakes. Reliability is improved when cross-checks can be made between the data of an individual nation's seismographic network and that of the networks of neighbouring States. According to Lynn R. Sykes[56], there is agreement among the international community of experts that, in cases where the explosive power is greater than 10 kilotonnes, it is possible to distinguish between a nuclear explosion (even one that is "de-coupled") and an earthquake, based purely on seismographic data available from outside the country where the disturbance occurs. If that country has its own national network, and makes the data available for comparison with that of external, or peripheral, networks, the threshold of discrimination is reduced to 1 kilotonne. Canadian Peter W. Basham and Swede Ola Dahlman are quite categoric: "the technology exists to develop an international seismological verification system ... , the system can be designed to meet any specified political requirements".[57]

International Efforts in Seismic Detection

It would appear that the problems of verification in the area of nuclear testing could be resolved by establishing an international verification system involving all the main countries concerned, to allow for data exchange in real time. The world is still far from attaining this objective, but progress in the negotiations is promising.

There were three main stages in the evolution of international efforts to ban nuclear testing. The first goes back to the Conference of Experts on Methods of Detecting Violations of an Agreement to Halt Nuclear Tests. This Conference was held in Geneva from 1 July to 21 August 1958. The conclusions reached at the Conference of Experts were re-examined at the tripartite (U.S., U.K., USSR) Conference on Halting Nuclear Weapons Tests which opened in Geneva on 31 October 1958 and which continued to function intermittently until the end of 1961. On 29 January 1962, the Geneva Conference was adjourned indefinitely and the issues which preoccupied it were referred, in March 1962, to a subcommittee of the Eighteen-Nation Disarmament Committee.

The joint Conference of Experts brought together eight nations[58], four from the West and four from the East. At this Conference, the suggestion was made that discrimination between earthquakes and 1 to 5 kilotonne nuclear explosions was possible using 170 land observation stations and a dozen or so maritime stations, complemented with an on-site inspection system for ambiguous cases.[59] In the interval between the first technical Conference and the tripartite political discussions, it was learned that new data had been obtained indicating that it was possible to disguise nuclear tests using "decoupling" techniques. At the time of the tripartite political meetings in March 1960, it was determined that an agreement in principle could be reached on (a) a draft treaty banning underground nuclear tests of magnitude greater than 4.75 (equivalent to an explosion of 20 kilotonnes), (b) a moratorium on underground nuclear tests less than this magnitude, and (c) the possibility of mounting a joint research program on identification and detection of underground nuclear tests.[60] The final obstacle concerned agreement on the number of on-site inspections required. The United States wanted seven per year, while the USSR was only ready to accept two or three.

This first stage of negotiations came to an abrupt end following the failure of the Paris Summit in 1960, the resumption of nuclear testing in 1961, the Cuban missile crisis in 1962 and the signing of the Partial Test Ban Treaty in 1963.

The second stage resulted from national efforts to develop seismic techniques. The United States developed the VELA satellite system and embarked on the Large Aperture Seismic Array (LASA) program. LASA was abandoned in 1978. The British, with stations in Canada, Scotland, Australia and India, decided to place primary emphasis on teleseismic detection (detection at distances in excess of 3,000 km). In addition, the World Wide Standardized Seismograph Network (WWSSN), involving 60 nations and 125 seismic observation stations, came on stream in 1967.

These initiatives were largely supported by nations like Sweden and Canada. Sweden convened a meeting of experts in Tällberg in 1968 at the invitation of the Stockholm International Peace Research

Institute (SIPRI). In 1969, Canada, in collaboration with a number of other countries, sponsored Resolution 2604 A (XXIV) which invited States to advise the Secretary General of their capabilities in seismological techniques with a view to the possible development of an international seismic detection network. Forty-five nations provided information on their facilities, and 22 nations informed the Secretary General[61] that they had no technical capability in this area.[62] Unfortunately, little information was provided by the Socialist Bloc on the technical capabilities of their seismographic stations.

In the wake of all these national efforts, Sweden developed its own seismic detection program. Norway, with its stable tectonic plates, instituted its NORSAR (Norwegian Seismic Array) program in 1971, which was recently complemented by the NORESS (Norwegian Regional Seismic System), capable of detecting magnitudes of about 2.5 on the Richter scale in the high frequency range, at thousands of kilometres from the origin of the disturbance. The number of seismological stations in Canada is over one hundred. Canada has two remote seismological detection units within the Regional Seismic Test Network (RSTN) based in Albuquerque, New Mexico. One is located at Red Lake, Ontario, and the other near Yellowknife in the Northwest Territories. All the seismic data is transmitted to Albuquerque by the WESTAR satellite.

Given that the structure of the Canadian precambrian shield is similar to the geological formations beneath the Eurasian continent, it is "therefore a testing ground where a great deal can be learned about close-in seismological techniques that might be applicable to a remotely controlled network within the USSR".[63] The achievements of other countries such as France, China, the Federal Republic of Germany, and Australia in the area of seismic detection must also be recognized.

The third stage in the negotiations to end nuclear testing started in 1976 with the Swedish initiative to create an *Ad Hoc* Group on Seismic Verification within the Conference of the Committee on Disarmament (CCD) based in Geneva. This group still exists today, and is better known as the Group of Scientific Experts (GSE). The GSE, which comprises 26 participating nations, usually meets for a two-week period in Geneva twice a year. The GSE submitted its first report[64] to the CCD in March 1978, its second report[65] in July 1979 and its third[66] and fourth[67] reports in March 1984 and August 1986 respectively. Two other progress reports were submitted by this same Group in 1987.

Presently, the GSE is proposing to establish a three-level international system of verification. The first level – a world system using remote sensing – would consist of fifty or more standardized "primary" stations. The second level would consist of regional networks which would analyze the results obtained from the level 1 stations. This stage is especially important in the process of discriminating between nuclear explosions and earth tremors. Finally, the third level would consist of the detection networks of the superpowers, involving special arrangements between them.[68] Several countries, including the FRG and Australia, have requested a full exchange of data between levels 2 and 3 to prevent the superpowers from considering their own facilities as purely national networks.

As an international organization comprising scientific experts, the GSE is in a position to propose the immediate implementation of levels 1 and 2 of an international verification system. Most countries would support this approach. Level 3 of this system could only be established within the framework of international negotiations on a Comprehensive Test Ban (CTB) Treaty. Bilateral discussions between Soviet and American negotiators resumed in 1987. In 1988, both sides were still evaluating the reliability of their respective networks based on joint experiments conducted at Semipalatinsk and in Nevada.

NEGOTIATIONS LEADING TO THE PARTIAL TEST BAN TREATY OF 1963

In view of the abundant literature in this area, brevity is compelling. Discussion will, therefore, be restricted to a brief history of the course of negotiations, followed by a study of pertinent Canadian policy.

Historical Review of Negotiations

The appearance of the thermonuclear bomb and the ballistic missile plunged the entire international system into disarray. These developments occurred during the period starting in the 1950s up to the time following the Cuban missile crisis in 1962. These were the darkest hours of the Cold War. The security of the two opposing blocs, East and West, took precedence over any other consideration. Moral and scientific arguments were of little avail in reconciling the differences between the superpowers. Propaganda was a way of life. On both sides, useless weapons[69] were developed in the name of security and deterrence. The Soviets tried to drive a wedge into the American empire, whether in Berlin or in Cuba. Both sides actively solicited the confidence of third party States, and the UN experienced one of the worst crises in its history.

Public protest was rampant, while the superpowers engaged in testing not only their warheads and missiles, but also their political will. Prime Minister Nehru of India was the first to propose, in April 1954, a "standstill agreement"[70] on nuclear tests. This matter was subsequently discussed regularly in the UN General Assembly. In July 1956, the British sought private discussions with the Americans on "test restrictions". According to Greb[71], this initiative was rejected by the United States. The issue of halting nuclear testing was amongst the ten collateral measures suggested within the framework of general and complete disarmament in the marathon proposal submitted[72] on 27 August 1957 by the Western nations to the Subcommittee of the Disarmament Commission in London. The issue, therefore, remained inextricably linked to broader general agreements. The United States held to this position until 31 October 1958, the date of the official opening of the Conference of Experts on Detection of Nuclear Tests. This Conference predicated its analysis on the basis of the Rainier series of tests. This somewhat tenuous basis was subsequently challenged by a number of observers[73] following the Hardtack series of tests in October 1958. At that point, it was discovered that it was possible to muffle the explosive power of a nuclear test.

On 8 April 1958, in a letter to Chairman Khrushchev, President Eisenhower asked for "technical discussions" on the matter. On 22 August 1958, in independent statements, the British and the Americans declared their desire for formal negotiations on the suspension of nuclear tests. The tripartite Conference opened in Geneva on 31 October 1958 in somewhat unfavourable conditions since the Soviets had resumed nuclear testing one month earlier. The Soviets continued testing until 3 November 1958, at which time they agreed to a halt. Britain had stopped testing on 23 September, and the United States on 30 October. Between November 1958 and September 1961, at which time the Soviets resumed testing, the world enjoyed the longest moratorium ever observed prior to the formal signing in 1963 of the Treaty Banning Nuclear Weapon Tests in the Atmosphere, in Outer Space and Under Water, generally known as the Partial Test Ban Treaty (PTBT).

The Soviet rationale for the resumption of testing in autumn 1961 was predicated on the French nuclear tests in the Sahara in 1960. The Americans, taken by surprise, were only ready to resume testing on 25 April 1962. These conditions hardly favoured the work of the Eighteen-Nation Committee which, at that point in time, had been charged with studying these problems. A few days earlier, on 16 April 1962, the eight Neutral and Non-Aligned (NNA) nations had presented their memorandum[74] against the wishes of the super-powers.[75] At first bluntly rejected, it was used later as a "basis for new negotiations". East-West divergence persisted over whether the provisions of the memorandum concerning on-site inspection were supposed to be compulsory or optional.

This question became the central issue of the debate. On three occasions the United States argued that underground tests should be segregated from the overall issue of suspension of nuclear tests in the other three environments: space, underwater and in the atmosphere. Proposals to this effect were submitted by President Eisenhower on 13 April 1959 and 11 February 1960[76], and were also integral to the Anglo-American proposals of 27 August 1962. At that time, the Soviets refused to consider these Western proposals on the pretext that underground nuclear tests were excluded. In July 1963, however, following discussions with u.s. negotiator Averell Harriman, Moscow came to accept them. Harriman, who was authorized to negotiate an overall suspension of nuclear tests, was thus only able to obtain Soviet agreement on a Partial Test Ban Treaty.[77]

As a result, the two superpowers finally decided to come to terms with reality. Following the Cuban missile crisis some compromise was necessary, and public opinion, which clamoured for a nuclear test ban, had to be appeased. We know today that, on both sides, the superpower agreement was authored by the politicians, against the advice of their respective military establishments. The testimony and depositions of experts, in the United States at least, showed clearly that Congress finally supported ratification of the Treaty only after receiving formal assurances from the u.s. Administration. The Treaty was signed in Moscow on 5 August 1963 and entered into effect on 10 October 1963 following the tabling of the instruments of ratification in the three capitals.

The Partial Test Ban Treaty (PTBT) resulted essentially from the political will of the two superpowers to reach agreement on a matter that was of paramount concern to pressure groups, pacifist movements such as the Campaign for Nuclear Disarmament (CND) and the Pugwash group (named after the location in Canada where scientists dedicated to peace first met), as well as the general public which was rightly concerned about the harmful and deleterious effects of "atomic poison". Following the Cuban missile crisis, the two superpowers became convinced of the need to avoid nuclear warfare. By signing the PTBT the superpowers finally recognized the merits of international moderation, but they still refused to move one inch on their need to maintain nuclear deterrence which, they believed, could alone guarantee their security.

Canada's Position between 1956 and 1963

In 1956, during debate in the UN Disarmament Commission, Australia, Canada, the United States, France and the United Kingdom proposed that any disarmament agreement be based on the three following principles:

The program should provide that, at appropriate stages and under proper safeguards, the build-up of stockpiles of nuclear weapons would be stopped, all future production of nuclear material would be devoted to peaceful uses and limitations would be imposed on the testing of nuclear weapons.[78]

At about this time, Canada undertook a comprehensive review of her general policies on the suspension of nuclear tests. Early in 1956, following a wave of world-wide protest against nuclear testing, External Affairs' Minister Pearson expressed his concern about the inadequacies of U.S. policy. John W. Holmes, in a note to Under-Secretary Léger, referred to Pearson's desire to halt nuclear testing, stating that it was "not good enough merely to argue that such a step must await an overall disarmament agreement".[79] For their part, the military establishments were unsympathetic to any constraint that would impact on the development of new weapons. On 4 April 1956, in a note to the Joint Intelligence Committee (JIC) prepared by the Defence Scientific Intelligence Division directed by J.C. Arnell, five key points were stressed: nuclear tests were essential for weapon development; the number of victims of these tests was negligible; the United Kingdom would not support a ban until the completion of its own thermonuclear test; it would be ludicrous to prohibit thermonuclear tests without including fission weapon tests[80]; and, there was little immediate danger of radioactive contamination, although the issue was continually under review.[81] In defence of the Scientific Intelligence Division, it must be admitted that the document also contained a good number of arguments for Canadian support of a possible test ban. On the whole, however, it was weighted squarely in favour of continued testing. The JIC concurred in the view of the Scientific Intelligence Division.

At about that time, Marcel Cadieux of the United Nations Division suggested opening up the Arctic to the Americans so that they could pursue nuclear testing with complete equanimity.[82] Cadieux sent a note to Jules Léger recommending that he adopt the position of the JIC which argued against Canadian support for a ban on nuclear tests. This note passed through the office of John W. Holmes, who made the annotation: "I am afraid I have not had time to study this carefully, but I do not want to delay it further".[83] Five days later, Jules Léger gave his opinion to External Affairs' Minister Pearson. He argued that, given the strong opposition in the United States to a nuclear test ban, it would be difficult not to support the position of the JIC, even though the JIC had not taken account of the proposals discussed in the UN Disarmament Commission. Although Léger felt that a test ban should continue to be an overall objective for the West, he suggested that it might be more appropriate in the circumstances for the Canadian Delegation to the UN to support the ideas of "monitoring" and "regulating" tests. These were two of the key ideas embodied in Phase One of the U.S. proposals to the London Subcommittee and in Phase Two[84] of the Anglo-French disarmament proposal. The British were strongly opposed to an early halting of the tests, since their testing program was scheduled to begin in the forthcoming months.[85]

Clearly, Léger was trying to keep everyone happy, avoiding serious dissent among the member nations of the London Subcommittee while stressing the need for the West to abandon the posture of "defensive diplomacy" in which it was locked. In his various notes to Pearson, Léger repeated all the humanitarian arguments which he found "authentic" among the nations. The position of Paul Martin, then Minister of Health and Welfare, was essentially the same. In a speech to the House on 17 July, Martin recalled that Canada was in favour of halting nuclear tests and of establishing a Committee of Experts "to consider a limitation on the number and nature of test explosions".[86]

One day later, Léger wrote a lengthy memorandum[87] to Pearson, stating:

A complete prohibition of tests of all kinds of nuclear weapons, standing alone, would present a number of substantial problems. It would raise Soviet political objections if its control were to be effective. It would involve technical control difficulties which might never be disposed of to the satisfaction of the United States. It might well be opposed by our combined Chiefs of Staff. And it would in all possibility be opposed by the United States and the United Kingdom.

An agreement on the limitation and regulation of test explosions would partly or wholly avoid each of these objections ... Limitations relating to size and frequency of explosions should not be open to the same objections on the part of our combined Chiefs of Staff as total prohibition. The United Kingdom and the United States have expressed themselves in favour of limitations in certain conditions. And the objectives which would be served by Canadian support of the total prohibition of tests can equally well be achieved by a policy of limitation.

Léger concluded by stating that Canada should persuade the United States and the United Kingdom of the validity of the Canadian position, and try to change the allied view which held that a test ban was possible only within the framework of an overall disarmament agreement. At the suggestion of Cadieux, and with the concurrence of John W. Holmes, this memorandum was sent not only to Pearson, but also to Paul Martin. The stage was set for a significant change in Canada's foreign policy. The phrase "self-denying ordinance for the nuclear powers" was used in later texts. Two reservations were, however, expressed. First, the Joint Chiefs of Staff should be consulted and, second, the British should be given time to conduct their planned nuclear tests.

During the third week of May 1956, Canada learned through the foreign press that the U.K. was thinking not only of holding trilateral negotiations on the subject, but also of separating it from the whole disarmament issue. Jules Léger was furious.[88] The Americans too were outraged, and reprimanded the British for this blatant lack of consultation. The British were actually thinking in terms of limitations, but not of overall prohibition of tests. This incident provided added impetus to the review of Canadian policy, and all else was subordinated to this end.[89]

The work continued throughout the whole summer. The policy review involved a number of government departments and agencies, foremost among which were the Department of National Defence, the Defence Research Board, the Atomic Energy Laboratories at Chalk River, the Department of Health and Welfare and, of course, the Department of External Affairs. There was a wide diversity of opinion, and this was characteristic of the times. The Minister of National Defence stuck solidly to his conservative position. Chalk River was reticent to make any definitive pronouncement on the dangers of radioactivity and the Department of Health and Welfare, in concert with the Department of External Affairs, displayed nothing but extreme circumspection.

The Defence Research Board (DRB) engaged in lengthy debates on radioactive contamination, and there was talk of "maximum permissible concentration". A.K. Longair of DRB stressed that there were "legitimate differences of opinion". Chalk River, in particular, was most reticent to minimize the long-term dangers of radioactivity. It was estimated[90] that, in 1954 alone, U.S. tests liberated at least 50 Mt of fissile matter in the atmosphere, perhaps even more. DRB proposed that an annual limit of 50 Mt, or 250 Mt over five years be adopted as an acceptable threshold, stating that it would be unrealistic to adopt a limit of 1 Mt for individual tests, since the danger to public health depended on the total accumulation of radioactivity. For this reason, if the threshold of 250 Mt were not reached in the first five-year period, the shortfall should not be added to the second five-year period. DRB was undoubtedly correct, but the procedure was artificial and hardly convincing.

In documents published later, it was stressed that these estimates were based on data received from Canada's allies. In point of fact, the only data provided by the allies came from the British in their Command Paper 9780 and from the Americans in the *Proceedings of the National Academy of Sciences*.[91] DND documents stressed the importance of nuclear weapons for strategic defence, both in air defence where the nuclear intercepting warheads would have yields of several hundreds of kilotonnes, and in anti-missile defence where interception could be effected at altitudes of some 20 miles with megatonnic yield warheads.[92]

These arguments were obviously staffed up the chain of military command to the Chairman, Joint Chiefs of Staff and thence to the offices of the ministers of primary interest.[93] The recommendations were finalized at the 597th Meeting of the Joint Chiefs of Staff on 3 October 1956: Canada should support a minimum test policy in order to ensure the effectiveness of weapons on which NATO depended; a global limit on testing should be accepted if it met the needs of NATO without endangering public health across the world; and, agreement in principle should be sought to establish a system of prior registration of nuclear tests with an international committee which would be responsible for subsequent verification.

On the face of it, three recommendations were made, but in fact there was really only one, for the other two simply echoed the agreement in principle of the Joint Chiefs of Staff to establish an international test surveillance system which would fix the annual upper limit of nuclear tests at 50 Mt. The first recommendation recognized the possible need for megatonne weapons for the defence of Canada, and called for a reappraisal of how this might affect previous policies on atomic requirements. The Department of National Defence thus succeeded in transforming a request for limitation of nuclear tests into a requirement for maximization of tests and a claim for more nuclear weapons.

In his report on this meeting to External Affairs' Minister Pearson, R.M. MacDonnell – who signed on behalf of Léger[94] – presented a rather dispassionate analysis of the issues:

It would appear that, according to the more conservative views, i.e., those which set the quantity of radiation added at a high figure and the danger threshold at a low figure, the point has already been reached at which nuclear explosions should cease. Even the more "optimistic" group would set this point only a few years in the future.

National Health and Welfare would prefer not to adopt a position immediately on these matters. During the next three or four weeks there will be a series of conferences – of Commonwealth experts in London beginning on October 9, of the United States, the United Kingdom and Canada in Washington about October 18 and of the United Nations Scientific Committee in New York beginning on October 22 ...

The root of the National Defence position is that only atomic weapons, perhaps of a very large size, can provide effective defences for Canada against certain forms of atomic attack now in the process of evolution ... And because of the lack of original Canadian data on the effects of nuclear explosions, they are inclined to think that we should go along with any specific recommendations from the United States and the United Kingdom.

No one was about to put his conscience up for auction, but there could not have been a more elegant way of confusing the issue. Diplomacy is surely an art, but the search for truth should take precedence over the expedient of camouflaging feigned ignorance as a conciliatory virtue. MacDonnell claimed that the meeting had sensitized the military to the need for placing greater emphasis on the dangers of radioactivity "as a proximate problem" in policy development. Policies could be revised as more information became available. Clearly, the military considered that security needs had a higher priority than moral and scientific needs. To conclude, however, that the military preferred to follow the party line of the Alliance because they had no first hand information on the effects of nuclear explosions is to provide an unnecessary alibi to the Department of National Defence which clearly had consolidated its position considerably earlier.

The Department of External Affairs, unable to obtain a consensus on proposals to limit the explosive power and frequency of nuclear tests, and faced with the uncertainties within scientific circles on acceptable levels of radioactive fallout[95], looked to foreign capitals before seeking any further advice from Canada's own Department of National Defence.[96] On 29 October 1956, Cadieux was asked by the Information Bureau of External Affairs whether the statement made before the House in July by Paul Martin, Minister of National Health and Welfare, was still valid. Cadieux responded that the Canadian position was unchanged, but that External Affairs' Minister Pearson had added a new element to the debate in the House on 1 August by adopting the British position that a global prohibition on testing should be part of a general disarmament agreement, lacking which, the negotiations would have to be limited.

That was about as far as the Canadian Government could go in 1956. The telegrams sent in November to the Canadian Delegation in New York in preparation for the UN General Assembly discussions referred to the "self-denying ordinance" and to Canadian support for a policy of restricted tests. Canada continued to follow the debates and to intervene as appropriate, but her position remained unchanged. Limitations and restrictions were desirable for humanitarian reasons. Nothing new appeared until the time of the breakthrough of the Conference of Experts on the Detection of Nuclear Tests and the tripartite Geneva Conference on the Halting of Nuclear Tests.

In the area of verification and control, Canada missed an unexpected opportunity. In 1958, the Defence Research Board conducted a lengthy study on this issue. DRB considered it equitable that Canada should maintain 5 of the 170 seismic detection stations that had been proposed in Geneva. Some thirty scientists would be assigned of each of these detection stations, together with the requisite support personnel. Canada wanted the organization responsible for monitoring nuclear tests to report to the UN rather than the IAEA, believing that it was better to report to the Secretary General of the United Nations rather than to an organization that was not a specialized institution of the United Nations.[97]

This position was also supported by the British, who sought to establish an international corps of technicians. Canada had nothing against that, on condition that their allegiance to the United Nations be clearly defined. On 12 November 1958, DRB Chairman Zimmerman stressed:

If we were to listen to the British, Canada would only contribute land and money to the system ... In addition, the seismic stations under national control would provide complementary information to that obtained by the "authorized detection stations". Would this mean that the existing national stations would continue to operate alongside the network planned by the

British? ... It would be more economical for the national networks to be integrated with the international system planned by the British, which was to be set up over a five-year period.

On 9 January 1959, Zimmerman elaborated further in a letter to Norman A. Robertson:

Canada should reserve the right to approve the kind of equipment that would be installed on her soil, and should be free to operate any other kind of technical equipment, provided that such equipment would not prejudice the effective operation of the planned verification and control system.

At this point in the studies, and with international negotiations at a standstill, External Affairs' Minister Green received a message from British Prime Minister Harold MacMillan dated 28 April 1960 inviting Canada to develop, in collaboration with the British, a "programme of coordinated research" aimed at improving seismic detection methods for nuclear tests registering less than 4.75 on the Richter scale. Howard Green faithfully transmitted the content of MacMillan's letter to Prime Minister Diefenbaker. On 14 May, he followed it up with a memorandum to Cabinet, in which he made an assessment of the British request.

Green considered that it essentially comprised two requests. First, that a major seismological monitoring station be established on Canadian soil to serve as an experimental facility. Second, the main monitoring station would be linked with some twenty mobile stations, in this instance trucks, each manned by three or four technicians. The main experimental station would be on a 24-hour vigil, and staffed by 16 technicians. The total cost of this system was projected as 2.5 million pounds sterling, or seven million dollars.

The snag was that nuclear tests would have to be conducted in order to prove the reliability of the system. Green reminded Diefenbaker of his statement in the House of 2 August 1958, to the effect that Canada would be willing to participate in the establishment of an international seismic detection network. Green went on to point out that this statement was made well before it was realized that additional nuclear tests would be required to prove the system and that Canada's policy was one of "unqualified opposition to all tests".

Green won his case in Cabinet. The question was considered at the end of May 1960, but no one wanted to follow up on any such request unless it had been formulated jointly by the United States, the United Kingdom and the USSR. Canada thus missed an unique opportunity to pursue dialogue leading to the establishment of the first bilateral seismological detection network, whose main elements would subsequently become multilateral in scope. By wishing to declare himself more orthodox than the Pope, Green forgot that the Church cannot operate without a Vicar. He preferred the status of apostolic nuncio to that of curate which the British legitimately required of him.

All indications point to the fact that the British were sincere. The records reveal nothing to indicate that it was a disguised attempt on the part of the British to make Green feel more comfortable about things nuclear, or to justify nuclear tests on the grounds that they were needed to demonstrate the effectiveness of detection devices. From 1958 onwards, bilateral agreements with the Americans allowed the British to make unmistakable progress in this area.

Between 1960 and 1963, Canada attempted to lay emphasis on the technical aspects of underground nuclear test detection, and to influence negotiations in the Eighteen-Nation Disarmament Committee. Until the demise of the Diefenbaker Government, the positions of the Departments of External Affairs and of National Defence were diametrically opposed. The Harkness-Green and Miller-Burns pairs were pulling against each other, while Diefenbaker, unable to resolve the conflict, became the fallen hero of the piece.[98]

Zimmerman, in the Department of National Defence, deeply regretted the lack of Canadian expertise. At the time, there was one former British scientist who had previously worked on nuclear weapon development, but he was not up to date on these issues. On such matters, Zimmerman sought tighter links with London and Washington. A policy of test limitation would not necessarily reduce the threat of war. Indeed, it could even have the opposite effect, since only a policy of deterrence could guarantee Western security. These considerations are documented in the paper *Disarmament and Deterrence* which was approved by the Joint Chiefs of Staff at their 662nd meeting partitioned between 9 and 13 June 1960. Canada was moving further and further away from the military policies of 1956.

On 30 January 1961, the Joint Chiefs of Staff produced an interesting report on the suspension of nuclear tests, which was revised and amplified on 30 June 1961. This document was the very model of an operational staff paper developed by a military organization working with clockwork precision. Many observers consider that the arguments advanced at the time are still valid today. The rationale for testing was strategic, economic and political in nature. From a strategic standpoint, information was needed for a number of reasons: to assess the effectiveness of ABM nuclear interceptors; to improve miniaturization techniques; to develop precision nuclear weapons (the "neutron" bomb is still a current topic); to understand better the effects of underwater nuclear explosions; to appreciate the effects of nuclear explosions on space-based warning and communications systems; to determine the effective lifetimes of nuclear weapons and the attendant need to replace them; to evaluate the reliability of "fail-safe" systems, specifically electronic locking and unlocking mechanisms; and, finally, to assess the resistance of concrete silos. From an economic standpoint, tests were needed to develop potential nuclear propulsion systems, to conduct experiments for peaceful purposes and to reduce the production costs of nuclear equipment by using less expensive materials and smaller amounts of fissile material. Nuclear tests were also required to improve the effectiveness of seismological detection systems. It was clear from this kind of thinking that the Department of National Defence was remarkably astute and well-informed on all the issues that it particularly espoused, but pleaded ignorance when proposals were made by other departments which were at variance with its views.

When the Soviets decided to slam the door[99], the Ten-Nation Committee on Disarmament found itself still-born, and was never able to consider the issue of a nuclear test ban. In 1960, there was talk of general and complete disarmament. The issue of a nuclear test ban became even more urgent when the Eighteen-Nation Disarmament Committee started its work in March 1962. The Soviets had resumed testing in 1961, and the Americans planned to resume testing off the Christmas Islands in April 1962. Washington was acutely conscious of the diplomatic difficulties that would arise, and tried to avert their impact by arranging consultations[100] between Secretary of State Rusk and Canadian Ambassador Heeney.

Rightly or wrongly, the Americans were concerned about the initiative taken by eight neutral countries on 16 April 1962. The U.S. and the USSR were forewarned of this initiative by Indian Delegate Arthur Lall, an initiative that was criticized subsequently by several non-aligned nations.[101] Washington also wondered whether Canada intended to co-sponsor a proposal made by Sweden, one of the eight non-aligned countries of the Eighteen-Nation Committee, on the issue of nuclear tests. Secretary Rusk had even discussed the matter by telephone with External Affairs' Minister Green during the preceding week. Heeney assured Rusk that Canada did not intend to co-sign the document even though the content appeared "constructive" and conducive to a *rapprochement* between the superpowers. Heeney also voiced Green's concerns that the resumption of testing would bring the world back to the worst hours of the Cold War, that the disarmament negotiations were at a "critical stage" and that it was essential, therefore, to reach speedy agreement even if only partial measures could be agreed upon.

For his part, Rusk stood behind U.S. policy. He reminded Canada that the United States had undertaken a major review of the issue in March 1961, and that the U.S. had significantly softened its requirements in the area of control at the risk of losing face before the Joint Committee on Atomic Energy. The U.S. had made over twenty changes to its draft, the most significant of which was U.S. support for a global ban on nuclear tests as expressed by President Kennedy in his statement of 2 March 1962. The result of this radical change was to reduce the number of inspections of suspect events from one in five to one in twenty. In addition, most seismological stations were to be relocated, and the larger part of the USSR would have only three seismological listening stations. In the event of inspection, there would be no more than two-thousandths of Soviet territory open to foreign eyes. Despite all these concessions, Gromyko apparently informed Rusk in Geneva that even one man "might bring back secret information damaging to the USSR."

The Rusk-Heeney discussions actually had two purposes. First, to inform Canada that a control system involving the participation of non-aligned countries would be unacceptable to the United States, a fact that was already known to Ottawa. Second, and more importantly, to seek means of preventing non-aligned nations from withdrawing from the Eighteen-Nation Committee once the United States resumed testing. The same message arrived from London on 11 April. It could be paraphrased, in somewhat undiplomatic terms, as follows: keep the non-aligned nations busy so that they don't panic! Canada did, in fact, seek the active support of the non-aligned nations in the Eighteen-Nation Committee during the 1960s. As it turned out, London and Washington were not completely wrong in counting on Canada's collaboration, which was particularly useful since the Soviets were trying to persuade the non-aligned nations to withdraw from the Eighteen Nation Committee.[102] In view of the lengthy memorandum that the non-aligned nations had prepared on a nuclear test ban, it is doubtful that they thought seriously of withdrawing from the Committee. It must be recognized, however, that the willingness of the superpowers to consider this document as a "basis for negotiation", given their violent opposition to its tabling, was surely a greater factor in keeping these non-aligned nations at the negotiating table than the modest influence that Canada could exert within the Committee.

When the Americans resumed nuclear testing on 25 April 1962, Prime Minister Diefenbaker expressed Canada's "profound regret". He argued strongly for the adoption of the memorandum of non-aligned countries which he viewed as a sincere effort to reach a compromise. The same sentiments were echoed by the UN General Assembly in Resolution 1762 B adopted at its 17th Meeting on 6 November when the memorandum of the eight non-aligned nations was accepted as a "basis for negotiation". The UN General Assembly insisted that the tests should cease immediately or, at the very latest, by 1 January 1963. Significantly, this resolution, which appeared just a few days after the Cuban missile crisis, was supported jointly by the United States and the United Kingdom. When the Eighteen-Nation Committee resumed its work in 1963, discussions centred on a complete test ban in all environments.

The Memorandum to Cabinet on nuclear testing dated 28 May 1963 has been mentioned previously in Chapter 6 in the section on "Continuity of Canadian Policy". This Cabinet Memorandum recommended that no undue pressure should be placed on the United States and the United Kingdom to accept Soviet proposals which they could not support. Ottawa thus tempered its position. Because Canada was kept informed of the American-Soviet dialogue, there was no longer any excuse to go off track. On 10 June, it was announced that the U.S., the U.K. and the USSR had agreed to meet in Moscow in mid-July ...

The trilateral negotiations in Moscow were completed in just ten days. The world had awaited international agreement since 1954, and the Partial Test Ban Treaty (PTBT) was finally signed in August 1963. After that, only a few explosions were felt around the planet, and they were modest compared with those produced earlier by the superpowers. As noted previously, the French and Chinese nuclear tests account for only 13% of the total megatonnic yield exploded in the atmosphere since 1945 and their impact is, therefore, small in relation to that caused by the superpowers. In a letter to General Burns in Geneva, A.K. Longair of the Defence Research Board estimated the amount of radioactive fallout in the atmosphere from the various sources as follows:

- up to 1958: 92 megatonnes of fission products;
- USSR (1961): 25 megatonnes of fission products;
- U.S. (1962): 10 megatonnes (May 1962 estimate, based on pessimistic assumptions concerning U.S. tests).

Longair also estimated that the total fallout from nuclear tests conducted between 1945 and the time of the moratorium in 1958 as

5% of all the natural radiation striking Earth from the environment.[103] Canada ratified the PTBT on 28 January 1964.

THE ELUSIVE CTB TREATY

Few issues have preoccupied the international community more than the quest for a Comprehensive Test Ban (CTB) Treaty. The UN General Assembly has regularly revisited this issue and it has been a perennial subject of multilateral negotiation. Many countries, including Canada, have always considered a CTB as a priority, and all the significant documents and treaties signed since 1963 have constantly reminded the superpowers of their responsibilities to bring to an end the development of nuclear weapons. There appear to be two alternatives: either the superpowers abandon nuclear technology as a means of ensuring their security, which would require a fundamental change in strategic thinking, or they seek other technological options to preserve the *status quo*, which would mean abandoning nuclear weapons that nobody wants anyway, and which are maintained only because of paralysis rooted in fear.

The threat of nuclear peril certainly invites wisdom, but the absence of such peril could just as easily lead to other types of threat, perhaps equally ruinous and onerous for humanity. There is, however, the subtle difference that the survival of the entire human race would not necessarily be in jeopardy.

Overview of Negotiations

Between 1963 and 1988, no effort was spared in encouraging the superpowers to abandon nuclear testing. Most of the discussions took place within the UN itself, or at the bilateral, trilateral or multilateral levels.

Starting in 1957, the issue of banning nuclear tests was added to the agenda of the UN General Assembly. Since 1963, when the PTBT was signed, up to the end of 1987, there was a plethora of almost 50 resolutions.[104] During this period, there were two significant developments. The first occurred on 16 December 1969 when, at the initiative of Canada and several other countries, the UN General Assembly asked the Secretary General to solicit the assistance of nations in providing certain information in the context of an international exchange of seismological data.[105] The second was the publication[106] on 16 April 1986 of a study sponsored by the UN Secretary General on a global nuclear test ban. The experts who participated in this study concluded that a total test ban should be considered as "the foremost and most urgent step" towards halting the nuclear arms race.

A UN *Ad Hoc* Working Group on banning nuclear tests was established by consensus[107] on 21 April 1982. By 1988, this Working Group had still not received a formal mandate to negotiate a global test ban treaty, despite continual exhortations from member nations. As early as 1980, UN member nations had argued that the Committee on Disarmament, the forerunner of the *Ad Hoc* Working Group, be given a formal mandate to negotiate a comprehensive test ban treaty. Conceivably, such a mandate could be accorded in future years if the superpowers follow through with their statements of 1987 and those made at the Moscow Summit in 1988 concerning a phased approach to the conclusion of a Comprehensive Test Ban (CTB) Treaty. For the moment, this is still far from reality, since neither West nor East can agree on the mandate for this organization. Perhaps the role of the *Ad Hoc* Group will be important only *a posteriori*, given that the superpowers will likely accept no more than has been previously agreed.

Amongst the various multilateral fora, the Group of Scientific Experts (GSE), responsible for studying verification issues, has made the most significant progress. The work of the other fora, specifically that of the Eighteen-Nation Committee on Disarmament and its successors (the Conference of the Committee on Disarmament, the Committee on Disarmament and the Conference on Disarmament), was clearly concerned with political rather than technical issues.

Over the years, the issue has received greater or lesser emphasis in concert with changes on the international scene. Following the signing of the Partial Test Ban Treaty, concern over nuclear proliferation became the order of the day. The preamble of the PTBT puts the onus on the superpowers to seek agreement on banning all nuclear tests in all environments and for all time. When the nuclear Non-Proliferation Treaty (NPT) was signed, the superpowers undertook to negotiate a halt to the arms race in good faith, which all concerned nations understood to mean a nuclear test ban. This aspect was continually at the fore throughout the three Review Conferences on the NPT.

Within the framework of the SALT negotiations in the late 1960s, interest shifted towards reducing offensive weapons. President Gerald Ford continued the work of his predecessor, Richard Nixon. Nixon was in favour of a CTB, but found that the SALT negotiations consumed all his time and energies.[108] The increasingly bilateral nature of the dialogue led to a series of summits and to the signing of the treaties negotiated under the Ford administration, specifically, the Threshold Test Ban Treaty (TTBT)[109] signed on 3 July 1974 which limited underground nuclear explosions to a ceiling of 150 Kt, and the complement of this treaty, the Peaceful Nuclear Explosions Treaty (PNET)[110], signed on 28 May 1976.

In 1974, the superpowers negotiated the TTBT in only five weeks during the hastily-called Moscow Summit, perhaps because there was little else on the agenda. The limit of 150 Kt would appear to be somewhat arbitrary, but was likely selected because it was about one-third of the actual expected yield of nuclear warheads currently in development.[111] Nevertheless, at that time, the USSR was pursuing a significant program of nuclear explosions for peaceful purposes. The two issues were thus viewed as clearly distinct, and bilateral negotiations on the second treaty began only in October 1974.

The same limit of 150 Kt was also accepted for individual nuclear explosions for peaceful purposes, except that the tests were to be conducted at test sites other than those identified in the TTBT of 1974. Essentially, this meant that such explosions could not be conducted in facilities that were normally used for military purposes. "Composite explosions" of total power greater than 150 Kt were also prohibited unless the nuclear devices were separated by at least 40 km[112] or that successive explosions were phased to occur over periods in excess of 5 seconds. Finally, the Protocol to the Peaceful Nuclear Explosions Treaty (PNET) specified that the Parties to the Treaty should not derive any military benefit from tests undertaken for peaceful purposes. Neither treaty was ratified by the United States, although both Parties respected the terms of the treaties for all practical purposes. In 1988, both superpowers were still conducting validation tests on their verification systems – the CORRTEX system – in Nevada and at Semipalatinsk, in order to provide the requisite follow-up to the two treaties with a view to their eventual ratification. In 1988, the verification protocol for the 1976 PNET was virtually completed, the Soviets having insisted that this be written before the protocol for the TTBT.

The international community was certainly encouraged by the new treaties, but most nations felt that they ran counter not only to the spirit of a CTB Treaty but to its eventual realization. Trilateral negotiations between the United States, the United Kingdom and the USSR resumed in the autumn of 1977. In his memoirs, ex-President Carter recalls that both he and Gromyko decided in September 1978 to proceed first with a SALT agreement before addressing the issue of a CTB Treaty. The events in Afghanistan in 1979, together with the internal difficulties experienced in the United States, led to a complete impasse in negotiations.

Nevertheless, important progress was made in these trilateral negotiations. In 1976, the USSR finally agreed to on-site inspections (OSI), and even to inspection on challenge. The three parties then jointly agreed to develop, test and produce "fool-proof" detection systems – the famous "black boxes" that were proposed by the Pugwash movement in the early 1960s. In the trilateral report[113] of the Committee on Disarmament, the three powers stated simply that they were "negotiating" the question of National Seismic Stations (NSS) but that exceptional progress had been achieved on the three important issues of global exchange of seismological data, the need for the Committee of Experts and OSI.

It is now known that the CTB treaty was first intended to be of indefinite duration, but that it was subsequently limited by Carter to five years and then to three years. The vacillations in U.S. policy and the pressures exerted by the bureaucracy and by the major research establishments finally "literally consumed" the CTB treaty.[114] For their part, the Soviets insisted that there be an equal number of seismological stations installed on the territories of the three parties. This implied ten seismological stations in the U.K., which was more than the British were willing to accept. Whether the Soviets intended to demonstrate that the real problem was political rather than technical, or were simply disinterested in negotiating a CTB while awaiting the inauguration of a new President in Washington, is a question which may never be answered.

In any event, negotiations were suspended in November 1980, and officially broken off in 1982 when President Reagan decided that underground nuclear tests were essential to U.S. security. In 1986, the superpowers re-established lines of communication on this subject, and a major breakthrough occurred with the meeting of Shevardnadze and Schultz in September 1987. At that point, the superpowers moved from a stage of consultation to one of formal negotiation. At least, that was the essence of the joint communiqué issued on 17 September 1987. In January 1988, technical teams visited the respective test facilities. In August 1988, the first joint tests were undertaken to assess the reliability of the respective detection systems. If the tests prove positive, the two superpowers should proceed to ratify the treaties of 1974 (TTBT) and of 1976 (PNET) as a matter of established protocol. According to the Moscow Declaration of June 1988, limitation and eventual banning of nuclear tests will have to follow a phased approach of international negotiation. One might expect, therefore, that the Protocols of the 1974 and 1976 treaties will be rapidly negotiated, and that subsequently the superpowers will conclude a START Agreement, followed by negotiations to eliminate underground nuclear explosions "for all time". In the interim, there might even be reason to hope that the thresholds of underground nuclear explosions could be reduced to levels below that of the Hiroshima bomb.

Canada's Position Between 1963 and 1978

Prior to the time of the first United Nations Special Session on Disarmament (UNSSOD I) in 1968, the Canadian position on a CTB Treaty changed several times. The three most important changes occurred in 1966, 1969 and 1974, and they may be characterized by three words: prudence, open-mindedness and compromise. In 1963 the Liberals seized power from the Conservatives. Following the somewhat smug optimism of Green, who was unable to appreciate the gulf separating reality from true international peace and security, a pragmatic policy began to emerge which built on progressively increasing Canadian competence in the area of seismic detection.

No real political progress was made on a nuclear test ban during the seven years that the Eighteen-Nation Committee was in existence. The neutral countries favoured some three or four inspections per year, which nowadays might be described as Confidence-Building Measures (CBMs).[115] In 1963, General Burns declared that the security of nations could not be ensured through two or three annual inspections.[116] In the years that followed, up to 1969, Canada's general position was to support all attempts to achieve a CTB through a framework of negotiation and an effective verification system.

The Phase of Prudence. During the 1960s, discussion centred on three main proposals: the principle of "inspection on challenge", the creation of a "seismic detection club", and the concept of "thresholds" proposed by the Pugwash movement in 1961 and 1962.[117] The first two were advanced by Sweden in 1965.[118] The third was championed by Ethiopia in 1964[119] and by Mexico and the UAR in 1965. Support from the UAR was essentially accorded to prevent Israel from testing its nuclear devices. The "threshold" concept was supported chiefly by the neutral countries apart from Sweden which, like many other countries, opposed it on the grounds that such measures only partly met the objective of a global nuclear test ban.

Sweden sought Canada's support against this idea of a "threshold". At the end of the 1965 session, General Burns said only that the concept was "attractive" but that "we would need to know a good deal more about the facts" before rejecting it.[120] The British found the idea "attractive" but foresaw "serious objections". The United States was ready to re-evaluate its position, albeit without much enthusiasm, but would make no concessions on inspection. Kosygin's position, according to Lord Chalfont, was that the Russians "were not interested in such refinements as a threshold".[121] The Delegation in Geneva considered it as a "fallback position"[122], since Burns rightly considered that such an approach would only encourage attempts to refine "de-coupling" techniques. Burns felt, nevertheless, that the Western position was becoming increasingly untenable and rigid.

In Ottawa, the issue was studied without much success. On 30 May 1966, D.M. Cornett, Director General of the Disarmament Division, following many discussions with the scientific community, concluded that no authoritative opinion could be advanced since there was no information that could confirm or invalidate the data provided by the United States. He noted that the pressures to change Canada's position came, understandably, from the Canadian Delegation in Geneva. In a memorandum to the Minister dated 14 June on the state of negotiations, Marcel Cadieux concurred:

Following a re-examination of Canada's policies, there is no reason to change the traditional position which calls for an effective verification system including on-site inspections. It would be unwise to act otherwise, given that Canada has no specific information on the matter, and that there is no strong public pressure for a CTB.

Actually, this re-examination was undertaken largely to satisfy Canadian desire to understand the situation better, particularly in light of persistent rumours abroad concerning progress in seismic detection technology. The reticence of Canadian public officials was well founded. On 22 March 1966, H.B. Robinson signed a series of letters, on behalf of the Under-Secretary of State for External Affairs, appealing for help. These letters were addressed to officials in the Department of National Defence[123] and to Dr. Kenneth Whitham, a seismologist of international repute, in the Department of Mines and Technical Surveys. The letter to the Chairman of the Joint Chiefs of Staff, Air Marshal Frank Miller, posed eleven questions. The first ten concerned detection techniques, while the eleventh sought his advice on the value of nuclear testing. In a second letter to Whitham, dated 26 April 1964, the Under-Secretary of State for External Affairs stated that the Canadian Government could not proceed "diplomatically" until the scientific context had been clarified.

Air Marshal Miller held to his arrogant position cited in epigraph – we should be careful about displaying our ignorance – and insisted on the need to conduct tests to develop weapons for the ABM mission.

He returned to this point in his letter of 18 April to the Under-Secretary of State for External Affairs. He argued that, on the subject of improving detection capabilities at the expense of on-site inspections, Canada should support the Americans rather than neutral countries, such as Sweden, so as not to sabotage the u.s. position.[124] Longair of DRB, in private discussions with D.M. Cornett on 15 April, was more prudent. He endorsed the same arguments for support of ABM defence, but stated that he thought that tests to improve the warheads on u.s. missiles were unnecessary, and felt that an effective ABM system against Soviet missiles was "unattainable".[125] Clearly, there was a divergence of opinion between the senior military and scientific staffs. Miller believed that an ABM system was definitely possible, and that its realization depended more on economic than technical constraints. Longair probably felt obliged to express his position verbally to External Affairs out of respect for the hierarchy.

J.M. Harrison, Assistant Deputy Minister (Research) at the Department of Mines and Technical Surveys, replied on 7 April to the 22 March letter from External Affairs, stating:

No research or evaluation program exists within our Department on such a complex subject. This is regrettable and the Department can respond only in general terms to the questions posed. In addition, we have no information on the merits of on-site inspection systems.

From a technical standpoint, the response from the Department of Mines and Technical Surveys was also a call for better equipment and greater investment:

Factors of 10 in capital cost, computing equipment and manpower are crudely equivalent to one-half magnitude, i.e., an increase in the total Western world effort by ten times might push the same identification probability down to magnitude 3.5, although this is not certain.

I quote from A.K. Longair, DRB, his understanding which is also that of the Observatories Branch "the pessimists in the u.s.a. say that of the possible 250 events annually in the ussr the use of LASA will reduce the number of unidentified events only from 80 to 55". This is a percentage change from 68% identification capability to 78% identification capability, or an improvement of 10 parts in 68 or 15%.

On 4 May, a meeting of Canadian and American experts[126] was organized in order to clarify the concepts in vogue at the time – inspection on challenge, the nuclear detection club and the idea of a threshold. On the American side, participants included Ambassador

C. Timberlake of the U.S. Arms Control and Disarmament Agency (ACDA), Dr. Robert A. Frosch of the Advanced Research Projects Agency (ARPA), Dr. Stephen Lukasik of the Seismic Detection Office of the U.S. Department of Defense, and John L. Gawf, First Secretary at the United States Embassy in Ottawa. The representatives of External Affairs included H.R. Robinson, D.M. Cornett, and J.P. Chioler. Also present were Alex Longair from DRB and Dr. Ken Whitham of the Dominion Observatory. In discussions on the seismic detection club, it became apparent that the United States would not oppose it on condition that the club would not make political judgements on underground tests, since according to the Americans this was the prerogative of national organizations. Before such a club could gather a data bank and undertake analyses, all the implications would have to be examined. These discussions were primarily aimed at alerting Canada to the U.S. position on seismic detection prior to the first meeting of experts scheduled for May 1966 in Stockholm.

On the technical side, it was learned that the United States counted heavily on its LASA system, which was theoretically capable of detecting disturbances of magnitude 2.6. It was also revealed that the VELA system absorbed between 80% and 85% of the U.S. research program on seismic detection. These revelations surprised everyone at the time, since the diplomatic circles in Geneva had hoped that a treaty banning nuclear tests below a 4.5 or 4.7 threshold would eventually be possible. It was learned much later, however, that the LASA system had not completely met U.S. expectations. When H.R. Robinson enquired about the implications of such a system, the U.S. advised him that it could contribute towards reducing the number of required on-site inspections and thus represented a step closer to a total ban.

Generally, the U.S. position was very clear. The U.S. was not opposed to the idea of increased international cooperation in the exchange of seismological data, provided that only those nations with the proper authority could make observations on the perceived events. Sweden, which had advanced this proposal in the first place, had no objection to this caveat. Concerning a treaty to permit tests below a given threshold – which remained to be determined – Washington agreed with Burns, believing that it would only encourage "decoupling". The idea of inspection on challenge was not popular either, since it would place the onus of proof on the wrong party, it would not solve the problems of on-site inspection and it would undoubtedly have been opposed by Moscow which had shown no interest in the idea whatsoever. The Americans were not totally opposed to an international seismological detection network since they sought support from their allies to install LASA equipment on allied soil.

Canada continued to support the United States. In June 1966[127], the principle of inspection on challenge was accepted on condition that it would not be viewed as a substitute for on-site inspections. This position was tantamount to advocacy of the *status quo*.

Following the Commonwealth First Ministers Conference in London in autumn 1966, attitudes started to change. British Foreign Secretary Brown favoured the scientific approach, believing that the U.S. position on on-site inspections was "indefensible and unnecessary".[128] Telex 288 from Ottawa to London, dated 28 September, reveals that the British position took Canada by "surprise", since the U.K. had not made any mention of this new direction at the time of the Conference of Experts in NATO. On 12 October, Ottawa came to accept the view that it appeared possible to discriminate between earthquakes and underground nuclear explosions.[129] The words on the lips of all seismologists at the time were "there are no Love waves in explosions".[130] Unfortunately, it was later discovered that such was not always the case. A Briefing Note to the Minister of External Affairs prior to his visit to Europe[131] recommended that Canada should not "out-herod Herod" and advised that, for several months, Canada had not insisted on on-site inspections in anticipation of a possible shift in the U.S. position. It also touched on the renewed interest in "black box" installations, in light of certain advances in technology.

The Phase of Open-Mindedness.   In January 1967, at a meeting[132] in Washington attended by General Burns and several high level U.S. policy-makers in the arms control field, Dr. Herbert Scoville, then Assistant Director of the U.S. Department of Science and Technology, confirmed that current technological progress in seismic detection made it possible to distinguish between earthquakes and explosions of magnitude 4.5, compared with 4.75 which was the previous threshold of discrimination. "Black boxes" were used in experiments conducted at various locations in New Mexico, Utah and Alaska. Scoville concluded that these devices should serve to keep the Soviets "honest" because, until then, it was relatively easy to falsify seismological data.

The Swedes took advantage of this information to reintroduce the idea of extending the PTBT of 1963 to underground tests. The Swedes essentially judged that the margin of error in discrimination could henceforth be considered negligible. Canada did not share this view.[133] In October 1967, Ottawa supported Washington in its proposal to accord responsibility for developing a seismic detection network[134] to the World Meteorological Organization (WMO), even though Whitham considered that this extra responsibility could seriously impede the communications capability of this organization.[135] For all intents and purposes, this proposal resulted from a certain *rapprochement* between various organizations in the United States responsible for seismic detection – the Environmental Sciences Agency (ESA) among others.

This proposal marked the beginning of the process of international sharing of seismic data. It allowed the USSR to participate at low cost and to have access to all the data in the public domain. Washington thus gave meaning to the idea of a "seismic detection club". At the Second Conference of Experts organized by SIPRI in July 1968 in Stockholm there was strong pressure for further research in seismic detection and for an international cooperative network. Prior to this Stockholm meeting, Canadian scientists had estimated that even with 5 or 6 on-site inspections annually, there was no more than a 10% probability of physically detecting an underground test in zones where 200 or more earthquakes occurred each year.[136] In addition, problems still remained in identifying explosions ranging "between 4 and 20 Kt at best, and between 20 and 60 Kt at worst".[137] Consequently, there was no reason to change Canadian policy on the need for on-site inspection in the event that a CTB were concluded.

In February 1968, Carlson stressed that Canada's position might be too closely aligned with that of the United States, arguing that a CTB was a collateral disarmament measure which should be discussed once the NPT was signed. No one wanted to see a "vacuum" develop in Geneva but, at the same time, the Americans did not want a CTB on the agenda. Carlson felt that Canada could support the Swedish position without upsetting the Americans, particularly since the British appeared to be somewhat flexible on the matter. Carlson's view proved to be correct. In 1967, the British Cabinet concluded that a CTB without inspection would be better than no CTB at all, for it would at least constitute a bridge-building exercise between East and West. Canada was made aware of the British position[138] only during November 1968. Publicly, the British continued to support the U.S. view, but privately they supported Swedish efforts towards negotiating a CTB.

This duality of British diplomacy did not go unnoticed and, in 1969, Canada followed Britain's approach. Starting in 1968, Canada sought answers to some of the more pressing questions. Following a meeting between Cornett, Whitham and Longair on progress in teleseismic detection and methods for identifying nuclear tests[139], Whitham concluded that Canada could make substantive progress in the area of "diagnostic aids". According to Whitham, the Americans would never be satisfied with identification methods based on probability techniques.[140] Whitham and the British seismologist, Thirlaway, thought that the margin of uncertainty for suspect events could be reduced to permit discrimination at magnitude 4 (1–3 Kt in granite) compared with the 20 to 60 Kt previously estimated, while the Americans calculated that this method of identification was not reliable below 10 Kt.[141] Whitham decided that it would be futile to engage in a battle over figures either with the United States, whose figures were "mathematically correct", or with other nations, particularly Sweden, whose figures were based on data at the tail of the probability distribution curve[142] where insufficient samples existed.[143] 1968 was, therefore, an eventful year. The Stockholm meeting seemed to convince Canadians that numerical data could be of some help in solving political problems.

At this same meeting, Whitham asserted that Canada was second to none in seismic detection. He stressed, however, that Canada's equipment was operating near the theoretical limit of detection, and that more funds would be needed if the momentum were to be maintained. The additional funds required were estimated at one million dollars over three years. On the essential issues, Whitham considered that any CTB would amount to no more than a political gesture, since the risks of detection were infinitely greater than the likelihood of a nation pursuing tests with impunity. No one thought that there was much chance of a change in U.S. policy, even in the post-Nixon era, in view of the intensive research conducted by Washington on the ABM program. Nevertheless, in 1963, Whitham thought that the risk of evading detection under a CTB treaty was no greater than the risk of evading detection of an atmospheric nuclear test. On this point, Longair of DRB disagreed. Longair thought, however, that it would be in American interests to conclude a CTB, since "freezing the situation" would allow Washington to keep its lead in the area of Multiple Independently-Targetable Reentry Vehicle (MIRV) warheads.

Canadian experts no longer had the same formal assurance as in 1966. A CTB was scientifically impossible in 1966, but in 1968 it afforded a conceivable and admissible political gesture. At the time of the general review of Canada's foreign policy under the Trudeau government, the Department of External Affairs essentially espoused

Whitham's views as a basis for policy change. In a document entitled *Disarmament Policy Review: Comprehensive Test Ban (CTB)*, the following statement by Whitham[144] appears:

In my opinion, much of the remaining controversy about a CTB is political ...

In summary, an act of political faith appears to me to be a reasonable scientific but not a quantitatively defined risk. I doubt if it is reasonable to continue to use seismology as a whipping-post to avoid this issue. There is no contradiction between these statements and formal unbiased advice on specific issues showing that the problem with low yield explosion is at present theoretically untractable without inspection. That is why the problem is so delicate.

On 12 February 1969, Whitham[145] suggested changes in the Memorandum prepared for Cabinet. In his view, an international seismic detection network could significantly enhance the chances of seismic detection because of the advances made in technology. He considered that the risks could be minimized if some form of international collaboration could be worked out. He suggested, therefore, that Canada should not hold rigid to her previous position on the issue of inspections. In view of the fact that the world was enjoying a period of *détente* and that the SALT negotiations were progressing well, the Department of External Affairs decided to strike while the iron was hot.

In May 1969, Atomic Energy of Canada Limited ran a rearguard battle on the issue of on-site inspections[146], but it was already too late in face of the combined pressure of the Department of External Affairs and the Department of Mines and Technical Surveys. Cabinet made its decision on 29 June 1969: Canada would continue to play a leading role in seismological verification. The requisite funds would be appropriated to facilitate research, Canadian territory could be used for "verification exercises"[147] and Canada would drop her insistence on on-site inspections as prerequisite to the negotiation of a CTB – albeit without advising her allies. The issue remained linked, however, to progress in the SALT negotiations because bilateral agreement between the superpowers was needed before a CTB could be surfaced as a priority.

This phase of open-mindedness was doubtless linked to the preoccupations of Prime Minister Trudeau who wanted to see Canada invest more resources in arms control. He saw no reason why Canada could not utilise her scientific resources to a greater extent in furthering progress towards a CTB (which Tucker[148] described as the "catalytic" aspect of Canadian diplomacy), even though the SALT negotiations certainly were of priority in the Prime Minister's mind. In short, the Prime Minister had no wish to jeopardize the SALT negotiations by stressing the need for a CTB.

The Phase of Compromise. The Cabinet decision was taken in 1969 following the departure of General Burns and prior to the arrival of George Ignatieff as Canada's new Ambassador for Disarmament. Ignatieff was unhappy that Canada had not supported Sweden in promoting negotiations for a CTB, and had instead adopted a policy of arguing for seismological verification as the best way of achieving a CTB. Nevertheless, it was in the area of seismological verification that Canada exerted her influence up to 1978.

In the years between 1969 and 1978, Canada presented a large number of working documents to the ENDC and the CCD (see Table 10). Two documents are worthy of note. The first, ENDC/251/Rev 1, dated August 1969, specified the kind of technical detail that should be included in the responses from nations to the request of the UN Secretary General for information on their seismological detection equipment and facilities (UN General Assembly resolution 2604 A (XXIV) of 16 October 1969). The second, CCD/305, dated August 1970, was an appreciation of the seismic detection capabilities of nations based on the responses to the Secretary General from 54 nations.[149] The most important conclusions of this appreciation were:

Briefly, this ensemble of stations can detect P waves (body waves) of both earthquakes and underground explosions down to body wave magnitudes m 4.0 to m 4.2 occurring anywhere in the northern hemisphere: the definition involves greater than, or equal to, 50 percent interval probability at a minimum of 5 stations, and with a corresponding location capability between 20 and 45 km. When conversion is made to 90 percent probability of detection of an event by at least 5 stations, the lower limit in the northern hemisphere is between m 4.5 and m 4.7.[150]

Identification is a much more severe problem: the *earthquake* [emphasis added] Rayleigh wave (surface wave) detection capability is generally between m 4.6 and m 5.0 in the northern hemisphere with an analogous 50 percent probability definition (we have converted in this statement to body wave magnitude). An improvement of 0.4 magnitude units is possible for some test sites and station paths, and matched filtering capability at certain stations can produce a further improvement of between 0.2 and 0.3 magnitude units. There is, therefore, a potential for a range m 4.0 to m 4.4 for earthquake Rayleigh surface wave detection at the 50 percent probability level, although this requires some relaxation of the definition used. Again, conversion to

90 percent probabilities increases this estimate to m 4.5 to m 4.9. The corresponding figures for the detection of explosion Rayleigh waves and thus for positive identification of *explosions* [emphasis added] are 1 magnitude higher, namely, between m 5.0 and m 5.4 at the 50 percent level and 0.5 magnitude units higher at the 90 percent level. Extensive research ... could produce a decrease estimated at 0.6 magnitude units in these figures provided some further relaxation in the rigour of the definitions used is accepted. Magnitude 4.75 can be equated with a yield between 8 and 20 kilotonnes in hard rock.[151]

It cannot be said that the Canadian scientists of the day erred on the side of popularization. The report stated first that detection *per se* of a seismic event must be established, and that positive identification techniques were then required to discriminate between earthquakes and nuclear explosions. Second, it had to be understood that any general assessment of the situation would be valid only insofar as it represented the aggregate of the analyses of national networks, which therefore explained the conservative nature of some figures. Third, and as a logical consequence of the second, positive discrimination between an earthquake and a nuclear explosion could only be established with certainty for magnitudes in excess of 4.75. This did not mean, in any way, that the more advanced detection systems such as those of the Americans could not obtain better results. The costs involved, however, would have been prohibitive for most nations. Fourth, Canada, unlike Sweden[152], abstained from correlating the magnitudes of Rayleigh surface waves with kilotonne threshold equivalents, for although seismological theories at the time would have allowed such a procedure, they were not based on empirically demonstrated data.[153]

There was, of course, one exception. This concerned the tectonic plates of North America, for it had been empirically established that an explosion between 8 and 20 kilotonnes in the granite of Nevada produced a body-wave magnitude of 4.75. Subsequently, in 1971, it was established that, using slightly improved seismological techniques[154], the positive detection method could yield a 90 percent probability for magnitude 4.2, or between 5 and 10 Kt in the northern hemisphere in cases where the explosion occurred in granite. Clearly, measurements varied from one country to another, and only a good knowledge of the region would permit meaningful estimates of probability. In addition, any comparison between body waves and surface waves at the time did not include the advantages of spectral analysis of high frequency waves.[155]

Table 10

List of Main Working Documents Presented by Canada during 1969–1978 to the Eighteen-Nation Committee on Disarmament and to the Conference of the Committee on Disarmament

ENDC 248	WP* Listing Canadian Seismological Research (21 May 1969) (revision, with summaries, of ENDC 244 tabled on 17 April previous).
ENDC 251 and Rev.10	WP on Requests to Governments for the Provision of Certain Information in the Context of Setting Up a World-Wide Exchange of Seismological Data (23 May 1969 and 18 August 1969).
CCD 305	WP on Seismological Capabilities in Detecting and Identifying Underground Nuclear Explosions (10 August 1970).
CCD 327	WP on Seismological Capabilities in Detecting and Identifying Underground Nuclear Explosions (29 June 1979; Add.1 presented on 7 July 1971).
CCD 336	WP on Possible Progress Towards the Suspension of Nuclear and Thermonuclear Tests (22 July 1971).
CCD 376	WP on Measures to Improve Tripartite Cooperation (Canada, Japan and Sweden) in the Detection, Location and Identification of Underground Nuclear Explosions by Seismological Means (20 July 1972).
CCD 378	WP Containing Bibliography of the Department of EMR Papers Relevant to Seismological Verification Problems (25 July 1972).
CCD 380	WP on an Experiment in International Cooperation: Short-Period Seismological Discrimination of Shallow Earthquakes and Underground Nuclear Explosions (27 July 1972).
CCD 406	The Verification of a Comprehensive Test Ban by Seismological Means (10 July 1973).
CCD 457	WP Reporting the Summary Proceedings of an Informal Scientific Conference held 14–19 April 1975 to Promote Canadian-Japanese-Swedish Cooperation in the Detection, Location and Identification of Underground Nuclear Explosions by Seismological Means (14 July 1975).
CCD 490	The Verification of a Comprehensive Test Ban by Seismological Means (20 April 1976).

* Working Paper.

When the United States and the Soviet Union signed the TTBT (Threshold Test Ban Treaty) in 1974, Canada, Sweden and Japan pointed out[156] that the information on calibration tests called for in the Protocol to the Treaty would be indispensable in improving seismological verification techniques. The three-level verification system envisaged by the CD[157] could produce important results provided that the Soviets collaborated. In the early 1970s, however, the immensity of the problem of seismological detection was only dimly visible. In 1976, Canada tabled another important document which included a survey of masking techniques.[158] There is no doubt that Canadian competence in this area was exceptional, and constituted, as Tucker observed at the time[159], "the keystone of our diplomacy". This expertise still exists today through funding appropriations, the steadfast cooperation of the Earth Sciences Division of the Department of Energy, Mines and Resources, and the decisions taken under the Trudeau Government to place emphasis on the verification aspects of arms control.

In the context of political efforts within the CCD, Canada reverted in 1971 to certain ideas advocated in 1956, specifically the possibility of opening the way for a CTB by reaching agreement on "interim measures" to limit tests of the highest explosive yield[160], while stressing the need to publicize tests in advance and to improve seismological verification techniques. The proposal was clearly aimed at reminding the superpowers of their responsibilities. The Soviets rejected this proposal[161] in September 1971. Canada thus held to her decision of 1969, which did not call for on-site inspection, since there was no difficulty in interpreting data in the high-yield explosion range.

Events started to move faster during 1971 and 1972. The superpowers showed no interest in a CTB. In their public statements, the Soviets stressed that they would only subscribe to this kind of treaty on condition that all the other nuclear powers would also be party to it. France and the PRC had always been kept out of the negotiations in Geneva and nothing indicated that they would be the least bit interested in participating. Moreover, the Americans were preparing for their ABM tests in Amchitka (specifically the Cannikin test) with the aim of developing a nuclear warhead for their Spartan missile. The French were conducting experiments in the Pacific, raising a wave of protests from Australia and New Zealand, while in Ottawa, on 15 October 1971, the House voted in favour of a resolution tabled by External Affairs' Minister Mitchell Sharp calling on the Americans to cancel their planned tests in Alaska. This latter resolution, which was adopted unanimously with the exception of one dissension[162], was subsequently communicated officially to Washington. Canada's opposition stemmed mainly from her frequently-stated aversion to nuclear testing and from her concern for the environment at the off-shore test location which was judged by many to be seismically unstable. On 22 February 1971, an official note of protest was delivered to Washington elaborating the Canadian position.[163]

At the 26th Session of the UN General Assembly in December 1971, Canada closed ranks with Australia and Sweden by supporting Resolution 2828 C which called upon the major powers, particularly the States Party to the PTBT, to take "restrictive measures" immediately, either unilaterally or following negotiations, to suspend, restrict or reduce the power of nuclear tests. Until that time, apart from the two resolutions that Canada tabled in 1969 and 1970 to facilitate technical studies on the problems of seismic verification, Canada's involvement in the debate on nuclear testing had been limited to voting in favour of all resolutions to suspend nuclear tests. Resolution 2828 C marked, therefore, a shift towards a harder Canadian position. From that time on, Canada agreed to play a leadership role amongst nations seeking a more definitive position. Canada's posture was maintained through 1972 with her support for Resolution 2934 B (XXVII), which called for a ban on testing in all environments, and which was a way of pointing the finger at France and the PRC.

The interventions of the Greenpeace Foundation in the Pacific in 1972, and the impassioned attitudes of the Australian and New Zealand governments against nuclear testing in the Pacific, provided an extra rung to the ladder of Canadian resolve. Following a recommendation from a high-level public official on 10 January 1973, Canada elected to mark the tenth anniversary of the PTBT by joining with Australia, Sweden and a number of Pacific rim countries in sponsoring Resolution 3078 B of 6 December 1973 at the UN General Assembly. In the text of this resolution, the sponsoring nations expressed profound concern at the continuation of nuclear testing, asking again that all nuclear testing be banned in all environments, and insisting that those nations which still conducted tests in the atmosphere – namely, France and the PRC – end such testing forthwith.

France, the United States, the United Kingdom and the USSR abstained from voting on the 1971 resolution. In the 1972 resolution, France and the PRC voted against, while the United Kingdom, the USSR and the United States abstained. In the 1973 resolution, the PRC and France voted against, 65 countries voted in favour, and the USSR, the United States, the United Kingdom and 53 other nations abstained. Faced with France's powerful diplomatic lobby in the United Nations, Canada suffered a bitter defeat. At least, such was the conclusion inferred by the Department of External Affairs.

Nevertheless, it remains that whenever Canada sponsored resolutions in the UN, it was because they were widely considered to be legitimate.

No one thought of pointing out that the Chinese tests in the atmosphere were infinitely more damaging for the northern hemisphere than the French tests in the southern hemisphere. At all events, France took offence at the double standard: why should France be singled out for testing in the atmosphere when the other major powers ceaselessly continued testing underground at a more forceful rate than that of France? Moreover, in 1973, the House of Commons condemned the French nuclear tests on three occasions but passed silently over those of the PRC, a gesture which France interpreted as unfriendly.

For some, that was the straw that broke the camel's back. Paris had no hesitation in adding fuel to the flames. France went so far as to question, in hardly veiled terms, the legitimacy of Ottawa to represent Québec abroad, and even opposed Canada's requests to negotiate an outline agreement with the EEC. The Europe Branch of the Department of External Affairs was strongly inclined to take French representations seriously, for Canada was keenly interested in negotiating contractual links with the EEC. At the time, Paris was fighting against all odds to have the French *force de frappe* recognized as a component of Atlantic Alliance deterrence – which was accepted at the North Atlantic Council Meeting held in Ottawa in 1974 – and was formally committed to the development of thermonuclear weapons during the 1970s.

In light of this diplomatic environment, Canada softened her position. Up to that point in time, the Canadian Government believed that the issues could be discussed in principle without jeopardizing Canadian interests, but soon discovered that such was no longer the case. In February 1974 the Government concluded that the risks to the environment from French nuclear tests were minimal compared with the political risks of maintaining a resolute attitude towards France. Even New Zealand and Australia seemed willing to subdue their strong protestations while awaiting the opinion of the International Court of Justice in The Hague on the legality of the French nuclear tests. Consequently, at the end of April 1974, Cabinet undertook to examine new policies.

In brief, Cabinet adopted a compromise. Canada obviously could not abandon general support for a complete cessation of nuclear tests by all the nuclear powers in all environments. It was necessary, therefore, to support this objective in the Conference of the Committee on Disarmament and to support UN resolutions aimed at this objective. Within this general framework, Canada was careful not to give disproportionate emphasis to the importance of ending testing in the atmosphere. In the area of arms control and disarmament, priority was accorded to the major strategic negotiations such as SALT and the strengthening of the nuclear Non-Proliferation Treaty. In essence, this meant that for all practical purposes there was less emphasis on a CTB than previously. In other words, the major strategic issues received greatest priority, rather than a CTB in isolation.

The somewhat reserved statement of Mitchell Sharp on 21 June 1974 expressed this new approach. The Canadian Government obviously deplored the nuclear tests that occurred in the atmosphere during the days preceding Sharp's statement, but found consolation in the fact that France announced that the offending series would be the last. Sharp also expressed hope that China would adopt a similar attitude in the future. In this way, the Canadian Government was able to make amends for singling out France in 1973. In addition, Canada invited the United States and the USSR to reach agreement on a CTB, thus reminding the superpowers of their responsibilities and reversing the discriminatory position held earlier against France and China. Evidently, the most banal communiqués are often steeped in the most subtle of diplomatic guile. On 9 December 1974, Canada withheld support for Resolution 3257 (XXIX) presented by Australia, Sweden and fourteen other countries condemning all nuclear tests in all environments. Nevertheless, during the 30th and 31st sessions of the UN General Assembly in 1975 and 1976, Canada continued to support the proposals of Australia and New Zealand[164], requesting the CCD to accord "the highest priority" to reaching agreement on a CTB.

Two important events intervened to relegate the issue of a CTB to the backdrop of the prevailing international scene: the nuclear explosion conducted by India in May 1974 and the surprise signing of the TTBT in July 1974. There was an urgent need to address the problems of peaceful nuclear explosions so as to plug the loopholes of the NPT and, at the same time, a need to respond to the goodwill of the major powers which, without advising any of their allies, adopted Canada's long-standing requests for a policy of restraint and restriction on underground nuclear tests.

The Cabinet decision of April 1974 was not merely taken for the sake of appearances. It followed a lengthy analysis of the situation and a review of Canadian policy on a CTB. This review[165] started modestly in 1972 and gained momentum during 1973. Several factors militated in favour of increased flexibility of Canadian policy.

From that time on, it was recognized that the problem was political in nature, and no longer depended on the goodwill of the small or middle powers. Technical studies on seismic detection had reached maturity, but the technological argument, which could have served as a "catalyst", was beginning to crumble in light of several factors, specifically the monolithic positions adopted by the superpowers, the determination displayed by France and China to pursue their tests, and the irrepressible need of the superpowers to perfect their weapons systems in the name of security and deterrence stability. As well, the United States insisted that nuclear tests were essential to the security of the Alliance.

Although it had been thought previously that a CTB would possibly pave the way for other more general agreements, it was then recognized that agreement on a CTB would likely be predicated on the outcome of the major SALT negotiations. Moreover, the formal links that earlier had been expected to bind a CTB with a possible NPT gradually lost precedence to other considerations, such as the need for third party countries to conduct peaceful nuclear explosions in order to alleviate the burden imposed by the 1973 oil crisis.

There was a progressive reversal in the formal logic and rationale of the Canadian position. Through the Cabinet decision of 1969, Canada had recognized that the SALT negotiations might well be determinant in the evolution of a CTB. There was, therefore, a return to the traditional strategic thinking which held that so long as the major powers were unwilling to make significant reductions in the quality and quantity of their strategic arsenals, the chances of reaching agreement on a CTB were somewhat slim, if not non-existent. In other words, the bull had to be taken by the horns. In 1974, Canada yielded to the pressures of France, but there is nothing to indicate that Canada would not have reached the same conclusions herself following an in-depth review of her foreign policy.

The logic which dictated the strategy of "suffocation" at the time of the first UN Special Session on Disarmament (UNSSOD I) in 1978 was precisely the same. The term "suffocation" was first coined by one of Canada's most brilliant diplomats, Klaus Goldschlag, during private discussions at a symposium attended by the Prime Minister. The Prime Minister was intrigued by this turn of phrase, and it became part of diplomatic usage. It stressed the urgent need to contain the arms race in all its global dimensions, and was one of the key ideas in the 1970 White Paper, which argued that Canada should not leave it to the superpowers alone to determine the pace of progress in the field of disarmament.

The Canadian strategy of "suffocation" was advanced in the hope that the SALT II agreements would soon be concluded and that a CTB would follow. The CTB thus headed the list of the four measures proposed. The other three measures included prohibition of flight-testing of new launch platforms, prohibition of the production of fissile materials for military purposes, and the freezing of military expenditures followed by progressive reductions. There was really nothing new in substance, but it was hoped that these various elements would interact to produce a progressive "suffocation" in the arms race, comparable to that of a "technological freeze". As G.H. Pearson later wrote, it was not a matter of "reversing" the arms race, but of "controlling" it.[166] In parallel, it was hoped that the East and the West would agree to stabilize the situation through reduced military spending and progressive reductions in their conventional forces.

Thus, between 1963 and 1978, there was an underlying internal logic in Canadian policy on a CTB. In the earlier years, seismic detection techniques were primitive. Prudence thus reigned until 1967–68. In 1969, following rapid advances in verification techniques Canada abandoned her pursuit of a foolproof verification system, considering that the security risks entailed were minimal in comparison with the political advantages that the West could gain through a global suspension of nuclear testing. Thus, there was a transition in thinking that might be likened to that which occurred from the Middle Ages to the Renaissance. Hopes that technology could resolve all problems were high, but it was soon realized that technology could not solve all the political problems engendered by nuclear testing. Canada later opposed all forms of nuclear testing as a matter of principle, and yielded too easily to the pacifist pressure groups throughout the world, without realizing that this particular form of discrimination would most offend those nations whose interests were essentially legitimate. In 1974, a reorientation of policy occurred, due largely to a re-evaluation of the general circumstances which had led Canada to the belief that the problem of achieving a CTB could not be approached in isolation. This logically led to the 1978 strategy of "suffocation" championed by Prime Minister Trudeau at the second United Nations Special Session on Disarmament.

Unwavering Canadian Support (1978–1988)

The strategy of "suffocation" lost its potential impact shortly afterwards with the belligerent rhetoric of the new administration in Washington. Trilateral negotiations, which had been adjourned in 1980, were suspended completely when U.S. President Reagan publicly announced that nuclear testing was vital to the security of the Alliance. Towards the end of 1982, a minister from the Canadian

West succeeded in convening a meeting of Cabinet on the issues raised by the peace movements in Canada. Steps were taken within the Prime Minister's Office to promote ideas that subsequently were embodied in the famous peace initiative of Pierre Elliott Trudeau.

The Department of External Affairs was justifiably concerned about the Western Canada initiative which, had it been pursued in isolation by its proponents, could have compromised Canada's international reputation. Secretary of State for External Affairs, Alan McEachen, saw fit to create a Task Force which developed the ten principles that would spearhead this initiative.[167] There is no doubt that Canada was seriously worried about the way that u.s. policy was developing. The Prime Minister's speech of 16 May 1982 to the University of Notre-Dame contained the germ of the political philosophy that was to inspire his peace initiative. In short, the Prime Minister feared that the superpowers would lose control in the many conflicts which divided them, and that the situation would degenerate into a violent East-West confrontation. He also expressed alarm at the deepening gap which divided the Atlantic Alliance on the issues of negotiations with the East and on the lack of progress on MBFR.

The Soviets were undoubtedly pleased to find such faithful support in Canada for an active disarmament policy. At the same time, it must be admitted that they were also trying to understand the u.s. political system, and particularly the thinking in Washington that made the Soviets subject to public obloquy and held them responsible for all the evils of the Cold War. Private contacts were even sought with former civil servants of the Prime Minister's Office who had been promoted to other positions within the bureaucracy. The objective was probably to determine whether a common ground existed for restoring East-West dialogue.

During the 1978–1988 period, Canadian support for a CTB was unwavering. Canada continued, as in the past, to seek avenues at all levels. In the early 1980s, the UN General Assembly made concerted efforts to achieve progress by forming, within the Committee on Disarmament, an *Ad Hoc* Working Group on Halting Nuclear Tests. On 17 July 1981, following a general review by Cabinet on security and arms control, Secretary of State for External Affairs, Mark MacGuigan, sent a letter to his u.s. counterpart, Alexander Haig, confirming Canada's commitment to the strategy of "suffocation", expressing the hope that the SALT negotiations would shortly resume, and that tripartite discussions on a CTB would re-open in the wake of such discussions. He also stressed that the CD should be accorded real power to negotiate. Despite opposition from the superpowers, the CD finally assumed the responsibilities conferred on it by paragraph 120 of the Final Document of UNSSOD I, by creating its own working group in April 1982. A few months earlier, Canada had stated that the CD should follow up on proposals "as a matter of procedure", or simply tackle problems that had not been discussed already at the bilateral level.[168] On 1 February 1983, McEachen[169] congratulated the CD on its initiative. Unfortunately, as it turned out, it was impossible to reach agreement even on the possibility of broadening the mandate of the *Ad Hoc* Group beyond the confines of the problems of verification. On 26 April 1984, the Canadian Representative to the CD, Ambassador Alan Beesley, concluded that "the debate mandate is so rarefied as to be almost artificial".[170]

Under these circumstances, Canada's only recourse was to fall back on her previous policy of supporting technical discussions within the GSE at the expense of the major political problems of the day. In his speech before UNSSOD II, Prime Minister Trudeau had asked that the International Seismic Data Exchange (ISDE) program be implemented prior to the potential signing of a CTB. This approach remained unchanged in Canadian diplomacy during the 1980s. Canada nevertheless suggested, in February 1982, that a "second-stage agreement" be reached aimed at establishing a threshold for underground nuclear explosions.[171] Ottawa applauded the TTBT and encouraged Washington to ratify it, despite the objections of some critics[172] who claimed that it would only legitimize underground nuclear explosions and undermine the very foundation of a CTB.

UNSSOD II afforded Canada the opportunity to "institutionalize and expand" her role in verification, a field that had been singled out in the 1980 Throne Speech. On 16 July 1982, in conformity with a Cabinet decision, the Secretary of State for External Affairs identified the main areas where Canada could develop specialized expertise, namely seismology, nuclear safeguards, remote sensing, communications satellites, toxicology and protective measures against chemical weapons. As early as June 1981, Cabinet decided to investigate the possibility of international collaboration to train specialists from developing countries in seismology, and thus to augment her verification programs at an estimated cost of 200,000 dollars annually.

In 1985, the Department of External Affairs granted a two-year contract to researchers at the University of Toronto to improve seismic detection in the high frequency range so as to facilitate discrimination between low amplitude nuclear explosions and small earthquakes.[173] In October 1986, the first workshop was held in Ottawa, involving 43 participants from 17 countries. This workshop focused on the development of a world seismic network, which would not be geared towards analyzing a particular seismic event, but rather towards sharing seismic information to facilitate verification of a CTB. Since 1986, the Soviets have become progressively more supportive of this idea.

Although chemical weapons assume first priority in Canada's verification program, nuclear weapons are a close second. This was the substance of the statement made on 4 April 1985 by Alan Beesley, Ambassador to the CD. To give action to words, the Canadian Government announced on 7 February 1986, in a speech by Secretary of State for External Affairs, Joe Clark, that the seismological facilities at Yellowknife would be modernized at a cost of 3.6 million dollars over the years 1986 through 1989. Needless to say, this action reflects Canada's desire to be first in the race to offer verification capabilities in the event that agreement on a CTB is reached.

At the two Review Conferences on the Non-Proliferation Treaty held in 1980 and 1985, Canada insisted vigorously on the need for a CTB.[174] The realization of a CTB Treaty has remained as one of Canada's basic foreign policy objectives since the time that one of Canada's ambassadors, in a speech to the CD, replaced the wording "possibly fundamental" by "fundamental". Perhaps the Ambassador was absent-minded, or had little care for adverbs, but in any event Canada has always been willing to exhibit some degree of deliberate flexibility. In this context, the Secretary of State for External Affairs, Joe Clark, in a speech delivered in August 1986 to the CD, stated: "In the Canadian view, a gradual incremental step-by-step approach will be required if a comprehensive test ban is to become a reality".[175] The same sentiments were echoed by Ambassador de Montigny Marchand before the same international forum on 10 March 1988 when he stressed the need for a step-by-step approach and for "further limitations on nuclear testing".

10 Canada and Outer Space

It is man's ineluctable fate to work on tasks which he cannot
complete in his brief span of years ...

Reinhold Niebuhr

The economic, military, strategic and legal implications of the use of
outer space (os) came to light with the spectacular launch of the first
Soviet satellite, Sputnik, in October 1957. The Soviet Union was the
first nation to orbit, in turn, a dog, a man and then a woman. In
1958, the first International Conference on Space Law was held at
The Hague.[1] That same year, following an initiative of u.s. Secretary
of State John Foster Dulles, the un General Assembly passed Resolution 1348 (XIII) which called for the creation of an *Ad Hoc* Committee on the Peaceful Uses of Outer Space. One year later it came
into being. In conformity with the mandate of the General Assembly,
under which the un is empowered to create any subsidiary organization necessary for its operation, the un established the Committee
on the Peaceful Uses of Outer Space (copuos) through Resolution
1472 (XIV) on 12 December 1959. Subsequently, copuos created
several subcommittees, the most important of which was, of course,
the Legal Subcommittee.

The economic significance of space needs no further demonstration. World expenditures on space activities for peaceful purposes
reached 55 billion u.s. dollars in 1987, and associated personnel
totalled in excess of one million.[2] That same year, the Committee on
Space Research (cospar) of the International Council of Scientific
Unions (icsu) submitted its report[3] on progress in space research to
the Scientific and Technical Subcommittee of copuos. In all the
various areas of research – Earth observation, solar system observation, astrophysics, plasma physics, life sciences, and material

manufacturing in space – the number of projects and associated countries involved was increasing at lightning speed. The same conclusions were also to be found in the report[4] on outstanding accomplishments in space technology in 1987 presented to COPUOS by the International Astronautics Federation (IAF) on 7 January 1988.

In 1986 Canada ranked eighth amongst nations in terms of space expenditures expressed as a percentage of Gross National Product (GNP), and was a prominent international partner in the peaceful uses of space. Canada is currently involved in some thirty[5] projects under both bilateral and multilateral agreements with essentially seven nations and the European Space Agency (ESA). This gives an indication of the economic importance of space for Canada, whose return on investment is expected to amount to some tens of billions of dollars over the next decade.[6]

In the strategic arena, space has become "the eyes and the ears" of the superpowers from where they observe everything of military interest that moves or stirs. Satellites that serve peaceful purposes – for instance meteorological and observation satellites – can also serve military purposes. Satellites that contribute towards strengthening means of verification are viewed as stabilizing, while those that serve purely offensive military purposes are destabilizing. As with any technology, it can only be termed aggressive or peaceful once its final application is known. The jurists have a difficult task regulating activities in space which are so delicate and controversial.

Our purpose here is not so much to focus on the strategic implications of space[7] which are well known and about which law can do little, but rather to highlight the close links that exist between international law and arms control. In the first part of this chapter we shall look at the scope of the main legal instruments that govern the activities of States in the peaceful use of space. We shall then extend this study to include the main agreements in effect on the control and limitation of military activities of States in outer space. Finally, we shall examine the extent of Canadian diplomatic action to prevent an arms race in space.

SPACE LAW

The main sources of space law are as follows: the Charter of the United Nations, the main documents and treaties which govern the activities of States concerning the peaceful uses of space, jurisprudence – which is practically non-existent in this area – and the general principles of international law that are recognized by civilized nations. The first two cover the most important aspects, while the fourth poses special problems in terms of the standards of law that are prescribed and those that are accepted by States in the conduct of their affairs.

All jurists agree that Articles 2(4) and 51 of the Charter of the United Nations are pre-eminent. Article 2(4) prohibits the use of force or any threat of resort to force. No act of aggression against space vehicles could, therefore, be committed by a member State of the UN. In addition, Article 51 accords to States the right of self-defence. In present international law, there is no legal provision to remove a State's right of retaliation or defence against acts of aggression. No such provision has ever been established by the United Nations. This would imply that any State attacked by another has the right to destroy the space assets of the attacker. Where the jurists do not agree, however, is whether the right to retaliate applies only to military space vehicles. Danielsson[8], for instance, finds it inconceivable that the right of self-defence should apply to non-military satellites. This view is not universally shared, for some satellites are seen to be "force multipliers" – for example, navigation and communications satellites – and hence the State which is attacked would feel free to make a highly subjective assessment of its right to retaliate. Other satellites, as we shall see in the following section, are protected under bilateral agreements.

Another aspect, specific to the UN, is the binding or non-binding nature of the provisions established by the UN itself or its subordinate organizations. In this context, the UN has recourse to only three kinds of intervention. The UN General Assembly has the right to make recommendations but not decisions – except on internal matters within its authority, such as its budget. Decision-making is the prerogative of the Security Council by virtue of the provisions contained in Chapter VII of the UN Charter. The UN Secretary General can, however, bring matters of arbitration, mediation or conciliation to the attention of the Security Council by virtue of the powers conferred on him by Article 99 of the Charter. In addition, matters can be referred to the International Court of Justice in The Hague which can render decisions. These decisions, however, are binding only if the contesting States agree beforehand to respect the judgement of the Court.

International law is founded on agreements between States. States can, therefore, reach voluntary agreement on any matter of mutual interest, for instance, a resolution of the UN General Assembly. Peace-keeping perhaps provides the best example. Thus, when the time came to establish the United Nations Emergency Force (UNEF) in Suez in 1956, two parallel series of agreements were concluded to give effect to the UN General Assembly resolution which otherwise had only the status of a recommendation. The Secretary General signed a bilateral agreement with the host country, in this case Egypt, since Israel would not accept to have a peacekeeping force on Israeli territory. The agreement defined the conditions of implementation and operation of the UNEF on Egyptian territory, and specifically the application of the Convention on Privileges and Diplomatic Immunities to the members of the UNEF. In addition, all the member States of the UNEF signed Participating States Agreements with the UN, which is a Party under international law. These aspects were important in 1967 when President Nasser asked for the withdrawal of the UN Blue Berets. Some jurists argued that the UN should maintain the Blue Berets in Egypt, while others maintained that once Egyptian consent for the UNEF presence was withdrawn, the UN had only to respond to Egypt's wishes, which indeed it did.

The same kind of debate exists today in respect of space law. What is the legal status, for instance, of resolutions adopted unanimously by COPUOS? One can only conclude that the authors of the Charter never thought of granting the UN General Assembly, or in this case its organizations, any legislative powers, and that despite the fact that some resolutions reflect the characteristics of universalism and world acceptance they cannot replace internationally-established practice whereby States are bound only by the agreements to which they freely subscribe. In this regard, the majority of world opinion does not constitute legal truth; it expresses only the general standards that it would be desirable for States to adopt, based on duly-signed accords or agreements.

Are things different, however, when a Declaration of Principles is involved, such as that[9] of December 1963 which was unanimously adopted by the UN General Assembly? Did Canada's statement that this Declaration "reflected international law as it was currently accepted by Member States"[10] constitute a codification of international law? Were not those States that came out in favour of this Declaration bound *inter se* since they voluntarily consented to the binding interpretation of this resolution? In fact, this Declaration of Principles would be binding not because it was accepted unanimously but because it constituted a "statement" of customary international law, which would make it binding even before it was adopted.

This perspective, which was held by the United States at the time, left the door open to a number of legal interpretations. Member States, therefore, undertook to codify through treaties most of the declarations contained in the three main resolutions of the United Nations on Outer Space. The first resolution 1721 (XVI) of

Table 11
Main Agreements and Resolutions on Outer Space Law

RESOLUTIONS

Res. 1721 A (XVI)   Use of Outer Space for the Benefit of Mankind and Non-appropriation by States (20 December 1961).

Res. 1884 (XVIII)   Prohibition of Placing into Orbit Nuclear Weapons or Other Weapons of Mass Destruction (17 October 1963).

Res. 1962 (XVIII)   Declaration of Legal Principles on the Use of Outer Space (13 December 1963).

TREATIES AND AGREEMENTS

Outer Space Treaty: Treaty on Principles Governing the Activities of States in the Exploration and Use of Outer Space, Including the Moon and Other Celestial Bodies (United Nations Res. 2222 (XXI), 14 December 1966).

Date of Signature	Date of Entry into Force
27 January 1967	10 October 1967

Rescue and Return Agreement: Agreement on the Rescue and Return of Astronauts and the Return of Objects Launched into Outer Space (United Nations Res. 2345 (XXII), 19 December 1967).

Date of Signature	Date of Entry into Force
22 April 1968	3 December 1968

International Liability Convention: Convention on International Liability for Damage Caused by Space Objects (United Nations Res. 2777 (XXVI), 29 November 1971).

Date of Signature	Date of Entry into Force
29 March 1972	1 September 1972

Registration Convention: Convention on the Registration of Objects Launched into Outer Space (United Nations Res. 3235 (XXIX), 12 November 1974).

Date of Signature	Date of Entry into Force
14 January 1975	15 September 1976

Moon Treaty: Agreement Governing the Activities of States on the Moon and Other Celestial Bodies (United Nations Res. 34/68, 14 December 1979).

Date of Signature	Date of Entry into Force
5 December 1979	11 July 1984

December 1961 affirmed that the UN Charter and international law applied to outer space and celestial bodies. The new aspect here was the clause that prohibited national appropriation of outer space and celestial bodies which could be "freely explored and exploited" by all nations for the well-being of all humanity. Hurwitz[11] maintains that the superpowers are bound by this resolution because they agreed to support it in the same way as other principles of customary law. The argument is clearly no longer at issue since the Outer Space Treaty of 1967 confirmed these principles. Resolution 1884 (XVIII) called upon nations to abstain from placing in orbit around the Earth any objects carrying nuclear weapons or any other kinds of weapons of mass destruction, from installing such weapons on celestial bodies, or stationing such weapons in outer space in any other manner. Since this resolution was not written in the form of a principle, it is doubtful whether it is binding. This provision was, however, repeated in Article IV of the 1967 Outer Space Treaty which makes it binding for all States Signatory to the Treaty.

Resolution 1962 (XVIII) of December 1963 is by far the most important, being a Declaration of Principles Governing the Activities of States in the Exploration and Use of Outer Space. It contained all the principles enunciated in earlier resolutions, as follows: space is the heritage of all humanity, space shall be explored freely based on equality and non-discrimination, nuclear weapons or other weapons of mass destruction shall not be placed in orbit, and nations shall respect the Charter of the United Nations and international law in pursuing activities in space. In addition, a number of new elements appeared: the need to assume international responsibility for activities deriving from national activities; the need to return space components recovered by a third-party State to the owner State; the principle of non-interference of States in space activities pursued by other States; and the principle of cooperation and mutual assistance in a context where astronauts are considered as "envoys of mankind". All these principles were repeated in the first Outer Space Treaty of 1967 which constituted the *Magna Carta*, or the constituent Charter, of Space Law.

The Outer Space Treaty[12] comprises 17 articles and a lengthy preamble which acknowledges the common interest of all mankind in making progress in the exploration and use of outer space for "peaceful purposes". All the principles of the December 1963 Declaration are to be found in the body of the text. The only article governing military activities in space is Article IV which repeats, in part, resolution 1884 of the UN General Assembly of October 1963, and which itself was taken from a previous agreement between the superpowers on the prohibition of placing in orbit nuclear weapons or other weapons of mass destruction. Given the importance of this article, it is quoted here *in extenso*:

States Party to the Treaty undertake not to place in orbit around the Earth any objects carrying nuclear weapons or any other kinds of weapons of mass destruction, install such weapons on celestial bodies, or station such weapons in outer space in any other manner.

The moon and other celestial bodies shall be used by all States Party to the Treaty exclusively for peaceful purposes. The establishment of military bases, installations and fortifications, the testing of any type of weapons and the conduct of military manoeuvres on celestial bodies shall be forbidden. The use of military personnel for scientific research or for any other peaceful purposes shall not be prohibited. The use of any equipment or facility necessary for peaceful exploration of the moon and other celestial bodies shall also not be prohibited.

The first sentence of Article IV prohibits the placing of nuclear weapons or weapons of mass destruction in orbit around the Earth, on celestial bodies or in outer space. The second paragraph of Article IV specifies that "the Moon and other celestial bodies" shall be used by States Party to the Treaty "exclusively for peaceful purposes". The establishment of military bases, installations and fortifications, as well as the testing of any type of weapons and the conduct of military manoeuvres are formally prohibited on "celestial bodies".

Some observers hold that this article, taken together with others in the Treaty, compels compliance with a "complete demilitarization of space". Aside from the fact that such an interpretation was not in the minds of the authors when they drafted the Treaty – otherwise they would not have taken the trouble to specify prohibitions applicable to "celestial bodies" – it must be understood that anything that is not formally prohibited by the Treaty is "permitted". Similarly, although the Preamble to the Treaty refers to the exploration of space for "peaceful purposes", the Article specifies that celestial bodies should be used for "exclusively peaceful purposes". Why was the adverb "exclusively" added, save to apply only to celestial bodies?[13]

Whether or not the Moon is a celestial body is also a relevant question, since a large number of the articles in the Treaty make reference to "the Moon and other celestial bodies". According to Hurwitz[14], this omission on the part of the Americans was deliberate. The ambiguity was removed with the 1979 Moon Treaty which specifies in Article 3(1) that the Moon should be used for "exclusively peaceful" purposes.

The Outer Space Treaty was largely negotiated within the COPUOS. Many other agreements have since been negotiated to complement it in the area of arms control. It should be noted, however, that this first Treaty prohibits any ABM or Anti-Satellite (ASAT) system, and indeed the testing of any weapon, including conventional weapons, on the Moon or other celestial bodies. One can only conclude that the superpowers never considered installing such systems beyond their "practical" range.

All the other legal agreements have served to complement or strengthen this first Treaty on space law. Thus, the 1968 Rescue and Return Agreement is essentially an elaboration of Articles V and VIII of the Outer Space Treaty; the 1972 International Liability Convention is an amplification of Articles VI and VII; the 1975 Convention on the Registration of Objects Launched into Outer Space is an elaboration of Articles V and VIII; while the 1979 Moon Treaty repeats certain articles of the 1967 Treaty with specific reference to the Moon and establishes a particular legal constituency for this Earth satellite. In the context of the 1967 Treaty and the other treaties that followed, Magdelénat[15] writes:

It should be noted that the first four texts are the products of agreements between the two space powers, exercising their supremacy in law as in technology. Admittedly, there was greater participation by other States in the case of the Moon Treaty. This last small step was certainly inspired by analogy with the Law of the Sea where the duopoly of the superpowers has been steadily eroding for a much longer time.

It should be added, however, that by 31 December 1987 only a few States[16] had signed and ratified the Moon Treaty. Based on the agreements to date, space law can be generalized as follows:

- the exploration and use of outer space should be carried out for the benefit of mankind and only for peaceful purposes;
- the rules of customary law in respect of terrestrial military activities and the Charter of the United Nations apply to space law;
- outer space and celestial bodies should not be subject to national appropriation, and should be free for exploration and use by all States;
- States should bear international responsibility for national activities in outer space and on celestial bodies, and should not interfere with the activities of other States;
- it is prohibited to place nuclear weapons or other weapons of mass destruction in orbit around the Earth, on the Moon or other

celestial bodies, and it is prohibited to establish military bases, installations and fortifications on the Moon or other celestial bodies;
• the use of military personnel in space is not prohibited.

Two schools of thought exist on the peaceful uses of space. The United States holds that "peaceful use" simply means "non-aggressive", while the USSR contends that the terminology means "non-military".[17] The document[18] tabled by Canada at the Conference on Disarmament in July 1986 argues that the concept of "militarization of space" lies somewhere between "military use of space", which some States find acceptable, and "weaponization of space", which other States find unacceptable. The concept of "militarization of space" seems to imply a military presence less pronounced than that of "weaponization of space" but more pronounced than that of "military use of space". For some States, however, militarization of space concerns any military use of space. Evidently, some clarification of the concepts is needed. In aerial law, the way that an aircraft is used is the "decisive factor".[19] By analogy, it would seem appropriate to question the ultimate purpose of military devices in space.

The semantic difficulty of defining binary or "dipolar" terms other than by relation of one to the other will remain unresolved, for it is always a question of degree. In other words, it is a question of ordinal measure rather than cardinal measure. One can only make judgements on devices in space according to their function and ultimate use. The fact that the superpowers, for example, have decided to protect their National Technical Means (NTM) through bilateral agreements and treaties is still the best proof that this is the only path open.

It could be argued that the militarization of space started with the launch of the first Soviet Sputnik. On the other hand, the items on the agendas of the UN General Assembly or the Conference on Disarmament attest to the "prevention of an arms race in space", which some observers contrast with the concept of "halting the arms race on Earth". The word "prevention" implies that militarization of space has not yet occurred. This is just as false as the notion of the "prevention of an arms race at sea", on the pretext that there have been no rivalries in this area that could constitute an arms race.

All that can be said is that demilitarization implies a process of retarding or reversing something that is already militarized. History has witnessed several demilitarization treaties. Non-militarization calls for an absence of weapons, and in this context the concept of "non-weaponization" of space has at least the merit of meaning something contrary to the vague term "militarization". But even then, we revert to concepts which themselves give rise to binary terms, for "non-weaponization" can only be defined relative to "weaponization", which raises all the questions of "more or less", "less than more", "more than less", "greater than" and "less than". It would be better here to accept the situation and to use these terms only when they can shed some light on the state of knowledge.

SPACE LAW AND ARMS CONTROL

Countless agreements have supplemented the provisions of international law on control of outer space. We apologize to the jurists for dissociating the general treaties governing space law from the more specific agreements concluded by the superpowers on arms control. We have done so in order to speak of "control regimes" for outer space. This terminology surely has a different connotation and meaning for the jurists who, until now, have been mainly used to the common terminology "legal regime" which is defined as the whole "corpus" of legal provisions applicable to a specific field. In this context, one may speak of the legal regime of the sea or the legal regime of space. By "control regimes" we understand the collectivity of political, economic or military provisions aimed at regulating activities in space of a technological, legal, economic or strategic nature.

Before speaking of "control regimes" we must first consider briefly the other legal provisions that affect the activities of States in space. Some military activities in space are prohibited, while others are tolerated. In describing them, the trend has been to discuss military activities consistent with international law.[20] Thus,

- the use of military personnel in space is permitted under the 1967 Outer Space Treaty:
- the use of military satellites for verification of arms control agreements is permitted under the 1972 ABM (Anti-Ballistic Missile) Treaty, the SALT I and SALT II Treaties; under the 1974 TTBT (Threshold Test Ban Treaty) and the 1976 PNET (Peaceful Nuclear Explosions Treaty) which complements it; and under the INF (Intermediate-range Nuclear Forces) Treaty signed on 8 December 1987 and ratified at the Moscow Summit in the summer of 1988;
- the use of early-warning, communications, navigation and meteorological satellites is also permitted or required under the 1971 and 1984 Agreements between the USA and the USSR on Measures to Improve the Direct Communications Link[21], the 1971 Agreement on Measures to Reduce the Risk of Outbreak of Nuclear War[22], the 1973 Agreement on the Prevention of Nuclear War[23] and the 1987 Agreements on Nuclear Risk Reduction Centers (NRRC).[24]

To the extent that some activities are prohibited by international agreements, Canada has taken the position that such activities are inconsistent with international law. Thus,

- testing of nuclear weapons in outer space, by virtue of the 1963 Partial Test Ban Treaty (PTBT);
- interference with space-based remote sensors used for verifying arms control agreements, consistent with the treaties and agreements defined above, and Article 35 of the 1973 Convention on International Telecommunications which was complemented by the 1982 Nairobi Convention;[25]
- placement of nuclear weapons or other weapons of mass destruction in orbit, by virtue of the 1967 Outer Space Treaty, the 1979 Moon Treaty and the 1979 SALT II Treaty (which includes FOBS – Fractional Orbital Bombardment System);
- hostile acts or use of force on the Moon or other celestial bodies in the solar system, or in orbits around them, consistent with the Moon Treaty;
- placement of military bases and conduct of military tests or manoeuvres on celestial bodies or in orbits around them, consistent with the 1967 Outer Space Treaty and the Moon Treaty;
- development, testing or deployment of space-based ABM systems or components, consistent with the 1972 ABM Treaty;
- mesological warfare, i.e., military or hostile use of environmental modification techniques, consistent with the Convention on the Prohibition of Military or Any Other Hostile Use of Environmental Modification Techniques (opened for signature in Geneva on 18 May 1977; entered into force 5 October 1978).[26]

Over the past thirty years, international law has witnessed a multitude of agreements governing the activities of States in space. Many significant problems remain unresolved, however, and the most thorny issues clearly reside in the area of arms control. Table 12 depicts the four specific "control regimes" which we consider currently apply to activities of States in space. They are: 1. the "permissions regime" which is governed essentially by technological evolution, 2. the "obligations regime" where law prevails, 3. the "exclusions regime" which depends largely on the political will of States, and 4. the "restrictions regime" which reflects the self-imposed restrictions of States in pursuit of their activities in space.

Space law obviously applies to all these regimes. Strictly speaking, law has no direct influence on the "permissions regime", unless of course a special legal dispensation has been introduced, such as, for instance, the use of military personnel in space. By analogy, there

Table 12

The Various Control Regimes of Outer Space

"NON-WEAPONIZATION"	
1. Permissions	*2. Obligations*
Nuclear energy sources	International responsibility
Use of military personnel	Rescue and return of astronauts
Military observation satellites	Non-interference
	Registration of space vehicles
	PAXSAT and other verification satellites
3. Exclusions	*4. Restrictions*
Military bases or manoeuvres on the Moon or other celestial bodies	1972 ABM Treaty
Placing in orbit of nuclear weapons or other weapons of mass destruction	
Mesological warfare	ASAT systems?
Nuclear tests in the atmosphere or in outer space	
Deployment of ABM systems in space	Exotic technologies?
"WEAPONIZATION"	

are few States which have tolerant abortion laws, but specific legislation can always be introduced should the practice become widespread. As circumstances dictate, States can either liberalize their laws or make them more restrictive. In international law, it is not possible to legislate in advance that which does not yet exist, but standards can be imposed or principles established to guide or direct the conduct of States in specific areas. Certain types of activity can also be prohibited. Such is the case for the Outer Space Treaty.

In Table 12, there is a natural cleavage between "weaponization" and "non-weaponization". We prefer this terminology to that of "peaceful" or "non-peaceful", for it is not certain that an ABM system would necessarily be non-peaceful in all circumstances[27], while it is certain that such a system would fall under the heading of "weaponization" of space. In defence of this terminology, "weaponization" implies something harmful for States and their environments, while "non-weaponization" has the connotation of something beneficial.

Law frequently lags practice, or, more specifically, technological development. It is, however, remarkably swift in codifying the transition from "permissions regime" to "obligation regime". Thus, jurists quickly recognized the need to hold States responsible for damage or harm caused to other States in pursuing space activities. Registration of space objects not only ensures some public knowledge of space activities but also facilitates identification of re-entering space objects and debris in the event of requests for compensation and damages. Interestingly enough, according to the registration reports sent to the Secretary General of the United Nations, all space vehicles serve only peaceful purposes!

When radioactive debris from Cosmos 954 fell on Canadian territory on the morning of 24 January 1978, Canada demanded compensation for "clean-up" operations and, in parallel, tabled a working document before the COPUOS Subcommittee calling for the development of international legislation to ensure the safe use of nuclear power sources in space.[28] In April 1981, the USSR agreed to contribute three million dollars in final settlement of all claims in respect of the disintegration of its Cosmos 954 satellite. Canada had to foot most of the bill. The costs of the "clean-up" operation were estimated at 14 million dollars, while the claim presented to the USSR was only for 6 million dollars.

The "obligations regime" is undoubtedly the area where the law envisages provisions beyond those that States are willing to accept in written agreements. For example, the French proposal to create an International Satellite Monitoring Agency (ISMA), the Soviet proposal[29] to create an International Space Agency, and the Canadian proposal on International Verification Satellites all comprise specific legislation which could have long-term benefit both for the stability of the international system as well as for all mankind. In this regard, no one has yet proposed a universal insurance plan to cover international responsibilities. Thirty years ago, such a proposal might have seemed totally "utopic", particularly since the superpowers had no wish to pay premiums comparable to the amounts they would have had to pay in compensation in the event of an accident. In the coming years, if the number of nations in space continues to increase at the same rate as in the 1970s, this kind of international liability insurance could become quite interesting. There is no suggestion here that Lloyd's of London be "nationalized", but rather that an equitable insurance scheme be established so that profits, if any, could possibly be used to support development of other space activities, particularly for those countries less well endowed with resources or technology.

The "restrictions regime" clearly defines the limitations that States are willing to accept in conducting their strategic space activities. The only instrument known in this area is the Anti-Ballistic Missile (ABM) Treaty signed by the U.S. and the Soviet Union on 26 May 1972.[30] The Treaty was complemented by the Protocol of 3 July 1974[31] which limited each superpower to a single ABM site instead of the two that were envisaged when the Treaty was drafted. Under the Treaty, the use of ABM systems was not prohibited, but simply restricted. Even though the duration of the Treaty is unlimited, either party can withdraw if it considers that its "vital interests" are threatened. Finally, the Treaty is open to amendment and review every five years (Article XIV).

The jurists would obviously like to change all the "restrictions" to prohibitions, or "exclusions" to remain faithful to our adopted terminology, but it is far from certain that the superpowers would be prepared to follow this path. They could abrogate the Treaty, amend it, complement it or even extend it for a new period of time. A new ABM Treaty could even emerge to include provision for the new "exotic" technologies. If that were to happen, the superpowers would likely agree once more to restrictions in respect of their strategic capabilities. Moreover, nothing prevents ABM issues from falling under two or other different conventions.

The same is true for anti-satellite (ASAT) systems which currently exist but which are not subject to any restrictions except those that derive from the ABM Treaty, despite continual efforts by the international community to persuade the superpowers to impose mutual restrictions on such ASAT systems. In this regard, it should be recognized that the issue concerns not only the security of the superpowers or the stability of East-West nuclear deterrence, but mainly the protection of third party satellites which could become ASAT targets. As we shall see, no particular approach will likely meet the security requirements that are sought in this regard. Perhaps a combination of the "obligations" approach and some restrictions freely accepted by the superpowers, together with some kind of ABM prohibition would still be the best way of resolving this delicate issue.

The "exclusions regime" is surely a commendable one, but in reality accommodates only those items that the superpowers had agreed to exclude in the first place. The only exclusion that is perhaps regretted by the superpowers today is the prohibition of ABM systems in space, because of the promise of new technologies which are appearing on the horizon and their impact on strategic posture. For this reason, it is difficult for the superpowers to reach agreement on an issue as highly contested as that of ABM.

In terminating this section on space law and arms control, it should be noted that the "permissions regime" often appears before law can utter a word on the subject. In the 1930s, the legal experts in public law never thought about prohibiting the atomic bomb. There is no assurance that a better interface between science and law would resolve many of the current problems, but it would perhaps stimulate discussion on the possible advances in science that will occur over the next twenty years, and lead to a better codification of the "permissions regime". The "exclusions regime" depends essentially on the political will of the superpowers. In this regard, if the jurists were to spend less time pondering the question of what should or could be prohibited and instead expend more thought on practical ways of giving meaning to the restrictions that everyone seeks, it might lead to a better balance between what "is" and what "ought to be", that is, between reality and the desired standards. It must be admitted that the INF Treaty has surpassed anything that the jurists dared to hope for in the area of verification. This means that serious studies are needed in the area of verification. The fact that Canada and the United Kingdom, to mention only two countries, have decided to establish institutes and to emphasize work in the verification area[32] is the most positive sign of progress in arms control. Similarly, the "obligations regime", understood to mean the rights and responsibilities of States, is the essential preserve of international law. We are not advocating that the jurists be restricted to a specific domain, but rather emphasizing the need for much greater interplay between science, politics and law.

ARMS CONTROL AND SPACE

Overview of Negotiations

For reasons of clarity, the issue of ASAT weapons will be separated from issues pertaining to the ABM Treaty or non-militarization of space. We should first, however, say a word about UN procedures, since these issues are closely related under the same agenda item.

At the UN itself, the issue of non-militarization of space recurs regularly since the Western nations requested that it be considered under the wider heading of "general and complete disarmament".

On 9 December 1981, the UN General Assembly adopted resolution 36/97 C on "the prevention of an arms race in outer space", which called on all States, and particularly those with major capabilities in space, to work towards this ideal end. The resolution also called upon the Committee on Disarmament to initiate studies in its 1982 session on means of negotiating effective and verifiable agreements aimed at preventing an arms race in outer space, "taking into account all existing and future proposals designed to meet this objective". Variations of this resolution have since been introduced at each meeting of the General Assembly[33] aimed at giving the Conference on Disarmament a true mandate for negotiation.

In 1983, the first obstacle was overcome when the United States and Great Britain agreed to create an *Ad Hoc* Working Group on this issue, provided it had a "pragmatic" mandate. Since, at the same point in time, the Eastern Bloc countries wanted the Conference on Disarmament to negotiate a binding treaty on the prevention of an arms race in space, no agreement was possible. Only on 29 March 1985 was an *Ad Hoc* Group finally struck within the Conference on Disarmament, in conformity with paragraph 120 of the Final Document of the first UN Special Session on Disarmament (UNSSOD I). The Conference on Disarmament thus went through the same procedure again that it had followed in establishing an *Ad Hoc* Group on halting nuclear tests.[34]

In its 29 March decision, the Conference on Disarmament specified that the *Ad Hoc* Group "will take into account all existing agreements, existing proposals and future initiatives" in developing its report on these matters. The socialist States and several non-aligned nations declared that they would only be satisfied with this process provided that it led to true negotiations in the shortest possible time. In its November 1987 resolution, the UN General Assembly noted that the Conference on Disarmament, as a organ for multilateral negotiations, "has the primary role in the negotiation of a multilateral agreement or agreements, as appropriate", to prevent an arms race in outer space.

In the period 9 to 21 August 1982 the Second United Nations Conference on the Exploration and Peaceful Uses of Outer Space (UNISPACE 82) was held in Vienna. The final report of the Conference stressed the danger of the arms race spreading to outer space, and exhorted all nations, and especially the superpowers, to work towards preventing it.[35] The Group of 77 in a separate Declaration stated "that the testing, stationing and deployment of any weapons in space should be banned", and invited "the two major space Powers" to initiate negotiations to that end.

One final point should be stressed. Although UN proposals on arms control in outer space have appeared relatively recently, it should not be forgotten that the first true Western effort dates back to 1957. In fact, in their marathon proposal of 29 August 1957 to the Subcommittee of the Disarmament Commission in London, the four Western powers proposed "the establishment of a technical committee to study the design of an inspection system which would make it possible to assure that the sending of objects through outer space will be exclusively for peaceful and scientific purposes".[36] This proposal, which was part of a dozen other collateral proposals at the time, would have rapidly fallen into oblivion – even though it contained the germ of an idea on registration of objects in space – had it not been for the launch of the first Soviet Sputnik a few months later.

The issue thus became one of paramount urgency at the 12th meeting of the UN General Assembly. The Canadian records on this subject are rather amusing. Before October 1957, the United States had wanted to include this element of the Western proposal in a resolution to be tabled before the 12th session of the General Assembly. The British were violently opposed to this suggestion, because the U.K. Ministry of Defence was afraid that such a proposal would leave Soviet superiority in space frozen for all time and possibly inhibit the development or use by the United Kingdom of Medium-Range Ballistic Missiles (MRBM). The United States, France and Canada did not subscribe to this British view but, faced with fierce opposition from the U.K., this element of the proposal was finally suppressed during an informal meeting of the Western Delegations. Sputnik obviously changed the American way of thinking. From that time on it was impossible to go to the General Assembly empty-handed, and it was only after lengthy discussions with the British that the original phrasing of the Western proposal of August 1957 was restored.[37]

Within the various multilateral negotiation organizations, the issue of limitations on space weapons has only been discussed sporadically and mostly in the context of general proposals on collateral disarmament issues. It may be recalled that, in his declaration of 27 March 1962, Minister of External Affairs Howard Green argued that space be used solely for peaceful purposes.[38] In an article published in *International Perspectives*[39], William Epstein concludes that Canada subsequently ceded her right to speak on these issues to the superpowers. This situation persisted right up to the time of the First UN Special Session on Disarmament (UNSSOD I). This somewhat severe judgement is historically correct for, at the time, space was the monopoly of the superpowers and, as of 1988, despite the unceasing efforts of States to obtain a mandate for the Conference on Disarmament to negotiate agreements on limiting weapons in space, this objective had still not been attained.

Negotiations on ASAT (1978–1985)

Some discussions on anti-satellite (ASAT) systems took place during the major strategic talks – the Strategic Arms Limitations Talks (SALT I, SALT II); the Strategic Arms Reduction Talks (START); and the Nuclear and Space Talks (NST) – and during other talks that were held during the time of the Carter Administration. But, strictly speaking, no bilateral negotiations have ever taken place between the superpowers on eliminating ASAT systems. The only significant agreement that indirectly touches on ASAT systems is the 1972 ABM Treaty which we shall examine in the following section. Although bilateral talks between the superpowers resumed in January 1985 following the Soviet withdrawal from other bilateral fora of negotiation in September and December 1983 (the INF and START negotiations), debate has centred essentially on the links to be established between the START Agreement and the ABM Treaty, and on the implementation of the Treaty.

Little, if anything, is generally known about the bilateral talks held between the USSR and the United States during 1978 and 1979. Three discussion sessions were held successively at Helsinki, Berne and Vienna.[40] In the course of these discussions some progress was made in defining a "no-hostile act" policy and the "rules of the road" which would apply to their respective space activities.[41] According to Stares, these talks ran into two major obstacles. First, the Soviets insisted on including the U.S. Space Shuttle within any agreement on ASAT systems and, second, on excluding the satellites of other nations (meaning China?) from the discussions. At the time of these discussions, the United States also proposed a moratorium of "limited duration" on ASAT tests, which the Soviets respected in large part between 1978 and 1980.[42] The Soviet intervention in Afghanistan and the election of Reagan to the U.S. Presidency put a temporary halt to these bilateral discussions.

Officially, negotiations did not resume on this subject until the opening of the Nuclear and Space Talks (NST) in March 1985. It is difficult to know the degree of importance attached to the ASAT debate within the NST, since the talks related essentially to START and the ABM Treaty. Since we have no privileged information on this matter, we must terminate any further analysis of ASAT discussions at this point. Before taking account of the evolution of NST negotiations, however, several points should be recalled which marked the ASAT debate between 1980 and 1985.

In 1981, the Soviets tabled before the UN their first Draft Treaty on the Prohibition of the Stationing of Weapons of any Kind in Outer Space.[43] Article I of the draft treaty stressed the prohibition of placement in orbit of weapons of any kind, including reusable manned space vehicles. This was the Soviet way of saying that the U.S. Space Shuttle was a potential ASAT weapon. In similar manner, the Soviets tabled a second draft treaty on 23 August 1983, broader in scope than the first, entitled: "Draft Treaty on the Prohibition of the Use of Force in Outer Space and from Outer Space to Earth".[44] Among the provisions under Article II of the draft treaty was the commitment that States would undertake "not to test or create new anti-satellite systems and to destroy any existing anti-satellite systems". Included in this draft treaty were not only weapons in space and space weapons directed at Earth but also land-based weapons directed at space, since the draft envisaged the elimination of land-based anti-satellite weapons.

Until the early 1980s, the Soviets maintained that these issues should be discussed within the framework of bilateral talks between the superpowers. At about that time, the Soviets modified their position and presented draft treaties to the UN which were manifestly aimed at influencing public opinion and embarrassing the United States for developing ASAT systems rather than at bringing about real negotiations on the subject. For their part, the Americans insisted, from January 1983 onwards, that ASAT discussions should take place within the framework of the Committee on Disarmament in Geneva rather than on a bilateral basis[45], which indicated that the United States had lost all hope of reaching rapid agreement on the matter. This impression was confirmed in the Reagan Administration *Report to the Congress on U.S. Policy on ASAT Arms Control, 31 March 1984*, which stated that prohibition of ASAT weapons was difficult to verify and that any proposal should be compatible with the "national security" interests of the United States.

Other political, economic and technological developments complicated considerably the debate on prohibition of ASAT weapons. The Strategic Defence Initiative (SDI) announced in March 1983 for all practical purposes tolled the knell on ASAT negotiations, for any ABM weapon that is capable of intercepting or destroying a ballistic missile in flight can obviously intercept, damage or destroy a satellite. This observation follows simply from the fact that there are less parameters to analyze for a satellite, whose orbit is predictable, than for a ballistic missile. From that time on, negotiations on space took a new turn. Conformity with the 1972 ABM Treaty became a priority objective in the search for arms control agreements.

The unilateral moratorium declared by the USSR on ASAT tests in August 1983 led Congress to tie ASAT tests to the arms control process.[46] Congress moved from a policy of limitation (imposition of quotas) to a policy of total prohibition on ASAT tests during fiscal year 1986 (this prohibition applied only to the F-15 ASAT tests and not to tests of other systems against real or fictitious targets in space), since the U.S. Administration maintained that no progress in ASAT negotiations was possible in the absence of binding verification procedures.

Most of the U.S. ASAT tests were conducted using the Miniature Homing Vehicle (MHV). The MHV system is based on small missiles launched at high altitude from specially modified F-15 aircraft. The missiles use infrared guidance to manoeuvre close to the satellite which is destroyed by purely conventional means, in this particular case by deploying a mass of metallic balls which impact directly on the satellite. The United States originally planned to equip two F-15 squadrons for ASAT missions, one on the East coast and the other on the West coast. Apparently only the Langley base on the East coast will be used, and the original number of 112 ASAT interceptors will be reduced to 35.[47] Some observers believe that Langley could never become operational given the refusal of Congress to authorize Air-Launched Miniature Vehicle (ALMV) tests against real targets.

In view of the technical difficulties encountered in this program, there is increasing interest in the development of land-based ASAT systems employing the "exotic" technologies presently being developed under the SDI, such as laser weapons and particle beam weapons. It should be noted that the United States is trying to perfect four other options: the Emerald project (laser-based), the Free Electron Laser (FEL) project, the Exo-atmospheric Reentry-vehicle Intercept Sub-system (ERIS) project which resulted from the Homing Overlay Experiment (HOE), and the Space-Based Kinetic Kill Vehicle (SBKKV) project. All these systems were developed under the SDI project, but undoubtedly could be used for ASAT missions.

For their part, the Americans view the Soviet Union as the only country to possess an operational ASAT system. Although some authors judge the system as rudimentary, the U.S. Department of Defense in its 1988 report *Soviet Military Power* claims that the system is "far from primitive". Whatever the truth of the matter, the Tyuratam space complex houses the SL-11 launch vehicle which can effect a co-orbital intercept and destroy the target satellite by means of a mass of metallic pellets. The disadvantage of this system is that intercept can usually only be accomplished on the second orbit. The u.s. believes that the ABM Galosh interceptor has a low altitude ASAT intercept capability and that the Soviets also have a land-based system capable of irradiating u.s. satellites in space, specifically at Sary Shagan[48] and perhaps also at Dushanbe near the Soviet-Afghan border, which has the closest geographical location in the USSR to the trajectories of satellites in equatorial orbit.

On the international scene, States did not remain silent as the u.s. SDI program was strengthened. Within the Atlantic Alliance, SDI gave rise to violent disagreements. On the question of the ABM Treaty, most allies demanded strict compliance from the Americans with the 1972 agreement. With regard to arms control proposals in space, several States were close to believing that it was essential to accord absolute priority to the prohibition of ASAT weapons. This attitude was characteristic of most of the Western nations which sat on the Committee on Disarmament, particularly between 1980 and 1984.

At the UNSSOD II in 1978 Canada proposed a prohibition on the development of ASAT systems designed to intercept satellites in high Earth orbit. Subsequently, in 1979, Italy tabled a draft treaty before the Committee on Disarmament which included a provision to prohibit "devices designed for offensive purposes" which probably was meant to include ASAT systems.[49] Later, in June 1984, France presented proposals to the Conference on Disarmament aimed at banning ASAT systems.[50] The main provisions proposed by Paris were:

- strict limitations on antisatellite systems, to include especially those capable of reaching satellites in high orbit, since such satellites are essential for maintaining the strategic balance;
- prohibition, on a five-year renewable basis, of any directed energy weapons, whether deployed on the ground, in the atmosphere or in space, which are capable of destroying ballistic missiles or satellites at long range and, as a corollary, prohibition of corresponding tests;
- strengthening of the disclosure procedures whereby all States or organizations launching objects into space would be required to provide much more detailed information on mission characteristics so as to improve opportunities for verification;
- commitment by the United States and the USSR to extend to other nations the same provisions which had been agreed bilaterally between them concerning the immunity of satellites and other space objects.[51]

In summer 1984, Canada wanted to table similar proposals in Geneva, but was prevented at the last moment by high level foreign pressures. At that point in time, those nations that wanted to make progressive proposals in Geneva ran into a number of problems, due principally to two reasons. First, the Conference on Disarmament had still not received an official mandate to negotiate "arms control" in outer space and, second, when the United States decided in 1983 to support the idea of the creation of an *Ad Hoc* Committee on the Prevention of an Arms Race in Outer Space, it expressed the condition that Western proposals should first be reviewed for comment (meaning for approval) before being tabled in public. France was severely called to order, while Canada dared not cross the bounds that had been set ...

In general, although most Western countries were justifiably concerned at the lack of progress within the Conference on Disarmament on outer space, the United States and the USSR nevertheless resumed their talks in the summer of 1984 on ways of preventing an arms race in space. The United States, however, insisted that the talks be unconditional while the USSR insisted that they be linked to a moratorium on ASAT weapons. The September meetings allowed both parties to "talk for the sake of talking", or "agree for the sake of agreeing", on the need to resume discussions. The real breakthrough occurred when Shultz met with Gromyko in January 1985. As a result of these discussions, both parties agreed that the negotiations would embrace issues in respect of both space and strategic nuclear weapons, and their attendant interrelationships. On 12 March 1985, the first phase of the NST opened in Geneva.

The NST and the ABM Treaty

The strategic arms reductions talks are beyond our current scope, and will not be covered here. Rather, we shall lay stress on the evolution of the 1972 ABM Treaty which still constitutes one of the main cornerstones of the legal architecture encompassing outer space.

Three major circumstances gave crucial meaning to the ABM Treaty during negotiations on the prevention of an arms race in outer space. The first, obviously, was the famous speech of President Reagan on SDI delivered on 23 March 1983. The second was a corollary to the first, and concerned the "strategic concept" of Presidential Advisor Paul Nitze, designed to enable a transition from deterrence based on offensive strategic nuclear weapons to deterrence based on defensive strategic weapons. The third, and most important, was the consequence of the second, namely that the Reagan Administration had abandoned the restrictive interpretation of the ABM Treaty.

We shall start by considering the first two elements, which are the easiest to grasp. President Reagan's speech of 23 March 1983 was largely improvised and based on the advice of a few presidential aides without any consultation with the Administration or the various departments of primary interest. President Reagan sought to render nuclear weapons "impotent and obsolete" through the use of advanced technology to develop a spatial shield capable of intercepting and destroying them. This far too optimistic vision of technology inspired Paul Nitze's famous "U.S. strategic concept". At the time, Nitze was advisor to Secretary of State, George Shultz, at the Geneva talks. The "strategic concept" was developed at the end of 1984 and officially announced in January 1985. Essentially, it consisted of the following four sentences:

During the next ten years, the U.S. objective is a radical reduction in the power of existing and planned offensive nuclear arms, as well as the stabilization of the relationship between offensive and defensive nuclear arms, whether on earth or in space. We are even now looking forward to a period of transition to a more stable world, with greatly reduced levels of nuclear arms and an enhanced ability to deter war based upon an increasing contribution of non-nuclear defences against offensive non-nuclear arms. This period of transition could lead to the eventual elimination of all nuclear arms, both offensive and defensive. A world free from nuclear arms is an ultimate objective to which we, the Soviet Union, and all other nations can agree.[52]

The United States had no hesitation in using this pretentious terminology in a four-page draft treaty tabled at the Nuclear and Space Talks (NST) in Geneva on 22 January 1988. The draft treaty was titled: "Treaty between the United States of America and the Union of Soviet Socialist Republics on Certain Measures to Facilitate Cooperative Transition to the Deployment of Future Strategic Ballistic Missile Defenses".[53]

As costly as it might be, this strategy has the undeniable advantage of not exposing the planet to total annihilation in the event of war between the superpowers. It does not solve, however, the problem of whether it would not simply be better to disarm or renounce the idea of making war, the second being a logical consequence of the first. The first would not necessarily be an essential condition for the second since, in time of crisis or conflict, either superpower could resume the arms race. This "strategic concept" depends essentially on the illusion that the promise of technology will solve all political problems. How can one feel secure with a new technology which replaces "unthinkable war" with the idea of security based on maximizing the benefits to one while minimizing the benefits to the other?

This strategy of transition obviously represents a unilateral redefinition of the "rules of nuclear play" which, in the long term, might serve the reciprocal interests of the superpowers. It nevertheless constitutes a reversal of the idea of deterrence founded on reciprocal vulnerability, namely mutual suicide. The thinkers of the Reagan Administration might reply that deterrence is no longer credible since it is absurd and hence irrational. But the reason that deterrence works is precisely because war is absurd and irrational. The theory of Mutual Assured Destruction (MAD), which was consecrated in SALT I, at least had the merit of projecting the USSR as a world power on an equal footing with the United States. This notion of nuclear parity in turn elicits the notion of nuclear responsibility. A shift from MAD to MAS (Mutual Assured Survival) would be feasible if the Soviets thought like the Americans, but that has never been the case. Thus, the Soviets continue to maintain that START negotiations are impossible in the absence of ABM agreements which restrict defence against ballistic missiles.

The world has come a long way since 1983 when the U.S. announcement of the Strategic Defense Initiative provoked a state of psychosis. This is not to say that the Soviets will not adopt more defensive technologies in the future, or that the superpowers will not eventually reach agreement on some form of limited strategic defence based on new technologies. Such a readjustment of their strategic postures, which could result from a relaxing of tensions and the active pursuit of positive *détente*, could eventually provide the superpowers with some kind of protection against technical accidents or the threats of other States.

Clearly, a complete reorientation of strategy towards purely defensive weapons would make no sense, for not only would it plunge the world into a new arms race but it would also have no valid basis in a world where all offensive strategic nuclear weapons had been eliminated. Any transition which is oriented towards escaping today's dominant paradigms can only be effected slowly and in small steps. In short, the outcome of the debate must lie between the two extremes of a transition involving cooperation or a transition involving conflict.

The style of language used by the U.S. Administration, which was admittedly designed to convince the American public, did little to facilitate things for the Soviets. The Strategic Defense Initiative Organization (SDIO) systematically set about to present a series of proposals which progressively became more grandiose, with the result that the Soviet adversary, who might have been expected to show some form of understanding, displayed only resentment, bitterness and lack of comprehension. In addition, the situation might possibly have remained tolerable if the proposals had remained as mere words without substance, but it lapsed into incoherence and provocation when the time came for reinterpretation of treaties which, until then, had been perfectly clear.

The debate can be summed up succinctly as follows: some maintain that any weapon can be developed which is not expressly forbidden by the Treaty, while others maintain that only weapons expressly permitted by the Treaty can be developed. The first line of reasoning falls squarely in the domain of laxity and permissiveness, allowing the text of the Treaty to be opened up for reinterpretation.[54] The second line of reasoning conforms with the spirit in which the Treaty was understood when it was signed.[55]

The essence of the ABM Treaty is embodied in Article 5: "Each party undertakes not to develop, test, or deploy ABM systems or components which are sea-based, air-based, space-based, or mobile land-based." Article 1 prohibits any ABM system "for the defence of the territory" or "an individual region" of either Party to the Treaty, but it provides for two exceptions. These concern the protection of national capital areas and/or ICBM silo areas, where, in both cases, the radius of the area is not to exceed 150 km. Evidently, these areas can only be protected using fixed land-based installations. A parallel examination of these two articles goes right to the heart of the debate. The ABM Treaty forbids ABM systems, but the treaty is "permissive" in that it allows for the two exceptions mentioned.

A Common Declaration D was, however, added to the Treaty concerning Other Physical Principles (OPP); meaning "exotic technologies". This particular Declaration served as a pretext for the U.S. to reinterpret the Treaty. The Declaration states that if ABM systems based on other physical principles ever see the light of day, "including components capable of substituting for ABM interceptor missiles, ABM launchers, or ABM radars", specific limitations would be imposed on such systems and components following discussions in compliance with Article XIII (consultation procedures) and Article XIV (amendment procedures). The text of Common Declaration D commences, however, with the phrase "in order to meet their obligations not to deploy ABM systems and their components, except as stipulated in Article III" of the Treaty. Article III does no more, therefore, than define the operational conditions of ABM systems for the areas permitted in Article I.

Up to that point, the situation is relatively clear. Exotic technologies are not prohibited, since they may be subject to discussion and agreement in meeting ABM requirements in the two permitted areas. For the most part jurists agree that exotic technologies are permitted, but they may be applied solely to systems used in the two permitted areas, namely land-based systems.[56] Jurists also agree that the use of exotic technologies is strictly subject to the framework of consultations and amendments provided for in the Treaty. The situation becomes cloudy, however, when the Common Declaration D is read in conjunction with Article II of the Treaty.

Abraham Sofaer, Legal Advisor to the U.S. State Department, contends that some negotiators tried to get the Soviets to accept the idea of a total ban on systems based on "other physical principles". In a statement of October 1985, Sofaer declared: "The record reflects that they (the negotiators) have failed to obtain the ban they sought, and that we could never have enforced such a ban against the Soviets".[57] In Sofaer's mind, exotic technologies are permitted because the Soviets refused to support the idea of banning them. Also, he considers that Common Declaration D must be read in conjunction with Article II of the Treaty which stipulates that an ABM system is "a system to counter strategic ballistic missiles or their elements in flight trajectory, currently consisting of ABM interceptors ..., ABM launchers ..., ABM radars". Here, the level of the debate changes, for the meaning of the phrase "currently consisting of" must be defined. Was it intended to apply only to systems existing at the time, or to all systems that are developed in the future?

It is fruitless to speculate further. The U.S. Administration has adopted a position on this issue, at least as far as the legal language of the Treaty is concerned. In its report to Congress dated April 1987, the U.S. Department of Defense stated that according to the *strict interpretation* of the ABM Treaty, "the development and testing of ABM systems based on other physical principles is only permitted for fixed land-based systems or their components".[58] In this regard, almost everyone agrees. The report also states that a *broader interpretation* of the Treaty would be as follows: "ABM systems based on other physical principles – that is, systems other than ABM interceptors, ABM launchers or ABM radars – as well as the components that could replace ABM interceptors, ABM launchers or ABM radars, can be developed and tested but not deployed, regardless of their basing mode".[59]

According to Strobe Talbott, the expression "currently consisting of" had been added at the request of Raymond Garthoff who was on the U.S. negotiating team when the ABM Treaty was signed.[60] Garthoff claimed that, at the time, this expression had a broad meaning, in that it applied to all future weapons. The Reagan Administration decided otherwise.

Finally with regard to the main provisions of the ABM Treaty, the conclusions drawn by Paul Nitze in a speech to a group of jurists in New York on 31 October 1986 are worth noting:

- First, the Treaty does not limit the development and testing of missiles that are neither components of ABM systems nor substitutes for these components.
- Second, the Treaty permits testing of missiles in a non-ABM mode, for instance, against satellites. The terminology "tested in ABM mode" was the subject of a secret agreement in 1978 within the Consultative Committee – established through the SALT agreements – in Geneva.
- Third, the Treaty permits testing of certain ABM systems of the 1972 generation.
- Fourth, the Treaty permits the testing of systems based on physical principles other than those in being in 1972. In other words, the Common Declaration D permits the development and testing of space-based ABM systems and their components that employ "other physical principles".

Supporters of the restrictive school, who base their conclusions on an analysis of the ABM Treaty, call for:

- prohibition of the development, testing and deployment of space-based ABMs and ABM components, whether dependent on existing or exotic technologies. This prohibition also applies to air-based, sea-based, and mobile land-based ABMs and ABM components, that is, to everything but fixed land-based systems and components;
- prohibition of the deployment of fixed, land-based ABM systems and components, except at a single designated site[61] not more than 150 kilometres in radius, centred on the national capital or a missile silo field, and containing not more than one hundred launchers;
- no prohibition of the development and testing of fixed, land-based ABMs and ABM components of traditional technologies at existing test ranges;
- prohibition of deployment of exotic technologies even if fixed and land-based, and even at the existing test ranges except after discussion and agreement with the other party;
- prohibition of upgrading non-ABM missiles, launchers and radars to an ABM capability, or in testing them in an ABM mode and,

arguably, by inference, restriction on upgrading components (that are not missiles, launchers or radars) of sub-ABM systems to ABM capability;
• no prohibition against research.[62]

Clearly, the ABM Treaty is one of the most ambiguous, if not the most badly written, instruments in the whole history of arms control negotiations since 1945. When it was signed in 1972, it at least had the merit of being an attempt to stabilize the balance between offensive and defensive weapons. The Treaty is open to review every five years. At the first review in 1977, the two parties agreed "that the Treaty is operating effectively ... serves the security interest of both parties, decreases the risk of outbreak of nuclear war, facilitates progress in the further limitation and reduction of strategic offensive arms, and requires no amendment at this time".[63] In 1982, although both parties reaffirmed their commitments to the aims and objectives of the Treaty, there was no joint appreciation, strictly speaking, of the effectiveness of the Treaty.

All that can be said about the 1987 review of the Treaty is that a working group was created within the framework of the NST negotiations to review questions of definition. This was a particularly delicate process given that the superpowers were close to agreement on strategic arms reductions and that the two questions – strategic arms reductions and the Strategic Defense Initiative – were intimately interlinked.

When President Reagan announced in early October 1987 that the United States would adopt a "wide" definition of the ABM Treaty, there was a general outcry of protests from around the world, and particularly from the NATO countries. In view of this violent allied criticism, the U.S. Administration gave way to pressure from the State Department and announced that it would hold to a strict interpretation of the ABM Treaty as a matter of policy but not as a matter of legal obligation.[64] In retrospect, one might wonder whether this reinterpretation of the Treaty was really necessary, since none of the ABM tests planned under the U.S. program up to 1989 contravened the ABM Treaty albeit at the cost of countless technological pirouettes.[65]

At Geneva in May 1986, the Soviets asked that the Parties not exercise the "withdrawal" clause in the ABM Treaty for a period of 15 to 20 years, although in private they admitted that non-withdrawal for a 10 to 15 year period would satisfy them.[66] In his letter of July 1986 to General Secretary Gorbachev, President Reagan proposed observing the broad interpretation of the ABM Treaty for a period of five to seven years, after which both Parties would be free to deploy antimissile defensive systems. In October 1986, at the Reykjavik Summit, President Reagan made substantially the same proposal, but agreed to extend the period of observation of the Treaty to ten years. In other words, as Admiral John Poindexter confirmed later, the United States offered not to withdraw from the Treaty for ten years on condition that the USSR accept a broader interpretation.[67] At the Washington Summit in December 1987 the two Parties agreed to respect the Treaty as signed in 1972 "while conducting their research, development and testing as required, which are permitted by the ABM Treaty". In addition, the USSR asked the United States not to avail itself of the withdrawal clause for "an agreed duration". All that the U.S. actually promised was not to withdraw from the Treaty before the end of 1994, while Moscow had asked that the period of non-withdrawal be extended to 9 to 10 years.

In Geneva, on 22 January 1988, the United States tabled a draft treaty on defence and space which incorporated, according to the Americans, the essential provisions that had been agreed in Washington. On 15 March 1988, the U.S. added a "predictability" Protocol to the draft treaty, under which the superpowers would exchange data annually on their space defence programs, arrange reciprocal visits to their respective facilities and observe tests conducted under their respective strategic defence programs. In early May 1988, the Soviets presented their own working paper which essentially reflected their former position on the link that had to be maintained between such a proposal and the signing of the START Agreements, and on adherence to the strict interpretation of the ABM Treaty. The Moscow Common Declaration put forward, at most, an account of progress towards development of the draft text which would become a Protocol associated with the 1972 ABM Treaty.

Meanwhile, Washington continued to adhere to the "broader" interpretation of the Treaty as far as legal contractual obligations were concerned. In 1986, the U.S. Government, in its Fiscal 1987 Arms Control Impact Statement (ACIS) declared, for the first time, that the "broad" interpretation was "perfectly justified". In the 1988 Defense Appropriations Bill, the House Armed Services Committee included a clause to the effect that expenditures would be authorized only for activities in strict conformity with the ABM Treaty. The past few years have, therefore, witnessed a latent conflict between Congress and the Executive over SDI.

The Soviets continue to hold firmly to the link between the START Agreement and the ABM Treaty, which they hope to introduce directly into the body of the text of the START Agreements. Thus, they seek to insert a clause which would render the START Agreements nul and void if one or other of the parties were to violate the ABM Treaty.[68]

The ASAT-ABM Linkage

The aim of this very brief section is only to highlight the links between ASAT and ABM systems so as to provide a better understanding of the political stakes involved, both for the superpowers and third-party States which have a legitimate right to ensure the security of their own satellites.

From the standpoint of international law, aside from the space debris that results from peaceful uses of space, there is also an accumulation of debris from most of the ASAT and ABM tests that are conducted in space, and which is a source of concern for both third-party States and the superpowers. In near space, there are presently some 7,000 objects greater than 20 cm in size. This is the smallest size that can be detected with existing radars. According to a report of the International Committee on Space Research[69], of these 7,000 objects:

about 23 percent correspond to satellite payloads, 10 percent to burnt-out rocket stages, 62 percent to fragments, and only 5 percent are "active" satellites; about 50 objects appear to contain radioactive material. Space debris consists not only of fragments of exploded rocket stages or broken-up satellites, but also a plethora of lens and instrument covers, clamps ... In addition to the larger fragments, there are at least 2,000 objects ranging in size from 10 to 20 cm and about 50,000 in the 1–10 cm range. Below this range there are estimates of millions to billions of metal and paint chips in the millimetre and submillimetre range. (It must be recognized that a 0.5 mm metal chip with an average speed of 30,000 km/hr could easily penetrate a space suit and even kill an astronaut).

The authors of this report concluded that the flux of anthropogenic debris is significantly greater than the flux of natural meteoroids. In addition, the largest concentration of fragments and debris is to be found between 350 and 1,250 km altitude where most Earth satellites, including the Space Shuttle and space stations, are orbiting. The test of the ASAT weapon which destroyed the SOLWIND satellite produced 257 "observable" fragments and a much larger number of "non-observable" fragments. Even if the probability of collision with micrometeorites is small, the chance of collision with space debris is far from negligible. On average, about a hundred satellites are launched annually, and at this rate our planet will become encircled with a massive accumulation of space debris before the end of the century. On many occasions, the International Astronomical Union (IAU) has denounced this situation as deplorable; space debris poses an immense obstacle to observation of space from the Earth.

We have quoted these few excerpts from the report to underscore the weakness of international law *vis-à-vis* the space activities of States. The Convention on Third Party Liability is a relatively useful instrument in cases where it is possible to identify, in the event of accident, the national origin of the debris falling back to Earth. When an accident occurs in space, however, it is obviously impossible to identify or register each flake of paint which floats freely in the space environment. A Convention on the Protection of the Space Environment would not solve all the problems, but it might perhaps set some limits on ABM, ASAT or other tests to reduce proliferation of anthropogenic space debris.

In the arms control area, some ASAT activities are already subject to some of the provisions of the legal instruments mentioned above. The 1963 PTBT, for instance, prohibits any nuclear explosion in space. Also, the 1967 Outer Space Treaty bans the placing of nuclear weapons in orbit, while the 1972 ABM Treaty bans the testing of ASAT systems in an ABM mode. Aside from these restrictions, there are few constraints on the development of ASAT systems.

It is improbable that a system designed for ASAT applications could be used in an ABM mode. On the other hand, laser weapons and directed energy weapons which may be developed for ABM purposes in the future could be formidable ASAT weapons. Such weapons are prohibited in the context of a strict interpretation of the ABM Treaty, but they could be admissible in the event of consultation and agreement between the two parties. Tests have already been conducted in the Homing Overlay Experiment (HOE). Other tests will also be conducted under the ERIS (Exo-atmospheric Reentry-vehicle Interceptor Sub-system) program, but with a single interceptor so as not to contravene the provisions of the ABM Treaty. It is quite possible that these tests could satisfy the needs of an ASAT program.

It is disquieting to conjecture that, prior to 1984, the U.S. Administration could, in part, conduct ABM tests under the cover of ASAT tests, and that after the prohibition of ASAT tests by Congress, SDI tests conducted within the broader interpretation of the ABM Treaty, could serve ASAT purposes. The official version, however, is that components of systems intended for ASAT missions can be tested in a non-ABM mode, whether the tests are land-based or space-based. In its report to Congress, the SDI Organization stated that "interception of certain orbital targets simulating antisatellite weapons is perfectly consistent with the ABM Treaty as long as the devices involved cannot substitute for ABM components or that they are not tested in an ABM mode".[70] The u.s. did exactly that with their test of 5 September 1986, better known as "Delta 180" or "Vector Sum". Durch concluded that this test simply showed that the United States possessed a co-orbital intercept capability similar to that of the Soviet Union. Part of this experiment consisted of studying the behaviour of "heavy" and "light" objects in space so as to develop a future capability for discriminating between "decoys" and "real targets" in space.

The superpowers are continuously striving to exploit future technologies. At the same time, the difficulties in distinguishing between ABM and ASAT technologies are increasing, particularly in respect of detection, target acquisition, tracking and destruction of targets in low earth orbit. As a working hypothesis, we consider it likely that the superpowers will accord first priority to problems associated with the START Agreements and ABM defensive systems, and that only afterwards will they address the question of imposition of possible restrictions on ASAT systems.

In parallel, the superpowers must take account of the increasing number of countries engaged in the peaceful use of space. These countries rightfully intend to ensure the safety of their satellites. There are a number of ways of achieving this, including restrictions on "lanes of access" to satellites by manned space vehicles, extension of the Convention on Third Party Liability to tests of a military nature, improvement of legal provisions on non-interference, and development of confidence-building measures to facilitate a greater degree of openness in space activities, for instance, by defining safety zones or maximum stay times for space vehicles in critical zones. In this regard, no single measure will likely be satisfactory, but a combination of measures could lead to more equitable sharing of responsibilities and duties in the field of space exploration.

THE CANADIAN POSITION

As in the previous section, we shall study separately Canada's position on the various issues of interest. First, we shall examine Canada's position on the control of antisatellite weapons. Next, we shall treat some broader issues, especially those related to SDI and the ABM Treaty. Finally, we shall consider space in the context of verification in arms control, a topic on which Canada has laid particular emphasis since the early 1980s.

Canada and ASAT Weapons

The first Canadian proposals of importance on the question of outer space date back to the 18 June 1982 speech of Prime Minister Trudeau to the Second United Nations Special Session on Disarmament (UNSSOD II). On that occasion, the Prime Minister expressed concern that the arms race might extend to space, and proposed that a treaty be drafted to prohibit the development and deployment of "any weapon intended for use in space". Evidently, Canada intended to oppose the development of any ASAT or ABM system which would employ new technologies, especially those of directed energy weapons.

The need to intensify Canadian efforts in arms control was well recognized in the Cabinet meeting held at Lake Louise in September 1980. The 1980 Speech from the Throne also acknowledged this issue as a "Government priority". On 23 April 1981, following an interdepartmental meeting of deputy ministers, it was agreed that the means for limiting or restricting the "military use of space" should be defined in consultation with the United States. On 12 May 1982, a Special Disarmament Advisory Session reinforced the substance of the Cabinet meeting at Lake Louise, concluding that "additional controls were necessary for outer space". Amongst the measures identified was the proposal to initiate a comprehensive research program on verification. This will be discussed more fully in the section on "Canada and Verification from Space".

Despite the statements, Canada had no real strategy for arms control in space. At its 8 June 1981 meeting, the Cabinet Committee on Foreign and Defence Policy still held fast to the strategy of "suffocation" developed in 1978. At the same time, the Committee stated that Canadian efforts should not be developed unilaterally, but within the framework of multilateral agreements. The 8 June meeting was nevertheless important, for it gave rise to collaborative studies, involving one or more companies, on the value of earth resources satellites in verifying arms control agreements. The interdepartmental committee meeting of April 1981 was also useful since it gave rise to a study which constituted one of Canada's main contributions to the Committee on Disarmament in 1982.

We refer, of course, to Canada's paper on "Arms Control and Outer Space"[71] which was tabled before the Committee on Disarmament on 26 August 1982. The paper was largely prepared by DND's Operational Research and Analysis Establishment, headed at the time by Dr. George Lindsey, and categorizes satellite systems as "stabilizing" or "destabilizing" in relation to arms control or crisis management. The paper argues that since the majority of military satellites are used as National Technical Means (NTM) and thus contribute to the stability of the nuclear balance, systems designed to destroy satellites, in particular ASAT systems, are "destabilizing".

At the Williamsburg Summit in May 1983, Prime Minister Trudeau told the Western powers "we should be busting our asses for peace". This prompted Mrs. Thatcher to remark that "Mr. Trudeau should be a comfort to the Kremlin".[72] The proposal to ban ASAT systems designed to attack satellites in high earth orbit was obviously earmarked as a dominant feature of Trudeau's peace initiative, although it did not appear as one of the five points in his speech to Guelph University on 27 October 1983. In fact, it was a few days later, on 13 November, that the Prime Minister chose to elaborate on the matter. In a speech delivered at the Queen Elizabeth Hotel in Montreal, Pierre Elliott Trudeau asserted:

I have in mind an agreement for banning the testing and deployment of high altitude antisatellite systems. Such weapons threaten the entire means of communication on which we depend for crisis management. During conflict, these weapons could deprive one or other of the opposing parties of its command and control network at the very instant when the maintenance of stability would be critically dependent on that party's ability to anticipate and react accordingly, rather than be panicked into blind retaliation.[73]

The main reasons underlying the Prime Minister's 1983 peace initiative were mentioned in Chapter 9. In his Montreal speech, he repeated the essential ideas that he expounded in Guelph:

But, if we succeed in giving political impetus to having the five major powers sit down together at the negotiating table; if we obtain a new political commitment to the Non-Proliferation Treaty; if we renew our efforts at the Vienna talks to achieve a balance of conventional forces and to raise the nuclear threshold in Europe; and if, finally, we apply ourselves to encouraging progress in strategic technologies only in those areas that will facilitate verification, then we shall have developed a truly global approach to the problems of peace and security.

To say that the Prime Minister's words met with mixed feelings in Washington would be an understatement. At the time, in December 1983, Washington was very cool towards negotiations on ASAT systems, since bilateral talks were breaking down and the Soviets were on the point of withdrawing from the negotiating table in Geneva.

As well, the ASAT systems under study in both the United States and the USSR were only capable of intercepting satellites in low earth orbit. There seemed to be little relationship between reality and a proposal to ban high earth orbit ASAT systems. Equally, such a proposal implied that space could be "fragmented", or "stratified", whereas no one had yet succeeded in even delineating the boundary between airspace and outer space.[74]

The truth of the matter is probably that the United States would not even consider this proposal for fear that it would open the way for more general discussions on ASAT systems. One high-ranking representative of the u.s. National Security Council (NSC) asked a Canadian top civil servant whether Canadians considered "the legs of astronauts" as ASAT systems, since they could effectively kick any low earth orbit satellite out of its orbit and, consequently, neutralize it.[75] It was quite evident that if the Americans could use their space shuttle to bring one of their satellites back to earth, they could equally well use it to de-orbit another country's satellite.

Moscow's enthusiasm for the Canadian proposal could hardly be described as delirious. At the Canadian-Soviet bilateral consultations held in June 1984, it was learned that Moscow had not accorded a warmer welcome to the Canadian proposal because of declining Soviet expectations in bilateral dialogue with the United States. The Soviets considered it useless to pursue dialogue under these circumstances, especially with a nation whose only ambition was to achieve strategic superiority.

Canada nevertheless was undaunted. Ottawa advised NATO of its proposal in February 1984, and lengthy consultations followed in Brussels on 11 April 1984. Ottawa was aware, however, from President Reagan's report to Congress on 31 March 1984, that the Canadian proposal would meet with stiff u.s. opposition in the area of verification because this issue was inextricably linked to ABM systems. Moreover, even if the United States acknowledged some merit in the Canadian proposal, an ASAT capability was deemed essential to ensure u.s. mastery of the seas and oceans in time of conflict.

Meanwhile, in the House of Commons on 9 February 1984, Prime Minister Trudeau announced his intention to table in Geneva the Canadian draft proposal to ban the development of high earth orbit ASAT systems. Although it was known full well that the Americans would oppose the proposal, it was considered that if the proposal were to be tabled anyway, it would be better to act speedily and minimize the time between tabling it and the start of the requisite consultations. The machinery was put into operation, despite an imbroglio between Geneva and the Department of External Affairs.

The confusion was of a purely semantic nature. Ottawa's instructions were to circulate the document; Geneva's response was that documents were tabled, not circulated! By then it was May 1984.

Some officials in the Department of External Affairs were afraid that such a proposal might jeopardize Canada-U.S. cooperation at a time when negotiations were in progress on the U.S. Space Station, when Washington was showing more than usual interest in Canada's geography (the possible deployment of an ABM system), and when NORAD was undergoing a significant reorganization through the establishment of a unified Space Command (SPACECOM) at Colorado Springs. On the whole, however, it was judged better to go forward because the two main departments involved – External Affairs and National Defence – were in perfect agreement on the "destabilizing" nature of high altitude ASAT systems.

On 10 July 1984, Cabinet approved the tabling of the Canadian document in Geneva. John Turner was the Prime Minister at the time, having replaced Pierre Elliott Trudeau on an interim basis following Trudeau's formal withdrawal as leader of the Liberal Party. In light of the contradictory reports from abroad, Turner was unwilling to make a firm decision. In Geneva, speed was of the essence. As the current session of the Conference on Disarmament drew to a close, swift action was required. The Canadian Delegation, recognizing that procedure called for a document to be circulated on the same date that it was to be formally tabled, tried to convince the Conference Secretariat to assign an agenda number ahead of time to the Canadian proposal. In this way, Canada would be able to intervene at the very end of the session, which would allow time for the Prime Minister to reach a decision. The disadvantage of this artifice was that it obliged Canada to give advance notice to her allies that she intended to table the document. We shall not elaborate on the sentiments of the Chairman of the Conference on Disarmament when faced with this ingenious Canadian procedure.

It was well known, however, in the Canadian Embassy in Washington that the Canadian proposal would not be appreciated by the Reagan Administration. The Embassy recommended against proceeding with the proposal since intense negotiations were in progress in the U.S. Congress concerning the assignment of quotas on the importation of Canadian steel. It was judged, therefore, that the time was not ripe for proceeding. In addition, a bilateral U.S.-Soviet dialogue was also in progress, and it was feared that the Canadian proposal might play into the hands of the Soviets.[76] On 6 July, Washington clearly expressed its position to the Canadian Prime Minister. On 7 August, in a second letter to External Affairs' Minister Jean

Chrétien, Washington apprised Ottawa of the latest developments in the u.s.-Soviet negotiations. Chrétien, supported by his principal advisors, became impatient with Canada's vacillations, and informed Prime Minister Turner on 14 August 1984 that the July decision of Cabinet had to be upheld, suggesting that Turner should not be too concerned about possible bad humour in Washington. This opinion was obviously not shared by the Minister of State for Science and Technology who, four days later, expressed to External Affairs, in no uncertain terms, his surprise at the absence of consultations between departments on the manner of proceeding in Geneva.

In Geneva, everything was set. The Canadian Ambassador proceeded in the manner described earlier. On 24 August, everyone waited with bated breath for the Prime Minister's instructions. On 26 August, the reply was given. The proposal would not be tabled. The telephone lines between Ottawa and Washington had been sizzling. Naturally, communications are simpler when only Bechtel to Bechtel are involved. Ottawa clearly considered it prudent to give in to Washington at a time when the federal election campaign was in full swing. In September 1984, the Conservative Party led by Brian Mulroney was elected with an overwhelming majority.

Nothing further was heard of the Canadian proposal. From that time on, Canada supported the international community within the Conference on Disarmament to develop agreements guaranteeing immunity to satellites[77], which, in itself, was far from a half-measure, since this was about the only available path to follow while awaiting the outcome of bilateral negotiations between the superpowers.

Canada, SDI and the ABM Treaty

The first position adopted by the Conservative Government on the issue of SDI and its impact on the ABM Treaty dates back to 21 January 1985. In the House of Commons, the new Secretary of State for External Affairs, Joe Clark, expressed pleasure that President Reagan had affirmed that the United States "would not go beyond pure research without discussions and negotiations".[78] The joint communiqué issued after the Shamrock Summit in Québec in March 1985 emphasized that u.s. research on SDI "would remain a cautious effort and respect the provisions of the Anti-Ballistic Missile Treaty ... "

These first two statements were made before the real intentions of the u.s. on SDI became known to the Canadian Government. On 26 March 1985, the u.s. Secretary of Defense officially invited all NATO allies to join the u.s. research efforts on SDI. The invitation contained a clause requiring that "action be taken" within 60 days. This unfortunate clause was subsequently withdrawn. The Atlantic Alliance supported the u.s. position, since most nations, including Canada, considered that research could not be subject to serious verification.

It appears that the Canadian Department of National Defence was alerted to u.s. intentions even before the u.s. invitation was made public, and was instructed to remain "tight-lipped"[79] on the subject. This typically American style of diplomacy, aimed perhaps at using Canada as a test platform prior to surfacing the proposal before all the NATO nations, proved to be a source of embarrassment for the Canadian Government. As soon as the offer became public, a top-flight civil servant, Arthur Kroeger, and several other public officials were hastily commissioned to provide their advice on SDI to the Prime Minister.[80] It was this style of u.s. diplomacy that forced the personal intervention of the Prime Minister. In the summer, following lengthy consultations with Washington and the main European capitals, the Kroeger report was submitted to the Prime Minister's Office.

The Kroeger report contained four fundamental options, ranging from a firm "No" to "full participation", the intermediate options comprising respectively minimal Canadian industrial participation in u.s. research, and Canadian specialization in space detection to supplement the future North Warning System (NWS).[81] Within the bureaucracy, it was impossible to reach interdepartmental agreement on a common draft of the fundamental problems raised by the u.s. invitation to participate in SDI research. To the best of our knowledge, no general document exists to explain the decision which was subsequently taken by Cabinet in September 1985. This might imply that Canada's decision was largely political. The absence of a consensus within the bureaucracy gave "elbow room" to the political authorities.

During the summer of 1985, a number of depositions were made at hearings across the breadth of the country. The large majority was against participation in SDI. Amongst the exceptions was the deposition of C.R. Nixon, former Deputy Minister of National Defence, who argued that there would be significant scientific and technological benefits to be derived from closer collaboration with the United States. The Special Joint Committee of the Senate and the House of Commons on Canada's International Relations submitted its report on 23 August 1985, recommending that Government "take no final decision ... before obtaining the necessary additional information on the strategic, financial and economic impact"[82] of SDI. On 7 September 1985, the Canadian Government made a Cabinet decision public in the House, at which time Prime Minister Mulroney declared:

the Canadian Government has reached the conclusion that the policies and priorities of Canada do not justify a government to government effort in support of SDI research.

This statement contained four noteworthy words: "policies and priorities", and "government to government". We shall return to this aspect later. Canada thus became the sixth country to decline the U.S. invitation to participate directly in advanced research work in the area of strategic defence, behind Norway, Australia, France, Denmark and Greece. In the interim, External Affairs' Minister Clark had already taken a stand in favour of a restrictive interpretation of the ABM Treaty before the Standing Committee on External Affairs and National Defence. In January 1986, Joe Clark vigorously reaffirmed that the ABM Treaty was to be strictly observed, and added: "We shall continue to exhort the Parties to this Treaty to do nothing to harm their integrity [and] to attempt to strengthen their provisions and their [value]".[83]

In its June 1986 report, the Special Joint Committee of the Senate and the House of Commons on Canada's International Relations (or Simard-Hockin Committee) stated that increased efforts were needed to establish "related measures" aimed at improving strategic stability. The Joint Committee adhered to a strict interpretation of the ABM Treaty, namely that the Treaty banned all work on defensive systems, "except for basic research".[84] This assertion obviously had no foundation since, by virtue of Article IV of the ABM Treaty, modernization of conventional systems – including test and development – is permitted at test ranges.

Six months later, in December 1986, External Affairs' Minister Joe Clark stated that the wording of the Treaty did not directly specify "research". According to Clark, it was up to the two Parties to agree on the true spirit of the Treaty. Until 1972, the U.S. interpretation of the research and development provisions of the ABM Treaty conformed to the 1972 interpretation of negotiator Gerald Smith given before the U.S. Senate Armed Services Committee:

The prohibitions on development contained in the ABM Treaty would start at the part of the development process where field testing is initiated on either a prototype or breadboard model. It was understood by both sides that the prohibition on "development" applies to activities involved after a component moves from the laboratory development and testing stage to the field testing stage, wherever performed. The fact that early stages of the development process, such as laboratory testing, would pose problems for testing by national technical means is an important consideration in reaching this definition. Exchanges with the Soviet Delegation made clear that this definition is also the Soviet interpretation of the term "development".[85]

Following the meeting in Reykjavik, Paul Nitze made his famous speech of 31 October 1986, which we have quoted *in extenso* in the section on "The NST and the ABM Treaty". Aside from the paragraph which deals with "other physical principles" and which broadens the interpretation of the ABM Treaty, there was little new in this speech. Paul Nitze did, however, state that research included "conceptual design and testing conducted both inside and outside the laboratory". It is hard to know whether or not this statement of Presidential Advisor Nitze was an attempt to erase the distinction between actual testing and field testing. It may be recalled that by the same occasion Nitze stated that experiments "in a non-ABM mode" had been the subject of a secret agreement in 1978.

At the end of 1986, the Canadian Government reiterated its wish that both Parties adhere to a strict interpretation of the ABM Treaty. External Affairs' Minister Clark added, however:[86]

There might be private documents in the hands of both the Soviet Union and the United States which might elaborate on other agreements that they made with respect to research. Only they can know that. All that we can ask is that the integrity of the ABM Treaty be respected and that there be a strict adherence to it. That is the position of the Government of Canada.

This statement came just at the right time to extricate the Canadian Government from an awkward situation. The Special Joint Committee of the Senate and the House of Commons on Canada's International Relations, and even the Government itself, had no authority to draw any firm conclusions from the set of provisions under the ABM Treaty, and Canada had made known its intention to adhere to the spirit, rather than the letter, of the ABM Treaty. Clark was probably trying to dissociate himself from a study undertaken at the end of 1986 by the Legal Affairs Bureau, which concluded that both sides had equally valid reasons for supporting their respective interpretations. Legally speaking, it could equally well have been argued that there was a noticeable absence of statements from other nations on the interpretation of the Treaty, which would have lead to the same ambiguity. Canada's official position was that it was not her lot to interpret treaties signed between other countries. As a rule, Ottawa advocates strict respect for treaties. In the case of SDI, Ottawa maintained right from the start that it was "prudent" to conduct such research, and the United States could only be appreciative of such support. The U.S. used SDI as a master card in negotiations with the USSR – a master card which, it must be said, was provided by the whole Atlantic Alliance. Perhaps the main purpose of the U.S. in promoting SDI was to obtain the support of the Atlantic Alliance in order to negotiate from a position of strength with Moscow.

Through a leak to the *Washington Post*[87] it was already known that External Affairs' Minister Clark, in his letter of 7 February 1987 to Secretary of State Shultz, had asked that existing agreements on arms control be strictly respected. He probably used this occasion also to emphasize that any space-based deployment would mean the end of the ABM Treaty. When U.S. Presidential Advisor Paul Nitze came to Ottawa in March 1987 to discuss the whole issue, External Affairs' Minister Clark grasped the opportunity to make the Canadian position clear to the United States. The discussion embraced more than just the legal aspect, for the following statement was added: "any unilateral action by either Party to the Treaty which could influence the present strategic balance would be of grave concern to Canada".[88] In this regard, it should be stressed that Clark had already asked the United States, on 5 January 1987, not to exceed the limits agreed upon in SALT II concerning the introduction into service of the B-52 bomber equipped with cruise missiles. In other words, Canada asked the U.S. government once more not to unilaterally change "the rules of the nuclear game" and to do nothing that would change the balance of forces in its favour.

Canada's position on the ABM Treaty remained essentially the same throughout all the debate in NATO, apart from a few nuances which were progressively introduced. At first, Canada asked the United States for "strict adherence" to the ABM Treaty. Later, Canada advocated "strict interpretation" of the ABM Treaty, without regard for legal arguments which favoured one interpretation or another, since that was the prerogative of the Parties signatory to the ABM Treaty. Finally, Canada sought to extend the debate to arms control as a whole, a process that had already started with the 1986 report of the Special Joint Committee of the Senate and the House of Commons which advocated "related measures" in the area of armaments. Canada thus remained faithful to a set of legal provisions which were viewed as specific "guidelines" that should not be modified.

The evolution of the SDI debate is more complex. The Cabinet decision of September 1985 revealed only the tip of the iceberg. It was clear that Canada wanted to refuse participation in SDI but, at the same time, minimize the adverse consequences of refusal. The "government to government" formula was therefore used to maintain Canada's virginity. At the same time, there was no wish to discourage Canadian industry as evidenced in a letter from the Minister of National Defence, Erik Nielsen, to his U.S. counterpart, Casper Weinberger, dated 7 September 1985, which stressed that "private companies and institutions interested in participating in the program will continue to be free to do so".[89] In addition, it was stated that the Government was determined to strengthen cooperation with the U.S. in the area of research, and would "continue to welcome further research arrangements with the United States, consistent always with Canada's national interest and its research and development priorities". Canada's position has not changed since.

It must be admitted, however, that the decision of September 1985 only sent the ball back into the court of the Department of National Defence, for who would decide the "policies and priorities" of Government? There is, of course, a close link between SDI and NORAD, if only because of their complementary technologies. There are cases where it is difficult to distinguish between strategic defence and tactical air defence. In this context, two problems arose. First, if Canadian industry could participate in research projects, would it mean that under no circumstances could the companies benefit from government funding support to achieve their research objectives, especially if those objectives concerned strategic defence or some area of air defence under NORAD? Second, given that the Government had decided not to participate in SDI, how would it be possible for Canada's military representatives in NORAD to distinguish, at the operational level, between activities that were SDI-related and those that were not?

In the first case, industry needed firm guidelines to know which way to turn, both in product planning and in research. But would the publication of such guidelines leave the Government open to criticism that while they were saying "No" they were also saying "Yes"? In the second case, it would be more than naïve to think that Canada's military representatives in NORAD could operate in any way other than on a "need to know basis". Presumably, all these problems were the subject of lengthy negotiation between the Departments of External Affairs and of National Defence during 1987 and 1988. The problem will become critical in the 1990s if the U.S. Government elects to deploy ABM systems to protect its silos, certain military bases or perhaps some nerve centres such as those dedicated to c^3i (Communications, Command, Control and Intelligence). In the meantime, the Canadian Government could continue to promulgate the fiction that SDI and NORAD are separate. So far, the Government has been rather successful ...

Canada and Verification from Space

Following the Lake Louise meeting in 1980, the Speech from the Throne in the same year and the Cabinet meeting of June 1981, several areas of arms control were selected by the Canadian Government for special emphasis. In particular, research programs on seismic detection and outer space were identified as key activities, subject to availability of the necessary funds to implement these programs. Canadian expertise would also be supplemented through advice from industry. At the Special Disarmament Advisory Session held at External Affairs on 12 May 1982, several suggestions emerged for consideration by Cabinet. One of these suggestions was the creation of an Verification Institute. The documentation indicated a sum of ten million dollars that could be appropriated for this purpose.

The priority sectors were identified by Secretary of State Mark Macguigan[90] in a speech to the Pugwash Conference on 16 July 1982. Prime Minister Trudeau, in a speech to the Second UN Special Session on Disarmament (UNSSOD II), had already expressed Canada's intention to "institutionalize and increase" her role in the area of verification. Unfortunately, circumstances prevented the release of the funds necessary to implement such a project that was so uncharacteristic of Canada's usual *modus operandi*. Instead, it was decided to establish an Interdepartmental Verification Program. Thus, on 20 February 1984, the Verification and Research Unit was created within the Arms Control and Disarmament Division of the Department of External Affairs. Special funds had been set aside at a meeting on 7 July 1983 to increase "Canada's growing role" in verification. In October 1983, the research program, to be conducted by the Verification and Research Unit, was approved with an annual budget of one million dollars.

In the area of verification from space, the first problem that Canada had to wrestle with was the proposal[91] submitted by France to UNSSOD I on the creation of an International Satellite Monitoring Agency (ISMA). Non-governmental organizations as well as several well-known Canadians, notably George Ignatieff, John C. Polanyi and Franklyn Griffiths of Toronto, were particularly interested in this French proposal. In External Affairs, interest in this proposal waned when it was learned that it was impossible to delegate an expert responsible for studying the French proposal to the Working Group in Geneva for fear that it would lead other nations (meaning USSR?) to seek similar status, or at least seek participation in all the working groups studying this proposal. Canada, of course, would have liked to send a technical expert to Geneva. The only request received by Canada was for a legal advisor, and that request was subsequently withdrawn, no doubt with some reluctance.

Canada did, however, have serious doubts about the feasibility of this undertaking. The overall costs of the project were estimated at six billion dollars. It was difficult, therefore, to imagine how the United Nations could undertake a project of such magnitude without the help of the superpowers. On the other hand, the superpowers could hardly be expected to finance the development of such a project given that their own verification satellites had detection capabilities far in excess of those that could be developed by other nations. The Department of Energy, Mines and Resources seriously proposed a verification system using aircraft, on the premise that satellites would doubtless be highly vulnerable in the future. The aircraft-based system would also be infinitely less costly.[92] History tells us nothing about the reaction of External Affairs to this proposal.

For all that, the advantages and disadvantages of the ISMA proposal were clearly identified in an External Affairs' document dated 15 October 1979. A particularly thorny problem was raised in an article which appeared in the *San Francisco Chronicle*[93], to the effect that any given State might be interested in obtaining photographs showing its geophysical characteristics, but not its military installations, while its neighbouring States were interested in just the opposite, namely intelligence of a military, rather than economic nature. The preliminary conclusions of the group of governmental experts in Geneva were forwarded to the UN Secretary General in a report[94] dated 14 August 1979. The final report, issued under the Chairmanship of Hubert G. Bortmeyer of France, was submitted to the Secretary General on 6 August 1981.[95] The ISMA project envisaged the implementation of an international program in three phases. Phase 1 was to be the creation of an Image Processing and Interpretation Centre (IPIC), Phase 2 the establishment of ground stations to receive and transmit data, and Phase 3 the construction of the necessary satellite launching facilities. At the time of UNSSOD II, France stated that she "would continue to work for a proposal ... that would contribute to technological development and the enlargement of the space club in the near term".[96]

Since the early 1980s, Canada had been interested in her own proposal on verification satellites. In May 1981, following an interdepartmental meeting at the deputy minister level, a submission was made to Cabinet proposing that a study be undertaken in concert with one or more industrial organizations on means of limiting or constraining the arms race in space. The PAXSAT (Peace Satellite) proposal resulted from these first contacts. It was subsequently divided into two sub-proposals: 1. PAXSAT A oriented towards space-space verification; and 2. PAXSAT B oriented towards space-ground verification. The brochure *Research on Verification*, published in December 1986 by the Department of External Affairs, concluded that space-based discrimination between civil and military satellites was possible, and that such a space verification satellite could be developed using "components already available to the civil space agencies of countries other than the superpowers".[97] The technical aspects of PAXSAT A have been described concisely in a brochure entitled *PAXSAT* published by SPAR Aerospace in November 1984. It states that studies of various treaties have shown the existence of scenarios "which could postulate the need for verification and the potential of a PAXSAT system".[98]

PAXSAT B was aimed at verification of regional disarmament agreements. In both cases, Canada made it known that these systems were proposed in the context of multilateral verification and that under no circumstances would Canada consider availing herself of any form of unilateral verification. These are two typical examples of science at the service of politics, involving the development of technical expertise which could serve to catalyse particular technical or multilateral discussions. Canada would obviously wait until requests for verification were formulated by the international community, even though the superpowers never entrusted other nations with the responsibility for verifying compliance with potential agreements, and even though malicious gossips claimed that PAXSAT A would be more of an ASAT weapon than a peaceful verification system.

Under this verification program, Canada funded important studies at the Institute of Air and Space Law (IASL) at McGill University. The two documents tabled in Geneva rank among the significant achievements of this Institute.[99] On 4 July 1985, Canada's Ambassador to the Conference on Disarmament, J. Alan Beesley, presented a compendium, in two volumes, of all the working papers and debates on outer space generated by the Conference.[100] Canada's contribution thus paralleled her earlier contribution in the area of chemical and bacteriological weapons.

In order to reconcile the legal and technical aspects of the problems of verification in space, Canada took the initiative to convene a workshop in Montreal of the Heads of Delegations and Observers at the Conference on Disarmament. This workshop was held in May 1987, and representatives of 35 other nations attended. At this meeting, Jean-Guy Hudon, Parliamentary Secretary to the Secretary of State for External Affairs, made the following declaration on 15 May 1987:

In October 1985, Prime Minister Mulroney identified the prevention of an arms race in outer space as one of Canada's six specific objectives in the arms control and disarmament field ... I would also like to reiterate the Canadian Government's view, recently made to the Conference on Disarmament by our Ambassador to that body, Mr. J. Alan Beesley, that the bilateral efforts by the u.s. and the ussr to prevent an arms race in outer space are not, and must not be, at cross-purposes with the multilateral efforts of the Conference ... Arms control in relation to outer space has always had an important multilateral dimension, and we believe this dimension is gaining in importance. Indeed, we believe this "two-track" approach to the issue to be a complementary one, of crucial importance to the international consideration of an issue vital to all mankind.[101]

In a speech in Edmonton on 8 November 1986, the Director of Arms Control and Disarmament, Ralph Lysyshyn, stated that Canada had opted for verification, "as a practical contribution to resolving arms control negotiations". In fact, this priority followed in the wake of long-standing efforts by Canada to have this issue placed before the United Nations General Assembly. Having vainly attracted attention to this issue in 1980 and 1984, Canada achieved success on 16 December 1985 with her draft resolution 40/152 (O) entitled "Verification in all its Aspects".[102]

This resolution invited all States to communicate their views and suggestions on the principles, procedures and techniques of verification to the Secretary General by 15 April 1986 at the latest. This resolution was adopted by consensus. In a letter dated 14 April 1986, the Canadian Government stated that verification should fulfil three functions: "deterrence of non-compliance, confidence-building and treaty assessment".[103] In this highly significant document, Canada identified three conceptual approaches to the problem of verification, without any expressed preference: 1. multilateral cooperation between nations having the means to conduct verification; 2. creation of an International Verification Organization (ivo) responsible for overall monitoring of existing international agreements; and 3. a specialized ivo according to specific monitoring function, for instance chemical weapons.

In order to make the transition from theory to practice, Canada suggested that it would be worth studying (i) the possibility of entrusting an increased role to the General Assembly and the Disarmament Commission, (ii) the hypothesis that countries or groups of countries having recognized expertise in verification offer their services to the international community for verification of multilateral agreements, and (iii) the issues of structures, procedures and techniques that could be designed or perfected to establish an IVO, "utilizing the rich body of documentation generated over the years in the Conference on Disarmament and elsewhere".

The issue has since been a regular topic of discussion in the UN General Assembly. Resolutions 41/86 Q of 4 December 1986 and 42/42 F of 30 November 1987 contained three important decisions: that the Disarmament Commission finalize its study on verification during the 1988 session, that delinquent nations submit their responses to the Secretary General in conformity with resolution 40/152 (O), and the item "Verification in all its Aspects" be put on the agenda of the 42nd session of the UN General Assembly.

On the issue of verification, either space-related or general, Canada has taken the lead amongst the group of nations seeking partial solutions to global problems. Clearly, any progress in this field will depend essentially on the political will of the States and the creativity that they can bring to the debate.

11 Of Turtles and Tanks: Canada and the MFBR Negotiations

> Diplomacy is the art of saying "nice doggy" until you can find a rock.
>
> Wynn Cotlin

From an arms control standpoint, Europe is a paradoxical place. Regarded since the start of the Cold War as the seat of East-West confrontation, the European peninsula – especially the central zone – boasts a concentration of military equipment and personnel unparalleled in the world. In monetary terms, this concentration accounts for roughly half of the world's total military expenditures. Yet war in central Europe is unthinkable both because of the unacceptable devastation it would cause and because of its likely escalation to nuclear proportions.

The situation in Europe is thus less of a military confrontation or aggressive encounter than a techno-strategic competition – a "strategy of means" – characterized by the incessant accumulation and improvement of weaponry, governed by the imperatives of diplomatic policy and budgetary constraints. The Old Europe is a fluid and complex political milieu; a continent of countries dominated by national egoism. In the timeless words of Lord Castlereagh:

It is impossible not to perceive that the settlement of a scale of force for so many powers, under such different circumstances as their relative means, frontiers, positions, and faculties for rearming, presents a very complicated question for negotiation.[1]

Yet despite the fact that, since 1945, the armed peace has provided a more viable security guarantee for Europe than for any other part of the world, and despite the Gordian knot of disarmament issues that it has engendered, the process of arms control has nevertheless flourished with unusual good fortune, even after the beginnings of the Cold War.

But the paradox does not stop there. Since the time that the major European negotiations "took off" in the mid-1960s, a complex structure of various arms control fora has emerged which, instead of evolving into an integrated system, continues to display all the characteristics of a disorderly and incomplete puzzle:

This disorderly pattern reveals the underlying truth that there is no integrating concept to hold together these diverse activities, no overall Western scheme of arms control negotiation with the East, and no comprehensive coverage in arms control negotiations of all important aspects of the East-West military confrontation.[2]

In 1988, five major sets of negotiations of regional scope were in progress in Europe. They concerned, in order: Mutual and Balanced Force Reductions (MBFR); Confidence-Building Measures (CBM) under the aegis of the Conference on Security and Cooperation in Europe (CSCE); Confidence and Security Building Measures (CSBM) at the time of the Conference on Disarmament in Europe (CDE) – the Stockholm Conference; Intermediate-range Nuclear Forces (INF); and, Chemical Weapons (CW) at the time of the Conference on Disarmament.

These five sets of negotiations differed, however, in terms of structure, regulations, participation and geographical scope. Some were multilateral in nature, some bilateral, while others were Alliance to Alliance. Some were restricted to zonal coverage, while others covered the whole of Europe from the Atlantic to the Urals, or even the entire planet. Some addressed the issue of military personnel, some military equipment, others military deployments, manoeuvres or again political behaviour.

But many issues were not addressed directly in any of these fora, such as the questions of naval and air forces, air defence, tactical nuclear weapons and nuclear-armed aircraft. As well, even though a global ban on chemical weapons was under active negotiation within the Conference on Disarmament, there was no purely European forum which addressed this issue despite the fact that the NATO and Warsaw Pact countries held the largest stockpiles of chemical weapons.

Finally, although the arms control process has been pursued in Europe for three decades, it has produced very few results. As Borawski observes:

Despite the conclusion of various agreements ... limiting nuclear weapons testing, basing, and vertical and horizontal proliferation, and despite a degree of East-West *rapprochement* arising in the late 1960s as a result of *Ostpolitik* and *détente*, the continent continues to host the most prodigious concentration of opposing firepower and military manpower on earth.[3]

The present Chapter is divided into three parts. The first part is devoted to the origin of the Vienna negotiations which were held from 1966 to 1973. The second discusses the main proposals introduced between 1973 and 1986, and is itself divided into three sections: the initial positions (1973–1976), the long march (1974–1979) and the demise of the negotiations (1980–1986). The third part of the Chapter presents an overall analysis of the negotiations.

The reader will quickly discover that Canada's presence at the MBFR, both in Brussels and Vienna, was relatively unobtrusive as far as substance, political initiative or even general management of the negotiations were concerned. We should stress at the outset, however, that the official diplomatic documents shed little light on Canada's official position on the MBFR. Even though the Chapter leans heavily on the records of the Department of External Affairs, Canada's influence is not readily apparent.

Canada's role in the genesis of the MBFR is described in the first part of the Chapter, and an overall assessment of Canadian policy on this issue is contained in the third part.

MBFR ORIGINS AND CANADA

The Beginnings of the MBFR

1966 was undoubtedly a key year in the history of European security. The Communist Party of the Soviet Union, at its 23rd Congress during March and April 1966, adopted the principle of a multilateral Conference on Security and Cooperation in Europe. President Johnson, in his speech of 7 October, proposed a number of measures conducive to *détente* in Europe, amongst them the proposal for Mutual and Balanced Force Reductions of the NATO and Warsaw Pact forces:

If changing circumstances should lead to a gradual and balanced revision in force levels on both sides, the revision could, together with the other steps that I have mentioned, help gradually to shape an entirely new political environment in Europe.[4]

These two events started the process which led, seven years later, to the MBFR and the CSCE negotiations.

Yet neither the principle of a European security system nor the notion of force reductions were really new concepts. Both formed part of the package of Soviet proposals on disarmament and arms control in the early 1950s. The precursor of the CSCE was the Soviet proposal for a Treaty on Inter-European Collective Security (1954–1955), which appeared again in modified form in Rapacki's speech to the UN in December 1964 and in a communiqué issued by the Political Consultative Committee (PCC) of the Warsaw Pact on 20 January 1965. Force reductions and weapons reductions in Europe had their origins in the Bulganin proposals to the Geneva Summit on 2 July 1955 and which were repeated in London in 1956.[5] These proposals were included in the famous Rapacki Plan of October 1957 and November 1958, calling for the denuclearization of the two Germanies and the reduction of armed forces in Central Europe.

By way of example, Khrushchev's proposal of 18 September 1959 to the UN General Assembly envisaged:

• the creation of a control and inspection zone and a reduction of foreign troops stationed in Western Europe;
•ʹ the creation of a denuclearized zone in Central Europe;
• the withdrawal of all foreign troops from the territories of European States and the closure of all military bases on foreign territory;
• the conclusion of a Non-Aggression Pact between the member States of NATO and the Warsaw Pact;
• an agreement to prevent surprise attack by any State against any other.

These themes – the denuclearization or disarmament of the two Germanies, the withdrawal of foreign troops, the dissolution of alliances, the *de facto* acceptance of the political *status quo* and agreements to ban the use of atomic weapons – recurred throughout the years. They were reiterated in the declaration of Bucharest on 8 July 1966[6] at the Warsaw Pact PCC meeting and again in the declaration of Karlovy Vary on 26 April 1967[7] at the time of the European Communist Party meeting. Logically, one can only conclude that the concepts of the Conference on Security and Cooperation in Europe (CSCE) and of balanced force reductions had their origins in East-European initiatives that remained invariant in Soviet policy on Europe. That these proposals were political in nature can hardly be doubted: the proposal concerning the withdrawal of foreign troops and the closure of foreign bases was clearly aimed at the United States. On the issue of foreign-based troops, the USSR affirmed:

> while their defensive role was negligible, they could be used for aggressive purposes, including surprise attack, they jeopardized the security of the host countries, and they constituted interference in the internal affairs of other States and served neocolonialist policies.[8]

The "neocolonialist" reference leaves no doubt as to the foreign military forces in question. In the same vein, the Soviet proposals for the disarmament of Germany, the dissolution of alliances and the acceptance of the political *status quo* were certainly political in nature and hardly realistic.

MBFR *Origins in the West*

Until the early 1960s, the West was unanimous in its refusal to consider any proposals for arms reductions in Europe, considering that territorial issues resulting from the Second World War took first priority.[9] Two factors intervened to cause the West to change its attitude. First, the shift towards *détente* between the Unites States and the Soviet Union increased NATO's awareness that significant changes bearing on European security were about to take place. The first arms control treaties surfaced and, in December 1967, the Atlantic Alliance accepted the Harmel report defining the future role of NATO. The report noted the new conditions of European security, stressed the complementary nature of security and *détente* and recommended the creation of a new peace-oriented European order based on East-West cooperation and force reductions by NATO and the Warsaw Pact. The MBFR talks were thus entrenched in Atlantic Alliance policy. The second factor was, however, more worrisome. Since 1966, the U.S. administration had questioned its policy of stationing U.S. troops in Europe, for a number of reasons:

* U.S. military involvement in South-East Asia;
* growing U.S. public opposition to military expenditures and over-commitment abroad;
* internal crises within the United States (the problem with the Black community and the protest movement among young people);
* the U.S. balance of payments problem;
* conflicts of jurisdiction between Congress (especially the Senate) and the Executive on security issues; and,

• criticism of the United States by the European members of the Atlantic Alliance (France's withdrawal in 1966).

The key catalyst in this crisis was undoubtedly the attitude adopted by the Senate. From August 1966 to 1977, Senator Mansfield, in particular, incessantly badgered the Executive to effect at least a partial troop withdrawal in Europe. During these years, the u.s. balance of payments was regularly in a deficit situation to the tune of some three billion dollars. To make matters worse, the outflow of u.s. currency incurred by the presence of u.s. troops in Europe amounted to some 1.28 billion dollars annually (700–900 millions for u.s. troops stationed in the FRG alone).[10] From 1961 onwards, the FRG attempted to compensate for this anomalous balance of payments by purchasing u.s. weapons on an annual basis valued at between 350 and 400 million dollars. From 1966 onwards, the FRG made an additional gesture by purchasing u.s. Treasury Bonds worth 500 million dollars[11] annually, which in fact amounted to a loan. These FRG actions did nothing to stave off the persistent attacks of Senator Mansfield who downplayed the Soviet threat and emphasized European ingratitude, nor did they prevent the unilateral withdrawal of u.s. troops stationed in Europe, from a total of 408,000 in 1962 to 310,000 in 1976.

In 1966, the European allies, and the FRG in particular, expressed their concern that the declining u.s. military presence threatened their defensive position by weakening one of the essential pillars of their security. At the time of the London Conference on Compensatory Measures[12], the FRG had already realized that the only alternative to unilateral u.s. troop withdrawals was mutually-agreed troop reductions for both the Warsaw Pact and NATO.[13] Following Johnson's speech, the Bonn Government became a staunch supporter of MBFR, as witnessed by the many statements of W. Brandt (then FRG External Affairs' Minister), who viewed MBFR talks as an extension of his policy of *détente* (*Ostpolitik*).

The u.s. government still refused to take the MBFR talks seriously. Curiously enough, Johnson's speech touched on MBFR only by accident. Z. Brzezinski had provided Johnson with an internal working document, and he found the example of mutual force reductions appropriate in the context of his speech, without realizing that such a reference, although made in a "climatic" sense, would be interpreted by the Europeans as a formal policy statement. The u.s. Government was torn by divergent opinion. It was preoccupied with the Vietnam problem and the preparations for the SALT negotiations, which had been going on since January 1967, and it had no wish to place them in jeopardy by opening a second forum of debate. Not surprisingly, the U.S. displayed great scepticism about the very viability of MBFR negotiations. On the other hand, U.S. leaders saw in these negotiations a weighty argument against the proponents of unilateral reductions and were impelled to adopt a conciliatory attitude in order to preserve good trans-Atlantic relations. As a result, the United States moved reluctantly towards the negotiations.

Within the Atlantic Alliance, the situation was hardly more clear.[14] Some member States, such as Belgium, the FRG and Italy, favoured the idea of MBFR, while others (the United Kingdom and the United States) were sceptical or even hostile (France, Greece and Turkey). By 1968, following studies within the Atlantic Alliance, there was still no clear consensus.[15] These studies underlined the military inferiority of NATO, thus providing arguments to those opposed to force reductions. Yet these same studies proposed models which were either advantageous for the Atlantic Alliance and non-negotiable for the Warsaw Pact or negotiable but detrimental to NATO. These purely military assessments, which highlighted the weaknesses of European defence, formed the underlying rationale for using the MBFR talks to resolve NATO's military problems. As R. Burt observed: "The concern for enhancing (or at least preserving) NATO's conventional posture therefore became the dominant aim of the West in pursuing MBFR".[16]

The support accorded to this "indirect" objective, coupled with the ambiguous results of analysis and the divergent political opinions on collective security, were hardly conducive to the emergence of a common Western strategy. The NATO foreign ministers met in Reykjavik in June 1968. Even before the NATO studies were completed, they announced to the Warsaw Pact countries that they were ready to engage in talks aimed at reducing the complement of foreign troops in Europe. Events in Czechoslovakia forced a delay but, in May 1970 in Rome, the NATO foreign ministers reiterated the key principles that should guide negotiations on MBFR:

- mutual force reductions should be compatible with the vital interests of Atlantic Alliance security and should not result in military disadvantages for either party, whether due to geographical or other differences;
- force reductions should be effected on a reciprocal basis, and be distributed over time and balanced in scope;
- reductions should be applicable to both national and foreign-based forces, as well as to the weapon systems deployed in the affected zones;

• appropriate verification and control procedures should be implemented to ensure respect for mutual and balanced force reductions.[17]

Although these principles constituted a first step towards a more unified conception of MBFR, they failed to address the basic differences which divided the Atlantic Alliance. The vital interests of the Atlantic Alliance were not defined. The FRG tried unsuccessfully to argue that neither the solidarity of Atlantic Alliance members nor European re-building should be adversely affected by MBFR. In the same vein, Bonn had suggested that the principles of *détente* and common defence be respected in the negotiations, that a tangible link be created between the CSCE and MBFR, that the concept of Confidence-Building Measures (CBM) be introduced and that priority be given to reducing offensive forces. Unfortunately, it proved impossible to reach agreement on these matters, and the Atlantic Alliance lacked unanimity in its approach to the MBFR negotiations.

Warsaw Pact Reactions

Warsaw Pact reaction to the Reykjavik communiqué was at first hostile. The East-German Ministry of Foreign Affairs accused the unfortunate Brandt of blatant militarism. As for European security, it could best be assured by "the disbandment of the most powerful and aggressive of all European armies, the West-German *Bundeswehr*, which was commanded by 'Nazi' [sic] generals".[18] In May 1969, the East-German *Dokumentation der Zeit* reiterated its observation that "the fundamental problem, as expressed at the 9th Plenary Session, remains the elimination of Bonn's expansionist [sic] *Ostpolitik* and its vengeful policies".[19] Later that month, Otto Winzer of the GDR declared:

We consider that the recognition of the territorial *status quo* resulting from the Second World War, the legal normalization of relations between European States, the duty of defending the rights of other peoples on the globe, as well as arms control and disarmament to be essential and indissociable elements of European security.[20]

The Budapest communiqué of 17 March 1969 was more moderate in tone. It called for a return to the security measures proposed in Bucharest two years earlier. The member States of the Warsaw Pact declared that they would reaffirm their position at the meeting of WP foreign ministers in Prague on 31 October 1969, to the effect that the CSCE had priority in matters of arms control. In other words, the Warsaw Pact adopted the very same attitude that the West-Europeans had espoused for over a decade – political settlement is prerequisite to disarmament. More characteristically still, the Eastern countries refused to consider the MBFR talks as the last manifestation of the Rapacki Plan – which was their own creation – although no one today would venture to contest their filiation. Obviously, the Warsaw Pact was not interested in changing a military situation that it dominated. On the other hand, it was certainly not indifferent to the issue of legal recognition of the 1945 boundaries, and hence the CSCE. Within this general framework, the MBFR could be of some tactical value. The Budapest Declaration of 22 June 1970, issued one month after the communiqué from Rome, was probably made in this context. Concerning the Western proposal, it called for:

a study to be conducted, either by the organization created at the Pan-European Conference or by any other organization acceptable to the interested parties, on the issue of reduction of foreign troops based on the territories of European States.[21]

Although cultural, economic and technological cooperation with the East was included as an item on the agenda for the NATO meeting of 5 November 1969, the member nations judged that the time was not ripe for the CSCE. In December 1970, the North Atlantic Council was content to reiterate the communiqués of Rome and Reykjavik, but also – and significantly – adopted the European Defence Improvement Programme (EDIP) aimed at rationalizing European defence. However, qualitative changes were already starting to take place following the signing of the Treaty between the FRG and the USSR on 12 August 1970 and the Treaty between the FRG and the Peoples' Republic of Poland on 7 December 1970, through which the Warsaw Pact – specifically the USSR and Poland – obtained FRG recognition of the boundaries established at Potsdam in 1945. The Quadripartite Agreement on Berlin of 3 September 1971 and, later, the Basic Treaty between the FRG and the GDR (21 December 1972) marked further evolutionary changes by recognizing the borders of the GDR and by opening up, after 25 years, the borders between "separated brothers". Thus, in 1970, the Warsaw Pact achieved its objective, but the CSCE and the lure of the MBFR remained important as a means of achieving multilateralization of *Ostpolitik*. In March 1971, at the 24th Congress of the Communist Party of the Soviet Union, Brezhnev revived the MBFR project by calling for the dismantling of foreign bases and the reduction of armed forces in Central Europe.

Brezhnev's speech at Tbilisi two months later was more revealing. The Nixon Administration faced a decisive Senate vote on 19 May 1971 on a proposal tabled by Senator Mansfield calling for a 50 percent reduction in u.s. forces stationed in Europe. Five days earlier, on 14 May, at Tbilisi, Brezhnev declared himself ready "to taste the wine of negotiations". The Mansfield proposal was subsequently defeated by 61 votes against 36. The correlation between the two events is impossible to deny. Paradoxically, had Brezhnev come to the aid of the u.s. Administration? Was it a coincidence or a premeditated gesture? Brezhnev's speech hardly seems to have been fortuitous. Logically, one is left to conclude that the Soviet Union had some interest in the mbfr and sought to avoid a unilateral and drastic withdrawal of American troops. There are some grounds for such speculation, for a sudden withdrawal of the United States could have forced the Europeans, and particularly the West Germans, to rearm and perhaps think of German reunification. Also, the Soviets possibly viewed the mbfr as a means of influencing Atlantic Alliance policy, while delaying agreement on force reductions. But that must remain as no more than a theory.

The Final Stages

On 11 June 1971, Brezhnev repeated his appeal. During the same month, the nato Council of Ministers in Lisbon responded to a joint Canadian, Danish and Dutch proposal to sound out the Warsaw Pact on its intentions. Manlio Brosio, a former Secretary General of nato, was chosen as the envoy. At that point in time, the United States was still not ready to negotiate, since the first serious study on force reductions was scheduled for completion only at the end of that year. Other nato nations were also sceptical of the degree of preparatory work undertaken by the Soviets. W. Brandt, during a visit to the Crimea in September 1971, succeeded in reaching agreement in principle with the Soviets on the following four points:

- all interested European countries should participate alongside the Soviets and the Americans;
- force reductions would not just be limited to the frg and the gdr;
- national troops would be included in the reductions;
- the final ratio of military forces on both sides would remain unchanged.[22]

The frg also sought a political extension of the mbfr talks to establish concrete links between the mbfr process and the csce. The

United States, preoccupied with the SALT negotiations which had opened in 1969, declined this FRG proposal, fearing that it would block future negotiations. During November and December 1971, the Warsaw Pact ratified the principles accepted in the Crimea, namely: the agreement would not preferentially favour either the Warsaw Pact or NATO; both national and foreign-based troops would be subjected to reductions; and, the negotiations would not be conducted on a military bloc-to-bloc basis, but on the basis of equal representation by participating States. As it happened, the Brosio mission was simply ignored, and precedence was still accorded to the CSCE. Clearly, the Soviets sought to make no commitments before President Nixon's visit to Moscow, scheduled for May 1972. The SALT agreements were of top priority, and they were signed on 26 May. Events unfolded quickly after that. On 30 May, U.S. Secretary of State Rogers announced to NATO that the two conferences – the CSCE and the MBFR – would be held in parallel. There would be no thematic link between them except, perhaps, in respect of Confidence-Building Measures which would be treated during the first round of CSCE negotiations on security issues. The second and third rounds of CSCE discussions would focus on economic and humanitarian issues respectively. The link between the CSCE and MBFR discussions would be purely chronological. In September 1972, during informal talks between Nixon, Brezhnev and Kissinger, the final details were spelled out: the preliminary talks on the CSCE would be held in the fall of 1972, while those on the MBFR would start in January 1973. On 15 November 1972, one week before the opening of the CSCE talks, NATO extended an official invitation to the Warsaw Pact countries to start the preliminary talks on the MBFR negotiations on 31 January 1973. The French, who were opposed to the MBFR talks as a matter of principle, dissociated themselves from this invitation. After much vacillation, Vienna was chosen as the site for the MBFR talks. The NATO invitation was accepted three weeks following the conclusion of the Bonn-Pankow fundamental agreement. The preparatory talks started on schedule and the negotiations proper started on 30 October 1973.

Canada's Position during the Preparatory Phase of Negotiations (1966–1973)

Despite Canada's manifest interest in East-West *rapprochement*, dating back to 1964, the first mention of conventional arms reductions in Europe appears in the official records only on 12 January 1967. The entry concerns a letter from General Burns to the Assistant Secretary of State for External Affairs. In the circumstances existing at the time, Burns was pessimistic about reaching a breakthrough, stating: "It doesn't seem that u.s. policy would allow for negotiations on mutual troop reductions in the near future".[23]

Burns' observation is noteworthy in light of Paul Martin's statement of 19 December 1966, made several days after the NATO foreign ministers' meeting:

I suggest that it might be useful to keep under review possibilities for gradual reductions in Western and Soviet forces in Central Europe. Then, if opportunities arise, we should know what was reasonable to propose on our side and what reciprocal action we might expect on the other side.[24]

To some extent, this vague rhetoric and the slowness of the Department in following the Minister's lead, point to the fact that Canada – after the fashion of most Atlantic Alliance members except for the FRG – was both sceptical and ill-prepared to respond to the u.s. initiatives of 1966. In retrospect, Canada's reluctance was quite natural, for she was a small player on the European military scene and considered that such an initiative was not properly her prerogative. Further, given Canada's modest military role in Europe, any hint of disengagement could have carried the risk of tarnishing her image and reputation which to that point were relatively intact.

Canadian policy on MBFR was thus characterized by discreet interest, tempered with scepticism and extreme caution.

1967 marked the appearance of the first controversies concerning the merits of a Canadian withdrawal from NATO. The debates intensified during the next four years, following the arrival in power of Pierre Elliott Trudeau and the unilateral withdrawal, in 1969, of half of Canada's land forces in Europe. As a result, the fluctuation and uncertainty of Canadian foreign policy during this period only served to accentuate further the circumspection of Canadian diplomats.

During the preparatory phase of the MBFR negotiations, other countries, such as the FRG, produced literally hundreds of specialized studies on the subject. Canada, however, remained a discreet spectator, content to participate in meetings of Atlantic Alliance experts without making any real commitments. As N. Bow judiciously pointed out in a letter dated 2 May 1969:

Balanced force reductions remain of special interest to Canada, but in order not to prejudice the proposal, we may have to let others take the lead in advocating it at a time when we may appear to have vested interests.[25]

In 1968, when the FRG introduced a resolution to prevent unilateral troop withdrawals from Europe, Canadian diplomats to NATO were forced to dissociate themselves from their allies. On 18 June 1968, an External Affairs' memorandum stressed – and for good reason – that Canadian policy did not exclude unilateral reductions. On 30 August 1968, Ambassador R. Campbell announced before the NATO Military Committee that Canada did not intend to freeze her forces at existing levels.[26] Several months later, he observed that Canada faced a dilemma. "How can we", he said, "play a significant role in mutual conventional force reductions if we act against the interests of the Atlantic Alliance?" Under these circumstances, Canada's problem was quite simply one of maintaining the confidence of her partners.[27]

Evidently, any researcher would be hard pressed to find anything in the records pertaining to a single Canadian initiative or even an important analysis on MBFR, at least prior to the fall of 1969. In the summer of that year, Cabinet conducted a review of Canadian arms control policy, and the Prime Minister asked for an assessment of Canada's position on conventional force reductions in Europe. In addition, U.S. pressure forced some movement in Brussels, and Canada had to take a stand prior to the December meeting of NATO foreign ministers.

The Department of External Affairs was, however, concerned that Cabinet might seize the opportunity to elaborate an "uniquely Canadian" posture that would not be well received in Brussels. This concern was eloquently expressed by Ross Campbell in a letter to N. Bow dated 14 November 1969. Amongst other things, Campbell stated:

There may be people who don't want to hear that NATO is a principal arms control and disarmament agency, but it is the Department's duty to see to it that they are told. The Government must accept this fact and not be afraid to work with and through NATO without trying to pretend that the issues are being dealt with somewhere else ... My whole point is that I want the Government of Canada to recognize that NATO is performing important functions in the arms control and disarmament field ... One of the policy decisions which emerged from the review earlier this year of our participation in NATO was that we would be actively participating in its disarmament activities. We have, in fact, been doing so, and in subjects which have a far more direct bearing on present peace than the long term activities of CCD. Why not let the Government in on the secret?[28]

The attitude of both the Prime Minister and Cabinet towards NATO was not, however, the only concern of the Department of External

Affairs. The Department of National Defence also seemed reluctant to support the project, as noted on 9 January 1970 by N. Bow, Under-Secretary of State for External Affairs:

We have come to the crunch with DND ... and they are unwilling to make officers available for a project about which their Minister appears to be unenthusiastic and to which our Department has been hesitant to assign an appropriate officer. Of course, the real inspiration of the increasing reluctance of DND and other interested departments and agencies is our own Department's failure to give priority and personnel consistent with our policies and positions in arms control and disarmament work.[29]

Canada's position on MBFR at the end of 1969 had evolved in a difficult context. Cabinet approved the adoption of a firm and favourable position on force reductions so that NATO would send a clear and unambiguous signal to the Warsaw Pact. Concurrently, coordination mechanisms were taking shape in Ottawa to define and monitor Canadian policy on MBFR. The Department of External Affairs and the Department of National Defence created three joint working groups: the MBFR Technical Working Group; the "Canadian Implications" Working Group; and, the Policy Committee.[30] This in no way implied that Canadian activities in Brussels would noticeably intensify, as reference to the records readily attests. The records show mainly that Canada was a spectator in the lengthy process which led to the negotiations in Vienna three years later. Until 1972, NATO was handicapped in developing a common position by allied hesitation and division, and even Washington seemed to be dragging its feet:[31]

The work lacked focus and direction ... Piecemeal approach to date has taken increasingly negative trend, partly because of domination of working group by military personalities inherently opposed to force reductions of any kind, but also because European member States have been so preoccupied with need to prevent early USA withdrawals that they have been unable to address themselves objectively to advantages of corresponding USSR withdrawals. Result of this situation is that ... major policy objectives which should govern approach to MBFR have been lost sight of.[32]

It was in this context – two months after Brezhnev's speech to the 24th Congress of the Communist Party of the Soviet Union – that Prime Minister Trudeau embarked on his visit to Moscow, amidst murmurings that Canada could play a decisive role at the opening of the MBFR negotiations. However, if the summary of the Prime Minister's discussions in Moscow is accurate:

The gist of conversations on MBFR and CSCE was a constant reiteration of Soviet proposals for talks on reductions in armed forces (which Kosygin described as "foreign armed forces" in his speech at the Kremlin luncheon). But in spite of numerous efforts it was impossible to tie Russians down to anything specific.[33]

Despite Prime Minister's very specific questions on Soviet position on troop reductions and next step which could be envisaged, no clearer picture emerged, although on all occasions, Prime Minister's interlocutors insisted on seriousness of Soviet proposals.[34]

Even though Pierre Elliott Trudeau had stated that he would not act as a mediator between NATO and the Warsaw Pact, his visit was disappointing, notwithstanding the joint communiqué issued at its conclusion.

Later that year, Canada took a second initiative through Mitchell Sharp's proposal to the NATO foreign ministers' meeting held in Lisbon during June 1971. At that time, the Minister proposed that a NATO representative be sent to Moscow to examine, with the USSR and other countries, "the possibility of holding [MBFR] negotiations as early as possible, based on agreed principles".[35] On 4 and 5 October, at a special meeting of the NATO deputy ministers, M. Brosio, the outgoing Secretary General of NATO, was nominated to undertake this exploratory mission. Despite intensified Canada-USSR contacts, Kosygin's visit to Ottawa in October 1971 and the Sharp-Gromyko meeting in New York on 2 October 1971, the Brosio mission was viewed by Moscow as "a clumsy attempt to drag things out".[36] In February 1972, the Canadian Ambassador to Moscow observed: "I think we can conclude that the Brosio mission is dead, if, in fact, it ever lived. Question is how to bury it!"[37]

The deadlock was broken in September 1972, without the benefit of Canadian intervention, when H.A. Kissinger obtained Soviet agreement on a date for opening the preparatory talks on MBFR and the CSCE.

A period of intense discussion ensued in Brussels. There were wide differences of opinion within the Atlantic Alliance on such issues as the geographical sectors where force reductions would be a priority, and the status of such countries as Greece, Italy and Turkey in future negotiations. There was also an obvious reticence to cooperate on the part of Warsaw Pact countries during the preparatory talks held in Vienna between January and May 1973. The Canadian Delegate observed at the time:

It is a scratchy and unhappy situation caused by the NATO tendency to leave serious decisions until too late. It must be admitted that there is no agreed NATO policy for MBFR, either in general or in detail.[38]

Nevertheless, as M. Tucker observed, this was the period during which Canadian intervention in the MBFR was most influential. Although the CSCE preparatory talks in Helsinki were nearing completion, the Soviets had not, as then, agreed to a date for the opening of negotiations in Vienna, and it was feared that their intent was to force a swift conclusion to the CSCE *before* the start of the MBFR negotiations. On 4 June 1973, the Canadian Delegation in Helsinki was informed that Canada would not approve the date of opening of the CSCE until the Soviets committed to the MBFR:

Canada's intervention on this matter in the North Atlantic Council and at Copenhagen represented, as far as is known, the first time this country took a firm stand on an MBFR issue over which the U.S. and West Europe were divided.[39]

Canada's position on the NATO guidelines for MBFR finally took shape, and was ultimately ratified by the Prime Minister on 1 June 1973. In essence, Canada's position was as follows:

- MBFR was probably the only mechanism for ensuring that the inevitable withdrawal of U.S. troops from Europe would be accompanied by an equivalent reduction of Soviet forces;
- the stability of the balance of forces in Europe was a guarantee of the climate of political *détente*, and nothing should be allowed to disturb this stability;
- it was in Canada's interests to ensure that her MBFR policies did not impact on her relations with her allies and that any form of unilateralism be avoided.

In this context, Canada was faced with two possible solutions: either Canadian forces could be withdrawn in parallel with U.S. forces or, as seemed to be advocated in Brussels, priority could be given to U.S. and Soviet troop withdrawals followed by withdrawals of other national contingents.

Canada could well have insisted that her troops be withdrawn in parallel with U.S. forces, but it was considered that:

Such a step – when we have only recently cut in half our forces in Europe – would undoubtedly raise doubts in NATO about the seriousness of our commitment to the collective defence of Western Europe. It could have highly unfavourable implications for our economic and political relations with our European allies, especially those members of the EEC.[40]

It was also considered that reductions in Canadian troops would only involve several hundred personnel, and that the savings would be insignificant. Canada thus elected not to participate in the first phase of MBFR. The Department of External Affairs, in conjunction with the Department of National Defence, developed a common position as follows: "We recommend in regard to our general approach to MBFR that we continue to pursue, in concert with our NATO allies, a positive but cautious approach to MBFR with limited objectives, to be implemented in phases".[41]

In other words, it would appear that the political decisions made in the summer of 1973 ended the period of unilateralism and hesitation which started in the spring of 1968. With the negotiations in Vienna due to begin within a few months, the Liberal Government apparently realized, perhaps in some confused way, that it could not pursue a viable arms control policy in Europe while at the same time neglecting its military responsibilities towards its allies:

Thus, in 1973, Canada heightened its appreciation of the need to return to its key "counterweight" policy of the Pearson era, and not just Western Europe in general but NATO Europe in particular, the *entrée* to which had always been a visible, if not substantial, Canadian military commitment.[42]

Canadian foreign policy during the MBFR preparatory period did not derive, therefore, from any special interest in the negotiations, but instead developed as a by-product of a broader debate between the atlantists and the unilateralists in Government. The MBFR undoubtedly served as an individual case to demonstrate to Cabinet that there was a fundamental relationship between the issues of military security, disarmament and economic relations with Canada's European partners which the Government simply had to respect if it wanted to promote its famous "third option". The irony of the situation was that this exercise in diplomatic pedagogy probably convinced the Department of National Defence that the negotiations in Vienna were of great interest, if only because they served to moderate the antipathy that the Trudeau Government had amply displayed towards the military.

THE VIENNA MARATHON:
MBFR PROPOSALS 1973−1986

Framework of the Negotiations

On 30 October 1973, five years after the Reykjavik communiqué was issued, negotiations started in Vienna "on mutual reductions in forces and armaments and associated measures in Central Europe". Not without a touch of optimism, the Dutch Delegate had stated, several months earlier:

Gentlemen, I am happy to report that we are now ahead of schedule of the famous Congress of Vienna of 1814. That Congress, sometimes called the "Dancing Congress", took nine months to reach a first plenary. Ours is definitely a work conference and took only three months to arrive at the same point.[43]

If the MBFR negotiations took some kind of lead over the illustrious Congress, they quickly lost it. As everyone knows, the Vienna negotiations persisted until 2 February 1989 ... but there was nothing to dance about.

There were 11 direct participants in the MBFR negotiations, 7 from NATO and 4 from the Warsaw Pact. Collectively, these nations covered the geographical extent of the Central European zone where force reductions would apply. As well, there were 8 other "indirect" participants (5 from NATO and 3 from the Warsaw Pact) who, while choosing not to have their territories subjected to possible reductions, considered that their security was at stake and that they should be active observers in the negotiations.

Although 19 individual States participated, the MBFR negotiations were essentially alliance-to-alliance in nature, rather than multilateral. In that context, the coordination mechanisms established in Vienna and Brussels are of great interest from the standpoint of process dynamics.

For instance, the North Atlantic Council (NAC), which comprised the 15 ministers of the NATO member nations, proved to be a supreme decisional organization. It was supported by the Political Committee at the Senior Level (PCSL), comprised of the Permanent Representatives (PERMREP) and the MBFR Working Group (WG). The MBFR WG itself consisted of specialist sub-groups. The PCSL was charged with coordinating NATO policy and with formulating directives to its various sub-organizations in Vienna. The MBFR Working Group and its sub-groups were charged with conducting technical military studies under the supervision of the NATO Military Committee. The MBFR WG was supported by the resources of the Supreme Headquarters Allied Powers in Europe (SHAPE), as well as those of the Supreme Allied Commander Europe (SACEUR) and of member nations. In Vienna, the *Ad Hoc* Group (AHG), comprising 12 NATO allies, developed day-to-day negotiation tactics based on NAC directives and instructions from the various capitals. The AHG met two or three times a week, and was supported by a working group whose main function was to review the speeches that would be made in plenary session.

In addition, unofficial and informal trilateral meetings were held from time to time between the key Western players: the FRG, the United Kingdom and the United States.

The Warsaw Pact established similar mechanisms for coordination, but the details are less well known. It had its own *ad hoc* group, and the WP negotiators met with it regularly in Moscow, or with the Political Consultative Committee, which was the WP counterpart of the North Atlantic Council.

MBFR negotiations took place at three levels. The Plenary Sessions commanded the highest visibility. One 1978 memorandum described the Plenary Session as follows: "It is a rather stylized and formal occasion with usually one prepared statement read each week by a Head of Delegation alternating between East and West".[44]

The Plenary Sessions actually provided a platform which allowed the two alliances to formalize their positions and prepare detailed statements for public consumption at press conferences.

The real work of the MBFR negotiators was achieved through informal meetings and bilateral contacts. Every week, some of the direct participants – mainly the United States, the USSR and four other selected countries – would meet to consider their respective positions in private, outside the formal rigid framework of Plenary Sessions. Bilateral contacts between representatives of the East and West were more discreet but no less important.

On the NATO side, the MBFR negotiation framework was thus a highly complex structure whose primary purpose was to ensure political unity within the Atlantic Alliance on arms control issues. It was an essential mechanism, for many profound differences of opinion existed between Western States at the time.

Initial Positions

When the talks opened in Vienna, the NATO nations had barely reached agreement on the set of common guidelines that were to shape the Western position for the next 13 years.

NATO resolved that the practical purpose of the MBFR talks was to minimize the extent of military confrontation between East and West, *but not to the detriment of NATO's defensive capability.* Central Europe would be the focus of any agreed force reductions, but associated measures, aimed at building confidence, could apply to a wider zone (including, for instance, Hungary). Even though reductions would apply to a restricted zone, care should be taken to avoid creating a particular zone in Central Europe (specifically Germany). The security of flank countries, such as Greece, Italy and Turkey, should not be neglected. The NATO objective in MBFR should be to reduce the quantitative asymmetries that favour the Warsaw Pact and minimize NATO's geographical handicap. Reductions should be effected in two phases, starting with the U.S. and the USSR, *but should not involve more that 10 percent of NATO forces.* Specifically, the objective of force reductions would be to achieve parity between NATO and WP forces at a mutually agreed ceiling of 700,000 personnel (land forces). The contingents concerned would be repatriated to their countries of origin except that, in the case of the United States, heavy equipment would be allowed to remain in the affected zone in light of the vast distances that separated the United States from Europe. In addition, the agreed ceiling of 700,000 personnel would constitute a numerical collectivity of forces from the various participants in each camp, so as to allow them total freedom of action. Finally, to ensure stability following troop reductions, certain restrictions would be imposed, including:

- constraints concerning the movements of troops towards and within the reduction zone;
- prior notification of manoeuvres or troop movements within the zone;
- limits on the scale of such manoeuvres; and,
- exchange of observers, etc.[45]

The U.S. proposal of 30 April 1973 comprised three options:[46]

- Option I: a phased reduction of NATO forces by 10 percent (roughly 80,000 personnel), starting with those of the United States, in concert with a phased reduction by 13 percent of Warsaw Pact forces (roughly 112,000 personnel), starting with those of the USSR;
- Option II: a 16.6 percent reduction of U.S. and Soviet forces to reach the famous common ceiling (representing reductions of 32,000 troops for the United States and 65,000 for the USSR);
- Option III: a complementary offer to Options I or II, involving mutual reductions in perceived offensive weapon systems comprising, for NATO, 1,000 nuclear warheads, 36 Pershing missiles and 54 F-4 Phantom jets and, for the Warsaw Pact, one armoured division of 1,700 tanks and 60,000 troops.

Several comments on these proposals and their underlying implications are warranted. First, Option I was clearly unacceptable to

NATO, in that the MBFR talks were aimed strictly at limiting, if not preventing, reductions in Western European forces and not at encouraging them. Option I would have reduced Western European forces by 60,000 personnel, while U.S. troops in Europe would have been reduced only by 20,000 personnel. Options II and III were, therefore, the only viable options open to NATO during the four years that were to follow.

NATO was not so much preoccupied with absolute numbers, but with the conclusion of a swift and modest agreement which, first and foremost, would be negotiable. This was the sense in which numbers, as opposed to weapons and equipment, had to be interpreted. From a practical standpoint, the NATO stance could not have included weapons and equipment without raising serious problems. Given the qualitative and quantitative asymmetries between the arsenals of the two alliances, there was little basis for meaningful comparison: could tanks equate to aircraft, or artillery to helicopters? If the Alliance sought speedy resolution of the problem, it would have to propose a simple and near-symmetric formula. In the area of manpower at least, there was approximate parity (NATO: 802,000; Warsaw Pact: 834,000). As observed in a Canadian commentary: "within the envisaged MBFR reductions area, the NATO/WPO asymmetry in manpower is negligible compared to that which exists in numbers of tanks, armoured troop carriers and artillery".[47]

In other words, on the basis of data available in 1973, NATO could have presented the Warsaw Pact with a proposal of negotiable proportions that required only one concession from the USSR: a modest reduction in Soviet military manpower representing some 65,000 personnel, compared with 32,000 personnel for the United States.

Instead, the Atlantic Alliance opted for a much harder line in its 22 November proposal. In essence, it called upon the Warsaw Pact to withdraw a full armoured tank corps, while NATO would not be required to reduce its forces on a unit-by-unit basis. Moreover, U.S. equipment would remain stockpiled *in situ*, while Soviet equipment would be withdrawn. The proposal was clearly geared to Option III, which specifically referenced 1,700 Soviet tanks.

Was it possible, as some observers claim, that the Atlantic Alliance was caught unawares by the Soviet proposal of 8 November, and fell victim to its own haste?[48] Had NATO's objective changed? The fact that Senator Mansfield succeeded, on 26 September 1973, in having the U.S. Senate vote in favour of an amendment to cut by half the number of U.S. troops deployed abroad lends credence to this hypothesis. The vote was quickly overturned, but it was clear that the attitude of Congress towards unilateral cuts had not been

Table 13A
Balance of Forces in the Reduction Zone, as of 30 April 1973
(Ground Forces)

	NATO	WARSAW PACT
Foreign troops	341,000	390,000
	(U.S.: 191,000)	(Soviet forces)
National troops	461,450	444,000
TOTAL:	802,450	834,000

* Source: Department of External Affairs, File 27–4–NATO-1–MBFR, 1973.

Table 13B
Balance of Forces in the Reduction Zone, as of 16 November 1973
(Ground Forces)

	NATO	WARSAW PACT
TOTAL:	777,000	925,000
	(U.S.: 193,000)	(Soviet 460,000)

* Source: Department of External Affairs, File 27-4-NATO-1-MBFR, 1973.

fundamentally affected by the prospect of an MBFR agreement. As Keliher observes: "Events in the summer and fall of 1973 clearly showed the NATO allies, and more importantly the East, that the administration would enter the MBFR negotiations with a congressional gun at its back".[49]

In other words, if the offensives of Senator Mansfield could not be tempered by a swift and modest agreement and if the Soviets, who were aware of the precarious nature of the U.S. situation, were awaiting further concessions from the West, it was imperative to block the negotiations instantly until such time as the political climate became more favourable.

The instrument invoked to serve this purpose was a revision of the data base on the ratio of troop deployments in the reduction zone. Until the summer of 1973, the data given in Table 13A had been accepted as representative of the near perfect balance between ground troops on both sides. But on 30 October and 16 November 1973, NATO revised its assessment as shown in Table 13B.

In specific terms, the Warsaw Pact was portrayed as having increased its ground forces by 90,000 personnel, of which 70,000 were Soviet troops.[50] Negotiations immediately became "much more difficult", since additional concessions were required from the East, as reflected in the tough initial Western proposal. In fact, a false start suited NATO perfectly. It is a matter of conjecture whether the Soviets themselves found it in their own interests to cooperate in this false start, if only to avert massive, unilateral withdrawals of U.S. troops, which could dangerously influence European perceptions of the military balance on the continent.[51]

The first Warsaw Pact proposal, tabled on 8 November 1973, contained nothing of interest to NATO, but essentially reflected the Soviet vision of the situation in Central Europe. It proposed overall force reductions for both alliances of 17 percent, to be effected in three stages, *but under one single agreement*. The Soviets contended that rough parity existed in the zone and that force reductions should be equivalent on both sides. Furthermore, the reductions for each alliance should be partitioned in proportion to the strengths of each component nation's troops deployed in the zone. In other words, if the FRG and the USSR accounted respectively for 50 percent of the NATO and Warsaw Pact troops in the reduction zone, each would have to make cuts amounting to 50 percent of the overall cuts envisaged for the zone. In addition, the troops withdrawn would be demobilized and their equipment stockpiled or destroyed. Thus, foreign-based troops together with their equipment, would be repatriated to their countries of origin and reductions would be effected by military unit rather than by general "thinning out". The Warsaw Pact proposal differed from that of NATO in the following four respects:

1   the reductions would be effected proportionately, on the premise that a balance of forces already existed at the time;
2   the reductions would apply to each nation individually, thus establishing *de facto* national levels;
3   all the reductions would be effected under one single agreement, rather than two for which the first would serve as a test case for the second; and,
4   weapon systems would be reduced in parallel with troop reductions.[52]

These provisions clearly demonstrated that the objectives of the Warsaw Pact (or rather the USSR) were essentially political in nature, as indeed were those of NATO. In this regard, and as a matter of principle, there was no question of acknowledging that NATO had any "rights of asymmetry" predicated on the geographical circumstances underlying Western security.

Irrespective of whether the Soviets wished to limit u.s. presence in Europe, their first objective was to constrain the *Bundeswehr*, as evidenced by their 8 November proposal which called for a 17 percent overall force reduction for all allied contingents in the reduction zone. In particular, for the FRG it would have involved 74,000 personnel.[53]

The "public relations" aspect of the whole operation came to the fore in mid-November when the Soviet proposal was leaked to the Western press, despite the fact that both parties had agreed in Vienna that all proposals and negotiations would be kept confidential. Starting in December 1973, the Eastern press published lengthy analyses of the virtues of the Warsaw Pact offer and the unacceptability of the Western proposal. As for the proposal itself, the Soviets acknowledged that the first phase of reductions (20,000 troops) was purely symbolic.[54] The same could be said of the verification measures that the Soviets envisaged, which were essentially discretionary and political, and contingent on the goodwill of both parties. The mechanisms for communication and consultation advocated by the proposal were aimed at stimulating public debate in favour of a "peace offensive". Clearly, such mechanisms would have provided the Warsaw Pact with the opportunity to criticize every NATO initiative to reorganize Western defence.

The initial positions adopted by the East and West were obviously incompatible, and it took seven long years before they were reconciled.

The Long March (1974–1979)

Minor amendments aside, the years between 1974 and 1979 witnessed only one proposal of substance from NATO and two from the Warsaw Pact. The NATO proposal amounted to little more than the Option III alternative which had been developed in the spring of 1973. It was formally tabled on 16 December 1975 and revoked in December 1979 when the Atlantic Alliance unilaterally decided to withdraw 1,000 nuclear warheads from Europe under the NATO force modernization program. From a military standpoint, the West continued to espouse the idea of withdrawal of a full Soviet tank corps or, at least, of five tank divisions (modified Western proposal of 19 April 1978).

On 19 February 1976, the Soviets responded to Option III with a counter-proposal in the form of a binding master agreement which envisaged a two-phase process. The first phase provided for troop reductions for both the u.s. and the ussr of 30,000 personnel, together with withdrawal of:

- 300 tanks;
- 54 nuclear-capable delivery aircraft (F-4 and Fitter);
- 36 surface-to-air missiles (Nike-Hercules and sam-2);
- an unspecified number of nuclear warheads.

Reductions under Phase 1 would involve the withdrawal of complete combat units and their subsequent disbandment – verification of this provision was impossible for the West. Agreement on Phase 1 would require implicit agreement on the provisions of Phase 2, namely a reduction by 15 percent of personnel and materiel for all nations of the respective alliances except for the u.s. and the ussr for which the reductions, of course, would be only 13 percent. Just as in 1973, the Soviet proposal was tabled in a highly-charged political climate orchestrated by an Eastern press campaign aimed at extolling the virtues of Warsaw Pact concessions. The proposal was tabled one week prior to Brezhnev's 24 February address to the 25th Congress of the Communist Party of the Soviet Union. Once again, the confidentiality of the negotiations was not respected. In its proposal, the East seized upon the Western nuclear formula (Option III) in order to acquire a political lever for insisting that nuclear weapons under the partial control of the *Bundeswehr* be included in the second phase of force reductions.[55] Moreover, despite numerical equivalences, there was no technological equivalence of materiel included under Phase 1 of the Soviet proposal. It would have been a fool's bargain – nato would have been subjected to severe capability cutbacks in exchange for Soviet withdrawal of obsolescent equipment. Moreover, although the United States was ready to accept a 15 percent force reduction, the European allies were not. At most, they were prepared to accept a reduction of 10 percent.[56]

On the other hand, the second proposal of the Soviet Union, tabled on 8 June 1978, was clearly more serious, perhaps in light of the prevailing political climate at the time (unssod i, salt ii and German-Soviet *rapprochement*). The main points may be summarized as follows:

- overall ground and air forces of nato and the Warsaw Pact would be reduced to 900,000 personnel;
- the 11 to 13 percent reduction (depending on country) would apply only to ground forces – the socialist States would cut their forces

by 105,000 and the Western States by 91,000 – resulting in a complement of 700,000 personnel for both sides;

- materiel reductions would apply only to certain types of equipment: the United States would withdraw 1,000 nuclear warheads and the weapon systems envisaged in the u.s. proposal of 16 December 1975, while the Soviet Union would withdraw 1,000 tanks and 250 infantry combat vehicles;
- initially, only the ussr and the United States would reduce their ground forces in proportion to their military personnel in Europe, specifically in a ratio of 2 to 1 (30,000 and 14,000 personnel respectively) while, during the second phase, all member States, including

the West-European States which provide ⅔ of nato's armed forces stationed in Central Europe would reduce their ground forces proportionately to conserve the current approximate balance at a much reduced level.[57]

It was clear, therefore, that although the East would never subscribe to the concept of asymmetry, the idea of equal and collective ceilings was acceptable. Symbolically, at least, the ussr was ready to accept force reductions that were twice those accepted by the United States. As well, the Warsaw Pact nations magnanimously offered to reduce their tank complement by 1,000, although they never specified the types of tank in question. The most important Eastern bloc concession was probably the acceptance of the principle that "the member States of each alliance will be free to balance any additional unilateral force reduction implemented by its allies on condition that no member State reaches, or exceeds, its previous force level".[58]

In sum, the Soviets were ready to accord some flexibility to the Atlantic Alliance in respect of adjustments to its various national contingents. The Warsaw Pact nevertheless continued to insist that:

- force reductions of individual States should be proportional to the contributions of the States in question to the collectivity of forces in their particular alliance;
- during the first phase, each State should announce the magnitude of its force reductions.

As always, the Soviets exploited all means of propaganda, and the period 1978–1979 was punctuated by a series of gestures visibly aimed at bringing the European disarmament question to centre stage. For instance, on 23 November 1978, the Political Consultative

Committee of the Warsaw Pact pronounced in favour of a Conference on Disarmament in Europe (CDE) and, one week later, on 30 November in Vienna, the East tried to block NATO's long-term planning by proposing a freeze on the collective forces of each alliance. On 5–6 December 1979, the Warsaw Pact reiterated its appeal for a CDE that would address confidence-building measures as its first priority. And finally, in Berlin on 6 December 1979, Brezhnev announced a series of unilateral measures including the withdrawal of 20,000 Soviet military personnel and 1,000 tanks from the GDR, together with measures to restrict military manoeuvres. The operation was conducted like a publicity stunt, and Western journalists were invited to witness the partial withdrawals.

This was the context in which the Atlantic Alliance introduced, on 17 December 1979, its first substantial modification to the position that it had held since 1973. After seven years of difficult negotiations in Brussels, the member nations of NATO reached agreement on a list of associated measures that they felt would constitute a viable proposal to the Warsaw Pact. These measures included, amongst others, the following:

1   prior notification of field exercises conducted by military units equal to, or in excess of, divisional strength (10,000 men);

2   mandatory exchange of observers in exercises for which prior notification is given;[59]

3   at least one month's notification of outside troop movements towards a given reference zone in cases where contingents would reach or exceed divisional strength;

4   permanent observers at fixed installations (ports, airports, road and rail junctions) to monitor troop entries and departures in the reference zone at specific, previously-determined access points;

5   the right to conduct inspections, either by mobile land groups or by low-level aerial observations, whenever suspicious activities were observed within the zone, to a maximum of 18 annually, with the proviso that they would be undertaken within hours following formal request.[60]

In addition,

6   both alliances would exchange detailed data on an annual basis concerning the structure and troop complements of their units down to the battalion level;

7   interference with "National Technical Means" (NTM) (surveillance satellites) would be prohibited; and,

8   a Consultative Committee would be established to discuss issues
   of adherence to the provisions of the Treaty.

The December 1979 proposal on force reductions was clearly more
modest than previous Western proposals. The first phase would affect
only 13,000 U.S. personnel and 30,000 Soviet personnel. On the
Soviet side, the reductions would be made entirely on a unit basis,
and three divisions would be affected. For its part, the United States
would make two-thirds of its cuts by eliminating whole units and
one-third by generally "thinning out". Phase 1 also called for residual ceilings on Soviet and American troops in the MBFR zone. In
Phase 2, which was also subject to a second agreement, NATO and
the Warsaw Pact would reduce their forces to a common ceiling of
700,000 (land forces) and 900,000 (land and air forces combined).
The linkage between Phases 1 and 2 would depend, as before, solely
on the promise of continued negotiations between the two alliances.

Overall, the basic principle of limited, symbolic force reductions
by the U.S. and the USSR remained unchanged, but the spotlight was
turned towards the associated measures that NATO was prepared to
adopt, undoubtedly in response to growing Western scepticism that
meaningful force reductions could be effected.

It is doubtful whether this new approach had any hope of influencing Warsaw Pact posture, for:

the USSR remained totally opposed to any form of control in the absence of
some form of disarmament. The Soviets interpreted this NATO proposal as a
Western subterfuge to acquire information on the strength of the Socialist
Bloc and, at the same time, to legalize espionage. It was inevitable, therefore,
that the Western proposal would elicit negative reaction.[61]

Demise of The Negotiations

There was no fundamental change in the situation between 1980
and the time of the Budapest Declaration in 1986. During that
period, nine "new" proposals or modifications were presented in
Vienna – six by the Warsaw Pact and three by NATO. For instance,
on 10 July 1980 (see Table 14), the Warsaw Pact modified its stance
on the force reduction proposal tabled in 1978, arguing that in light
of Soviet unilateral force withdrawals effected the preceding year,
Phase 1 would henceforth comprise cuts of 13,000 U.S. personnel
but only 20,000 Soviet personnel. Drawing on a West-German concept, the Warsaw Pact proposed further that, once Phase 2 was
completed, the total complement of national and foreign-based

Table 14
The Vienna Negotiations: MBFR and Associated Measures

Genesis: Following preliminary consultations between January and June 1973, negotiations started on 30 October 1973; they ended on 2 February 1989.

Mandate: To negotiate reductions in armed forces and certain so-called associated measures applicable within the Central European zone, comprising Belgium, Czechoslovakia, FRG, GDR, Luxembourg, Netherlands and Poland.

Composition:
• Direct participants: Belgium, Canada, Czechoslovakia, FRG, GDR, Luxembourg, Netherlands, Poland, United Kingdom, United States and USSR.
• Indirect participants: Bulgaria, Denmark, Greece, Hungary, Italy, Norway, Romania and Turkey.

Frequency and Duration:
Three sessions annually, of approximately two months each.

Principal Location: Hofburg Palace, Vienna.

MAIN PROPOSALS EXCHANGED IN VIENNA (1973–1986)

NATO	WARSAW PACT
Proposal of 22 November 1973	Draft Treaty of 8 December 1973
Proposal of 16 December 1975 (Option III)	Proposal of 19 February 1976
Proposal of 19 April 1978	Proposal of 8 June 1978
Proposal of 20 December 1979	Proposal of 10 July 1980
Proposal of 21 July 1981	Proposal of 18 February 1982
Draft Treaty of 12 July 1982	Proposal of 17 February 1983
Proposal of 19 April 1984	Draft Treaty of 23 June 1983
Proposal of 5 December 1985	Proposal of 14 February 1985
	Proposal of 20 February 1986

17 February 1987 marked the start of discussions within the Group of 23 aimed at developing another mechanism to replace the talks in Vienna. There was a proposal to enter into Conventional Stability Talks (CST) which were planned for the spring of 1989. The acronym CST was short-lived, as was its successor CAFE (Conventional Armed Forces in Europe) which was changed quickly to CFE, perhaps because it was felt in some circles that the Vienna CAFE could hardly be taken seriously.

troops on a sovereign State's soil would not be permitted to exceed 50 percent of the total forces of the alliance to which that State belonged. This softening in the Soviet approach was likely aimed at exploiting divergence of opinion within the Bonn Government. On 9 March 1979, West German Chancellor Helmut Schmidt surfaced this idea during a debate in the *Bundestag*, but it was immediately repudiated by his Foreign Affairs' Minister, H.D. Genscher, who refused either to adopt it or to transmit it to the NATO allies.[62]

In November 1980, the Warsaw Pact attempted to consolidate its stance by proposing that Phase 1 reductions should span a three-year period during which time the remaining forces on both sides would be collectively frozen. Evidently, the aim of this manoeuvre was to halt any qualitative or quantitative development of NATO forces over this three-year period in exchange for symbolic reductions. In short, it represented, once again, nothing short of a fool's bargain.

Finally, on 19 December 1980, the Warsaw Pact responded to NATO's proposed associated measures through its own reformulation, specifically:

- mutual notification of the start and completion of reductions;
- exchange of inventories of residual units and residual forces within the two alliances;
- creation of temporary observation posts to monitor reductions;
- exchange of information to verify and ensure strict adherence to the provisions of the Treaty;
- exchange of data on U.S. and USSR forces which would be reduced during Phase 1;
- regular updating of data;
- 30-day prior notification of manoeuvres involving 20,000 or more troops;
- prior notification of troop movements involving more than 20,000 military personnel;
- prior notification of military inflow and outflow in the reduction zone;
- limitations on major manoeuvres (restricted to 40,000 or 50,000 military personnel);
- provisions to permit verification through the use of "National Technical Means" (NTM) and to prohibit interference with those means;
- establishment of a consultative mechanism to resolve differences in respect of adherence to the Treaty;
- the creation of a Consultative Commission to this effect.[63]

Once again it became clear that although the Warsaw Pact was prepared to make a positive move towards the position of the Atlantic

Alliance by accepting the principle of associated measures, it refused to accept the basic Western tenets of on-site inspection and the establishment of permanent observations posts. The above-mentioned modifications were incorporated into a draft treaty tabled by the Warsaw Pact in February 1982. Compared with the 1978 Soviet proposal, it contained no new ideas, apart from that of requiring guarantees that troops affected by force reductions would not be redeployed in the vicinity of flank countries.

On 12 July 1982, NATO responded to these Warsaw Pact initiatives. NATO's draft treaty, the first since 1973, deviated little from its 1979 proposal. The now-familiar objective of establishing troop ceilings at 700,000 and 900,000 was reiterated, but the reductions to achieve these levels would be effected in four phases over a seven-year period. The provisions of Phase 1 were also retained, namely a reduction in Soviet and U.S. personnel by 30,000 and 13,000 troops respectively. The NATO draft treaty was, therefore, nothing more than a reincarnation of its 1979 strategy which was pursued until 1985. It was simply a matter of making the Soviets accept a series of associated measures which would give NATO a greater in-depth appreciation of the deployment of Warsaw Pact forces in Central Europe and in the European sector of the Soviet Union. The absence of innovation is understandable if the draft treaty was introduced as a short-term political move aimed primarily at negating Warsaw Pact initiatives taken during the two preceding years.

Clearly, the Vienna negotiations had run out of steam, and the Eastern responses of 17 February and 23 June 1983 seemed to indicate growing Soviet disinterest in the Vienna forum and increasing pessimism in the prospects for an MBFR agreement. The Warsaw Pact had practically lost all hope of negotiating significant reductions in West German forces. The only consolation was a vague NATO promise that "proportionality" would be respected in any troop reductions of its member States. The East, in turn, sought to avoid the most restrictive aspects of a formal treaty, proposing that the reductions in Phase 1 (concerning only the U.S. and the USSR) be effected only "to set an example" and not as a formal provision within the framework of a treaty. This approach would effectively deflect the issue of an agreement to provide data on the armed forces of each alliance, and leave in limbo the issue of the true balance of forces in Central Europe. The means of verification proposed by the Warsaw Pact were, once again, no more than symbolic. For example, observers would be invited *on a voluntary basis* to monitor reductions, four permanent control posts would be established *following the period of force reductions*, and inspections would be *subject to a right of refusal*.

On the other hand, there was a hint of flexibility in the Western offer of 19 April 1984. Although the main thrust of the 1979 proposal was maintained, the requirement for data exchange was limited to U.S. and USSR combat and combat support troops. Moreover, NATO dropped its insistence that the data be absolutely precise, and agreed that accuracies to within 10 to 15 percent in American and Soviet troop strengths would be acceptable. Finally, the West agreed that 90 percent of the troop reductions on both sides should be effected by unit. However, as Jean Klein noted, NATO's liberalism was tempered by firm adherence to the need for agreement on associated measures which was the West's main battle-horse.[64]

Neither should it be forgotten that these events occurred during a period of significant cooling in East-West relations, and that the arrival of the Ground-Launched Cruise Missile (GLCM) and the Pershing missile in Europe towards the end of 1983 was a major snub to the Soviets who had struggled for five years to avert modernization of NATO's nuclear forces.

It came as no surprise that a further hardening in the position of the Warsaw Pact ensued. The socialist countries rejected the latest Western proposal out of hand, and their response, on 14 February 1985, represented a step back in the negotiations in every respect. In particular, it called for the revival of a Phase 1 with no specific agreement on numbers of deployed forces, to be negotiated within the framework of a treaty and no longer "to set an example". In addition, the freeze on armed forces, which would occur prior to Phase 2, would be accompanied by a commitment to halt the deployment of intermediate-range nuclear missiles. This was a highly irregular proposal, in that the deployment of such missiles was outside the scope of the discussions in Vienna.

Following Mikhail Gorbachev's election to power, and in the context of the first U.S.-Soviet summit held in November 1985, there was a modest attempt at *rapprochement*. On 5 December 1985, NATO tabled its last MBFR proposal which contained, among other things, a suggestion to effect a symbolic reduction of American and Soviet forces by 5,000 and 11,500 personnel respectively during Phase 1, without specific agreement on overall force data. These reductions would be accompanied with a freeze on all remaining personnel for a period of two years. In the absence of any agreement concerning the exchange of data on residual forces, NATO insisted on this occasion on the right to conduct 30 on-site inspections during the period of reductions.

On 20 February 1986, the Warsaw Pact responded to this initiative and accepted the general principles for Phase 1, namely the size of the reductions, the duration of the interim period and the freeze on residual forces. The Warsaw Pact insisted, however, on the withdrawal of heavy equipment from downsized units and refused on-site inspections on demand as well as the exchange of detailed data which the West considered prerequisite to agreement on Phase 2. The East rationalized this refusal by arguing that the means of verification should be related to the size of reductions, and since these reductions would be symbolic in Phase 1, so the means of verification would also be symbolic. The Eastern proposal, in common with all Warsaw Pact proposals since 1983, reflected Soviet pessimism towards any prospect of reaching agreement.

By early 1986, the MBFR negotiations were virtually dead, and discussions on conventional arms control in Europe subsequently resumed in another forum in the spring of 1989. The issue of military stability in Europe entered a new phase which bore the stamp of a new Soviet leadership, and it is still too early to assess its final outcome. For the moment, therefore, attention will be restricted to an analysis of the talks in Vienna which took place between 1973 and 1986.

ANALYSIS OF NEGOTIATIONS: THE MBFR AND CANADA'S ROLE

"Why is arms control such a boring subject?" This ironic remark of L. Freedman could well serve as the epitaph for the MBFR. For the past fifteen years, these negotiations, which still have not been finally laid to rest, have provided the world with an image of a "slow motion" diplomatic duel. The only result has been a long series of thrusts and parries of ambiguous proposals lacking any meaningful substance. The official Canadian records show clearly that both the East and West were equally responsible for these disappointing results.

The records also show that, apart from very rare exceptions, no one, either in the East or West, believed that agreement could be reached, even in the very modest form of a traditional SALT agreement. Consequently, the MBFR soon became a slow ritual whose only purpose was to create the illusion of progress.

Retaining the tactical advantage became the *leitmotif* of the two parties, and this presented a particular problem for NATO in view of the lengthy consultative mechanisms of the Alliance and the divergent policies of Western Europe.

There was an inherent risk in such tactics. Arguments that were repeated year after year progressively became worn out, thus undermining public credibility in the negotiations. The real danger was

that the MBFR talks would reach an impasse, not due to any deterioration in East-West relations, but simply for lack of good argument
or new ideas.

The way that the Vienna talks developed, and apparently drifted,
calls for a deeper explanation. Why did the MBFR negotiations become
an interminable ritual? And why were the initial positions of both
sides maintained with such rigidity?

The intentions of the Soviets were quite clear. According to one
Canadian Delegate:

I continue to believe that the MBFR talks have never had in them the potential
for more than what the Russians have long since offered us, namely a small,
politically symbolic but militarily insignificant, unbalanced reduction without
proper verification; that MBFR is not like SALT, that is, that it is not a process,
and that the reason is that the Russians are obliged to maintain, as a matter
of what they considered to be their fundamental security interests, forces in
Central Europe large enough to ensure that Germany is kept permanently
divided and that the strategic lands on the historic invasion routes from
Central to Eastern Europe remain permanently under Soviet control. Any
major reduction of Soviet forces in Central/Eastern Europe would place the
strategic advantages gained by the USSR at a horrible blood price in the
Second World War in jeopardy, and the USSR is unlikely in any foreseeable
future to be willing to take any such risk. On this analysis, MBFR has been
misconceived from the beginning, and I do not wish to be asked to agree to
advising Ministers to justify the negotiations, or our participation in them,
on the grounds that they will ever lead to mutual and balanced force reductions in Central Europe.[65]

In this context, Western data showed that, in 1981, the Warsaw
Pact would have had to reduce its forces by 280,000 personnel to
reach the collective ceilings of 700,000 (land troops) and 900,000
(land and air forces combined). The reductions required of the West
were only one-third of those required of the Warsaw Pact. Consequently, the asymmetry and extent of the cuts required of the socialist
countries would have raised serious problems. In particular, the
Soviet share of the reductions would have amounted to 130,000
troops in their land forces alone. If these reductions had been made
by unit – as NATO insisted – it would have required the withdrawal
of 13 of the 26 Soviet divisions in the reduction zone. Such a move
would have meant a radical lessening of the USSR's military and
political power in Central Europe, involving long term risk. Clearly,
such a demand was not negotiable during the period of the MBFR
talks.

It should be noted also that, even if the Western intelligence estimates had been incorrect by 30 percent, the Warsaw Pact would still have had to withdraw 200,000 personnel, of which the Soviet share would have been 100,000 troops, or 10 divisions. In other words, for obvious military and political reasons, the USSR, and hence the Eastern countries, could not accede to such demands.

Given their geopolitical vulnerability, the Western nations had just as much reason for not abandoning the rigid and paradoxical principles that they had adopted in 1973. Indeed, the military authorities in NATO were highly sceptical right from the start about the viability of the reductions, whatever form they took. As one official of the MBFR Working Group stated: "There is doubt whether any acceptable form of MBFR can be discovered because the existing disparity in strengths is so great".[66]

It might be added, without entering into detail on the balance of forces in Europe, that NATO's perception of its military weaknesses became more acute during the 1970s.

It was, therefore, fundamentally important for the West not to yield to the temptation of hasty reductions. One is left to wonder why NATO offered to open negotiations in a position of weakness when the situation undoubtedly called for greater defence rather than arms control.

The reasons for such a decision are clearly evident in the Canadian records, and they correspond directly with what was already known in well informed circles:

• The MBFR talks, which were launched following the publication of the Harmel report, were clearly conceived as the Western response to the proposal for a Conference on European Security which had no military context. As such, the talks were aimed at identifying the real causes of insecurity in Europe, from a Western perspective.
• More importantly, the Western initiatives at the time were motivated by strong political pressures for *détente* and East-West *rapprochement*.
• Lastly, Senator Mansfield's offensives in the U.S. Senate had pushed the American President to adopt the MBFR route to avoid the unilateral reductions that Congress seemed to wish to impose on him. It should be added that U.S. troops in Europe had already been cut from 416,000 in 1962 to 296,000 in 1970, and that Belgium, Canada, the Netherlands and the U.K. had followed suit. The threat of further withdrawals thus constituted a disquieting prospect, and the MBFR talks paradoxically offered a practical means of "stopping the rot in NATO".

Thus, in contrast to the Warsaw Pact, whose policies and strategies in the MBFR talks remained relatively stable, the Atlantic Alliance had to contend with military, economic and political factors which made its policies in the Vienna negotiations more complex and more contradictory:

Right from the start of MBFR it has been recognized that there was a fundamental difficulty in accomplishing *all* the aims of MBFR as set out in the so-called "Rome Criteria". It has proved impossible to obtain agreement in NATO as to how reductions could be "substantial and significant" and still have NATO in a position of undiminished security; and this position has been made more difficult still by the interpretation of the Rome criterion of "undiminished *military* security" ... The various studies that have been presented in NATO have shown that reductions to NATO forces, unless they were accompanied by far larger reductions by the WPO, would result in NATO's position being worsened. If these studies were basically sound – which they were on that point – the decision-makers should have realized that it was impossible to achieve both substantial and significant reductions and still have undiminished security.[67]

The initial directives of the Atlantic Alliance on MBFR (document 83 of the Military Committee of NATO, 1973) clearly show the contradictions and ambiguities that have influenced NATO's negotiation strategies right from the beginning. For instance, one might question an arms control policy which at once specifies that one of its main objectives is the improvement of the defensive capabilities of the Atlantic Alliance. One might also wonder how it is possible to confine the zone of reductions while, at the same time, taking into consideration the security of flank countries. It should also be remembered that the associated measures, which became a central issue for NATO during the 1980s, were left rather vague for six years due to reticence on the part of some allied nations.

It would not be unreasonable, therefore, to suggest that NATO entered into the Vienna negotiations on the wrong foot. NATO was badly prepared and even divided. Some nations, such as the United States, were ready to cut corners so as to hasten the negotiations, while others, such as Italy, Turkey and the United Kingdom were, to say the least, reticent. Nations such as Canada and the FRG positioned themselves somewhere between these two extremes. National positions have, of course, evolved over time, but discussions on form and substance continued until the 1980s. For that reason, the allies found it increasingly difficult first, to define their position concerning the parameters of the negotiation, second, to deviate from the 1973 directives, flawed as they were, and third, to proceed to a detailed review of their policy.

As a result, the Canadian negotiators in Vienna, often left in a vacuum on account of disagreement in Brussels, lost tactical control of the talks to the Warsaw Pact which, without even breaching the Western positions, scored more than one point in "public diplomacy". As one poetic Canadian diplomat put it:

> The *Ad Hoc* Group turned their eyes to Brussels,
> Although it is not known for speedy hustles,
> Spare us, we cried, this Brussels bickering
> Western hopes are faintly flickering
> Send us guidance – we'll always deliver
> But give us a tank and not a flivver.[68]

Alas, for most of the time the instructions never arrived from Brussels and when, on rare occasions, the North Atlantic Council reached consensus it was scarcely helpful to Western negotiators. Indeed, the impression that one gains from the endless stream of memoranda and official telegrams is that of a fastidious repetition of hackneyed facts and arguments. And that reflects, in a sense, the lack of leadership in the Atlantic Alliance, if not the paralysis of its policies on MBFR, until the beginning of the 1980s. As summarized by our diplomatic poet, at the end of the 25th Session of negotiations, in December 1981:

> A weary round, flat and zero
> Without a cause or a hero ...
> Face facts, council, and not theory
> The ammo's gone, troops are weary
> We've said it all, ambitions gone
> It's two years since the sun last shone.[69]

Thus, during the period in question, the divergence of views between allies became more pronounced, for many of them had the feeling that they were in a blind alley. Some nations, like the FRG, which sought at any price to protect what they considered to be vital interests, toughened their positions while others, such as the Netherlands, favoured *rapprochement* with the Eastern countries and were ready to make concessions towards that end which were deemed unacceptable by other allies. As noted in the report of the 26th

Session, which was produced immediately following the tabling of the February 1982 Warsaw Pact proposal:

If the East intended to use the February 18 proposals primarily as a divisive device they hit the target. A great many hours of work and all too many minutes of acrimony were spent in working groups and *ad hoc* groups on assessment and detailed analysis of Eastern draft texts. Both reports caused the AHG to divide along traditional lines with the more conservative group led by the U.K. and Italy. The Netherlands were strongly in front of the less conservative forces who saw more virtue in the Eastern draft text than did others; Canada was somewhere in the middle through conviction as well as desire to play an active conciliation and chairmanship role.[70]

It is easy to imagine the difficulties that Canadian diplomats encountered in presenting the appearance of a united front and in countering, as best they could, the tactics of the opposing party, especially within the framework of the complex consultation system of the Atlantic Alliance and of the no less complex system of the negotiations themselves.

It should also be stressed that the main themes upon which NATO had based its strategy for the previous fifteen years proved less solid than they appeared. Indeed, the concept of phased reductions, the principle of collective ceilings, the data question, the associated measures, verification, and so on, were not, as it turned out, impregnable fortresses of logic, but vulnerable glacis wide open to the diplomatic offensives of the Warsaw Pact.

On the question of armaments, for instance, why should the East withdraw its tanks and allow NATO to leave its equipment in the reduction zone? Why exchange a tank corps for a few obsolete nuclear systems? Why could NATO simply reduce its force levels when the Warsaw Pact had to withdraw its troops by unit? What would guarantee a second agreement on force reductions following Phase 1? And what assurance would the Warsaw Pact have that all the member nations of NATO would assume an equitable share of the reductions? All these weaknesses in NATO logic clearly provided ammunition to the socialist bloc, and the data question was certainly no exception. Of course, NATO assessments of Warsaw Pact strength were relatively reliable. There was truly an asymmetry in favour of the East, and Western intelligence estimates do not seem to have been artificially inflated.[71] NATO appears to have had very solid data for arguing its case, and for getting the Warsaw Pact to acknowledge its military superiority. Unfortunately for the Atlantic Alliance, the problem was more complex. The issue of numbers plagued the negotiations like a Pandora's Box which might be opened at any time.

First of all, it should be emphasized that despite the general agreement which existed in Brussels on Warsaw Pact strengths, intelligence estimates are never totally reliable, as pointed out by J. Dean: "Despite the highly professional care with which data on Eastern forces have been compiled, they nevertheless contain a considerable margin of error".[72] This margin of error was estimated to be about ten percent, so that the Warsaw Pact "superiority" could have been anywhere between 50,000 and 150,000 men. Consequently, the socialist camp had no trouble in contending that the NATO figures were wrong, for the force levels of the Warsaw Pact had been overestimated.

Secondly, it was difficult for NATO to point out errors in the data provided by the Warsaw Pact, since NATO was reluctant to provide its own data. To illustrate the point, the Warsaw Pact provided NATO with a general picture of its force levels in February 1976. It took NATO 11 months to respond in kind, and 7 months to table the Western estimates of Eastern force levels. As late as March 1981, when Ambassador Tarasov renewed his proposal to analyze in detail NATO's figures on Warsaw Pact strengths, the West agreed to discuss only ten figures relating to Soviet forces and, even then, on a one-by-one basis.

NATO's reticence to discuss these matters stemmed as much from fear of revealing its intelligence sources as from hesitancy on the part of some NATO nations to submit national data to scrutiny by the Warsaw Pact. For instance, to disclose detailed figures on German forces would have been tantamount to giving the Soviets the right to examine the forces of the *Bundeswehr*. The Atlantic Alliance was faced with a thorny choice, and the resulting compromise unfortunately took the edge off the West's argument on the numerical superiority of the East.

Overall, even if one were to concede that the basic principles underlying NATO's policy on MBFR were in some way imposed by circumstances, it would be hard to claim that the tactics and strategies of negotiation employed by the Atlantic Alliance represented the model of effectiveness. Nevertheless, in the final analysis, the MBFR talks constituted a kind of victory for the Atlantic Alliance, in that the West maintained its unity, as best it could, for 15 years. For all that, the Vienna talks were a shining example of the lack of Western leadership. Apart from very brief periods, the MBFR talks were far from centre stage on the political scene. They were "forgotten" negotiations, left in the hands of "technicians" and lacking political guidance.

In light of the above, an observer might be led to question the general usefulness of the Vienna talks. Did the negotiators waste their time for fifteen years? We would have to say not, for five reasons.

First, from a Western standpoint, the allies learned a great deal about the Eastern concept of conventional defence, which had been a closed book before the talks began. Not that any real secrets were exchanged, but each side acquired a better understanding of the perceptions and preoccupations of the other. It could even be argued that if the military doctrines and deployments of the two camps progressively became more in line, leading to greater military stability in Europe, it was due to the dialogue which started in Vienna in 1973.

Second, even though the MBFR talks rarely made the headlines, they were covered regularly, especially in Europe. A greater part of the public was thus kept informed of the military problems and issues underlying European doctrine. The public became increasingly aware of the strategies and strengths of the two alliances, and the MBFR talks certainly contributed to this growing awareness.

Third, the Vienna talks provided the opportunity for in-depth, and sometimes difficult, consultations between allies on their defence policies and their respective approaches to arms control. In this regard, the Atlantic Alliance was forced to develop common positions, strategies and tactics of negotiation. All constituencies in the Atlantic Alliance – politicians, diplomats and the militaries – were thus involved in a common effort to identify priorities and define approaches. In short, the MBFR talks proved to be a very useful exercise in political coordination.

Fourth, the negotiations led to a detailed examination of the military balance in Europe. Whereas previously the West had been satisfied with imprecise data, the MBFR talks forced a detailed analysis of the "threat". In turn, this led to a review of the methods used in Brussels for intelligence assessments, with a view to making them more rigorous. It might even be added that the West was forced to develop a better understanding of its own forces in order to make meaningful comparisons with those of the East.

Fifth, still from the Western standpoint, NATO certainly learned a great deal about the art of negotiating collectively as a single entity. It seems that this was most predominantly noticed "on the spot" in Vienna; according to the records, the members of the MBFR *Ad Hoc* Group were generally impressed with the degree of cohesiveness that the NATO team succeeded in maintaining.

Finally, 20 years after the signal from Reykjavik, political pressures for unilateral reductions continue to exist in the United States as well as in several other nations. It can reasonably be argued that if these pressures have been to no avail, it has been due, in large part, to the Vienna negotiations. The MBFR talks raised publicly a question that is still relevant in the West today: why should one member of the Atlantic Alliance rather than another be authorized to reduce its forces? Fortunately, the unilateralists have not yet found a satisfactory answer to this question.[73]

Canada's Role in the Vienna Negotiations (1973–1985)

The first part of this chapter has attempted to demonstrate that Canada, mainly because of changing internal politics, played only a minor role during the preliminary phase of the MBFR talks, that is, from the time of the signal of Reykjavik until October 1973 when the curtain first rose in Vienna. There was little change in Canada's stance during the period that followed, between 1973 and 1985.

Politically, the MBFR talks had never commanded primacy in Ottawa's foreign policy except in the initial stages. In this respect, Canada was no different from most of the nations within the Atlantic Alliance. The MBFR talks scarcely attracted the attention of the Canadian Government which, right from the start, confined itself to a general policy of support for the negotiations, without any distinctive particularity.

A memorandum to the Prime Minister, prior to his European tour in 1974, summarized the situation as follows:

Canada has been among the foremost advocates of MBFR negotiations for several reasons. First, the Canadian Government considered that the negotiations would allow for the development of an East-West dialogue on military security in Europe, which in itself could promote political understanding; MBFR negotiations could complement political *détente* and their outcome could constitute a test of the viability of *détente*. Secondly, Canada regarded MBFR as the best means available of ensuring that the perhaps inevitable withdrawal of some USA forces from Europe would be reciprocated by the USSR and would take place in a multilateral framework designed to reassure the USA's European allies. Finally, Canada saw the NATO discussions of MBFR and the MBFR negotiations themselves as forums within which it could complement its bilateral endeavours to strengthen its relations with the countries of Western Europe.[74]

In the main, the MBFR negotiations were considered as a complementary adjunct to Canada's European policies. At the same time, it was recognized that they were of primary concern to the Europeans themselves:

In determining the attitude we should adopt towards MBFR proposals, it would seem desirable to bear in mind not only Canada's commitment to both NATO security and East-West *détente*, but also the following considerations:

a   the USA administration is under Congressional pressure to reduce USA forces in Europe;

b   our European allies, given their proximity to the line of military confrontation, may feel more directly affected by the outcome of MBFR than the USA or Canada;

c   a major purpose of our role in NATO is to complement our economic and political ties with Europe; and

d   of the NATO military forces affected by MBFR, Canada's are the smallest but for Luxembourg's. In light of these considerations ..., we think it would be appropriate that we continue to act in accordance with the following guidance provided us by Cabinet:

In regard to our own part in the formulation of Alliance views on MBFR, Canada should pursue a constructive but "low profile role", making thoughtful substantive contributions where the opportunity offers, but avoiding taking sides on matters of controversy between the USA and our European Allies.[75]

On this basis, Canada thus excluded herself from the most substantial MBFR debates. Canada's role was clearly that of promoting unity within the Atlantic Alliance and not that of defending interests that she might have deemed vital. In other words:

Canada is seeking to contribute constructively to the formation of a consensus, but has not any specific suggestions for changes in the Allied position because it considers that initiatives in this area can more appropriately be taken by NATO countries which have more directly at stake in the MBFR, both politically and militarily, than does Canada.[76]

This does not mean, however, that Canada remained indifferent for 15 years. In fact, it was just the opposite. The diplomatic record shows that Canada's representatives often adopted a critical stance in an attempt to instill some dynamism into discussions, both in Brussels and in Vienna. Canada was amongst the first in the North Atlantic Alliance to insist that the Alliance position *vis-à-vis* MBFR negotiations be reviewed regularly and critically to preserve the credibility of NATO's policies in the public eye.[77]

On at least two occasions during the course of negotiations, the Prime Minister intervened directly to encourage new political thinking on MBFR. For instance, during the NATO Summit in the spring of 1978, Pierre Elliott Trudeau vigorously supported the initiative of his British counterpart in order to "breathe new life" into the Vienna negotiations. In substantive terms, it was a matter of convening a meeting of Atlantic Alliance foreign ministers as soon as there was any meaningful progress in the talks. Needless to say, there was no progress.

In the fall of 1983, following the "walk out" of Soviet negotiators in Geneva and Vienna, the Prime Minister again put forward the idea of a Summit of NATO ministers on the MBFR issue, to be held in Canada in the spring of 1984. It was unanimously rejected, however, by all the governments consulted; it was a worn-out theme, lacking political interest, since the negotiations were due to resume, without external intervention, in April 1984.

Overall, despite the lack of success of these modest initiatives, it cannot be said that Canada remained politically inactive. On the other hand, it would be wrong to pay excessive homage to Canadian leadership during this period. Ironically, one of the major interests of the Prime Minister in the Vienna negotiations was that they provided him with a possible reason to reduce further the Canadian contingent assigned to NATO. Thus, in 1973, when the Prime Minister was asked to abandon the idea of reducing Canada's contribution to NATO's forces in Europe during the first phase of an MBFR agreement, he stated that he had no objection providing that it was clear to all concerned that by 1976 all Canadian tanks would be replaced by light mobile ground forces, compatible with those stationed in Canada, and that Canada would not be precluded from considering reductions of Canadian forces during subsequent phases of negotiations.[78]

The irony of the situation is that Canadian tanks were still in Europe in 1988 and that, had the reductions been made at the time, they would only have affected some 300 Canadian troops.

On a more serious note, however, while Canada's political commitments to the MBFR talks can be debated, the technical work performed by Canada's diplomatic team in Vienna, Brussels and Ottawa was far from negligible. Briefly, this team essentially consisted of the Defence Relations Division of the Department of External Affairs (which replaced the Defence Liaison Division), the Directorate of Nuclear and Arms Control Policy (DNACPOL) in the Department of National Defence, Canada's Permanent Representatives to NATO and the negotiating team in Vienna. In total, the Canadian team comprised, and still comprises, a half dozen persons, compared with a complement of some twenty persons in the u.s. Delegation to Vienna alone. It should be emphasized, moreover, that the Defence Relations Division, which coordinated the entire MBFR effort, had only one specialist in the public service at its disposal and no "think tank" to analyze the substance of the negotiations.

It is remarkable that with such a limited team Canada could follow up so faithfully on the MBFR talks in Vienna. Its work is reflected in the sheer size of the MBFR records – some 200,000 pages of documentation in the archives of the Department of External Affairs.

Furthermore, the practical importance of Canada's role in diplomatic management and in logistic and administrative support was clearly recognized by NATO's diplomats in Vienna.

Even though the impact of Canada's policies on the MBFR negotiations is impossible to quantify, it is certainly true that the work of Canada's diplomats deserves some measure of praise, which has never been accorded by the media.

12 A Matter of Confidence: Canada and the Military Aspects of the CSCE

All is afar –, and nowhere does the circle close.

R.M. Rilke, *Sonnets to Orpheus*

As we have seen in Chapter 11, the MBFR talks were only a diplomatic exercise of limited scope that served mainly to discipline the Atlantic Alliance for 15 years in the matter of conventional arms control. The Conference on Security and Cooperation in Europe (CSCE), which has now concluded its fourth Review Conference – Helsinki-Geneva, Belgrade, Madrid and Vienna – is a richer and more evolutionary exercise (see Tables 15 and 16).

Fifteen years after the process started in Helsinki in the fall of 1972, the CSCE has produced significant agreements in areas that are as diverse as human rights, economic cooperation, information dissemination and confidence-building measures – agreements which involve all 35 European States from the "Atlantic to the Urals".

As such, the CSCE can probably be considered as one of the rare fora of productive East-West negotiation in the post-war period, one which best addresses the larger concept of security that integrates interstate cooperation in all its aspects. It might even be argued that the CSCE, given its endurance and flexibility, forms the embryo of a true European security system embracing an evolutionary set of principles and standards, or a code of interstate behaviour, for the purpose of controlling conflict within the framework of interdependence.[1]

This chapter does not attempt to recount the history of the CSCE. Several excellent texts have been written on this subject, to which the interested reader is referred.[2] Also, the origins of *détente* in

Europe (1966–1972) have already been discussed in detail in the context of the Vienna negotiations.

Instead, we shall focus attention on the development of one of the themes of the CSCE, known as Confidence-Building Measures (CBMS). These measures constitute the only strictly military element in the negotiations, and form, therefore, a concrete linkage to the arms control process in Europe. Moreover, there are very few texts which deal in depth with the evolution of the military aspects of the CSCE from Helsinki (1972) to Vienna (1989). This Chapter and the one that follows (Chapter 13) attempt, therefore, to redress certain deficiencies, particularly with regard to the development of diplomacy, and attempt to provide a synthesis of the negotiations and accomplishments of the CSCE in the military context from a Canadian diplomatic perspective.

The approach adopted herein follows closely the chronology of the CSCE and is organized in three parts covering successively the negotiations leading to the Final Act of Helsinki (1972–1975), the Belgrade Conference (1977–1978) and the Madrid Conference (1980–1983). Chapter 13 deals with the Stockholm negotiations (1984–1986), which were essentially a follow-on to the Madrid negotiations and a prelude to the Vienna Review Meeting (1986–1989) which opened the door to future talks on reductions of Conventional Armed Forces in Europe (CFE).

This analysis will focus essentially on three aspects:

- the development of Atlantic Alliance positions on Confidence-Building Measures (CBMS);
- the evolution of the negotiations themselves, in terms of tactics and strategies;
- the development of Canadian positions, and the Canadian input to these negotiations.

These three aspects give rise to a number of questions which reappear on several occasions throughout our discussion, and we draw attention to them immediately:

- What was the status of CBMS in relation to arms control in Europe? Did they constitute a prelude, a complement or a substitute for arms reductions? Did they provide a solution to all the impediments facing arms control in Europe?
- In contrast to State-to-State negotiations (SALT or INF) or alliance-to-alliance negotiations (MBFR), did the CSCE, which was perceived

Table 15
The CSCE and Follow-up Meetings

THE HELSINKI CONFERENCE
Preparatory Meeting: 22 November 1972 to 8 June 1973, in Dipoli;
Phase I: 3 to 7 July 1973, in Helsinki;
Phase II: 18 September 1973 to 21 July 1975, in Geneva;
Phase III: 30 July to 1 August 1975, in Helsinki;
Final Act of Helsinki: 1 August 1975.

THE BELGRADE CONFERENCE or the First Follow-up Meeting
Preparatory Meeting: 15 June to 5 August 1977;
Conference: 4 October 1977 to 9 March 1978.

THE MADRID CONFERENCE or the Second Follow-up Meeting
Preparatory Meeting: 9 September to 10 November 1980;
1st Session: 11 November to 22 December 1980;
2nd Session: 17 January to 8 April 1981;
3rd Session: 4 May to 28 July 1981;
4th Session: 27 October to 18 December 1981;
5th Session: 9 February to 12 March 1982;
6th Session: 9 November to 17 December 1982;
7th Session: 8 February to 25 March 1983;
8th Session: 19 April to 9 September 1983.

THE VIENNA CONFERENCE or the Third Follow-up Meeting
Preparatory Meeting: 23 September to 6 October 1986;
1st Session: 4 November to 19 December 1986;
2nd Session: 27 January to 10 April 1987;
3rd Session: 5 May to 31 July 1987;
4th Session: 27 September to 18 December 1987;
5th Session: 22 January to 25 March 1988;
6th Session: 5 May 1988 to 19 January 1989 (closing document
                        approved 15 January 1989).
Fourth Follow-up Meeting of CSCE scheduled for 24 March 1992, in Helsinki.

---

as a multilateral forum, really promote the influence of the lesser and middle powers in security matters?

In other words, did the CSCE process provide for a broader expression of international viewpoint? Did it improve the flexibility of negotiations and therefore promote compromise with the East? For

Table 16
Conference on Security and Cooperation in Europe (CSCE)

Genesis and Evolution: Following preliminary consultations (the Multilateral Preparatory Talks in Dipoli) between November 1972 and July 1973, the CSCE opened in July 1973 and concluded in the summer of 1975. Three Follow-up Meetings were held successively in Belgrade (1977–1978), Madrid (1980–1983) and Vienna (1986–1989).

Mandate: To discuss and negotiate European security issues (the principles of interstate relations and confidence-building measures); economic, scientific and technical cooperation, including environmental problems; cooperation in the humanitarian and other fields (final recommendations of the Helsinki consultations; Dipoli, June 1973).

Composition: The 33 European countries less Albania, plus the United States and Canada.

Main Proposals:

A. *Helsinki-Geneva (1972–1975)**
1   Multilateral Preparatory Talks (MPT) in Dipoli (proposals tabled 1 February 1973):

CSCE/HC/10, Switzerland;   CSCE/HC/21 corr. 1, Sweden;
CSCE/HC/11, USSR;   CSCE/HC/22, Switzerland;
CSCE/HC/28, USSR;   CSCE/HC/23, Yugoslavia;
CSCE/HC/28 add., GDR;   CSCE/HC/24, Netherlands;
CSCE/HC/13, Romania;   CSCE/HC/25, Spain;
CSCE/HC/17, Belgium;   CSCE/HC/26 rev. 2, Spain;
CSCE/HC/20, Austria;   CSCE/HC/29, Turkey.

2   Phases I and II (July 1973 – July 1975)
CSCE/I/3 (4 July 1973), USSR;
CSCE/I/18 (5 July 1973), U.K.;
CSCE/I/30 (7 July 1973), Turkey;
CSCE/II/C/4 (26 September 1973), Norway.
CSCE/II/C/8 (28 September 1973), Romania;
CSCE/II/C/9 (23 October 1973), Sweden;
CSCE/II/C/11 (21 January 1974), FRG;
CSCE/II/C/12 (4 February 1974), U.K.;
CSCE/II/C/13 (19 February 1974), NNA;
CSCE/II/C/14 (7 March 1974), comparison of Soviet, Western and NNA proposals;
CSCE/II/C/16 (8 March 1974), Spain;

Table 16 (continued)

B. Belgrade (1977–1978)

CSCE/BM/11 (2 November 1977), Canada, Netherlands, Norway and U.K.;

CSCE/BM/6 (24 October 1977), NNA: Austria, Cyprus, Finland, Liechtenstein, Sweden, Switzerland and Yugoslavia;

CSCE/BM/5 (24 October 1977), USSR;

CSCE/BM/S/1 (24 October 1977), Romania;

CSCE/BM/9 (28 October 1977), USSR;

CSCE/BM/14 (4 November 1977), Western nations less Greece and Turkey;

CSCE/BM/18 (4 November 1977), NNA;

CSCE/BM/40 (11 November 1977), Czechoslovakia and GDR;

CSCE/BM/41 (11 November 1977), Czechoslovakia;

CSCE/BM/45 (11 November 1977), Bulgaria;

CSCE/BM/46 (11 November 1977), Bulgaria;

CSCE/BM/50 (11 November 1977), GDR;

CSCE/BM/56 (11 November 1977), Romania;

CSCE/BM/67 (12 November 1977), Western nations less Austria, France, Liechtenstein, Sweden and Switzerland.

C. Madrid (1980–1983)

CSCE/RM/6 (8 December 1980), Poland;

CSCE/RM/7 (9 December 1980), France;

CSCE/RM/17 (11 December 1980), Yugoslavia;

CSCE/RM/18 (11 December 1980), Yugoslavia;

CSCE/RM/21 (12 December 1980), NNA;

CSCE/RM/27 (12 December 1980), Yugoslavia;

CSCE/RM/31 (15 December 1980), Romania;

CSCE/RM/33 (15 December 1980), Romania;

CSCE/RM/34 (15 December 1980), Sweden;

CSCE/RM/39 (16 December 1981),NNA;

CSCE/RM/39 rev. (15 March 1983), NNA.

---

* This list was produced using documents available in the DEA archives.

nations like Canada, did a multilateral forum such as the CSCE offer a political platform that was more promising in terms of opportunities for initiatives? And specifically, how did Canada attempt to exploit these opportunities?

In the context of these questions, the main body of our analysis will, therefore, attempt to substantiate certain hypotheses as follows. The set of Confidence-Building Measures developed during the 1970–1980 period represented neither a new "theory" nor a new mechanism of arms control, but rather an area of politico-symbolic negotiation which permitted East-West dialogue on European military security. As such, the CBMs offered the precise advantage of being flexible, evolutionary and yet technical, which permitted their progressive adaptation to the requirements of negotiations. It would, therefore, be wrong to attempt to analyze CBMs outside the diplomatic context which gave them birth. Above all, they provided 35 European nations with an indirect strategy of negotiation which allowed them to deal with military issues without becoming embroiled in the multiplicity of problems faced by the negotiators in Vienna. It should be added that, even though the genesis of the CBMs remains somewhat uncertain, they nevertheless worked mainly to the advantage of the Western nations. For over ten years, the CBMs enabled the Western nations to keep the focus on Soviet responsibilities in respect of the armed confrontation in Europe. They afforded a means of stressing the lack of openness of Soviet military activities while avoiding the issue of the balance of forces in Europe. Because of their "technical" or concrete nature, the CBMs served to counterbalance the strictly declaratory measures proposed by the East. Contrary to the theories advanced by a number of authors, the CBMs had little chance of preventing surprise attack, of reducing the risk of accidental war or even of impeding the implementation of the Brezhnev doctrine. They were neither a substitute nor a complement to the arms control process. At most, they could be considered as a prelude to the later CFE talks.

Concerning the process of the CSCE, and still within the context of the CBM negotiations, we shall attempt to show that far from being a multilateral forum, the CSCE remained as a forum for negotiation between the two blocs. The only difference between the CSCE and the MBFR talks was that the CSCE allowed the participation of countries such as France and the Neutral and Non Aligned (NNA) nations within the broadened Western bloc. In other words, although the CSCE provided for the expression of diverse viewpoints, it was nevertheless supervised, refereed and oriented in a conclusive way by the decisions taken within the Atlantic Alliance. Its merits lay in the fact that the Western groups (NNA, EEC and NATO) were able to pursue negotiations which overcame the contradiction existing between a wide diversity of positions on the one hand and an excess of discipline on the other. Thus it was possible to pursue a set of "independent" initiatives which corresponded, nevertheless, to the criteria agreed to and understood by the majority of Western countries. By avoiding the rigidities of U.S.-Soviet confrontation, the CSCE was able to establish room for negotiation which left an appreciable margin of manoeuvre to the Europeans and allowed them to present a relatively flexible and reasonably united front to the Eastern bloc.

Finally, one might have expected that Canada's diplomats would have taken advantage of the flexibility of the CSCE to promote Canadian initiatives and competence in arms control matters. Surprisingly enough, such was not the case, at least as far as the CBMS were concerned, and although Canada generally played her traditional role of mediator brilliantly, she scarcely exhibited her creativity or technical expertise. In fact, there is reason to believe that Canada realized only belatedly the importance of the CBMS and that her general attitude in this regard bore the same mark of discretion as had characterized Canadian participation in the MBFR talks. After all, military issues remained the prerogative of the major military powers and Canada did not count in the European context. It would be wrong to conclude, therefore, that the margin of manoeuvre afforded by the CSCE allowed Canada to define her role in arms control. In fact, Canada showed a greater interest in human rights issues, and this seems to indicate that Canadian policy concerning the CSCE was influenced to a greater extent by the Canadian public than by the freedom of diplomatic action or any "specific idea" of Canada's mission in arms control.

FINDING THE KEY IN HELSINKI (1972–1975)

Origins of the Notion of CBMS: An Idea in Search of a Theory

Unlike some other policy themes, the theme of Confidence-Building Measures (CBMS) which developed during the 1970s and 1980s does not appear to have had its origins in a set of basic precepts designed to guide its logical evolution. This, in itself, is interesting to note. The idea of CBMS, which appeared during the 1950s, did not follow from any specific theory aimed at promoting the confidence that was to develop continuously from that time on. CBMS were rather the product of diplomatic interaction and might be regarded as technical adjuncts to the disarmament plans of the period. Their rapid, and relatively unnoticed appearance on the scene can be summarized as follows. The Soviets were the first to propose, within the framework of a complete and general disarmament plan tabled on 10 May 1955, that weapons reductions should be accompanied with the implementation of a system of "control posts at major ports, railway junctions, highway intersections and airports". In addition, an international control organization, established by the signatories, "would have the right to require States to provide all the necessary information on the implementation of weapons and armed forces reduction measures and would have unhindered access to documents concerning the funds allocated by States to military purposes". Finally, the control organization would have permanent inspection rights "to the extent necessary to ensure that all States implemented the disarmament program".[3] These complementary proposals were explicitly aimed at redressing the "lack of international confidence" by permitting the verification of disarmament measures. They are to be found in one form or another in many of the Soviet proposals developed between 1955 and 1964.

On the Western side, the idea of CBMs appeared implicitly in the so-called Open Skies proposal presented on 21 July 1955 by President Eisenhower to the Subcommittee of the Disarmament Commission. According to this proposal, the United States and the USSR:

were to exchange information about the strength, command structure and disposition of personnel, units and equipment of all major land, sea and air forces, as well as a complete list of military plants, facilities and installations with their positions. Verification of information was to be accompanied by ground observers as well as unrestricted, but monitored, aerial reconnaissance.[4]

In addition, although these measures were designated as means of control, they would constitute the *prerequisite* to any disarmament agreement. These measures again appeared in Proposal 914 (X), which was adopted by the General Assembly of the United Nations on 16 December 1955. This proposal thus included, for the first time, an item entitled "measures aimed at creating a climate of confidence".[5]

Although the idea of promoting international confidence at the height of the Cold War appears somewhat ludicrous, the notion of CBMs was nevertheless born and low-key debates on this subject continued until the early 1960s, initially at the Geneva Conference on Experts on the Prevention of Surprise Attack (1958) and subsequently within the Ten-Nation Committee and the United Nations. The U.S. plan of 25 September 1961 on general and complete disarmament thus envisaged prior notification of military movements and manoeuvres, and the draft treaty of 18 April 1962 added to it an element concerning the exchange of military missions.

In July 1962, within the framework of a similar draft, the Soviets introduced the ideas of prohibiting large-scale international military movements and manoeuvres, providing prior notification of major national manoeuvres and exchanging military missions.

Finally, on 2 December 1962, the Americans tabled a proposal before the Eighteen-Nation Committee which advanced the idea of a set of measures aimed at reducing the risks of accidental war. These measures deserve mention for they anticipated the kind of measures that would be considered ten years later by the CSCE. Among other provisions they included the following:

1   notification, with seven days prior notice, of major military manoeuvres and movements on land, at sea and in the air. These notifications were to include information on the type of military activities, the size of units, the start and end dates, the geographical location and, in the case of movements, the destination;
2   creation of a centre for information exchange;
3   establishment of fixed observation posts in the main ports, railway junctions, main highway intersections and airports, as well as occasional visits to transportation centres where fixed posts would not be established;
4   measures for aerial observation;
5   mobile land observation teams;
6   radar observation systems;
7   direct contact between the militaries, including exchange of military missions for observing certain specific activities;
8   establishment of a government-to-government emergency communications system.[6]

By the start of the 1960s, the CBM concept had thus acquired some stature within the disarmament discussion framework. CBMs offered a means of control or verification to be used in parallel with or as a follow-up to any arms reductions (Soviet version), or as a prelude or even prerequisite to disarmament for the main purpose of limiting the risks of involuntary or accidental war (U.S. version). A set of assorted, and more or less clear, measures had been developed, but it still remained to be proven that the techniques so defined could fulfil the specific functions for which they were designed. These measures, in themselves, represented only secondary elements in the Soviet and Western disarmament plans and, in this regard, it is significant to note that the Open Skies proposal and the Conference of Experts on the Prevention of Surprise Attack had been rapidly relegated to the status of museum pieces. The CBM concept was thus fated to disappear as quickly as it had appeared, without its name even having been perpetuated in the sole agreement that it had inspired, specifically the agreement to install a "hot line" in June 1963. At the end of the first phase of its existence, the CBM concept seemed, therefore, to merit only footnote mention in the annals of disarmament.

The Development of CBMs Following the Harmel Report (1968–1971)

Having fallen into oblivion for several years, confidence-building measures reappeared timidly within the Atlantic Alliance during the discussions that accompanied and followed the preparation of the Harmel Report. Thus, during a meeting of disarmament experts in March 1967, the representatives of Belgium, the FRG and the Netherlands stressed that any agreement on reductions in armed forces should be accompanied by certain measures designed to alleviate the possible instability that might result. They suggested that such measures should take the form of a system of observation posts, installed on each side of the demarcation line.[7]

In the NATO studies on future MBFR negotiations, mention is made of confidence-building measures such as exchange of observers, prior notification of military movements or manoeuvres, an emergency communications system, exchange of military missions, information exchange and the establishment of a system of observation posts.[8] However, due to the problems encountered by the Atlantic Alliance in defining its policy on *balanced reduction* of military forces in Europe, the confidence-building measures theme seemed not to arouse as much attention as the reduction models themselves. Only the Belgians, according to available documentation, appeared to have studied the issue more seriously. Following discussions with Polish experts, they introduced a plan for freezing force levels that would be accompanied by:

1   negotiation of *ad hoc* agreements aimed at settling international differences by peaceful means and at ensuring respect for the principles of non-recourse to force or to the threat of force in international relations and of non-interference in the internal affairs of other States, in conformity with the Charter of the United Nations;
2   prevention of the risk of accidental warfare in Europe following miscalculation or surprise attack, by establishing *ad hoc* means, including an adequate system of observation posts.[9]

The idea of freezing force levels, however, scarcely appealed to allied interests and the concept of political agreements on non-recourse to the use of force seemed distinctly inspired by the East. The Belgian proposal was not, therefore, adopted. CBMs again disappeared from the major preoccupations of the Atlantic Alliance – apart from a brief mention in the NATO communiqué of 5 March 1969 – and reappeared only in 1971. From that time on, CBMs evolved along two lines: in the form of "collateral measures" within the MBFR talks and under the heading "some military aspects of security" in the context of the CSCE (see following section on "The Emergence of CBMs in the CSCE (1971–1972)").

The development of CBMs within the MBFR framework was inspired by the German idea of a *building block model*. According to this idea, the reductions themselves would follow prior agreement on the principles of negotiation and on the constraints affecting movements of military forces. In other words, it became increasingly apparent for the Atlantic Alliance that reductions which were both advantageous and negotiable would be very difficult to define. As noted in a June 1971 memorandum: "As it is obvious that NATO cannot change the geography of Europe to its own advantage, it is incumbent upon NATO planners to develop collateral measures or constraints, or both, that will serve to minimize the 'geostrategic' asymmetries that exist".[10]

In the following year, the United States thus proposed that emphasis should be placed on the development of such measures:

We should seek agreement on appropriate collateral constraints which would enhance stability and reduce the danger of either side miscalculating the intentions of the other and also reduce the risk of surprise attack. Such constraints could provide a yardstick for more confident, more timely interpretation by each side of military activities by the other. These constraints would be valuable in themselves and would also increase confidence that a reduction agreement was being observed.[11]

Such measures were specifically aimed at preventing the Soviets from sidestepping an eventual MBFR agreement by redeploying their forces outside the reduction area. These measures were also aimed at counterbalancing the advantages of the geostrategic situation that was enjoyed by the Warsaw Pact in terms of its potential for rapid mobilization and also at providing a prior indication of its mobilization intentions. As was stressed in the NATO guidelines on the eve of the MBFR talks:

Such measures could include advance notifications of movements of forces, and limitation of their size and the duration of their stay. Force reductions on their own, even if adequately verified, would need to be supported by measures of this type governing entry of forces into the reduction area. Movement constraints could also play an important role in the pre-reduction phase.[12]

Consequently, the Atlantic Alliance gradually developed four related themes under the heading of "associated measures":

1 *Pre-reduction stabilizing measures* to build confidence by reducing the risk of misunderstanding and ambiguous military activity, thus facilitating agreement on other measures ... i.e.,
   a pre-announcement of movements of USA and Soviet forces into area, including rotations;
   b pre-announcement of major exercises by all forces;
   c limits on size, location, number and duration of major exercises by all forces;
   d exchange of observers at major exercises by all forces.

2 *Stabilizing measures to accompany reductions* and to make reduction provisions effective (applicable to USA and Soviet ground forces only), including:
   a limitation on movements of forces into the area;
   b limitation on movements of forces across national boundaries within the area;
   c agreement to respect the new overall relationship in the levels of USA and Soviet ground forces established by the reduction agreement.

3 *Non-circumvention provisions* to ensure that any agreement will not be circumvented by an increase of Soviet forces in Hungary.

4 *Verification measures* to ensure that the provisions of the agreements are being carried out, to build mutual confidence and to enhance warning in the event of a Pact build-up.[13]

The Atlantic Alliance thus seemed to have developed and refined its approach to CBMs. Their justification was clearer, their definition relatively more precise and they had been integrated into the whole approach adopted by NATO on MBFR.

However, according to available data, no basic study had been undertaken on this subject and the allies do not seem to have realized that some of the measures envisaged would be difficult to accept for the Alliance itself and that they would require, in any case, significant modification and elaboration. It is not surprising, therefore, that NATO took over five years to agree on the package of associated measures, even though it was more modest than that originally envisaged. It would be wrong to assume that the consideration accorded by NATO to the associated measures could have fostered or stimulated Western efforts to develop CBMs within the CSCE framework. In fact, it was just the opposite. Given the priority accorded by NATO to the MBFR talks, as well as allied reticence to discuss arms control within a forum of 35 nations, it appeared necessary, as will be seen, to avoid proposing substantial CBMs within the CSCE framework in order not to interfere with the Vienna talks. The link between Vienna and Helsinki was, therefore, severed for political reasons and it can only be regretted that the most dynamic elements of the CBMs remained the prerogative of the stillborn MBFR talks. These last observations require some historical clarification, as discussed in the following sections.

The Emergence of CBMs in the CSCE (1971–1972)

The idea of addressing "certain military issues" within the CSCE was advanced by the Belgian foreign minister during the NATO ministerial meeting of December 1971. The suggestion was accepted by the North Atlantic Council and the communiqué issued at the end of the meeting made due reference to the conduct of studies on the subject.[14]

The divergent viewpoints in the North Atlantic Council were reflected by the extremely vague title adopted for this agenda item. Most allies agreed that a Conference on *security* in Europe would make little sense if it failed to address the military situation. But for Belgium and several other members of the Atlantic Alliance, this required the creation of a direct link between the CSCE and the MBFR process. This link could take the form of a common declaration on MBFR and the principles of future negotiations in Vienna, or again, more simply, of a "blessing" from the 35 nations in favour of disarmament in Europe. The United States was highly sceptical and France, which refused right from the start to participate in the Vienna talks, was absolutely opposed to the idea.

For other nations, military issues had to be addressed by the CSCE through confidence-building measures, in particular:

• notification of military manoeuvres and movements;
• exchange of observers during manoeuvres;

- constraints on force movements in certain areas;
- various surveillance measures.[15]

But the two differing approaches posed certain problems. It seemed unacceptable to empower the NNA – nations that were not members of the either of the two alliances – to dictate the principles of the MBFR, and it was out of the question to negotiate, within the CSCE, certain CBMS that could influence Western defence capabilities.

Following debate, the U.S. Delegation in Brussels circulated a draft directive which formed the basis of the allied position within the CSCE. It was drafted in the summer of 1972 and stressed that certain CBMS could be studied profitably in the CSCE. The United States considered that CBMS of modest scope could serve to promote stability and cause the Soviets to be more open in respect of their military activities in Europe. Tactically, if the Atlantic Alliance were to favour CBMS, it could encourage the NNA and allow some Eastern countries to play a more independent role. Finally, this would lead to a more balanced agenda for the CSCE. Although the U.S. draft acknowledged the usefulness of CBMS it nevertheless stressed that such measures should meet a set of nine criteria:

1   undiminished security;
2   strengthened confidence and stability, promotion of *détente*, improved relations with the East;
3   consistency with measures that may be agreed in MBFR talks;
4   applicability to the whole of Europe, not just selected areas;
5   sufficiently simple to obviate lengthy negotiations;
6   non-interference with NATO reinforcement plans and exercises;
7   minimal verification requirements;
8   no follow-on machinery;
9   clarity of wording to avoid misunderstanding.[16]

Various CBMS were examined within NATO during the summer and fall of 1972, but most were rejected since they failed to meet the above-mentioned criteria. Two measures were, however, adopted. They concerned prior notification of large-scale military manoeuvres and movements, and exchange of observers during manoeuvres on an equitable basis. These two concepts were extremely modest in scope but, once again, precise definition remained problematic. What was meant by "large-scale" manoeuvres? What was the difference between a manoeuvre and an exercise? What constituted a movement? And what was the definition of "equitable" in the context of exchange of observers? NATO's position was far from clear on these particular points and indeed on many others. The Atlantic Alliance was, therefore, drawn into preliminary CSCE talks without being properly prepared. But this was not unprecedented; recall the MBFR talks ...

The Multilateral Preparatory Talks at Dipoli
(November 1972 – June 1973)

On 22 November 1972, the curtain rose on the CSCE talks in Dipoli, a suburb of Helsinki. For the first time since 1945, all the European nations, as well as the United States and Canada, tried to define the overall principles of their future relations. This was a new experience from more than one standpoint. To be more precise, confusion – in appearance at least – was to become, from the outset, the diplomatic hallmark of the CSCE process. As one Canadian diplomat observed:

[At Dipoli, 35 nations] meet daily without any agenda, speaking order nor defined goal other than to discuss what matters of security and cooperation in Europe can be identified as suitable for consideration at a Conference on Security and Cooperation in Europe. These talks are, therefore, highly unstructured and it is most difficult to convey a feeling of what is going on to anyone who has not visited the site ... The daily drama of observing some 100 diplomats enter, sit, and the Chairman ... call for anyone to speak bears witnessing: will it be the representative of Liechtenstein? San Marino? The Holy See? The excruciating nature of these meetings is best exemplified by a 30 minute debate at a plenary concerning whether or not to have a debate about dates to take a break.[17]

The negotiations continued, however, despite confusion and slow progress. The numerous proposals on security were grouped into one of the four "baskets" that would serve to structure the future negotiations. Basket One contained, apart from the CBMs already mentioned:

• principles to guide interstate relations;
• means of implementing these principles;
• linkages between the CSCE and the MBFR process;
• peaceful settlement of differences;
• Mediterranean and Middle East security;
• several proposals on arms reductions.

By February 1973, Basket One contained 16 proposals advanced by 12 nations.[18] Although only a small number survived the

Multilateral Preparatory Talks (MPT), they provided a very clear indication of the main orientations of certain participants. For instance, the Soviet Union and the other members of the Warsaw Pact seemed to have accepted the principle of CBMS (the GDR proposal mentioned them explicitly). The Eastern bloc insisted, however, that these measures were secondary in relation to the principles of interstate relations. Moreover, the Eastern bloc clearly indicated that the CBMS considered in the CSCE should contain neither constraints nor reduction proposals. NATO and the Warsaw Pact seemed, therefore, to agree on the nature of the measures to be considered as well as on the distinction between the Helsinki and the Vienna talks.[19]

The main NNA countries – Sweden and Yugoslavia with the support of Romania – while accepting the idea of CBMS, regretted the absence of a more substantial link between the political and military aspects of security. For the NNA, the proposed CBMS were inadequate, and they wanted to consider some constraints or limitations on movements of military forces as well as a firm commitment towards arms reductions in Europe. The Swedes, in particular, favoured such an option, and even indicated their interest in military constraint measures for the Baltic sector. Yugoslavia, for its part, proposed that the CSCE should study restrictive measures such as:

• a ceiling on the size of manoeuvres;
• prohibition of manoeuvres near national borders;
• a freeze on foreign troops based on European territory.[20]

Some European countries raised the thorny problem of extending the CBMS to the Mediterranean, and this issue haunted the CSCE until 1983. Despite these differences, it soon became apparent that only those measures that were acceptable to the two alliances would be retained, and on 30 March 1973 a text to this effect was accepted *ad referendum* by all participants and finalized two months later. From that time on, the CSCE agenda included proposals on prior notification of large-scale manoeuvres and on exchange of observers "under mutually acceptable conditions", but was limited to a study of the issue of prior notification of military movements.[21] The position shared by the two superpowers was thus imposed on the 35 nations.

Canada remained relatively silent during the earlier debates. As one diplomat observed in a May 1973 report:

I believe it would be correct to say that up to now we have not discussed in depth a Canadian policy on CBMS in the CSCE. We have instead been content to accede to policy developed in Brussels, and we have reacted on an *ad hoc* basis to particular points as they have arisen.[22]

Furthermore, the Canadian attitude reflected a certain disinterest or scepticism in respect of CBMS within the CSCE framework:

Canadian performance so far suggests that we have been adhering to about four basic precepts in discussions of CBMS to date. Foremost has been the maintenance of a low profile in recognition of the greater need that European States have for increasing confidence among themselves. This low profile could also be considered desirable in order to retain Canadian clout for use on matters of greater interest to Canada such as encouragement of human contacts including reunification of families. Secondly, it has been assumed, probably rightly, that there is a greater opportunity for tangible progress in disarmament through MBFR negotiations, and we have therefore adopted a view that any factor that could conceivably impede progress in MBFR should be excluded from CSCE if possible. The last two precepts seem to arise in part from the first two: we apparently would not like to expand CBMS beyond those tabled in Helsinki, and we would like to see CBMS limited in their application as much as possible (indeed it would appear that some have a rather unformulated view that any CBMS that emerge from CSCE should be largely anodyne anyway). In sum, the Canadian approach seems to be primarily negative except for a passive recognition of the more vital interests of the Europeans.[23]

Two years after the start of allied discussions on CBMS in preparation for the CSCE, Canadian diplomats realized the lack of a clear national policy on the matter and, even though the Canadian position was not altogether atypical, one is led to wonder how many Western governments shared this attitude, which was both apathetic and indifferent. According to the records, the level of political and military activity in NATO on the eve of the formal opening of the CSCE was limited to a single study on CBMS that was in progress, but nothing else was planned at that time.[24]

From Helsinki to Helsinki: Negotiations on CBMS (1973–1975)

Phase I of the CSCE: Helsinki (3 to 7 July 1973).   The inaugural phase of the CSCE opened in Helsinki on 3 July 1973. Despite the formal nature of this occasion, several substantial proposals were advanced in the area of CBMS.

The British, who took the initiative for the Western camp, justified the importance of CBMS by stressing that the aim of prior notification of military manoeuvres and movements was to clarify the intentions of States which engaged in such activities and to allow other States to distinguish between military operations of a routine nature and those that might be interpreted as threatening. The British proposal also attempted to detail the topics for discussion during the second phase of the CSCE which would open in Geneva in September. Finally, the British proposal pointed out that the envisaged CBMS probably could not be subjected to verification given that any agreement reached by the CSCE would not be legally binding, and that the implementation of CBMS would be contingent on the moral and polit-ical commitments of participants (CSCE/I/18, 5 July 1973).

For their part, the Soviets proposed a "general declaration on the fundamentals of European security and the principles of interstate relations in Europe" (CSCE/I, 4 July 1973). This declaration appeared in the form of a final act, drafted in extremely general terms, and contained an article on CBMS. This article, however, only repeated the terms of the proposal introduced by the GDR during the preparatory talks and suggested that notification of manoeuvres would be nec-essary only "in certain specified areas" and not for the European theatre as a whole.

The Soviets, however, were not the only ones to dismiss the results of the Dipoli discussions. Yugoslavia, supported by Romania, ques-tioned the issue of constraining measures, and Finland raised the issues of nuclear-free zones and weapon reductions, insisting that these matters be studied during Phase II.

Four countries – Norway, Belgium, Spain and Romania – were ready to discuss concrete disarmament measures within the CSCE. As one observer ironically noted:

Of these, Romania was by far the most wide ranging and unreal. The Romanians mentioned every form of disarmament that anybody has ever thought of and stopped just short of suggesting that the CSCE replace every other forum in the world. (I half expected them to throw in limitations on kitchen sinks).[25]

At the end of the second brief encounter between the Soviets, NATO and the NNA, the differences were not resolved despite nine months of preparatory discussions, and the second phase of the CSCE promised to be long and difficult.

Phase II of the CSCE: Geneva (18 September 1973 to 21 July 1975). The real work phase of the CSCE opened in Geneva in mid-September 1973. It lasted for roughly 22 months and resulted in the Final Act of Helsinki which, to this day, constitutes the cornerstone of East-West relations in Europe. Negotiations on CBMs were held within one of the 11 special subcommittees created during the preparatory talks (subcommittee No. 2).

From the outset, discussions focused on the three CBMs originally proposed by NATO. The other discussion items were rapidly relegated to a secondary status. The positions of the participants crystallized on the application of the CBMs, specifically in respect of prior notification of military manoeuvres and movements. The following questions in particular had to be answered:

1   *What would be the area of application of prior notification?*
    Should it cover all European territory, as NATO and the NNA demanded, or should it be limited to border areas as suggested by the Soviets (50 kilometres, according to their initial position)?
2   *Who should be notified?*
    All the participants, as proposed by the NNA and NATO? Or only the immediate neighbouring States as proposed by the Soviets?
3   *For what kinds of manoeuvres and movements would prior notification be required?*
    Manoeuvres involving more than one division, or 10,000 troops (NATO)? More than one reinforced division, or 18,000 troops (NNA)? More than one army corps, or between 40,000 and 50,000 troops (USSR)?
4   *How much advance notice should be given?*
    Five days (USSR)? Two months (NATO)? Fifty days (NNA)?
5   *For which elements of the armed forces would prior notification apply?*
    Land forces, air forces, combined forces?
6   *What kind of information should be contained in the notification?*
    Detailed information on the purpose of the manoeuvre, its duration, the number of troops involved, the area of operations, the designations of the units, the start and end points (NNA, NATO)? Or minimal information on the purpose, duration and area involved (USSR)?
7   *How should notification of manoeuvres be given?*
    Should notification of manoeuvres and movements be dealt with under the same umbrella, according to the same parameters (NNA, NATO)? Or should notification concentrate on manoeuvres and the issue of movements be deferred to future negotiations (USSR)?
8   *When should the observers be invited?*
    Under what circumstances and conditions should observers be invited to monitor manoeuvres?

As these eight questions suggest, debate was focused on a limited number of very precise points. From the outset, the issues concerning military movements and observation of manoeuvres did not receive the same attention as the other points. It was quite clear that the Soviets were categorically opposed to prior notification of movements. The United States held the same position, and for this reason refused to support the British proposal (CSCE/II/C/13) submitted to NATO on 4 February 1974.[26] The issue of observation was clearly subordinated to that of prior notification of manoeuvres, since it was implicitly acknowledged by all concerned that observers would only be invited to activities for which prior notification had been given. This particular point was amongst the first to be recognized in an agreement signed in the summer of 1974. Finally, it should be stressed that the positions of NATO and the NNA were extremely close on the issue of prior notification. As one Canadian observer noted in October 1973: "Most NATO nations and the NNA are as one on CBMS ... although Yugoslavia, Sweden and to a lesser extent Switzerland would go further on [certain] matters than would NATO".[27]

In other words, despite certain fundamental differences that had divided NATO and the NNA during the preparatory talks and during Phase I, the West was able to maintain a common front before the seven Warsaw Pact nations on the issue of CBMS, obliging the Soviets to adopt an entirely defensive position which was static and therefore diplomatically uncomfortable.

Some authors and diplomats contend that the issue of CBMS was substantially "one of the most thorny subjects addressed during the talks".[28] Nevertheless, since the measures that were under *serious* consideration were purely symbolic in nature, only three major questions remained to be resolved: the areas to which prior notification applied; the size of manoeuvres involved; and the advance notice that had to be given. These three issues quickly became the subject of intensive bargaining.

In the winter of 1974, the Soviets relaxed their initial position concerning the area for which prior notification was required. As a Canadian report of 25 February noted:

While the Soviets continue to claim publicly that they can only accept a shallow zone along frontiers, there are indications ... that it may be possible to get a [larger] zone inside the Soviet Union ... It would seem unlikely that we would gain agreement to include all Soviet European territory but it should not be difficult to hold firmly to a position that all the rest of Europe must be included.[29]

In June 1974, the Soviet Delegate announced that the USSR would be ready to provide prior notification of major manoeuvres within a border zone of 100 kilometres inside its territory (instead of 50 kilometres), and that the timeframe for prior notification would be extended from five to ten days. On 26 June, through a British announcement, the NATO nations stated that the force level of manoeuvres requiring prior notification would be extended from 10,000 to 12,000 troops and that the timeframe for notification would be reduced from 60 to 49 days. In addition, the West indicated that it would be ready to make exceptions in the case of certain countries concerning the notification zone.[30]

In early summer 1974, the draft text on CBMS was nearing finalization, and six of the eleven paragraphs of the preamble had already been agreed upon in principle. In particular, the subcommittee had agreed to invite observers to manoeuvres[31] and to exchange military personnel (Spanish proposal, CSCE/C/16 of 8 March 1974). This latter element constituted the only confidence-building measure that was not part of the original NATO package. Besides, it was the only concession that the Atlantic Alliance made concerning the "other CBMS" that the subcommittee had examined.

Following the summer break, which lasted from July to September 1974, negotiations resumed and discussions focused on the idea of "exception zones". In other words, it was understood from then on that the principle of prior notification of manoeuvres would apply to *the whole of Europe*, except for the countries whose territories extended beyond the continent.[32] Such States, specifically the USSR and Turkey, would only have to announce certain military activities within a limited border zone. A text to that effect was adopted at the end of September. A Canadian report on this matter states:

Attention is now focused exclusively on [this text] and no others are really in play despite their registered status. The Soviets have accepted the wording in principle but reserved the right to return to any particular word in the future should they feel it necessary. (Interpretation: it looks good; Moscow's happy, but since it is a Western formulation, maybe we are being diddled and don't know it).[33]

At the end of September, however, the Warsaw Pact seemed to indicate that the time for concessions was over. The military authorities in the Kremlin were absolutely opposed to any relaxation of the Soviet position on the parameters of notification. Negotiations were thus deadlocked until the spring of 1975. To complicate matters further, the Greco-Turkish conflict of the previous summer had caused a hardening in the positions of these two States within the

CSCE and this posed a direct threat to Western unity on CBMS. Turkey, in view of its geographical position, had insisted that part of its territory be exempt from the requirements of prior notification, and there was a significant risk that Greece would react adversely and demand, in turn, compensatory measures.

This was the context in which Canada abandoned her traditional discretion and developed an initiative that would certainly play a significant role in breaking the deadlock. As it was described in a February 1975 memorandum:

In searching for ideas on a way around the stalemate, [External Affairs] devised a chart dealing with the parameters of notification of manoeuvres. Essentially, the chart provided, within the framework of a firm commitment to notify, a sliding scale for the parameters of notification, e.g., the greater the number of troops engaged in manoeuvres, the more stringent the notification would have to be with reference to time, area and content of notification. It was our hope that such a "matrix approach" might allow more positions to be accommodated in some degree, thereby allowing the USSR scope for compromise without the NATO participants abandoning their basic objectives. Our chart was not designed to promote particular parameters as the final desired outcome, but rather to suggest a way to break the impasse and open negotiations.[34]

The Canadian matrix, as it became known, was developed and discussed within the Atlantic Alliance between November 1974 and March 1975. This provides some indication of Canadian prudence and the lengthy procedures of consultation between allies. The draft was very well received and was presented unofficially to the NNA nations on 18 March 1975. However, the Canadian initiative progressed no further. On 13 March, under pressure from the Western and neutral countries[35], the Soviets agreed to reconsider their position on the parameters on condition that notification be given "on a voluntary basis". Moreover, they accepted unconditionally to notify all participants and not only their immediate neighbours. This was not really a concession. The Canadian matrix was thus overtaken by events but, as was stressed in its "eulogy":

While it never actually entered the wider negotiations ring as a formal proposal, its presentation to and discussion among the nine, the fifteen and the neutrals must be seen as having been useful, both tactically and substantively. The matrix idea may still be useful at some future time should deadlock return. Perhaps the greatest contribution of the Canadian matrix was that it represented a necessary and realistic attempt to break out of a deadlocked situation, and it showed the possibility of devising sensible alternatives to bargaining positions which had, perhaps, been too simple and inflexible. In doing so, presentation of matrix seems to have focused attention of interested officials here and elsewhere on CSCE circuit on details of a complex problem and to have stimulated an extensive quote rethink unquote.[36]

By mid-April 1975, negotiations on CBMS were progressing slowly but surely towards their conclusion. The Soviets had realized apparently that they would only obtain final agreement by showing flexibility. Further delays threatened to damage the mechanisms of *détente* in Europe, and the Soviets had invested too much in the process to allow that to happen. As a result, having indicated their willingness to move closer towards the Western position on parameters, the Soviets tried to reach direct agreement with the Americans. At his May 1975 meeting with Kissinger in Vienna, Gromyko offered to provide 18–day notice of manoeuvres involving over 30,000 troops within 150 kilometres of the USSR borders. The Soviets, at a meeting in Washington in early June, expanded the zone to 250 kilometres. Even though these "Washington parameters" satisfied the U.S. Secretary of State, they did not satisfy the Europeans who insisted on a ceiling of 22,000 troops, a zone of 300 kilometres and advance notice of 21 days.

At the end of June 1975, the NNA adjusted these figures and on 31 July the USSR accepted a final compromise of 25,000 troops, 250 kilometres and 21 days. Phase II of the CSCE was, therefore, completed after painful bargaining and one can only wonder whether the results obtained were worth all the efforts. The measures agreed upon really had no military significance. They were rather symbolic in nature, of limited scope, and their implementation depended on the goodwill of the participants (see Table 17).

A careful study of the texts and of their official interpretation reveals, however, that the gains obtained by the West were much more tangible than would appear at first sight.

The Final Act of Helsinki: Assessment from a CBM Standpoint

First of all, it should be recognized that, from a CBM standpoint, the main merit of the Final Act of Helsinki was in gaining Soviet acceptance of the Western "philosophy". The lengthy preamble of the document on CBMS establishes their autonomous status. This shows implicitly that, in terms of security, the CBMS were just as important as the principles of interstate relations. Significantly, the Soviets

Table 17
Parameters for Notification of Major Military Manoeuvres

Size	Time	Area	Content of notice	Addressees
1. One division or 12000 troops.	Minimum 10 days.	Europe as now mentally registered including an area within 100 kms of European frontiers of the USSR.	1. Dates; 2. Purpose; 3. General geographical location; 4. Scale.	All participating States.
2. Reinforced division or 18000 troops.	Minimum 30 days.	Europe as now mentally registered including an area within 350 kms of European frontiers of the USSR.	1. Designation if any; 2. Number of troops and nature of units; 3. Purpose 4. Geographic location; 5. Dates.	All participating States.
3. Army corps and higher.	Minimum 49 days.	Europe as now mentally registered including an area within 700 kms of European frontiers of the USSR.	1. Designation if any; 2. Number of troops; 3. Purpose; 4. Geographic location; 5. Dates points of departure; 6. Final points of departure and destination of units; 7. Unit designation; 8. Periods of absence from normal duty stations; 9. Other relevant information.	All participating States.

wanted only one document in "Basket One" and were opposed to a substantial preamble on the military aspects of security. Moreover, a large part of the preamble repeated the substance of British texts and reflected clearly the objectives of the Western countries as they had appeared in the initial proposals. Paragraphs 2, 4 and 9 in particular stressed the determination of participating nations to "strengthen confidence between each other", to "reduce the risks of armed conflict and misunderstandings" and, in this regard, recognized "the political importance of prior notification of large-scale military manoeuvres". In other words, the Soviets had been brought to admit explicitly the principle of CBMS and their role in the framework of *détente* in Europe. In addition, they had accepted the diverse and evolutionary nature of such measures. On several occasions the text mentions "other confidence-building measures", stating that the participants could unilaterally go further than the recommendations of the Final Act of Helsinki. Finally, in the context of "other confidence-building measures", it was stated that "the experience acquired during the implementation of the provisions could, with much effort, provide for the development and extension of confidence-building measures". Thus, the Soviets admitted unambiguously that the measures accepted in Helsinki were only a first step and that they should be developed further.

The USSR had insisted, of course, on the voluntary nature of the CBMS, but this weakening of the measures adopted in Helsinki was largely balanced by the terms used in the preamble. Although the words "voluntary basis" appeared in paragraph 11, their context indicated that it could not be an arbitrary measure or one left to the discretion of nations, nor was it an occasional act. Rather, it was because of its political nature that this confidence-building measure was established on a voluntary basis. In addition, the political importance of the measure was explicitly stated, as well as the responsibilities of nations in implementing it and in respecting the specified procedures. The Soviet negotiators admitted to such an interpretation on several occasions, both in formal meetings and in informal discussions.[37]

It is also important to note that the Soviets finally had to relinquish any mention of the "voluntary basis" in the key part of the text dealing with notification of manoeuvres and only the preamble made mention of it. In contrast, the beginning of the text uses the words "they will notify", which underlines clearly the compulsory nature of the measure. Finally, although the Soviets tried to limit the definition of CBMS to notifications of large-scale manoeuvres within a limited zone of their territory, they eventually agreed that provisions for the invitation of observers, notification of smaller scale manoeuvres and of movements should also form part of the CBMs. The geographical limitation of notification was identified as a clear exception, the principle being that notification applied to the whole of European territory.

The outcome of the CSCE could not, therefore, be construed as a Soviet victory, a perception that was widely held at the time. The Final Act of Helsinki, and especially the CBM document, provided considerable gains for the West. In his final report, the Head of the Canadian Delegation stated:

In spirit and outlook, as well as in balance of content and in form of expression, [the Final Act] is distinctly Western-type text. One of the mysteries of the CSCE is how and why the Soviets allowed themselves to lose control of areas they feared, letting the West and Neutrals put forward extensive demands, and contenting themselves with inserting safeguards rather than attempting to recast the whole exercise in the spirit and terminology of State control. This was a bad and very profound error on their part, but its full implications did not/not become apparent to Eastern bureaucracies until fairly late in the game – too late, in fact, to change the basic nature of what was going to emerge from Geneva. The excruciatingly tiresome CSCE negotiations may have taught the Soviets something about Western solidarity and about the strength of Western determination to impart a meaningful human dimension to *détente*.

In my view, the Conference as a process has been at least as important as the convoluted text it has produced, and probably even more important than the striking symbolism of the Helsinki summit. For almost three years it has been possible to remind the Russians day by day at formal and informal meetings, over lunch and at working dinners, that their view of the world of Europe is becoming outdated and that many aspects of their increasing interaction with countries having different systems are simply not/not tolerable any longer. I may be wrong, but I suspect that it was this very process, this stream of telegrams going back to Moscow from Geneva that ultimately got under their skin and convinced them ultimately that they were paying too high a price for too little. I suspect the Russians left Geneva feeling disappointed, even cheated, and it was only their sense of urgency (for other reasons) to achieve a summit meeting that made the final compromises palatable.[38]

It would be wrong, however, to judge Helsinki strictly in terms of gains and losses. For all the participants, the CSCE had been first and foremost a learning process, and the Final Act constituted no more than a provisional ratification of the first stage of the process.

In this regard, the Western Europeans had learned two important lessons:

- Western unity was an essential asset *vis-à-vis* the East;
- this unity did not preclude expression of individual differences as long as the Western bloc was in agreement on a set of common denominators.

From the perspective of the Soviet Union and the East in general, the outcome was not totally negative. The CSCE, together with the agreements that preceded it, recognized *de facto* the existence of post-war realities and the impossibility of changing them through the use of force. Moreover, the CSCE replaced the politico-military gesticulations of the Cold War with a modest but productive dialogue that was no longer totally controlled on the Western side by the United States. For the Soviets, therefore, Helsinki symbolized some important gains and a diplomatic overture to Western Europe that remained to be exploited.

In sum, for both sides, but especially for the West, the value of the CSCE lay in the future, and the first test of renewed hope was to take place in Belgrade two years later.

HOPES FADE IN BELGRADE

The preparatory talks of the Belgrade Conference opened on 15 June 1977. At first sight they promised a favourable political and diplomatic climate. The Democrats, who formed the new administration in the United States, favoured arms control and *détente*, and it was expected that they would demonstrate initiative and flexibility in the CSCE. In addition, and most importantly, two years of experience showed that, in the particular field of CBMs, both the West and the East had respected the letter, if not the spirit, of the Final Act of Helsinki. The NATO countries in particular had interpreted and applied the Helsinki provisions in a very liberal fashion. In some 13 cases they had provided prior notification of manoeuvres involving over 25,000 troops, and on several occasions had advanced the time-frame for notification from 21 days to 24 or even 34 days. The NATO countries had also taken pains to transmit as much information as possible, and had increased the content of notifications to include the designations and objectives of the manoeuvres, the participating countries, as well as the type and size of units, the duration of manoeuvres and, where applicable, their relationship with other allied manoeuvres. In addition, the allies had given prior notification of 13 smaller scale manoeuvres (10,000 to 25,000 troops), and Norway had given notification of two manoeuvres involving only 8,000 troops. Finally, the West had invited representatives of the CSCE Group of 35 to observe 9 of the 13 large scale manoeuvres and 6 of the 15 smaller scale manoeuvres.

In most cases, these invitations were extended to all the participants in the CSCE. The allies did their utmost to facilitate the work of the observers by providing them with all the necessary means – briefings, guides, observation posts, contacts with government officials and military personnel, and permission to use binoculars and cameras. The NNA had applied the Helsinki provisions in the same spirit. Switzerland provided notification of one large scale manoeuvre and four other countries provided notifications on smaller exercises involving between 8,000 and 24,000 troops (Yugoslavia 2, Sweden 2, Spain 1, and Austria 1). Observers were treated according to the same criteria as those respected by NATO.

As for the Warsaw Pact countries, the area of CBMS was one of the few in which their performance could be judged satisfactory. In 9 instances they had provided notification of all large scale manoeuvres exceeding a threshold of 25,000 personnel, and in September 1978, the USSR even went so far as to provide notification of a manoeuvre in the Caucasus, an area which was not covered by the Final Act. When providing notification of these manoeuvres, the Warsaw Pact countries strictly respected the parameters established in Helsinki. In April of 1976, and again in September of the same year, Hungary even gave notice of two smaller scale manoeuvres involving between 10,000 and 15,000 troops, but failed to respect the deadlines established for larger scale manoeuvres. As for observers, the Warsaw Pact invited certain CSCE countries to observe five of their nine large scale manoeuvres. However, between 1975 and 1977 these invitations were limited to a small number of countries neighbouring the USSR which were close to the location where the manoeuvres were conducted. In passing, it should be noted that the invited observers did not enjoy the same treatment as that accorded by the West to Eastern observers. In many cases, observation of manoeuvres was very limited, the briefings were minimal and the freedom of movement restricted. As well, the Eastern countries systematically declined Western invitations until June 1977. This likely reflected the desire of the East not to accord any kind of legitimacy to NATO military activities, which featured among the favourite targets of Soviet propaganda. The situation progressively improved, however, once the preparatory talks started in Belgrade.

Overall, the implementation of CBMS showed that the pertinent provisions of the Final Act of Helsinki could be respected without difficulty, and that these measures permitted some progress, even without modification of the terms of the Helsinki agreement.

In light of these most encouraging elements, many countries – including Canada – tried to define constructive strategies in anticipation of the main meeting of the CSCE which was scheduled to begin in the fall of 1977 in the Yugoslavian capital. For Canada in particular: "the objective of Belgrade should be to advance the practical implementation of the provisions in the Final Act where deficiencies and shortcomings can be identified, without attempting to enlarge the scope of the Final Act itself which is, in any case, beyond the mandate given to the Belgrade meeting".[39]

In order to achieve this end, Canadian diplomats considered that even if it were necessary to criticize the way in which some countries had applied the Helsinki agreement, "[they] should couch [their] interventions in objective and dispassionate terms and seek to contribute to the maintenance of an atmosphere in which the dialogue [could] be conducted without polemic or confrontation".[40]

In this spirit, Canada had already prepared several thematic proposals within the Atlantic Alliance, one of which was on CBMs and their possible development. This particular proposal stressed that the CSCE participants could contribute to promoting the objectives of the CBMs if they adopted a more liberal attitude when putting them into practice. It was specifically suggested that nations:

- give notification of smaller scale manoeuvres involving less than 25,000 personnel;
- provide more than 21 days notification;
- increase the content of their notifications;
- improve the treatment of invited observers;
- give notification of military movements associated with manoeuvres;
- take account of CBM objectives while conducting their various military activities;
- develop closer contacts through exchange of military personnel.

These various measures could, moreover, be adopted in the form of a general agreement to improve the implementation of the provisions of the Final Act of Helsinki, or through a formal commitment by both parties.[41] Unfortunately, the Canadian initiative, modest as it was, fell flat in an atmosphere that was both sceptical and confused. The preparatory talks had, in fact, been marked with several important events which determined how the Belgrade talks would unfold.

On the Eastern side, the Soviets seemed to adopt an extremely defensive position, probably because of their painful experiences in Helsinki and Geneva. In addition, in light of the whimsical initiatives of President Carter on the SALT issue, the Kremlin was worried about the new orientation of U.S. policy on arms control. As Tom Delworth notes:

[The] line taken by the Warsaw Pact Delegations can be seen as the product of Soviet anxieties on two scores: a) fears that open-ended non-stop meeting might confront them with same difficulties as had Geneva phase with comparably unpleasant results; b) uncertainty as to how USA, under Carter, would approach main Belgrade meeting. Warsaw Pact strategy throughout preparatory meeting could be described as containment designed to limit duration and scope of activity of main meeting to greatest extent possible in order to avoid potential threats to Soviet interests and Soviet concept of *détente*.[42]

On the Western side, the U.S. Delegation to Belgrade had also opted for prudence, but for different reasons. The State Department feared the untimely interventions of Congress and the White House and, for this reason, refrained from taking the lead in the NATO preparatory work. As well, contrary to their attitudes in Helsinki and Geneva, the NNA and the nine EEC members seemed to wish to affirm their political autonomy, and it was, therefore, to be expected that the differences in the Western group would be more marked than in the past.

For all these reasons, the diplomatic situation in the summer of 1977 could be described as "fluid and uncertain", which explains "the absence of any coherent collective view of broad Western objectives for main Belgrade meeting [which] inevitably added to intrinsic difficulties in achieving agreement on pursuing objectives and tactics for preparatory conference".[43]

The members of the Atlantic Alliance were still able to reach agreement on a two-stage strategy which would lay emphasis on the implementation of the Helsinki measures and defer consideration of new proposals until later, even though such proposals were extremely modest.

When the Belgrade Conference opened in the fall of 1977 the positions of the various groups were as follows: NATO, in a proposal presented by Canada, Netherlands, Norway and the United Kingdom (CSCE/BM/11) suggested:

• prior notification of manoeuvres of lesser scale (10,000 to 25,000 personnel);

- extension of timeframe for prior notification to 30 days;
- improvement of the treatment of observers; and chiefly,
- prior notification of military movements in excess of 25,000 personnel "if they move for 30 consecutive days and traverse a distance of over 200 kilometres as the crow flies from the point of departure of the movement".

The NNA adopted a posture very close to that of NATO, although less clear, concerning movements of lesser scale. The Swiss were firmly opposed to lowering the threshold for notification below 18,000 personnel and consequently the NNA were obliged to adopt a complex formula which called for notification of small, combined manoeuvres in cases where the total troop complement exceeded 25,000 personnel. The NNA also suggested that notification should be given in respect of naval manoeuvres and that military budgets should be given greater visibility (CSCE/BM/6, 24 October 1977).

The Soviet proposal (CSCE/BM/5, 24 October 1977) was like a "cold shower" to those who still espoused any hope that the Belgrade Conference would make even modest progress in the area of CBMS. In its Action Plan to consolidate military *détente* in Europe, the USSR suggested that the CSCE participants conclude a Treaty on No First Use of Nuclear Weapons (NOFUN) and also commit not to enlarge the military alliances. Into the bargain, the Soviet Union proposed to renounce manoeuvres of over 50,000 military personnel and to extend the application of CBMS to nations bordering the Mediterranean. In the view of the Soviets, these proposals could be negotiated by the Group of 35 within the framework of "special consultations".

Of course, the first two elements of the proposal fell outside the sphere of jurisdiction of the Belgrade Conference and the two others posed thorny technical and political problems. The USSR did not, therefore, seem ready to negotiate seriously.

From the outset, the Belgrade Conference was doomed to be dominated by polemics, arguments and recriminations, particularly in the areas of human rights and CBMS: "The discussion on CBMS gave the impression of two separate Conferences taking place in the same room, one of the East Europeans speaking about *détente*, disarmament, the right to love and the other Delegations discussing CBMS".[44]

The period for reviewing the implementation of the Helsinki measures extended over eight sessions which were entirely dominated by the West. The NNA contributed very little to the discussions and the Eastern countries refused systematically to enter into debate. In all, there were five new proposals: the Western proposal (BM/11); the two NNA proposals (BM/6 and BM/18); the Romanian proposal (BM/s1);

and the Soviet proposal (BM/5). Although a potential basis for discussion existed, the Warsaw Pact countries could not be moved. They were unable to prevent discussion on the proposals, but maintained that only the Soviet proposal was worthy of discussion. Following the Christmas break, the Soviets declared peremptorily that no new proposal would be accepted and that it would be inadvisable to enter into real negotiations on the matter.

In view of this deadlock, discussions during the final phase of the Belgrade Conference focused on a proposal to convene a meeting of experts on CBMS. This last minute proposal was advanced by Sweden, Romania and Yugoslavia, but it was received indifferently by both the East and West, despite its relationship with the Soviet concept of "special consultations" on security issues.

The Belgrade Conference drew to a close on 9 March 1978 without any tangible results on the matter of CBMS. This missed opportunity did not, however, imply total failure, for it showed the CSCE participants that there was no alternative solution to the process entered into in Helsinki, even though it was unable to provide in the short term all the solutions that both sides had anticipated. Belgrade brought into sharp focus the limitations of dialogue between different political systems. The West had to abandon the idea of using the CSCE as a public stage for nailing the USSR to the wall, or as an instrument for effecting drastic changes to the Soviet social system. The USSR, in turn, could not expect to see a change in attitude by the West if it refused to accept constructive criticism and proposed only measures that were either unrealistic or devoid of any substance.

The lessons of Belgrade were learned only with difficulty, and it took six more years, until the last stages of the Madrid Conference, for attitudes to change and for the CSCE to resume a more normal course.

A NEW BID IN MADRID

At the close of the Belgrade Conference it was apparent to all participants that, although hostile confrontation had been tolerated during the meeting, the experience could not be repeated in Madrid without causing irreparable harm to the CSCE process. To avert this danger, both sides had to show initiative and plan properly for the Madrid Conference. On the Western side, preparations followed two approaches which gradually converged: one was inspired by a French initiative launched in 1978, while the other was pursued internally within NATO.

The French Initiative for a Conference on Disarmament in Europe (1977–1979)

Since the early 1960s, France had remained absent from the major debates on arms control and disarmament for very specific reasons pertaining mainly to a certain perception of national independence and a Gaullist hostility towards NATO and the United Nations. From the very beginning, France had categorically refused to participate in the MBFR negotiations, considering that the framework was too constraining and the perspectives too limited. In 1977, the doctrinal rigidity of hard and fast Gaullism gave way to a more flexible concept of European security. This change came about both through the evolution of mentalities in the political elite and through an increased awareness of the risks engendered by an "empty chair" policy. Indeed, in the event that agreement was reached on arms limitations in Europe – or elsewhere – France's security could be threatened even without her participation in the debate. Besides, the disarmament negotiations provided a legitimate diplomatic forum in which France could exert influence and defend her interests.

In the summer of 1977, a communiqué was issued by the French Council of Ministers announcing, therefore, that the French Government "would give careful thought to the issue of disarmament and would present an overall plan at the appropriate time".[45] The plan was released in January 1978 and presented to the UN Special Session on Disarmament on 25 May 1978. France proposed that "a conference be convened – a Conference on Disarmament in Europe (CDE) – [which became the Conference on Confidence and Security Building Measures and Disarmament in Europe (CCSBMDE)] to which all European countries as well as the United States and Canada would be invited".[46] These new negotiations would be a follow-up to the CSCE, but in a different framework, since their scope would extend beyond the confines of the Final Act of Helsinki. The negotiations would be aimed at improving the security of the whole European continent from "the Atlantic to the Urals" (and not just for a limited area as considered in the MBFR or envisaged in the Final Act of Helsinki). The negotiations would encompass two stages:

• adoption of confidence-building measures (CBMs);[47]
• institution of a process of conventional disarmament involving land forces but excluding nuclear weapons and naval forces.

Immediately following the presentation of the proposal, France entered into bilateral consultations with the FRG and with the USSR which led to the Franco-Soviet declaration of 28 April 1979. In parallel, multilateral consultations were held to exchange views with the nine EEC countries and the fifteen NATO countries. Despite the fact that there was considerable interest in the French proposal, a year passed without the appearance of a consensus to convene the CDE. In the West, Canada, the United Kingdom and the United States had serious reservations for fear that the CDE would interfere with the MBFR and the CSCE, and saw no need to create a new forum for disarmament negotiations.

The Eastern European countries, including the Soviet Union, remained very reticent on the issue of CBMS, and favoured the extremely abstract idea of "military *détente*". They showed no interest in confidence-building measures except insofar as they could incorporate into them "declaratory" proposals which were inherited from the old idea of establishing a "collective security system" in Europe (non-expansion of alliances, non-aggression pact, treaty on no first use of military force). In addition, they refused to accept the idea of a zone extending to the Urals since they viewed it as "asymmetric".

The NNA countries wanted the CDE to cover nuclear weapons as well as naval forces, but they were also concerned about the impact of the proposed CDE on the CSCE. Overall, the French proposal was accorded a rather lukewarm reception. Nevertheless, whether by design or by accident, the French proposal came one year before a major Soviet initiative, and it therefore commanded considerable political importance.

On 16 May 1979, during the Warsaw Pact Meeting of Foreign Ministers in Budapest, the East proposed a Pan-European Conference on Military *Détente*. Its content was very different from that of the CDE, and it introduced no new ideas, for it was implicitly linked to the Belgrade "platform" (BM/5), the 23 November 1978 declaration of the Warsaw Pact Political Consultative Committee and Brezhnev's speech of 2 March 1979. However, through skilful wording, which resembled the language of the Franco-Soviet program, the "new" Soviet plan appeared to reflect a certain similarity with the French idea on the need for a forum of 35 to discuss security and develop confidence.

In actual fact, the purpose of the Conference proposed by the East was to create an alternative solution to the CSCE. For the Soviets, the CSCE had become the Way of the Cross and they sought to pursue European "*détente*" in a more favourable context. In all likelihood, the Soviet aim was to circumvent the French proposal; the Soviets would be content to accept CBMS that were "inoffensive", amongst which were the declaratory measures discussed previously. It should be stressed, however, that many of the CBMS mentioned in the Budapest Communiqué – prior notification of aerial and naval movements and manoeuvres, extension of CBMS to cover the Mediterranean region, and so on – were drawn from former proposals made by the NNA and were, therefore, clearly included as bait.

In July 1979, the Soviets proposed that a preparatory meeting be held to establish the conditions of a mandate, which would be adopted in Madrid, for a Conference to be held later. This, of course, required that the results of the preparatory meeting had to be available prior to the opening of the Madrid Conference which, therefore, put "pressure" on the work at the preparatory meeting.

In parallel, some Western and NNA nations indicated their desire to achieve concrete progress on CBMS at the Madrid Conference itself. This was the context in which the French, in the early fall of 1979, proposed their approach through a memorandum detailing the first phase of the CDE.

France was especially interested in a Conference on Disarmament in Europe since it allowed her to place the CBM issue in a political context. Up to that time, the Soviets had always countered Western demands for CBMS by claiming that the proposed measures were technical and too limited, and that they would contribute little to *détente* and disarmament. The CDE would reverse the situation by integrating confidence-building measures into the disarmament process during the first phase. The French memorandum also stressed that the CDE would provide the West with the opportunity:

- to pursue a program of progressive implementation of concrete measures, as opposed to declaratory measures;
- to defer consideration of the Eastern proposals until after the Madrid Conference, subject to prior implementation of Western counter-proposals;
- to obtain from the East, in return for such Western consideration, a reformulation of the declaratory measures in such a way that they would not appear as a political instrument to serve the *status quo*, but rather as an explicit recognition of progress in *détente*, resulting from the satisfactory implementation of the program.

In other words, as the Eastern countries were trying to put the West on the defensive, the onus would be on them to demonstrate good faith in the area of security and disarmament.[48]

In addition, the French judged it essential to retain the central role played by the CSCE in promoting *détente* in Europe *in all its aspects*. In this regard, while remaining autonomous, the CDE would be placed *under the aegis of the* CSCE. The advantages of such an arrangement would be as follows:

1   the link with the CSCE would allow the concept of *détente* to retain its integrity as symbolized by the equivalence of its three "baskets", namely security, economic cooperation and human rights. The CDE would thus remain as one of the major elements of the CSCE, and progress in disarmament would always be linked to progress in the other two areas. Meetings of the kind held in Madrid would act as "anchoring points" for the CDE, and the Group of 35 would be able to sanction the results obtained by the CDE in relation to progress achieved in the other two "baskets";

2   the CSCE-CDE link would also preserve the benefits of the CSCE, particularly the principle of discussion amongst 35 nations, the recognized role of the NNA, the idea of a homogeneous area covering the whole geographical extent of European territory and, lastly, tacit approval on the desired nature of a Conference of the Belgrade or Madrid kind which would meet at regular intervals and provide "anchoring points" for the proposed process;[49]

3   by establishing the CDE as an *extension* of Madrid (that is, the CSCE) but *outside* the Conference proper, the West would be able to:
   • *obtain certain fundamental concessions from the Warsaw Pact* (enlargement of the zone, agreement on criteria for future CBMs, etc.), without even having to negotiate the confidence-building measures themselves, which would be addressed exclusively by the CDE; and, therefore,
   • *avoid the prospect of a compromise in Madrid which, because of the diverse opposing initiatives, would necessarily be predicated on the lowest common denominator*, a compromise under which confidence-building measures of limited scope, unrestrictive and applicable to a minimal geographic area would be exchanged for the declaratory measures proposed by the East; but also
   • *prevent the major part of the Madrid debate from becoming bogged down in considering a long series of* CBM *proposals for which there would likely be no counterpart in the other "baskets".*

Finally, still concerning principles, the French proposal stated that the transition to the second phase of the CDE (disarmament) would not be automatic but would depend on the results of the first phase and would be subject to approval by the 35 nations within the CSCE framework.

On the basis of these principles, France proposed that the West should restrict discussions in Madrid to negotiation of the mandate of the CDE which would include, of course, the linkage between the two Conferences, but also, and most importantly, the criteria that new CBMS should satisfy. Specifically, for the CDE measures to attain their goals, they should apply to the whole of Europe's territory without exception – from the Atlantic to the Urals – and should be militarily significant. They should, therefore:

- permit true knowledge of military situations and activities;
- concern those military activities deemed to be particularly threatening;
- not be limited to notification procedures, but also provide for restrictions, and indeed prohibitions of some military activities;
- be legally binding; and, finally
- be subject to adequate observation and verification measures.[50]

The detailed French plan thus offered many advantages, not the least of which was that it placed the Warsaw Pact in the position of petitioner. In the fall of 1979, the Warsaw Pact confirmed its interest in a Conference on Military *Détente*. In a speech delivered in East Berlin on 6 October, Brezhnev announced that the USSR was prepared to consider any suggestion which might lessen the degree of military confrontation in Europe and offered, at the same time, a few proposals of his own including a unilateral withdrawal of 20,000 Soviet troops from East Germany.[51]

The *Quai d'Orsay* expressed its satisfaction with the Soviet gesture on 7 November 1979. France continued to score points in the Western camp. The Group of Nine showed marked interest in the French proposal and, on 20 November 1979, the NATO Foreign Ministers issued a statement which stressed that:

the Nine support ... an approach aimed at adopting, in Madrid, a mandate specifying the conditions under which negotiations could start to establish common agreement on militarily significant CBMS which are verifiable and applicable to the whole of the European continent, and which, by contributing to the security of States, are likely to create the climate for a later process of arms limitations and reductions in the same geographic sphere.

The French proposal was also viewed favourably by other nations, including the NNA (Statement of the Ministerial Committee of the Council of Europe, Strasbourg, 22 November 1979). The United States was also interested, but had reservations about the second phase.[52] On

20 December, however, the United States accepted the communiqué issued in Brussels at the end of the ministerial session of the Atlantic Alliance. The communiqué was in favour of the principle of negotiating a mandate for the CDE, but specified that "this process should take account of the various aspects of the existing security situation as well as the negotiations in progress on other aspects of disarmament and arms limitations on the European continent".

The French proposal had made some headway. NATO's decision to modernize its deterrent force and the Soviet intervention in Afghanistan in December 1979 were but chance mishaps on the road to Madrid. NATO's preparatory work in 1979 had demonstrated that there was a fundamental convergence of strategy between France and the Atlantic Alliance – it happens once in a while. The Western camp started to prepare a common negotiating strategy of a detailed and long-term nature.

The Work of the Atlantic Alliance in Preparation for the Madrid Negotiations (1979–1980)

In the spring of 1979, the NATO nations had started to reflect on CBMs and how they should be developed for Madrid. As mentioned earlier, the Atlantic Alliance had realized that a new Belgrade would be unacceptable. Consequently, "some concrete results had to be achieved at Madrid lest the CSCE process lose its dynamism and political credibility".[53]

The first contributions to the NATO studies were, however, disappointing. For example, Canada proposed that a new type of CBM be introduced at Madrid concerning chemical weapons. Although the idea was original, it was nevertheless unrealistic in the prevailing circumstances.[54]

For its part, the United Kingdom provided a general survey of the CBMs discussed in various fora[55], and Norway suggested a simple rearrangement of the allied proposals at Belgrade (BM/11), with the addition of:

- prior notification of independent naval and aerial manoeuvres and movements;
- restriction of movements near borders;
- imposition of a ceiling on the size of manoeuvres.[56]

Finally, the Netherlands timidly suggested that notification of "large" aerial and naval manoeuvres might be considered (to satisfy the NNA) as well as the issue of a ceiling on the size of manoeuvres.[57]

After some nine months of futile attempts, the allies had to face facts: the "classical" CBMs had lost their appeal. As one informed observer noted:

As to the value of existing CBMs, I confess to some disappointment. No military movements have been notified; Eastern performance when hosting observers remains no better today than it was four years ago; the East has not given any meaningful notification of a manoeuvre below the 25,000 man threshold; efforts to "develop and enlarge" CBMs (as called for in the Final Act) at Belgrade were unsuccessful. The only measure being correctly implemented by the East therefore is that concerning the notification of major manoeuvres and even here the information provided is the bare minimum called for in the Final Act notwithstanding the review at Belgrade on this aspect and the much more forthcoming notices issued by the West. In fairness, though, I also acknowledge that without the Final Act there would not even be these few steps toward confidence building. Nevertheless, it is clear that it would be highly desirable to gain from the Soviets a firm commitment to fuller implementation. This leads to the following question: are there other prospects for the improvement of existing CBMs? As already discussed I do not believe that the prospects for negotiating improvements in any field at Madrid are good. It is also relevant to note in this regard that the recent WPO communiqué makes no mention of strengthening the existing CBM regime insofar as notifying ground force manoeuvres and exchanging observers are concerned. Their previous proposal at Belgrade was cast in the context of the special consultations to follow that meeting: the same is true for the proposals in the communiqué and indeed the Norwegian proposal is also linked to follow-up expert groups. It would seem therefore that a strengthening of the CBM regime will have to be considered as work to be undertaken outside the main meetings of the CSCE in some fashion or other.[58]

Despite their perceptible reticence, the allies recognized the advantages of the French proposal, and NATO progressively moved towards consensus on the CDE and its underlying principles.

In parallel, the French plan had opened another door by facilitating the development of a "package" of confidence-building measures to meet the criteria described above. The French memorandum of 12 September had already proposed a set of 16 measures which were grouped into four categories:

A   *Information Measures*
      A1:   development of services accorded to the military attachés;
      A2:   development of means of communication;

A3:   publication of annual programs of main military activities;

A4:   exchange of military information and data.

B   *Notification Measures*

B5:   notification of land/air manoeuvres;

B6:   notification of movements:

1   in constituted units;

2   of personnel;

3   of materiel;

B7:   notification of certain other military activities:

1   simultaneous small manoeuvres and combined exercises;

2   emergency drills;

B8:   notification of aerial exercises;

B9:   notification of mobilization exercises.

C   *Stabilization Measures*

C10:   annual limitation on number and duration of main military activities;

C11:   ceiling on land/air manoeuvres;

C12:   ceiling on simultaneous manoeuvres and combined exercises;

C13:   limitation on certain activities in certain zones;

C14:   prohibition of certain military activities.

D   *Observation and Verification Measures*

D15:   observation of notified military activities;

D16:   verification of limited or prohibited military activities.[59]

The French, not content with their innovative idea of the CDE, thus proposed, for the first time in the CSCE context, a structured and integrated conceptual framework for CBMs. On 25 September 1979, the Political Committee of NATO created an *Ad Hoc* Working Group on CBMs to study the French "package" and any other suggestions put forward by the allies. On 19 December 1979, after nine sessions of the *Ad Hoc* Working Group, the Military Committee of NATO was able to report on a final set of 25 proposed measures which comprised essentially a slightly modified French package together with five CBMs of Soviet inspiration: 1. prohibition on establishment of new military bases; 2. extension of CBMs to cover the Mediterranean; 3. Non-aggression Treaty; 4. non-expansion of alliances; and 5. freeze on military budgets.[60]

It was clear from the report that the allies rejected three kinds of measures, namely:

- notification of independent naval and aerial manoeuvres (measures 7, 8, 10 and 11);
- constraining measures including limitations and prohibitions (measures 14 to 18);
- measures of Soviet inspiration (measures 19 and 22 to 25).

In addition, the questions of verification and of notification of movements required more detailed study.[61]

NATO's work was thus well under way but, somewhat surprisingly, certain allies still dragged their feet – and particularly Canada. In March 1980, there was still criticism of the CDE concept, which showed that some Canadian officials had not really understood the situation. Specifically, there was concern about the absence of the nuclear dimension in the French plan, and it was criticized for having excluded the declaratory measures favoured by the Soviets. As well, there was fear that a CDE "separated" from the CSCE would "balkanize" *détente*, and there was regret that the French proposal excluded the "traditional" CBMs, namely those that were voluntary and limited.[62]

In short, Canada was obviously not abreast of things, as the remarks and suggestions made by the Delegation during March and April 1980 readily attest. The traditional CBMs from Helsinki had to be saved for fear of dropping the substance for the shadow.[63] Canada was not alone in defending this position, and it may be noted that Norway persisted until October 1980 in its desire to present, at Madrid even, a set of "neo-classical" CBMs.[64]

It was obvious that the introduction of a proposal on the CDE mandate in parallel with a proposal on a package of traditional CBMs would provide the East with an easy way out, thereby reducing the chances of success of the French plan.

Fortunately, the Canadian arguments were quickly cast aside, as was an attempt to introduce a distinction between compulsory CBMs and voluntary CBMs.[65] Finally, in July 1980, the Atlantic Alliance agreed on a conceptual approach to CBMs. The criteria for future measures to be developed by the CDE were then accepted. They were to be of a compulsory nature (but not necessarily legally binding), militarily significant and verifiable, and they would apply to the whole of the European continent. Their objectives were also clarified:

- it was essential that the CBMs should preserve the freedom of action of NATO, both in terms of training of its military forces and its capability to react to events which threatened allied security;
- CBMs had to promote greater openness, and prevent the East from keeping its military activities secret;

- they should promote stability and prevent the use of military force as a means of political intimidation;
- they should lead to the establishment of accepted standards for routine military activities;
- they should contribute to reducing the risk of surprise attack;
- they should facilitate decision-making in NATO in times of tension or crisis.

The *Ad Hoc* Working Group on CBMS concentrated on 11 measures which were grouped according to the four categories proposed in the French plan (see Appendix II of this Chapter). In this context, it should be noted that a new concept emerged during the preparatory debates for Madrid. When the allies were searching for a verifiable notification criterion to cover all military activities, they had developed the idea of Outside-of-Garrison (OOG) activities. This concept related to any military activity which took place outside the location where troops were usually based, if such activity involved:

- a number, X, of units (divisions);
- a number, Y, of troops;
- a quantity, Z, of heavy equipment (tanks, artillery and armoured infantry vehicles) under a single command.

The concept of Outside-of-Garrison activities held greater potential for discussion than the concepts of manoeuvres, exercises or movements, all of which posed considerable definitional problems. As well, the introduction of a divisional threshold increased significantly the possibilities for detecting any infraction of a notification agreement. As noted in one report:

Existing intelligence sources available to the Alliance including National Technical Means, permit the rapid identification of units and formations deploying out of garrison. Potential violations of a threshold expressed in terms of combat units or divisions could therefore be identified rapidly and unambiguously and appropriate overt verification procedures set in hand. The same is not true of a numerical threshold, since, in general, it takes longer to obtain intelligence estimates of numbers of troops involved in a particular deployment. Such estimates are, in any event, less precise than the identification of units and formations. This point has recently been well illustrated by Alliance intelligence information on the progress of the Soviet unilateral withdrawals from the GDR, on the possible restructuring of Soviet divisions ... and on the monitoring of Soviet forces in connection with Afghanistan. In every case, the identification of formations and units has been possible earlier and with greater precision than any estimation of the number of personnel involved. This is particularly true for forces located in Eastern Europe, where organization and garrison locations of specific units are, in general, well known to the Alliance intelligence community. National Technical Means will give a rapid indication of the locations from which units are deploying and their identity can therefore be established almost immediately. Hence it is difficult to envisage a situation in which the Alliance was not able to establish whether a divisional threshold has been violated, and, in many cases, preparations by particular units would be detected in advance of any deployment.[66]

The work of the Atlantic Alliance progressed at a high pace and on 9 December 1980 the final package of future CBMs for the CDE was approved by the North Atlantic Council. The most significant change made to the set of measures envisaged in the summer of 1980 was the complete suppression of constraining or limiting measures. The stabilization measures included notification and exchange of annual programs of notifiable activities (see Appendix III of this Chapter). The confidence measures adopted were, therefore, fewer in number (seven in all) and more modest than at the start, but they constituted no less a coherent and articulated set based on in-depth technical and political analysis. Evidently, all the details were not settled but, in contrast to the situation that had prevailed in Helsinki and Belgrade, a considerable amount of collective work had been accomplished and consensus had been reached on Western objectives and strategies for the Madrid Conference.

The Madrid Conference and the CDE Mandate

The Madrid Conference opened on 11 November 1980. Despite the positive nature – from a Western perspective – of all the elements discussed above, negotiations took place in a very unfavourable political climate. The invasion of Afghanistan, the missiles-in-Europe debate, the events in Poland and the arrival at the White House of an openly anti-Soviet President all served to poison the atmosphere. For the diplomats facing each other, Madrid quickly became a Calvary. As J. Sizoo and T. Jurrjens noted:

The personal feelings of relief experienced by more than one Madrid diplomat when the final consensus was reached deserve every sympathy. What had seemed to be a never ending litany could at last be rounded off with an "Amen" ... but for the future, they hoped that never again would they have to go through such an experience: MADRID, NEVER AGAIN![67]

Technically speaking, the Madrid Conference lasted for 33 months. It consisted of eight negotiating sessions and was suspended on two occasions for several months (three months in July 1981 and eight months in March 1982). It was the longest CSCE meeting to date, and the most stormy. Essentially, the Madrid Conference can be segregated into two phases, the first covering the period from November 1980 to December 1981, and the second from November 1982 until the close of the Conference. In other words, negotiations really took place during two work periods of six to eight months each, excluding the usual Conference breaks. Attention will be focused, therefore, on these two main periods of work.

The Middle of the Road (November 1980 – December 1981).   The preparatory meeting which took place between 8 September and 10 November 1980 was marked with stormy debate, and the first session of the Madrid Conference was devoted almost entirely to reviewing the implementation of the Final Act of Helsinki. Generally, the Soviets and the Eastern countries submitted to stinging charges made not only by the West but also by the NNA. The NNA nations deplored the obstructive attitude of the USSR during the preparatory meeting and had drawn closer to the views of the West, to the point where one could speak about the Group of 28 within the Group of 35. These criticisms essentially concerned Afghanistan and the issue of human rights. As for the military aspects of security, an assessment of the practice followed since Belgrade in applying the CBMs of the Final Act of Helsinki provided the West with the opportunity:

- to develop the thesis that traditional or "classical" CBMs had no military significance;
- to convince the NNA, who were the harshest critics of the practice followed by the East in applying CBMs, that the Helsinki CBMs were essentially inadequate;
- to place the Eastern countries on the defensive, for they had no argument for refusing passage of the new types of measure.[68]

From December onwards, however, the new proposals on CBMs and on the CDE mandate took the limelight. Nine proposals were tabled in rapid succession:

- CSCE/RM/6 (8 December 1980), Poland, *in favour of a Conference on Military Détente and Disarmament in Europe* (CMDDE);
- CSCE/RM/7 (9 December 1980), France, *in favour of the CDE*;

- CSCE/RM/17 (11 December 1980), Yugoslavia, *concerning the promotion of peace and security in the Mediterranean region*;
- CSCE/RM/18 (11 December 1980), Yugoslavia, *promoting the process of détente*;
- CSCE/RM/21 (12 December 1980), NNA, *concerning CBMs*;
- CSCE/RM/27 (12 December 1980), Yugoslavia, *in favour of the CDE*;
- CSCE/RM/31 (15 December 1980), Romania, *in favour of a Conference on CBMs and Disarmament in Europe*;
- CSCE/RM/33 (15 December 1980), Romania, *concerning CBMs*;
- CSCE/RM/34 (15 December 1980), Sweden, *in favour of the CDE*.

Thus, of the nine proposals, five concerned a future Conference on Disarmament in Europe, two concerned the development of confidence-building measures and the remaining two concerned related aspects (peace and security in the Mediterranean and the process of *détente*). Discussion immediately focused on the CDE – its purpose, mandate and its relationship with the CSCE.

All the proposals were consistent on one point – the CDE should be a phased process of negotiation which should concentrate first on the development of CBMs and then on conventional weapons reductions. But the consensus stopped there (see Table 16). For instance, the Warsaw Pact (RM/16) proposed: that the CDE should negotiate relatively simple political and legal measures in addition to the CBMs;[69] that the 35 nations in Madrid should simply reach agreement on the principle of the CDE; that the mandate of the CDE should be decided later, and there was no question of accepting the preliminary conditions at Madrid. Moreover, according to the East, the linkage between the CDE and the CSCE should not be spelled out and the CDE "should not compromise the success of negotiations taking place in other fora".[70]

France (RM/7) proposed: that the CDE should not consider political measures or nuclear weapons; that the precise mandate of the CDE (CBM criteria and area of application) should be determined at Madrid, and the CDE should only move to the reductions phase once the results of the first phase had been approved by the CSCE; and that a tight linkage be maintained between the CDE and the CSCE.

Yugoslavia (RM/27) proposed: that the CDE should deal with nuclear weapons and its precise mandate should be defined at the preparatory meeting; that the linkage between the CDE and the CSCE should be guaranteed, and that the CDE should be allowed to provide input to other fora on disarmament.

Romania (RM/31) proposed: that nuclear matters and political measures should also be discussed by the CDE; that the CDE should not pass to the reductions phase before the results of the first phase had been studied (although it was not specified whether the CDE mandate should be negotiated at Madrid); that the CSCE should examine the results of the first phase of the CDE; that there should be a linkage between the CDE and the CSCE, and that the participants of the CDE should be informed of progress in other negotiations which were of interest to all parties.[71]

Finally, Sweden proposed: that the CDE should deal with issues of nuclear weapons; that its mandate should be agreed in Madrid and that the CBM criteria and the area of application should be specified; that the link between the CDE and the CSCE should be deemed essential, and that the participants of the CDE should be informed of progress in the work of other relevant negotiations.

The situation at the end of the first session at Madrid was thus:

- the Western proposal (RM/7) had been tabled and it had received explicit support from NATO (with the exception of Norway, which clung to the idea of developing traditional CBMs, but this did not pose a major problem);
- the positions of NNA, and particularly Sweden, were very close to that of the Atlantic Alliance, but the NNA appeared to be divided between those who were pro-CDE (Switzerland and Austria) and those who were not (Finland, Yugoslavia and Sweden), although the latter countries had already indicated avenues of compromise (deferment of the nuclear debate; preparatory meeting to decide upon the mandate of the CDE; and, development of traditional CBMs at Madrid);
- for the Warsaw Pact, the difficulties had been clarified: the nuclear problem had receded, but the Eastern countries all declared that the enlarged zone was unacceptable and, moreover, they rejected the mandatory and verifiable nature of the measures).

In general, other difficulties stood out:

- other proposals of a declaratory nature (Poland and Romania);
- the question of the transition from the first to the second phase of the CDE and the CDE-CSCE linkage;
- the idea of adopting, in Madrid, "transitional" measures between the CBMs of the Final Act of Helsinki and the CBMs of the CDE (Norway, Sweden, Austria, Yugoslavia and Romania), which was not conducive to the process of securing a precise mandate for the CDE in Madrid.[72]

Obviously, the first session already signalled that debate would focus on a few key issues in connection with the parameters of the

CDE mandate. Following the resumption of work and the examination of the various proposals – between 27 January and 11 February 1981 – the situation quickly clarified.

On 16 February, the new U.S. Administration accorded "full and entire support" for the French proposal (RM/7), and the firmness of this support ended Soviet attempts to split up support among both the West and the NNA nations. As a result, the NNA nations, which were worried about the rigidity of the Soviet position, moved closer to the French position on three essential points:

- there should be a linkage between the CDE and the CSCE, and the CDE mandate should be decided in Madrid;
- the transition from the first phase of the CDE to the second disarmament phase should not be automatic;
- the mandate for the first phase should be explicit.

Agreement between NATO and the NNA was thus achieved, and the French proposal acquired factual pre-eminence in the short span of three months. Moreover, the NNA compromise proposals lost any meaning, and the NNA proposals on classical CBMs were eclipsed.

On 23 February, the USSR made an important first concession. Brezhnev announced before the 26th Congress of the CPSU that the Warsaw Pact was ready to extend significantly the area of application of CBMs to all of the European part of the USSR, on condition that the area be enlarged in a corresponding manner by the Western nations. The Soviets thus gave up the special consideration that they had been accorded at Helsinki. But for all that, they refused to recognize the equality between all European States, since they demanded a "compensation" from the West even though coverage of all European territory had already been conceded.

One was left to speculate on what the expected compensation might be. The possibilities included:

- North American territory (the United States and Canada), which seemed unlikely; or
- the waters and airspace adjoining Europe (the Atlantic, the North Sea and the Mediterranean), which would have given the Soviets the right to monitor all the activities of U.S. forces deployed in Europe and around its periphery, including those of U.S. naval forces and the Rapid Deployment Force.

But the Soviets remained vague when asked to clarify this point. On the other hand, they indicated on 3 March that two of the Western criteria for CBMS – specifically, that CBMS should be verifiable and compulsory – might be accepted or at least studied. Then, bowing to pressure from the NNA and the West, the Eastern nations accepted the wording on the future CDE to the effect that it would constitute "a substantial and integral part of the CSCE process". The link with the CSCE was thus established.

In addition, there was progress in drafting the terms of the CDE:

• a near-final wording was adopted on the objectives of the first phase;
• the problem of "transitional measures" raised by the Yugoslavs was resolved by giving the new name "Confidence- and Security-Building Measures" (CSBMS) to the confidence measures of the future CDE.

Finally, the question of a mechanism for transition from the first to the second phase was addressed on 19 March, and the East recognized for the first time:

• the role that the next meeting, of the kind held in Madrid, would have to play in defining the linkage between the CDE and the CSCE;
• the need to take into account other negotiations affecting Europe in the disarmament field before committing to the second phase.

Despite the difficulties, the work had progressed considerably, and the NNA tabled a final draft document on 31 March. On the question of security, it included:

• a draft mandate for the Conference on CBMS and Disarmament in Europe, which eclipsed the original proposals of Yugoslavia and Sweden (RM/27 and RM/34);
• two proposals on traditional CBMS which replaced the eight measures proposed in RM/21.

Overall, the NNA proposal was favourable to the Western position, particularly concerning the area of application of the CBMS. As well, there was an ingenious formula for transition from the first to the second phase. To circumvent U.S. prejudice against a firm commitment to disarm, the NNA proposed that the second phase be deferred indefinitely since the decision to pass to a second phase would be taken at "one" meeting in the CSCE series and not necessarily at the meeting immediately following the one in Madrid. Lastly, the question of holding a preparatory meeting for the CDE would depend on

approval of its mandate, and this essentially constituted a renunciation by some NNA nations (Yugoslavia, amongst others) of their dangerous compromise suggestion.

The positions of the West Europeans were clarified and firmed
up, but the Soviets remained inflexible on the issue of an enlarged
zone. In addition, they demanded a precise definition of the objectives of the second phase – which obviously was too sensitive an issue
to be discussed at Madrid – and they insisted on an "escape clause"
in respect of the verifiable and compulsory nature of the CBMs.

Due to lack of progress on these points, negotiations at the third
session – from May to July – focused on the issue of transition
between the two phases. After many fruitless attempts to resolve the
issue, it was finally settled on 13 July to the satisfaction of the West
based on the formula proposed by the NNA.

On 28 July 1981, the Madrid Conference was interrupted at
the suggestion of the Swiss for a period of three months, until
27 October. On that date, the main elements of the CDE mandate
that had been agreed upon were:

- the title of the Conference, namely the CCSBMDE in Stockholm;
- its relationship with the CSCE;
- the content of the first phase;
- the three criteria other than that pertaining to the area of application itself, specifically verification, political commitment and military significance (the problem of the escape clause, however, still
  remained);
- the transition from the first to the second phase, conditional upon
  three factors: the decision to be taken at a later meeting of the
  CSCE, the results of the first phase and consideration of progress
  in other negotiations.

In addition, the subsisting difficulties were clearly identified. They
concerned the zone of application and the "escape clause" through
which the East sought to circumvent the other criteria. The question
of the zone itself was the most important point, and the positions of
the East and the West remained hard and fast:

- the Americans had proposed that the CBMs would apply first of all
  to the European continent, but would also apply to its adjoining
  waters and airspace when the forces operating there formed an
  integral part of notifiable activities on the continent (functional
  definition of the enlarged zone);

- the Soviets had proposed, on 20 July, that the zone should include all of Europe with its adjoining waters and airspace to a corresponding extent, as well as the territories of non-European States participating in activities covered by the measures (geographical definition of the enlarged zone, with compensatory clause). In addition, the Soviets held that the provisions should be developed at the CDE on a reciprocal and balanced basis, taking into account the commitments undertaken in conformity with the Final Act of Helsinki.

Despite a highly-charged political climate – the Polish crisis was strongly in evidence – the negotiations progressed remarkably well. It should be mentioned also that the results achieved in the other "baskets" alone rendered the overall accomplishment at Madrid superior to that at Belgrade: about two-thirds of all the proposals in the other "baskets" were incorporated into a provisional agreement at the end of this third session.

Work resumed in October 1981, but the results did not however meet the expectations that were engendered by previous success. Placed on the defensive by the Western and NNA nations, which demanded concessions in respect of the area of application, the Soviets returned to the most rigid of positions and referred back to the 250 kilometre border zone which, according to them, constituted the "political and strategic balance" established once and for all in Helsinki. In addition, the compensations that they demanded were to include U.S. military forces deployed throughout Europe, their bases, and their armaments, including nuclear weapons and delivery vehicles.

In light of such a clearly unacceptable position, the Western and NNA nations re-doubled their efforts to reach an agreement, if only to avoid carrying the responsibility for a deadlock. The Finns, in particular, with the support of most Western nations, tried to formulate a compromise concerning the zone, but their attempt ended in failure. The NNA met in Zurich on 5 and 6 December to develop a procedural formula which provided for:

- adoption of a final compromise document for the non-military aspects of the negotiations;
- a decision to convene the CDE based on elements already agreed upon;
- a preparatory meeting of the CSCE, of six weeks' duration, to settle contentious points;

• a resumption of the debate at the following CSCE meeting in the event that the preparatory meeting ended in failure.

This formula was rejected immediately by the Western nations which refused to consent to the CDE until its mandate was precisely determined. In order to demonstrate their magnanimity, the Soviets amended, on 8 December, the definition of the zone that they had proposed on 20 July, and suppressed the phrase concerning the inclusion of North American territory. But the withdrawal of this demand, which no one had taken seriously anyway, was not considered as a concession. The Soviets continued to claim "geographical compensation" for the inclusion of their territory, and insisted that the independent aerial and maritime activities which occurred in this additional zone be the subject of future CBMs. This contravened not only maritime law (freedom of movement on the high seas) but also the principle of equality of States in the framework of the CSCE. It was in this very difficult context that the Austro-Swiss draft of the final document was presented, in the wings, on 9 December. Within a few days it won the support of the NNA. The draft proposed a formula for the zone which was the most skilful up to that time. The second paragraph drew on the Western formula concerning the functional concept of adjoining areas, but the first paragraph, in compensation, adopted a Soviet formulation: "on the basis of equality of rights, equal security and respective obligations of all the participating States of the CSCE concerning CSBMs and disarmament in Europe, of balance and reciprocity, these CSBMs will cover ...".

Encouraged by the initial Soviet reaction, the NNA and NATO decided to adopt a positive attitude towards this initiative. On 16 December, following discussion of the proposal, the amended draft (RM/39) was tabled officially in Madrid under the sponsorship of the NNA.

An important step on the path towards an overall solution had thus been taken, even though the draft RM/39 was not as clear as the 9 December document. Concerning the CDE, the paragraph on the functional approach had been modified under pressure from the Soviets. It stated that the activities to be included in the adjoining areas should "constitute a part of the activities in Europe for which States decide to provide notification".[73] In other words, the activities notifiable in the areas adjoining Europe would only be defined at the CDE itself. In addition, in the first paragraph (see above), the words "balance and reciprocity" were placed before – and not after – "in Europe", in order to avoid any new demands for "compensation".

Negotiation on these various points was scheduled to take place after Christmas in an attempt to reach overall agreement. But the Polish crisis, which erupted on 13 December, had a crushing impact on the problem. From 18 December onwards, and again at the reopening of the fifth session in February 1982, Poland essentially became the focus of attention. No negotiations took place during this period and, on 12 March 1982, the Madrid Conference was adjourned until 9 November.

The Final Rounds. Despite the international situation, which remained of concern during the summer and fall of 1982, negotiations resumed in November in a climate of cautious optimism. Although the CSCE had afforded the West with a choice platform for flaying the socialist countries on the occasion of the Polish crisis, the pursuit of polemics could only lead to, at best, an insignificant final document, similar to that of Belgrade. Clearly, the technical advances that had been made in the work held the promise of a better result, particularly in "Basket One", in view of the fact that the USSR continued to show great interest in the CDE. Brussels decided, therefore, to pursue the negotiations seriously with a view to achieving a "substantial and balanced" final document.[74]

The Western position concerning the mandatory nature of future CBMs was, moreover, strengthened by a Soviet blunder. It happened during the summer of 1981 when the Soviets directly violated, for the first time, the provisions of the Final Act of Helsinki. They failed to notify "Zapad 81" which was the largest manoeuvre (100,000 troops) organized by any of the Group of 35 since 1975. During November and December 1982, the sixth session proceeded at a slow pace, and no new drafts were written. In the course of informal contacts on 6 December, the Soviets indicated that they would be willing to accept enlargement of the zone if it would encompass "all the activities affecting the security of Europe" and include "adjoining waters and airspace". It was clear to the West that this formulation would:

- give the East the right to monitor all allied military activities including nuclear-related activities and independent maritime operations in the Atlantic and the Mediterranean; or
- allow the East to refer the precise definition of adjoining areas and of notifiable activities to the CDE.[75]

The NATO nations thus reformulated the definition of the zone as follows:

As far as application to the adjoining sea area and air space is concerned, the measures will be applicable to the military activities of forces of all the participating States operating there whenever these activities constitute an integral part of the activities on land in Europe which the participating States will agree to notify. Necessary specifications will be made through the negotiations on the confidence- and security-building measures at the Conference.[76]

Clearly, the discussion had become very semantic, and the sixth session ended in December without any significant progress having been realized. There was, however, evidence of political will to disentangle the impasse. On 5 January 1983 in Prague, following the pattern set by NATO, the Warsaw Pact stated that "the East sought a fruitful conclusion of the Madrid Conference and the adoption of a substantial and balanced closing document".[77] It fell to the NNA, which met in Berne in January, to take up the initiative.

When the seventh session opened on 8 February 1983, Finland suggested that the participants establish informal mini-groups and use, as a basis for their work, the NNA document tabled in December 1981 (RM/39) as well as the proposals of NATO. Then, on 15 March, the NNA tabled a revised version of RM/39 which proposed a compromise formula for the zone. In particular, it stated that "with respect to the adjoining sea and air space, States must notify those activities which affect security in Europe and constitute a part of such activities taking place in the whole of Europe" (RM/39 rev., 15 March 1983).

The revised version thus contained the words used by both NATO and the Warsaw Pact. As one observer said: "the last ten minutes of the Madrid Conference had just started".[78] For reasons relating to "Basket Three", however, the RM/39 (rev.) document did not satisfy the West, and the United States in particular. Nevertheless, the U.S. yielded to pressure from its allies and, following the Easter break, the curtain rose on the final act of the Madrid Conference.

By April, the NATO nations had reached agreement on six essential amendments to the revised document (RM/39, rev.). Concerning the CDE, two semantic changes were made: suppression of the word "such" in the phrase "constitute a part of such activities" and suppression of the word "ocean" in the phrase "adjoining sea, ocean and airspace". The minor nature of these changes did not seem to pose a problem. Then, on 17 June, the Spanish Prime Minister suggested a final compromise. It related mainly to the issue of human rights, but three changes had been made concerning the CDE:

- its opening would be postponed until January 1984 so that the Conference could not be used as an opportunity for condemning the deployment of missiles in Europe, which was scheduled to occur in the fall of 1983;
- as compensation, it was proposed that a preparatory meeting of the CDE be held in the fall of 1983;
- one of the two semantic changes proposed by NATO was suppressed (the word "ocean" was re-inserted in the above-mentioned phrase).

After a brief period of hesitation, the Spanish compromise was accepted and all the Delegations, except that of Malta, gave their assent to the final document on 15 July. It was signed on 7 September 1983.

For most Western nations, including the NNA, the outcome of the Madrid Conference was generally judged to be a considerable, if not a major, success, especially given the difficult political context in which the Conference took place. As the Canadian Ambassador noted in his final report:

The Madrid Follow-up Meeting of the CSCE produced a Concluding Document which can fairly be said to represent a substantial improvement and even expansion of the Final Act of Helsinki (1975). In this sense the Madrid Meeting must be seen as a distinct success, especially when it is viewed in light of the deterioration of East-West relations which has proceeded steadily since the signature of the Final Act. According to the statements of the Warsaw Pact Delegations themselves, the Concluding Document is more than 80 per-cent Western in content; in fact, the percentage is probably even higher.[79]

Despite the compromise wording that had been adopted, the West made some significant gains in areas as diverse as trade-union law, terrorism, religious rights, access to diplomatic missions, family reunification, trade, and the work conditions of journalists.

Most of the Western objectives for the CDE had already been attained in the summer of 1981, and the Final Document reflected the views of the NATO allies on the zone of application of CBMs even though it was more ambiguous than they would have wished. But over and above the semantic differences concerning the "zone" or the "mandate", the Madrid Conference – and especially the period of thought which preceded it – engendered the emergence of a coherent approach to the development of confidence- and security-building measures and led to a new framework for conventional arms control in Europe. That was the great success of Madrid.

Finally, to return to our original hypothesis, the diplomatic history of the CSCE, specifically in the area of CBMs, shows clearly:

- that the CSCE process, although sometimes giving the appearance of multilateralism, has been dominated, on the one hand, by the dialogue of the two superpowers and, on the other, by a handful of "star players" including France, Germany, the United Kingdom and a few temporary associates; that apart from the NNA nations, which have played a technical role of mediation aimed at maintaining Western unity, the role and the importance of the other participants have been only marginal; that the CSCE has been a hierarchical decision-making process, dominated by a "board of directors" which, paradoxically, has had to respect the rule of consensus amongst 35 participating nations;
- that before the preparatory meetings of the Madrid Conference, the concept of confidence-building measures and the vision of how they would be applied in practice were largely embryonic; that in the strictest sense there existed no theory of CBMs and that their value lay mainly in the diplomatic use to which they were put; and, finally, that it was the thinking which preceded the Madrid Conference, and specifically the French initiative, which led to the emergence of a theory of confidence-building measures that was integral to a coherent approach to stability and arms reductions in Europe.

Undoubtedly, the reader will have noticed the lack of any reference to Canada in the above account of the Madrid Conference. In contrast to the first two phases of the CSCE, where Canada played a minor but visible role in respect of security issues, she appears to have stayed in the background completely during the negotiations on the CDE. One might speculate that Canada, without too much regret, relinquished her role to France, a European power which undoubtedly was much better placed to accomplish the task. It should be stressed, however, that although Canada proposed no significant initiatives on the CDE, she was very active in other areas. For instance, the meeting of experts on human rights was a Canadian proposal which found its place in the Final Document. As T. Delworth noted:

In a day-to-day sense our role is important. We have a function to perform between Europe and the United States in the CSCE which is difficult to define but very important: we can say things which will satisfy the requirement for a transatlantic voice which the Americans cannot say precisely because they are too important. We can try to bring Europeans and Americans to see the point of view of the other, and whether we lean one way or the other on a given issue in the CSCE process can have a great deal of influence at critical moments. These facts were demonstrated by the way in which the West found agreement to resume negotiations in November 1982, and the way in which they were resumed in the light of events in Poland. Both then, and again in May 1983, it was the Canadian Delegation which was asked to present the Western packages of amendments to the meeting as a whole, while the EEC Ten satisfied themselves with a symbolic role to emphasize their identity. It is not possible to say without qualification that Canada always plays a vital role in the CSCE process, but it is possible to say that it plays a role which is vital at times.[80]

From this perspective the Canadian diplomat was certainly not absent in Madrid, but one wonders nevertheless whether the growing europeanization of the CSCE process carries the risk that Canada might see herself edged out of transatlantic dialogue. According to the Department of External Affairs, this is certainly not the case. The Final Report states:

So long as Canada wishes to have some say in the avoidance of a war between the two systems, it will have to continue to participate in this process. Canadian withdrawal from it would also risk having isolationist effects on the United States. Do we want to be embraced in Fortress America? There is no doubt that our presence in the CSCE system, like our presence in NATO, is valued by the Europeans. Either of these systems, with Europeans on one side and the Americans alone on the other, would be agonizing for the Europeans and perhaps fatal to the maintenance of the present world balance. In this sense our role is a vital one.[81]

It might be added that, although it is not difficult to accept the fact that Canada needs Europe to ensure some measure of autonomy in her foreign policy, it is difficult to convince oneself that the Europeans could not, one day, do without Canada.

APPENDIX I
THE 25 CBMS STUDIED BY NATO

1   Development of services accorded to military attachés.
2   Development of means of communication.
3   Publication of annual programs of main military activities.
4   Exchange of information and military data.
5   Notification of land/air manoeuvres.
6   Notification of simultaneous and combined manoeuvres.
7   Notification of naval exercises.
8   Notification of aerial exercises.
9   Notification of military movements (land).
10 Notification of naval movements.
11 Notification of aerial movements.
12 Notification of emergency drills.
13 Notification of mobilization exercises.
14 Annual limitation on the number and duration of main military activities.
15 Ceiling on manoeuvres.
16 Ceiling on simultaneous manoeuvres or combined exercises.
17 Limitation of certain activities in certain zones.
18 Prohibition of certain military activities.
19 Prohibition on establishment of new military bases in Europe, and ceiling on foreign-based troops stationed in Europe.
20 Observation of military activities.
21 Verification of limited military activities.
22 Extension of CBMS to Mediterranean region.
23 Treaty on No First Use of Nuclear or Conventional Weapons.
24 Non-expansion of alliances and political associations in Europe.
25 Freeze on military budgets.

APPENDIX II PACKAGE OF WESTERN
CBMS IN SUMMER 1980

A *Information*
1 Periodic exchange of information on:
  • military budget and other pertinent financial resources;[1]
  • command organizations;[1]
  • basing, designation and composition of forces.[1]

B *Notification*
2 Publication of annual programs of main notifiable activities.
3 Notification of military activities, namely:
  • out-of-garrison land activities, either independent or combined with aerial or amphibious support;[2]
  • emergency drills, from the time of initiation;
  • mobilization activities.

C *Constraints and Stabilization*[3]
4 Limitations on military activities:
  • limitation on number of out-of-garrison divisions that a participant can deploy simultaneously in a zone located outside the participant's territory (suggested ceiling of five divisions);
  • limitation on mobilization activities involving over 50,000 personnel or five divisions.
5 Limitation on increase of main military activities over a certain period (number of manoeuvres, emergency drills or mobilization exercises).[4]

D *Observation and Verification*
6 Development of services accorded to military attachés.
7 Invitation of observers to notifiable military activities.
8 Codification of a means of verification including the possibility of inspections.[5]
9 Non-interference with National Technical Means (NTM).[6]
10 Exchange of liaison groups between major military formations.[7]
11 Development of means of communication.

Notes
1 These three elements had been added to give greater precision to measure A4 of the French plan.
2 Opinions differed on the definition of the criterion to be proposed for notification of land activities (10,000 troops, one division, number of tanks, etc.)
3 These measures were far from gaining acceptance by the allies.
4 Corresponding to French measure C10.
5 The issue of inspections was not settled.
6 A new measure that posed no problem given that it was part of the SALT principles.
7 A new measure which had not yet been discussed within the Atlantic Alliance.
Source: DEA, file CSCE.

APPENDIX III   PACKAGE OF MEASURES
FOR A CDE MANDATE

A   *Information Measures*
1   Exchange of information on military command organization (location, identification and composition of main land and air units).

B   *Stabilization Measures*
2   Exchange of annual programs on notifiable military activities, viz:
   • land force activities;
   • mobilization exercises;
   • activities of amphibious forces.
3   Notifications:
   • prior notification:
      • of military out-of-garrison land activities;
      notification period: 45 days in advance;
      notifiable threshold: one division, its equivalent or the major fraction of its operational elements.
      • of mobilization exercises:
      notification period: 45 days in advance;
      notifiable threshold: 25,000 troops or 3 or more divisions.
      • of amphibious activities:
      notification period: 45 days in advance;
      notifiable threshold: all these activities are notifiable.
   • notification of emergency drills at time of initiation.

C   *Observation and Verification*
4   Development of services accorded to military attachés.
5   Observation:
   • observation of activities subject to prior notification (see "prior notification");
   • definition of standards for treatment of observers.
6   Verification of Adherence to CBMS:
   • non-interference with National Technical Means (NTM);
   • development of a means for obtaining information, for consultation or for clarification of ambiguous events;
   • development of an inspection procedure.
7   Development of Means of Communication in order to:
   • facilitate exchange of information;
   • transmit notifications;
   • transmit requests and responses concerning verification of adherence to the agreement.

13 From the Megaphone to the Boudoir* Canada and the Stockholm Conference (1983–1986)

One waits. Most of the great moments in history are ever and everywhere spent in waiting.
                                        Marguerite Yourcenar, *Quoi? l'Éternité*

On 23 November 1983, scarcely two months after the close of the Madrid marathon and a few weeks before the Stockholm Conference opened (see Table 18), East-West relations hit an icy low. NATO had just deployed the first Pershing II missiles in Europe. For the Soviets it was a significant defeat because NATO had held fast to its decision of December 1979. Also, the Soviet "withdrawal" from the negotiations in Geneva and Vienna proved to be a gross miscalculation. As J. Dean notes:

The public could not understand why the Soviet Union, since its establishment the most consistent proponent of arms control and disarmament, was sulking like Achilles in his tent, while the conservative president of the United States smilingly proclaimed his willingness to negotiate further. In the West, the Soviet Union was threatened with the loss of its influence over public opinion and over European governments.[1]

For the West, the deployment of missiles in Europe had not been a cut and dried blessing. Despite the collapse of the anti-nuclear movement, some of the main European social-democratic parties had taken up the torch of disarmament thus threatening consensus within the Atlantic Alliance. In short, despite the situation, or perhaps even because of it, the East and the West had to resume dialogue. At the

---

* Phrase coined by a Swiss diplomat to describe the evolution of superpower negotiations at the CDE (J. Klein, *Sécurité et désarmement en Europe*, p. 222).

end of 1983, most of the talks on disarmament had been suspended. Only one link remained – the Stockholm Conference which was scheduled to open on 17 January 1984. From then until 1985, the Conference on Confidence- and Security-Building Measures and Disarmament in Europe (CCSBMDE) – to give it its official title – was the touchstone of East-West dialogue on disarmament. It might even be said, without exaggeration, that Stockholm became the springboard of a new *détente* which progressively developed between Washington and Moscow. The Stockholm Conference, or CCSBMDE, like its predecessors in Madrid and Belgrade, was characterized by a bilateral Soviet-American diplomacy which gradually abandoned the use of the megaphone in favour of private summits. As the Canadian Delegate humorously observed at the signing of the Stockholm Accord in September 1986:

The press photographers (bless their hearts) snapped at least a million candid shots of Barry and Grinevski leering amiably at each other as if the multitude of other champagne guzzlers were but a bunch of minor lords swelling a scene or two.[2]

The CCSBMDE had several other things in its favour in addition to the intensified Gorbachev-Reagan dialogue. The purpose of the negotiations was not to reduce the number of weapons and troops in Europe, but to adopt a set of measures that were more political than military in nature without upsetting the balance of forces by even one iota. Correspondingly, the Stockholm Conference did not address what might be called the vital interests of the participating States – their military arsenals – and did not have to face the technical obstacles which characterized other negotiations such as those in Geneva or Vienna. In a way, Stockholm served as a testing ground and as a prelude to renewed efforts in conventional arms control which ultimately led to the Treaty of Washington in December 1987.

Because the confidence measures negotiated in Stockholm were rather political and ambiguous in nature, the CCSBMDE did not attract the attention of the media in the same way as the INF or START negotiations. According to T. Delworth, there was certainly an advantage in being able to negotiate this Accord in relative obscurity, "away from the klieg lights of public opinion and domestic controversy".[3]

Diplomatic experience shows that whenever public opinion dictates the agenda it complicates rather than facilitates negotiations. According to many accounts, the Stockholm Conference gained from the semi-obscurity which characterized the course of negotiations.

Table 18
Conference on Confidence and Security Building Measures and
Disarmament in Europe

Genesis and Evolution: Founded on the basis of the mandate adopted at
the Madrid Conference of the CSCE. The Stockholm Conference opened on
17 January 1984 and was adjourned on 19 September 1986.

Mandate: To negotiate a set of militarily significant, politically constraining
and verifiable confidence- and security-building measures applicable to the
whole of the European continent.

Composition: The 35 States participating in the CSCE.

Main Proposals:
• SC1 NATO: 24 January 1984;
• SC2 Romania: 25 January 1984;
• SC3 NNA: 9 March 1984;
• SC4 USSR: 8 May 1984;
• SC5 Malta: 8 November 1984;
• SC6 USSR: 29 January 1985;
• SC1 (Amplified) NATO: 30 January 1985 and 27 February 1985;
• SC7 NNA: 15 November 1985;
• SC9 (Final Document): 19 September 1986.

Dates of Sessions:
Opening Date: 17 January 1984.
    1st Session: 17 January to 16 March 1984;
    2nd Session: 8 May to 6 July 1984;
    3rd Session: 11 September to 12 October 1984;
    4th Session: 6 November to 14 December 1984;
    5th Session: 29 January to 22 March 1985;
    6th Session: 14 May to 5 July 1985;
    7th Session: 10 September to 18 October 1985;
    8th Session: 5 November to 20 December 1985;
    9th Session: 28 January to 14 March 1986;
    10th Session: 15 April to 27 May 1986;
    11th Session: 10 June to 28 July 1986;
    12th Session: 19 August to 19 September 1986;

Final Stockholm Document: 22 September 1986, dated 19 September.

Unlike the preparations made by the West for other negotiations, the preparations for the CCSBMDE had been made long in advance, and the set of confidence-building measures tabled in Stockholm had been developed, in large part, at the time of the Madrid Conference.

Despite the favourable circumstances, the Stockholm negotiations were neither swift nor easy. They required 12 sessions, each of 6-weeks' average duration, and were spread over a period of 3 years. The drafting of the Final Accord was only seriously undertaken in 1986, after 2 years of complex pussyfooting around, the logic of which often escaped the most informed observer. Although at first sight this state of affairs may seem surprising, it must be remembered that Stockholm inherited the apparent confusion and slowness which had characterized the CSCE process from the beginning. In addition, after five years of tension and polemic, it was not to be expected that East-West relations would be normalized from one day to the next. In this context, the slowness of the Stockholm talks reflected the caution and progressiveness of the changes in direction made in the White House and the Kremlin.

Perhaps it should also be added that the confidence-building measures considered for adoption in Stockholm were no longer the same as those of Helsinki. They had to be compulsory, militarily significant, verifiable and more rigorous in terms of their parameters. Also, they were to constitute the first step on the path towards conventional arms reductions in Europe. In practical terms, the Stockholm confidence-building measures were important stakes; technically, they were more tricky to negotiate because the East and West – as we shall see – had fundamentally different conceptions of their nature.

PRELUDE TO STOCKHOLM: THE
POSITIONS OF THE PARTICIPANTS
DURING THE SUMMER AND FALL OF 1983

The mandate for Stockholm was agreed at the Madrid Conference in July 1983. It is important to fix in mind the initial positions of the main political groups which were to dominate the debate during the course of the CCSBMDE.

NATO apparently found itself in an excellent diplomatic position. The Atlantic Alliance had already agreed upon the objectives to be sought in Stockholm and upon the main elements of the proposal which the West was to table in January 1984. NATO's position was based on the seven confidence-building measures defined on 9

December 1980 (document no. 63 of the NATO Military Committee, see Chapter 12). Amongst these measures, three elements were especially important: 1. the exchange of annual programs of notifiable military activities; 2. the strengthening of measures for notification and observation of military activities; and 3. the verification measures associated with the Accord as a whole. In concrete terms, these three types of measure clearly illustrate the fundamental objectives of the Atlantic Alliance, namely: to anticipate, at least one year in advance, the major fraction of normal training activities of the Warsaw Pact; to increase the "visibility" of these activities through observation; and, to ensure the reliability of the system through regular inspections. Also, the technical importance of the concept of out-of-garrison activities contained in the Atlantic Alliance proposal should not be forgotten. This concept covered, for the purpose of "notification and observation, any military activity (movement, exercise or manoeuvre) involving more than one division". It envisaged opening up for observation the majority of the territory of the Warsaw Pact States, as far as the Urals. The scope of this concept can be appreciated when one remembers that East Germany, for instance, had taken steps to prohibit access by foreign observers – military attachés in particular – to 40 percent of its territory.[4]

Several months before the negotiations opened in Stockholm, NATO had developed an approach which appeared convincing, practical and coherent. This solid initial position undoubtedly lent credibility to the allied proposals that were to be advanced over the three-year duration of the Stockholm Conference. The situation proved, however, to be more complex than it appeared at first sight. The diplomatic correspondence at the time shows clearly the divergence of opinion between the NATO allies, particularly in respect of Western strategy. For example, Washington appeared rather sceptical and seemed to want to define the CDE as "a damage-limiting exercise". In this regard, the tactical objectives that the United States suggested to NATO were:

- to ensure and maintain Western domination of the negotiations;
- to ensure Atlantic Alliance unity;
- to promote cooperation with the neutral countries;
- to educate the Western public on the basic facts of European security; and
- to ensure that the CCSBMDE would not interfere with other negotiations, specifically the bilateral negotiations in Geneva and the MBFR talks.[5]

The attitude of the United States was hardly encouraging for those who viewed the CCSBMDE as a positive enterprise which could lead to a significant agreement. At the end of the summer, some observers even went so far as to suggest that the Americans had no interest in the negotiations and that they might well introduce, at the last minute, a proposal unacceptable to the Soviets so as to force them to reject it publicly.[6]

In retrospect, the negative American attitude might have been aimed at moderating the enthusiasm of some allies, such as Canada, who wanted to "enrich" the NATO proposal by re-examining the 25 confidence-building measures initially studied in 1979, and who wanted to study some of the suggestions put forward by the East or by the neutral countries. As well, it will be recalled that, in his peace initiative, Pierre Elliott Trudeau had even suggested to Swedish Prime Minister Olof Palme that arms limitation or disarmament measures be introduced immediately in Stockholm, a suggestion that ran counter to the very mandate of the CDE which was approved in Madrid. As M. Shenstone noted: "Any attempt to compress the phases (of the CDE) into one ... would unravel the consensus upon which the mandate of the CDE is based and would cause major problems with our allies, particularly the United States".[7]

In view of the serious risk that anarchical initiatives of this kind posed for Atlantic Alliance unity, one might logically conclude that the initial negativism of Washington was aimed at avoiding a premature internal debate which could only have weakened NATO's position. Moreover, by implicitly threatening the "radicals" with sabotaging the negotiations, the Americans reminded them that an Accord could not be reached without their concurrence and that a realistic compromise would, therefore, be necessary. Finally, American scepticism would obviously be leaked to the East and would clearly show the Soviets that the United States was not a petitioner in Stockholm and that it had no intention of accepting an Accord at any price.

On the eve of the preparatory talks in Helsinki, from 25 October 1983 to 11 November 1983, Brussels acceded to the American position. The Atlantic Alliance would adopt a cautious approach structured around the objectives defined by Washington, and based exclusively on the measures contained in document no. 63 of the NATO Military Committee issued in 1980. The United States stubbornly refused to consider any kind of confidence-building measure which could constrain the military activities of the Atlantic Alliance, as well as any notification measure which could embrace American forces in transit in Europe. As a result, NATO discussions focused on precise parameters for the set of Western measures, which was not an easy task given the differences between the Western nations on points of detail.[8] Agreement was finally reached in Brussels on 10 January 1984, two weeks before the NATO proposal was tabled in Stockholm.

Despite friction between the allies, the NATO proposal was solid. But on the Soviet side, the political conditions which existed in 1983–1984 were rather sombre. The USSR was in the middle of a leadership crisis following the death of Brezhnev and then of Andropov, and it was not until 1985, when Gorbachev arrived in the Kremlin, that the situation stabilized. It is not surprising, therefore, that the Soviet diplomatic machinery was in no position to take the initiative in Stockholm.

In the fall of 1983, the Soviets shot down, by accident, a Boeing civil airliner belonging to the Korean Air Lines (KAL). This incident, following in the wake of Afghanistan and Poland, simply added to the long list of events which had tarnished the reputation of the USSR on the international scene. The Kremlin was clearly on the defensive and, on the eve of the Stockholm Conference, the Soviets wanted to maintain dialogue as a first priority. According to T. Delworth:

It was clear that the Russians, who were undoubtedly looking forward to the Stockholm Conference as a forum to publicize their special views on arms control, did not want anything to happen that would cast them in the spoiler's role, especially so soon after the KAL incident and against the longer term background of Western criticism of Soviet policies towards Poland and Afghanistan.[9]

In substance, the specific proposals that the Soviets wanted to introduce in Stockholm – despite the uncertainties that still surrounded them at the end of 1983 – hardly held the promise of surprise. Judging by the Declaration of Prague on 5 January 1983, the Warsaw Pact proposal would contain, in particular, one of the traditional elements of Soviet policy since 1954, namely a multilateral Non-aggression Treaty. The Kremlin's attitude towards confidence-building measures still appeared very woolly although, quite obviously, Soviet ideas on these matters went far beyond the technical definition proposed by NATO. Following the declarations made by the GDR in the fall of 1983, it was clear that the East viewed confidence-building measures rather as declaratory measures of a political nature, to include, for instance, non-use of force and no first use of nuclear weapons.

On the other hand, the position of the Neutral and Non-Aligned (NNA) nations seemed to be more innovative than that of the East.

Sweden, in the person of its prime minister, Olof Palme, distinguished itself in 1982 through its participation in the independent Commission on Disarmament and Security. Concerning the Stockholm negotiations, the Commission suggested that the work of the CCSBMDE should concentrate on measures aimed at reducing the dangers of surprise attack. Amongst other things, the Palme Report stated:

The specific measures to be discussed should relate to information, notification, observation and stabilization. The approach should strive to develop standards for routine military activity through agreed guidelines for reporting, observing and limiting the size and scope of these activities. They may in the future extend also to such areas as budgeting, planning and [military] R and D.[10]

The approach of the NNA, as reflected in the Palme Report, was generally in line with NATO's philosophy on many points, and the importance that the Palme Report accorded to the principle of verification could only satisfy the Atlantic Alliance. Some of the confidence-building measures envisaged by the NNA were, however, more ambitious than those of NATO. The Palme Report included amongst its suggestions the possibility of establishing Nuclear-Free Zones (NFZ) in Europe. In the fall of 1983, Austria had expressed interest in this idea, but the concept was obviously unacceptable for the allies. As well, as stressed earlier, measures aimed at limiting military activities met with firm opposition from the United States.

But the most serious problem of the NNA did not concern these differences. When the preparatory talks opened in Helsinki it was apparent that, although the NNA were in agreement on the general orientation of their policies for Stockholm, they were far from unanimous on the specific measures that should be adopted. As the Head of the Canadian Delegation observed:

The NNA group will have realized that the forthcoming negotiations will be a new ball game for them. Their security interests are so totally different one from the other that they will not be a cohesive group in Stockholm. They will probably not be able to play the same kind of institutionalized role between East and West to which they have aspired in the past and to which they have sometimes been successful. ... In Stockholm, the NNA will be a much looser group than they have been in the past; they will have more scope for individual or national initiative, but the weight and influence of the neutrals will be less than in the past.[11]

This prediction, which proved to be remarkably accurate, was based on the observation that many of the neutral countries had already realized that some of the most radical confidence-building measures could have a negative impact on their security and that, consequently, prudence was the order of the day. For example, Sweden and Switzerland – two countries which saw to their own defence – were not slow in adopting more moderate positions, thus opposing the more rebellious nations of the NNA such as Malta and Finland.

From a political standpoint, even though neither the East nor the NNA were ready to assume the initiative on the eve of the Stockholm Conference, both groups of nations nevertheless wanted the negotiations to take place, but for different reasons. The preparatory talks in Helsinki were, therefore, concluded without major incident. The 35 participants agreed on the opening formalities of the Stockholm Conference, comprising ceremonies, speeches and presentation of proposals. They also adopted a work schedule for the first year (1984) and decided to defer the matter of follow-up actions to the Stockholm Conference to a subsequent meeting of the CSCE – either in 1986 in Vienna, or later.

The apparently anodyne nature of these decisions masked, however, the real stakes at the Helsinki talks. Progress in the negotiations would depend in large part on the specific schedule of the Stockholm Conference but, most of all, on the underlying organizational structure. In other words, in the absence of a work and drafting structure, the Stockholm Conference would be condemned to plenary sessions which would hardly be conducive to progress in sensitive negotiations leading to a possible Accord. And indeed, the Helsinki talks left the responsibility for establishing a work structure and schedule to the Stockholm Conference itself:

The Conference thus had no precise negotiating agenda. It would also have to decide on the timing of the sessions for 1985–1986 ... and the Conference would have to agree periodically on its work programs. In other words, Stockholm would have to make up much of its procedure as it went along.[12]

The absence of organizational structures allowed the main players in Stockholm – the United States and the USSR – to dominate the negotiations much as they pleased, without having to intervene in any negative way as far as the substance of the talks was concerned. It must be said that this situation suited the Americans very well, since they had no wish to negotiate seriously until after the presidential elections in

November 1984. The Soviets were still digesting the consequences of the deployment of missiles in Europe and were waiting for a new leader to take the helm in the Kremlin, but this happened only in March 1985. Procedural decisions – acting as "locks" to the negotiations – would thus dominate the Conference until its final phase which was to commence in 1986. The history of the negotiations can thus be divided into three phases: the first, which led to the formation of working groups in December 1984; the second, which resulted in the formation of drafting teams; and finally, the third, which concluded in September 1986 with the Stockholm Document itself.

THE PLENARY PHASE: JANUARY TO DECEMBER 1984

Despite the prudence and slowness which characterized the first four sessions of the CCSBMDE it was clear, from the time of opening of the negotiations on 17 January 1984 and throughout the subsequent talks, that both the East and the West had the will to maintain dialogue by avoiding the polemics of Belgrade and Madrid. To demonstrate this will, the foreign ministers of all 35 nations, including in particular Mr. Gromyko and Mr. Shultz, participated in the first sessions of the CDE. Even though the opening speeches again revealed the fundamental differences between the Warsaw Pact and the West, the climate was not one of direct confrontation and tensions remained latent. The message was clear. The deployment of missiles in Europe did not mean a break in East-West dialogue and, even if the participants were not ready to "sit at the table", it was still possible to "consult the menu".

Aside from the oratorical exchanges which occurred during the month of January, the first sessions of the Stockholm Conference witnessed the tabling of the main preliminary proposals, specifically those of NATO on 24 January 1984, Romania on 25 January 1984, the NNA on 9 March 1984, the USSR on 8 May 1984 and Malta on 8 November 1984.

Exchange of Proposals

The NATO Proposal. The NATO proposal (SC1) was both brief and precise. It pointed out that the Stockholm Conference formed part of the CSCE process and that the fundamental objective was to adopt a set of complementary confidence-building measures that would increase the visibility of military activities, reduce the risk of surprise attack and lower the threat of armed conflict in Europe. In addition, it stated that the implementation and verification of these measures would facilitate progress in disarmament.

Within this framework, six particular measures were proposed:

1   annual exchange of information on the structure of land and air forces of the participating States in the area agreed under the Madrid mandate, namely from the Atlantic to the Urals;[13]
2   exchange of annual calendars describing notifiable military activities planned to be conducted in the zone of application;
3   notification, 45 days in advance:
   • of out-of-garrison ground activities at or over the divisional level of 6,000 troops under the same command;
   • of mobilization exercises involving 25,000 troops or over, or the major elements of 3 divisions;
   • of landing exercises involving 3 battalions or over, or 3,000 troops; in this regard it was specified that some activities such as emergency drills, which could not be announced within the expected timeframes, would be subject to notification as soon as they commenced;
4   invitation of observers by the participating States to all notifiable activities, on a universal basis;
5   verification measures including:
   • national technical means;
   • inspections on demand;
6   development of means of communication between the participating States.

The main quality of the Western proposal was its simplicity. It represented a substantial improvement over the measures adopted in Helsinki in 1975, while remaining technically modest and politically negotiable. The notification and observation measures were designed to develop and systematize the measures already adopted, and thus promised to provide much greater visibility of military activities in Europe. The notification threshold was lowered from 25,000 to 6,000 troops so as to include divisional activities, and the timeframe for notification was increased from 21 to 45 days. In addition, the definition of notifiable activities was broadened to include manoeuvres, exercises, movements, partial mobilizations and emergency drills. The addition of landing exercises to the number of notifiable activities was a significant gesture by NATO to address the specific concerns of the Scandinavian countries.

For purposes of negotiation, the NATO proposal afforded some flexibility, and some elements appeared less important than others.

In particular, measure 1 (annual exchange of information) could be viewed as redundant and measure 6 (development of means of communication) was only symbolic, given that intergovernmental means of communication already existed. As well, the threshold for notification, fixed by the Atlantic Alliance at 6,000 troops for ground activities, left wide room for bargaining, given that the Warsaw Pact divisions usually comprised 11,000 troops.

Within the Atlantic Alliance some contentious issues still remained, which explains some of the imprecisions of the sc1 proposal. Turkey in particular was reluctant to provide the information called for in measure 1, having no wish to disclose the deployment of its forces at the proposed threshold of 6,000 personnel. Also, the allies were unable to reach agreement on the notification threshold for equipment (battle tanks, armoured vehicles, etc.) and on the number of annual inspections that States would have to accept for verification purposes. Agreement on these particular points was not reached until the fall of 1984, but the essential outcome was that NATO was able to take a significant diplomatic lead over the other political groups at the opening of the Stockholm Conference.

The four other proposals tabled in 1984 showed that neither the Warsaw Pact nor the NNA were in a position to compete seriously with NATO on the substance of the confidence-building measures.

The Romanian Proposal. The Romanian proposal (sc2), which was tabled one day after NATO's, was hardly credible. It presented a disorderly set of measures including the creation of nuclear-free corridors, a ban on transporting nuclear weapons along land and sea boundaries, a ban on establishing new military bases in Europe, a pan-European Non-aggression Treaty, a freeze on military expenditures and a ban on warmongering propaganda.

Obviously, Romania played its traditional role of singularity in the Warsaw Pact, but to the detriment of a few elements in the proposal which, when considered in isolation from the others, might have constituted a serious basis for negotiation. In this regard, the sc2 proposal suggested:

1   notification, 30 days in advance, of:
    - ground or combined manoeuvres above a threshold of between 18,000 and 20,000 troops;
    - manoeuvres of some special forces (paratroops or landing troops) involving over 5,000 personnel;
    - independent naval manoeuvres exceeding 10 to 12 vessels or a total tonnage of between 50,000 to 60,000 tonnes;

- independent aerial manoeuvres involving 45 to 50 aircraft;
2 notification, 30 days in advance, of military movements involving two or more divisions or their equivalent, and of movements of weapons and heavy equipment to these divisions;
3 notification, as early as possible, of military alerts that could occur in times of crisis;
4 limitations on ground manoeuvres to between 40,000 and 50,000 troops, and similar limitations on naval and air manoeuvres.

Despite the conspicuous absence of observation and verification measures, the Romanian proposal revealed that there was a basis for dialogue on the parameters of notification. It was nevertheless clear from proposal sc2 that the East would base its diplomatic counter-offensive on two "shortcomings" of the Western proposal, and would pursue the concepts of constraints on military manoeuvres and of notification of independent naval and air manoeuvres. It will be recalled that, because of the multinational nature of its forces, NATO traditionally organized manoeuvres that were larger than those of the Warsaw Pact. A 50,000 troop ceiling on ground manoeuvres would, therefore, exert an asymmetric impact on the training capabilities of the two alliances. As well, the requirement to give notification of independent naval and air manoeuvres would again raise the question of the geographic definition of the area encompassed in the Stockholm negotiations. In this case, the inclusion of independent naval manoeuvres would extend the area from the Atlantic to the Mediterranean and would imply the possible notification of manoeuvres unrelated to European security itself. The Western allies could not, therefore, afford to make concessions on these two specific points, which would have allowed the East nations to exploit them to their advantage. But the Warsaw Pact still pursued them to the bitter end in the negotiations.

The NNA Proposal. Despite the many difficulties encountered by the NNA in harmonising a collective position, they were the third to enter the lists. The NNA proposal (sc3) was tabled on 9 March 1984. It reflected a position that was very close to that of the Atlantic Alliance, and contained 12 confidence-building measures. The terse manner in which they were expressed showed that there was no NNA consensus on the specific parameters which should govern their application. After a very verbose preamble, the sc3 proposal advocated:

1 improving the parameters for notification of manoeuvres which appeared in the Helsinki Accord (longer notification times and more specific content);

2   providing notification of smaller manoeuvres when the total number of troops involved exceeded a threshold that was indicated in the measure;

3   providing notification of airborne and air exercises and amphibious exercises;

4   providing notification of large-scale military movements;

5   providing notification of significant military activities in the sea areas and airspace adjoining Europe when such activities could affect the security of the continent and formed part of the activities in progress on the continent itself;

6   inviting observers to notifiable manoeuvres and movements, and optimizing the conditions for observation;

7   providing notification of redeployments of major units as well as any significant rotation of military personnel;

8   providing notification of some other military activities, specifically emergency drills and mobilization exercises (the parameters for such exercises could not be agreed amongst the NNA);

9   exchanging annual calendars on main military activities;

10 imposing quantitative ceilings on major military manoeuvres as well as on smaller scale manoeuvres occurring at the same time or in the same area of operation;

11 imposing a ceiling on airborne and air activities and amphibious exercises;

12 establishing areas where the deployment of military units, weapons and offensive equipment would be restricted.

In addition, sc3 emphasized the importance of the verification measures underlying the Accord and noted that the adoption of a coherent set of confidence-building measures could create a favourable climate for reaffirmation of the principles of non-use of force and of peaceful settlement of differences. Apart from the constraining measures (10 and 11) and the idea of special areas (measure 12), the sc3 proposal clearly showed that the allied and neutral positions were very close. It augured well for the emergence of a coalition of interests between the Western groups during the opening months of the Stockholm Conference, and hence a consolidation of the already favourable position of NATO.

The Soviet Proposal.   Given the political context (Andropov had just died on 9 February 1984), it is not surprising that the Soviets took a long time in responding officially to the Western proposals. Their proposal was tabled only on 8 May 1984, five months after the start of the negotiations. It was disappointing from more than one standpoint; it brought nothing new to the debate beyond the statements of Gromyko at the opening of the Stockholm Conference, and it had very few points in common with the Western proposals. In particular, the Soviet proposal (SC4) suggested that the CCSBMDE participants:

1 commit to no first use of nuclear weapons;
2 conclude a Treaty on Non-Use of Force which would include a commitment to no first use of nuclear or conventional weapons;
3 commit to freeze and subsequently reduce military expenditures in order to promote economic and social development and to increase assistance to the Third World;
4 prohibit chemical weapons in Europe;
5 support the establishment of nuclear-free zones in Europe.

Obviously, none of these measures was responsive to the Stockholm Conference mandate which was established in the summer of 1983. On the other hand, the sixth element of the SC4 proposal addressed the issue of confidence-building measures. In essence, it proposed:

• imposing a ceiling (unspecified) on ground manoeuvres;
• providing notification of independent or combined ground, sea and air manoeuvres in Europe and its adjoining sea areas and airspace;
• providing notification of large-scale military movements (ground and air) and transfers within or towards the zone of application;
• developing the practice of inviting observers to major military manoeuvres.

Finally, a symbolic comment in favour of verification supplemented the Soviet text.

Overall, most of the SC4 proposal was inspired by the Prague Declaration, and it clearly demonstrated the incompatibility between Soviet and Western approaches towards meeting the objectives of the Stockholm Conference. The Soviets obviously were inclined towards declaratory and political measures (five out of six) while NATO favoured measures of a military and technical nature. The sixth element of the Soviet proposal was still extremely vague and contained so many "thorns" for NATO that it was practically useless as a platform for negotiation. According to one Canadian observer:

[Soviet comments] which elaborated on the measures suggested they are designed to restrict NATO's military flexibility of reinforcement during periods of crisis, cover independent naval, amphibious, airborne and air exercises, limit forward-based systems (nuclear) deployment, as the USA rapid deployment force staging through Europe, and limit NATO exercises.[14]

The Maltese Proposal.   The last official proposal of 1984 was tabled by Malta on 8 November. Following Romania's example, Malta also sought to express its independence from the political group to which it belonged (the NNA), and manifested its frustration at the exclusion of the Mediterranean area from the preoccupations of the CCSBMDE. It was, of course, a lone rearguard battle, since neither the CCSBMDE nor the CSCE could deal with Mediterranean issues without becoming embroiled in the thorny political problems of the Maghreb and the Middle East. As in former years, the Maltese proposal (SC5) was judged unacceptable and was ignored by all the participants. It did, however, contain five confidence-building measures:

1   information measures providing for the annual exchange of data on military forces deployed by the participants in the Mediterranean area;
2   notification of military manoeuvres and movements in that area;
3   limitation on the size and frequency of manoeuvres in the Mediterranean;
4   observation and verification of notifiable activities and of agreed limits;
5   commitment by the participants not to resort to the threat or use of force against States bordering the Mediterranean.

The Nature of the Problem

By mid-May 1984, following the tabling of the most important proposals, it became possible to assess the nature of the negotiations to come.

The main problem for the Atlantic Alliance was to determine whether the Eastern and Western positions could be made more compatible. The Eastern approach was based on a set of political and declaratory measures, while that of the West was geared to measures that were both technical and concrete. The problem for NATO was to know whether it could, in principle, find place in the future Accord for one or two of the measures proposed by the East in exchange for corresponding Eastern concessions on the set of measures proposed by NATO. Specifically, the only element of the SC4 proposal for which the Atlantic Alliance could envisage such a compromise was the principle of non-use of force which had already been recognized in the Final Act of Helsinki in 1975. There was no question of reaffirming this principle in a treaty, for such a legal formulation would weaken the Charter of the United Nations which already included the same commitment. In legal terms, a negative obligation such as non-use of force could neither be developed nor repeated without being qualified and hence weakened.[15]

In addition, the insertion of a non-use of force provision in a treaty would accord this principle a particular status in relation to the other elements of the Final Act of Helsinki. The only solution would consist, therefore, of a simple reaffirmation of non-use of force and, in the spring of 1984, several nations of the Atlantic Alliance, including Italy, Belgium, Denmark and Canada, tried to stimulate discussions to this end. In March 1984, the Canadian Delegation suggested to Ottawa that the principle of non-use of force might be linked to the principle of peaceful settlement of differences so as to temper Soviet enthusiasm for a treaty. In effect, the two principles were opposite sides of the same coin, but the idea of peaceful settlement of differences was resisted strongly by the Kremlin for it implied the possibility of arbitration by a third party (Final Report of the Canadian Delegation, Section 3). In late May 1984, Canada even suggested that the allies develop a counter-draft of the treaty in a form unacceptable to the Soviets in order to lead them to a compromise. These initiatives met with opposition in the Western caucus which, while admitting that the principle of non-use of force should be discussed within the Atlantic Alliance, had no wish to adopt a specific strategy on the matter. NATO took a year and a half to define its position on non-use of force, by which time the Soviets had already abandoned the idea of a treaty.

There was, however, some logic in the Atlantic Alliance's "wait and see" policy. A formal concession to the Soviets at that stage of the negotiations carried some risk, as noted in a report issued by the NATO Secretariat in April 1984: "There is a risk that engaging in negotiation on a declaratory Soviet proposal would so dominate the CDE that the possibility of specific and concrete CSBMs would be lost in favour of agreement on a general concluding single declaration".[16]

Tactically, it was preferable for the Western nations to ensure that their set of measures remain at the centre of negotiations before approaching the subject of non-use of force. In other words, although it was appropriate to indicate Western goodwill to the Soviets on the matter of non-use of force, there was no question of officially approaching the subject in Stockholm until the Soviets themselves had agreed to negotiate seriously the Western proposal in its entirety. The problem was, therefore, fundamentally a matter of procedure: how could the West organize a balanced discussion between non-use of force and the set of Western measures so as to ensure that agreement was not reached on the Soviet proposal for an Accord before the conclusion of discussions on the Western set of confidence-building measures? The search for a satisfactory solution kept the Stockholm Conference occupied until the end of 1984.

In a speech in Dublin on 4 June 1984, the u.s. President clearly indicated to the East that NATO was ready to consider the modalities of reaffirming the principle of non-use of force on condition that the Warsaw Pact countries would agree to debate the concrete measures which gave real substance to this principle. The President's statement was not really productive for it injected confusion into the ranks of the Atlantic Alliance, several of whose members had not been informed of the American initiative. As one Canadian observer noted:

Overnight, and without any prior consultation with the Allies, Western policy had changed ... While we welcomed this move ... as a way of moving the conference forward, it was an obvious electoral ploy ... and belittled by the Russians who claimed that it had no real implications for the American position at the Conference.[17]

Consequently, although the American gesture was perfectly justified from a tactical standpoint, it hardly made the negotiations easier.

The central issue of the status, within the negotiations, of the principle of non-use of force was thus resolved at the Stockholm Conference itself where a complex debate developed on the modalities that should govern the organization of Working Groups or Discussion Groups. Inside the Atlantic Alliance, there were two opposing views. The French favoured the constitution of three Working Groups. The first would deal with Western measures, the second with limitations and constraints while the third would deal with declaratory measures including the principle of non-use of force. This approach was not particularly satisfactory in light of NATO's reluctance to discuss constraining measures. At best, such an organizational structure would have given equal weight to the Soviet and Western proposals. For this reason, the United States instead suggested that a single Working Group be formed in the hope that this would avoid any parallelism between declaratory and concrete measures. France, however, refused to abandon its position, thus delaying the decision of the Western caucus.

As a result, the NNA took the initiative in June 1984 and proposed the creation of two Working Groups, one to deal with measures provided for in the Final Act of Helsinki (notification and observation) and the other to debate "new" measures (verification, information, constraints and declaratory measures). This ingenious formula, which was aimed at ensuring that the lion's share of attention would be given to the Western measures, unfortunately arrived too late in the session to become the subject of a detailed Accord before the summer break in negotiations. The Finns nevertheless refined the formula at the last minute to guarantee to the Soviets that the principle of non-use of force would have an equitable place in the discussions. In return, the Soviets would implicitly abandon the other "unorthodox" measures in proposal sc4. These latter measures could only be dealt with in plenary session once a week and would, therefore, for all practical purposes, be eliminated from the negotiations.

The Finnish initiative was at the centre of the debate for the last two sessions in 1984. Finally, after interminable discussions, both within the Atlantic Alliance and with the Soviets, agreement was reached and recorded in the proceedings of the Conference on 3 December 1984. The agreement provided for the constitution of two Working Groups. Working Group A would deal with:

- non-use of force (Subgroup A1);
- calendars of, and constraints and limitations on, military activities (Subgroup A2);
- information and verification measures (Subgroup A3).

Working Group B would discuss:

- notification measures (Subgroup B1);
- observation measures (Subgroup B2).

Under the agreement, the elements of the five official proposals (sc1 through sc5) were broken down in detail and divided between the various subgroups, and a weekly schedule of meetings for each of the subgroups was established.

After a full year of protracted and trivial manoeuvres, the Stockholm Conference finally showed signs of movement.

THE WORKING GROUP PHASE: JANUARY TO DECEMBER 1985

Despite the agreement on procedure of 3 December 1984 and the subsequent transition to working discussions, the pace of the Stockholm Conference hardly picked up.

On 29 January 1985 the Soviets tabled a Treaty on Non-Use of Force (sc6) which contained a clause on no first use of nuclear weapons. This provoked a strong reaction from the allies and, faced with this let-down, the Head of the Soviet Delegation sharply declared to his Canadian counterpart: "Until I am convinced that you are seriously interested in negotiating on Non-Use of Force I can guarantee that this Conference will go nowhere".[18]

The principle of non-use of force continued to haunt the Stockholm Conference. But it is striking to note that the Soviets themselves discreetly abandoned the idea of a Treaty in April and gradually relegated the reaffirmation of non-use of force to the bottom of their list of priorities while, in parallel, the principle of non-use of force became a bone of contention for the West.

Starting in February 1985 the focus of discussion shifted and the debate centred mainly on the confidence- and security-building measures (CSBMs). In the fall of 1984, the Atlantic Alliance had finally reached agreement on the detail of the six previously described measures and, between 30 January and 27 February 1985, the allies introduced, element by element, the improved version of their proposal (sc1 Amplified). The specifics were as follows:

INFORMATION MEASURES

1   The following military information would be exchanged at the start of each calendar year by the participating States with forces deployed in the zone of application:
    • the command organization;
    • the usual location of the headquarters and the composition of ground and air forces. (It was agreed that this information should be exchanged down to the divisional level, but not down to the battalion level or lower).

CALENDARS

2   The annual projections of notifiable military activities that were to take place in the zone of application would be communicated at latest by 15 November for the following calendar year and consist of quarterly listings. Each quarterly list would include the following information:
    • the designation, including the name of the exercise, if appropriate;
    • the general purpose of the activity;
    • the month in which the activity would start;
    • the list of participating States;
    • the planned area of activity;

- the duration of the activity;
- the planned total of all participating forces, including the directing group and the refereeing body;
- the types of forces involved.

NOTIFICATION MEASURES

3 Out-of-garrison military activities in the area, whether independent or combined with airborne or amphibious support, would be subject to notification by the participants when they were conducted:
- by one or more divisions of ground forces or equivalent formations, whenever they reached the thresholds mentioned below;
- by a temporary formation having a structure comparable to a divisional formation, whenever it reached the thresholds mentioned below:
  - half or more of its main combat elements (brigades and regiments of battle tanks, infantry, motorized infantry or airborne troops or formations of equivalent size) and with at least one out-of-garrison artillery, engineer or helicopter support element;
  - 6,000 or more troops; or
  - 240 battle tanks (minimum number); or
  - 615 armoured transport vehicles (minimum number).
- by elements of ground combat forces that are not organized in a divisional formation, whenever they reached the following thresholds:
  - 6,000 troops;
  - 240 battle tanks (minimum number); or
  - 615 armoured transport vehicles (minimum number).[19]

4 Mobilization activities, including recall of reservists, would be subject to notification 45 days in advance, whenever:
- 25,000 troops or more participate in the zone of application;
- the majority of the main combat elements of three divisions or more participate there.

5 All amphibious landings in the CCSBMDE area would be subject to notification whenever they reach the following thresholds:
- 3 battalions or more;
- 3,000 troops or more.

6 In the case of a notifiable activity conducted without prior notice, such as an emergency drill, notification would be given as soon as troops receive the order to conduct the activity in question.

7 All notifications would include the following information:
- the description of the activity, including the name of the exercise, if appropriate;

- the general headquarters responsible for the activity;
- the general purpose of the activity, including its relationship with any other notifiable activity;
- the planned date and duration of the activity, indicating the precise dates of the first deployments, the active phase of the exercise and the return to garrison;
- the names of the participating States;
- the precise geographical delineation of the zone of activity;
- the number of participating forces;
- the types of ground divisions;
- the types of other forces involved (airborne, airmobile, naval, amphibious forces);
- additional information if the activity were to deviate from the original plan or had not been included in it.

OBSERVATION MEASURES

Each State participant in the agreement could send up to two observers to activities notified by the other States, except for emergency drills of less than 48 hours' duration. In this context, the host State would:

- ensure that the observers could communicate rapidly with their diplomats (embassy or consulate);
- allow observers to use their own optical equipment as deemed necessary for accomplishing their missions;
- provide observers with all the requisite details on the notified activity;
- provide observers with the opportunities to observe directly all units participating in the activity;
- allow observers direct access to all phases of the activity in the zone between the garrison and the deployment location, etc.[20]

EXECUTION AND VERIFICATION

Each State would be allowed two inspections annually for purposes of verifying conformity with the agreement. No State would have the right to refuse a request for inspection, but it would be allowed to designate a certain number – as limited as possible – of prohibited areas (military installations, bases, garrisons, military industrial installations, scientific laboratories, and so on). Inspection teams would be permitted to enter the territory of the host State no later than 36 hours after having made the request, and their missions would have to be accomplished within a 48-hour period. Inspections could be conducted using aircraft, or land vehicles that could be provided by the inspecting State. Inspection teams could use their own maps, observation instruments, photographic equipment, tape recorders and telecommunications equipment.

DEVELOPMENT OF MEANS OF COMMUNICATION

Improving means of communication was never a central element of the negotiations. In comparison with the sc1 proposal, this aspect of the sc1 (Amplified) proposal was without consequence.

Although the set of Western measures had thus become definitive in form, it was no more convincing in the eyes of the Soviets than the sc2 proposal. The East had taken its own initiative in respect of "technical" measures and tabled five working documents on the subject between February and May 1985. The substance was, however, disappointing. The Warsaw Pact proposed to limit the size of manoeuvres to 40,000 troops (CSCE/WGA1, 7 February 1985).[21] The Warsaw Pact also proposed that ground manoeuvres above a threshold of 20,000 troops should be notifiable 30 days in advance (CSCE/SC/WGB1, 20 May 1985)[22] and that independent naval and air manoeuvres should also be notifiable above thresholds of 30 ships and 50 aircraft respectively (CSCE/SC/WGB2 and WGB3, 20 May 1985).[23] Finally, the Warsaw Pact suggested that notification should be given of movements and military transfers above a threshold of 20,000 troops *towards* the zone of application (CSCE/SC/WGB4, 21 June 1985).[24] The zone of application was obviously that contained between the Atlantic and the Urals, and notification would apply to movements from country to country within the zone of application and to movements from the outside towards the zone of application.

The Eastern position thus seemed to have changed little by the end of June, except in two respects: the East was now negotiating in terms of concrete measures and according symbolic support to the principle of verification. On the other hand, the NATO measures continued to be viewed by the East as some form of legalized espionage. Many observers felt that the Soviets were tightly limiting their concessions so that the final outcome of the Conference would be a mini-set of measures differing little from those of Helsinki.

For instance, in the context of verification, the Soviets seemed to favour the use of national technical means and a system of consultation without inspections. This position was different both from that of NATO, which called for inspection quotas, and from that advanced by Sweden in early June which proposed inspection on demand, but with the right of refusal. The Swiss, for their part, had introduced the idea of a "*salon des ambassadeurs*" which would study inspection demands. The Eastern countries were warm to these latter suggestions, but there remained a considerable divergence of view between the Warsaw Pact and the West, including the NNA nations, on the issues of non-use of force, notification thresholds, the definition of notifiable activities, observation of manoeuvres, inclusion of air and naval activities, verification, exchange of information and constraining measures.

By the summer of 1985, the situation was still not especially encouraging. The Ottawa meeting on human rights became deadlocked on 17 June, and there was fear that the Stockholm Conference might suffer a similar fate. The tone of the Canadian report issued at the end of the session on 9 July 1985 reflected a sense of great anxiety: the 6th session – from 14 May to 5 July – had been barren, for the East had firmed up its position and had gradually gained the initiative while the allies were increasingly divided on their strategy. Atlantic Alliance policy remained confused on the issues of non-use of force and constraining measures, and many technical anomalies were apparent in the set of Western measures. The Canadian Delegation feared that a gulf might develop within NATO between the "maximalists", such as the United States, which seemed prepared to accept a deadlock at the Stockholm Conference unless the set of Western measures were accepted in entirety, and the "minimalists", such as Norway, which favoured the adoption of a mini-set of Soviet measures rather than allow the CCSBMDE to end in failure. According to the Head of the Canadian Delegation, the main problem of the Atlantic Alliance in this situation was diplomatic apathy:

The articulation of one hundred good reasons for doing nothing is, for diplomats, the most important "*déformation professionnelle*". It is probably as deeply rooted in the human character as it is in national political realities, and there is unfortunately not much that can be done about it by way of corrective action.[25]

The Canadian message was clear – the allies had to regain the initiative by re-formulating their strategy and by being prepared, especially, to make changes to their proposal.

In late summer, anticipating pressure from the allies, the Americans relaxed their position and concluded an agreement which extricated the Stockholm Conference from the quagmire. Following a meeting in Moscow between the Heads of the American and Soviet Delegations, agreement was reached on a formula to allow the CCSBMDE to move on to the drafting stage. The agreement was announced at the closing of the 7th session which lasted from 10 September to 18 October 1985. It accorded responsibility to Working

Group B for drafting confidence measures on observation and notification as well as on related verification, information and communication means. This implied that verification and information measures would be limited to the specific context of notifiable activities. The Western annual information measures were thus implicitly abandoned. Working Group A, for its part, would concern itself with reaffirmation of the principle of non-use of force and with constraining measures, including the annual calendar of manoeuvres. The Americans had succeeded in having calendars take the place of constraints. In addition, the Soviets themselves recognized that from among all the declaratory measures, only the principle of non-use of force would form part of the final Accord.

This agreement thus went much further than a simple agreement on procedure which, in fact, was the form that it took. It reflected the resolve of the superpowers to make the Stockholm Conference the first stage of the *détente* that was progressively emerging. The statements of Gorbachev at the French National Assembly on 3 October 1985 and the dialogue at the u.s.-Soviet summit in Geneva in November, echoed the new climate. Events started to move faster during the 8th session which was held between 5 November and 20 December. On 15 November, the NNA nations tabled a new proposal (SC7) in the hope that it would serve as a base document for the final Accord. The SC7 proposal contained, in particular, the following measures:

1　*Notification measures.*
   Notification of ground manoeuvres involving one division or more would be given 42 days in advance.
2　*Annual calendars.*
   Every participant would provide an annual list of ground manoeuvres involving one division or more.
3　*Observers.*
   Observers from each country would be invited to all notifiable manoeuvres; they would have the right to ascertain that the manoeuvres in question were conducted in conformity with notifications and that they posed no threat.
4　*Notification and observation of military activities conducted without advance notice.*
   On the subject of military activities conducted without advance notice, the NNA nations proposed that notification of emergency drills and mobilization exercises would be given "as quickly as possible", but that observation of such activities would not be a requirement unless they "took the form of manoeuvres" and that

even then the requirement for observation would only apply to manoeuvres extending beyond a certain period (unspecified).

5 *Constraints.*
- no manoeuvre could exceed the threshold of 5 divisions or last longer than 17 days;
- no country could host more than five manoeuvres of less than two divisions or participate in them, and only one manoeuvre of less than two divisions could take place at the same time (these restrictions would not apply if notification of the activities were given in the annual calendar);
- no State could host more than five manoeuvres at the two-division threshold or participate in them; notification of manoeuvres exceeding this threshold had to be given in the annual calendars. No more than two manoeuvres of this type could be conducted at the same time, but once a year such manoeuvres could be combined provided that a threshold of seven divisions would be respected.

6 *Observation on demand.*
The participating States could request that a neutral observation team be sent at short notice to the territory of another participating State if they felt that their security was at risk. However, the participating State receiving such a request could refuse for reason of State.

7 *Communication.*
It was planned to install a facsimile communications system for transmitting texts, maps and graphics to the various participating States; in addition a transmission band on the Eurovision and Intervision networks would be reserved for the use of the CCSBMDE.

8 *Mode of consultation.*
In exceptional circumstances, diplomatic mini-meetings between parties concerned could be convened at short notice.

9 *Non-use of force.*
It was proposed that the principle of non-use of force be reaffirmed and that the threat of force be condemned; the text of the NNA nations also contained a paragraph reaffirming the importance of basic human rights and freedoms; moreover the participating States would also commit not to assist terrorists.

Overall, despite its late arrival on the scene, the document showed clearly that the position of the NNA nations was very close to that of NATO, although there were some differences in respect of constraints and inspections. Proposal sc7 was thus received favourably in Stockholm. In December 1985, the Head of the u.s. Delegation stated optimistically that the chances of reaching successful agreement during the following year were rather good. But some friction appeared in the Atlantic Alliance in late 1985. At that stage in the Stockholm Conference, the main decisions had been taken bilaterally between the United States and the ussr and, throughout the year, the allies had shown little spirit of collective initiative.

NATO's policies on constraints and non-use of force remained confused and the NNA nations, despite their own difficulties, were ahead of the Atlantic Alliance on these two issues. It was in this already unsatisfactory climate that the allies again showed division within their ranks, this time concerning the closing date of the Stockholm Conference. The French wanted to fix the date of 18 July 1986 in order to instil a sense of urgency in the political climate. In view of the monumental amount of work that remained to be done, the July date was simply unrealistic. The French were also out of order since the csce rules of procedure require that all Conference participants agree by consensus on the date of adjournment. The majority of the Western caucus, not without some difficulty, eventually made the French see reason and the closing date of the Conference was set as 19 September 1986. This episode, although minor, nevertheless demonstrates the internal problems experienced by the NATO group and foreshadowed the ups and downs and the setbacks that were to mark the course of the CCSBMDE during the following year.

These were the circumstances in which Canada again became the spokesman for the most spirited of the allies by urging the Atlantic Alliance to regain the unity that had dissipated since 1984. Although it would probably be an exaggeration to affirm that Canada's role was a determining one, it nevertheless became apparent that NATO could no longer content itself with a policy of maintaining the *status quo*.

THE DRAFTING PHASE:
JANUARY TO SEPTEMBER 1986

The 9th session of the CCSBMDE, held between 28 January and 14 March 1986, brought optimistic expectations for a favourable outcome of the Stockholm Conference. In a matter of just a few weeks, the Soviets removed most of the obstacles that had blocked the negotiations up to that time.

On 15 January, in a keynote speech on disarmament, Gorbachev announced that the Eastern countries were ready to relinquish their demands on the notification of independent naval manoeuvres. On 10 February, the Poles, speaking for the Warsaw Pact countries, accepted the principle of inviting observers to all notifiable activities on a universal basis. On 6 March, the drafting group reached agreement in principle on the matter of calendars. Finally, on 13 March, in a move towards *rapprochement* with the NNA nations, Bulgaria proposed limiting the scope of military activities to five times the notifiable level (five divisions) and limiting their duration to 15 days. On this occasion, the Warsaw Pact also offered to impose a ceiling of 7,000 troops on airborne and amphibious activities.

On the matter of constraints, the most significant event of the 9th session was, without question, the Irish proposal on "time constraints". Under this proposal, no activity involving over 75,000 participants could take place unless announced in an annual calendar submitted two years in advance. For activities involving over 100,000 participants, the calendar would have to be submitted three years in advance. The idea opened the way for one of the most important compromises of the negotiations.

In brief, at the end of the session, only four essential matters remained to be settled:

- the threshold for notifications;
- the content of notifications and the matter of independent air manoeuvres;
- the conditions for observation;
- the matter of inspections.

Through Soviet concessions, considerable progress had been made in a relatively short time, but NATO was very slow in attuning to the new climate.

The first reason stemmed from what might be called the "crisis of non-use of force". At the end of 1985, despite initiatives from many of the allies, the Western caucus had still not defined its position on reaffirmation of the principle of non-use of force. In February 1986, and with much fanfare, France presented the Atlantic Alliance with the proposal of the Twelve, being careful not to divulge the origin of this "independent" initiative but insisting on its importance. In addition, the French demanded that their proposal be accepted in caucus without amendment and without discussion of other options. Not surprisingly, this led to another "family squabble" during which the French Delegation was publicly accused of concealment and crookedness. It was only in mid-March that NATO presented the general position of the Sixteen on non-use of force. Internal disputes over the details of the proposal nevertheless continued until 18 June 1986. Ironically, the East seemed to have lost all interest in the matter, and the Atlantic Alliance made a spectacle of itself over insignificant stakes.

The second reason for the slowness of the Atlantic Alliance in adjusting to the new climate concerned the matter of constraints. Although many analyses had been conducted in Brussels, the allies remained unconvinced of the NATO options that emerged, considering that any form of constraint would have negative consequences for the West. For this reason, the main Western players at the meetings of the Atlantic Alliance in March 1986 resisted even harder. The Americans, in particular, opposed constraints for reasons of principle, considering that constraints were foreign to confidence-building measures *per se*.

This atmosphere of total stagnation in the debate persisted until after the break in the proceedings which took place from 15 March to 14 April 1986. And it was only in August, five weeks before the Stockholm Conference was to close, that the allies were ready to start drafting a constraining measure.

The United States, far from facilitating agreement within NATO, threw oil on the fire through the suggestion of Max Kampelman that the results of the Stockholm Conference be referred to a subsequent CSCE meeting in order to "balance" them in relation to concessions on human rights. In other words, the Stockholm Accord would not become executory until after the results of the CSCE Follow-Up meeting, scheduled to open in Vienna in November 1986, had been judged satisfactory. And only God knew how long that would take. Shocked by such a heretical suggestion, which incidentally contravened the Stockholm Conference mandate, the allies pointed out to the Americans that such a formula could delay things for several years and that it would pose many "public relations" problems. Max Kampelman refused, however, to debate the issue and simply repeated that "to allow the CCSBMDE to acquire an autonomous existence would be a mistake".

In light of the difficult and confused context, the 10th session of negotiations – from 15 April to 23 May – was not expected to become the decisive phase of the Stockholm Conference. A Canadian memorandum dated 10 April 1986 confirmed this impression: from the Western standpoint, there was no prospect of breaking the deadlock before the summer. Yet the tone of the memorandum was still confident: "If common political will exists in Washington and Moscow, agreement will be reached". On 23 May, in a continuing show of good faith, the Soviets proposed lowering the threshold for notification of manoeuvres from 20,000 to 18,000 troops and, in addition, stated that notifications should specify the number of divisions participating in the manoeuvres. It was the first sign that the Warsaw Pact was ready to accept a divisional threshold for notification. Finally, the East proposed that air manoeuvres involving over 700 flights and 350 aircraft should be notifiable. In this context, the West responded to the gesture by accepting the principle of notification of air manoeuvres, but only when conducted in concert with military ground activities. Negotiations progressed in tiny steps but, with the closing of the Stockholm Conference just a few months away, some Western nations expressed concern that a race against the clock would allow the Soviets to reduce to nothing the concessions already made by linking them with unacceptable conditions. According to the Head of the Canadian Delegation:

The Soviet tactic is to squeeze the negotiating agenda which is unquestionably Western in content by avoiding real negotiations as long as this can be done, and when this posture is no longer tenable they will make a few concessions ... to give a measure of satisfaction to Western negotiators and more importantly to achieve an agreement that will look credible to Western opinion.[26]

Soviet goodwill was not without its ambiguities. For instance, as T. Delworth noted, despite Gorbachev's 15 January speech the Soviet negotiators did not drop their insistence on notification of independent naval manoeuvres until the end of the 10th session, some five months after the concession had been publicly announced.

Canadian fears eased during the 11th session which extended from 10 June to 19 July. On 19 June, the Soviets proposed that notification should be given, in addition to manoeuvres, of military movements above a threshold of 18,000 troops and of amphibious manoeuvres involving over 5,000 personnel.[27] As for constraints, the Soviets suggested that the limit of 40,000 troops for ground manoeuvres might be exceeded once every three years. Then, following the Gorbachev-Mitterand meeting in Moscow on 8 and 9 July, the Soviets announced that they would drop their insistence on notification of independent air manoeuvres and that they would accept the principle of inspections. In the final analysis, France had successfully completed a prestige operation, even though the Kremlin had already decided to make these concessions one month earlier. On 11 June, in Gorbachev's Budapest declaration – his second major initiative – he had clearly indicated the desire of the Soviets to move to phase 2 of the CCSBMDE which concerned disarmament issues. The Stockholm Conference was thus "fated" to end in success.

At the same time, NATO started to move and, on 30 June, T. Delworth officially announced that:

- the threshold of 6,000 troops for notification of manoeuvres could be raised;
- mobilization activities would no longer be part of the notifications;[28]
- the timeframe for observations would be limited to the execution phase of the manoeuvres, when the threshold for notification is exceeded;
- the quota of active inspections could be limited to 1 per year, that is, 7 for the Warsaw Pact countries and 28 for NATO and the NNA nations.

In parallel, Ireland continued to pursue its initiative and proposed that activities not listed in the calendar should not involve more than a certain number of troops and that the number of such activities should not exceed a fixed proportion of the activities listed. Participants would have to give two years' advance notification of military activities involving over 75,000 troops and three years' advance notification of activities involving over 100,000 troops. In the absence of such notifications, the activities and manoeuvres in question would be forbidden, except for those of emergency drills.[29]

In his reply of 18 July, the Head of the Soviet Delegation confirmed that the USSR was prepared to accept inspections on its territory on an experimental basis, and on 23 July it was announced unofficially that the East would drop its demand for notification of military forces in transit through Europe to other destinations.

By the beginning of August, the main obstacles had been removed, and the path towards reaching agreement seemed clear. As T. Delworth observed in his report at the end of the session: "The avalanche has just begun". He added, however, that if the closing date of 19 September were to be respected it would require a monumental effort by all the participants. The 12th and last session of the Stockholm Conference would not open until 19 August, which left barely five weeks for the drafting of the Accord. In view of the number of problems that still remained to be settled, it was difficult to imagine how the Atlantic Alliance would be able to coordinate its strategy among its 16 member nations. In mid-August, at the NATO meeting in The Hague, Canada suggested that the responsibility for the key decisions be accorded to the "main players" – the United States and the USSR – on condition that the allied caucus would be kept informed. Thus, the final negotiations in Stockholm took place in the "boudoir" of the superpowers, but not without several blasts of the "megaphone".

These bilateral discussions focused mainly on the procedures for inspections and the kinds of activity that would be notifiable. In the case of inspections, the Soviet-American talks had revealed that the Soviets were opposed to a multilateral verification system in which the NNA nations would necessarily participate. The Soviets were also opposed to a retrospective examination of inspections by the 35 participants of the Stockholm Conference. In other words, the Soviets wanted a limited and discreet inspection system. As one Canadian memorandum noted: "The Soviets really seem to want something they can call inspections but, like the USA, they do not want anybody to pass judgement on the results of the inspections".[30]

As for activities which would be notifiable, the Soviets appeared reluctant to accept the Western idea of out-of-garrison activities, for it would open up to observation too many military zones where access was forbidden. Instead, they proposed that notification and observation should pertain to situations involving troop concentrations, either during manoeuvres or military movements.

Following these discussions, Ambassador Grinevski announced on 19 August 1986 that the East would accept a quota of one or two passive inspections annually. The idea of out-of-garrison activities was rejected. Two days later, on 21 August, the Soviets proposed a "two-gear" system of observation and notification under which observation of notifiable activities would only be mandatory above a threshold of 20,000 troops. On 22 August, the USSR confirmed that notification of troop transfers towards Europe would only be given if the troops were to be deployed in the CCSBMDE zone. Then, on 26 August, Soviet-American agreement was reached on the types of activities to be notified: the concept of out-of-garrison activities would be discarded in favour of the ideas of concentration and transfer.

On 28 August, following the meeting of its member States in The Hague, NATO proposed that two years' advance notice should be given for activities involving over 75,000 troops. The requirement for two years advance notice would also apply to activities involving over 40,000 troops, except that such activities would not be prohibited in the event that circumstances prevented notice from being given within this timeframe.

At the beginning of September, despite the complex implications of the mutual concessions that had been made, negotiations entered their final phase. As T. Delworth noted:

With a month left to go, the Conference has moved into high gear, at least in terms of speed if not in terms of registering results. There is in fact a frenetic air to the whole business, with working groups, coffee groups, contact groups, cluster caucuses, teams, troikas and heaven only knows what other combinations of Delegates discussing the issues before us virtually non-stop from eight in the morning right through until midnight, with the working day climaxing at working dinners. So hectic is the pace that many of us, including Grinevski, complain bitterly that it is difficult for Heads of Delegations to have regular staff meetings and to keep themselves informed because all staff members are so fully occupied.[31]

In this frenzied atmosphere, it was inevitable that clashes would occur. Ironically, these were not provoked by the Soviets but by the Western nations themselves. One of these clashes – and a major one at that – concerned the procedures for inspections. On 28 August, the Soviets had proposed that aerial inspections should be performed using aircraft provided by the inspected State. The Americans preferred another solution whereby the neutral and non-aligned nations would provide the aircraft and the pilots to fly inspection flights. Washington thus supported a Swiss initiative (itself supported by Austria, Finland, Sweden and Ireland), which resulted in a visit by the Swiss foreign minister, P. Aubert, to Moscow on 5 and 6 September 1986. Aubert announced somewhat prematurely on 7 September that the Soviets were prepared to accept the NNA proposal. At that juncture, during a restricted meeting of the Atlantic Alliance caucus on 15 September, the United States revealed a "major revision" to its policy: should the NNA proposal be rejected by the USSR, Washington was prepared to see the Stockholm Conference end in failure.[32] This last minute manoeuvre obviously provoked a general outcry in the Atlantic Alliance, and the U.S. President, pressed by Germany and the United Kingdom, tried to reassure his allies by stressing that this "initiative" was purely a tactical manoeuvre to wrest one last concession from the Soviets but there was no question, of course, of allowing the negotiations to end in failure. American support for the NNA initiative proved, in fact, to be no more than a bluff. This was leaked to the *New York Times* on 17 September and, as J. Klein noted: "The reversal of the NATO nations on the issue of aerial inspection and the dropping of the NNA solution in the absence of any clear Soviet responsibility were strongly resented by the NNA nations whose mediation role had been demolished".[33]

In parallel with this rather unedifying episode, the last haggling started on the thresholds for notifications and the precise number of inspections to which each participant would have to submit annually. Following an avalanche of proposals and counter-proposals, agreement was finally reached on 21 September (the clocks at the Stockholm Conference had been stopped at 10:55 p.m. on Friday 19 September to avoid a technical adjournment of the Conference). It was agreed that concentrations and transfers of troops would be subject to notification above thresholds of 13,000 troops and 300 tanks, that such activities would be subject to observation above a threshold of 17,000 troops and that the quota of inspections would be fixed at three per calendar year. At 9:30 a.m. on 22 September 1986, the CCSBMDE came to a close. The first arms control agreement since June 1979, when SALT II was signed, had just been concluded.[34]

THE STOCKHOLM ACCORD: A SUMMARY

The Final Document of Stockholm, even more than the Helsinki (1975) and Madrid (1983) agreements, constituted a clear victory of Western philosophy on confidence-building measures. A cursory survey of the main sections of the Document shows that, for the most part, NATO requirements were satisfied.

1   Refraining from the Threat or Use of Force.

This section reaffirms the commitment of the participating States to refrain from the threat or use of military force in their relations, not only between themselves, but with any State "regardless of that State's political, social, economic or cultural systems and irrespective of whether or not they maintain with that State relations of alliance". This constituted, therefore, the first implicit condemnation of the Brezhnev doctrine that the Soviets were to sign. The Document also stresses "the universal significance of human rights and fundamental freedoms" and reaffirms that respect for, and the effective exercise of, these rights and freedoms "are essential factors for international peace". The text continues by emphasizing the need "to take resolute measures to prevent and to combat terrorism". In addition, the preamble to this section clearly indicates that the confidence-building measures should "give effect and expression to the duty of States to refrain from the threat or use of force in their mutual relations".

Overall, the initial Soviet proposal for a Treaty on Non-Use of Force accompanied with a commitment to no-first-use of nuclear weapons had been completely neutralized and transformed into an inoffensive document that mainly reflected Western preoccupations.

2   Prior Notification of Certain Military Activities.

The participants undertook to give prior notification, 42 days in advance, of the following four types of military activity when occurring in the zone extending from the Atlantic to the Urals:

- exercise activities of land forces involving at least 13,000 troops or 300 battle tanks if organized into a divisional structure;
- amphibious landing activities involving at least 3,000 troops;
- parachute drop activities at or above the same threshold;
- troop transfers in or towards the zone of application when these forces are concentrated to participate in an exercise involving at least 13,000 troops or 300 battle tanks.

If such activities were carried out without advance notice to the troops involved, an "alert" notification would be given at the time that such activities commenced.

Despite the more modest and perhaps more ambiguous wording of the Stockholm Document, the notification measures approved in Stockholm were a significant improvement over those adopted in Helsinki. They provided for a more complete vision of standard military activities and were tied to an acceptable threshold, requiring that prior notification be given of any military exercise, manoeuvre or movement at or above the standard divisional level. The notification also had to contain more information, specifically;

- the designation of the military activity;
- its general purpose;
- the names of the States participating in the activity;
- the level of command, organizing and commanding the activity;
- the start and end dates of the activity;
- the total number of troops taking part, by category (ground troops, amphibious troops, airmobile and airborne troops, etc.) and by State, if applicable;
- the number and type of divisions participating for each State;
- the number of battle tanks participating for each State;
- the total number of anti-tank guided missile launchers mounted on armoured vehicles;
- the total number of artillery pieces and multiple rocket launchers (100 mm calibre or above);
- the total number of helicopters, by category;
- the envisaged number of sorties by aircraft;
- the purpose of air missions;
- the categories of aircraft involved;
- the level of command, organizing and commanding the air forces;
- naval ship-to-shore gunfire support, if applicable;
- indication of other ship-to-shore support;
- the level of command, organizing and commanding the naval force participation;

- the engagement of amphibious or airborne troops in these activities;
- the total number of such amphibious or airborne troops;
- the points of embarkation of these troops, if in the zone of application;
- the transfers of troops within or towards the area of application to participate in these activities;
- the total number of troops transferred;
- the total number of battle tanks participating in a notifiable arrival or concentration;
- the geographical coordinates for the points of arrival and for the points of concentration of the troops;
- the area of the military activity delimited by geographical features together with geographical coordinates;
- the start and end dates of each phase (transfers, deployment, concentration, etc.) of activities as well as the tactical purpose and corresponding geographical areas for each phase.[35]

3   Observation of Certain Military Activities.

In this area, progress in Stockholm was particularly noticeable. The Final Act of Helsinki had made observation of military activities a voluntary practice, left to the good grace of the States participating in the CSCE. The Stockholm Document makes this practice mandatory when notifiable activities exceed a threshold of 17,000 troops in ground manoeuvres and 5,000 troops in landing exercises. In addition, the 1986 Document creates a true observation system which obliges the host State to satisfy a certain number of requirements. The host State must allow the observers to use their own observation equipment and, of course, must provide them with food, lodging and transportation. The host State must also provide observers with appropriate topographical maps, with specific information on the activity subject to observation and with opportunities for timely communication with their diplomatic missions. The host State will:

provide opportunities to observe directly forces of the State/States engaged in the military activity so that the observers get an impression of the flow of the activity; to this end, the observers will be given the opportunity to observe major combat units of the participating formations of a divisional or equivalent level and, whenever possible, to visit some units and communicate with commanders and troops; commanders or other senior personnel ... will inform the observers of the mission of their respective units.[36]

Each participating State may send up to two observers to all noti-fiable activities – including emergency drills lasting over 72 hours – but it may also decline invitations without prejudice to its rights.

4   Annual Calendars.

Measures concerning annual calendars were not included in the Final Act of Helsinki. The Stockholm Document makes provision for the annual exchange, between participating States, of calendars of all notifiable military activities. Calendars are exchanged no later than 15 November to cover activities for the following year. The informa-tion included in the calendars is less detailed than that in the noti-fications. Notifiable activities not included in the annual calendar must be communicated as soon as possible and no later than the date of the appropriate notification.

5   Constraining Provisions.

The constraining provisions prescribe that information on military activities involving more than 75,000 troops must be communicated to all other participating States two years in advance. If this require-ment is not respected the activities will be prohibited. The same two-year advance notice provision applies to activities involving over 40,000 troops, although they may be permitted if the activities are included in the annual calendar. If military activities subject to prior notification are carried out in addition to those contained in the annual calendar, the participating States must make sure that they are as few as possible.

6   Compliance and Verification.

Certainly the most novel element of the Stockholm Document is the set of provisions on verification. After 40 years of refusals, the USSR finally agreed to the principle of inspections. Any participating State may submit a request for inspection to another participating State if in doubt about compliance with the agreed CSBMS. No participating State is obliged to accept more than three such requests per calendar year. It is agreed, however, that States will not artificially fill this quota by soliciting requests for inspection from States with whom they are allied (see Annex IV of the Stockholm Document). A State receiving a request for inspection – if its quota is not filled – must respond within 24 hours and allow the inspection team (four persons at most) to enter its territory within 36 hours of the issuance of the request. The inspection, which can be conducted on the ground or from the air, must be terminated within 48 hours of the arrival of the inspection team at the specified area. This specified area is designated by the inspecting State; its dimensions can vary, but it may not exceed the area required for an army level military activity. Although the inspection team is permitted access, entry and unobstructed survey in the specified area, it may not have access to areas and sensitive points such as military installations, naval vessels, military vehicles, etc.; the number and extent of the restricted access areas must be, however, as specified in the Document, "as limited as possible". Ground and air transportation is provided by the State receiving the request for inspection, but the inspection team is permitted to use its own maps, photo cameras, binoculars and dictaphones, as well as its own aeronautical charts. In the case of aerial inspections, the inspection team may have access to the on-board navigational equipment to make sure that the aircraft is following the filed flight plan. Finally, the inspection team must have continuous access to appropriate telecommunications equipment. After the inspection is completed, the inspecting State must prepare a report and send a copy to all participating States.

Unquestionably, the Stockholm Accord represents a significant qualitative leap forward in the arms control process in Europe. The first confidence-building measures of Helsinki were largely superseded and replaced by measures that are verifiable, systematic, much more detailed and politically constraining. But perhaps the great success of Stockholm lies less in the details of the final Accord than in the practice which it engendered; the exchange of annual calendars and the conduct of observations and inspections now form part of a system which seemingly satisfies all participants. In 1987, for instance, the Warsaw Pact gave notification of 32 activities, or a number roughly equal to the total number of manoeuvres announced by the East in the preceding decade. In 1988, notification of 34 activities was given, and 15 observations and 8 inspections took place without incident. The Warsaw Pact has also exhibited more flexibility in respect of observations, and observers at the Friendship 88 exercise, which took place in the GDR in April 1988, were allowed for the first time to photograph activities as they pleased, which is more than required under the terms of the Accord. The implementation of the Stockholm Document has thus created its own dynamics, and the internal reports of NATO express satisfaction with its success.

The remaining prejudices against the Stockholm Document should, therefore, dissipate even if the arsenals of the two alliances remain intact and threatening. The issue now faced by the 35 States of the CSCE is how to follow up on the process started in Helsinki two decades ago. Would it be appropriate now for the Western nations to address the issue of arms reductions, or should they content themselves with perfecting the confidence-building measures established in Stockholm?

Following the logic ratified at Madrid, the 35 CSCE participants had reason to tackle these two questions head on at the close of the Vienna Conference in January 1989. Given the insoluble problems posed by the MBFR, the traditional waverings of NATO and the NNA, and the uncertainties surrounding superpower politics, one is led to wonder whether such undertakings are not, for the moment, premature. Whatever the risk, we do not believe that the arms control process started in Stockholm in 1986 and pursued in Washington in 1987 should be stopped, even though prudence may dictate that it be slowed. As a means of managing international relations, the Cold War has had its day, and it is time that the United States along with Europe adapt to a climate in which the weight of diplomacy and dialogue is more important than the weight of arms. Viewed from this standpoint, some myths should be discarded, and it can only be hoped that the United States will respond soon to the superb challenge thrown down by Arbatov: "We are going to do something terrible to you Americans. We are going to deprive you of an enemy."

Conclusion

Negotiating ceaselessly, openly and secretly, in every place ...
is vital for the well-being of States.

Cardinal Richelieu, *Testament politique*

The foregoing thematic chapters are aimed at providing the reader with an understanding of the essential elements of arms control and disarmament and the related decision-making process. We shall, therefore, restrict discussion here to a few general observations on the nature of the process, on problems of decision-making, and on political power and influence.

In an article published in 1989[1], we have focused attention on the premises of the two predominant schools of thought on the theory of international relations, specifically those that subscribe to the ideas of "peace through force" and "peace through law". The first derives from scientific positivism and the industrial revolution, and the second from the great Judeo-Christian traditions of social justice and of peaceful settlement of differences.

The realist or neo-realist school of international relations occupies a privileged position within the "peace through force" school, whose strategists are essentially concerned with maximizing the benefits to the State, often at the expense of the best interests of the international community. The strategy is first and foremost nationalistic and secondarily "internationalistic". The "peace through law" school on the other hand is primarily "internationalistic" and secondarily nationalistic. But within each of these two paradigms there are wide variations. The "peace through force" school extends from one extreme of "brutal and total" force – the two world wars, for instance – through nuclear deterrence as a means of preserving the system, to the other extreme of exploitation of conflicts involving third parties. The "peace through law" school extends from legal idealism embracing plans for perpetual peace (the Abbé de Saint-Pierre, and Kant in particular), through open parliamentary diplomacy as typified by the League of Nations, to oligarchical management of the system as exemplified by the Security Council of the United Nations.

There have been differences in the intensity and importance of these variations within each of these paradigms. Now, as in the past, there is a continuing search for ways of sustaining world peace. But neither force nor law can, by themselves, eliminate inequalities between States or the "desperate causes" of terrorism. Transformation of the international system requires a harmonious mix of these two approaches. Everyone is aware of the problems of general disarmament. It is not simply a matter of progressively reducing the military equipment and forces of adversaries, but of building, at the same time, a mechanism for positive cooperation between them founded on the principles of law and social justice.

Canada's foreign policy has traditionally drawn from both these schools. At the height of the Cold War, during Diefenbaker's term in office, Canadian parliamentarians were as much concerned with disarmament, the United Nations and the Third World as they were during the Trudeau era.[2] During these two periods, however, Canada consistently thought that she could best influence the international system through her military alliances. This is not to say that Canada neglected the United Nations or the other major international fora for negotiation, but rather that Canada recognized that she alone did not possess the key for transforming the international system. One gains the impression that Canada was always reluctant to be party to a military alliance, which she views as a necessary evil until such time as the international system adjusts to her political ideals.

Under these circumstances, it is not therefore surprising that Canadians progressively came to view both the United States and the USSR in a negative light, considering them jointly responsible for the arms race. This was the most striking conclusion of the opinion polls conducted by Don Munton,[3] and was subsequently confirmed through our own research.[4] In short, Canada strived to develop a foreign policy which minimized the most harmful aspects of "peace through force" and maximized the most beneficial aspects of "peace through law".

Before summing up the Canadian diplomatic efforts on arms control and disarmament, it would be useful to keep in mind the three major channels of negotiation on the international diplomatic scene. The first embraces all the work of the United Nations from 1945 to 1957, from the time that the UN Atomic Energy Commission was created to the time that the work of the Subcommittee of the Disarmament Commission was completed in 1957. The second channel comprises the functional negotiations on the major topical issues: nuclear non-proliferation, halting of nuclear tests, elimination of biological and chemical weapons, and the so-called problem of non-militarization of space. The third and last channel includes the alliance-to-alliance negotiations and specifically the MBFR talks, the CSCE and the CDE.

During the first 12 years of the UN's existence, covering the first period of negotiations within the major fora for discussion created by the UN, Canada's contribution lay more in promulgating her particular vision of the international system than in developing the specific substance of disarmament proposals themselves. Canada was neither enamoured by the way in which the Soviets negotiated nor by their proposals, but had no wish to add fuel to the fire. Within the UN Atomic Energy Commission, Canada sought to reach a compromise with the Soviets on the right of veto, but in vain. Towards the end, Canada threw her support behind the Baruch Plan, probably because of the wishes of Mackenzie King. Canada's vision of a well-policed international system and her desire to reap the economic benefits of the peaceful use of atomic energy led her to advocate a non-discriminatory system of controls on technology development, whether linked to civil or military purposes.

Within the Commission for Conventional Armaments, Canada played a very small role since her troops had long been demobilized and she was not generally regarded as a military power. Canada's approach was basically similar to that of the United Kingdom – she refused to play propaganda games and sought to end discussions that seemingly led nowhere. Ottawa displayed the line of thinking that would subsequently be followed by Canadian delegates in the Subcommittee of the Disarmament Commission. During the 1950s, disarmament was nothing more than a name. The battle was conducted by means of propaganda, marathon proposals aimed at transferring responsibility for failure or refusal to the other party, and by the classical discourse of the Cold War. The Geneva Summit in 1955 shed new light on the discussions, for at this point the Americans first started to talk of arms control. In this climate, there was no further mention of disarmament. The death knell for the "disarmament enterprise", as Jean Klein put it so well, was sounded in 1957 at the time when the London Subcommittee completed its work.

The main issues addressed in the functional negotiations at the first Conference of Experts in Geneva in 1957 have persisted up to the present day. Negotiations have been pursued on a sector-by-sector basis on the major problems concerning military relations between States in the international system. The problems have been dissected one by one against a backdrop of much wider strategic considerations. The issue of non-proliferation acquired stature in 1965 when Moscow and Washington deemed that it was more important to deny the FRG access to nuclear weapons than to focus exclusively on their own bilateral relations, particularly in light of the Chinese problem which was not totally absent from their preoccupations.

During the 1970s, the important issue of a Convention on the Prohibition of Bacteriological and Toxin Weapons came to the fore, mainly in response to persistent criticisms from States which considered that the multilateral negotiations were going nowhere. The 1971 Convention on the Prohibition of Bacteriological and Toxin Weapons was a great step forward in itself, but it followed in the wake of bilateral efforts to rejuvenate a process that had long been paralysed. One year later, the first SALT agreements were signed along with a whole series of cooperative agreements with the East to give substance to *détente*.

On the other hand, the eternal issues of a comprehensive nuclear test ban and the problem of non-militarization of space continue to remain right at the centre of the superpower struggle for technological superiority. These are major problems, for they bear the stamp of the epic struggle to develop new weapons, to perfect counter-weapons, counter-counter-weapons, and so on. The spiralling arms race can only be ended through the political will of the superpowers, despite the efforts of the other States to have them exercise restraint in their technological flights of fancy. The two chapters that deal with these issues (Chapters 9 and 10) illustrate the major technological steps that marked the merciless struggle waged between the superpowers during the most tense periods of the Cold War, a struggle deemed exhausting and futile in peacetime.

Every analysis of the alliance-to-alliance negotiations shows that they were primarily dominated by the will of the superpowers and only secondarily by that of their allied States. This is not to minimize the role of the allied States, but rather to highlight the fact that the multilateral negotiations, which themselves were rich in content, ensued from bilateral dialogue. Although it may be premature to think in terms of a new way of managing military relations between the East and the West, it remains no less that these multilateral discussions were the formative stage of a long process of East-West management in which the main third-party States came to occupy a privileged position. This would have occurred earlier had it not been for the stubborn opposition to change that was exhibited by the superpowers on some very important issues.

Concerning Canadian diplomacy *per se*, we have pointed out that the responsibility for managing security is shared between the Department of External Affairs and the Department of National Defence. We believe that this division of responsibility has been well reflected in the first chapter where we spoke of the "bees" and the "ants". It should be added, however, that the stereotype image of a bureaucracy in which these two departments are necessarily dedicated to pulling in opposite directions is not a strict reflection of reality. Although it is rare to find "peaceful bees" in the Department of National Defence and "warlike ants" in the Department of External Affairs, there is a remarkable diversity of opinion within each of the departments. The Department of National Defence is, by nature, much more monolithic, but appropriate solutions have appeared whenever interdepartmental moderation has prevailed.

For the "ants", Canadian security required a close alliance with the United States, a firm stance towards the USSR and nuclear warheads for the Canadian Armed Forces. This attitude prevailed until the beginning of the 1960s. Significantly, Diefenbaker's Conservative Government is the only Canadian government which has fallen over defence issues.

Since that time, the Department of National Defence lost some of its importance in matters of arms control and disarmament, particularly following the integration of the Canadian Armed Forces. The participation of new departments, such as the Department of Energy, Mines and Resources, and the increased role of the Operational Research and Analysis Establishment of the Department of National Defence, have contributed to the "depolarization" of a needlessly tense or ill-perceived situation. Efforts to reorganize the Department of External Affairs together with the creation of appropriate interdepartmental committees have also facilitated better coordination of policy, if only because all points of view are represented.

In the Department of External Affairs, Canadian policy has changed frequently. Legal and political idealism reached its height with the Green-Burns combination. The Department of External Affairs has, however, followed the median line of the "peace through law" school for most of the time, but has sometimes revised its basic policies in deference to military considerations linked to the maintenance of strategic dialogue between the superpowers. Such was the case in the 1970s during the debate on a Comprehensive Test Ban

Treaty when interest in this subject declined following the resumption of strategic dialogue between the superpowers.

The dichotomy of functional responsibilities for security, necessarily shared between different departments, naturally gave rise to more than one paradox. In the mid-1960s Canada was conscious of the considerable benefits that could be derived from participation both in military alliances and in the major fora for multilateral negotiations on arms control. Canadian expertise acquired through collaboration in military alliances played an important role in multilateral negotiations. This expertise was most evident in debates on chemical weapons and the use of outer space, while the Canadian contributions of primary importance were on the stabilizing and destabilizing effects of technology[5] and on seismic detection. Some authors incorrectly contend that the bureaucratic conflicts between the Department of National Defence and the Department of External Affairs abated in 1965 because of the involvement of the Department of Energy, Mines and Resources (EMR). In point of fact, between 1965 and 1968, EMR and DND worked in close collaboration, and it was only in 1968 that an important breakthrough was made in seismic detection.[6] Only from that time on was Canada able to exert her full influence in the multilateral negotiations, and precisely because of her technical expertise.

Exerting influence through technical expertise was characteristic of the lesser or middle powers in the multinational negotiating fora. All these States, with Canada in the fore, wanted to use science to serve politics. Some, in Canada, have termed this approach "catalytic",[7] in that it utilizes all the scientific means available in support of the diplomatic mission. The superpowers might have found this approach troublesome, but on occasion they had no hesitation in adopting it. At least it had the merit of putting the philosophy adopted in proper perspective, unlike other approaches used by the superpowers and which served as convenient alibis when they decided to place politics at the service of science in order to exploit technology to their advantage. In other words, in the "peace through force" philosophy military projects that are often destabilizing and sometimes fanciful are justified in the name of technological progress while, in the "peace through law" philosophy, science is used to slow the spiralling arms race and not to fuel it. We are now clearly in the realm of metaregulation, or of finalities which should govern the aims of politics and not its instruments of exploitation.

Since the early 1980s, the Department of External Affairs has placed emphasis on the technical problems of verification, which provides further proof of Canadian efforts to use science to advantage in support of politics. Even within this area, Canada intends to specialize in certain "niches" where her technical expertise can be most effectively used to shelter some issues from political conflict. Canada would be the first to acknowledge the limitations of this approach, but she cannot be faulted for diversifying her efforts in this area.

Diplomatically, Canada has surely played a useful interpretive role in the Atlantic Alliance. In the mid-1950s, when Canada had the privilege of participating in the Subcommittee of the Disarmament Commission in London, she was conscious of the disarray within the Atlantic Alliance, of the limits of her influence, of the determining nature of the policies of Washington and of the dangers that certain choices could entail. In some instances, Canada was afraid of being caught in the middle between the Americans and the Europeans. Probably with good reason, Canada preferred to let her allies decide between themselves on major issues rather than promote disunity or isolate the United States, even on matters about which Canada felt strongly.[8] In this regard, the political testament of the Canadian negotiator in London, Norman A. Robertson, is revealing. Canada's contribution was small, quite simply because Canada had little influence.

On other matters, and the MBFR talks in particular, Canada largely followed the party line of the Atlantic Alliance. These circumstances probably contributed to Canada's late appreciation of the dynamics of the major transformations that were occurring in Europe when it came time to define Canadian policy on, amongst other things, confidence-building measures during Phase 1 of the CDE. Overall, however, Canada has always tried to keep both sides happy, simply because her policies, like those of most of her allies, must accommodate her own security needs as well as contribute to the management of peaceful relations between States. In Geneva in 1984, when Canada felt a strong need to present a proposal prohibiting anti-satellite systems, she chose from amongst all the Canadian proposals the one that was least "offensive" to the United States. But even this insignificant proposal was judged too "progressive" by Washington. In this regard, Canada might be reproached for having taken a "prime-ministerial" decision, even though Cabinet had given the green light for tabling the Canadian proposal in Geneva.

As for the U.S. Strategic Defense Initiative, Canada was commended by Washington for her support of "research" which, incidentally, represented the common position of the Atlantic Alliance. Perhaps this was all that Washington looked for, because it gave the

United States a general position for negotiating with the Soviets. In parallel with many other nations, Canada refused to participate officially in the project. The problem remains, however, that it is difficult to dissociate SDI from NORAD, and decisions in this area will probably be hard to take in future. With the improvement in Soviet-American relations, Canada may be able to avoid having to decide. If, however, a decision has to be made in the name of American national security, Canada would obviously have to determine how much further she could go, and if she were not prepared to go further, it could possibly threaten the security of the United States.

Considerable progress has been made in the management of disarmament issues. Since the start of the 1960s, significant human and financial resources have been progressively accorded to the Public Service for administration of these increasingly complex issues. This has led to the creation of interdepartmental committees whose composition varies in accordance with the items on the agenda. This approach does not necessarily lessen the bureaucratic conflicts between departments, but it ensures a thorough study of the issues most of the time.

The appearance of State negotiators of stature added a new dimension to the development and planning of Canadian policy. The role of the Government Advisor on Disarmament has evolved over time. Only General E.L.M. Burns had direct access to Cabinet, and his successors have reported to Cabinet through the Secretary of State for External Affairs. The other negotiators, and George Ignatieff in particular, did not benefit from such acknowledged privileges. It is difficult to assess the difference that this could have made, for when we examine the issues addressed during the period of transition between the Pearson and Trudeau years it appears that the bureaucracy itself was largely responsible for effecting it. In some documents and speeches, Ignatieff later denounced the ponderousness of the bureaucracy, especially that of the Department of National Defence. Perusal of the records shows, however, that the proliferation of opinion was much greater than some were inclined to believe.

Moreover, the role of the Canadian Ambassador for Disarmament evolved as that of "mediator" between the Government itself and the peace movements, as progressive democratization of the debate on these issues ensued in Canada. By force of circumstance, the bureaucracy again inherited the fundamental responsibility for the formulation and development of general policy. In general, it may be observed that the formulation of policy was more solid and coherent during periods when there were not too many changes in portfolio in the Department of External Affairs. In this context, perhaps one of the most appealing virtues that could be claimed by the Mulroney Government was the constancy of office during the period that the Department was under the leadership of Joe Clark. One cannot say as much for the Trudeau period when numerous changes of portfolio occurred and which allowed each of the new ministers to advance his own priorities at the expense of a more cohesive or constant policy.

As Middlemiss and Sokolsky have pointed out, the bureaucracy has since truly acquired "a considerable latitude in determining the general strategies" of government,[9] but this is inescapable given the growing complexity of some issues and the need for better integration of communications between allies. In fact, only the Government and the Cabinet can compensate, politically, for the natural caution and inertia of bureaucracies that are too often turned inwards rather than outwards.

This leads us naturally to a discussion of public figures and their political leadership. At the end of the Second World War, a handful of individuals who knew each other and who more or less came from the same school, quickly decided Canadian policy in a world where Canada had scarcely any influence. According to the late John W. Holmes, the country had to try to intervene in situations where national interests had to be defended.[10] In this regard, the political knowledge of ex-General McNaughton, former Minister of National Defence during the Second World War, was of invaluable assistance to Canada. A nationalist at heart and a staunch defender of Canadian diplomatic integrity, McNaughton was a monument of Canadian determination in resisting the immoderate ambitions of u.s. advisor Bernard Baruch.

Under Louis Saint-Laurent's leadership, Lester B. Pearson, the Secretary of State for External Affairs, had relative autonomy of action. Under Pearson, Paul Martin enjoyed a kind of "monitored freedom", since Pearson preferred to keep control of policy for himself. It was only during Diefenbaker's Conservative interlude that Canada found herself in quite an unique and atypical situation. At the height of the Cold War, with the two poles of the system firmly hardened along opposing lines, the ministers of the two departments of concern were each ready to resign should the policies of one assume ascendancy over those of the other. In these circumstances, which were hardly conducive to decision-making, the situation deteriorated and the prime minister of the time was incapable of resolving the conflict or even of making a decision. It took a general election to resolve the situation. Nevertheless, it is difficult to believe that a personality as strong as that of Pearson could not have resolved it if he had been in power at the time. Obviously, this is not a productive hypothesis since no one can rewrite history.

The Green-Burns combination has never been equalled in Canadian diplomatic history. A man who was austere *par excellence*, Green believed that come hell or high water he could change the world by his incessant appeals for negotiation and disarmament. Doubtless, he found it more important to talk to a brick wall than to relinquish his right to speak. An incalculable number of his efforts were aimed at procedure rather than substance, and this could only offend Canada's main allies. Admittedly, on matters of substance, he was supported by a man of remarkable stature, General E.L.M. Burns. Burns was an excellent diplomat who championed proposal after proposal, and was really the first to create a true core of experts on disarmament. He was not always supported, because some of his proposals were either highly vague, such as his proposal for de-nuclearizing Europe, or hastily written and improvised. Because of his deep-rooted opposition to nuclear weapons, which caused havoc within the alliances, Burns found it difficult to persuade the bureaucracy and even the government to share his ideas. His sense of political reality was much more acute on the humanitarian law of war, that is to say on the prohibition of chemical and biological weapons, on major visionary proposals for general and complete disarmament and on transfers of conventional weapons. Moreover, he was faced with an unprecedented barrage of opposition from his peers in the Department of National Defence, whose intransigence only fuelled his visionary drive.

The eminent public servant, Norman A. Robertson, was undoubtedly one of the major unknown figures on disarmament in Canada. Robertson's work, in his capacity as Under-Secretary of State for External Affairs, went largely unrecognized. Yet his tireless work in the Subcommittee of the Disarmament Commission in London, his sense of realism, his loyalty to Green during the worst moments of the quarrel between National Defence and External Affairs, his sense of compromise – which he maintained despite ridicule from Green – and his firm desire to halt nuclear proliferation rank him amongst the greatest personalities in the disarmament field in Canada.

George Ignatieff, another dominant individual, who judged that Europe could not be defended without nuclear weapons – and he was right at the time – was undoubtedly another key figure on disarmament issues in Canada. His main achievement was his active contribution in the process of concluding the Convention on the Prohibition of Bacteriological (Biological) and Toxin Weapons, and in formulating related Canadian policy. When he relinquished his duties, he judged, probably incorrectly, that the prerogative for developing Canadian policy had been passed to the bureaucracy. In fact, neither Trudeau nor the Cabinet could keep abreast of the range of issues, particularly that of reaching agreement on a Comprehensive Test Ban Treaty. The records show that neither on this issue nor on the issue of chemical and biological weapons was there any "ditching" of Canadian policy either by the Department of National Defence, by the Department of Energy, Mines and Resources or by the Department of External Affairs.

Another person who ranked at the fore was William Barton who, at the time of writing, was still performing his duties as Chairman of the Board of Directors of the Canadian Institute for International Peace and Security in Ottawa. In all likelihood this diplomat was responsible for averting certain failure of the first Review Conference on the Nuclear Non-Proliferation Treaty in 1975.[11] In a private interview, he also confided that, of all his efforts, the most rewarding were those which led France to resume her place on the Committee on Disarmament in Geneva in 1979.

Of all Canadian prime ministers, Pearson was likely the most unpredictable. As one Australian diplomat said: "He runs with the hare and hunts with the hounds!" His special relations with the United States, his determination to do nothing rather than play "musical chairs" in London, his refusal to take a position on basic issues between allies and mainly his desire to show consideration for the United States, together with his sense of realism on peace issues (at the time, peace was based on deterrence rather than disarmament), made him one of the most characteristic representatives of the schools of "peace through force" and "peace through law". This was undoubtedly the most "realist" period of Canada's history. His Liberal successor, P.E. Trudeau, who was traditionally anti-military, anti-nuclear and a fierce defender of human rights, was one of the most typical representatives of the "peace through law" school. His interest in these issues was, however, more occasional than permanent. The interest that he showed in the Nuclear Non-Proliferation Treaty was clearly aimed at keeping Canada free of nuclear weapons and, similarly, his interest in the MBFR talks was one way of pursuing his aim of withdrawing Canadian troops from Europe. When he appointed a Minister of National Defence, he made it clear that he had no wish to hear about the problems of the Department,[12] and it appears that the Deputy Minister at the time, C.R. Nixon, was advised not to present any request for supplementary funds to Treasury Board.

Trudeau's peace initiative dates back to the Williamsburg Summit in May 1984 when he decided that there should be an all-out effort for peace. It was doubtless the main intervention of this prime minister in favour of peace and disarmament. It had a profound impact on the Canadian public, and one of its main consequences was the creation of the Canadian Institute for International Peace and Security. According to some sources, the history of this initiative remains to be written. In this context, it should be noted that we have not had access to the bountiful records of the Prime Minister's Office. We must, therefore, wait for the historians to ponder this subject, for we have no more significant detail to add than has been discussed in Chapter 9 or published in the striking article by Riekhoff and Sigler.[13] All that is known is that Reagan's little phrase to the effect that "a nuclear war can neither be fought nor won", which was first used in Tokyo and subsequently repeated in Washington, was a determining one for the Soviets, if not to induce them back to the negotiating table then at least to convince them that the United States was ready to discuss.

One cannot say that Prime Minister Mulroney has truly become involved in the issues of arms control and disarmament. His main intervention is limited to the speech he made on 31 October 1985 in Ottawa, in the presence of his Ambassador for Disarmament, Doug Roche. This speech consisted of a general statement on the major priorities of the Government in this area. The hottest issue that Brian Mulroney had to deal with was the u.s. invitation to participate in sdi research. The Prime Minister was exasperated with the way in which the matter was presented to Canada, and he subsequently gave Arthur Kroeger the responsibility of writing a report on the subject. Canada then adopted a hard line, inviting the u.s. government to hold to the strict interpretation of the ABM Treaty and not to take any initiative which could undermine its foundations. By officially refusing government participation but unofficially sanctioning Canadian industrial participation, the Government has embarked on a process that will be difficult to maintain in an honest way, for the technology underlying NORAD and sdi is common and unbounded. Contrary to what some observers claim, the Cabinet decision of September 1985 was not taken to prevent a loss of Canada's credibility in arms control and disarmament, but simply because Canada wanted "to say 'no' without feeling that she had said 'no'". It goes without saying that this decision only threw the ball back into the court of the Department of National Defence which was then alone in trying to extricate itself from the hornet's nest that encircled it as a result of governmental policy.

On the major fundamental issues, it can likely be concluded that Canada's influence on arms control and disarmament went much further than might have been expected from a country both as small and as large as Canada. This was particularly true after 1945 and during the 1950s, when Canada continued to enjoy the status of a privileged ally from the Second World War. Subsequently, nuclear non-proliferation was one of her main battle horses. This issue continues to attract the constant attention of Canadian diplomats. Chemical weapons and a comprehensive nuclear test ban still figure amongst Canadian priorities. And as the fora for negotiations were progressively enlarged – the Ten-Nation Committee on Disarmament, the Eighteen-Nation Committee on Disarmament, the Conference of the Committee on Disarmament (CCD), the Committee on Disarmament and the Conference on Disarmament – other nations such as Japan, the FRG and France added the full measure of their weight to the negotiations. Canada nonetheless continued to maintain special bilateral relations with Sweden, Japan and Australia – to name but three – and continued to develop her technical competence, particularly in the areas of verification and international law in general. Concerning the peaceful uses of outer space, Canadian competence, whether legal or technical, took a back seat to no one. Several European countries even seek "information sessions" with Canada on these important issues of the day.

In the major European fora, Canada perhaps has greater need of Europe than Europe has of Canada. In this context, the efforts of Canadian diplomacy are unfortunately not well known to the public, perhaps because the subjects of negotiation are complex and multiform, especially the confidence-building measures. The CFE negotiations, which started in 1989, will pose difficult choices for Canada. Doubtless the problems will be addressed in the future as they were in the past, with much tact and patience, recognizing that Canada is only one player amongst others but one which is frequently expected to set the tone of leadership. Canada can be proud of her accomplishments. In the future, she can best make her influence felt through the "peace through law" approach, both for historical and cultural reasons.

"Negotiating ceaselessly, openly and secretly, in every place ... " as Richelieu maintained in his *Testament politique*, "is vital for the well-being of States". Never was such a maxim so true as in the nuclear age. Canada, at the fore, has never lost hope. She has pursued, for forty-three years, a diplomacy of hope. It is indeed a short period in the annals of human history with its sombre procession of bloody memories. If the climate moves towards one of "growing charity", as some philosophers point out, one can only hope that the great negotiators can progressively find a way to transform the system of conflict which has darkened the world since 1945 into a system that is more open, more cooperative and hence less armed and more secure.

Appendix A

PRIMARY SOURCES

DEPARTMENT OF EXTERNAL AFFAIRS

Docket 1: 201 F
            Meetings of the Advisory Panel on Atomic Energy
            Years 1946 to 1954

Docket 2: 50219-A-40
            Atomic Energy Advisory Panel

Docket 3: 211 G
            UN Discussions on Disarmament
            Vols. 1 and 2

Docket 4: 50189–40
            UN Discussions on Disarmament
            Vols. 1 to 9.

Docket 5: 50271-A-40
            United Nations Disarmament Commission
            Vols. 1 to 32

Docket 6: UN Discussions on Disarmament

Docket 7: 50189-B-40
            UN Discussions on Disarmament
            Vols. 1 to 8

Docket 8: 50189-C-40
            UN Discussions on Disarmament
            Vols. 1 and 2

Docket 9:   50189-D-40
             UN Discussions on Disarmament
             Vols. 1 and 2
Docket 10:   50271-B-40
             Interdepartmental Working Party on Disarmament
             Vols. 1 to 3
Docket 11:   50271-H-40
             Proposals for Joint Handling of Atomic Energy and Related
             Matters
Docket 12:   50271-K-1–40
             Ten-Nation Disarmament Committee (Administrative and
             Financial Arrangements)
Docket 13:   50271-K-2–40
             Ten-Nation Disarmament Committee
             a) Conventional Arms b) Military Manpower and Armaments
Docket 14:   50271-K-40
             Ten-Nation Disarmament Committee
             Vols. 1 to 16
Docket 15:   50271-N-40
             Nuclear Free Zone in Europe
             Vols. 1 and 2
Docket 16:   50271-U-40
             Disarmament and the Swedish Resolution
Docket 17:   50271-S-40
             Disarmament – USA Revised Plan
             Vols. 1 and 2
Docket 18:   50271-T-40
             Eighteen-Nation Committee on Disarmament
             Vols. 1 to 15
Docket 19:   28-4-ENCD
             Eighteen-Nation Committee on Disarmament
             Vols. 1 to 21
Docket 20:   28-4-CCD
             Conference of the Committee on Disarmament
             Vols. 1 to 9
Docket 21:   28-4-COD
             Committee on Disarmament
             Vols. 1 to 11
Docket 22:   28-6-6 CBW
             Chemical and Bacteriological Weapons (Reduction and Elimi-
             nation of ...)
             Vols. 1 to 22

Docket 23:   Disarmament and Outer Space
             Vols. 1 to 10
Docket 24:   28-7-5 (microfilms)
             Nuclear Safeguards – Prevention of Further Spread of Nuclear
             Weapons – Draft Treaties on Non-Proliferation (U.S. and USSR)
             Files 1 to 20
Docket 25:   28-7-5-1 (microfilms)
             Ibid.
             Files 1 to 11
Docket 26:   28-7-5-1-6
             Review Conference of the Non-Proliferation Treaty (1975)
             Vols. 1 to 7
Docket 27:   8-7-5-1-7
             Review Conference of the Non-Proliferation Treaty (1980)
             Vols. 1 to 3
Docket 28:   28-7-5-1-8
             Review Conference of the Non-Proliferation Treaty (1985)
             Vols. 1 to 5
Docket 29:   28-8-4-2-CTB
             Nuclear Tests and Comprehensive Test Ban
             Files 1 to 18; Vols. 9 to 11
Docket 30:   28-West-1-CDA
             Canada (Policy and Statements)
             Vols. 1 to 22
Docket 31:   27-4-NATO-1-MBFR
Docket 32:   20-4-CSCE
Docket 33:   20-4-CSCE-MDRID-1
Docket 34:   28-4-6-CDE

Appendix B

Main Topics Discussed by the Canadian Representatives before the Eighteen-Nation Disarmament Committee, the Conference of the Committee on Disarmament, the Committee on Disarmament and the Conference on Disarmament (1962–1985)

Date	Serial	Topic	Speaker
EIGHTEEN-NATION DISARMAMENT COMMITTEE (ENDC)			
1962			
19 Mar 1962	PV 4	Committee of the Whole	H. Green
25 Mar 1962	PV 8	Informal discussions with non-aligned countries	H. Green
27 Mar 1962	PV 10	Outer space	H. Green
	PV 11	Establishment of a subcommittee	H. Green
29 Mar 1962	PV 15	Comparative analysis (US-USSR draft treaty)	E.L.M. Burns
10 Apr 1962	PV 17	General and complete disarmament (GCD)	E.L.M. Burns
12 Apr 1962	PV 19	Cessation of nuclear tests	E.L.M. Burns
16 Apr 1962	PV 21	Agenda	E.L.M. Burns
19 Apr 1962	PV 24	Cessation of nuclear tests	E.L.M. Burns
24 Apr 1962	PV 26	Article II (GCD draft treaty)	E.L.M. Burns
25 Apr 1962	PV 27	Article III (GCD draft treaty)	E.L.M. Burns
26 Apr 1962	PV 28	Cessation of nuclear tests	E.L.M. Burns

3 May 1962	PV 30	Nuclear weapons launchers	E.L.M. Burns
8 May 1962	PV 33	Working method (subject: GCD)	E.L.M. Burns
11 May 1962	PV 35	Nuclear weapons launchers	E.L.M. Burns
14 May 1962	PV 36	Definition of launchers	E.L.M. Burns
16 May 1962	PV 38	*Ibid.*	E.L.M. Burns
21 May 1962	PV 40	Outer space	E.L.M. Burns
28 May 1962	PV 43	Definition of launchers	E.L.M. Burns
29 May 1962	PV 44	War propaganda	E.L.M. Burns
31 May 1962	PV 46	CD report	E.L.M. Burns
1 Jun 1962	PV 47	Opposition to adjournment	E.L.M. Burns
6 Jun 1962	PV 50	International police force	E.L.M. Burns
8 Jun 1962	PV 52	Request for informal consultations before adjournment	E.L.M. Burns
14 Jun 1962	PV 56	Criticism of Soviet attitudes	E.L.M. Burns
18 Jul 1962	PV 59	Risks of war and arms limitations	E.L.M. Burns
24 Jul 1962	PV 60	Opening speech for second session of the ENDC	H. Green
27 Jul 1962	PV 62	Comments on request for adjournment	E.L.M. Burns
30 Jul 1962	PV 63	Analysis of phase one of Soviet GCD draft treaty	E.L.M. Burns
6 Aug 1962	PV 66	Definition of launchers (GCD)	E.L.M. Burns
8 Aug 1962	PV 67	*Ibid.*	E.L.M. Burns
15 Aug 1962	PV 70	Canadian opposition to adjournment	E.L.M. Burns
20 Aug 1962	PV 72	*Ibid.*	E.L.M. Burns
22 Aug 1962	PV 73	Nuclear weapons launchers	E.L.M. Burns
27 Aug 1962	PV 75	Cessation of nuclear tests (US-UK draft)	E.L.M. Burns
7 Sep 1962	PV 82	Summary of second session	E.L.M. Burns
30 Nov 1962	PV 85	Nuclear tests	E.L.M. Burns
17 Dec 1962	PV 93	Launchers (problems of control)	E.L.M. Burns
19 Dec 1962	PV 94	Lack of consensus concerning resumption of session for 1 Jan 1963	E.L.M. Burns

1963

14 Feb 1963	PV 97	Kennedy-Khrushchev correspondence	E.L.M. Burns
22 Feb 1963	PV 101	Nuclear tests	E.L.M. Burns
1 Mar 1963	PV 104	*Ibid*	E.L.M. Burns
11 Mar 1963	PV 107	*Ibid.*	E.L.M. Burns

13 Mar 1963 PV 108	On-site inspections	E.L.M. Burns
18 Mar 1963 PV 110	Agenda for Committee of the Whole	E.L.M. Burns
20 Mar 1963 PV 111	On-site inspections	E.L.M. Burns
22 Mar 1963 PV 112	Comparison of the US-USSR draft treaties	E.L.M. Burns
3 Apr 1963 PV 117	Gromyko proposal (launchers)	E.L.M. Burns
5 Apr 1963 PV 118	Risks of war	E.L.M. Burns
10 Apr 1963 PV 120	Opposition to adjournment	E.L.M. Burns
17 Apr 1963 PV 121	Discussion of the Gromyko proposal	E.L.M. Burns
24 Apr 1963 PV 124	Limited balanced nuclear deterrence	E.L.M. Burns
3 May 1963 PV 127	Non-aggression pact and non-use of foreign bases	E.L.M. Burns
6 May 1963 PV 128	Nuclear free zone (Latin America)	E.L.M. Burns
8 May 1963 PV 129	Gromyko proposal	E.L.M. Burns
10 May 1963 PV 130	Non-aggression pact	S. Rae
15 May 1963 PV 132	Gromyko proposal	E.L.M. Burns
17 May 1963 PV 133	Non-aggression pact	E.L.M. Burns
22 May 1963 PV 135	Gromyko proposal	S. Rae
7 Jun 1963 PV 141	Non-aggression pact	E.L.M. Burns
12 Jun 1963 PV 143	Elimination of nuclear weapons	E.L.M. Burns
21 Jun 1963 PV 147	Program and work agenda	E.L.M. Burns
30 Jul 1963 PV 148	Opening statement	E.L.M. Burns
1 Aug 1963 PV 149	Cessation of nuclear tests	E.L.M. Burns
14 Aug 1963 PV 151	GCD draft treaties (US-USSR)	E.L.M. Burns
16 Aug 1963 PV 152	Risk of war	E.L.M. Burns
27 Aug 1963 PV 155	Elimination of military bases	E.L.M. Burns
29 Aug 1963 PV 156	Summary of second session	E.L.M. Burns

1964

4 Feb 1964 PV 163	Gromyko proposal	E.L.M. Burns
18 Feb 1964 PV 167	*Ibid.* (control)	E.L.M. Burns
5 Mar 1964 PV 172	Reduction of military budgets	E.L.M. Burns
12 Mar 1964 PV 174	*Ibid.* and atomic energy (control)	E.L.M. Burns
17 Mar 1964 PV 175	Gromyko proposal	E.L.M. Burns
23 Mar 1964 PV 177	Opening speech	E.L.M. Burns
26 Mar 1964 PV 178	Collateral measures	P. Martin
7 Apr 1964 PV 181	Gromyko proposal	E.L.M. Burns
9 Apr 1964 PV 182	Risks of war	E.L.M. Burns
14 Apr 1964 PV 183	Gromyko proposal (control)	E.L.M. Burns

16 Apr 1964	PV 184	Reduction of military budgets	E.L.M. Burns
21 Apr 1964	PV 185	Reduction of fissile material	E.L.M. Burns
28 Apr 1964	PV 187	Summary of session	E.L.M. Burns
16 Jun 1964	PV 190	Agenda and procedural outlines	E.L.M. Burns
25 Jun 1964	PV 193	Halting production of fissile material	E.L.M. Burns
7 Jul 1964	PV 196	Working Group (terms of reference)	E.L.M. Burns
14 Jul 1964	PV 198	*Ibid.*	E.L.M. Burns
16 Jul 1964	PV 199	Destruction of bombers	E.L.M. Burns
23 Jul 1964	PV 201	Non-proliferation and the MLF	E.L.M. Burns
28 Jul 1964	PV 202	Working Group (terms of reference)	E.L.M. Burns
30 Jul 1964	PV 203	Reduction of military budgets	E.L.M. Burns
6 Aug 1964	PV 205	First anniversary of the PTBT	E.L.M. Burns
18 Aug 1964	PV 208	Working Group (deadlock)	E.L.M. Burns
20 Aug 1964	PV 209	Cessation of nuclear tests	E.L.M. Burns
25 Aug 1964	PV 210	Comments on balance of forces by way of response to the USSR	E.L.M. Burns
1 Sep 1964	PV 212	UN international police force	E.L.M. Burns
8 Sep 1964	PV 214	Working group on conventional weapons	E.L.M. Burns
15 Sep 1964	PV 216	Collateral measures	E.L.M. Burns

1965

5 Aug 1965	PV 221	CTB and World Conference on Disarmament	E.L.M. Burns
24 Aug 1965	PV 226	NPT (US and non-aligned proposals)	E.L.M. Burns
9 Sep 1965	PV 231	CTB and non-proliferation	E.L.M. Burns
16 Sep 1965	PV 234	Non-aligned proposal (NPT)	E.L.M. Burns

1966

3 Feb 1966	PV 237	CTB, NPT, and GCD	E.L.M. Burns
17 Feb 1966	PV 241	NPT	E.L.M. Burns
22 Feb 1966	PV 242	NPT	E.L.M. Burns
3 Mar 1966	PV 245	NPT, CTB, and weapons freeze	E.L.M. Burns
17 Mar 1966	PV 249	Nuclear disarmament and review of various proposals	E.L.M. Burns
4 Apr 1966	PV 254	Article II of the NPT draft treaty	E.L.M. Burns
19 Apr 1966	PV 257	Collateral measures	E.L.M. Burns
21 Apr 1966	PV 258	*Ibid.*	E.L.M. Burns

26 Apr 1966 PV 259 *Ibid.*   E.L.M. Burns
 5 May 1966 PV 262 Nuclear safeguards   E.L.M. Burns
10 May 1966 PV 263 NPT and FRG   E.L.M. Burns
 5 Jul 1966 PV 270 NPT   E.L.M. Burns
12 Jul 1966 PV 272 NPT, CTB, GCD   E.L.M. Burns
21 Jul 1966 PV 275 Comparative analysis of US-USSR   E.L.M. Burns
                      NPT draft treaties
 9 Aug 1966 PV 280 CTB and control   E.L.M. Burns
24 Aug 1966 PV 285 Nuclear tests, NPT and NFZ   E.L.M. Burns

1967
28 Feb 1967 PV 289 NPT (Statement of Paul Martin)   E.L.M. Burns
 9 Mar 1967 PV 292 PNE   E.L.M. Burns
25 May 1967 PV 299 NPT   E.L.M. Burns
 1 Jun 1967 PV 301 NPT and procedures   E.L.M. Burns
20 Jun 1967 PV 306 NPT (reciprocity of obligations)   E.L.M. Burns
 6 Jul 1967 PV 311 Conventional arms transfers   E.L.M. Burns
 3 Aug 1967 PV 319 NPT, PNE, and nuclear safeguards   E.L.M. Burns
10 Aug 1967 PV 321 NPT   E.L.M. Burns
12 Sep 1967 PV 329 NPT   E.L.M. Burns
21 Sep 1967 PV 332 Cessation of nuclear tests   E.L.M. Burns
 5 Oct 1967 PV 336 NPT   E.L.M. Burns
12 Oct 1967 PV 338 NPT and Articles I and II   E.L.M. Burns

1968
23 Jan 1968 PV 358 NPT   E.L.M. Burns
21 Feb 1968 PV 368 PNE   E.L.M. Burns
28 Feb 1968 PV 371 NPT   E.L.M. Burns
13 Mar 1968 PV 378 NPT   E.L.M. Burns
18 Jul 1968 PV 382 NPT   E.L.M. Burns
23 Jul 1968 PV 383 NPT and Canada's signature   E.L.M. Burns
13 Aug 1968 PV 389 Cessation of nuclear tests   E.L.M. Burns
15 Aug 1968 PV 390 Halting the nuclear arms race   E.L.M. Burns
22 Aug 1968 PV 392 Non-Use of nuclear weapons (sub-   E.L.M. Burns
                     ject: Resolution 2289)
27 Aug 1968 PV 393 NPT   E.L.M. Burns

CONFERENCE OF THE COMMITTEE ON DISARMAMENT (CCD)

1969
20 Mar 1969 PV 396 Disarmament and arms control   G. Ignatieff
17 Apr 1969 PV 404 CTB   G. Ignatieff

29 Apr 1969 PV 407 US proposal on control and verifi- G. Ignatieff
cation
13 May 1969 PV 410 Sea-bed draft treaty G. Ignatieff
23 May 1969 PV 415 CTB, presentation of ENDC 251 G. Ignatieff
8 Jul 1969 PV 417 Chemical weapons G. Ignatieff
31 Jul 1969 PV 424 Chemical weapons and Sea-bed G. Ignatieff
draft treaty
13 Aug 1969 ? CTB: request for informal meeting G. Ignatieff
19 Aug 1969 PV 429 Revision of ENDC 251 G. Ignatieff
26 Aug 1969 PV 431 Working Group on General G. Ignatieff
Assembly resolution on chemical
weapons and on the exchange of
seismic data
8 Oct 1969 PV 441 Discussion of Article III of Sea- G. Ignatieff
bed draft treaty
30 Oct 1969 PV 447 Sea-bed treaty G. Ignatieff

1970
24 Mar 1970 PV 460 Chemical weapons (1925 Geneva G. Ignatieff
Protocol)
28 Apr 1970 PV 468 Sea-bed treaty and chemical G. Ignatieff
weapons
25 Jun 1970 PV 473 Seismic data G. Ignatieff
23 Jul 1970 PV 481 Freeze of military expenditures G. Ignatieff

1971
25 Feb 1971 PV 496 CTB, seismic data and chemical G. Ignatieff
weapons
6 Apr 1971 PV 507 CTB G. Ignatieff
11 May 1971 PV 515 CTB G. Ignatieff
29 Jun 1971 PV 517 CTB G. Ignatieff
22 Jul 1971 PV 523 CTB: presentation of CCD 336 G. Ignatieff
10 Aug 1971 PV 528 Chemical weapons G. Ignatieff
7 Sep 1971 PV 536 CTB and non-proliferation M. Sharp
28 Sep 1971 PV 542 Chemical weapons (CW) G. Ignatieff

1972
2 Mar 1972 PV 546 CTB: two Canadian proposals G. Ignatieff
27 Apr 1972 PV 560 Chemical weapons and CTB G. Ignatieff
22 Jun 1972 PV 562 CTB G. Ignatieff
25 Jul 1972 PV 571 CTB G. Ignatieff
10 Aug 1972 PV 576 Chemical weapons G. Ignatieff

| 22 Aug 1972 | PV 579 | General questions | G. Ignatieff |
| 29 Aug 1972 | PV 581 | CTB | G. Ignatieff |

1973

13 Mar 1973	PV 591	Chemical weapons	W. Barton
3 Jul 1973	PV 609	CTB	W. Barton
21 Aug 1973	PV 623	Chemical weapons: presentation of CCD 414	W. Barton

1974

21 May 1974	PV 637	Indian nuclear test	W. Barton
23 May 1974	PV 638	*Ibid.* and TTBT	W. Barton
16 Jul 1974	PV 643	Chemical weapons and documents CCD 433 and 434	A. Rowe
20 Aug 1974	PV 653	Chemical weapons	W. Barton

1975

6 Mar 1975	PV656	NFZ and PNE	W. Barton
24 Jun 1975	PV 666	NPT and Review Conference	W. Barton
15 Jul 1975	PV 672	NPT and PNE	A. Rowe
5 Aug 1975	PV 678	Environmental modifications	A. Rowe
26 Aug 1975	PV 685	Chemical weapons and discussion of CCD 473	W. Barton

1976

1 Apr 1976	PV 699	Environmental modifications	W. Barton
20 Apr 1976	PV 703	NPT and CTB	W. Barton
22 Apr 1976	PV 704	Exchange of seismic data	W. Barton
22 Jun 1976	PV 705	Welcoming address	W. Barton
24 Jun 1976	PV 706	CTB (terms of reference of the Group of Experts)	W. Barton
29 Jun 1976	PV 707	*Ibid.*	J. Simard
6 Jul 1976	PV 709	Chemical weapons	J. Simard

1977

22 Feb 1977	PV 731	CTB	R.H. Jay
29 Mar 1977	PV 740	Chemical weapons	R.H. Jay
21 Aug 1977	PV 746	CTB and PNE	R.H. Jay
9 Aug 1977	PV 760	CTB and Chemical weapons	R.H. Jay

1978

| 28 Mar 1978 | PV 782 | CTB | R.H. Jay |
| ? 1978 | PV 799 | Strategy of suffocation | R.H. Jay |

COMMITTEE ON DISARMAMENT (CD)

1979

25 Jan 1979 PV 4	CTB and halting production of fissile material	G.A.H. Pearson
29 Mar 1979 PV 23	Chemical weapons	R.H. Jay
5 Jul 1979 PV 39	Canada and SALT II	R.H. Jay
17 Jul 1979 PV 42	Radiological weapons	J. Simard
26 Jul 1979 PV 45	Chemical weapons	J. Simard
2 Aug 1979 PV 47	CTB	J. Simard

1980

12 Feb 1980 PV 58	Disarmament and arms control	G.A.H. Pearson
4 Mar 1980 PV 65	CTB	D.S. McPhail
27 Mar 1980 PV 73	Conventional weapons and Peacekeeping	D.S. McPhail
1 Apr 1980 PV 74	Radiological weapons	D.S. McPhail
17 Apr 1980 PV 79	Fissile material and discussion of CD 90 (with Australia)	D.S. McPhail
12 Jun 1980 PV 83	Chemical weapons and verification	D.S. McPhail
8 Aug 1980 PV 99	CTB Treaty	J. Simard

1981

19 Feb 1981 PV 108	CTB Treaty	G.R. Skinner
26 Mar 1981 PV 118	CW and presentation of CD 167	D.S. McPhail
3 Apr 1981 PV 121	Elimination of chemical weapons	G.R. Skinner
16 Apr 1981 PV 125	Discussion of agenda items	D.S. McPhail
11 Jun 1981 PV 128	CW, CTB and presentation of CD 183	D.S. McPhail
16 Jul 1981 PV 138	Discussion of CD 173	D.S. McPhail
21 Jul 1981 PV 139	Chemical weapons	D.S. McPhail

1982

18 Feb 1982 PV 156	CTB	D.S. McPhail
21 Apr 1982 PV 173	Chemical weapons and control	D.S. McPhail
3 Aug 1982 PV 175	Chemical weapons and CTB	D.S. McPhail
31 Aug 1982 PV 183	Presentation of CD 320	G.R. Skinner

1983

1 Feb 1983 PV 189	CTB, CW, and NPT	A. MacEachen
17 Feb 1983 PV 195	Chemical weapons	D.S. McPhail
28 Feb 1983 PV 198	Procedural questions	D.S. McPhail
28 Apr 1983 PV 216	CTB and Outer space	D.S. McPhail

23 Aug 1983 PV 236 Chemical weapons and presenta-   D.S. McPhail
                      tion of CD report 416

CONFERENCE ON DISARMAMENT (CD)

1984
21 Feb 1984 PV 243 Chemical weapons   J.A. Beesley
26 Apr 1984 PV 262 CW, CTB, Outer space, and Radio- J.A. Beesley
                      logical weapons
 3 Jul 1984 PV 269 Need to negotiate   J.A. Beesley

1985
 4 Apr 1985 PV 306 Chemical weapons   J.A. Beesley
23 Apr 1985 PV 310 *Ibid.*   J.A. Beesley
18 Jun 1985 PV 313 *Ibid.*   J.A. Beesley
23 Jul 1985 PV 323 Outer space   R. Rochon

Appendix C

Texts and Documents submitted by Canada before the Eighteen-Nation Disarmament Committee, the Conference of the Committee on Disarmament, the Committee on Disarmament and the Conference on Disarmament (1962–1985).

Date	Serial	Topic

EIGHTEEN-NATION DISARMAMENT COMMITTEE (ENDC)

Date	Serial	Topic
28 Mar 1962	ENDC 17	Peaceful use of outer space
6 Apr 1962	ENDC 19/Rev.1	Comparative analysis of U.S. and USSR draft treaties
4 May 1962	ENDC 36	*Ibid.*
1 Aug 1963	ENDC 36/Rev.1	*Ibid.* (revised)
3 Apr 1963	ENDC 79	Comparative analysis of salient features of U.S. and USSR draft proposals (1960–1963)
20 Aug 1963	ENDC 36/Rev.1	*Ibid.*
16 Aug 1963	ENDC 110	*Ibid.*, particularly concerning risks of war by accident or misunderstanding
4 Jul 1966	ENDC 175	Summary of U.S. and USSR draft proposals
17 Apr 1969	ENDC 244	Working paper listing Canadian scientific papers concerning the detection and identification of underground nuclear explosions by seismological means
21 May 1969	ENDC 248	*Ibid.*, with summaries
23 May 1969	ENDC 251	Working paper: Comprehensive Test Ban

| 18 Aug 1969 | ENDC 251/Rev.1 | Requests to Governments for information about exchange of seismological data |
| 26 Aug 1969 | ENDC 266 | Canadian draft resolution to UN General Assembly on chemical and bacteriological warfare |

CONFERENCE OF THE COMMITTEE ON DISARMAMENT (CCD)

8 Oct 1969	CCD 270	Working paper on Article III of draft Sea-bed Treaty
6 Aug 1970	CCD 300	Working paper on the verification of prohibitions of the development, production, stockpiling and the use of chemical and biological weapons
10 Aug 1970	CCD 305	Seismological capabilities in detecting and identifying underground nuclear explosions
29 Jun 1971	CCD 327	Seismological detection and identification of underground nuclear explosions
7 Jul 1971	CCD 327/Rev.1	*Ibid.*, with explanatory comments
8 Jul 1971	CCD 334	Atmospheric sensing and verification of a ban on chemical weapons
22 Jul 1971	CCD 336	Working document on possible progress towards the suspension of nuclear and thermonuclear tests
28 Sep 1971	CCD 353	Revised draft convention on the prohibition of bacteriological (biological) and toxin weapons, presented jointly with 11 other Delegations
20 Jul 1972	CCD 376	Measures to improve tripartite cooperation among Canada, Japan and Sweden in the detection, location, and identification of underground nuclear explosions by seismological means
25 Jul 1972	CCD 378	EMR working paper relevant to seismological verification problems
25 Jul 1972	CCD 380	Joint working paper (Canada and Sweden) on an experiment in international cooperation (short-period seismological discrimination)
24 Aug 1972	CCD 387	Working paper on toxicity of chemical substances
10 Jul 1973	CCD 406	Nuclear testing and verification
21 Aug 1973	CCD 414	The problem of defining chemical substances
16 Jul 1974	CCD 433	The problem of defining compounds as irritating and incapacitating agents

	CCD 434	Destruction and disposal of Canadian stocks of World War II mustard agent
14 Jul 1975	CCD 457	Summary proceedings of informal tripartite conference on seismological cooperation (Canada, Japan, and Sweden)
4 Aug 1975	CCD 463	Preliminary approach to a convention on environmental modifications for military or other hostile purposes
26 Aug 1975	CCD 473	Use of measurements of lethality for definition of agents of chemical warfare
20 Apr 1976	CCD 490	Verification of a comprehensive test ban
2 Feb 1978	CCD 549	Draft program of action for UNSSOD I

COMMITTEE ON DISARMAMENT (CD)

17 Apr 1979	CD 90	Prohibition of the production of fissionable material for weapons purposes (Australia and Canada)
10 Jun 1980	CD 99	Verification and arms control
9 Jul 1980	CD 113	Organization and control of verification within a chemical weapons convention
10 Jul 1980	CD 117	Range and scope of a chemical weapons convention
26 Mar 1981	CD 167	Verification and control requirements for a chemical arms control treaty
3 Apr 1981	CD 173	Disposal of chemical agents
12 Jun 1981	CD 183	Conceptual paper on arms control verification
7 Apr 1982	CD 275	Compendium of arms control verification proposals, second edition
16 Apr 1982	CD 313	A proposed verification organization for a chemical weapons convention
26 Aug 1982	CD 320	Arms control and outer space
8 Feb 1983	CD 342	Report of the *Ad Hoc* Working Group on Chemical Weapons
21 Feb 1983	CD 348	Progress report of the *Ad Hoc* Group of Scientific Experts to consider international measures to detect and identify seismic events
22 Jul 1983	CD 399	*Ibid.*, Progress report, 16th session
17 Aug 1983	CD 413	Draft mandate for *Ad Hoc* Working Group on the Prevention of an Arms Race in Outer Space
18 Aug 1983	CD 414	Report of the *Ad Hoc* Working Group on Radiological Weapons (see also Doc: CD/RW/WP. 3)

22 Aug 1983	CD 416	Report of the *Ad Hoc* Working Group on Chemical Weapons
7 Feb 1984	CD 429	*Ibid.*
9 Mar 1984	CD 448	Progress report of the *Ad Hoc* Group of Scientific Experts to consider international measures to detect and identify seismic events

CONFERENCE ON DISARMAMENT (CD)

20 Jul 1984	CD 521	Draft mandate for the *Ad Hoc* subsidiary body relative to item 1 entitled "Nuclear Test Ban" (submitted with eight other Delegations)
30 Jul 1984	CD 527	Draft mandate for an *Ad Hoc* Committee on item 5 entitled "Prevention of an Arms Race in Outer Space" (submitted with eight other Delegations)
10 Aug 1984	CD 535	Progress report of the *Ad Hoc* Group of Scientific Experts to consider international measures to detect and identify seismic events
31 Aug 1984	CD 539	Report of the *Ad Hoc* Working Group on Chemical Weapons
1 Feb 1985	CD 546	*Ibid.*
4 Jul 1985	CD 606	Report of the *Ad Hoc* Committee on the Prevention of an Arms Race in Outer Space
23 Jul 1985	CD 618	Survey of main texts and agreements on the prevention of an arms race in outer space

Notes

1 See especially P. Lyon (1963) and J.W. Holmes (1979).

2 See S. Clarkson (1968).

3 See T.C. Hockin (1968 and 1969).

4 M. Tucker (1977).

5 J. Eayrs, 1972, p. 67.

6 This section draws on the *Grand Dictionnaire universel du XIXe siècle* (Larousse) and the following works: concerning bees, *La vie des abeilles*, by B. and R. Darchen, Paris, Éditions Nathan, 1985, and, concerning ants, *Le peuple des fourmis*, by F. Ramade, Paris (Collection "Que Sais-Je?"), PUF, 1972.

7 See G. Dumézil (1968).

8 See M. Crozier and E. Friedberg (1977).

9 DEA, F-3/2). See Appendix A, "Primary Sources" concerning records cited. The designation F-3/2 here means File 3, Vol. 2 and refers to series 211G.

10 DEA, F-5/9.

11 DEA, F-5/8.

12 DEA, F10/1.

13 DEA, F-10/1.

14 DEA, F-10/1.

15 DEA, F-10/1.

16 DEA, F-10/1.

17 DEA, F-11.

18 DND, Acc.73/1223.

19 P. Stursberg, 1975, p. 168.

20 P. Stursberg, 1975, p. 177.

21 J.L. Granatstein, 1986, p. 119.

22 DEA, F-12.

23 DEA, F-10/3.

24 DEA, F-12.

25 3 officers of classes 6, 4 and 2 respectively and 12 support staff).

26 DEA, F-11.

27 DEA, F-11.

28 DEA, F-11.

29 Authors' note: the French text talks of "*la responsabilité des dossiers sur la suspension des essais nucléaires.*" The French text appears to us to be more correct, unless allied nuclear tests had been planned on Canadian territory, of which we are not aware.

30 DEA, F-10/3.

31 J.A. Munro (1975).

32 J.L. Granatstein (1986).

33 DND, Acc.73/1223.

34 Quoted in J.A. Munro, 1975, p. 81.

35 J.L. Granatstein, op. cit., 1986, Ch. 5.

36 DND, Acc.73/1223.

CHAPTER 2

1 DEA, File 7-DA.

2 J.W. Holmes, 1979, p. 197.

3 J. Klein, 1964, p. 40.

4 J. Goldblat, 1982, p. 13.

5 AEC/31/Rev. 1.

6 AEC/8.

7 *The United Nations and Disarmament, 1945–1970*, p. 25.

8 A/658.

9 J. Klein, 1964, p. 54.

10 S/C. 3/SC. 3/21/Rev. 1/Corr. 1.

11 J. Eayrs, 1972, p. 141.

12 J. Eayrs, 1972, p. 159.

13 Quoted in J. Eayrs, 1972, p. 35.

14 J.W. Holmes, 1979, p. 221.

15 Quoted in J. Eayrs, 1972, p. 295.

16 Quoted in J. Eayrs, 1972, p. 99.

17 Quoted in J. Eayrs, 1972, p. 335.

18 D.C. Thomson, 1967, p. 197.

19 Quoted in J. Eayrs, 1972, p. 147.

20 J. Eayrs, 1972, p. 286.

21 The Conference was held between 29 July and 15 October.

22 The Scientific and Technical Sub-Committee.

23 M.J. Tucker, 1985, p. 12.

24 J. Swettenham, 1973, p. 108.

25 G. Ignatieff, 1985, p. 93.

26 J. Eayrs, 1972, p. 291.

27 J. Swettenham, 1973, p. 117.

28 J. Eayrs, 1972, p. 293.

29 J.W. Holmes, 1979, p. 208.

30 DEA, D-3/1.

31 Telex Atom 184 of 30 November.

32 DEA, D-3/1.

33 A/C. 1/Sub. 3/4.

34 Interview with the authors.

35 Under serial 211 G.

36 J. Eayrs, 1972, p. 11.

37 Interview with the authors.

38 J. Eayrs, 1980, p. 51.

39 J. Eayrs, 1980, p. 18.

40 P.N. Baker, 1958, p. 193.

41 J. Laloy, 1966, pp. 23–24.

42 J. Eayrs, 1972, p. 37.

43 DEA D-3/2, 8 March 1948.

44 Ibid.

45 The historical comparison is strange. The nomination of Litvinov as Soviet Foreign Minister marked the occasion on which the Soviet Union became a member of the League of Nations and the beginning of Soviet *rapprochement* with the West. It was nevertheless under Litvinov that a series of regional security agreements with the majority of neighbour States of the Soviet Union were signed.

46 Report of McNaughton, dated 29 July 1948.

47 Despatch of Starnes, dated 13 May.

48 S/1372.

49 S/1405.

50 Quoted in J.W. Holmes, 1979, p. 219.

51 DEA, D-2.

52 Unless otherwise mentioned, all the quotations of this section were drawn from series 50219-A-40 of File 2.

53 J.W. Holmes, 1979, p. 202.

54 Vol. 9, 1942–1943.

55 Minutes of CPC, 8 December 1949.

56 J.W. Holmes, 1979, p. 203.

57 Minutes of CPC, 8 December 1949.

58 J. Eayrs, 1972, p. 308.

59 At the time of the CPC meeting on 4 April 1949, C.J. Mackenzie advised his colleagues of the potentialities of the second Chalk River reactor. It would cost 30 million dollars to construct, and would produce 60 kilograms of plutonium annually, representing a tenfold increase over the production capacity of Chalk River at the time. The production of an atomic bomb requires 5 to 7 kilograms of plutonium 239.

60 J. Eayrs, 1972, p. 303.

61 J. Eayrs, 1980, p. 240.

62 On the evolution of U.S. strategy and U.S.-Canada negotiations, see J. Eayrs, 1980, Chapter 4.

63 J. Eayrs, 1980, p. 242.

64 Minutes of CPC, 11 November 1950.

65 Minutes of CPC, 16 June 1951.

CHAPTER 3

1 Unless otherwise noted, all the Canadian quotes in this chapter are taken from the 36 volumes of the 50271-A-40 series.

2 J. Klein, 1964, p. 64.

3 DEA, 25 April 1952.

4 DEA, 2 April 1952.

5 Johnson's despatch of 26 May 1952 to the Department of External Affairs.

6 Letter No 527, 7 May 1952, from Johnson to DEA.

7 Despatch from Johnson to the Department of External Affairs, 25 April.

8 Despatch from Canadian Delegation to the Department of External Affairs, 6 May.

9 Despatch from Johnson to the Department of External Affairs, 25 April.

10 Despatch from the Commonwealth Relations Office in London to Ottawa, 19 August.

11 Authors' note: terms borrowed from a prior report by John Halstead.

12 See Chapter 1.

13 Despatch from Ambassador Wrong to the Department of External Affairs, 16 September.

14 Despatch from the Canadian Delegation to the Department of External Affairs, 19 September.

15 Note from Roger Chaput to S. Morley Scott, 25 May 1953.
16 A/C. 1/L. 74, 9 November 1953
17 S.F. Rae to the Acting Under-Secretary, 5 April 1954.
18 DEA memorandum, 7 April 1954.
19 Despatch from New York to Ottawa, 1 November 1954.
20 See Chapter 1.
21 J. Klein, 1964, p. 96.
22 *The United Nations and Disarmament, 1945–1970*, p. 56.
23 Undated report on the Third Session of the Subcommittee by L. Saint-Pierre of the United Nations Bureau.
24 Report of 06 June from Ottawa to New York on Subcommittee meetings, 19 April – 18 May 1955.
25 Despatch from New York, 4 August.
26 Despatch from Ottawa to London, New York and Washington, 1 September.
27 Despatch from Ottawa to New York, 20 October 1954.
28 The 27 October resolution of the Subcommittee of Five adopted by the First Committee.
29 Authors' note: the text speaks of the French Accords!
30 Despatch from Ottawa to New York, 27 October 1954.
31 Authors' note: in the event of withdrawal of the American bases.
32 Authors' note: ICBM, or Intercontinental Ballistic Missile, in today's language.
33 United Nations Division, note of 25 April 1955.
34 Pearson to Robertson, 2 March 1955.
35 Series 50189–40.
36 Interview with Geoffrey Pearson.
37 Interview with Jean Chapdelaine.
38 J. Klein, 1964, p. 117.
39 Minutes of the 10th Meeting of Foreign Ministers.
40 Despatch from Ottawa to all NATO missions, 24 October 1955.
41 Conversations between Messrs. Holmes, Martin and Cadieux, 12 September 1955.
42 Resolution 914 (X).
43 Despatch from Ottawa to London, 25 August 1955.
44 Cited in Klein, 1964, p. 128.
45 Despatch from London to Ottawa, 20 March 1956.
46 London to Ottawa, 6 April 1956.
47 London to Ottawa, 7 June 1956.
48 J. Klein, 1964, p. 141.
49 DND, 1644–1, Vol. 8, 29 August 1957.
50 Telex from Selwyn Lloyd to Gladwyn Jebb in Paris, 20 March 1956.

51 Holmes for the UN Division, 4 April 1956.

52 Authors' note: the Committee of the Wise Men on consultations concerning Article 2 of NATO.

53 Léger to Pearson, 6 July 1956.

54 S.F. Rae to Ottawa, 14 March 1956.

55 Robertson to Ottawa, 14 March 1956.

56 Cadieux to Chaput, 28 March 1956.

57 Report of Brigadier-General Robert P. Rothschild to Marcel Cadieux, 20 April 1956.

58 Telex 298 from London to Ottawa, 14 March 1956.

59 Ignatieff to Holmes, 3 April 1956.

60 Memorandum from John W. Holmes to Pearson, 3 April 1956.

61 DC/SC. 1/PV. 82.

62 Ottawa to London, 27 April 1956.

63 5th Meeting of the Joint Planning Committee, June 1956.

64 Telex from Ottawa to London, 10 April 1956.

65 Despatch from Moscow, 18 May 1956.

66 Authors' note: a proposal that we did not believe useful to record here in light of Washington's clear rejection of it.

67 Authors' note: the least that can be said.

68 Memorandum from Ford to the United Nations Division, 4 July 1956.

69 See telex from Ottawa to London, 22 May.

70 Correspondence with authors, 28 January 1987.

CHAPTER 4

1 See Chapter 3.

2 Unless otherwise indicated, all the dates of reports and letters cited were drawn from the following records: 50271-B-40; 50271-K-40; 50271-N-40 and 50271-T-40. Alphabetic letters refer to specific volumes.

3 Record B, letter from Holmes to Léger dated 2 June.

4 Record B, 12 June 1957.

5 DND record.

6 Report on "Aerial Reconnaissance as a Method of Inspection Against Surprise Attack", dated 9 October.

7 Report on "Telecommunications in Polar Regions", dated 15 October.

8 Report on "Ground Controls: Mobile and Static", dated 17 October.

9 Bardufoss, or Bodo in Norway, Thule in Greenland, Resolute Bay in the Northwest Territories, Fairbanks and Point Barrow in Alaska.

10 DND letter from Foulkes to Wilgress, dated 31 October.

11 Klein, 1964, p. 194.

12 Ibid., p. 197.

13 A/4078 and S/4145, 5 January 1959.

14 Klein, 1964, p. 199.

15 Record B, 2 June 1958.

16 See in particular the despatch of 28 May 1958 from Washington to Ottawa, not cited herein.

17 On this subject, see Chapter 1.

18 Record B, 13 June 1958.

19 A bomb in a briefcase, for example.

20 Record B.

21 Hansard, 6 June 1960.

22 See Chapter 3.

23 Despatch from Washington to Ottawa, 26 April 1960, Record K.

24 In the area of disarmament, nothing has been found in the Canadian records concerning private conversations that supposedly took place in the UN at the end of 1957 between Lange of Norway, Sydney Smith and Polish Foreign Minister Rapacki. The other participants were John W. Holmes and Manfred Lachs. Lachs is today a judge in the International Court of The Hague, and was formerly closely associated with the development of the Rapacki Plan. In correspondence with the authors (4 January 1987), John W. Holmes recalled that during these discussions the Poles assured the Canadians that the Rapacki Plan was truly a Polish plan and had not been imposed in any way by Moscow. Manfred Lachs and Polish Foreign Minister Rapacki allegedly went to Moscow in order to convince the Soviet leaders of the merits of their proposal. During the meeting in New York, Lange and Rapacki mostly spoke German, both having suffered the unfortunate experience of German concentration camps during the War. The Canadians and the Norwegians insisted on voicing their views in the names of their own countries, and not in the name of the Atlantic Alliance. It was probably during this meeting that the Poles received Canadian support for their proposal. Holmes stressed that one of the objectives of the meeting was to avoid the possibility that a White House spokesman would dismiss the Plan out of hand simply because it originated in the East, without any prior consultation from member nations of the North Atlantic Alliance. Finally, it is possible that the minutes of this meeting are contained in the Canada-Poland archives, which the authors did not research.

25 Klein, 1964, p. 183.

26 Despatch from Ottawa to Geneva, 12 April 1962, Record T.

27 Correspondence with J. Klein, 13 October 1987.

28 Authors' note: the date of this text was incorrectly cited as December 1958.

29 Record B.

30 No record number.
31 See Chapter 1.
32 Record K.
33 Record K.
34 See Chapter 1.
35 Note to Ignatieff, dated 11 May 1961.
36 Record N.
37 Conceived by L.J. Byrne of the same Bureau.
38 Record N.
39 Record N.
40 See Klein, 1964, pp. 188 and 190.
41 Record N, 31 August 1961.
42 Record T.

CHAPTER 5

1 A. Fontaine, 1967, p. 380.
2 L.P. Bloomfield, W.C. Clemens Jr and F. Griffiths, 1966, p. 92.
3 Despatch from Heeney to Robertson, 10 November 1960, volume B. Unless otherwise indicated, all the documents cited are taken from volumes 50189 A-40, B-40, C-40 and D-40, or from files 50271-B-40, H-40, K-40, K-1-40 or K-2-40. The 50189 series is designated by the term "volume" followed by an alphabetical letter; the 50271 series is designated by the term "file" followed also by an alphabetical letter.
4 All these elements were extracted from the despatch from Burns to Ottawa, 30 January 1960, file K? [illegible].
5 File K.
6 File K.
7 See J. Klein, 1964, p. 241.
8 Ibid, p.243.
9 In another document, the date of 21 January is mentioned.
10 File K.
11 File K, 4 April 1960, despatch from R.M. Tate to Ottawa.
12 File K, 6 April 1960, New York to Ottawa.
13 Specifically item 4 on the list approved by Cabinet on 25 January.
14 Authors' note: Foulkes was wrong in this respect. The United States, under the Kennedy Administration, agreed that all the technical details to prevent unauthorized missile launch should be discussed at a Pugwash meeting, and that the Russians should thus be informed of the findings.
15 Authors' note: this is not discussed in the document.
16 File 50271-K-2-40, 8 March 1960.
17 File K.

18 File K, 27 April 1960.

19 File K.

20 File K, 7 June 1960.

21 Volume B.

22 Volume B, 26 October 1960, Miller to Robertson.

23 Volume B.

24 A National Defence text references 6 December.

25 File K, 11 March 1960.

26 Meeting of 14 November, Volume C, 16 November 1961, report to the Prime Minister.

27 Specifically, the Disarmament Commission.

28 File K, Murray to Robertson, 6 July 1960.

29 The Disarmament Commission met on 16 August to review the work of the Ten-Nation Committee.

30 A/C. 1/L. 255/Rev. 1.

31 Volume B, note from Murray to Robertson, 3 November 1960.

32 Volume B, note from Halstead to Ritchie, 11 October 1960.

33 Volume B, 7 September 1960.

34 File K, note from Burns, 11 August.

35 Harry Jay of the UN Bureau and Fochin of the Soviet Embassy.

36 Volume B, Robertson to Green, 2 September 1960.

37 Volume B.

CHAPTER 6

1 See Chapter 7.

2 ENDC/30.

3 ENDC/2.

4 Taken from *The United Nations and Disarmament, 1945–1970*, pp. 137–173.

5 See Chapter 1.

6 M. Tucker, 1967.

7 File T, 11 May 1962. The 50189 series is designated by the term "volume" followed by an alphabetic letter, and the 50271 series is designated by the term "file" followed also by an alphabetic letter. Other records are cited under their particular serial numbers.

8 File T.

9 See Chapter 1.

10 File 28-West-1-CDA.

11 Authors' note: those of Hellyer.

12 File 28-West-1-CDA, 20 August 1963.

13 It was signed by Martin on 17 September and sent to Hellyer on 23 September.

14 28-West-1-CDA, 2 February 1967.
15 28-West-1-CDA, 5 April 1967.
16 28–4-ENDC.
17 The evaluation was conducted by B.A. Keith during 19 - 22 March 1968.
18 28–4-ENDC.
19 File T.
20 File T, 19 January 1962.
21 File T, 15 February 1962.
22 Authors' note: the text is anonymous, but we believe it was written by Sutherland. The text was attached to a letter from the Department of National Defence dated 23 June 1964, File 28-West-1-CDA.
23 File T.
24 File R, 15 January 1962.
25 ENDC/17, 28 March 1962; ENDC/19/Rev. 1, 6 April 1962; ENDC 36/Rev. 1, 20 August 1963; ENDC/79, 3 April 1963.
26 For a complete description, see Appendix II of *The United Nations and Disarmament, 1945–1970.*
27 File T.
28 File T.
29 ENDC/PV 40, 27 May 1962, pp. 9–11.
30 28–4-West-ENDC, 15 April 1970.
31 Volume D, 7 December 1962.
32 File S, 17 May 1962.
33 File T, memorandum of George Murray, 4 July 1962.
34 File T, 20 June 1962.
35 Volume D, 19 June 1962.
36 Authors' note: the Soviet proposal spoke also of frontier police.
37 Quoted in R. Sutherland, 23 June 1964, 28-West-1-CDA.
38 File T, 7 June 1962.
39 Memorandum from G. Murray to the Under-Secretary, 12 June 1962.
40 File T, 6 December 1962.
41 28–4-West-CDA, 11 August 1965.
42 24-West-1-CDA, 5 January 1966.
43 27° longitude.
44 See the Burns Plan discussed in Chapter 3.
45 28-West-1-CDA, 27 January 1966.
46 ENDC/17.
47 File T.
48 See the Burns report, File T, 3 May 1962.
49 File T, 22 June 1962, Robertson to Green.
50 ENDC/PV 178.

51 Freeze on delivery vehicles, destruction of bombers, non-dissemination, halting of production of fissile materials, establishment of observation posts, comprehensive test ban treaty and strengthening of the UN peacekeeping ability.

52 ENDC/110.

53 DND, *Disarmament Progress Report No. 36*, 4 February 1964.

54 File T, 18 February 1963, Chairman Joint Chiefs of Staff to Under-Secretary of State for External Affairs.

55 ENDC/60, *The Technical Possibility of International Control of Fissile Material Production.*

56 File T, letter from A.K. Longair, Defence Research Board, 12 February 1963.

57 See Chapter 7.

58 ENDC/PV 143, p. 5.

59 ENDC/PV 167, 175, 181 and 183.

60 ENDC/PV 285, 24 August 1966.

61 ENDC/PV 172, 184 and 203.

62 28–4-West-CDA, memorandum to Martin, 1 June 1964.

63 *Canadian Reply to Polish Memorandum*, Appendix B, CSC 1644–1 [JS/DSS], 29 April 1964.

64 File T, 13 March 1963, letter from the Under-Secretary to the Chairman, Joint Chiefs of Staff.

65 File N.

66 File U, 22 February 1962.

67 File U.

68 File U.

69 J. Klein, 1964, p. 285.

70 J. Klein, 1964, p. 286.

71 File N, 14 November 1962.

72 File N, 11 June 1963.

73 File N.

74 Directives to the Canadian Delegation, 10 December 1964, 28–1-West-CDA.

75 File T, 11 April 1963, Ottawa to the Geneva Delegation.

76 28-West-1-CDA, 6 January 1966.

77 ENDC/PV 319.

CHAPTER 7

1 Title of a collective work published by Plon in 1985 on behalf of the Charles de Gaulle Institute.

2 W. Schütze, 1987, p. 24.

3 J. Klein, 1987, p. 249.

4 *IAEA Bulletin* (hereinafter referred to as *Bulletin*), Vol. 29, No. 2, 1987, p. 40.

5 *Bulletin*, Vol. 29, No. 3, 1987.

6 Specifically the processes of Atomic Vapour Laser Isotope Separation (AVLIS) and Molecular Laser Isotope Separation (MLIS), the latter being dependent on the differing nuclear resonance frequencies of individual atoms.

7 "Breeders" produce more plutonium than "spent" fuel which, if recovered, can be used again in the nuclear fuel cycle, whence the term "breeder".

8 *Bulletin*, Vol. 29, No. 3, 1987, p. 32.

9 B.M. Mazer, 1980–1981, p. 91.

10 W. Schütze, 1987, p. 24.

11 ENDC/152.

12 A/5763.

13 CD/224.

14 *The United Nations and Disarmament, 1945–1970*, p. 199.

15 A/5976.

16 ENDC/157.

17 Res. 2028 (XX).

18 ENDC/178.

19 ENDC/152/Add. 1.

20 ENDC/192 and 193.

21 Authors' note: opinions differ here, for this clause continues: "and which possesses overall characteristics applicable to warfare".

22 M. Willrich, 1969, p. 68.

23 Ibid., p. 69.

24 Ibid., p. 97.

25 ENDC/192/Rev. 1 and ENDC/193/Rev. 1.

26 ENDC/225 Annex A.

27 See section on "Evolution of International Nuclear Safeguards".

28 R.M. Lawrence and J. Larus, 1974, p. 21.

29 R. Pendley, L. Scheinman and R. Butler (1975).

30 Authors' note: this proposal was probably dead anyway in light of the reticence of some U.S. experts and the progressive tempering of Bonn's enthusiasm following widespread criticism.

31 A. Kramish, 1967, p. 2; and R. Pendley, L. Scheinman and R. Butler, 1975, p. 604.

32 R. Pendley, L. Scheinman and R. Butler, 1975, p. 607.

33 M. Willrich, 1969, p. 114.

34 A. Kramish, 1967, p. 4.

35 R. Pendley, L. Scheinman and R. Butler, 1975, p. 606.

36 Implying Japan: see R. Imai, 1972, p. 14, who argues that credibility is, above all, a political phenomenon, and is not the same as a "level of confidence" which depends on statistical probabilities.

37 Cited in R. Pendley, L. Scheinman and R. Butler, 1975, p. 607.

38 Interview.

39 See Charlotte S.M. Girard, *Canada and World Affairs, 1963–65*, pp. 214–224.

40 Interview.

41 R. Pendley, L. Scheinman and R. Butler, 1975, p. 607.

42 According to paragraph 2 of this Resolution, some States will provide or lend immediate assistance, in conformity with the Charter, "to any non-nuclear-weapon State Party to the Treaty ... subject to an act of aggression, or threat of aggression, involving nuclear weapons".

43 R. Pendley, L. Scheinman and R. Butler, 1975, p. 609.

44 ENDC/167.

45 R. Imai, 1972, p. 30.

46 The OAU, the OPANAL, the Council for Mutual Economic Assistance (CMEA), EURATOM, etc.

47 The International Labour Organization (ILO), the Food and Agriculture Organization (FAO), the World Health Organization (WHO), the United Nations Industrial Development Organization (UNIDO), etc.

48 For instance, the European Atomic Forum, the European Confederation of Agriculture, the International Air Transportation Association, etc.

49 R. Pendley, L. Scheinman and R. Butler, 1975, p. 603.

50 *Bulletin*, Vol. 29, No. 3, 1987, p. 30.

51 *Bulletin*, Vol. 24, No. 2, June 1982, p. 46.

52 L. Scheinman , 1977, p. 71.

53 For greater technical detail, see B. Sanders (1975), and particularly D. Fischer and P. Szasz, 1985, pp.79–80.

54 J. Jennekens, 1987, p. 77.

55 R. Imai, 1972, p. 10.

56 *Bulletin*, Vol. 24, No. 2, June 1982, p. 47.

57 See Chapter 1.

58 Authors' note: it was a time of private discussion and agreement between heads of State. In return for the Canadian decision in March 1964 to provide a military contingent for UN peacekeeping in Cyprus, President Johnson asked L.B. Pearson what his country could do to assist Canada. Pearson replied that important trade negotiations were underway between the two countries, and that he was particularly interested in the establishment of a free trade agreement for

automobiles. The Prime Minister's son, Geoffrey A. Pearson, suggested in an interview with the authors that this was the moment at
which the Auto-Pact was born.

59 Speech before the House of Commons, 7 June 1963.

60 28–7–5, telex of 17 November 1964 to Foreign Missions.

61 28–7–5, Geneva Delegation to DEA, 27 August 1964.

62 28–7–5, 11 August 1965.

63 28–7–5, 29 March 1965.

64 28–7–5, 10 March 1965.

65 28–7–5, 30 May 1966, R.D. Jackson to D.M. Cornett.

66 28–7–5, telex from Washington to DEA, 19 August 1966.

67 28–7–5–1, 19 August 1966.

68 28–7–5–1–4, letter to Trudeau dated 18 December 1968.

69 28–7–5–1–1.

70 The agreements of 16 August 1963 and of 17 September 1965 supplemented the original agreements.

71 28-West-1-CDA, letter from M.N. Bow to Mitchell Sharp, 22 May 1969.

72 Specifically, the need to halt the production of fissile materials for
military purposes and the need to reach agreement on a treaty to ban
underground nuclear tests.

73 A "notational" document, i.e., for discussion purposes.

74 Authors note: The United States declared that it would not contravene Resolution 1665, and invited the USSR to make a similar declaration; see *The United Nations and Disarmament, 1945–1970*, p. 197.

75 See the statement of External Affairs' Minister Martin to the House
on 20 May 1963, and his statement to the Eighteen-Nation Committee
on 26 March 1964, ENDC/PV/178.

76 See the 23 July 1964 statement of the Canadian Delegation to
the Eighteen-Nation Committee on Disarmament in Geneva, ENDC/PV/
201.

77 The text uses the expression "about-face".

78 Letter from Under-Secretary Marcel Cadieux to the Joint Chiefs of
Staff, 23 April 1965.

79 28–7–5, 31 May 1965, Paul Martin to Foreign Missions. All these elements were reintroduced by Martin in his testimony of 18 June before
the Parliamentary Committee on External Affairs.

80 28–7–5–1.

81 28-West-1-CDA, Burns to Ottawa, 18 April 1966.

82 28-West-1-CDA, 13 April 1967.

83 28–7–5, Disarmament Division, L. Houzer, 18 December 1964.

84 28–7–5, 8 January 1965.

85 28–7–5, Joint Report to the North Atlantic Council, period 20 February to 3 March 1966.

86 ENDC/165. Authors' note: shortly after the Chinese nuclear explosion of 1964, President Johnson made a similar declaration, as did U.S. Ambassador Goldberg before the 20ᵗʰ Session of the UNGA.

87 ENDC/167.

88 28–7–5–1, 26 October 1966, New York Delegation to DEA.

89 Document prepared by D.M. Cornett of the Disarmament Division in anticipation of the visit of V. David, Czechoslovakian Minister of Foreign Affairs, scheduled for 6–11 December 1966.

90 A/C. 1/L. 371.

91 28–7–5–1, DEA to New York, 8 November 1966.

92 Joint Canada-USA Ministerial Committee Meeting, 20–22 June 1967, no file number, 26 May 1967.

93 *The United Nations and Disarmament, 1945–1970*, p. 284.

94 28–7–5, 8 June 1966.

95 "Canadian Mission to the United Nations", *Press Release*, No. 68, October 1966, p. 4.

96 R.D. Jackson, Disarmament Division, 14 August 1967, no file number.

97 28-West-1-CDA, 23 February 1968; see also the Departmental Memorandum of 15 February 1968.

98 For the full text of the statement, see *Canadian Foreign Policy Texts* (hereinafter referred to as *Texts*), DEA, May 1982, p. 7.

99 Interview with the IAEA Director of Nuclear Safeguards, February 1978.

100 Interview.

101 See section on "Nuclear Safeguards".

102 The CIRUS reactor.

103 The 40-megawatt TRR (Taiwan Research Reactor).

104 The 137-megawatt KANUPP reactor.

105 RAPP-1 (Rajasthan Atomic Power Plant No. 1).

106 RAPP-2 (Rajasthan Atomic Power Plant No. 2).

107 The 600-megawatt CANDU reactor.

108 L. Scheinman, 1971, p. 638.

109 See discussion in first section of this Chapter.

110 Australia ratified the Treaty only in 1973.

111 28-West-1-CDA, 18 March 1969.

112 *Texts*, 1982, p. 10.

113 The Joint Intelligence Committee and the Directorate of Scientific and Technical Intelligence of DND.

114 28–7–5–1, 5 April 1967.

115 28–7–5, 28 November 1966.

116 Interview.

117 *A Background Paper on Nuclear Safeguards and Canadian Safeguards Policy*, 1976, p. 17.

118 H. Galarneau, 1979, p. 110.

119 *Texts*, 1982, p. 10.

120 CIRUS, RAPP-1 and RAPP-2.

121 Assistance would be provided either by the Canadian International Development Agency (CIDA) or the Export Development Corporation (EDC).

122 H. Galarneau, 1979, p. 135.

123 With Spain in July 1975 and Sweden in September 1977, these two agreements replacing those of 1965 and 1962 respectively; with South Korea and Argentina in January 1976; with Finland in March 1976; and with Romania in October 1977.

124 *Texts*, 1982, p. 15.

125 See *Canada Treaty Series*, 1977, No. 35, especially paragraph 4.2.

126 Authors' note: see *Texts*, 1982, for more details; and the article of J.J. Noble (1978) concerning the difficulties in renegotiating the agreements between 1974 and 1977.

127 *Canada Treaty Series*.

128 Interview with William Barton.

129 See D.B. Dewitt, 1987, p. 167.

130 See *SIPRI Yearbook*, 1976, p. 391.

131 CCD/PV/653.

CHAPTER 8

1 A/7575 and S/9292.

2 See *The Problem of Chemical and Biological Warfare*, Vol. 1, Stockholm International Peace Research Institute (SIPRI), Stockholm, 1971, p. 304.

3 E.M. Spiers, 1986.

4 *SIPRI Yearbook*, 1986, Chapter 8.

5 See J. Kraus, 1986.

6 *SIPRI Yearbook*, 1986, p. 168.

7 North Atlantic Assembly, Military Committee, November 1986, pp. 13–15.

8 *SIPRI Yearbook*, 1987, p. 102.

9 The famous document MC 14/3 approved by NATO on 22 September 1967 and since revised and corrected on several occasions.

10 Sometimes known as the Australian Group since it was convened by Australia and is still chaired by an Australian.

11 Estimates vary between 20 and 40 countries.

12 11 January 1988, p. 24.

13 R. Ranger, 1976, p. 22.

14 Memorandum to Cabinet, 23 August 1968, file 28–6–6.

15 File 28–6–6.

16 A/37/259.

17 J.J. Norman and J.J. Purdon, 1986.

18 SIPRI Yearbook, 1986, p. 163.

19 *An Epidemiological Investigation of Alleged CW/BW Incidents in South East Asia*, Ottawa, NDHQ, Surgeon General Branch, August 1982.

20 T. Seeley *et al.* (September 1985).

21 J.J. Norman and J.J. Purdon (1986).

22 M. Meselson, J. Guillemin and J.P. Perry Robinson (1987).

23 P. Gizewski (September 1986).

24 See *The Arms Control Reporter*, 701.B.31.

25 For a more detailed study of Canada's position during these two Review Conferences, the reader is referred to the previously mentioned study of Gizewski (September 1986). An analysis of the main elements of the Second Review Conference is also given by J. Goldblat in the *SIPRI Yearbook* of 1987, pp. 409–414.

26 ENDC/231.

27 28–6–6), 1 April 1968.

28 28–6–6, H. Sheffer to D.M. Cornett, 4 September 1968.

29 28–6–6, A.K. Longair to M. Bow, 11 February 1969.

30 28–6–6, Disarmament Division to Legal Bureau, 20 February 1969.

31 See section on Legal Considerations.

32 28–6–6.

33 Authors' note: the Eastern Bloc plan submitted to UNGA on 19 September 1969.

34 CCD/PV/460, pp. 14–15.

35 Authors' note: the Canadian Forces would have to draw from U.S. stockpiles in wartime in order to exercise the right of chemical retaliation.

36 R. Ranger, 1976, p. 46.

37 Authors' note: the WHO separates chemical weapons into three classes: lethal weapons, incapacitating weapons and irritants. In the body of the text, a fourth chemical category is expressly added: herbicides.

38 CCD/338 and 337.

39 CCD/353, see Table 8.

40 P. 515.

41 Ignatieff, 9 January 1988.

42 G. Ignatieff, 1985, pp. 251–252.

43 See G. Ignatieff 1985, p. 252.

44 CCD/361.

45 CCD/420.

46 CCD/512.
47 CD/48, the text of which is reproduced in *SIPRI Yearbook*, 1980, pp. 373–375).
48 G.K. Vachon, March 1982, p. 105.
49 CD/416 of 23 August 1983 which was also incorporated in the final report CD/421.
50 CD/PV 195.
51 CD/343 and CD/294.
52 The famous CD/500 which is always on the agenda in Geneva.
53 CD/715.
54 France mainly stresses the dangers of terrorism and her desire to maintain security stocks.
55 See Chapter 6.
56 File 50271-K-40.
57 Letter from G.S. Field to Director of JBMDS dated 11 February 1960, (see Chapter 1 on the JBMDS), no file number.
58 No file number, but the letter is dated 12 February with the serial CSC 2196–2 (JBMDS) and, according to a hand-written note, could have been attached to the letter from Miller, Chairman of the Joint Chiefs of Staff, to DEA.
59 No file number, but the proposals are under the same serial as that of DND.
60 See Chapter 4.
61 See Chapter 6.
62 See *SIPRI Yearbook*, 1980, p. 373.
63 See A. Crawford *et al.*, (1987).
64 CD/333.
65 CD/113.
66 CD/PV 262, p. 50.
67 CD/677.
68 CD/689.
69 This report was subsequently forwarded to the Conference on Disarmament on 10 July 1987, see CD 770.
70 CD/679.

CHAPTER 9

1 *Nuclear Energy in Canada*, 1975, p. 10.
2 *Radiation – A Fact of Life*, IAEA, 1979, p. 6.
3 *Nuclear Energy in Canada*, 1975, p. 11.
4 Roughly half of those exposed to this level of radiation die within thirty days; at a level of 1,000 rems, there is no chance of survival.
5 S. Glasstone, 1964, p. 592.

6 J.M. White, 1983, pp. 14–15.

7 In J. Goldblat and C. Cox, 1988, hereinafter referred to as Goldblat-Cox, pp. 83–84.

8 *Comprehensive Study on Nuclear Weapons*, 1981, p. 86.

9 UNSCEAR: United Nations Scientific Committee on the Effects of Nuclear Radiation.

10 Authors' note: the total megatonnage of nuclear test explosions should not be confused with the megatonnage of fission products released; also it should be remembered that fission products are released by the detonation devices of fusion bombs.

11 The unit of "collective dose" is based on the product of mean dose received and the number of persons exposed: thus, 10,000 manrad is equivalent to 1 rad received by 10,000 persons, or 10 rads received by 1,000 persons.

12 Heavy water (deuterium oxide) which has been irradiated.

13 J.-C. Roy, 1987, p. 7.

14 R. Latarjet, 1986, p. 673.

15 *New York Times*, 16 February 1987, p. 10.

16 *New York Times*, 26 April 1987, p. 31.

17 United States 824; USSR 606; United Kingdom 40; France 144; PRC 30; India 1.

18 The proportions for the United Kingdom, France and China are 4.3, 9.2 and 4.4 percent respectively.

19 See R.S. Norris and R. Ferm in Goldblat-Cox. The data of Norris and Ferm are based on the U.S. Department of Energy publication "Announced United States Nuclear Tests, July 1945 through December 1986".

20 R.S. Norris, T.B. Cochran and W.M. Arkin, 1986, p. 56.

21 Estimated at 138 Mt.

22 J.I. Sands, R.S. Norris and T.B. Cochran, 1986, p. 49.

23 The effective yield of the Hiroshima bomb was actually 13 Kt.

24 In Goldblat-Cox, p. 112.

25 In Goldblat-Cox, p. 151.

26 The overall project was abandoned only in 1977, see I.Y.P. Borg in Goldblat-Cox, p. 66.

27 The last Chinese test in the atmosphere occurred in 1980.

28 R.S. Norris and R. Ferm, in Goldblat-Cox, p. 401.

29 Quoted in J. Klein, 1964, p. 298.

30 R.S. Norris, T.B. Cochran and W.M. Arkin, 1986, p. 55.

31 In Goldblat-Cox, p. 37.

32 According to Norris, Cochran and Arkin, 33 tests out of the total number conducted between 1945 and 1986, or less than 1 per year on average.

33 According to D.R. Westervelt, in Goldblat-Cox, p. 49.

34 See Goldblat-Cox, p. 36.

35 In Goldblat-Cox, p. 56.

36 The fission-fusion-fission bomb consisting of an outer envelope of uranium 238 which is fissile when bombarded with the extremely fast, and hence highly energetic, neutrons released in the fusion reaction; or alternatively consisting of a fission bomb in which gas capable of sustaining a fusion reaction is injected.

37 J.C. Mark in Goldblat-Cox, p. 39.

38 Multiple Independently-Targetable Reentry Vehicle (MIRV).

39 R.S. Norris and R. Ferm in Goldblat-Cox, p. 401.

40 T.B. Taylor (1987).

41 On this topic, see Chapter 10.

42 In Goldblat-Cox, p. 231.

43 See following section.

44 In Goldblat-Cox, p. 334.

45 Or "volume waves".

46 Authors' note: the seismological facility at Yellowknife is situated less than 10,000 km from the main nuclear test sites in Nevada (United States), Novaya Zemlya and East Kazakhstan (USSR), Lob Nor (China) and the Mururoa Atoll (French Polynesia). See B. North (1987).

47 See E. Johannisson in Goldblat-Cox, pp. 384–385.

48 See S. Ortoli, 1986, p. 25. Note that the largest earthquake of the century in Canada (magnitude 8) occurred in the Queen Charlotte Islands of British Columbia on 22 August 1949.

49 Ibid.

50 DEA, Seismic Verification, 1986, p. 38.

51 L.R. Sykes and J.F. Evernden, 1982, p. 141.

52 J.K. Leggett, in Goldblat-Cox, p. 217.

53 S. Ortoli, 1986, p. 25.

54 L.R. Sykes, in Goldblat-Cox, p. 149.

55 D.C. Fakley, in Goldblat-Cox, p. 163.

56 In Goldblat-Cox, pp. 150–151.

57 In Goldblat-Cox, p. 187.

58 The United States, Great Britain, France and Canada from the West, and the USSR, Poland, Romania and Czechoslovakia from the East.

59 Basham and Dahlman, in Goldblat-Cox, p. 171.

60 Ibid.

61 Report of the Secretary General, A/7967.

62 Basham and Dahlman, in Goldblat-Cox, p.173.

63 DEA, Seismic Verification, 1986, p. 48.

64 CCD/558.

65 CD/43.

66 CD/448.

67 CD/720.

68 For a description of the operation of these three levels see Basham and Dahlman, in Goldblat-Cox, pp. 180–186.

69 For instance, the 58 Mt Soviet bomb of 1961. Authors' note: Soviet Ambassador A. Arutunian, in a meeting with George Ignatieff in Ottawa, stated that nuclear weapons constituted a much more effective deterrent than the deployment of U.S. tanks to Berlin. File 50271-M-40, 9 May 1962.

70 Or an agreement to maintain the *status quo*.

71 G.A. Greb, 1988, p. 96.

72 See Chapter 3.

73 G.A. Greb, 1988, p. 99.

74 ENDC/28.

75 S. Ahmed, 1967, p. 65.

76 G.A. Greb, 1988, p. 102.

77 Ibid.

78 Cited in *The United Nations and Disarmament, 1945–1970*, p. 140.

79 File 50271-A-40, 20 January 1956.

80 Authors' note: the record does not indicate how the Defence Scientific Intelligence Division reached this conclusion. As will be seen shortly, perhaps the Canadian policy of imposing quotas on the number and explosive power of nuclear tests was interpreted as applicable only to thermonuclear tests.

81 JIC 174/1 (56), 4 April 1956.

82 See Chapter 3, section on "Canadian Reactions".

83 File 50271-A-40, 12 April 1956.

84 Authors' note: this varied with the official proposals; during discussions in the Subcommittee, Great Britain talked on some occasions of phase "three" and on others of phase "one".

85 File 50271-A-40, 16 April 1956.

86 *Hansard*, p. 6050.

87 File 50271-A-40, 18 July 1956.

88 Memorandum from Léger to Pearson, dated 26 July.

89 Letter from E.H. Gilmour of the United Nations Bureau to Captain F.W.T. Lucas of the Joint Staff, dated 3 August 1956.

90 Memorandum from the Defence Research Board (DRB), 31 August 1956, no file number.

91 *Proceedings of the National Academy of Science*, June 1956.

92 Authors' note: we retain the expression "megatonnic yield" originally used in the texts and subsequently replaced with "large yield atomic warheads" by the Chairman of the Joint Chiefs of Staff, General Charles Foulkes.

93 50271-B-40, 14 September, entitled "Canadian Atomic Weapons Requirement Policy".

94 File 50271-B-40, 5 October 1956.

95 Authors' note: debates over strontium apparently posed few difficulties, but there were many uncertainties concerning the dangers of cesium.

96 Note from Cadieux to Léger dated 1 October.

97 Letter from M. Zimmerman, Chairman DRB, to John W. Holmes, dated 7 October 1958, DND file 1644–1.

98 See Chapter 1.

99 See Chapter 5.

100 Telex from Washington to DEA, 12 April 1962, no file number.

101 S. Ahmed, 1967, p. 29.

102 See Chapter 6.

103 File 50271-T-40, 22 May 1962, to which is attached the letter of 9 May.

104 27 November 1963, 1910 (XVIII); no resolution in 1964 on account of difficulties with Article 19 of the Charter; 3 December 1965, 2032 (XX); 5 December 1966, 2163 (XXI); 19 December 1967, 2343 (XXII); 20 December 1968, 2455 (XXIII); 16 December 1969, 2604 A/B (XXIV); 7 December 1970, 2663 A/B (XXV); 16 December 1971, 2828 A/B/C (XXVI); 29 November 1972, 2934 A/B/C (XXVII); 6 December 1973, 3078 A/B (XXVIII); 9 December 1974, 3257 (XXIX); 11 December 1975, 3478 (XXX); 10 December 1976, 31/66, and 14 December 1976, 31/89; 12 December 1977, 32/78; 14 December 1978, 33/71 C; 11 December 1979, 34/73; 12 December 1980, 35/145/A/B; 9 December 1981, 36/84; 9 December 1982, 37/72 and 37/73; 15 December 1983, 38/62, 38/63 and 38/72; 12 December 1984, 39/52, 39/53 and 39/60; 12 December 1985, 40/80 A/B, 40/81 and 40/88; 3 December 1986, 41/46 A/B, 41/47 and 41/54; 30 November 1987, 42/26 A/B and 42/27. For an analysis of the resolutions of the General Assembly between 1963 and 1979 see the Report of the Secretary General of the United Nations A/35/257, 23 May 1980, p. 18.

105 See Section on "International Efforts in Seismic Detection".

106 A/35/257 and CD/86.

107 Authors' note: following resolutions 35/145 A, 36/84 and 36/87 which repeatedly called for the creation of such a working group.

108 See G.A. Greb, 1988, p. 104.

109 This document was published under two covers: A/9698 of the UNO and CCD/431 of the Conference of the Committee on Disarmament.

110 A/31/125.

111 Authors' note: most of the weapons developed by the United States at the time were designed for yields of between 350 and 450 Kt.

112 Specifically, all the straight line segments connecting pairs of points.
113 CD/130, 30 July 1980, p. 10.
114 G.A. Greb, 1988, p. 109.
115 See the 10 June 1963 memorandum of three non-aligned countries, Egypt, Ethiopia and Nigeria, ENDC/94.
116 ENDC/PV/104: see M. Tucker, 1982, p. 123.
117 ENDC/PV/98, p. 16.
118 See C/C/1/PV 1385 and report A/35/257, p. 21.
119 ENDC/144, p. 11.
120 File 28–8–4–1, 25 April 1966.
121 Telex 79 from Geneva dated 28 February 1966.
122 File 28–8–4–2, letter from Burns to Ottawa, 27 March 1966.
123 To Miller and Longair.
124 File 28–8–4–2.
125 File 28–8–4–2, 18 April 1966.
126 File 28–8–4–2.
127 "Preparations for Resumed Session of ENDC", 8 June 1966, no file number.
128 Telex 4027 from London to Ottawa, 28–8–4–2.
129 Authors' note: based on the classic distinction between body waves (P and S) and Love (or Rayleigh) waves; see Section on "Seismic Detection".
130 See S. Ortoli, 1986, p. 21.
131 File 28–8–4–2, for the planned visit of the Minister to Europe, 4–16 November.
132 28 West-1-Can, report from A. de W. Mathewson to D.M. Cornett, 13 January 1967.
133 28–8–? (illegible), discussions between Canada and Sweden, see memorandum of 31 August 1967.
134 File 28–8–4–2, 19 October 1967.
135 For further detail, see Section on "Seismic Detection".
136 File 28–8–4–2, memorandum from S.F. Carlson to Cornett, 2 February 1968.
137 File 28–8–4–2, undated memorandum from A.D. Morgan to Cornett, *CTB: Next Steps*.
138 Telex 5570, 21 November 1968.
139 Authors' note: this meeting resulted from a letter from Whitham to Cornett enclosing a study on the problems of seismic detection at a distance.
140 Authors' note: the technique was that of examining the general map of a given region (master earthquake) in relation to a number of isolated suspect events. In this regard, the seismological data varied from one site to another.

141 28–8–4–2, 15 July 1968.

142 28–8–4–2, letter to Bow dated 7 May 1969.

143 In this context, see CCD/306.

144 File 28–8–4–2, undated.

145 28-West-1-CDA, Whitham to Mac N. Bow, Director General of the Disarmament Division.

146 28–8–4–2, 5 May 1969.

147 Authors' note: this decision clearly reversed the Green-Diefenbaker decision of May 1960.

148 M. Tucker, 1982, p. 123. Authors' note: this aspect, which Tucker ascribes to the early 1960s, and which he borrowed from George Ignatieff (1974), only truly conformed to Canadian diplomacy starting in 1968 and 1969.

149 Actually, the responses came from 48 nations since 6 nations had made it known that they preferred to exchange seismological data on a voluntary basis.

150 Authors' note: the definition in the report uses a 50 percent probability interval, or one half-magnitude, with a maximum of 5 stations having a corresponding location capability between 20 and 45 km.

151 CCD/305, pp. 2–3.

152 In their document CCD/306.

153 Authors' note: which, at the same time, allowed some flexibility in cases where theoretical progress was more rapid than anticipated.

154 See CCD/327.

155 See Section on "Seismic Detection".

156 In document CCD/457.

157 See Section on "International Efforts in Seismic Detection".

158 On multiple explosions and masking techniques see CCD/490.

159 M. Tucker, 1981, p. 648.

160 See CCD/336, p. 2.

161 Ignatieff, G., 1974, p. 707.

162 38 Liberals, 11 Conservatives, 7 New Democrats and 2 Social Creditists.

163 Cf. *International Canada*, March 1971, p. 68.

164 Resolutions 3478 and 31/89.

165 In particular, "The Comprehensive Test Ban – Its Possible Significance for Nuclear Arms Control", March 1972.

166 G.H. Pearson (1985).

167 In this regard, see the noteworthy article of H. von Riekhoff and J. Sigler (1985).

168 CD/PV 156, pp. 9–10.

169 CD/PV 189, p. 20.

170 CD/PV 262, p. 53.

171 CD/PV 156, p. 11.
172 W. Epstein (1985).
173 See Section on "Seismic Detection".
174 See Chapter 7.
175 DEA, *Disarmament Bulletin Supplement*, Ottawa, Winter 1986 – Spring 1987.

CHAPTER 10

1 J.-L. Magdelénat, 1980, p. 63.
2 A. Simon, (1988).
3 A/AC. 105/399, 16 December 1987.
4 A/AC. 105/400.
5 These projects are listed below, and appear in an undated publication of the Interdepartmental Committee on Space entitled *Canada's Place in Space*: with the *United States*: Alouette, ISIS (International Satellite for Ionospheric Studies), CTS (Communications Technology Satellite), LANDSAT (Earth observation satellite), meteorological satellites, MSAT (mobile services satellite), COSPAS/SARSAT (search and rescue satellite SARSAT, Soviet equivalent COSPAS), CANADARM (Canada Arm on the Space Shuttle), RADARSAT, UARS (Upper Atmosphere Research Satellite), space science and the Space Station; with *Japan*: EXOS-D (physics of the magnetosphere and polar auroras), JERS-1 (Earth Resources Satellite), MOS-1 (Maritime Observation Satellite), and remote sensing; with the *USSR*: COSPAS/SARSAT and INTERBALL (studies of the magnetosphere – Canada provides the ultraviolet imagery from polar aurora studies); with the *ESA*: CTS, OLYMPUS (communications technology satellite), ERS-1 (remote sensing), PSDE (Payload and Spacecraft Development and Experimentation Program), EOPP (Earth Observation Preparatory Program) and HERMES (French space shuttle); with the *United Kingdom*: Canada participates in joint studies on RADARSAT; with *France*: SPOT (*Satellite Probatoire d'Observation de la Terre* – Earth geodesic observation satellite), WIND II/UARS (wind imagery device which will be integrated with UARS) and COSPAS/SARSAT; and, finally, with *Sweden*: VIKING (Swedish space science satellite) and GEODE (experiment on fabrication of materials in space).
6 A. Legault, 1988, p. 431.
7 See G. Lindsey (1988).
8 S. Danielsson, 1984, p. 1.
9 See Table 11.
10 Cited in B.A. Hurwitz, 1986, p. 24.
11 B.A. Hurwitz, 1986, p. 19.
12 See Table 11 for its official title.

13 On this lengthy legal debate, see the Canadian paper "Terminology Relevant to Arms Control and Outer Space", CD/716, 16 July 1986.

14 B.A. Hurwitz, 1986, p. 61.

15 J.-L. Magdelénat, 1981, p. 63.

16 Chile, Netherlands, Philippines and Uruguay.

17 B.A. Hurwitz, 1986, p. 59.

18 CD/716, p. 4.

19 D. Goedhuis cited in B.A. Hurwitz, 1986, p. 71.

20 See *SIPRI Yearbook*, 1986, p. 463.

21 30 September 1971.

22 30 September 1971.

23 22 June 1973.

24 15 September 1987. Authors' note: this list was largely drawn from the Canadian paper CD/618 which we have taken the liberty of updating by including the INF Treaty and NRRC Agreements. The NRRC Agreements reaffirm the obligations of the superpowers in respect of the 30 September 1971 Agreement on the Improvement of Teletypes between Moscow and Washington, and the 25 May 1972 Agreement Between the Government of the United States and the Government of the Union of Soviet Socialist Republics on the Prevention of Incidents on and over the High Seas.

25 See T. Beer, 10 September 1985, p. 196, and S. Danielsson, 1984, p. 2.

26 *Convention on the Prohibition of Military or any other Hostile Use of Environmental Modification Techniques*, 18 May 1977, entered into force 5 October 1978.

27 Authors' note: for an interesting discussion on stabilizing and de-stabilizing influences, see article by G. Lindsey (1983).

28 See J. Reiskind (1981) and J.A. Beesley, D.W. Sproule and M. Collins (1988).

29 A/40/192, 16 August 1985.

30 Entered into force on 3 October 1972.

31 Entered into force on 24 May 1976.

32 See J.K. Leggett and P.M. Lewis (1988).

33 9 and 13 December 1982, Res. 37/83 and 37/99D: 15 December 1983, Res. 38/70; 12 December 1984, Res. 39/59; 12 December 1985, Res. 40/87; 3 December 1986, Res. 41/53; 30 November 1987, Res. 42/33.

34 See Chapter 9.

35 A/conf. 101/10 and Corr. 1 and 2.

36 See Chapter 3 on the Western proposal of August 1957.

37 Authors' note: all the above events are recounted in a memorandum from the United Nations Division to Alan Gotlieb of the Legal Affairs Bureau dated 16 January 1958, file 50189–40; the memorandum con-

cluded with the observation that: "in future, it would be desirable for the Western powers to discuss this issue again, not as a legal problem but as a political problem in the broader context of disarmament agreements!" At about the same time, General Foulkes presented the same arguments to Léger on the virtues of MRBMS (see letter of 5 September 1958 from General Foulkes to Jules Léger, file DND, CSC 16444, volume number illegible).

38 See Chapter 6, section on "Partial Measures of Disarmament".

39 March-April 1980.

40 8–19 June 1978 in Helsinki; 23 January – 19 February 1979 in Berne; 23 April – 17 June 1979 in Vienna.

41 We are grateful to P.B. Stares (1983) for some of the historical details.

42 Ibid., p. 6.

43 Annexed to letter of 10 August 1981 to UN Secretary General, A/36/192.

44 Annexed to letter from Foreign Minister Gromyko to UN Secretary General dated 23 August 1983, A/38/194; see also CD/476.

45 Statement of ACDA Director Kenneth Adelman; see *The Arms Control Reporter*, p.104.347.

46 CD/420.

47 See *SIPRI Yearbook*, 1987, p. 68.

48 *Soviet Military Power*, 1988, p. 65.

49 See S. Danielsson, 1984, p. 4.

50 CD/PV/263, 12 June 1984.

51 See *The United Nations Disarmament Yearbook*, Vol.9, 1984, p. 362.

52 P. Nitze, 1985, p. 372.

53 See *The Arms Control Reporter*, p. 575.B.292.

54 See article by U.S. State Department Legal Advisor Abraham Sofaer (1986).

55 Authors' note: on this latter point, see the lucid analysis of A. Chayes, A.H. Chayes, and E. Spitzer (1986).

56 Note, however, that paragraph (d) of the Common Declaration does not specify the deployment environment – air, sea, land or space.

57 Deposition before the Arms Control International Security and Science Subcommittee of the Foreign Affairs Committee of the House of Representatives.

58 P. 1 of Appendix D of the report.

59 Authors' note: this definition is a bold interpretation of Article V of the Treaty which prohibits the development, testing or deployment of "ABM systems or components which are sea-based, air-based, space-based, or mobile land-based". We shall not deal with these aspects here, which would entail lengthy development, but we shall touch on them again in the section on "Canada, SDI and the ABM Treaty" which

deals with the provisions of the ABM Treaty concerning research activities.

60 *Times*, 23 March 1987.

61 Authors' note: this analysis obviously includes the provisions of the 1974 Protocol to the Treaty which limits ABM systems to one single site; see Chapter 9.

62 A. Chayes, A.H. Chayes and E. Spitzer, 1986, pp. 214–215.

63 Communiqué of 21 November 1977 of the Permanent U.S.-USSR Consultative Commission established under the SALT Agreements.

64 See, in this regard, the analysis of W.J. Durch, 1987, p. 23.

65 Ibid., p. 29.

66 Ibid., p. 24.

67 Ibid.

68 R. Einhorn, 1988, p. 395.

69 COSPAR, A/AC.105/403, p. 3.

70 W.J. Durch, 1987, p. 34.

71 CD/320.

72 See J.J. Noble (1989). Authors' note: Noble also considers the Trudeau peace initiative to have started on this same date.

73 *Statements and Speeches*, 83/20, 13 November 1983, p. 6.

74 See, in this regard, I. Vlasic (1988).

75 External Affairs' document dated 30 January 1984.

76 See section on "Negotiations on ASAT (1978–1985)".

77 See CD/PV/347, 13 March 1986.

78 *House of Commons Debates*, 21 January 1985, p. 1502.

79 Interview, and *New York Times*, 29 March 1985.

80 Statement of Prime Minister Brian Mulroney to the House, 18 April 1985.

81 Interview.

82 Interim report of the Special Joint Committee of the Senate and of the House of Commons on Canada's International Relations, 23 August 1985, p. 125.

83 *House of Commons Debates*, 23 January, 1986, p. 10101.

84 Special Joint Committee of the Senate and of the House of Commons on Canada's International Relations, *Interdependence and Internationalism*, June 1986, p. 54.

85 U.S. Senate Armed Services Committee, *Hearings on the Military Implications of the SALT Agreements*, 92nd Congress, 2nd Session, 18 July 1972, p. 377.

86 *House of Commons Debates*, 1986, p. 581.

87 8 February 1987.

88 *Statements and Speeches*, 87/14, 5 March 1987.

89 Statement of 7 September 1985, *Disarmament Bulletin*, Autumn 1985, p. 7.

90 See Chapter 9, section on "Unwavering Canadian Support (1978–1988)".

91 A/S-10/AC. 1/7.

92 Letter of 20 August 1979, addressed to G.H. Pearson.

93 29 November 1978.

94 A/34/540 Appendix.

95 A/AC. 206/14.

96 *SDEDSI*, 1983, pp. 69–70.

97 See page 37 of the brochure.

98 See page 7 of the brochure.

99 CD/618 of 23 July 1985, and CD/716 of 16 July 1986.

100 CD/606.

101 Cited in *Disarmament Bulletin*, Summer-Autumn 1987, p. 15.

102 Draft supported by: Australia, Belgium, Cameroon, Costa-Rica, Federal Republic of Germany, Italy, Japan, New Zealand, Turkey and the United Kingdom.

103 *Disarmament Bulletin*, Summer-Autumn 1986, p. 9.

CHAPTER 11

1 Quoted in L. Brady and J. Kaufman, 1985, p. 189.

2 J. Dean, 1987, p. 93.

3 L. Brady and J. Kaufman, 1985, p. 189.

4 *Keesing's Contemporary Archives*, 1965–66, p. 21672.

5 *The United Nations and Disarmament, 1945–1970*, 1971, pp. 57–62.

6 B. von Rosenbladt, 1971, p. 28.

7 Ibid.

8 *The United Nations and Disarmament, 1945–1970*, 1971, p. 99.

9 B.M. Russet and C.C. Cooper, 1966–1967, p. 37.

10 J. Newhouse et al., 1971, pp. 106 and 128.

11 H. Haftendorn, 1974, p. 468, note 25.

12 Ibid., pp. 242–243.

13 Ibid., pp. 243–245.

14 Ibid., pp. 256–257.

15 Ibid., pp. 247, 251–255.

16 R. Burt, 1976, p. 20.

17 *White Paper* (FRG), 1971–1972, p. 11.

18 *NATO-Einmischung in DDR Angelegenheiten rechtswidrig*, p. 238.

19 H. Blaesio and K. Wohlgemut, 1969, p. 10.

20 O. Winzer, 1969, p. 9.

21 A. Legault and M. Lachance, 1978, p. 248.

22 H. Haftendorn, 1974, p. 249.

23 DEA, File 27–4-NATO-1-MBFR, 12 January 1967.

24 House of Commons Debates, 19 December 1966, p. 11281.

25 DEA, File 27–4-NATO-1-MBFR, 2 May 1969.

26 DEA, File 27–4-NATO-1-MBFR, 30 August 1968.

27 DEA, File 27–4-NATO-1-MBFR, 28 April 1969.

28 DEA, File 27–4-NATO-1-MBFR, 14 November 1969.

29 DEA, File 27–4-NATO-1-MBFR, 9 January 1970.

30 DEA, File 27–4-NATO-1-MBFR, 27 October 1972.

31 DEA, File 27–4-NATO-1-MBFR, 29 March 1971.

32 DEA, File 27–4-NATO-1-MBFR, 23 March 1971.

33 DEA, File 27–4-NATO-1-MBFR, 20 May 1971.

34 DEA, File 27–4-NATO-1-MBFR, 20 May 1971.

35 M. Sharp (1971).

36 DEA, File 27–4-NATO-1-MBFR, 15 October 1971.

37 DEA, File 27–4-NATO-1-MBFR, 9 February 1972.

38 DEA, File 27–4-NATO-1-MBFR, 15 May 1973.

39 M. Tucker, undated, p. 38.

40 DEA, File 27–4-NATO-1-MBFR, 1 June 1973.

41 Ibid.

42 M. Tucker, undated, p. 40.

43 DEA, File 27–4-NATO-1-MBFR, 14 May 1973.

44 DEA, File 27–4-NATO-1-MBFR, 4 July 1978.

45 DEA, File 27–4-NATO-1-MBFR, 18 October 1973.

46 DEA, File 27–4-NATO-1-MBFR, 1 June 1973.

47 DEA, File 27–4-NATO-1-MBFR, June 1973.

48 J. Keliher, 1980, p. 53.

49 Ibid., p. 48.

50 J. Dean, 1987, p. 15.

51 J. Keliher, 1980, p. 48.

52 J. Dean, 1987, p. 158.

53 J. Keliher, 1980, pp. 64–65.

54 Ibid., p. 54.

55 Ibid., p. 103.

56 Ibid., p. 70.

57 J. Klein, 1987, p. 81.

58 Ibid.

59 These two measures applied to the whole of Europe, so as to accommodate the security of the flank countries.

60 J. Klein, 1987, pp. 85–86.

61 Ibid., p. 84.

62 T. Hirschfeld, 1986, p. 9; and J. Klein, 1987, p. 88.

63 See S. Canby, in E.C. Luck, 1983, p. 201.

64 J. Klein, 1987, p. 98.

65 DEA, File 27–4-NATO-1-MBFR, 29 June 1981.

66 DEA, File 27–4-NATO-1-MBFR, 5 November 1970.

67 DEA, File 27–4-NATO-1-MBFR, April 1973.

68 DEA, File 27–4-NATO-1-MBFR, Final Report of the 1981 Session.

69 Ibid., (concerning NATO's last initiative in December 1979).

70 DEA, File 27–4-NATO-1-MBFR, Final Report of the 26ᵗʰ Session, February 1982.

71 DEA, File 27–4-NATO-1-MBFR, 3 December 1981.

72 DEA, File 27–4-NATO-1-MBFR, 15 October 1981.

73 DEA, File 27–4-NATO-1-MBFR, 22 May 1976.

74 DEA, File 27–4-NATO-1-MBFR, 7 October 1974.

75 Ibid.

76 Ibid.

77 DEA, File 27–4-NATO-1-MBFR, 5 December 1974.

78 DEA, File 27–4-NATO-1-MBFR, 1 June 1973.

CHAPTER 12

1 K. Möttöla, 1986, pp. 12–14.

2 L. Ferraris (1979); J. Maresca (1985); J. Sizoo and Th. Jurrjens (1984); R. Spencer (1984); and J. Klein (1987).

3 UNO, 1971, p. 56.

4 Ibid., p. 58.

5 Ibid., p. 61.

6 *Documents on Disarmament 1962*, 1963, pp. 1214–1224.

7 DEA file 20–4-CSCE, 22 March 1967.

8 DEA file 20–4-CSCE, 7 March 1968.

9 DEA file 20–4-CSCE, 5 March 1968.

10 DEA file 20–4-CSCE, undated.

11 DEA file 20–4-CSCE, 31 July 1972.

12 DEA file 20–4-CSCE, 19 December 1972.

13 DEA file 20–4-CSCE, 7 August 1973, pp. 1–3.

14 DEA file 20–4-CSCE, 26 July 1972.

15 DEA file 20–4-CSCE, 26 July 1972.

16 DEA file 20–4-CSCE, 31 July 1972.

17 DEA file 20–4-CSCE, 22 March 1973.

18 Specifically the following:

CSCE/HC/10 Switzerland;

CSCE/HC/11 USSR;

CSCE/HC/28 USSR;

CSCE/HC/28 add. GDR;

CSCE/HC/13 Romania;

CSCE/HC/17 Belgium;

CSCE/HC/18 Italy;

CSCE/HC/20 Austria;

CSCE/HC/21, corr. 1 Sweden;

CSCE/HC/21 add. 1 Sweden;

CSCE/HC/22 Switzerland;

CSCE/HC/23 Yugoslavia;

CSCE/HC/24 Netherlands;

CSCE/HC/25 Spain;

CSCE/HC/26 rev. 2 Spain;

CSCE/HC/29 Turkey.

19 DEA file 20–4-CSCE, 25 June 1973.

20 Ibid.

21 J. Klein, 1987, p. 173.

22 DEA file 20–4-CSCE, 23 May 1973.

23 Ibid.

24 DEA file 20–4-CSCE, 14 June 1973.

25 DEA file 20–4-CSCE, 17 July 1973.

26 DEA file 20–4-CSCE, 18 March 1974; and J. Maresca, 1985, p. 170.

27 DEA file 20–4-CSCE, 30 October 1973.

28 J. Klein, 1987, p. 139.

29 DEA file 20–4-CSCE, 25 February 1974.

30 J. Maresca, 1985, p. 172.

31 DEA file 20–4-CSCE, 30 August 1976.

32 J. Maresca, 1985, p. 172.

33 DEA file 20–4-CSCE, 26 September 1974.

34 DEA file 20–4-CSCE, 24 February 1975. See Table 17 of this Chapter.

35 J. Maresca, 1985, p. 135.

36 DEA file 20–4-CSCE, 7 April 1975.

37 DEA file 20–4-CSCE, undated.

38 DEA file 20–4-CSCE, 21 August 1975.

39 DEA file 20–4-CSCE, 1 August 1977.

40 Ibid.

41 DEA file 20–4-CSCE, 12 July 1977.

42 DEA file 20–4-CSCE, 8 August 1977.

43 Ibid.

44 DEA file 20–4-CSCE, 20 March 1978.

45 J. Klein, 1987, p. 160.

46 DEA file 20–4-CSCE, January 1978.

47 By way of example, France suggested ten CBMs grouped into three categories (see J. Borawski, 1988, pp. 20–21). They formed the first version of the French package presented to NATO in September 1979.

48 DEA file 20–4-CSCE, 12 September 1979.

49 Ibid.

50 These elements were taken from *Chronology of Negotiations on the CDE at the Madrid Meeting*, undated, and DEA file 20–4-CSCE, 12 September 1979.

51 J. Klein, 1987, p. 163.

52 See J. Borawski, 1988, pp. 25–26.

53 DEA file 20–4-CSCE, 25 April 1979.

54 DEA file 20–4-CSCE, 20 February 1979.

55 DEA file 20–4-CSCE, 31 July 1979.

56 DEA file 20–4-CSCE, 4 July 1979.

57 DEA file 20–4-CSCE, 1 October 1979.

58 DEA file 20–4-CSCE, 28 September 1979.

59 DEA file 20–4-CSCE, 12 September 1979.

60 See the package of 25 measures at Appendix I.

61 DEA file 20–4-CSCE, 19 December 1979 and 4 February 1980.

62 DEA file 20–4-CSCE-MDRID-1, 26 March 1980.

63 DEA file 20–4-CSCE-MDRID-1, 14 March 1980 and 16 April 1980.

64 DEA file 20–4-CSCE-MDRID-1, 28 November 1980.

65 DEA file 20–4-CSCE-MDRID-1, 19 May 1980.

66 DEA file 20–4-CSCE-MDRID-1, 27 August 1980.

67 J. Sizoo and T. Jurrjens, 1984, p. 18.

68 DEA file 20–4-CSCE-MDRID-1, undated.

69 J. Klein, 1987, p. 166.

70 Ibid.

71 Ibid., pp. 169–170.

72 DEA file 20–4-CSCE-MDRID-1, undated.

73 Authors' note: the absence of an adjective before "part", the fact that land activities are not specifically mentioned, the ambiguity of the relative pronoun "which" (that could refer either to "part" or "activities in Europe") could lead to the following interpretation: "inasmuch as these activities are part of the activities in Europe for which the participants decide to notify the CDE".

74 J. Klein, 1987, p. 179.

75 DEA file 20–4-CSCE-MDRID-1, 18 December 1982.

76 DEA file 20–4-CSCE-MDRID-1, 9 December 1982.

77 J. Klein, 1987, p. 180.

78 *Arms Control Reporter (The)*, 1983. p. 402.B.19.

79 DEA file 20–4-CSCE-MDRID-1, 5 December 1983.

80 DEA file 20–4-CSCE-MDRID-1, final report.

81 Ibid.

CHAPTER 13

1 J. Dean, 1987, p. 138.

2 DEA file 28–4–6 CDE, 25 September 1986.

3 DEA file 28–4–6 CDE, 26 September 1986.

4 J. Klein, 1987, p. 219.

5 DEA file 28–4–6 CDE, 25 August and 20 September 1983.

6 DEA file 28–4–6 CDE, 23 August 1983.

7 DEA file 28–4–6 CDE, 6 October 1983.

8 Particularly with regard to exchange of information (measure 1) on deployment of forces down to regimental level (opposed by Turkey) and the number of inspections that each country had to accept (measure 5).

9 DEA file 28–4–6 CDE, 15 November 1983.

10 *Common Security: A Programme for Disarmament* (Palme Report), 1982, pp. 117–118.

11 DEA file 28–4–6 CDE, 15 November 1983.

12 DEA file 28–4–6 CDE, Final Report of the Canadian Delegation, Autumn 1986, Section 10, p. 1.

13 This information also included specific regulations applying to foreign military personnel – the military attachés – accredited to the governments of States participating in the CDE.

14 DEA file 28–4–6 CDE, 6 July 1984.

15 DEA file 28–4–6 CDE, 14 March 1984.

16 DEA file 28–4–6 CDE, 26 April 1984.

17 DEA file 28–4–6 CDE, Final Report of the Canadian Delegation, Autumn 1986, Section 3, p. 3.

18 DEA file 28–4–6 CDE, 31 January 1985.

19 These figures are not mentioned in the SC1 (Amplified) proposal, but they constituted the threshold envisaged in document no. 2 of the Military Committee of NATO, dated 2 November 1984. These figures also applied to the previously mentioned element, namely at the divisional formation level.

20 For the sake of brevity, several items have been omitted herein in the description of the SC1 (Amplified) proposal.

21 This proposal had been introduced in Belgrade in 1977; it was reintroduced in the Soviet proposal of 6 October 1979.

22 This offer had already been made on 6 October 1979.

23 These proposals were already contained in Brezhnev's 1979 statement.

24 Repetition of the offers made by Romania in Belgrade in 1977, and by Brezhnev on 6 October 1979.

25 DEA file 28–4–6 CDE, 21 August 1985.

26 DEA file 28–4–6 CDE, 28 May 1986.

27 This concession took account of the particular concerns of the NNA.

28 See preceding remark.

29 J. Borawski, 1988, p. 91.

30 DEA file 28–4–6 CDE, 25 July 1986.
31 DEA file 28–4–6 CDE, 27 August 1986.
32 DEA file 28–4–6 CDE, 15 September 1986.
33 J Klein, 1987, p. 221.
34 J. Borawski, 1988, p. 100.
35 See Articles 34 to 37 of the Stockholm Document.
36 See Article 53.4 of the Stockholm Document.

CONCLUSION

1 A. Legault, M. Fortmann, F. Fâché and J.-F. Thibault (1989).
2 Ibid.
3 D. Munton (1988).
4 See Note 1.
5 See Chapter 10.
6 See Chapter 9.
7 See Chapter 1.
8 See Chapter 3.
9 D.W. Middlemiss and J.J. Sokolsky, 1989, p. 78.
10 See Chapter 2.
11 See Chapter 7.
12 "No news, good news", quoted in D.W. Middlemiss and J.J. Sokolsky (1989).
13 H. von Riekhoff and J. Sigler (1985).

Bibliography

A Background Paper on Nuclear Safeguards and Canadian Safeguards Policy. Ottawa: Department of External Affairs, 30 January 1976.

Ahmed, Samir. "The Neutrals and the Test Ban Negotiations: An Analysis of the Non-Aligned States' Efforts between 1962–1963". *Occasional Paper No. 4*. New York: Carnegie Endowment for International Peace, 1967.

Arms Control Reporter (The). Brookline (Mass.): various issues.

Baker, Philip Noel. *The Arms Race*. New York: Oceana Publications Inc., 1958.

Beer, Thomas. "Arms control in Outer Space – Military Technology vs. International Law". *Arms Control*. Vol. 6, September 1985, pp. 153–202.

Beesley, Alan J., D.W. Sproule and Mark Collins. "L'apport du Canada au droit spatial et au contrôle des armements dans l'espace extra-atmosphérique" [Canadian Support for Space Law and Arms Control in Outer Space]. *Études Internationales*. Vol. XIX, No. 3, September 1988, pp. 501–517.

Blaesio, H., and K. Wohlgemut. "Sozialistische Staaten und Europäische Sicherheit". *Dokumentation der Zeit*. Vol. 21, No. 12, May 1969, p. 10.

Bloomfield, Lincoln P., Walter C. Clemens Jr., and Franklin Griffiths. *Khrushchev and the Arms Race: Soviet Interest in Arms Control and Disarmament, 1954–1964*. Cambridge (Mass.): The MIT Press, 1966.

Borawski, J. *From the Atlantic to the Urals*. London: Brassey's, 1988.

Brady, L., and J. Kaufman. *NATO in the 1980s*. New York: Praeger, 1985.

Burns, E.L.M. *Megamurder*. New York: Pantheon Books, 1967.

Burt, R. "New Weapons' Technologies: Debate and Directions". *Adelphi Paper*. No. 126, 1976, p. 20.

Butler, G.C. *Report on Use of Chemical Warfare in South-East Asia*. Note to Department of External Affairs, 2 December 1981.

Canadian Foreign Policy Texts. Ottawa: Department of External Affairs, May 1982.

Canby, S. "Arms Control, CBMS and Verification", in E.C. Luck, *Arms Control, The Multilateral Alternative*. New York: New York University Press, 1983, p. 201.

Chayes, Abram, Antonia Handler Chayes and Eliot Spitzer. "Space Weapons: The Legal Context", in Long, Franklin A., *Weapons in Space* cited below, pp. 193–218.

Chronology of the Negotiations on the CDE at the Madrid Meeting. Canadian Archives document, undated.

Clarkson, Stephen. *An Independent Foreign Policy for Canada*. Toronto: McClelland and Stewart, 1968.

Common Security: A Programme for Disarmament. The Report of the Independent Commission on Disarmament and Security Issues under the Chairmanship of Olof Palme. London and Sydney: Pan Books, 1982.

Crawford, Alan, Gregor MacKinnon, Lynne Hanson and Ellis Morris. *Compendium of Arms Control Verification Proposals*. 3 Vol. Ottawa: Operational Research and Analysis Establishment (ORAE), July 1987.

Crozier, Michel and Erhard Friedberg. *L'acteur et le système*. Paris: Seuil, 1977.

Danielsson, Sune. "Examination of Proposals Relating to the Prevention of An Arms Race in Outer Space". *Journal of Space Law*, 12, Spring 1984, pp. 1–11.

Darchen, Bernadette and Roger. *La vie des abeilles*. Paris: Éditions Nathan, 1985.

Dean, J. *Watershed in Europe*. Lexington (Mass.): Lexington Books, 1987.

Dewitt, David B. *Nuclear Non-Proliferation and Global Security*. London & Sydney: Croom Helm, 1987.

Documents on Disarmament 1962. Washington: Arms Control and Disarmament Agency, 1963.

Doern, Bruce G., and Robert W. Morrison. *Canadian Nuclear Policies*. Montreal: Policy Research Institute, 1980.

Dumézil, Georges. *Mythe et Épopée*. Vol. 1: *L'idéologie des trois fonctions dans les épopées des peuples indo-européens*. Paris: Gallimard, 1968.

Durch, William J. "The Future of the ABM Treaty". *Adelphi Papers No. 223*. London: IISS, Summer 1987, p. 80.

Eayrs, James. *In Defence of Canada*. Vol. III: *Peacemaking and Deterrence*. Toronto: University of Toronto Press, 1972.

– *In Defence of Canada*. Vol. IV: *Growing Up Allied*. Toronto: University of Toronto Press, 1980.

Einhorn, Robert. "Strategic Arms Reduction Talks: The Emerging START Agreement". *Survival*. September-October 1988, pp. 387–401.

Epstein, William. "Test Ban – First Step to Disarmament". *International Perspectives*. May-June 1985, pp. 21–24.

Ferraris, L. *Report on a Negotiation*. The Hague: Sijthoff-Nordhoff, 1979.

Fischer, David and Paul Szasz. *Safeguarding the Atom*. London: Taylor and Francis, 1985.

Fontaine, André. *Histoire de la guerre froide, 1950–1967*. Paris: Fayard, 1967.

Galarneau, Hélène. "La politique du Canada en matière de contrôle des exportations nucléaires" [Canadian Policy on Control of Nuclear Exports]. Master's Thesis. Québec: Laval University, 1979.

Girard, Charlotte S.M. (Dir.) *Canada in World Affairs, 1963–1965*. Toronto: Canadian Institute of International Affairs, 1980.

Gizewski, Peter. "Biological Weapons Control". *Issue Brief No. 5*. Ottawa: Canadian Centre for Arms Control and Disarmament, September 1986.

Glasstone, Samuel. *The Effects of Nuclear Weapons* (rev. ed.) Washington: USAEC, 1964.

Goldblat, Jozef. *Agreements for Arms Control*. London: Taylor and Francis, 1982.

Goldblat, Josef and David Cox (eds). *Nuclear Weapon Tests: Prohibition or Limitation?* Oxford: Oxford University Press, 1988 (A CIIPS-SIPRI Study).

Granatstein, J.L. *Canada 1957–1967: The Years of Uncertainty and Innovation*. Toronto: McClelland and Stewart, 1986.

Greb, G. Allen. "Survey of Past Nuclear Test Ban Negotiations", in Goldblat and Cox, *Nuclear Weapon Tests: Prohibition or Limitation?*, pp. 95–117.

Haftendorn, H. *Abrüstung und Entspannungspolitik*. Düsseldorf: Bertelsmann Universitätsverlag, 1974.

Hirschfeld, T. "MBFR in Eclipse". *Arms Control Today*. October 1986, p. 9.

Hockin, Thomas C. "Federalist Style in International Politics", in Stephen Clarkson, *An Independent Foreign Policy for Canada*, pp. 119–135.

– "Domestic Setting and Canadian Voluntarism", in Lewis Hertzman, John Warnock and Thomas C. Hockin, *Alliances and Illusions: Canada and the NATO-NORAD Question*. Edmonton (Alberta): M.G. Hurtig, 1969.

Holmes, John W. *The Shaping of Peace: 1943–1957*. Toronto: University of Toronto Press, 1979.

Hurwitz, Bruce A. *The Legality of Space Militarization*. Amsterdam: North-Holland, 1986.

IAEA. *Radiation – A Fact of Life*. Vienna: 1979.

IAEA Bulletin. Vols. 25–30, 1983–1988.

Ignatieff, George. "Canadian Aims and Perspectives in the Negotiation of International Agreements on Arms Control and Disarmament", in R.S.T. Macdonald et. al. (eds), *Canadian Perspectives on International Law and Organization*. Toronto: University of Toronto Press, 1974, pp. 690–725.

– *The Making of a Peacemonger*. Toronto: University of Toronto Press, 1985.

Imai, Ryukichi. "Nuclear Safeguards". *Adelphi Papers*. No. 86, March 1972.

Jennekens, Jon. "The IAEA, International Safeguards and the Future of the NPT", in David B. Dewitt, *Nuclear Non-Proliferation and Global Security*, pp 73–85.

Keesing's Contemporary Archives, 1965–1966. New York.

Keliher, J. *The Negotiations on MBFR*. New York: Pergamon Press, 1980.

Klein, Jean. *L'entreprise du désarmement, 1945–1964*. Toulouse: Cujas, 1964.

— *Sécurité et désarmement en Europe*. Paris: Éditions Economica, 1987.

Kramish, Arnold. "The Watched and the Unwatched: Inspection in the Non-Proliferation Treaty". *Adelphi Papers*. No. 36, June 1967.

Krause, J. *Optionen chemischer Kriegsfürung in der Strategie des Warschauer Pakts*. Ebenhausen: Stiftung Wissenschaft und Politik, Report No. SWP-AZ 2481, August 1986.

Laloy, Jean. *Entre guerres et paix*. Paris: Plon, 1966.

Latarjet, Raymond. "Sur l'accident nucléaire de Tchernobyl". *Politique Étrangère*. No. 3, 1986, pp. 669–677.

Lawrence, Robert M., and Joel Larus (eds.) *Nuclear Proliferation, Phase II*. Lawrence (Kansas): The University Press of Kansas, 1974.

Legault, Albert and M. Lachance. "Les MBFR". *Études Internationales*. Vol. 9, Nos. 2–3, June-September 1978, p. 248.

Legault, Albert (ed.) "L'espace extra-atmosphérique et le Canada" [Outer Space and Canada]. *Études Internationales*. Vol. XIX, No. 3, September 1988.

Legault, Albert, Michel Fortmann, Françoise Fâché and Jean-François Thibault. "La paix par la force et la paix par le droit", in Charles-Philippe David (ed.), *Les études stratégiques: approches et concepts*. Montreal: Éditions Méridiens, 1989.

Leggett, Jeremy K., and Patricia M. Lewis. "Verifying a START Agreement". *Survival*. Vol. XXX, No. 5, September-October 1988, pp. 409–429.

Lindsey, George. "L'espace: rôle auxiliaire ou quatrième arme?" *Études Internationales*. Vol. XIX, No. 3, September 1988, pp. 451–467.

— "The Military Uses of Outer Space and Arms Control". *Canadian Defence Quarterly*. Vol. 13, No. 1, 1983, pp. 9–14.

Long, Frank A., Donald Hafner and Jeffrey Boutwell (eds.) *Weapons in Space*. New York: W.W. Norton & Company, 1986.

Lyon, Peyton V. *The Policy Question: A Critical Appraisal of Canada's Role in World Affairs*. Toronto: McClelland and Stewart, 1963.

Magdelénat, Jean-Louis. "Perspectives du droit spatial", [Perspectives in Space Law], in *International Law and Canadian Foreign Policy in the 1980s*. Ottawa: United Nations Association in Canada and Canadian Council on International Law, 1981, pp. 63–72.

Maresca, J. *To Helsinki*. Durham and London: Duke University Press, 1985.

Mazer, Brian M. "The International Framework for Safeguarding Peaceful Nuclear Energy Programs". *Saskatchewan Law Review*. Vol. 45, 1980–1981, pp. 83–102.

Meselson, Matthew, Jeanne Guillemin and J.P. Perry Robinson. "Yellow Rain: The Story Collapses". *Foreign Policy*. No. 68, Fall 1987, pp. 100–117.

Middlemiss, D.W., and J.J. Sokolsky. *Canadian Defence: Decisions and Determinants*. Toronto: Harcourt Brace Jovanovich, 1989.

Morrison, Robert W., and Edmond F. Wonder. *Canada's Nuclear Export Policy*. Ottawa: The Norman Paterson School of International Affairs – Carleton University, coll. "Carleton International Studies" III, 1978.

Möttölä, K. *Ten Years After Helsinki*. Boulder (Col.): Westview Press, 1986.

Munro, John A., and Alex I. Inglis. *Mike: The Memoirs of the Right Honourable Lester B. Pearson*. Vol. 3. Toronto: University of Toronto Press, 1975.

Munton, Don. "Peace and Security in the 1980s: The View of Canadians". *Working Paper*. Ottawa: Canadian Institute for International Peace and Security, 1988.

NATO-Einmischung in DDR Angelegenheiten rechtswidrig, *Aussenpolitische Korrespondenz*. Vol. 12, No. 28, July 1968.

Newhouse, J., et al. *U.S. Troops in Europe*. Washington (DC): Brookings Institution, 1971.

Nitze, Paul. "The Objectives of Arms Control", in Small, Melvin and David J. Singer, *International War: An Anthology and Study Guide*. Illinois: Dorsey Press, 1985, pp. 363–376.

Noble, John J. "Canada's Continuing Search for Acceptable Nuclear Safeguards". *International Perspectives*. July-August 1978, pp. 42–48.

– "La politique étrangère américaine de 1980 à 1988: l'héritage Reaganien", [American Foreign Policy from 1980 to 1988: the Reagan Heritage". *Actes du XXe Congrès du Centre québécois de relations internationales*. Québec: 1989 (forthcoming).

Norman, J.J., and J.J. Purdon. *Final Summary Report on the Investigation of "Yellow Rain" Samples from Southeast Asia*. Ottawa: Defence Research Establishment Ottawa (DREO), February 1986.

Norris, Robert S., Thomas B. Cochran and William M. Arkin. *Known U.S. Nuclear Tests: July 1945–October 1986*. Washington: Natural Resources Defense Council, 1986.

North Atlantic Assembly (NAA) Military Committee. *Interim Report of the Subcommittee on Conventional Defence: New Strategies and Operational Concepts*. Brussels: November 1986.

North, Bob. "Pour mieux détecter les explosions nucléaires". *GEOS*. Vol. 16, No. 1, Winter 1987, pp. 1–5.

Nuclear Energy in Canada. Toronto: Canadian Nuclear Association, 1975, 47p.

Ortoli, Sven. "Essais nucléaires: le détecteur de mensonges des géophysiciens". *Science et Vie*. No. 829, 1986, pp. 16–26 and 175.

Pearson, Geoffrey H. "Trudeau Peace Initiative Reflections". *International Perspectives*. March-April 1985, pp. 3–6.

Pendley, Robert and Lawrence Scheinman, with the collaboration of Richard W. Butler. "International Safeguarding as Institutionalized Collective Behaviour". *International Organization*. Vol. 29, No. 3, 1975, pp. 585–616.

Pike, John. "Anti-Satellite Weapons and Arms Control". *Arms Control Today*. Vol. 13, No. 11, December 1983, pp. 1–7.

Ramade, François. *Le peuple des fourmis*. Paris: PUF, coll. "Que sais-je?", 1972.

Ranger, Robin. "The Canadian Contribution to the Control of Chemical and Biological Warfare". *Wellesley Paper*. No. 5. Toronto: Canadian Institute of International Affairs, 1976.

Reiskind, Jason. "Toward a Responsible Use of Nuclear Power in Outer Space – The Canadian Initiative in the United Nations", in Matte, Nicolas Mateesco, *Annales de droit aérien et spatial*. Vol. VI, 1981, pp. 461–474.

Riekhoff, Harald von and John Sigler. "The Trudeau Peace Initiative: The Politics of Reversing the Arms Race", in Brian W. Tomlin and Maureen Molot (eds.), *Canada Among Nations 1984: A Time of Transition*. Toronto: James Lorimer and Company, 1985, pp. 50–69.

Rosenbladt, B. von. *Die Haltung der DDR in der Frage der MBFR*. SWP-AP 1063. Eggenberg: photocopy, 1971.

Roy, Jean-Claude. *L'accident nucléaire de Tchernobyl et son impact sur la région de Québec*. Québec: Laval University, Department of Chemistry, 1987.

Russet, B.M., and C.C. Cooper. "Arms Control in Europe". *Monograph Series in World Affairs*. Vol. 14, No. 2, 1966–1967, p. 37.

Sanders, Benjamin. *Safeguards Against Nuclear Proliferation*. Stockholm: Almqvist & Wiksell, 1975.

Sands, Jeffrey I., Robert S. Norris and Thomas B. Cochran. *Known Soviet Nuclear Explosions: 1949–1985 (Rev. 2, June 1986)*. Washington: Natural Resources Defense Council, June 1986.

Scheinman, Lawrence. "Safeguarding Reprocessing Facilities: the Impact of Multinationalization", in Abram Chayes and Lewis W. Bennett, *International Arrangements for Nuclear Fuel Reprocessing*. Cambridge (Mass.): Balinger Publishing Company, 1977, pp. 65–79.

– "Security and a Transnational System: The Case of Nuclear Energy". *International Organization*. Vol. 25, No. 3, 1971, pp. 626–649.

Schiefer, H.B. *Study of the Possible Use of Chemical Warfare Agents in Southeast Asia: A Report to the Department of External Affairs*. Ottawa: 1982.

Schütze, Walter. "France and Germany: Cooperation and Conflict in Defence and Security". *PSIS Occasional Papers*. No. 2, 1987.

Seeley, Thomas D., Joan W. Nowicke, Matthew Meselson, Jeanne Guillemin and Pongthep Akratanakul. "Yellow Rain". *Scientific American*. Vol. 253, No. 3, September 1985, pp. 128–137.

Seismic Verification. Brochure on Verification No. 1. Ottawa: Department of External Affairs, 1986.

Sharp, Mitchell. "Maintaining the Solidarity of the North Atlantic Alliance". *Statements and Speeches*. 71/24, 27 September 1971.

Simon, Alain. "L'importance économique de l'espace: situation internationale" [The Economic Importance of Space: the International Situation]. *Études Internationales*. Vol. XIX, No. 3, September 1988, pp. 435–450.

SIPRI. *The Problem of Chemical and Biological Warfare: The Rise of CB Weapons*. Vol 1. Stockholm: Almqvist & Wiksell, 1971.

SIPRI Yearbook. Stockholm: Almqvist and Wiksell, various issues.

Sizoo, J., and Th. Jurrjens. *CSCE Decision Making: The Madrid Experience*. The Hague: Martin Nijhoff, 1984.

Société pour le développement des études de défense et de sécurité internationale (SDEDSI). "La crise du désarmement; la deuxième session extraordinaire de l'Assemblée générale des Nations Unies sur le désarmement" [The Disarmament Crisis: Second UN Special Session on Disarmament]. Grenoble: SDEDSI, 1983.

Sofaer, Abraham. "The ABM Treaty and the Strategic Defense Initiative". *Harvard Law Review*. Vol. 99, No. 8, June 1986, pp. 1972–85.

Spencer, R. *Canada and the CSCE*. Toronto: Toronto University Press, 1984.

Spiers, Edward M. *Chemical Warfare*. London: MacMillan Press, 1986.

Stares, Paul, B. "Déjà vu: The ASAT Debate in Historical Context". *Arms Control Today*. December 1983, pp. 2–7.

– "Outer Space: Arms or Arms Control?" *Arms Control Today*. Vol. 11, No. 6, July/August 1981, pp. 1–3.

Stursberg, Peter. *Diefenbaker – Leadership Gained: 1956–1962*. Toronto: University of Toronto Press, 1975.

Swettenham, John. *McNaughton*. Vol. III. Toronto: Ryerson Press, 1973.

Sykes, Lynn R., and Jack F. Evernden. "The Verification of a Comprehensive Nuclear Test Ban". *Scientific American*. October 1982, pp. 139–147.

Taylor, Theodore B. "Third-Generation Nuclear Weapons". *Scientific American*. Vol. 256, No. 4, pp. 30–39.

Thomson, Dale C. *Louis St-Laurent, Canadian*. Toronto: MacMillan of Canada, 1967.

Tucker, Michael. *Canada's Role in the Disarmament Negotiations*. Doctoral Thesis. Toronto: University of Toronto, 1977.

– "Canada and the Test Ban Negotiations: 1955–71", in Kim Richard Nossal, *An Acceptance of Paradox: Essays on Canadian Diplomacy in Honour of John W. Holmes*. Toronto: Canadian Institute of International Affairs, 1982, pp. 114–140.

– *Canadian Foreign Policy: Contemporary Issues and Themes*. Toronto: McGraw Hill and Ryerson, 1980.

– "Canada and Arms Control: Perspectives and Trends". *International Journal*. Vol. 36, No. 3, Summer 1981, pp. 635–656.

– "General Tommy Burns". *Bout de papier*. Vol 3, No. 3, Fall 1985, pp. 11–12.

– "Canada and MBFR". Unpublished, undated.

United Nations Association in Canada. *International Security and Outer Space*. Proceedings of a Conference held at McGill University on 16–17 March 1984. Ottawa: United Nations Association in Canada, 1984.

United Nations Organization. *Comprehensive Study on Nuclear Weapons*. Study Series 1. New York: UNO, 1981 (A/35/392).

United Nations Organization. *The United Nations and Disarmament, 1945–1970*. New York: UNO, 1971.

Vachon, G.K. "Le contrôle des armements et les armes chimiques". *Études Internationales*. Vol. XIII, No. 1, March 1982, pp. 97–109.

Vlasic, Ivan. "Le droit international et les activités spatiales: le point de la situation" [International Law and Space Activities: the Current Situation]. *Études Internationales*. Vol. XIX, No. 3, September 1988, pp. 467–477.

White Paper (FRG), 1971–1972, Ministry of Defence, Bonn.

White, J.M. *An Introduction to Radiation Protection Principles*. Chalk River: Chalk River Nuclear Laboratories, 1983.

Willrich, Mason. *Non-Proliferation Treaty: Framework for Nuclear Arms Control*. Charlottesville (Virginia): The Michie Company, 1969.

Winzer, Otto. "Die DDR: ein Stabiler Faktor für Frieden und Sicherheit". *Dokumentation der Zeit*. Vol. 21, No. 14, July 1969, p. 9.

Index

Departments, agencies and organizations of the Government of Canada appear as main entries. In all other cases, departments and agencies appear under the main entries for the particular nations and/or organizations listed.

accords, agreements, conventions and treaties: *see* Agreement on Measures to Improve the Direct Communications Link (1971, 1984); Agreement on Measures to Reduce the Risk of Outbreak of Nuclear War (1971); Agreement on Nuclear Risk Reduction Centres (1987); Agreement on the Prevention of Nuclear War (1973); Anti-Ballistic Missile (ABM) Treaty (1972); Berlin, Treaty of (1921); Biological and Toxin Weapons Convention (BTWC) (1972); Bonn-Pankow Fundamental Agreement (1973); Brussels, Treaty of (1948); Chemical Weapons Convention (CWC); Convention on Assistance in Case of Nuclear Accident or Radiological Emergency (1987); Convention on Early Notification of Nuclear Accident (1987); Convention on International Telecommunications (1973); Convention on Mesological Warfare (1987); Convention on Physical Protection of Nuclear Material (1987); Convention on Privileges and Diplomatic Immunities; Convention on the Registration of Objects Launched into Outer Space (1976); Final Act of Helsinki (1975); Franco-German Cooperation Treaty (1963); FRG/GDR Basic Treaty (1972); FRG/Poland Treaty (1970); FRG/USSR Treaty (1970); Geneva Protocol (1925); INF Agreements (1987); Intermediate-Range Nuclear Forces (INF) Treaty (1988); International Liability Convention (1972); London and Paris Accords (1954); Moon Treaty (1984); Moscow, Tripartite Treaty of (1963); Nairobi Convention (1982); Non-Proliferation Treaty (NPT) (1970); Outer Space Treaty (1967); Paris Accords (1954); Partial Test Ban Treaty (PTBT) (1963); Peace Treaties (1919); Peaceful Nuclear Explosions Treaty (PNET) (1976); Quadripartite Agreement on Berlin (1971); Rarotonga, Treaty of (1986); Rescue and Return Agreement (1968); SALT I Treaty (1972); SALT II Treaty (1979); Sea-Bed Treaty; Threshold Test Ban Treaty (TTBT) (1976); Tlatelolco, Treaty of (1967); Versailles, Treaty of

atom 10, 41, 44, 45, 47, 49, 58, 62–64, 70, 71, 102, 230, 233, 235, 288, 315, 316, 320; alpha particle emission 316; beta particle emission 316, 319; fission 235; fusion 316, 319; ionizing radiation 44, 314–319, somatic and genetic effects of 315–320; isotopes 316, 319; mass of 315; radioactive decay 316; radioactive half-life 316, 319; radioactivity, maximum permissible concentration 342; structure of 315, 316

atomic bomb, *see* nuclear weapons

atomic energy 45, 46, 78; Advisory Panel on (1946) 77, 78, 270; control of 13, 45–47, 49, 52, 60, 62, 65, 68, 72, 87, 88, 92, 94, 99, 102, 104, 106, 114; peaceful uses of 44–47, 58, 62–65, 71, 77, 79, 81, 102, 232, 233, 248, 566, *see also* Atoms for Peace Plan

Atomic Energy Control Board (AECB) 15, 16, 58, 78, 126, 268

Atomic Energy of Canada Ltd (AECL) 22, 268, 342, 362

Atoms for Peace Plan (Eisenhower, 1953) 87, 92, 101, 103, 248

Attlee, Clement 45

Aubert, P. 557

Austin, Warren 66

Baker, Philip Noel 68

Barry 526

Barton, William 19, 140, 225, 277, 280, 574

Baruch, Bernard 46, 57–60, 66–68, 87, 106, 121, 125, 303, 566, 572

Baruch Plan 13, 46, 55, 60, 65, 87, 102, 103, 106, 112, 121, 125, 303, 566

Basham, Peter W. 334

Battaglini, Giovanni 216

Bean, W.W. 155, 265

Bechoeffer, B.H. 98

Beesley, J. Alan 312, 373, 374, 419, 420

Bergson, Henri 195

Berlin blockade 67

Berlin Conference (1947) 66

Berlin crisis (1958) 161, 167, 171, 194, 337

Berlin, Treaty of (1921) 283

Berlin Wall 171, 172

Bevin, Ernest 42, 45, 65, 66

Bindt, M. 193

Biological and Toxin Weapons Convention (BTWC) (1972) 281, 282, 285, 290, 292–294, 296, 298, 300, 302, 303, 308, 567, 573; proposals 291; 1st Review Conference (1980) 282, 294, 295; 2nd Review Conference (1986) 282, 295; 3rd Review Conference (1991) 282

Bonaparte, Napoléon 5, 6, 13

Bonn-Pankow Fundamental Agreement (1973) 432

Borawski, J. 423

Bortmeyer, Hubert G. 418

Bow, Mac N. 209, 433–435

Bowie, R. 165

Bradley, Omar 67

Brandt, W. 223, 427, 429, 431

Brewin, Andrew 299

Brezhnev, Leonid Ilyich 430–432, 435, 446, 448, 471, 499, 502, 531, 558